A History of the Prophets of Islam

Derived from the Quran, Ahadith and Commentaries

Vol. I

Suzanne Haneef

Library of Islam

Library of Congress Cataloging in Publication Data

Bibliographical references.
1. Prophets, Pre-Islamic. I. Author. II. Title.
BP137.T331997 297'.1224 77-25941
ISBN: 1-871031-11-4

Published by
Library of Islam

Distributed by
KAZI Publications, Inc.
3023 W. Belmont Avenue
Chicago, IL 60618
(T) 773-267-7001; (F) 773-267-7002
email: info@kazi.org online catalog: www.kazi.org

Other Books by the Author

What Everyone Should Know About Islam and Muslims

(also available in Russian)

Islam, the Path of God

Dedication

To the honored memory of Sayyidina 'Abdullah ibn 'Abbas,
may God be pleased with him,
the chief of the interpreters of the Qur'an,
by whose inspired understanding of the stories of the prophets
the writing of this book has been guided,
I humbly and gratefully dedicate this work.

Volume One

ADAM THROUGH SHU'AYB

A HISTORY OF THE PROPHETS OF ISLAM

Derived from the Qur'an,
Ahadith and Commentaries

ACKNOWLEDGEMENTS

With deep gratitude, I acknowledge the following authors' and publishers' permissions to cite material from the works listed below:

Abul-Qasim Publishing House, Jeddah, Saudi Arabia, publisher of *The Qur'an, Arabic Text with Corresonding English Meanings*, English revised and edited by Saheeh International (1997).

Shaykh Muhammad al-Akili, translator and editor of *The Beauty of the Righteous and Ranks of the Elite* (1996).

Hakim Investment Holdings (M. E.) Limited, U.K., publisher of *The Commentary on the Qur'an*, by Abu Ja'far Muhammad b. Jarir al-Tabari, translated by J. Cooper, published by Oxford University Press (1987).

Material quoted from *The History of al-Tabari, Volume I: General Introduction and From the Creation to the Flood*, translated by Franz Rosenthal, is reprinted by permission of the State University of New York Press © 1989, State University of New York. All rights reserved.

Material quoted from *The History of al-Tabari, Volume II, Prophets and Patriarchs*, translated and annotated by William M. Brinner, is reprinted by permission of the State University of New York Press © 1986, State University of New York. All rights reserved.

Material quoted from *The History of al-Tabari, Volume III, The Children of Israel*, translated by William M. Brinner, is reprinted by permission of the State University of New York Press © 1991, State University of New York. All rights reserved.

Material quoted from *The Qur'an and Its Interpreters, Volume One*, by Mahmoud M. Ayoub, is reprinted by permission of the State University of New York Press © 1984, State University of New York. All rights reserved.

Material quoted from *The Qur'an and Its Interpreters, Volume Two*, by Mahmoud M. Ayoub, is reprinted by permission of the State University of New York Press © 1992, State University of New York. All rights reserved.

Maps were created by Yusuf Siddiqui using data from the USGS and ESRI, Inc.

I am deeply indebted to Dr. M. Salih Bayraktutan, Director of the Earthquake Research Center at Atatürk University, Erzurum, Turkey, and head of a research project entitled "The study of the pre-Sumerian inscriptions and remains of civilizations in the Ararat region (SEPAC)," which is concerned with finding the remains of Noah's Ark, for making available to me the outline and findings of his research.

My warmest thanks go to my friend, Salma al-Houry, translator of *Selection of Prophetic Hadiths & Muhammadan Wisdoms*, by as-Sayed Ahmad al-Hashimi, published by Dar al-Kutub al-Ilmiyah, Beirut, for her invaluable help in translating *ahadith*.

TABLE OF CONTENTS

The Story of Hud (A)

The Story of Saleh (A)

The Stories of Abraham, Ishmael, Isaac and Jacob (A)

Part One

Part Two

The Story of Lot (A)

The Story of Joseph (A)

The Story of Job (A)

The Story of Shu'ayb (A)

List of Maps

SOURCES

THE QUR'AN AND COMMENTARIES

Abdullah Yusuf Ali. *The Holy Qur'an: Text, Translation and Commentary*

A. J. Arberry. *The Koran Interpreted*

Muhammad Asad. *The Message of the Qur'an*

Mahmoud Ayoub. *The Qur'an and Its Interpreters, Volumes One and Two*

Abdalhaqq and Aisha Bewley. *The Noble Qur'an, A New Rendering of its Meaning in English*

Muhammad Taqi-ud-Din al-Hilali and Muhammad Muhsin Khan. *Interpretation of the Meaning of the Noble Qur'an in the English Language*

Ibn Kathir, *Al-Tafsir Ibn Katheer* (*The Commentary of Ibn Kathir*) (Urdu)

Ibn Kathir. *Tafseer Ibn Katheer: Juz' 'Amma* (*Part 30 of the Qur'an*), translated by Sameh Strauch

S. Abul A'la Maududi. *The Meaning of the Qur'an*

Marmaduke Pickthall. *The Meaning of the Glorious Qur'an*

Saheeh International. *The Qur'an, Arabic Text with Corresponding English Meanings*

Abu Ja'far Muhammad b. Jarir al-Tabari. *Commentary on the Qur'an, Volume One*, translated by J. Cooper

HADITH

Sahih al-Bukhari, translated by Dr. Muhammad Muhsin Khan, 1974

Sahih Muslim, translated by Abdul Hamid Siddiqi, 1971

Sunan Abu Dawud, translated by Ahmad Hasan, 1990

Mishkat al-Masabih, translated by James Robson, 1963

Al-Muwatta, translated by 'A'isha 'Abdarrahman at-Tarjumana and Ya'qub Johnson, 1982

Al-Hadith al-Qudsiyah, published by Dar al-Fikr, Beirut, 1988

Selection of Prophetic Hadiths & Muhammadan Wisdoms, by as-Sayed Ahmad al-Hashimi, translated by Salma al-Houry, 1993

COMMENTARIES ON STORIES OF THE PROPHETS

Ibn Kathir. *Qasas al-Anbiya'* (*Stories of the Prophets*) (Arabic)

Abdul-Wahhab an-Najjar. *Qasas al-Anbiya'* (*Stories of the Prophets*) (Arabic)

Muhammad Ali as-Sabuni. *An-Nubuwwah wal-Anbiya'* (Arabic)

Al-Tabari. *Qasas al-Anbiya'* (*Stories of the Prophets*) (Arabic)

Al-Tabari. *The History of al-Tabari, Volume I: General Introduction and From the Creation to the Flood*, translated and annotated by Franz Rosenthal

Al-Tabari. *The History of al-Tabari, Volume II: Prophets and Patriarchs*, translated and annotated by William M. Brinner

Al-Tabari. *The History of al-Tabari, Volume III: The Children of Israel*, translated and annotated by William M. Brinner

Al-Tabari. *The Ancient Kingdoms, Volume IV*: The Ancient Kingdoms, translated by Moshe Perlmann

REFERENCE WORKS

Shaykh Muhammad al-Akili. *The Beauty of the Righteous and Ranks of the Elite*

The Holy Bible, New International Version

Rev. W. M. Clow. *The Bible Reader's Encyclopaedia and Concordance*

Muhammad bin 'Uthman adh-Dhahabi. *The Major Sins*, translated by Mohammed Moinuddin Siddiqui

Cyril Glasse. *The Concise Encyclopedia of Islam*

Ibn Ishaq. *The Life of Muhammad*, translated by A. Guillaume

Edward William Lane. *An Arabic-English Lexicon*

Martin Lings. *Muhammad, his life based on the earliest sources*

Ahmad ibn Naqib al-Misri. *The Reliance of the Traveller*, translated by Noah Ha Mim Keller

Abdullah Abbas Nadwi. *Vocabulary of the Holy Qur'an*

Syed Muzaffar-ud-din Nadvi. *A Geographical History of The Qur'an*

John Penrice. *A Dictionary and Glossary of the Qur'an*

William Smith. *Smith's Bible Dictionary*

Merrill C. Tenney, ed. *Handy Dictionary of the Bible*

Hans Wehr. *Arabic-English Dictionary: The Hans Wehr Dictionary of Modern Written Arabic*, edited by J. M. Cowan, Third Edition

SPECIAL SOURCES FOR THIS VOLUME

Eli Barnavi, General Editor. *A Historical Atlas of the Jewish People from the Time of the Patriarchs to the Present*

Tosun Bayrak al-Jerrahi al-Halveti. *The Most Beautiful Names*

Friedrich Bender. *Geology of the Arabian Peninsula: Jordan*

Edwin Bernbaum. *Sacred Mountains of the World*

James Henry Breasted, Ph.D. *A History of Egypt from the Earliest Times to the Persian Conquest*

David J. Burdon. *Handbook of the Geology of Jordan*

David Daiches. *Moses, the Man and His Vision*

Al-Ghazali. *Freedom and Fulfillment*, translated by Richard Joseph McCarthy

Al-Ghazali. *Ihya 'Ulum a-Din, Kitab al 'Ilm* [*Revival of the Religious Sciences, Book One: The Book of Knowledge*] (Arabic)

Al-Ghazali. *The Remembrance of Death and the Afterlife: Kitab dhikr al-mawt wa-ma ba'dahu. Book XL of The Revival of the Religious Sciences (Ihya 'ulum al-din)*, translated with an introduction and notes by T. J. Winter

T. G. H. James. *Ancient Egypt, the Land and Its Legacy*

Kenneth MacLeish. "Abraham, the Friend of God," *National Geographic Magazine*, Dec. 1966

Pierre Montet. *Lives of the Pharaohs*

P. H. Newby. *Warrior Pharaohs, The Rise and Fall of the Egyptian Empire*

Sayyid Qutb. *The Islamic Concept and Its Characteristics*, translated by Mohammed Moinuddin Siddiqui

William Ryan and Walter Pitman. *Noah's Flood*

Ayman Taher. *Sinai, Guide of the Peninsula and the Red Sea*

Tony Wheeler. *Sri Lanka, a Travel Survival Kit*

KEY TO ABBREVIATIONS OF SOURCES FOR THIS VOLUME

THE QUR'AN AND COMMENTARIES

The Holy Qur'an: *Q*

Abdullah Yusuf Ali translation: Ali/*Q*

Muhammad Asad translation: Asad/*Q*

Mahmoud Ayoub, *The Qur'an and Its Interpreters*: Ayoub/*Q*, volume:page

S. Abul A'la Maududi translation: Maududi/*Q*, chapter:verse

Ibn Kathir, *Tafsir* (*Commentary*): Ibn Kathir/*T*, chapter:verse

Ibn Kathir, *Tafseer Ibn Katheer: Juz' 'Amma*: Ibn Kathir/*Juz' 'Amma*

Al-Tabari, *Commentary*: Tabari/*C*, I:page

HADITH

Sahih al-Bukhari: *Bukhari*, volume:*hadith* number

Sahih Muslim: *Muslim*, *hadith* number

Sunan Abu Dawud: *Abu Dawud*, *hadith* number

Mishkat al-Masabih: *Mishkat*, *hadith* number

Al-Muwatta: *Muwatta*, *hadith* number

Al-Houry, Selection of Prophetic Hadiths & Muhammadan Wisdoms: Al-Houry, *Hadiths*, *hadith* number, page

COMMENTARIES ON STORIES OF THE PROPHETS

Ibn Kathir, *Qasas al-Anbiya'*: Ibn Kathir/*Q*, prophet's name, page number

An-Najjar, *Qasas al-Anbiya'*: An-Najjar/*Q*, prophet's name, page number

Al-Tabari, *Qasas al-Anbiya'*: Tabari/*Q*, prophet's name, page number

Al-Tabari, *History of al-Tabari*: Tabari/*H*, volume:page number

OTHER WORKS

Al-Akili, *Beauty of the Righteous and Ranks of the Elite*: Akili/*B*

Barnavi, *A Historical Atlas of the Jewish People from the Time of the Patriarchs to the Present:* Barnavi/*Atlas*

Breasted, *A History of Egypt from the Earliest Times to the Persian Conquest*: Breasted/*History*

Daiches, *Moses, the Man and His Vision*: Daiches/*Moses*

Glasse, *Concise Encyclopedia of Islam*: Glasse/*E*

Ibn Ishaq, *The Life of Muhammad*: Ibn Ishaq/*M*

James, *Ancient Egypt, the Land and Its Legacy*: James/*Egypt*

Keller, *Reliance of the Traveller*: Keller/*R*

Lane, *An Arabic-English Lexicon*: Lane/*L*

Lings, *Muhammad, his life based on the earliest sources*: Lings/*M*

Montet, *Lives of the Pharaohs*: Montet/*Pharaohs*

Nadvi, *A Geographical History of the Qur'an*: Nadvi/*History*

Newby, *Warrior Pharaohs*: Newby/*Pharaohs*

Sayyid Qutb, *The Islamic Concept and Its Characteristics*: Qutb/*Concept*

Hans Wehr, *Arabic-English Dictionary:* Wehr/*D*

In the name of God, the Merciful, the Compassionate

PREFACE

As-salamu 'alaikum — may God's peace be upon you. And congratulations!

For what? Because, by opening this book, you are about to embark on a fascinating voyage of discovery — of the roots of Islam, its message, and its messengers and their continuity through time.

Through this series of stories of the prophets of Islam, you will be introduced, first, to the Islamic concept of God. This quite naturally constitutes the central theme of the Islamic teachings, since sound belief, as well as sound values, morals and behavior, obviously rests on a sound understanding of God's nature and reality.

Afterwards, we will speak of the diversity of God's creation and will then focus on ourselves, mankind — our origin, relationship with God, and special destiny. Central to this discussion will be Islam's view of God's all-inclusive plan for humankind and the role of His specially-appointed messengers in carrying out this plan. This will hopefully enable us to come to a clearer understanding of two essential matters: Islam's view of God and of ourselves, mankind, in the totality of His divine scheme. The remainder of this work will be devoted to exploring the lives and missions of God's prophet-messengers in historical order.

The stories in this work are based primarily on the narratives contained in the Holy Qur'an, but three other sources have been utilized as well. These include, firstly, the ***ahadith*** (the plural of ***hadith***) or sayings of Prophet Muhammad (S)[1] regarding the topics under discussion. The second supplementary source is the interpretations of the early classic Islamic commentators, traditionists and scholars. Among these, we have relied primarily on the interpretations of the most illustrious of the Qur'anic interpreters, the Prophet's cousin, 'Abdullah ibn 'Abbas (R),[2] about whom we speak in detail in Appendix A. And our third supplementary source is the work of present-day translators and scholars of the Qur'an.

According to a ***hadith***, God sent 124,000 prophets and messengers to various peoples of the earth (***Mishkat***, 664w). The first in the prophetic line was

[1]This symbol stands for "***Sallallahu 'alayhi wa sallam***, God's peace and blessings be upon him," an invocation used by Muslims whenever Prophet Muhammad (S) is mentioned.

[2]This symbol means "***Radi-Allahu 'anhu***, may God be pleased with him," an invocation used by Muslims whenever the name of a Companion of the Prophet is mentioned.

Adam (A),[3] and the last and final one was Muhammad (S), the Seal of the Prophets. In between these first and last, the following prophets are mentioned in the Qur'an: Idris [Enoch?], Noah, Hud, Saleh, Abraham, Ishmael, Isaac, Jacob, Lot, Joseph, Job, Shu'ayb, Aaron, Moses, Samuel, David, Solomon, Elijah, Elisha, Dhul-Kifl, Jonah, Zechariah, John the Baptist, and Jesus, God's peace and blessings be upon them all. All these prophets — those who made the greatest and most lasting impact upon humanity — lived and carried out their missions in the Middle East, the birthplace of the three monotheistic faiths, Judaism, Christianity and Islam.

If you are familiar with the prophets of the Bible, the names of most of these prophets will be familiar to you, for with the exception of the four Arabian prophets — Hud, Saleh, Shu'ayb and Muhammad, God's peace and blessings be upon them — they are the same. As you read, you will note that their stories as told in the Qur'an have many similarities to the Biblical text. But there is a major difference that you may want to keep in mind.

In the Islamic understanding, the prophets were, without exception, men of the highest character and morals, free of major sins — the most perfect among mankind. They were individuals who surrendered their own personal wills to their Lord in order to manifest His divine Will, which they knew through revelation and the inspirations coming to their hearts.

Now, no one can become a prophet by wishing to or trying to be, for prophethood is granted by divine appointment. Each prophet was specially chosen by God Most High, and then trained and nurtured, guided, directed and inspired until he was prepared to carry the responsibility of prophethood and to convey God's Message to his people — or, in the case of the Last Prophet, peace be upon him and upon them all, to all mankind. Thus, in contrast to the Biblical understanding, the Islamic understanding of prophethood is not based primarily upon propheseying the future, although God indeed gave His prophets such knowledge of the Unseen as He willed.

As you read, it should become apparent to you that the teachings conveyed through all the prophets, from the first to the last, constitute a single, uniform, unvarying Message, whose consistency and continuity is one of its most striking features. This Message firstly affirms God's existence, reality and Oneness, emphasizing that the sovereignty and control of all things rests with Him, and that no one else is worthy of the human being's submission,

[3]This symbol means "'*Alayhi-s-salam,* peace be upon him," the invocation used by Muslims whenever an angel or a prophet other them Muhammad (S) is mentioned.

worship and obedience. Secondly, it proclaims that each individual bears responsibility for his or actions in front of God. Thirdly, it declares that each of us will return to Him for judgment and for a life of eternal duration in which the fruits of our earthly deeds will become manifest.

It is God Himself who gives a name to this Message, this faith, calling it ***al-islam***, the state of surrender or submission to Him. Apart from the beings who possess free will, this state is shared, involuntarily, by the universes and whatever they contain, according to His words,

> **Then is it other than God's religion they desire, while whoever is in the heavens and earth has submitted to him, willingly or unwillingly, and to Him they will be returned? (Holy Qur'an, 3:83)**

As for the possessors of free will, they are likewise governed by that divine Will which is above their wills. However, unlike the rest of God's creation, they possess freedom to choose whether to ***voluntarily*** submit their wills to Him or not. It is this state of voluntary submission or surrender to God that constitutes ***islam***, the primordial faith of mankind since the very beginning of human life on earth, according to God's words: —

> **Assuredly, the religion in the sight of God is Islam. (3:19)**

And its followers are called Muslims, for

> **He [God] named you Muslims beforehand and in this [Qur'an]. (22:78)**

You will note the common letters, "s," "l" and "m" in the words "Islam" and "Muslim," for both words are derived from the same three-letter Arabic root. This root — and hence the word "Islam" itself — means "peace," "submission" and "surrender". A Muslim is, therefore, by definition, one who is at peace — with God, with himself or herself, with other human beings, and with the totality of God's creation; who submits to His laws and guidance as conveyed by His prophets; and who surrenders to His divine Will as it manifests itself in the unfolding of events.

In this sense, all the prophets from Adam up to the Last Prophet, Muhammad (S), and those who believed with them and followed them, were ***muslims,*** surrendered to God. However, in order to maintain a distinction between Islam and its followers before and after its final revelation, brought by Muhammad (S), we have used "***islam***" to denote the true, pristine faith of the pre-Muhammadan period and "***muslim***" for the believers who followed it, and, according to common usage, the terms "Islam" and "Muslim" for the faith and its followers after the coming of Muhammad (S).

Now, there are two basic ways to approach the telling of the prophets' stories. One is to cite all the Qur'anic verses concerning a given prophet together, interspersed with commentary — the method of the classic commentators and most other writers. However, the problem with this approach is that verses concerning individual prophets are found scattered throughout the Qur'an, sometimes with many repetitions or variations. This leaves a writer of these stories with the question of which Qur'anic passage to cite and which to omit where there is overlapping, as well the matter of the historical ordering of material, leading to many difficulties in presenting the basic story, together with its commentary, in a coherent and connected manner.

Another method is to combine and interweave all the verses relating to a given story in a continuous narrative, supported by commentary. The problem with this approach is that the majesty and compelling quality of the Qur'anic passages is often lost by being reduced to quotations interspersed with other material. Nonetheless, as this seemed the more readable of the two approaches, this is the method I have chosen to follow.

The translations of the Qur'anic verses are derived primarily from the recently-published Saheeh International translation, which I have found to be by far the most accurate and understandable of English texts, in consultation with the translations of Yusuf Ali, Arberry, Asad, Abdalhaqq and Aisha Bewley, Hilali/Khan, Maududi and Pickthall. Quotations from the Qur'an are given in boldface throughout this work to set them off from other material. Verses pertaining to each prophet are also cited in full in the "Qur'anic References" section at the end of each story. I encourage you to refer to these complete Qur'anic passages to access the full context and flow of verses which have been quoted in small segments throughout the narrative.

The present work is divided into two volumes. The first half of Volume One covers the prophet Adam, his immediate successors Seth and Idris, Noah, and the Arabian prophets Hud and Saleh. The second half concerns the family of Abraham: the patriarch himself, his sons Ishmael and Isaac, his grandson Jacob, his nephew Lot, his great-grandson Joseph, and his later descendants, Job and Shu'ayb. In Volume Two, the first half is comprised of the stories of Moses and Aaron and the later prophets of the Israelites: Joshua, Samuel, David, Solomon, Elijah (Ilyas), Elisha (Alyasa'), Dhul-Kifl and Jonah, while the second half concerns the family of 'Imran: Zechariah, John, Mary and Jesus, God's peace and blessings be upon them all.

Many new terms and key words will be presented in this series. These are terms with which Muslims living in the Muslim world generally become familiar during their religious training in childhood. But if you happen to be either a non-Muslim or a non-Arabic-speaking Muslim, many of these terms may be new to you. In order to call such terms (whether Arabic or English) to your attention, they are given in boldface the first time they are introduced. If you are able to learn them as you read, they will be useful in helping you gain an understanding of basic Islamic concepts and terminology.

Numerous footnotes have been added to clarify the text. For additional detail, material not immediately related to the story has been presented in appendices at the end of some stories. If you are someone who likes as much detail as possible, you may benefit from these notes and appendices. If not, you may prefer to stick to the text and ignore the explanatory material altogether, or to refer to it only when you need clarification on a specific matter.

At various points in the text where discussion is called for, relevant questions are posed, material related to the story is discussed, and attempts are made to arrive at lessons and draw conclusions. Although these conclusions will be those of Islam, it is hoped that these discussions will stimulate further reflection and exploration by readers of any path.

Perceiving a critical lack in the Islamic literature in English in this area, I began this work in the winter of 1992. The stories were built little by little on the resources available to me in English, with constant consultation and help from my husband, may God bless and reward him, in translating other source materials from Arabic and Urdu. Readers who are interested in further information on particular points are encouraged to seek out other authoritative sources in Arabic or other languages.

My approach has been to keep as much as possible to interpretations that are clear and definitive, while omitting questionable or ambiguous material. However, due to my own limitations and a dearth of English sources, certain omissions or errors may have found their way into this work. May God Most Gracious forgive my unintentional mistakes and accept this very humble effort, which has been a joy and a source of light to me during the years of my work on it. Endless glory and praise be to Him who made it possible, and may He bless you and everyone who reads these pages.

The Story of Adam and His Descendants, Seth and Idris

peace be upon them

Indeed, God chose Adam and Noah and the family of Abraham and the family of ‘Imran over all mankind, descendants of one another. And God is Hearing and Knowing. (3:33-34)

In the name of God, the Merciful, the Compassionate

PART ONE: AT THE BEGINNING

1. BY WAY OF INTRODUCTION

There is certainly a lesson in their [the prophets'] stories for those of understanding. Never was it [the Qur'an] an invented narration, but rather a confirmation of what was before it and a detailed explanation of all things, and a guidance and mercy for people who believe.
(Holy Qur'an 12:111)

Islam is a vast, endlessly deep, wide ocean of knowledge related to matters both spiritual and temporal. In this ocean, the histories of the prophets is a specialized area of knowledge about which countless volumes have been written over the centuries by Islamic scholars in the various languages of Muslim peoples, but most commonly in Arabic, the language of revelation.

The story of Adam, God's peace and blessings be upon him, is the entry into that ocean of knowledge. It introduces us, firstly, to the realm of Islamic concepts and understandings of Reality, addressing such questions as, *What is it all about, this life that we are in? Who are we as a species and who am I as an individual? Where did I come from and how did I get from "there" to "here"? Where am I going and how will I reach the final destination?*

Adam's story is secondly a history of our species. Adam (A) is both the first man and ancestor of the human race, as well as the prototype of the human being, the archetypal Man. More than that, he is also the first prophet. But at a deeper level, his story is also a subtle allegory concerning mankind and the human condition, both before and after the Fall.

Consequently, the purpose and deeper significance of the story of Adam (A) is to inform us of our true origin, nature and identity, information that in turn enables us to put the various stages of our existence and the elements of our being into perspective so that we can know who we truly are and where we belong in the divine scheme of things.

2. Allah

He is Allah in the heavens and the earth. He knows your secret and your open matters, and He knows what you earn. (6:3)

He is Allah, the One besides whom there is no other deity, Knower of the Unseen and the Witnessed. He is the Most Merciful, the Compassionate. He is Allah, the One besides whom there is no other deity, the Sovereign, the Holy One, the Source of Peace, the Bestower of Safety, the Guardian, the Exalted, the Irresistible, the Supreme. Glory be to Allah above whatever they associate with Him! He is Allah, the Creator, the Maker, the Fashioner. To Him belong the beautiful Names. Whatever is in the heavens and on earth glorifies Him, and He is the Exalted, the Wise. (59:22-24)

These verses describe Allah — God Most High, the Lord of the universes, the Lord of the heavens and the earth, the Lord of every creature, the Lord of mankind. And belief in Him is the first article of faith in Islam.

From ancient times, the name of God in Arabic, the language of the Qur'an and Islam, has been "Allah". Indeed, to this day, most Arabs, both Christians and Muslims, refer to God as "Allah"

Allah is a name that cannot be applied to anyone except Him, the Most High. It has no plural form — that is, there are no "*allahs*" in the sense of "gods."[1] And although we have used the word "God" in the place of "Allah" throughout this text for the sake of familiarity, Allah is the name by which He calls Himself in thousands of verses of the Holy Qur'an.

The Source of the Knowledge of God

A discussion of the concept of God in any faith tradition logically begins by asking certain key questions, such as, *What are this faith's sources of information about God? What sort of a nature and characteristics does it attribute to Him? And how does it regard the human being's relationship with Him?*

Islam's answer to the first of these questions is quite simple: that the source of knowledge of God is God Himself, and from this answer all other answers follow. On their own, finite, created beings can never arrive at a correct understanding of the Creator and Sustainer of endless universes and all they contain; although we can and do speculate about Him, this can in no way be imagined to represent the truth about Him. Consequently, unless God Himself informs us

[1]However, the Arabic word *ilah* (as in the Declaration of Faith, *"La ilaha illa-Llah*, there is no deity except God") is used to refer generally to any deity or object of worship.

about Himself, He will remain the Ultimate Unknowable and our speculations concerning Him will be mere guesswork — and, given our limited capability of understanding infinity, much more likely to be wrong than right.

But God Most High created us with enquiring minds and yearning hearts so that we might seek to know Him and search for Him, the Source from whom we come and to whom we will return. He therefore informed us about Himself through His prophets throughout the ages — especially through His Last Prophet, Muhammad (S), in His Last Testament, the Holy Qur'an, which, for historical reasons, is our most accurate, definitive and trustworthy source of information concerning Him.

And what does God say about Himself in the Qur'an? He informs us, firstly, that He is one God and that no one shares in His divinity in the minutest degree; that is, no one other than He can be God or gods: —

> **If there had been deities besides God in them [the heavens and the earth], they [the heavens and earth] would both have been ruined. Then glorified be God, Lord of the Throne above what they describe! He is not questioned about what He does, but they will be questioned. Or have they taken deities besides Him? Say, [O Muhammad:] "Produce your proof. This [Qur'an] is the message for those with me and the message of those before me, but most of them do not know the truth, so they are turned away." And We did not send any messenger before you [Muhammad] but that We revealed to him that there is no deity but Me, so worship [and serve] Me.** (21:22-25)

Second, God is not similar to anything created, for although created beings such as humans and angels may possess attributes mirroring His, His divine nature is absolutely unique. Third, He informs us that He is entirely self-sufficient and totally independent of all His creation; He does not need anything but everything needs Him. He is God, the uncreated Creator, the lordless Lord, the masterless Master who is in absolute control of all things: —

> **Say, [O Muhammad:] "He is Allah, One; Allah, the Self-Sufficient. He does not father [anyone] nor is He fathered, and it is not for Him to have any equal."** (112:1-4)

Without any beginning or end, without parents or any other source, Allah or God, the Source of all things, has always been and will always be. Even if this universe, and whatever other universes there may be besides it, were to continue for billions or trillions of years, He would be; even if nothing else were in existence, He would remain forever. He is outside time and space, unbounded by any of the limitations which apply to created beings: —

He is the First and the Last, and the Outward and the Inward, and He is Knower of all things. (57:3)

Allah, God Most High, does not have a body with a form like a created being; likewise, He is not a substance, finite and measurable, nor are substances part of Him. Nor is He to be imagined in human terms, for to do so is bound to result in falsehood and is moreover degrading to His exalted divine Reality. Consequently, Muslims are not permitted to speculate on God's beginning,[2] nor do they ever ascribe to Him a relationship with or incarnation in any created being, such as a wife, mother or son: —

God has not taken any son, nor has there ever been any deity with Him. [If there had been,] then each deity would have taken away whatever it created and some of them would have sought to overcome others. Far removed is God from what they attribute [to Him]! Knower of the Unseen and the Witnessed, exalted is He above whatever they associate with Him. (23:91-92)

Muslims are also very cautious about interpreting Qur'anic verses or *ahadith* in which God speaks of His divine "Face," "Eyes" and "Hands," or His "Throne" or "Chair". Since the nature and attributes of God, the Unique and Exalted, are far removed from and infinitely greater than anything pertaining to His creation, such words are not to be taken in a literal sense which would liken Him to any created being.[3] Therefore, when God says that He created Adam (A) with His own Hands (38:75) or that cattle are among the things which His Hands have created (36:71); when He speaks of the building and floating of Noah's ark under His Eyes (11:37, 23:37, 54:14) or assures Prophet Muhammad (S) that he is under His Eyes (52:48); or when He speaks of His divine Face (2:272, 6:52, 18:28, 28:88, 55:27), Muslims do not try to interpret, imagine or speculate on what these words mean but simply accept them as they are. "Ponder over God's creation," said Prophet Muhammad (S), "but do not ponder over God because you will not be able to comprehend His power" (Mishkat, 202w). For God, who is unimaginably, incomparably greater than anything anyone can conceive of — indeed, infinitely greater than the sum-total of all human thought concerning Him — can never be imagined or described.

There is nothing whatsoever like Him, and He is the Hearing, the Seeing (42:11).

[2]Prophet Muhammad (S) said, "Satan comes to one of you and says, 'Who created such-and-such?' until he [the person] says, 'Who created your Lord?' Therefore, when he [Satan] inspires such a question, one should seek refuge with God and give up such thoughts" (*Bukhari*, 4.496). He also said, "People will not stop asking questions until they say, 'This is God, the Creator of everything, but then who created God?'" (Al-Houry, *Hadiths*, #963).

[3]In other religions, such anthropomorpic and literal notions about God have resulted in the making of pictures and statues 'depicting' Him, the Most High, and then attributing reality and power to these depictions and worshipping them. See Keller/*R*, v1.2- v1.7.

Glorified be God, the Lord of Power, above whatever they ascribe to Him. (37:180, 159; 21:2; 43:82)

And they have not assessed God according to His true assessment. . . . Glorified and exalted is He above the partners they ascribe to Him! (39:67; 22:74)

Muslims express God's unimaginable greatness by the often-repeated phrase, "***Allahu akbar*** — God is Most Great." And because of the unbounded adoration and reverence they feel toward their Lord, they often follow His Name by titles expressing glorification and praise.[4]

The Divine Attributes

At the same time, the Islamic understanding of God or Allah is far removed from the concept of an abstract power or force, such as "the First Cause," "Universal Intelligence," "the Ultimate Reality" or "Ground of All Being" of the theologians and philosophers. Rather, God Most High is the Divine Being, who speaks of Himself alternately using the three personal pronouns, "We," "He" and "I".

But while the Lord of all creation is beyond imagination and description, nonetheless we can know something about His exalted divine attributes — His power, glory, knowledge, wisdom, mercy, beneficence, and love — from the beauty, creativity and wisdom we see manifested throughout His creation and within our own selves. Indeed, in numerous verses of the Qur'an, God Most High appeals to us to observe His creation and then use our minds to understand who its Creator is. For example:

In the creation of the heavens and the earth, and the alternation of the night and the day, are signs for those of understanding. (3:190; also 10:6)

On the earth are signs for the certain [in faith], and in yourselves. Will you not then understand? (51:20-21)

He brings forth the living from the dead and brings forth the dead from the living, and He brings the earth to life after its death. And thus will you be brought forth. And among His signs is that He created you from dust, whereupon you are human beings, scattered about. And among His signs is that He created spouses for

---

[4]Among these are *Allah Ta'ala* (God Most High), *Allah Subhanahu wa Ta'ala* (God, the Glorified and Most High), *Allah 'Azza wa Jall* (God, the Mighty and Glorious), *Allah Jalla Jallalahu* (God, may His glory be exalted), *Allah Jalla Shanahu* (God the Sublime), and *Allah Jalla wa 'Ala* (God, the Sublime and Most High).

you from among yourselves, that you might find tranquility in them, and He put love and mercy between you; surely in that are signs for people who reflect. And among His signs is the creation of the heavens and the earth, and the diversity of your languages and colors; surely in that are signs for the knowing. And among His signs is your sleep by night and day, and your seeking of His bounty; surely in that are signs for a people who listen. And among His signs is that He shows you lightning, [causing both] fear and hope, and He sends down rain from the sky by which He brings the earth to life after its death; surely in that are signs for a people who use reason. And among His signs is that the sky and the earth stand by His command; then, when He calls you with a [single] call, from the earth you will at once come forth. And to Him belongs whomsoever is in the heavens and earth; all are devoutly obedient to Him. And it is He who begins creation, then repeats it, and that is [even] easier for Him. His is the highest similie in the heavens and earth, and He is the Almighty, the Wise. (30:19-27)

In the Holy Qur'an, God informs us of ninety-nine of His attributes or ***sifat***, known as ***al-Asma' al-Husna***, the Excellent or Beautiful Names (given in Appendix B at the end of this volume). These are mentioned in such verses as the following:

Allah — there is no deity but He. To Him belong the beautiful Names. (20:8; also 7:180)

Say, [O Muhammad:] "Call upon Allah or call upon the Most Merciful [*ar-Rahman*]. Whichever [name] you call, to Him belong the beautiful Names." (17:110)

To Him belong the beautiful Names. Whatever is in the heavens and on earth glorifies Him, and He is the Exalted, the Wise. (59:24)

And Prophet Muhammad (S) said:

Allah has ninety-nine Names, one less than one hundred. Whoever memorizes them will enter Paradise. (*Bukhari*, 8:419; *Mishkat*, 2285)

These holy Names or attributes describe Allah or God. Certain of these Names, such as the One, the Living, the Eternal, the Most High, the Almighty, the Glorious, the Majestic, the Self-Subsistent, are related to His divine Essence. These are known as the Attributes of Transcendence (*Sifat Tanzihi*).

Other holy Names refer to God's relationship with His creation, and these are divided into two groups. Some, such as the Compassionate, the Merciful, the Forgiving, the Gentle, the Loving, the Kind, the Tolerant, the Provider, the Source of Peace, the Benefactor, the Generous and many others, reflect His attributes of mercy, compassion, forgiveness, gentleness and love toward His creation; these are known as the Attributes of Beauty (*Sifat Jamali*). Other holy Names, such as the the Strong, the Powerful, the Just, the Irrisistible, the Overpowering, the Possessor of Majesty and Honor, relate to His qualities of sovereignty, strength or severity in relation to His creation, and these are called the Attributes of Majesty (*Sifat Jalali*).

These two sets of attributes are not opposite but rather are complementary. For example, while God is the Giver of Life, He is also the Giver of Death, since whatever is born must die; while He is the most Merciful, He is also the absolutely Just, since mercy involves doing justice to those who have been wronged. Taken all together, these attributes or *sifat* of beauty and majesty point to the absolute perfection of the Lord of creation. He is perfect in goodness, in mercy and compassion, in kindness and love; in strength, power, majesty, glory; in justice, wisdom, knowledge — in every good and holy attribute, and in all He does or wills. Without such perfection, He would not be God, nor would there be divine perfection in whatever He wills, decrees and plans.

To God Most High belongs absolute control, power and dominion over all things, both in the physical and the spiritual realm. He wills, decrees, forms, guides and directs what He has created, and nothing takes place in any part of His creation without His knowledge, decree and will.

> **Whatever is in the heavens and the earth glorifies God, and He is the Almighty, the Wise. His is the dominion of the heavens and earth. He gives life and causes death, and He is powerful over all things.** (57:1-2)
>
> **Blessed is He in whose hands is the dominion, and He is powerful over all things — who created death and life that He might test you as to which of you is best in deed, and He is the Almighty, the Forgiving, who created seven heavens in harmony. You do not perceive any inconsistency in the creation of the Most Merciful. Then return the glance again; do you perceive any rift? Then return the glance yet again: the glance will return to you diminished and weary.** (67:3-4)

Because God Most High describes Himself in the Qur'an as the self-sufficient Divine Being who is unlike any of His creation, people sometimes suppose that Islam fosters a concept of a God who is completely remote and removed from His creation — especially from us, mankind. But nothing could be more inaccurate.

As the Creator and Sustainer of all things, God is absolutely independent and **free from need of all the worlds** (3:97, 29:6; also 35:15, 60:6; 14:8). At the same time, He is ever involved and concerned with His creation. Thus, He says, **He is with you wherever you are** (57:4), fully **Knowing of whatever is within the breasts of His servants** (35:38), and **closer to him** — the human being — **than** his **jugular vein** (50:16), **the Forgiving, the Loving, the Merciful** (85:14, 11:90).

Indeed, the two attributes or Names of God most often mentioned in the Qur'an are ***al-Rahman*** and ***al-Rahim***,[5] both derived from the same root, "*r-h-m*," denoting compassion, beneficence and mercy. ***Rahman*** refers to one who is intensely merciful beyond the level of human capacity. This word, which is used only to describe God, occurs in the Qur'an no less than fifty-seven times. ***Rahim*** denotes one who is continually merciful; it may be used to describe someone other than God. Mentioned in the Qur'an 115 times. the divine Name *al-Rahim* is usually paired with the Name, ***al-Ghafur***, "the Forgiving," which is mentioned in the Qur'an ninety-two times.

Now, God Most High was obviously not under any obligation or constraint to inform mankind about Himself. Yet He revealed Himself to us through His prophets so that we might know Him, according to His saying by divine inspiration through the mouth of His Holy Prophet, Muhammad (S),[6] "I was a hidden treasure and desired to be known." This one ***hadith*** alone informs us that it is within the capability of each one of us to come nearer and nearer to our Lord through sincere worship and service, until eventually we become like a mirror of His exalted divine attributes.

---

[5] ***Ar-Rahman*** is variously translated as "the Beneficent/Most Beneficent," "the Merciful/Most Merciful/All-Merciful," "the Compassionate/Most Compassionate," or "the Gracious/Most Gracious". ***Ar-Rahim*** is translated as "the Merciful," "the Ever Merciful," "the Mercy-Giving" or "the Beneficent".

[6] That is a ***hadith qudsi***, meaning a ***hadith*** in which the Prophet (S) speaks about God through divine inspiration.

3. God's Creation

Indeed, in the heavens and the earth are signs for the believers. And in the creation of yourselves and [in] what He scatters about [upon the earth] of moving creatures are signs for people of certainty. And [in] the alternation of the night and the day, and [in] what God sends down from the sky as provision and thereby gives life to the earth after its lifelessness, and [in His] directing the winds, are signs for people who reason. (45:3-5; also 3:190; 42:29)

Do they not contemplate within themselves? God has not created the heavens and the earth and whatever is between them except in truth and for a specified term. (30:8)

Endless eons before earthly time began, God Almighty created the universes and the worlds, both those we know about and others about which we have no information, and everything between them and in them. According to His infinitely great and wise plan, He created all things in the best of forms, with infinite wisdom, knowledge, skill and artistry.

Because God created us human beings with enquiring minds, we naturally wonder *how* He created all this. But only He knows how. None of us can fully understand the process of creation, which lies outside of time and space, since we ourselves are part of that creation. Anything we may say about it is bound to be largely guesswork and theorizing, arrived at from our exceedingly limited and finite perspective. What we do know with certainty that it all happened according to the design of the Best of Planners, whose unfathomable wisdom, knowledge and creativity are manifested at every level and in every atom of His creation, and whose endless glory and greatness are reflected throughout the heavens and the earth and in our own selves.

Nevertheless, the Creator has thrown out some tantalizing hints about the origins of creation, such as the following, upon which Muslim astronomers and physicists, combining divine revelation with their scientific disciplines, built their knowledge-base:

> **Then He directed Himself to the firmament while it was vapor, and said to it and to the earth, "Become, willingly or unwillingly!" They said, "We have become, willingly."** (41:11)
>
> **And it is He who created the night and the day and the sun and the moon; all of them are floating in an orbit.** (21:34; also 36:40)
>
> **Have those who disbelieved not considered that the heavens and the earth were joined and We separated them, and We made every living thing from water? Will they not then believe? And We placed upon the earth firmly set mountains, lest it should shift**

with them, and We inserted therein passes [as] roads, that they might be guided. And We made the sky a well-guarded canopy; but they are turned away from its signs. And it is He who created the night and the day and the sun and the moon; all of them are floating in an orbit. (21:30-34)

He created the heavens without supports that you can see and has put firmly-set mountains upon the earth lest it should shift with you, and dispersed therein something of every creature. (31:10)

God created every [living] creature from water. (24:45)

It is He who has released the two seas, one fresh and sweet, and one salty and bitter, and He placed a barrier and a prohibiting partition between them. It is He who created the mortal from water. (25:54)

God Most High has also detailed the stages of the creation of the human being from conception to death:

We certainly created the human being from an extract of clay. Then We placed him as a sperm-drop in a firm lodging [the womb]. Then We created of the semen-drop a clinging clot [the embryo] and created of the clot a lump [the fetus], and We created of the lump bones and clothed the bones with flesh. Then We developed it into another creation. So blessed be God, the Best of Creators! Then indeed, after that you will die. Then indeed, on the Day of Resurrection you will be raised. (23:14)

We surely created you from dust, then from a drop of sperm, then from a clinging clot, then from a lump of flesh, [both] complete and incomplete, in order that We may make clear to you [Our power and creativity]. And We lodge whomever We will in the wombs for a specified term; then We bring you forth as a child, then [develop you] that you may reach your maturity. And among you is the one who is taken [early] in death, and among you is the one who is returned to the most abject [old] age so that, after knowledge, he knows nothing. (22:-5)

As the Creator, **God creates whatever He wills, and He is the Knowing, the Omnipotent** (30:54; also 24:45, 42:49). Moreover, as the Guardian and Sustainer of His creation, He knows the purpose and directs the destiny of all things, down to the most minute particle — seeing, hearing, protecting, guiding and caring for all of His creatures, including each one of ourselves, mankind.

But we must not be simplistic enough to suppose that God's creation includes only those creatures that inhabit our planet Earth, on which alone there is such an immense variety of species. The fact is that we human beings are such insignificant, limited creatures that even with the help of the most sophsticated scientific instruments, we can know only about the most minute portion of God's endlessly vast and complex creation. For that creation includes both the part that we can perceive or observe through our senses or technology, as well as the unseen, spiritual realm and all it contains, including two species of invisible beings about whom we will speak shortly, angels and jinn.

The invisible, spiritual world is known as ***al-Ghayb***, the Unseen. Impressive as the material universe is in its complexity and majesty, we may assume that the spiritual realm is infinitely more awe-inspiring and complex, if we could but perceive. And this spiritual realm continually interacts and interfaces in a subtle manner with the visible, material world, known as ***al-Shahadah***, meaning the realm of what can be witnessed.

As we know, the visible realm includes billions of huge stars or suns, planets and other celestial bodies floating along in space so vast that no one can imagine any limit for it, among which are those that are essential to human life: —

> **And the sun runs [on its course] toward its resting-place [at sunset]. That is the determination of the Almighty, the Knowing. And the moon — We have determined phases for it until it returns like an old curved date stalk. It is not allowable for the sun to reach the moon, nor does the night overtake the day, and each swims in an orbit.** (36:38-40)

However, God Most High did not simply initiate creation, setting off the "Big Bang," and then withdraw from His role as creator and sustainer, while it all somehow evolved on its own into whatever it was to become. On the contrary, God ever continues the work of creating and sustaining, shaping, evolving and supporting what He has made. The words,

> **Have they not considered how God begins creation and then repeats it? Indeed, that is easy for God** (29:19);
>
> **Each day He is at His business** (49:29);

inform us that He is ever active and involved with His creation, not a tired or a *re*tired God, but the all-aware, ever-creative Lord empowering all things, planning, willing, originating, bringing into fruition, and guiding each atom to the specific destiny He has decreed for it.

In the Holy Qur'an, God Most High informs us that He created seven heavens, one above the other. These heavens belong in part to the visible world, that part of creation that we are able to observe and study, and in part to the unseen realm, and they include Paradise and its inhabitants. And as one minute part of the heavens, God created the earth, with all its natural features: its oceans and mountains, its spread-out plains and deserts and forests and poles, and its varied climates and natural phenomena: wind and clouds and lightning, life-giving rain and snow, and destructive floods, storms, earthquakes and volcanoes. And He created seven Hells, with their eternal fires, as well.

God Most High then populated this earth with millions of plant and animal species, mostly in complementary pairs. As we saw in the verses cited earlier, God Himself informs us of the origin of life from water (21:30, 24:45), confirming the fact that living creatures' bodies are composed largely of water, upon which they depend for the sustaining of their life. Summarizing the whole spectrum of what He has created as it relates to us, mankind, He says:

> **Indeed, God is the splitter of the grain and the date seed. He brings forth the living from the dead and brings forth the dead from the living. That is God, so how are you deluded? Cleaver of the daybreak, and He has made the night for rest and the sun and the moon for calculation. That is the determination of the Almighty, the Knowing. And it is He who has appointed the stars for you, that you may be guided by them through the darknesses of the land and sea; We have detailed the signs for a people who know. It is He who produced you from a single soul and [granted you] a place of settlement and lodgement; We have detailed the signs for a people who understand. And it is He who sends down rain from the sky, and We produce thereby the growth of all things. Then We produce thereby verdure, from which We bring forth grains arranged in layers. And among the palm trees, from their emerging fruit, are clusters hanging low, and gardens of grapevines and olives and pomegranates, similar yet varied. Look at the fruit of it when it bears and [at] its ripening. Indeed, in that are signs for a people who believe.** (6:95-99)

REFERENCES: Qur'an: The seven heavens: 2:29; 23:17; 65:12; 67:3; 71:15; 78:12. Hell: 2:39, 81, 257; 3:116; 4:14; 9:63, 68, 109; 10:7-8, 27; 22:72; 27:90; 32:20; 33:64; 35:36; 38:27; 47:12; 52:13; 57:19; 64:10; 66:6; 70:15; 72:23; 83:16; 98:6; 102:5-7 and dozens of others. Natural phenomena: 2:22, 164; 6:99; 7:57; 13:12-13; 14:32; 15:19, 22; 16:10, 65; 20:53; 24:43-45; 25:54; 27:60-61; 30:24, 46, 48; 35:27-28; 39:21; 41:39; 42:32-34; 43:11; 77:27; 78:14-16; 80:25-32 and many others. Living creatures: 13:3; 35:11; 36:36; 42:11; 43:12; 45:4; 50:7, 9-11; 51:49; 53:45; 71:14, 17; 78:8.

4. Angels

Praise be to God, Creator of the heavens and the earth, who made the angels messengers having wings, two or three or four. He adds to creation as He wills. Indeed, God is powerful over all things. (35:1)

Among all living beings about whom God Most High has informed us, He granted minds and intelligence to three species: ourselves, mankind, and angels and jinn. And belief in angels is the second article of faith in Islam.

Angels, who are created of light, belong to the unseen world. Neither male nor female, they are spiritual beings who have no physical needs or functions; they do not eat, sleep, marry or reproduce. Although God endowed them with intelligence, they do not possess freedom of will or choice. Rather, in complete obedience to the holy Will and command of their Lord, they worship and serve Him in countless different ways.

At each moment, innumerable angels are worshipping and glorifying their Lord, the Praised and Exalted. Prophet Muhammad (S), whose spiritual vision enabled him to see that which others cannot see and who often relayed information about the workings of angels, stated that there is not a space equal to four fingers in the seven heavens which is not occupied by angels prostrating to God (*Mishkat*, 406[R]).

> **To Him belongs whosomever is in the heavens and the earth. And those before Him are not prevented from His worship by arrogance, nor do they tire. They glorify Him night and day, and do not slacken.** (21:19-20)

Angels have numerous other functions, acting as their Lord's agents throughout the visible and unseen realms of His creation, for **God chooses emissaries from among angels and from among mankind** (22:75). He created angels for His pure worship and service, putting them in charge of revelation, natural places and events, and whatever else He wills. Although by God's command angels may sometimes appear in human form, ordinarily they are invisible to us. However, the task of some angels is to guard us humans, pray for God's forgiveness and mercy upon us, and help and support us.

God Most High has informed us about the identities and roles of the following individual angels:

(1) **Gabriel** (Arabic, Jibril) is the angel who conveys his Lord's revelations and messages to His prophets and to others whom He wills. God refers to Gabriel (A) in the Qur'an variously as **the spirit** (70:4; 78:38; 97:4); **Our spirit** (19:17); **the holy spirit** (2:87, 253; 5:110/113; 16:102); and **the trustworthy spirit** (26:193).

It was Gabriel (A) who came to Prophet Muhammad (S) while he was in seclusion in Hira' cave near Mecca, conveying to him the first revelation of the Qur'an and informing him that he was the messenger of God. Gabriel (A) continued to convey the verses of the Qur'an to Muhammad (S) during the next twenty-two years until its completion. He also reviewed the entire Qur'an with the Holy Prophet (S) each year during the month of Ramadan.

Numerous *ahadith* make it clear that Gabriel (A) was very often with the Prophet (S), instructing him in his faith. And once, as is mentioned in a well-known *hadith*, when Gabriel (A) suddenly appeared in the form of a man to question and instruct Muhammad (S), he was also seen by a number of the Prophet's Companions (*Bukhari*, 6:300; *Muslim*, 1).

(2) **Michael (Mika'il),** who is mentioned once in the Qur'an, is the angel in charge of safety, fertility, rain and provision.

(3) **Israfil** is the angel who will blow the trumpet heralding the Day of Resurrection.

(4) **'Azra'il** is the Angel of Death who takes people's souls when their allotted span on earth is finished.

(5 and 6) **Munkar** and **Nakir** are two awesome angels who come to the soul after death to question it concerning its beliefs and faith.

(7) **Ridwan** is the angel who guards the gates of Paradise.

(8) **Malik** is angel who is in chage of Hell.

(9 and 10) **Al-Kiraman Katibin, the Honored Scribes**, are two recording angels who accompany each human being. One of them records our good deeds and the other our evil deeds, to be presented before God Most High in a complete, unalterable record on the Day of Judgment. (Further details concerning the recording angels and their manner of inscribing our deeds is presented in Appendix C.)

Besides the recording angels, two other angels, one in front and one behind us, protect us from harm, except as God wills. Thus, each of us has four angels with us at all times, a different set for daytime and for nighttime.[7]

In addition to these, there are angels who are entrusted with the development of the fetus in the womb (*Bukhari*, 8:543-:544; *Muslim*, 6392). The angels of *dhikr*, the remembrance of God, go in search of those who have gathered to remember Him, and when they find such a group, they report it to their Lord, who grants forgiveness to those who are among them (*Bukhari*, 8:417).

---

[7]This is mentioned in *Bukhari*, 1:530, 1:621, and *Muwatta*, 19.24.85. It is these unseen angels, as well as their fellow-worshippers, whom Muslims greet when they turn their faces to the right and the left at the conclusion of their prayers, offering them the Islamic greeting of peace, "*As-salamu 'alaikum wa rahmat-Allah* — peace be upon you and God's mercy."

Yet other angels give glad tidings to believers at the time of their death and resurrection (41:30-32). There are also beneficent angels who welcome the souls of the righteous to Paradise (13:23; 16:32; 21:10) and angels who are its custodians (39:71). At the same time, in Hell there are terrible angels of punishment who carry out their Lord's orders and never fail in their appointed task (66:6; 74:30-31; 96:18). And besides these, there may be many other ranks and functions for angels which we do not know, for indeed, **No one knows the hosts of your Lord except Him** (74:31).

REFERENCES: Belief in angels as an article of faith: Qur'an, 2:177, 285; 4:136. The worship and obedience of angels: Qur'an, 2:34; 4:172; 7:206; 13:13; 15:8; 16:49; 19:64; 21:19-20; 22:75; 25:25; 37:164-166; 39:75. The responsibilities of angels toward humans: Qur'an, 3:124-125; 8:9; 13:11; 16:2; 25:25; 33:43; 41:30-3; 42:5; ***Bukhari***, 1:530, 8:594; ***Muslim***, 830, 6226, 6392, 6590; Keller/*R*, w22.2. Individual angels: Keller/*R*, u3.3. Gabriel: Qur'an, 2:97-98; 66:4; also 53:4 ff, 81:19-21; ***Bukhari***, 1:2-3, 1:345, 1:5, 1:794, 4:431, 4:827, 6:448, 6:7, 6:300, 6:378, 6:520, 8:220, 9:547, 9.608; ***Muslim***, 0333, 1694; ***Muwatta***, 5.4.7; ***Mishkat***, 6056; Keller/*R*, x126. Michael: Qur'an, 2:98; ***Bukhari***, 1:794; ***Muslim***, 1694; ***Mishkat***, 6056; Keller/*R*, x239. Israfil, the Blower of the Trumpet of the Last Day: Qur'an, 6:73; 18:99; 20:10; 23:102; 27:87; 36:51; 39:68; 50:20; 69:13; 74:8; 78:18; Keller/*R*, x197. 'Azra'il, the Angel of Death: Qur'an, 4:97; 6:61, 93; 8:50; 16:28; 32:11; 47:27; 79:1; ***Muslim***, 5920; ***Mishkat***, 162; Keller/*R*, x97. Munkar and Nakir, the Questioning Angels: ***Bukhari***, 2:422, 2:450; ***Mishkat***, 130; Keller/*R*, g5.6(1), v2.2, w32.1(1 and 2), x270, x281. Ridwan, the Guardian of Paradise: Keller/*R*, x305. Malik, the Keeper of Hell: Qur'an, 43:77; ***Bukhari***, 4:462, 4:608, 9:171a; ***Muslim***, 328; Keller/*R* x229. The Honored Scribes and their recording of deeds: Qur'an, 10:61; 17:14, 71; 19:79; 21:94; 23:62; 36:12; 43:77, 80; 45:29; 50:17-21; 69:19, 25; 83:7-9, 18-21; 84:7-12; ***Bukhari***, 4:462, 4:608, 9:171a; ***Muslim***, 233, 235, 328, 7079; ***Muwatta***, 15.7.25; ***Mishkat***, 1559-1560, 1579.

5. JINN

We created the jinn previously from scorching fire. (15:27)
He created the jinn from a smokeless flame of fire. (55:15)

The third order of intelligent beings about whom we are informed are jinn, whom God created from fire. Belief in jinn is obligatory in Islam.

The word "jinn" comes from the Arabic verb "*janna*," which means "to be concealed, covered or veiled from sight," for jinn belong to that category of beings known as *al-jinnah*, which also includes the angels, meaning those who are concealed from human senses.

Jinn are of both sexes and they reproduce. Together with intelligent minds, God granted them free will. Therefore, like humans, jinn have the ability to choose to obey or disobey Him; they are accountable for their deeds and will pass on to the Eternal Life together with humans. Some jinn are good — in fact, some are Muslims (46:29-31; 72:1-32) — while others are evil and rebellious. Satan or Iblis is the chief of the evil jinn or devils.

The Prophet (S) said, "With each of you there is a companion from the jinn and a companion from the angels" (*Muslim*, 6757, 6759), meaning that each human being is accompanied throughout his or her life by a personal satan, as well as by personal angels. Jinn can take various forms and can sometimes be seen or heard. Often understood as spirits, demons or extraterrestrial beings, jinn may have extensive, although covert dealings with human beings.

And that brings us to how we, humankind, began and where we fit into the total scheme of things. We therefore begin the story of the first man, who was also the first prophet — Adam, may God's peace and blessings be upon him.

REFERENCES: Qur'an: 6:112, 130; 7:12, 38, 179; 11:119; 32:13; 38:76; 46:18, 67; 72:15; 114:4-6. Commentaries: Tabari/*C*, I:212; Tabari/*H*, I:252; Ibn Kathir/*T*, 15:27, 55:15; Asad/*Q*, 6:fn. 86, 15:fn. 25, 37:fn. 67, 55:fn. 6, Appen. III, pp. 994-995; Keller/*R*, o8.7(18), w22.1-2.

PART TWO: ADAM (A)

6. IBLIS

And [mention, O Muhammad,] when We said to the angels, "Prostrate to Adam," then they prostrated, except Iblis. He was of the jinn, and he deviated from the command of his Lord. (18:50)

In approaching the story of Adam, God's peace and blessings be upon him, it is important to keep in mind that it has two aspects, both equally important. While it is firstly the actual life-story of the first man, it is at the same time an allegory concerning mankind's role, place in the scheme of creation and ultimate destiny, as is clear from God's saying,

We certainly created you [all], then formed you. Then We said to the angels, "Prostrate to Adam," whereupon they prostrated, except Iblis. He was not among those who prostrated. (7:11)

Adam's story begins in the spiritual world, in the timeless, spaceless realm of God and His angels. And while Adam (A) is obviously the most important character in his own story, there is another character who is also of great importance — **Iblis** (Ib-*lees*), the arch-villain.

The name Iblis is derived from the Arabic verb *ablasa*, meaning "to despair, feel remorse and grieve." However, the real name of the being known as Iblis was 'Azazil or al-Harith. And as the Qur'anic passage cited above informs us, although Iblis was present among the angels in Paradise, he was actually of the jinn.

The classical Qur'anic commentators have given differing explanations of the nature of Iblis, his relationship to both the jinn and to the angels, and the reason for his presence among the angels. From among the various interpretations of the early Qur'anic commentators, we present what seems to us the most authoritative view from our trusted mentor and guide to the Holy Qur'an, 'Abdullah ibn 'Abbas (R).

As we saw earlier, God Most High states that **He created the jinn from a smokeless flame of fire [*marijin min nar*]** (55:15), which is said to mean the fire at the tip of the flame when it flares up, and also that He **created the jinn previously from scorching fire [*nari samum*]** (15:27). From this, it is clear that jinn are created from both these different types of fire, perhaps some jinn from one kind and others from the other. However, God's saying that He created jinn from these two kinds of fire does not exclude the possibility that He may have created something besides jinn from them.

The interpretation of Ibn 'Abbas (R) is that among the angels there was an angelic tribe known as ***al-Hinn*** (sometimes given as ***al-Jinn***), who were the guardians of Paradise. These angels were created from the flames of fire, ***nari samum*** (15:27), a scorching fire different from the fire that we know. Apart from this tribe of angels, all the other angels were created from light, according to the Prophet's ***hadith:***

> The angels were created from light and the jinn were created from smokeless fire [***marijin min nar***], and Adam was created from what has been described to you [in the Qur'an]. (***Muslim***, 7134)

Iblis or 'Azazil was one of the noblest among the ***Hinn***, belonging to their most honored tribe. God Most High had granted him vast authority, making him a keeper of Paradise who ruled over the lower heaven as well as the earth. Among the angels, he was one of the most knowledgeable. Moreover, he was also one of the most zealous worshippers of his Lord.

Ibn 'Abbas (R) informs us that the jinn who were mentioned in the Qur'an as being created from smokeless fire were the first to live on the earth. They caused corruption upon it, shed blood and killed one other. God then sent 'Azazil against them with an army of angels who belonged to his own kind. The angelic troops killed and routed the wicked jinn, eventually banishing them to islands in the oceans and to mountains.

Because of his role in this, Iblis became haughty and self-important. He was so proud of his accomplishments that he considered himself to be better than anyone else. And while the angels had no idea of what was going on within the heart of Iblis, God Most High, who is absolutely **knowing of that which is within the breasts** (3:119, 154 and many others), knew it perfectly.

REFERENCES: Qur'an: 15:27; 18:50; 55:15. Commentaries: Tabari/*C*, I:212-215, 238-242; Tabari/*H*, I:249-257; Ibn Kathir/*T*, 15:27, 55:15; Ayoub/*Q*, I:73-76, 91-92; Keller/*R*, x321.

7. The New *Khalifah*

[Mention, O Muhammad,] when God said to the angels, "Indeed, I am going to appoint a *khalifah* on the earth." (2:30)

In the timeless, spaceless spiritual world, God Almighty, the Lord of the worlds and all the beings they contain, made an announcement to His angels. According to the interpretation of Ibn 'Abbas (R), this announcement was not made to all the angels but only to the angels who were with 'Azazil.

"Indeed, I am going to appoint a *khalifah* — meaning a successor, substitute, deputy or vicegerent — **on the earth"** (2:30), the Lord Almighty said. **"I am surely going to create a human being from ringing clay, coming from altered mud"** (15:28, 58:71).

Hearing this, the angels reacted with surprise and concern. **"Will You place on it someone who will cause corruption on it and shed blood,"** they asked their Lord, adding, **"while we extol Your glory with praise and sanctify You?"** (2:30).

The addressing of such a question to God Most High by the ever-obedient, perfectly devout angels may surprise us. The explanation of the classical Qur'anic commentators is that the angels had witnessed the earlier wicked behavior of the evil jinn upon the earth. Consequently, they were afraid that any successor to these jinn on earth would be as corrupt as their predecessors had been, while they themselves, the nearest beings to God, were constantly occupied with their Lord's praise, worship and service.

We may wonder how anyone, especially the holy angels, would presume to question God the Exalted. But He, the Subtle and All-Aware, knew with perfect knowledge that the angels neither intended to contradict Him nor to express enmity toward His new creation. Rather, out of their boundless love for Him and protectiveness of His sanctity and majesty, they were simply asking to be informed about what they did not understand. Hence, God Most High was not angry with His angels for expressing their uneasiness. Rather, He merely said to them, **"Indeed, I know what you do not know"** (2:30).

Now, what was this knowledge of the All-Knowing Lord's that His angels did not possess? It was, firstly, that although the angels claimed to be totally devoted to God, there was one among them who was not — 'Azazil or Iblis. Having no knowledge except what was imparted to them by God, the angels could have no idea that one of their Lord's most ardent worshippers and honored servants was now full of secret arrogance and conceit over his own importance and accomplishments. Therefore, one meaning of God's saying, **"Indeed, I know what you do not know,"** was, "I surely know the state of Iblis' heart, whereas you do not."

Secondly, the angels were certainly correct in their understanding that among this new species there would be those who would cause corruption on the earth and shed blood. Indeed, some would descend to an unprecedented level of wickedness, to become **the lowest of the low** (95:9). But what the angels did not know was that among them there would also be individuals of the highest standard of excellence: prophets and messengers, testifiers to the truth, martyrs, saints, ascetics, scholars, worshippers, and large numbers of righteous believers who would be true to their Lord, obedient to His commands, and who would live for His pleasure, their hearts trembling with fear and love of Him. And from among these would eventually come the most perfect of all creation, Muhammad (S), whose blessed seed would be carried in the body of the new ***khalifah*** and transmitted, through him, to the unbroken line of all the prophets to come.

REFERENCES: Qur'an: 2:30; 15:28; 58:71. Commentaries: Tabari/*C*, I:208-227; Tabari/*H*, I:254, 257-258, 266, 270-271; Ibn Kathir/*T*, 2:30; Ayoub/*Q*, I:73-77.

8. The Creation of Adam

Such is the Knower of the Unseen and the Witnessed, the Almighty, the Merciful, who perfected everything that He created, and who originated the creation of the human being from clay. Then He made his reproduction out of the extract of a lowly fluid. Then He proportioned him and breathed into him of His Spirit, and He made for you hearing and vision and hearts; little are you grateful. (32:6-9)

We certainly created the human being from ringing [potter's] clay [coming] from altered mud. (15:26)

Thus it was that God Almighty created the first man, Adam, peace be upon him, who is mentioned by name eighteen times in eight *surahs* or chapters of the Qur'an.

Several *ahadith* speak of the day and time of Adam's creation. "The best day on which the sun has risen is Friday," said the blessed Prophet (S), speaking out of his immense ocean of knowledge of the spiritual world. "On it, Adam was created and on it he was made to enter Paradise and on it he was cast out of it. And the last Hour will not take place on any day other than Friday"[8] (*Muslim*, 1857, 1856). And as is suitable for the most perfect and developed of God's creations, Adam (A) "was the last creation at the last hour of the hours of Friday, between afternoon and night" (*Muslim*, 6707; *Mishkat*, 1363, 1365) — that is, during the most blessed hour among the daylight hours of the week. The Prophet (S) also said:

> God created Adam from a handful [of clay] which He took from the whole of the earth; so the children of Adam are in accordance with the earth, some red, some white, some black, some a mixture, also smooth and rough, bad and good.[9] (*Mishkat*, Book I, "Faith," Chapter IV)

This clay, both sweet and salty, was brought to the Lord God at His command by the Angel of Death — or, according to some commentators, by Iblis.

---

[8]Another version adds, "On it, his [Adam's] repentance was accepted and on it he died, and on it the Last Hour will take place" (*Abu Dawud*, 1042).

[9]God says, **From it [the earth] We created you, and into it We shall return you, and from it We shall bring you forth another time** (20:55). In other verses not connected with the creation of Adam, He says, **It is He who created you from clay** (6:2); **He originated the creation of the human being from clay** (32:7); **We surely created them [human beings] from sticky clay** (37:11); **He created the human being from clay like pottery** (55:14). A detailed description of the stages of creation in the womb also begins with the words, **We certainly created the human being from an extract of clay** (23:12). This indicates that the substance or basic element of each human being's creation is the same, from Adam, who was created as a mature adult, without parents and without going through the stages of a fetus in the womb, up to all his descendants until the end of time.

The clay was of three kinds: thick, **sticky clay (*teen lazib*)** (37:11); **clay like pottery (*salsal*)** (55:14), meaning dry clay like unfired potter's clay, which makes a sound when struck; and **ringing [potter's] clay [coming] from altered black mud (*salsalin min hamaim masnun*)** (15:26, 28, 33), which is described as slimy mud. And from this clay God Most High created the first human being, Adam, so named, it is said, because he was made from the skin [*adim*] of the earth.[10]

Describing the creation of the first man, the blessed Prophet (S) said:

> God created Adam (A) in his [finished] form,[11] and his height was sixty cubits [about 41 meters or 126 feet]. . . .Therefore, all who enter Paradise will be of the form of Adam, and people have not stopped decreasing in stature up to the present. (*Bukhari*, 8:246, 4:543; also 4:544)

The Prophet (S) also said:

> When God had fashioned Adam in Paradise, He left him as He willed to leave him. Then Iblis went around him to see what he was. And when he found him hollow, he recognized that he had been created with an uncontrolled disposition. (*Muslim*, 6319)

Ibn 'Abbas (R) adds that when the angels passed by Adam (A), they were frightened of him. So was Iblis. He would kick the body, which would give forth a hollow sound like pottery makes when it is struck, according to God's words, **He created man from clay like pottery** (55:14). At that, Iblis would say, "What were you created for?" and, "You are nothing. You were not created for anything!"

Iblis repeatedly went in through Adam's mouth and came out through his posterior. Then he said to the angels, "Do not be afraid of this one, for your Lord is solid but this body is hollow." Then, addressing the lifeless body of Adam (A), he said, "If I am given power over you, I will destroy you utterly, but if you are given power over me, I will surely disobey you!"[12]

Having formed Adam (A), God Most High then **breathed into him from His Spirit** (32:9; also 15:29, 38:72). The breath came from the front of Adam's

---

[10]In the various languages of Muslims, such as Arabic, Farsi, Urdu and Turkish, the word *adam* and its variations denote a human being or man.

[11]The meaning of "in his [finished] form" (*suratihi*) is said to refer to the fact that Adam did not go through the stages of a fetus in the womb but was created in his mature, adult form by the divine act of creation.

[12]That is, at that point, Adam's body, made of clay, lay inert and lifeless, for the spirit had not yet been breathed into it. All that Iblis perceived, therefore, was a hollow clay form, through whose top and bottom openings he was able to come and go, suggesting lack of solidity and firmness, and consequently easy mastery.

head, says Ibn 'Abbas (R), and everything that flowed from it within his body became flesh and blood.

When the breathing reached his navel, Adam looked at his body and marveled at the beauty of what he saw. He then tried to get up but could not. This is the meaning of God's words, **The human being is created of haste** (21:37), meaning that he is restless and impatient in both pleasure and hardship.

Then, the Prophet (S) informs us, when the breath in his body was complete, Adam (A) sneezed and by divine inspiration he said, ***"Al-hamdu lil-Lahi Rabbi-l-'alamin*** — all praise is for God, Lord of the worlds,"[13] the words which were to become the opening verses of the Qur'an.

Thus, Adam (A) praised God by His own permission. And his Lord replied to him, *"Yarhamak-Allah, Adam* — may God have mercy on you"[14] (*Mishkat*, 4662).

The Prophet (S) further said that when God had created Adam, He said to him, "Go and greet that group of seated angels and then listen to what they will greet you with, for that will be your greeting and the greeting of your descendants."[15]

So Adam said to the angels, "*As-salamu 'alaikum* — peace be upon you all," to which they replied, "*As-salamu 'alaika wa rahmat-Allah* — peace be upon you, and God's mercy," thus adding, "*Wa rahmat-Allah* — and God's mercy," to the words of the original greeting (*Bukhari*, 8:246, 4:543; *Mishkat*, 4662).

And so it is up to this day. The greetings which Muslims exchange when they meet and part, and the blessings they invoke upon themselves and one

---

[13]The word "'***alamin***" (sing., "'***alam***," meaning "world") has several interpretations. One is that it refers to all the worlds, known and unknown, which God, who is able to actualize all possibilities, may have created. Another is that it indicates the world of all rational beings, or all beings other than God, or those things which are known. Ibn 'Abbas states that it refers to the communities of humans and jinn; other commentators add to this the community of angels (in this sense it is used, as in 29:10 and 29:28, to denote everything and everyone). The classical commentator al-Qurtubi states that "the people of every age are a world (***'alam***)." The expression "***Rabbi-l-'alamin*** — Lord of the worlds," occurs in the Qur'an forty-two times, underscoring the primal importance of the fact that, as the great Qur'anic commentator al-Razi put it, "The Lord of the words is the Lord of all things; things which can be seen and imagined and things which can neither be seen nor imagined" (Ayoub/*Q*, I:47-48; also Tabari/*C*, I:64).

[14]The Holy Prophet (S) instructed Muslims, when they sneeze, to praise God with the same words which Adam was instructed to say above, and those around the sneezer to respond as the angels responded to Adam (*Bukhari*, 8:242, 8:243, 8:244, 8:245).

[15]Thus, God says, **When you enter houses, give greetings of peace upon each other, a greeting from God, blessed and good** (24:61).

other when they sneeze, all originated with the first man, our grandfather Adam (A), to be taught by his noble descendant Muhammad (S) to his ***ummah*** or community in time to come.

REFERENCES: Qur'an: 6:2; 7:12; 15:26, 28-29, 33; 17:61; 20:55; 23:12; 32:6-9; 37:11; 38:71-72, 76; 55:14. Commentaries: Tabari/*C*, I:212-216, 222-223, 228; Tabari/*H*, I:258-266, 286-287; Ibn Kathir/*Q*, "Adam"; Ibn Kathir/*T*, 2:30; *Al-Hadith al-Qudsiyah*, pp. 96-99; Ayoub/*Q*, I:75.

9. ADAM IS TAUGHT THE NAMES

And He taught Adam the names, all of them. (2:31)

Then, as the above verse informs us, the Lord God taught His brand-new servant the names — all of them.

What were these "names" that God taught Adam (A)? Various interpretations have been given by the classical Qur'anic commentators. Some affirm that Adam was taught the names of the angels; others say that the names were the names of his own descendants, and still others that the names were the holy Names of God Himself, by which Adam (A) was granted knowledge of his Lord. But the majority of commentators, including Ibn 'Abbas (R), are of the opinion that the "names" were the names of all things, living and non-living.[16]

Like the faculty of free will, the ability to give names to things relates to a unique human attribute: the capacity to observe the characteristics of objects and then name them, and by this means to relate the parts to the whole. For example, when a little child is learning to talk, a parent points out to him a "tree," an "apple," or a red-colored object. In this way, the developing human being learns to recognize and classify all objects that look like trees or apples or that are colored red under the same headings. This is the basis of the ability to form concepts out of particularities, which in turn forms the basis of language — that is, the entire process of "naming" things.

And when God had imparted the "names" to Adam (A), **He presented them** — the things that had been named — **to the angels,** saying, **"Inform Me of the names of these, if you are truthful"** (2:31).

God's words, **"If you are truthful,"** convey a subtle meaning. According to the most widely accepted interpretation, they refer to the truthfulness of the angels' claim of possessing knowledge that their Lord's new creation would cause corruption and shed blood on the earth, and that they themselves, as the most obedient and worshipful among His creatures, were the most deserving of filling the role of His ***khalifah***. It is thus as if God were saying to them, **"Inform me of the names of these, if you are truthful** in your claim that if I place a deputy of another order of creation on earth, his descendants will spread corruption and shed blood."

[16]This interpretation can be inferred from the wording of 2:31. That is, God **taught Adam the names, all of them. Then He presented them** — obviously referring not to the names but to the things named — **to the angels and said, "Inform me of the names of these [things that were to be named,] if you are truthful"** (2:31).

This passage again demonsrates how gentle and forbearing God Most Gracious is with His servants. He did not reproach the angels for their previous question about His placing a creature on the earth whose race would become a source of trouble, nor did He tell them directly that they were wrong — although, according to His perfect knowledge, they partially were. For since the angels were unaware of the totality of their Lord's divine plan and knew nothing of what was to come, they were at a loss to grasp the divine wisdom behind the creation of this new being whom He was going to place on the earth. All they were able to see was that they themselves were the most suitable ones to be God's deputies and agents, and the potential of any other beings to whom He might entrust the earth for causing corruption and shedding blood.

Now, by teaching Adam the names of all things, God Almighty was indirectly replying to His angels' question. For how could they claim to understand what they had not been informed about — that is, God's plan for Adam and his kind — if their knowledge did not include the knowledge that He had granted to this new *khalifah*, by means of which he and his kind would administer the affairs of the earth? By means of this subtle lesson, God made clear to them that Adam possessed certain characteristics and knowledge which they themselves did not possess, and that, because of this, he would have a very different role and destiny from theirs. Yet the race of Adam would not be the angels' rivals in nearness to God, for He had created His angels to be always near Him, while human beings would have to constantly strive for that nearness.

In this indirect and subtle manner, then, God Most High informed His angels that He was aware of their concerns and reservations. At the same time, He reminded them of the limitations of their knowledge, while assuring them that, according to His infinite knowledge and wisdom, His creating Adam as His *khalifah* on the earth was entirely good, right and proper.

The angels now realized that they could know nothing about the divine wisdom behind the creation of this new being. But since their Lord had seen fit to create him and honor him, they accepted it with total acceptance and respected him as their Lord had commanded them to do. As obedient servants, their task would be to support the members of this new species and help them reach the high destiny for which God had created them — not as rivals, but side-by-side with themselves.

Accordingly, they now voiced their submission. **"Glory be to You!"** they said humbly. **"We have no knowledge except what You have taught us. Indeed, it is You who are the Knowing, the Wise!"** (2:32).

God Almighty then addressed His new creation. **"O Adam,"** He ordered, **"inform them of their names"** (2:33).

And Adam (A) did so. From the special knowledge that God had granted him, he told the angels the names of the things that God had presented to them, names which the angels themselves did not know. And when he had finished, the Lord Almighty again addressed the angels.

"Did I not tell you that indeed I know the Unseen of the heavens and the earth," He said, **"and I know what you disclose and what you conceal?"** (2:33).

Here, **"Did I not tell you?"** refers to God's previous words, **"Indeed, I know what you do not know"** (2:30). **"What you disclose"** is understood as referring to the angels' words concerning the corruption the new *khalifah* would make on earth. **"What you conceal"** has been variously interpreted as referring to the angels' secret sense of the superiority of their essence over Adam's because of their purity and sanctity, or, again, to the arrogance and envy in the heart of Iblis which was concealed from the angels. In a broader sense, it may also refer to God's perfect knowledge, which the angels did not share, of the final destiny of His creation, in which Adam and his descendants would play a major role.

REFERENCES: Qur'an: 2:30-33. Commentaries: Tabari/*C*, I:229-238; Tabari/*H*, I:266-272; Ibn Kathir/*T*, 2:31-33; Ayoub/*Q*, I:79-81.

10. THE COMMAND TO HONOR ADAM

We certainly created you, then formed you. Then We said to the angels, "Prostrate to Adam," whereupon they prostrated, except Iblis. He was not among those who prostrated. (7:11)

When God Almighty had announced to the angels — those angels who were with Iblis, not those who were in the heavens, according to the interpretation of Ibn 'Abbas (R) — that He was creating a human being, He followed His announcement with an order:

"Then, when I have formed him and breathed into him of My Spirit, fall down in prostration to him" (15:29, 38:72). And, as their Lord commanded, **the angels prostrated, all of them together, except Iblis. He refused to be among those who prostrated** (15:30-31, 2:34, 17:61, 18:50, 20:116), and **was arrogant and became among the disbelievers** (38:74, 2:34).

Now, the Arabic word for "prostration" is "*sujud*" or "*sajdah*". Muslims prostrate in their prayers, bowing down to the ground as the highest expression of adoration, respect and humility toward their Lord, the Most High. But here we see that God Himself ordered His angels to prostrate to a being whom He had created.

What was the meaning of that order? Obviously it was not so that the angels might worship Adam (A), for no one may be worshipped except the Creator of all things, may His glory be exalted. Rather, the angels were commanded to prostrate as a mark of respect to the one whom their Lord in His infinite wisdom had seen fit to create as their superior and whom they were destined to help, support and serve. This understanding is borne out in *ahadith* which we will cite later, in which Adam (A) is mentioned as the father of mankind, whom God created with His own Hand, into whom He breathed from His Spirit, to whom He ordered the angels to prostrate, and to whom He taught the names of all things (*Bukhari*, 6:236, 9:507, 9:532C).

But this respect was not only for Adam, the first human individual who was now before the angels. As is clear from God's words, **We created you and then formed you**, using the collective plural "you," followed by the words, **Then We said to the angels, "Prostrate to Adam"** (7:11), it was for all of us, the entire race of humankind. That is, the angels were to prostrate to Adam, the Original Man, as the prototype and representative of mankind, who carried within himself the seeds of all his descendants-to-come.[17]

---

[17]See the *hadith* cited on pages 80-81 concerning God's bringing forth and addressing the descendants of Adam.

From God's order to the beings closest to Him, His holy angels, to show such respect to Adam (A), we can understand how greatly our Lord has honored and respected all of us, mankind, about whom He says,

> **We have certainly honored the children of Adam . . . and preferred them over much of what We have created with [special] preference** (17:70).

Why? we may ask We can understand why the angels were asked to respect Adam (A), whom God created in such a unique manner. *But why should God, the Creator and Lord of all things in existence, the Glorious, the Exalted, the Holy, give honor and respect to such limited, finite, faulty creatures as human beings?*

The answer is contained in the words of God Himself: **"I . . . breathed into him of My Spirit"** (15:29, 38:72-73). It is further clarified by the Prophet's saying,

> When God created Adam and his descendants, the angels said, "O Lord, You created them to eat and drink and marry and travel. Therefore, make this world for them and the Hereafter for us." God Most High said, "Shall I make the one whom I created with My Hands and into whom I breathed from My Spirit [Adam] like one whom I created by 'Be!' [that is, the angels] and he was?" (*Mishkat*, 662W)

This *hadith* informs us that, while the angels were created by the divine word of command, "Be," God Most High created Adam (A) in a unique and special manner, peculiar to the human species.[18] The secret of our uniqueness therefore lies in the fact that we carry something of our Lord's divine Spirit within us — our souls. No matter how wrong, sinful or even terrible our actions may be, this eternal divine spark is nonetheless alive within us. Even though we may deny it, ignore it, violate it or try to crush it, nothing can ever take it from us, since it relates to our essence. Our Lord Himself is its Creator and He, the **Guardian over all things** (11:57), protects it.

---

[18] The following *ahadith* (and several others of similar meaning, reported in various *hadith* collections) confirm this uniqueness of the creation of the human being:

> Indeed, each one of you is assembled in his mother's womb for forty days. Then he becomes a clot for the like of that [period]; then he becomes a lump for the like of that. Then God sends an angel to him with four words, whereupon he writes his deeds and his life-term and his provision and [whether he will be] wretched or happy. Then the spirit is breathed into him. (*Bukhari*, 4:549, 8:593; *Muslim*, 6390)

> God assigns an angel to the womb and he [the angel] says, "O my Lord, a sperm drop! O my Lord, a clot! O my Lord, a lump!" Then, if God wishes to complete its creation, he [the angel] says, "O my Lord, a male or a female? Wretched or happy? What will its provision be? What will its term of life be?" So that is written [for it while it is] in its mother's womb. (*Bukhari*, 8:594)

This, then, is the meaning of God's command to the angels to prostrate to Adam (A): respect for a being who was created in a special manner, who carried a special light within himself, and who, as a result, would also have a very special destiny. This fact should give us an idea of how much we must respect one another, and also how much we must respect our own selves.

REFERENCES: Qur'an: 2:34; 7:11; 15-29-31; 17:61; 18:50; 20:116; 38:73-74. Commentaries: Tabari/*C*, I:213, 215, 222-223, 238-243; Tabari/*H*, I:263-266; Ibn Kathir/*T*, 2:34, 7:11, 38:71-85; Ayoub/*Q*, I:76.

11. Iblis Rebels Against God

And [mention, O Muhammad,] when We said to the angels, "Prostrate to Adam," and they prostrated, except Iblis. He refused and was arrogant, and became of the deniers. (2:34)

God Most High, the All-Powerful, the Glorious, the Majestic, had given an order, and all those who heard it had obeyed without question except one among them.[19] When this occurred, therefore, the previously unsuspecting angels became aware of what had been concealed in Iblis' heart.

We may wonder how anyone could anyone be given a direct order by God Almighty, the Creator of all things, and have the unspeakable boldness to reject it. But Iblis was among those whom the All-Wise Lord had granted free will,[20] and God does not cancel out an attribute that He has granted by compelling those to whom He has granted it to obey His orders. Moreover, envy,

---

[19]God's command to the angels to prostrate to Adam and Iblis' refusal are mentioned seven times in the Qur'an in the following verses:

> **We certainly created you, then formed you. Then We said to the angels, "Prostrate to Adam," whereupon they prostrated, except Iblis. He was not among those who prostrated.** (7:11)
>
> **And when We said to the angels, "Prostrate to Adam," they prostrated, except Iblis. He refused.** (20:116)
>
> **"Then, when I have formed him and breathed into him from My Spirit, fall down in prostration to him." Then the angels prostrated, all of them together, except Iblis. He refused to be among those who prostrated.** (15:29-31)
>
> **When We said to the angels, "Prostrate to Adam," they prostrated, except Iblis. He refused and was arrogant, and became of the deniers.** (2:34)
>
> **"Then, when I have formed him and breathed into him from My Spirit, fall down in prostration to him." Then the angels prostrated, all of them together, except Iblis. He was arrogant and became of the deniers.** (38:72-74)
>
> **And when We said to the angels, "Prostrate to Adam," they postrated, except Iblis. He said, "Am I to prostrate to one whom You created from clay?"** (17:61)
>
> **And when We said to the angels, "Prostrate to Adam," they prostrated, except Iblis. He was of the jinn and he deviated from the command of his Lord.** (18:50)

It will be seen that in each of these passages, Iblis' refusal is followed by a different qualifying statement. Taken together, these statements form a series, each a little stronger than the previous one, describing Iblis' behavior, attitude and the reason for his disobedience

[20]Previously we mentioned the difference of opinion among the early Qur'anic commentators concerning the nature of Iblis: whether he was a true jinn (based on God's saying, **He was of the jinn** [18:50]); an angel (based on the words, **The angels prostrated, all of them together, except Iblis** [15:30-31, 38:73-74]); or an angel-jinn (according to the opinion of Ibn 'Abbas). But since angels, unlike humans and jinn, do not possess the attribute of free will, Iblis' deliberate decision to rebel against God's order suggests a major difference between his nature and that of an angel.

pride, arrogance and enmity are very powerful emotions, so powerful that, in the case of Iblis, they enabled him to defy his Lord's command — deliberately, intentionally and with full knowledge of the consequences.

Now, since God Almighty plans and decrees all things down to the minutest detail, He obviously knew that Iblis would disobey His order and all that would follow as a result. And although He was perfectly aware of everything that was going within the heart of that rebellious servant, nevertheless, in His infinite divine justice, He gave Iblis a hearing, a chance to explain his behavior, to say whatever he wished and to repent, even after his act of deliberate disobedience.

"O Iblis," God said, **"what is with you that you were not among those who prostrated? What prevented you from prostrating, when I commanded you, to what I created with My Hands? Were you arrogant, or were you of the self-exalted?"** (7:12, 15:32 and 38:75).[21]

However, instead of showing remorse, Iblis attempted to justify his blatant rebellion against the divine command. **"Am I to prostrate to one whom You created from clay?"** (17:61), he demanded impertinently. **"I am better than he! You created me from fire, while You created him from clay"** (7:12, 38:76), he went on, giving vent to the fiercely negative emotions which filled his being. **"It is not for me to prostrate to a human being whom You created from** mere **ringing clay** derived **from altered mud!"** (15:33).

"Then go down from it" – that is, Paradise — **"for it is not for you to be arrogant in it. Then go forth! Indeed, you are of the debased"** (7:13), God Almighty commanded. **"Go out of it, blameworthy and cast out! Whoever follows you among them, I will surely fill Hell with you, all together** (7:18). **Indeed, you are damned, and My curse will be surely upon you until the Day of Recompense!"** (15:34-35, 38:77-78).

"Do You see this one whom You have honored above me?" (17:62), Iblis retorted, shamelessly trying to shift the blame for his sin onto his exalted Lord. A plan then came to his mind by which he could avenge himself upon Adam's descendants up to the end of time.

"My Lord," he said, **"then defer me until the day they are resurrected** (7:14, 15:36, 38:79). **If You defer me until the Day of Resurrection, I will surely destroy his descendants, except a few!"** (17:62).

With what may seem like surprising readiness, God Most High granted Iblis' request, saying, **"Then indeed You are of those deferred until the Day of the well-known time"** (38:80-81, 15:37-38; also 7:15).

---

[21]Please see "Qur'anic References – Adam" at the end of this story for a complete citation of these and other verses.

"**My Lord,**" Iblis went on unabashedly, "**because you have let me fall into error, I will surely make evil and disobedience attractive for them on the earth, and, by Your might, I will surely mislead them all, except Your sincere servants among them!**" (7:16, 15:39-40, 38:82-83).

"**This**" — the way of singlemindedness and commitment of the sincere — "**is the straight path to Me,**" God Almighty declared. "**Indeed, My faithful servants — You will have no authority over them, except those who follow you among the misguided. And Hell is surely the promised place for them all!**" (15:41-43).

But the prospect of Hell did not move Iblis, inflamed by the heady prospect of destroying the race of the one on whose account he had gone astray. "**I will certainly lie in wait for them on Your straight path,**" he vowed to his Lord. "**Then I will come upon them from the front of them and from behind them, and at their right and at their left, and You will not find most of them thankful!**" (7:16-17). And, he boasted, "**I will surely take an appointed share of Your servants, and I will mislead them and will arouse desires in them, and I will command them so they will slit the ears of cattle**[22] **and will command them so they will alter God's creation**" (4:118-119).

"**Go!**" the Lord God ordered. "**And whoever follows you among them, indeed, Hell will be your recompense, an ample recompense! And incite whomever you can among them with your voice, and assault them with your cavalry and your foot-soldiers, and become their partner in wealth and children, and make promises to them. But,**" He added, warning all mankind to come, "**Satan promises them nothing but delusion. Indeed, You will have no authority over My servants**" — those who would be faithful and steadfast. "**And your Lord is sufficient as Guardian**" (17:64-65).

And God Almighty banished Iblis from Paradise, saying, "**Then this is the the truth, and the truth I do speak — that I will surely fill Hell with you and those of them who follow you, all together!**" (38:84-85).

The transition from the ardent worshipper and teacher of the angels, excelling in divine knowledge and the praise of his Lord, to the abased, accursed Tempter of mankind was now complete. Stripped of all the high honors and ranks he had been granted, accursed and outlawed, Iblis is known to us as Satan or Shaytan, the Evil One, the Devil, the leader of the forces of evil whom we call demons, devils or evil ones — that is, those who intice and incite God's servants to wrong-doing and disobedience to Him.

REFERENCES: Qur'an: 4:118-120; 7:12-18; 15:32-43; 17:61-65; 38:75-85. Commentaries: Tabari/*C*, I:213, 216, 223, 238-243, 245; Tabari/*H*, I:255-257, 263-265, 272-273; Ayoub/*Q*, I:92, Asad/*Q*, 4:fn. 141.

---

[22]The pre-Islamic pagan Arabs used to dedicate certain of their cattle to their idols by cutting off or slitting the animal's ears, after which the animal was regarded as sacred.

12. Eve

It is He who created you from a single soul and from it made its mate, that he might find tranquility in her. (7:189, 39:6)

Thus it was that, while Iblis was cast out of Paradise, an abode filled with blessings and favors beyond imagination, our forefather Adam (A) was settled in it. His sacred soul dwelt there amidst divine realities and endless beauties in his Lord's holy Presence. Everything he could desire, every kind of pure pleasure and wholesome satisfaction was his. He did not experience hunger or thirst, fatigue or boredom, cold or heat, but was always comfortable and in pleasure. He had no responsibilities or burdens, and all that he desired was instantly provided without his having to make the slightest effort. There was no suffering, pain or sadness, no evil or ugliness or anything unpleasant which could annoy or disturb his being.

But, says Ibn 'Abbas (R), Adam (A) went about in the Garden alone, the only one of his kind. There was a sort of emptiness within him as if something were missing, and his heart yearned for a thing that he was unable to name to make himself complete.

That yearning had been put into the heart of the first man by God Himself — the longing for a mate of his own species who would fulfill the deep need for completeness that is an inherent part of our humanity, by means of which another part of the Lord's great, wise plan would be fulfilled.

Then Adam (A) fell asleep, Ibn 'Abbas (R) continues. And when he awoke, he found a woman, whom God had created from his rib, sitting beside his head.[23]

"Who are you?" he asked her.

"A woman," she replied.

"Why were you created?"

"That you might find tranquility in me," she replied.

---

[23]The Holy Prophet (S) said, "I advise you to be good to women, for they have been created from a rib, and the most curved part of the rib is its upper portion. Consequently, if you try to straighten it you will break it and if you leave it it will continue to remain curved. Therefore, I advise you to be good to women" (*Bukhari*, 4.548, 7:114). This is understood as meaning that woman's nature has its particularities, which are different from those of men. Consequently, if a husband tries to change his wife's nature by force, relations between them will become strained, resulting in a rupture of their relations, while if he accepts her as having a nature which differs from his own, they can live together in harmony.

Then, to test the extent of Adam's knowledge, the angels asked him, "What is her name, O Adam?"

"Hawwa," he replied — that is, "Eve."

"Why is she called Hawwa?" the angels asked him.

"Because she was created from something living [*hayy*]," Adam (A) replied, meaning that she had been created from his own living self.

REFERENCES: Tabari/*C*, I:245; Tabari/*H*, I:273; Ayoub/*Q*, I:82.

13. The Forbidden Tree

Then Satan whispered to him, saying, "O Adam, shall I direct you to a tree of immortality and a dominion that will never decay?" (20:120)

Thus it was that Adam (A) and Eve began their life together in the blessed Garden. Everything their souls could desire was instantly theirs without any effort on their part. As innocent as new-born babes, they knew nothing about sin or evil. It did not occur to them that they were being tested by their Lord, and that soon their condition would change dramatically.

God Most High, however, warned Adam (A) of the vulnerability of their position. **"O Adam,"** He said, **"dwell, you and your wife, in Paradise, and eat from it in abundance, as you will. But,"** He said, imposing only a single condition for their continuance in their present state, **"do not come near this Tree, lest you be among the wrong-doers"** (2:35; 7:19).

What was that Tree (***shajarah***)? The early commentators differed widely concerning it. Since the word "***shajarah***" denotes anything having a stalk, some considered it a plant rather than a tree; in the opinion of Ibn 'Abbas, it was the wheat plant. Be that as it may, what is important is to understand the properties of this plant or tree.

One of the early Qur'anic commentators, Abu al-'Aliyah, says, "It was a tree which moved the bowels of whoever ate it. It was not seemly that there should have been excrement in Paradise" (Tabari/C, I:253). This is supported by the Prophet's statement that in Paradise there will be no urination or defecation (***Muslim***, 6798). From this, it may be inferred none of the food of Paradise, apart from the fruit of this Tree, produced bodily waste. In other words, that one Tree, among all the plants of Paradise, possessed earthly rather than heavenly characteristics. Consequently, eating its fruit would lead to the process of digestion and elimination, and, because food is needed for sexual activity, it may also have had a connection with the first sexual desire.

God Most High also issued a second warning, designed to make the new couple aware of the existence and enmity of Iblis. **"O Adam,"** the Lord God said, **"indeed, this is an enemy to you and your wife. Therefore, do not let him oust the two of you from Paradise so that you become miserable. It is surely granted to you not be hungry therein or unclothed, or to be thirsty therein or affected by heat"**[24] (20:117-119).

---

[24]These words refer to the basic needs of humankind for food, drink, clothing and shelter. God's warning thus implies that, while these were quite perfectly provided for Adam and Eve in Paradise, disobedience to the divine command would result in their having to provide all these necessities for themselves through their own efforts.

No warning could have been more clear or direct. But the expelled, debased Iblis had formulated a plan — a quite simple one, in fact. Having noted that Adam was hollow inside, he had already drawn the conclusion that he could be easily overcome and ruined. And Iblis now employed the same keen intelligence he had used previously for good actions to destroy his new enemy.

Up to that time, it is said, Adam and Eve were totally unaware of their private parts, which were concealed by a covering like fingernails or horn. However, Satan knew of the existence of these parts from reading the books of the angels. His intention was therefore to trick the two into eating the fruit of the Tree, resulting in their becoming aware of what had been concealed from them and thus losing their heavenly innocence. Disobeying God would render them unfit to dwell in Paradise, forever putting an end to their high station and blissful life, and their Lord would cast them out, Iblis assumed, as utterly disgraced and accursed as himself.

Ibn 'Abbas (R) and other Companions of the Prophet (S) inform us that when God said to Adam, **"O Adam, dwell, you and your wife, in Paradise, and eat from it in abudance, as you will. But do not come near this Tree, lest you be among the wrong-doers"** (2:35, 7:19), Iblis wanted to enter Paradise with them. But the guardians of Paradise prevented him.

Iblis then approached various animals, proposing to them that they should take him into the Garden so that he could speak to Adam (A) and his wife, but they all refused. Finally, Iblis persuaded the snake, who was then an animal with four feet like a camel and one of the most beautiful of beasts, to let him enter its mouth and so take him in to Adam (A). Permitting Iblis to enter it by the side of its mouth, the snake passed by the guardians of Paradise and, as God willed, went in without their noticing.[25]

Just as, in this world, the wicked one is cunning, clever, underhanded and treacherous in his dealings, while the good one is sincere, trusting and expects only goodness from others, Satan approached the untried, innocent couple with craftiness and deceit. At first, it is said, he spoke to Adam (A) from the side of the snake's mouth. Then, when Adam (A) did not pay attention to what he said, Satan went out and spoke to him.

"O Adam," he whispered, **"shall I direct you to a tree of immortality and a dominion that will never decay?"** (20:120), meaning, "Shall I direct you to a Tree such that, if you eat from it, you will become a sovereign like God,

---

[25]A tradition cited from Ibn 'Abbas states that after the snake allowed Iblis to use it to deceive Adam, God cursed it, cutting off its legs and leaving it to crawl around on its belly. Because of its role in the destruction of Adam, it is regarded as the enemy of mankind (Tabari/*C*, I:251-252; Tabari/*H*, I:277-278; Ayoub/*Q*, I:84).

or the two of you will become immortal and never die?" **And Satan whispered to them to make apparent to them what was concealed from them of their private parts, and he said, "Your Lord only prohibited you from this tree lest you become angels or become of the immortal," and he swore to them, saying, "I am surely among the sincere advisors to you"** (7:20-21).

As Adam and Eve listened to Satan's evil suggestions and lying promises, they forgot their Lord's clear warnings — both about the Tree and about their enemy, Iblis. Completely innocent and free of ill intentions, they could have no suspicion of the intense envy and enmity that burned in the heart of the Arch-Deceiver, concealed from all except his Lord.

Iblis continued his attack on the unsuspecting pair until they believed his lies and fell headlong into his trap. **Thus, he caused them to fall by deceit** (7:22). By being forgetful and heedless, they were tricked and made to slip into disobedience to their Lord's command, according to His words,

> **And We had previously enjoined [an obligation] on Adam, but he forgot and We did not find firmness in him.** (20:115)

The ultimate catastrophe then occurred. Ibn 'Abbas tells us that at first Adam (A) refused to eat from the fruit of the Tree but Eve came forward and ate. She then said, "Adam, eat! I have eaten and it has not done me any harm."[2] **And Adam disobeyed his Lord and erred** (20:121). **Thus, Satan caused them to slip out of it** — their innocence — **and removed them from that in which they had been** (2:36), meaning their blessed state in Paradise.

REFERENCES: Qur'an: 2:35-36; 7:19-22; 20:117-121. Commentaries: Tabari/*C*, I:251-257; Tabari/*H*, I:275-281, 299-300, fn. 677; Ibn Kathir/*Q*, "Adam"; Ayoub/*Q*, I: 83-84.

---

[26]Although the Prophet's saying, "If it had not been for Eve, no woman would ever have acted unfaithfully toward her husband" (***Muslim***, 3471-3472; ***Bukhari***, 4.547), confirms Ibn 'Abbas' statement that Eve was the first to eat of the prohibited Tree and that she encouraged Adam to do likewise (Tabari/*C*, I:252), the words, **Thus, he [Satan] caused them to fall by deceit** (7:22), and, **He caused them to slip out of it and removed them from that in which they had been** (2:36), make it clear that it was a mutual act in which both participated. The Qur'anic account contains no suggestion that Eve was to blame for Adam's sin. Rather, God's words, **We had previously enjoined [an obligation] on Adam, but he forgot and We did not find firmness in him** (20:115), and, **Adam disobeyed his Lord and erred** (20:121), make it clear that Adam was responsible for his own sin — and indeed, perhaps indirectly for Eve's as well, as is suggested by God's saying to Adam, **"O Adam, dwell, you and your wife, in Paradise. . . . But do not come near this Tree, lest you be among the wrong-doers"** (2:35, 7:19), and, **"O Adam, indeed, this is an enemy to you and your wife. Therefore, do not let him to get the two of you turned out of Paradise so that you become miserable"** (20:117).

14. The Expulsion from Paradise

Thus, he caused them to fall by deceit. And when they tasted of the Tree, their private parts became apparent to them, and they began to fasten together [something] of the leaves of Paradise upon themselves. And their Lord called to them, [saying,] "Did I not prohibit you from that Tree and tell you that Satan is a clear enemy to you?" They said, "Our Lord, we have wronged ourselves, and if You do not forgive us and have mercy upon us, we will surely be among the lost." (7:22-23)

The eating of the fruit of the forbidden Tree brought about a sudden transformation in the new couple. By disobeying their Lord, they had made an abrupt transition from pure spiritual beings, dwelling with the Holy One and His blessed angels in Paradise, to humans with wills of their own, which they had now exercised. Under the sway of physical needs and desires, they were now fit for life on earth but not in Heaven.

Obviously, none of the promises that Satan had made to them came true. They had not become gods or angels by eating from the Tree, and since they were now mortals, there was no question of their living forever. Instead, by listening to their enemy, they had forfeited all the boundless favors and blessings their Lord had granted them.

Just as Satan had planned, once the two had tasted the fruit of the Tree, **their private parts** — the parts involved in the elimination of food and sexuality — **became apparent to them** (7:22). And out of shame at their strange and unaccustomed state of nakedness, **they begin to fasten together** something **of the leaves of Paradise upon themselves** (7:22, 20:121). Thus originated the virtually universal habit of covering the private parts of the body, suggesting that modesty and a sense of shame are an inherent part of the basic nature with which God endowed mankind. This is confirmed by His saying,

> **O children of Adam, We have bestowed upon you [the use of] clothing to conceal your private parts and as adornment. But the clothing of mindfulness of God [*taqwa*] — that is best. That is among the signs of God, that perhaps they may remember. O children of Adam, do not let Satan seduce you as he ousted your parents from Paradise, stripping them of their garments in order to show them their private parts. Indeed, he sees you, he and his tribe, from whence you do not see them. We have surely made the evil ones allies of those who do not believe.** (7:26-27)

And God Most High called to the pair, saying, **"Did I not prohibit you from that Tree and tell you that Satan is a clear enemy to you?"** (7:22).

"Our Lord, we have wronged ourselves," they said, deeply remorseful. **"And if You do not forgive us and have mercy upon us, we will surely be among the lost"** (7:23).

Here we may note that although the first human pair had disobeyed God's order as well as Iblis, their case was entirely different from his. For while Iblis had disobeyed purposefully and with full understanding of the consequences of his action, Adam and Eve (A) had disobeyed through simple forgetfulness and heedlessness, without premeditation. And while Iblis arrogantly continued to defy his Lord, refusing to admit his wrong-doing, defending his action, and even making long-range plans for doing every possible evil up to the Last Day, Adam and Eve were intensely, desperately sorry for their sin, humbly repenting and beseeching God for forgiveness.

Then Adam received words from his Lord (2:37), meaning that He, the All-Merciful, presented Adam (A) with certain words which were acceptable to Him, by which to express his repentance.

What were those **"words"**? The early Qur'anic commentators held differing views on this point. Ibn 'Abbas (R) says that Adam spoke to God, saying, "O Lord, did You not create me with your own Hand?" and God replied, "Yes."

"O Lord, did You not breathe something of Your Spirit into me?" and God replied, "Yes."

"O Lord, did You not give me an abode in your Paradise?" and again God replied, "Yes."

"O Lord, does not Your mercy overcome your anger?" and again God replied, "Yes."

Adam (A) then said, "What is Your judgment if I repent and improve — will You return me to Paradise?" and God said, "Yes." "This," added Ibn 'Abbas (R), "is [the meaning of] His words, **'Then Adam received words from his Lord'"** (Tabari/*C*, I:263).

Other commentators hold that these **"words"** were what is mentioned in the Qur'an — that is, the saying of Adam and Eve mentioned above: **"Our Lord, we have wronged ourselves, and if You do not forgive us and have mercy upon us, we will surely be among the lost"** (7:23). But whatever the phrasing of these words may have been, the common understanding is that God Himself presented Adam (A) with that by which he expressed his remorse. Adam (A) accepted these holy words, turning to his Lord in deep and sincere repentance for his sin. And the Most Gracious Lord turned to Adam (A) because of the latter's acceptance of the words he had received from Him and his remorse for his sin, and **He accepted his repentance. Indeed, He is the Acceptor of Repentance, the Merciful** (2:37).

However, forgiveness does not cancel the consequences of actions. Now, in spite of their repentance and God's acceptance of it, once Adam and Eve had disobeyed their Lord, there was no easy way back for them. Just as Iblis had been cast out of Paradise for his disobedience, so were they also to be cast out.

Pronouncing His divine judgment upon all those connected with the first sin of mankind, God Almighty expelled them collectively from Paradise. **"Go down from it, all,"** He commanded, **"enemies to one another"**[27] (20:123; 2:26; 7:24; 2:38). Then, addressing Adam (A) and Eve and all their descendants-to-come, He said, **"And on the earth will be a dwelling-place and means of enjoyment for you for a time. On it you will live and on it you will die, and from it you will be brought forth"** (7:24-25).

At the same time, the Most Merciful Lord issued a promise which softened His judgment and made it more bearable, saying, **"But if there comes to you guidance from Me"** — meaning the guidance that I shall reveal through My prophets — **"then whoever follows My guidance will not go astray nor be miserable, and no fear shall be upon them nor shall they grieve"** (20:123, 2:38).

This statement of mercy was, however, followed by a stern warning to those who would choose unbelief over faith: **"Those who disbelieve and deny Our revelations, those will be the company of the Fire; they will remain therein** (2:39). **And,"** God Most High declared, pointing to the eternal difference between the state of believers and unbelievers, **"whoever turns away from My remembrance, he will surely have a narrowed-down life, and We will raise him up blind on the Day of Resurrection. He will say, 'My Lord, why have You raised me up blind, whereas before I used to see?' He [God] will say, 'Thus did Our revelations come to you but you forgot them, and thus will you be forgotten this Day'"** (20:124-126).

Here ends the Qur'anic narrative concerning Adam (A), and we are left to ponder its meaning. Our instinct tells us that in this story we are face to face with something whose significance and importance extends far beyond the account of the life of the first man — indeed, something of such magnitude that our minds can hardly fathom all its meanings and implications. It is these that we will explore in next section.

REFERENCES: Qur'an: 7:22-26; 2:36-39; 20:121-126. Tabari/*C*, I:253-268; Tabari/*H*, I:275-281, 299, 302-303; Ibn Kathir/*T*, 20:123-126; Ayoub/*Q*, I:84-85.

---

[27]Here, **"enemies"** has been variously interpreted as referring to the enmity between Adam, who represents the human race, and Iblis, the father and chief of the tribe of evil jinn, or to the enmity between Adam, Eve, Satan and the snake.

Part Three: Time Out for Reflection

15. Islam and Original Sin

Has he not been informed of what was in the scriptures of Moses and Abraham, who fulfilled [his obligations]: that no bearer of burdens shall bear the burden of another; and that man shall have nothing except what he strives for; and that his effort will be seen, and then he will be recompensed for it with the fullest recompense; and that to your Lord is the final end? (53:36-42)

The seriousness of the consquences of our first parents' sin, both for themselves and for each one of us, their descendants, does not require comment. At the same time, just as if it had been committed by any other human beings, it was their own individual sin for which each was personally responsible, and which God also forgave individually.

This is such a central point in the Islamic teachings that it is reiterated again and again in verses such the one cited above and the following:

> **God does not charge a soul except with its capacity. It will have whatever [good] it has gained and it will bear whatever [evil] it has earned.** (2:286)
>
> **Whoever earns a sin earns it only against itself. And God is ever Knowing and Wise.** (4:110)
>
> **Each soul earns only for itself, and no bearer of burdens shall bear the burden of another.** (6:164, 35:18, 39:7)
>
> **Whoever is guided, is guided only for his own soul, and whoever errs, errs only against it. And no bearer of burdens shall bear the burden of another.** (17:15)
>
> **God created the heavens and the earth with truth, and that each soul may be recompensed according to what it earned, and they shall not be wronged.** (45:22; also 2:281, 40:17)

Consequently, in Islam there is no question of the sin of Adam and Eve being 'inherited' by their descendants, or of anyone's being put into Hell for eternity for the so-called original sin of the first man or woman. As mentioned earlier, God repeatedly speaks about Himself in the Qur'an as "the Most Merciful (*ar-Rahman*)," "the Compassionate (*ar-Rahim*)," and "the Forgiving (*al-Ghafur*)." And He says:

> **Your Lord has prescribed mercy upon Himself.** (6:12, 54)
>
> **Inform My servants that it is I who am the Forgiving, the Merciful.** (15:49)

The one who does a wrong or wrongs himself but then seeks forgiveness of God will find God forgiving and merciful. (4:110)

But indeed, I am surely the Forgiver of the one who repents and believes and does righteous deeds and then continues in guidance. (20:82)

It is therefore not to be imagined that God would be so unjust, merciless, cruel, and at the same time so illogical and unreasonable, as to send anyone to Hell because of what the first individuals of our species did eons before we were born. Also unimaginable in the Islamic frame of reference is the notion that we need a 'savior' to save us from the consequences of our sins, when only God can save us from Himself.

No one can possibly know our nature, a nature prone to sin and error, as our Creator does. And since, by His own ordaining and wisdom, **the human being was created weak** (4:28), He is ever willing and ready to forgive our sins and faults. Various small and large acts by which one may obtain forgiveness of sins are mentioned in dozens of *ahadith*. And speaking about forgivness generally, the Holy Prophet (S) said:

Every son of Adam is a sinner, and the best sinners are those who repent. (*Mishkat*)

If you did not sin, God would take you away and bring [in your place] a people who would sin and then seek God's forgiveness, and then He would forgive them. (*Muslim*, 6621-6622; also 6620)

If this is not sufficient evidence of God's boundless mercy and forgiveness, we may recall His saying, **We surely honored the children of Adam** (17:70). This is an unqualified, inclusive statement, embracing all humanity. If we were miserable sinners, condemned to burn in Hell for all eternity unless we accept the mediation of some authorized mediator or savior, He would not have said this, nor would He have given those who believe in Him and turn to Him such a promise as is contained in the words,

Hasten to forgiveness from your Lord and a Paradise as wide as the heavens and the earth, prepared for the God-conscious. (3:133)

Nor would He have proclaimed to mankind in His Last Testament, the Qur'an:

O My servants who have transgressed against their souls, do not despair of God's mercy. Indeed, God forgives all sins. Indeed, it is He who is the Forgiving, the Merciful. (39:53)

Neither would He have permitted His angels to pray for our forgiveness, according to His words:

The heavens almost break apart from above them [from God's grandeur], and the angels glorify in praise of their Lord and ask for forgiveness for those upon the earth. Unquestionably, it is God who is the Forgiving, the Merciful. (42:5)

Those [angels] who carry the Throne and those around it extol their Lord with praise and believe in Him and ask for forgiveness for those who believe, [saying,] "Our Lord, You have encompassed all things in mercy and knowledge, so forgive those who have repented and followed Your way, and preserve them from the punishment of the Fire; Our Lord, and admit them to gardens of Paradise which You have promised them and whomever was righteous among their fathers and their spouses and their offspring. Indeed, it is You who are the Almighty, the Wise. And preserve them from the evil consequences [of their deeds]. And the one whom You preserved from evil consequences that Day, You will have shown him mercy. And that is the temendous achievement." (40:7-9)

Islam is therefore free of anything remotely resembling the doctrine of Original Sin, insisting on the wholesomeness and goodness of human nature and the inherent purity of each soul created by the Most Merciful Lord.

16. The Question of Free Will

O mankind, assuredly God's promise is true, so do not let the life of this world delude you and do not let the Deceiver deceive you about God. Indeed, Satan is an enemy to you, so take him as an enemy. He only calls his party to be among the companions of the blazing fire. (35:5-6)

O you human being, what has deceived you concerning your Lord, the Generous, who created you, then proportioned you, then balanced you? (82:6-7)

Among the issues raised by the story of Adam (A) is the question of why God, the Most Just, would have granted Satan's request for deferral so that he could attack us humans in order to divert us from His straight path. *Why did He not simply put the arrogant, rebellious Iblis into Hell (which was in any case promised as his final abode) and thus be done with him forever? But* — even more importantly — *why would He permit one of His creatures to deceive, confuse and misguide others, leading them to destruction?* Taken a step further, this ultimately leads us to a question that troubles the hearts of many people in our time: *Why would the good God permit evil to exist?*

Now, God Most High does not tell the stories of His prophets in the Qur'an as entertainment. In addition to conveying otherwise unknowable information about the lives and missions of His messengers, many of these stories — most notably Adam's — also contain profound lessons and precious wisdoms concerning the human condition. And the story of Adam (A) deals head-on with the issue of human free will in relation to God's Will, a matter that has puzzled some of the wisest scholars and theologians throughout history.

Among the creatures of whom we have knowledge, free will is an attribute that God has granted only to two species, jinn and humankind. Free will is, therefore, part of the definition of being human.

At the same time, free will does not really come 'free'. It inevitably carries a pricetag: responsibility, for the freedom to choose means that we are responsible for the consequences, immediate or long-term, of any choices we make. And it is precisely because of the moral responsibility this free will entails that we humans have been granted a rank higher even than that of the angels, who, not possessing free will, do not carry such responsibility.

In our desire for a world in which there is no evil, we often overlook an essential point: that free will means the ability to make choices without constraint or compulsion. Hence, if we are free to choose good, we must also be free to choose evil. If God were to routinely 'interfere' with and set aside our bad choices and their consequences, free will would obviously have no meaning, nor would we bear that moral responsibility which is an integral aspect of our humanity.

Thus it was that the Lord Almighty left Iblis free to choose to disobey Him in the matter of prostrating to Adam (A). God then granted Iblis' request to be given respite until the Last Day in order to carry out his scheme against Adam's descendants (another choice on Iblis' part). At the same time, God granted Adam and Eve, and with them their entire species, the freedom to choose to follow Iblis or to keep to *His* way, warning of serious consequences for those who make the former choice, and protection and mercy for those who make the latter.

17. The Divine Decree

It is He who created you from clay and then decreed a term and a specified time [known] to Himself; yet you are in dispute. (6:2)

Taking the story of Adam (A) at face value, it may seem as though God left Satan totally free to inflict whatever harm he wished upon the new creatures whom He had honored even above the angels — and, after them, upon their descendants. But this is only an appearance, for in reality God's permitting Satan to carry out his scheme was actually a part of what He Himself willed — that is, of His all-embracing divine plan for His creation for all eternity.

Perhaps this may give us a clue as to how immensely wide and all-embracing God's plan is — and, at the same time, how subtle: For it was God who gave Satan respite to become the tempter of mankind, and, while it was God who commanded Adam and Eve (A) not to eat the fruit of the Tree, at the same time it was God who permitted Satan to seduce them, and who allowed them to disobey Him and thus commit the first sin. It was, again, God who willed that they turn to Him in repentance, and even more than that, it was God Himself who gave Adam (A) the words of repentance that were acceptable to Him, and then **chose him and turned to him in forgiveness and guided [him]** (20:122).

These seeming contradictions may be reconciled by understanding that there is God's Will and there is His command, but His Will is above His command. Thus, God commanded Adam and Eve not to eat, but His Will permitted them to exercise their own personal freedom of choice and eat. Perhaps the secret is contained in His words, **And you do not will except as God wills** (76:30, 81:29).

This in turn is linked to the sixth Article of Faith in Islam, known as ***Qada wa Qadar***, or the Divine Decree. This is the belief that that all things, both good and evil, proceed from one divine Will and Decree, that of Him who possesses absolute knowledge of all the secret, subtle interconnections among whatever He has created. Noah Keller concisely sums up the meaning of this article of faith in the following words:

> To believe in ***destiny, its good and evil*** means to be convinced that Allah Most High has ordained both good and evil before creating creation, and all that has been and all that will be only exists through Allah's decree, foreordinance, and Will. Early Muslims used to answer whoever asked about destiny by saying, "It is knowing that what hits you was not going to miss, and what misses you was not going to hit." (Keller/*R*, u3.7, p. 813)

This vitally important concept is mentioned in verse after verse of the Qur'an, such as the following:

Say, [O Muhammad:] "Never will anything befall us except what God has decreed for us; He is our Protector." And let the believers rely upon God. (9:51)

Say, [O Muhammad:] "Even if you had been in your houses, those for whom killing was decreed would have come forth to their death beds." (3:154)

For each nation is a term. Then when their time comes, they will not remain behind an hour nor will they precede [it]. (7:34; also 10:49)

We did not destroy any city but that it had a known decree. No nation will precede its term, nor will they remain thereafter. (15:4-5)

Do they not see that God, who created the heavens and the earth, is able to create the like of them, and He has set a term for them, concerning which there is no doubt. (17:99)

God takes the souls at the time of their death, and those which do not die, [He takes] during their sleep. Then He retains those for whom He has decreed death and releases the others until an appointed term. In that are surely signs for a people who reflect. (39:42)

With Him are the keys of the Unseen; none knows them except Him. And He knows what is in the land and the sea. Not a leaf falls without His knowing it, nor is there any grain within the darkness of the earth, nor anything wet or dry, but that it is in a clear register. (6:59)

This register or record of God's decrees for eternity is known as ***al-Lawh al-Mahfudh***, the Preserved or Guarded Tablet. Concerning it, God says:

Do you not know that God knows whatever is in the heaven and the earth? Indeed, that is in a register. Indeed, that is easy for God. (22:70)

Nor is anything of an atom's weight on earth or in heaven absent from your Lord, nor what is smaller than that or greater, but that it is in a clear register. (10:61, 34:3)

There is no creature on earth but that its provision rests on God, and He knows its dwelling-place and its repository. All is in a clear register. (11:6)

Indeed, your Lord knows what their breasts conceal and what they reveal, and there nothing hidden in heaven and earth but that it is in a clear register. (27:74-75)

God created you from dust, then from a sperm-drop; then He made you [male and female] pairs. And no female conceives nor gives birth except with His knowledge, nor is any aged person granted

> **[further] life, nor is his lifespan lessened, but that it is in a register. Indeed, that is easy for God.** (35:11)

> **No disaster befalls on the earth or among yourselves but that it is in a register before We bring it into being — indeed, that is easy for God — in order that you may not despair over what has eluded you, nor exult in what He has given you.** (57:22-23)

Indeed, the very Qur'an, in which all this information is contained, is itself inscribed in this eternal Book of Decrees, as is stated in the words,

> **This is an honored Qur'an, [inscribed] on a Preserved Tablet.** (85:22)

18. The Life-to-Come

He is the Dominant over His servants, and He sends guardians [angels] over you until, when death comes to one of you, Our messengers [the angels of death] take him, and they do not fail. Then they are returned to God, their true Lord. Unquestionably, His is the judgment, and He is the swiftest of accountants. (6:61-62)

And be mindful of a Day when you will be returned to God. Then each soul will receive in full what it earned, and they will not be wronged. (2:281; 3:25, 161; also 16:111, 45:22, 46:19)

You may recall God's saying to the angels, **"Indeed, I am going to appoint a *khalifah* on the earth"** (2:30), thus making it clear that the abode which He intended for Adam and Eve (A) from the beginning was earth, not Paradise.[28] It may therefore logically be asked, *If it was their destiny to live on earth, why did God not create them on it from the beginning instead of sending them to earth from Paradise?*

The answer is, simply, so that they would be aware, through their own personal experience, of their origin and homeland in the spiritual world. For while it is a characteristic of humans to be attached to their homelands, in order for such an attachment to form, one must have lived in that homeland, or, at the very least, must know something about it and have some sort of tie to it.

The true, original homeland of Adam and Eve was Paradise. And while it was their destiny to leave it and dwell upon the earth, the earth was nevertheless to be only a place of temporary sojourn for them, from which they would return to their place of origin. Therefore, by giving Adam and Eve a taste of Paradise, the All-Knowing Lord established a firm, unbreakable connection between their hearts and the spiritual world which would be their eternal home.

What is true of our first parents is also true of each one of us. We are souls originating in the spiritual realm, housed temporarily in physical bodies. When God decrees that our souls become attached to and manifested in a material form, they are put into our developing fetuses in our mothers' wombs. Soon

---

[28]The Prophet (S) said: "Adam and Moses met. Then Moses said to Adam, 'Are you the one who caused people to be miserable and got them ousted from Paradise?' Adam said to him, 'Are you the one whom God selected for His Message and whom He chose for His own Self and to whom He revealed the Torah?' He said, 'Yes.' He [Adam] said, 'Did you find that decreed for me before my creation?' He [Moses] said, 'Yes.' Thus Adam defeated Moses [in argument by pointing out that what happened to him had been eternally decreed by God]" (*Bukhari*, 6:260, 6:262, 4:621, 8:611, 9:606; *Muwatta*, 46.1.1).

afterwards, we come into this life as helpless infants who little by little grow to maturity, inhabiting the body God gives us for as long as He wills. Then, when the Angel of Death comes to to take our soul, the light that animates our body is switched off, and we pass on to another state of existence in our journey from God to God.

Where does our soul go then? Islam's answer is that it goes to an intermediate existence known as ***barzakh***,[29] awaiting the Day of Resurrection, which will mark the end of this world and of the entire universe, according to God's words, **Behind them** — those whose souls have passed on — **is a barrier [*barzakh*] until the day they are resurrected** (23:100).

When that end comes, everyone living on this planet will die. Then, at God's command, all human beings will be raised again in a new creation and assembled before Him for judgment. Hence, belief in a life after this life, preceded by the Day of Resurrection and the Last Judgment, is the fourth article of belief in Islam. This belief is so essential that it is mentioned repeatedly in the Qur'an as a corollary to belief in God.

A great portion of the Qur'an's verses, far too many even to list here, deal with the theme of the Last Day and the Afterlife. What is striking about many of these verses is their intensely earnest tone. Extraordinarily compelling, not to be denied, they convey a sense of the absolute inevitability of what they speak of. We cite here only a few examples.

> **O mankind, be mindful of your Lord. Indeed, the convulsion of the [Last] Hour is a tremendous thing. On the Day you see it, every nursing mother will be distracted from what she was nursing and every pregnant one will abort her pregnancy, and you will see people [as if] drunk while they are not drunk, but God's punishment is severe.** (22:1-2)
>
> **Then, when there comes the deafening blast, on the Day [when] a man will flee from his brother and his mother and his father and his wife and his children, each one of them, that Day, will have concern sufficient for himself. [Some] faces, that Day, will be shining, laughing, rejoicing at good news, and [other] faces, that Day, will have dust upon them; darkness will cover them. Those are the disbelievers, the wicked!** (80:33-42)
>
> **When the sky ruptures and when the stars fall, strewn about, and when the seas burst forth and when the [contents of] the graves**

[29]Literally, a bar, obstruction, or a thing that intervenes or makes a separation between two things.

are scattered, a soul will know what it has sent ahead and kept back. (82:1-5)

O you human, you are surely toiling toward your Lord with [heavy] toil, and you will meet Him! Then, as for him who is given his record in his right hand, he will be judged with an easy accounting and return to his people in happiness. But as for him who is given his record behind his back, he will cry for destruction and burn in a blaze. Indeed, he had been among his people in happiness; indeed, he had thought that he would never return [to God]. No, but his Lord was ever seeing of him! So I swear by the glow of twilight, and the night and what it envelopes, and the moon when it is full:[30] **you will surely travel from stage to stage.** (84:6-19)

When the earth is crushed, ground-up, and your Lord comes,[31] **and the angels, rank upon rank, and Hell, that Day, is brought [within sight] — on that Day the human being will remember; but of what use will the remembrance be to him? He will say, "If only I had sent ahead [something] for my [future] life!" Then, on that Day, none will punish as He punishes, and none will bind [as severely] as He binds. O you serene soul, return to your Lord, pleased and well-pleasing. And enter among My slaves and enter My Paradise!** (89:21-30)

When the earth is shaken with its [ultimate] quaking and the earth sends forth its burdens,[32] **and the human being says, "What is the matter with it?" — on that Day it will tell its news, because your Lord has inspired it.**[33] **That Day people will go forth, dispersed, to be shown their deeds. Then whoever does an atom's weight of good will see it and whoever does an atom's weight of evil will see it.** (99:1-8)

And in heaven is your provision and what you are promised. Then, by the Lord of heaven and earth, it is as surely the truth as [the fact] that you can speak. (51:23)

---

[30]Here, as in many verses of the Qur'an, God Himself is swearing an oath of great solemnity.

[31]This has been understood by many of the classical commentators as referring to the manifestation of God's transcendental majesty and the materialization of His judgment.

[32]That is, the dead buried within it.

[33]Once the Prophet (S) recited the verse, **On that Day it [the earth] will tell its news** (99:4). He then told those around him, "Its news is that it will testify against every man and woman concerning what he or she did on earth. It will say that he or she did this and this on such-and-such day. This will be its news" (*Mishkat*, 408[R]).

Why is belief in the Day of Judgment and the Hereafter so strongly stressed in Islam? The answer is, first, *because it is a reality; it is going to happen.* And because it relates to our personal future existence, it is that event, among all the events that concern us, for which we need most to prepare. Consequently, the Holy Prophet (S) strongly stressed the importance of remembering death often (*Mishkat*, 2168, 5352).

The second reason is that belief in accountability is a corollary to belief in God. It is not enough simply to believe that God exists, for the mere fact of His existence does not in itself require any response from us. However, if we know that He sees, hears and knows everything we do and that we are accountable to Him for all our actions, then His existence takes on a vital importance related to ourselves and our final destiny.

In this life, there is always room for apologies and excuses, for repentance and reparation and new efforts, even new beginnings. But once this life finishes, the time for that will be over; the record will be closed and sealed, and the Judgment will be upon us. And when it takes place, each of us will be shown our life's 'journal,' completely accurate, absolutely fair, which was kept throughout our lives by our recording angels. **"Read your record,"** we will be told. **"Your self is sufficient against you as an accountant this day"** (17:14).

God Most High will then weigh each person's life-product in the balance, taking into consideration even the smallest details of our situation in this world — genetic factors, environmental constraints, socio-economic aspects and all the rest, according to His words:

> **And the earth will shine with the light of its Lord, and the record [of deeds] will be placed, and the prophets and witnesses will be brought, and it will be judged between them in truth and they will not be wronged. And every soul will be fully compensated for what it did, and He is most knowing of what they do. (39:69-70; also 10:54)**
>
> **And the weighing that Day will be the truth. Then those whose scales are heavy, it is they who will be the successful. And those whose scales are light, they are the ones who will lose themselves because they did wrong regarding Our signs. (7:8-9)**
>
> **Then today no soul will be wronged at all, and you will not be recompensed except for what you used to do. (36:54)**

That, then, will be the ultimate moment of truth, the moment of coming face-to-face with our sum-total life product, good or bad, the moment about which God informed mankind through all His prophets from the beginning of our history. It will be the moment when every good effort — all our worship, service, efforts and even good intentions — will be given its due payment, according to His promise:

> **Never will I permit the work of any worker among you to be lost, whether male or female; you are of one another.** (3:190)

It will also be the time when justice will be done on behalf of those who were wronged or harmed by others.

Those whose balance of good outweighs the bad will then be rewarded with a life so exquisitely beautiful and blessed that even the best things in this life are nothing in comparison, and in which the highest pleasure, the greatest satisfaction for the purified soul, will be the vision of God, the Blessed and Exalted. And while God speaks about the life of the Hereafter using words drawn from human experience (since those are the only words we understand), it is in reality a beatific spiritual state beyond description in language and beyond the mind's ability to imagine: —

> **No soul knows what has been kept hidden for them of satisfaction for the eyes, as a recompense for what they used to do.** (32:17)

> **For those who do good in this world there is good, but the Home of the Hereafter is better. And how excellent is the home of the God-conscious — gardens of Paradise which they will enter, under which rivers flow! They will have therein whatever they wish. Thus does God reward the God-conscious — the ones whom the angels take in death as good; they [the angels] will say, "Peace be upon you! Enter Paradise because of what you used to do."** (16:30)

> **On the Day you see the believing men and women, their light running in front of them and at their right, [it will be said to them,] "Good tidings for you today — gardens under which rivers flow, abiding in them forever. That is the tremendous achievement!"** (57:12)

> **And hasten to forgiveness from your Lord and a Paradise as wide as the heavens and the earth, made ready for the God-conscious, who spend [in charity] in ease and hardship, and who restrain anger and pardon people — and God loves the doers of good; and those who, if they do something indecent or wrong themselves, remember God and seek forgiveness for their sins — and who can forgive sins except God? — and do not persist in that which they have done, while they know. Those — their reward is forgiveness from their Lord and gardens under which rivers flow, abiding in them forever, and excellent is the recompense of the workers!** (3:133-136; also 57:21)

And Paradise will be brought near to the righteous, not distant. [It will be said,] "This is what you were promised, for each returner [to God] and keeper [of His way], who feared the Most Merciful unseen and came with a heart returning [in repentance]. Enter it in peace! This is the Day of Eternity." They will have whatever they wish therein, and with Us is [still] more. (50:31-35)

At the same time, as a requirement of God's perfect justice, the deeds of those who consistently denied Him, rejected His guidance, allowed themselves to engage in immorality or evil, or inflicted harm and suffering on others will also be recompensed.[34] Indeed, the doers of such deeds will have brought the punishment upon themselves by their own persistent wrong-doing.

In numerous verses of the Qur'an, God speaks of every kind of wrong-doing, generically known as ***dhulm***,[35] regardless of whom it may be directed against, as being in reality wrong-doing against our own selves or souls. Thus, He says, **They did not wrong Us, but [rather] they wronged themselves**[36] (2:57). And, making it clear that not the least injustice will be done to a single soul, He reiterates again and again, **God did not wrong them but [rather] they wronged themselves** (3:117, 4:64, 7:160, 9:70, 10:44, 14:45, 16:33, 16:118, 29:40, 30:9). He further says:

Whoever works righteousness, it is for his soul, and whoever does evil, it is against it. And your Lord is never unjust to His servants. (41:46)

For all are there are ranks in accordance with what they did, and so that He may fully compensate them for their deeds, and they shall not be wronged. (46:19)

---

[34]See 6:120; 10:8, 27; 14:18; 18:58; 27:90; 39:24, 48, 50-51; 42:22, 30, 34; 45:10; 78:30.

[35]*Dhulm* is a key Islamic term for which there is no single English equivalent. It means injustice, oppression, tyranny, transgressing proper limits, or doing something inappropriate or incorrect — in short, wrong-doing. *Dhulm* is of three kinds. One of these is between a person and himself/herself; it consists of harming one's own self by doing what is evil, prohibited or degrading to one's rank as a human being whom God has honored. Another kind of *dhulm* is between a person and God, and it consists of refusing to acknowledge Him, ascribing partners to Him or worshipping something other than Him, being ungrateful for His favors, rejecting His revelations and His messengers, and disobeying His commands. As for the third kind of *dhulm*, it is between one individual and another, and it consists of everything, great or small, by which one may harm others.

[36]Concerning this, al-Tabari says:

> Thus no one's disobedience harms our Lord, no one's injustice encroaches upon His reserves, nor does anyone's obedience benefit Him, nor anyone's justice increase His Kingdom. The unjust person wrongs but himself, the disobedient diminishes his own portion, the obedient benefits his own self, and the just gains his own portion. (Tabari/*C*, I:333)

Thus, it will be said to those who deserve punishment, **"That is for what your hands have sent ahead, and because God is never unjust to His servants"** (22:9-10; also 8:51), and they will be admitted to Hell. And although judgment will be given according to God's absolutely perfect justice, it will be tempered by His endless mercy, according to His saying in a ***hadith qudsi*** through the tongue of His Holy Prophet (S):

> When God created creation, He wrote in His Book [of decrees] — and He wrote [that] concerning Himself, and it is placed with Him on the Throne — "Indeed, My mercy takes precedence over My anger." (***Bukhari***, 9:501)

Does Islam teach that Hell is eternal? Yes, it does. However, not everyone who enters it will remain it eternally. Rather, the experiences of Hell are intended to serve both as the recompense of one's sins and the means of cleansing from them. Therefore, once sins have been expiated by punishment, their doer may be released and admitted to Paradise. This understanding is summarized by the classic scholar Ahmad ibn Naqib al-Misri in ***The Reliance of the Traveler*** in the following words:

> It is obligatory to hold that true believers in the oneness of Allah . . . will be taken out of hell after having paid for their sins, through the generosity of Allah Mighty and Majestic. No one who is a true monotheist will abide in the fire forever. (Keller/*R*, v2.7, p. 824)

It is also obligatory for Muslims to believe in the intercession of those whom God will authorize to intercede on the Day of Judgment: firstly, the prophets — particularly the Last Prophet (S)[37] — then the righteous, martyrs, scholars and finally other believers, the intercession of each being directly related to his standing with God. Writes al-Misri:

> Any believer remaining in hell without intercessor shall be taken out of it by the favor of Allah, no one who believes remaining in it forever, and anyone with an atom's weight of faith in his heart will eventually depart from it. (Keller/*R*, v2.8, p. 824)

---

[37]This is mentioned in numerous ***ahadith,*** such as the following:

> I shall be chief among the children of Adam on the Day of Resurrection, and I shall be the first whose grave will be split open and the first intercessor and the first whose intercession will be accepted [by God]. (***Muslim***, 5655)

> For each prophet there is a supplication with which he supplicates for his community [***ummah***] and then it is granted to him, and I have reserved my supplication to intercede for my community on the Day of Resurrection. (***Muslim***, 390, 392, 396, 389; also 385-388, 391. Other related ***ahadith*** are ***Bukhari***, 2:553, 2:636, 6:242, 6:243, 8:317B, 9:507, 9:532B, 9:532C; ***Muslim***, 367, 371, 373, 377, 378, 380, 381)

19. The Purpose of Life

Say, [O Muhammad:] "Indeed, my prayer [*salat*] and my rites of sacrifice and my living and my dying are for God, Lord of the worlds, who has no partner. And this I have been commanded, and I am foremost of the Muslims." (6:162)

Probably each person on this planet has some idea or privately-held understanding concerning the purpose of life. Naturally, these ideas are as varied as the beliefs and understandings of individual human beings. For some, life is centered around the relationship with God or family or service to humanity. For others, life's purpose may be achievement, production or material success; for still others, it may be the pursuit of power, success, fame, wealth, pleasure and happiness. For the less fortunate, it may be the daily struggle merely to exist and to avoid suffering. The list could go obviously go on and on.

These are our human notions about what our purpose is. But they may differ from God's. We may therefore ask, *What was God's purpose in creating us? For what were we created?*

God's answer is contained in His clear, direct statement, **I did not create jinn and humankind except to worship Me [*illa li-ya'buduni*]** (51:56), the words **"*li-ya'buduni*"** meaning both "to worship Me" and "to serve Me". And while this answer may not fit with our personal understanding, or even with the understanding of most of the people living on earth at the present time, because it is *God's* answer, it is the standard by which we must measure our own answers.

But it must be emphasized that God's creating us for His worship and service is not because He needs it or anything else from us or from any of His creatures. As Creator and Sustainer of everything in existence, He is totally free of all needs and wants, absolutely self-sufficient, as the following verses proclaim:[38]

---

[38]This is also stated as part of a ***hadith qudsi***, in which God says, through the tongue of His beloved Muhammad (S):

> O My slaves, you can never attain [the level of] harm so you would harm Me, nor reach the level of benefit so you would benefit Me. O My slaves, if the first of you and the last of you, your humans and your jinn, were to be as God-conscious as the most God-conscious heart of any one man among you, that would not increase My dominion in anything. O My slaves, if the first of you and the last of you, your humans and your jinn, were to be as wicked as the most wicked heart of any one man among you, that would not decrease My dominion in anything. O My slaves, if the first of you and the last of you, your humans and your jinn, were to rise up in one place and make a request of Me and I were to grant each individual what he requested, that would not decrease what I have any more than a needle decreases the ocean if put into it. (***Muslim***, 6246; ***Mishkat***, 2344)

If you disbelieve, indeed, God is free of need of you. (39:7, 3:97)

Whoever strives, strives only for himself. Indeed, God is free of need of all the worlds. (29:6)

O mankind, you are those in need of God, while God is free of need, the Praiseworthy. (35:16)

I do not desire any provision from them, nor do I desire them to feed Me. Indeed, it is God who is the Provider, possessor of firm strength. (51:57-58)

Rather, our creation for God's worship and service is related to our identity and role in the scheme of things. Again and again, God refers to human beings in the Qur'an as His slaves or servants, and this is confirmed in numerous *ahadith*. And this servanthood (Arabic, *"'ubudiyat,"* from the root, *"'a-b-d"*) is entirely unrelated to our worldly rank, our standing with God, or any other consideration. Instead, it is an inherent, unescapable part of who we are.

As created beings, we cannot claim to be masters of anything. We did not ask to be born nor do we choose when or if to die, and even the richest, most powerful people are not masters of their own destinies. We do not control so much as our own breathing or the beating of our hearts, what comes up to us out of the earth or down from the sky, or what happens to us from one moment to the next. Consequently, we do not have a choice about whether or not to be servants of our Creator. Like it or not, He is our Master and we, needy and totally dependent upon Him, are His servants and cannot possibly be anything else. Indeed, although it may be a little too difficult for our egoes, "slaves" is a more accurate term, and hence we use the two terms interchangeably.

There are no exceptions, not even among the beings who are closest to God — the angels, who are the slaves (*'ibad*) of the Most Merciful (43:19; also 4:172), for there is no one in the heavens and the earth but comes to the **Most Merciful as a slave [*'abd*]** (19:93).[39]

To Him belongs whomsoever is in the heavens and the earth. And those before Him are not prevented from His worship by arrogance, nor do they tire. They glorify Him night and day, not slackening. (21:19-20)

The prophets, the most perfect among mankind, were, all of them, also slaves to their Lord — including Jesus Christ (A), about whom God says, **Never would the Messiah disdain to be a slave to God, nor the angels, near [to**

---

[39]Thus, the name 'Abdullah is actually *'abd-Allah*, meaning the slave of God; 'Abdur-Rahman is *'abd al-Rahman*, the slave of the Most Merciful; 'Abdul-Karm is *'abd al-Karim*, the slave of the Most Generous, and so forth.

Him] (4:172), and, **He [Jesus] was nothing but a slave upon whom We bestowed favor** (43:59). Speaking in infancy, Jesus (A) himself proclaimed, **"Indeed, I am the slave of God. He has granted me the scripture and made me a prophet"** (19:30).

Servanthood was also the most noteworthy characteristic of the Last Prophet, Muhammad, God's peace and blessings be upon him, as mentioned in the following verses:

> **If you are in doubt about what We have sent down [that is, the Qur'an] upon Our slave [Muhammad], then produce a *surah* like it. (2:23)**
>
> **Praise be to God, who has revealed the Book to His slave and has not placed therein any crookedness. (18:1)**
>
> **Blessed is He who sent down the Criterion [the Qur'an] upon His slave, that he may be a warner to the worlds. (25:1)**
>
> **He [the angel Gabriel] revealed to His slave that which he revealed. (53:10)**
>
> **It is He who sends down verses of clear evidence upon His slave, that He may bring you out of [multiple] darknesses into the light. (57:9)**

Thus, in spite of his clear awareness that he was the chief of the prophets, who had been granted the highest rank among all mankind with his Lord, God's beloved, Muhammad (S) never thought or spoke of himself as anything but His most humble slave, saying,

> Do not praise me as Jesus son of Mary was praised, but [rather] say, "God's slave and His Messenger."[40] (*Bukhari*, 8.817)

Similarly, when he wrote letters to the rulers of neighboring countries, inviting them to accept Islam, he would sign himself simply as "Muhammad, the slave of God and His messenger" (*Bukhari*, 1.6, 4.191). He also instructed Muslims to refer to him in the same way while invoking blessings upon him (*Bukhari*, 8.369; *Muwatta*, 3.13.56, 3.13.58, 3.13.59).

This is such a vitally important point that God has included it in the *Shahadah* or Testification of Faith — ***"Ashhadu an la ilaha illa-Llah wa ashhadu anna Muhammadan 'abduhu wa rasulihu,"*** meaning, "I testify that there is no deity except God and that Muhammad is God's slave and His Messenger" — which

---

[40]The Prophet (S) also said, "Whoever testifies that there is no deity except God, having no partner, and that Muhammad is His slave and His Messenger, and that Jesus is God's slave and His messenger and His word which He bestowed upon Mary and a spirit from Him, and that Paradise is real and Hell is real, God will admit him into Paradise, whatever deeds he may have done" (*Bukhari*, 4.644). This will be discussed further in the story of Jesus in Volume Two.

constitutes the foremost act of worship in Islam. These are words that are pronounced by anyone who embraces Islam and that are repeated by Muslims during every *salat*, the ritual prayer that was taught to Muhammad (S) by the angel Gabriel (A), to be observed by his followers in the same form up to the end of time.

All this makes clear the critical importance of never losing sight of the distinction between the Creator and His creation, even in its highest manifestation. And by Muhammad's emphasis on his servanthood, he also taught us the importance of our own, for when we accept our servanthood to our Lord, we align ourselves with His Will, with the purpose for which He created us, and with our own intrinsic nature and reality.

20. Testing, Testing . . .

It is He who has made you successors upon the earth and has raised some of you above others in rank, that He may test you in what He has given you. (6:165)

This brings us to the subject of testing. Again and again, God speaks about the fact that this life constitutes a trial period, an unbroken examination, which begins from the time we reach mature consciousness and continues up to our death.

> **And know that your possessions and your children are only a test, and that with God is an immense reward.** (8:28)
>
> **Indeed, We have made that which is upon the earth as adornment for it, that We may test them as to which of them is best in deeds.** (18:7)
>
> **We test you with evil and good as a trial, and to Us you will be returned.** (21:35)
>
> **Do people suppose that they will be left at [merely] saying, "We believe," while they will not be tested? And We certainly tested those before them, and God will surely make evident those who are truthful and will surely make evident the falsifiers.** (29:3)
>
> **We will certainly test you until We make evident those who strive among you and the patient, and We will test your affairs.** (47:31)

Throughout this examination, we are free to exercise our uniquely human attribute of free will, except as it is limited by God's Will, which is above ours. And it is our performance during this life-test that determines our ultimate destiny.

Now, when we think of a test, we naturally think of something difficult, troubling and oppressive. But our life-test embraces the totality of our situation, both the good and the bad of it, ease and hardship, happiness and sorrow. In other words, we are tested as much by the blessings God grants us — health, strength, youth, talents, status, power, wealth, and so on — as we are by difficulties and sufferings, for the one who has been granted more carries more responsibility. *So then what does passing the test depend on?*

Again, God Himself supplies the answer: **The pleasure of God is the greatest. It is that which is the tremendous attainment**[41] (9:72). From this

---

[41]See also 2:207; 3:15, 162, 174; 5:16/18, 119/122; 9:21, 109; 48:29; 89:27-28; 98:7-8. The word ***"rida,"*** which we have translated as "[God's] pleasure," also means acceptance, approval, satisfaction and contentment.

we know that our success or failure in the test depends on whether we have made Him pleased with us or not — that is, on what kind of servants we have been to Him, for while everyone is a servant, some are willing, faithful, devoted servants and others serve by default. And ***how*** we make Him pleased — by acknowledging Him, worshipping Him, being grateful to Him, keeping Him in our hearts, trying to follow His guidance, and accepting His Will for ourselves as it manifests itself in the unfolding of our lives — is the subject matter of much of the Qur'an and the Prophet's ***ahadith***.

God Most High declares repeatedly that making Him pleased is the highest posssible success or attainment imaginable; in comparison to it, nothing else matters. Conversely, if we have not managed to make Him pleased, when He sends us repeated opportunities by day and by night to do something that He likes, that will be the ultimate disgrace, humiliation and source of regret. For regardless of how high a status we may attain according to this world's evaluation, those who **followed what displeased God and disliked His pleasure** will ultimately find that **He made their deeds worthless** (47:28).

> **The punishment will be multiplied for him on the Day of Resurrection and he will remain in it, humiliated, except those who repent and believe and do righteous deeds. For them, God will replace their evil deeds with good, and God is ever Forgiving and Merciful.** (25:69-70; also 19:60)

Truly, God's mercy is so vast that He gives people every possible opportunity to enter Paradise and stay out of Hell. This is clear from His manner of recording and recompensing our deeds:[42] —

> **Indeed, God does not do [even] an atom's weight of injustice, while if there is a good deed, He multiplies it and gives, from Himself, a great recompense.** (4:40)

> **Those who come [on the Day of Judgment] with a good deed will have ten times like it, while those who come with an evil deed will not be recompensed except with the like of it, and they shall not be wronged.** (6:160)

The Prophet (S) elaborated on this by saying that when a person thinks of doing a good deed but does not carry it out, God records it as a good deed, while if he actually carries it out, God records from ten to seven hundred or more goodnesses for him. If, on the other hand, he thinks of doing a bad deed

---

[42]For details concerning the recording of deeds, see Appendix C, "The Recording and Guardian Angels," at the end of this story.

but does not carry it out, God records it as a good deed (because of the evil he avoided), while if he does a bad deed, it is recorded only as one[43] (*Bukhari*, 8:498, 9:592; also 1:40, 4:629; *Muslim*, 233, 235).

The Holy Prophet (S) also reported, through divine inspiration, that God said,

> O son of Adam, as long as you supplicate Me and hope in Me, I shall pardon you in spite of what you have done, and I do not care. Son of Adam, if your sins reached up to the sky and then you asked me for forgiveness, I would forgive you and I do not care. Son of Adam, if you were to meet Me with sins enough to fill the earth and then you met Me, not setting up any partner with Me, I would bring you as much pardon as would fill the earth. (*Mishkat*, 2332, 0442R)

All this brings us back to our earlier theme: the divine wisdom of Satan's role among mankind.

On an allegorical level, the angels' question, **"Are You going to place on it one who will cause corruption on it and shed blood?"** (2:30), represents the age-old query of everyone who is troubled and perplexed by the existence of evil and suffering on this earth. At the same time, God's reply, **"Indeed, I know what you do not know"** (2:30), provides a clear answer for those who believe in an eternal, all-embracing divine plan by which all things are governed.

By means of this statement, God Most High indirectly informed His angels, and with them ourselves, mankind, that He was aware of all that was to come. His infinite knowledge included the fact that great numbers of the children of Adam would commit all kinds of sins — firstly against Him by not acknowledging and obeying Him. They would also work corruption on earth and shed blood, as the angels had predicted, causing their fellow humans to suffer and fall into error.

At the same time, there would be others who would reach the highest level among creation. Unlike Iblis and his followers who used their wills to disobey, rebel against God and harm His servants, such individuals would use their wills to choose to do God's Will, thereby materializing the purpose of their creation. Out of love for Him and the desire for His pleasure, they would voluntarily surrender to Him the free will He had granted them to use in any way they pleased, so that they might manifest *His* Will alone, thus comprising

---

[43]The full text of this *hadith* is given in Appendix C. The Prophet also said, "When the slave [of God] accepts Islam and makes good his [practice of] Islam, God pardons all the sins that he used to do, and after that the requital of the good deed is from ten like it up to seven hundred times, and of the bad deed [only] the like of it, unless God disregards it [altogether]" (*Bukhari*, 1:39A).

the people of certainty and determination, the highest rank among created beings.

As long as we are in this world, God sends us, His servants, repeated opportunities to prove who we are — opportunities for those who choose goodness over evil and opportunities for those who choose evil over good. Satan is an essential part of our test, God's secret 'testing agent,' who is attached to us from the moment of our birth, causing the first cries of the newborn infant.[44] But if we understand God's purposes correctly, we will realize that Satan is the means, the 'ladder,' by which we can rise to our fullest potential — or, if we choose, descend to become **the lowest of the low** (95:5). Without Satan, there would be no test, no gain, no high ranks for us to strive toward, and, with God's help, to reach.

[44]The Prophet (S) said, "No child is born but that Satan touches it when it is born, whereupon it starts cryng because of Satan's touch, except Mary and her son" (*Bukhari*, 6.71; also *Muslim*, 5837-5838, 6429).

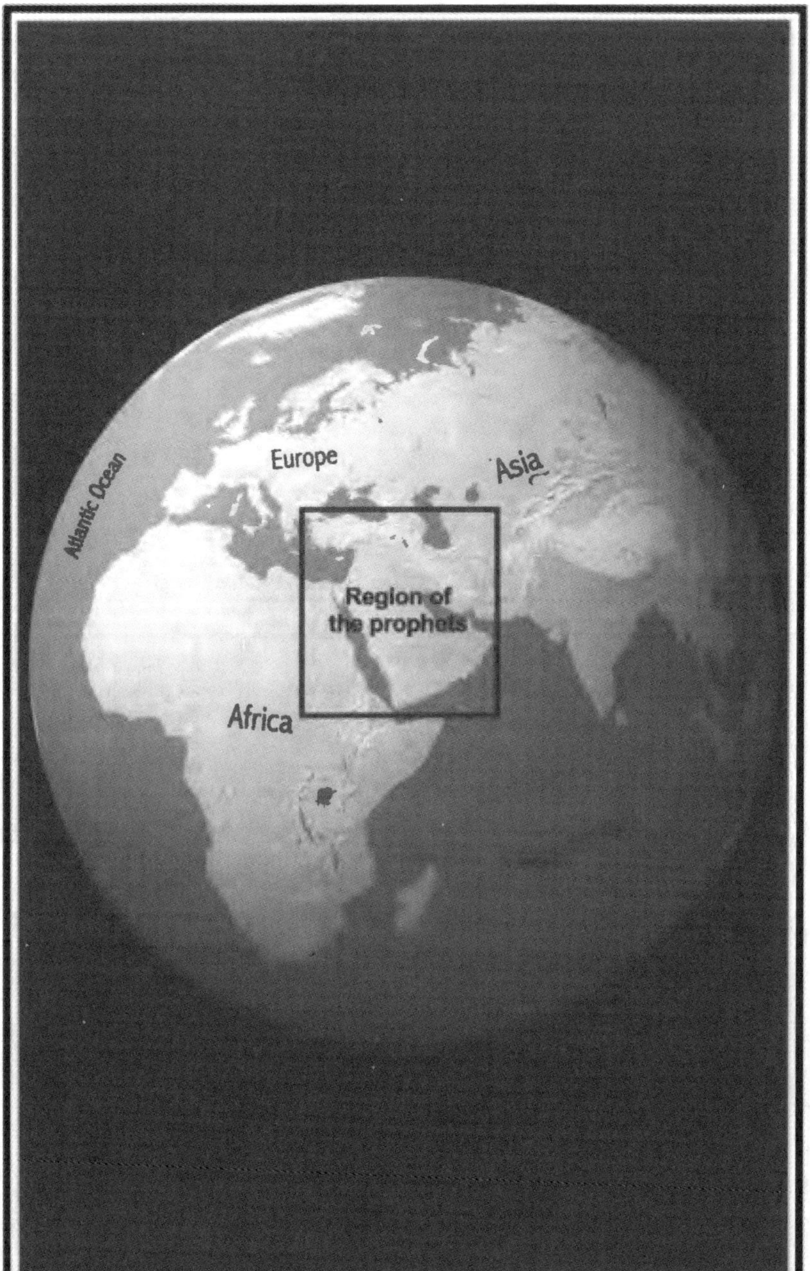

Map 1. The Eastern Hemisphere

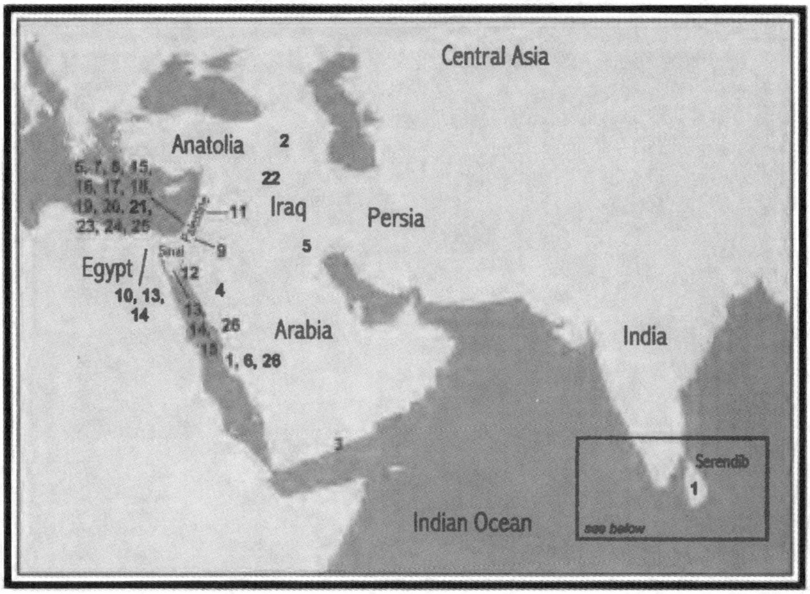

KEY

1 - Adam				21 - Dhul-Kifl
2 - Noah	7 - Isaac		16 - Samuel	22 - Jonah
3 - Hud	8 - Jacob	12 - Shu'ayb	17 - David	23 - Zechariah
4 - Saleh	9 - Lot	13 - Moses	18 - Solomon	24 - John
5 - Abraham	10 - Joseph	14 - Aaron	19 - Elijah	25 - Jesus
6 - Ishmael	11 - Job	15 - Joshua	20 - Elisha	26 - Muhammad

Map 2. The Middle East, home of the prophets

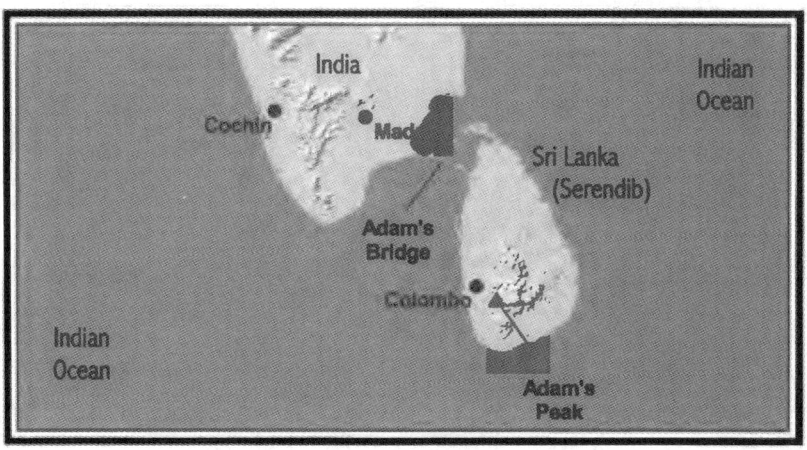

Map 3. The region of Adam's descent on earth

Part Four: The New Homeland, Earth

21. Settling-In

He produced you from the earth and caused you to dwell therein. (11:61)

From it [the earth] We created you and to it We shall return you and from it We shall bring you forth another time. (20:55)

It is God who made the earth a place of settlement for you and the sky a structure, and formed you and perfected your forms, and provided you with good things. That is God, your Lord. Then blessed be God, Lord of the worlds! (40:64)

Many are the reports of the classical Qur'anic commentators about the descent and settling-in of our first parents upon this earth.

Several *ahadith* report that Adam (A) came to earth on a Friday, the same day of the week on which he was created and the most excellent day among the seven.[45] Ibn 'Abbas (R) and other commentators report that Adam (A) was sent down upon a mountain called Budh or Nudh in India. He brought with him the scent of Paradise, which clung to India's trees and river valleys, filling them with perfume.[46]

---

[45]The Prophet (S) mentioned the importance of Friday in connection with Adam, saying:

> Friday is the foremost of days and the greatest of them in God's sight, being greater in God's sight than the Day of Sacrifice [*'Eid al-Adha*] and the Day of Fast-Breaking [*'Eid al-Fitr*]. It has five attributes: On it God created Adam; on it God sent Adam down to the earth; on it God took Adam in death; in it is an hour such that, if a servant asks for something in it, it will be given to him as long as he does not ask for anything prohibited; and on it the Last Hour will take place. There is no angel near [God,] nor heaven nor earth nor winds nor mountains nor ocean, that is not in awe of Friday. (*Mishkat*, 1363; also 1365)

> The best day on which the sun has risen is Friday. On it Adam was created, on it he was sent out [of Paradise], on it his repentance was accepted, on it he died, and on it the Last Hour will take place. On Friday, every beast is on the lookout from dawn to sunrise in fear of the Last Hour, apart from jinn and men, and it contains a time during which no Muslim prays and asks something from God without His giving it to him. (*Abu Dawud*, 1041; *Muslim*, 1856)

Concerning this special time of supplication on Friday, the Prophet (S) said, "Seek the time in which hope is placed on Friday from after the afternoon prayer [*'Asr*] until sunset" (*Mishkat*, 1360). And because of these special excellences of Friday, he said, "Invoke more blessings on me that day, for your blessings will be submitted to me." When he was asked, "O Messenger of God, how can it be that our blessings will be submitted to you while your body is decayed?" he replied, "God the Exalted has prohibited the earth from consuming the bodies of prophets" (*Abu Dawud*, 1042).

Other traditions hold that Adam (A) came down to earth in Serendib — that is, Ceylon or Sri Lanka. Because of the variance between these two reported sites of Adam's coming to earth, it may be speculated that Sri Lanka was once connected to India. This supposition is borne out by the fact that a chain of islands, known as Adam's Bridge, links Sri Lanka to India, and by the fact that the highest point on the island of Sri Lanka, Mount Budh (elevation 7360 feet), is popularly known as Adam's Peak.

According to local traditions, Adam (A) descended from Paradise to this mountain, at whose summit there is a depression in the rock, roughly shaped like a huge foot. Muslims as well as some Christians believe it to be Adam's footprint (other Christians believe it to be the footprint of St. Thomas of India, Buddhists believe it to be Buddha's, and Hindus believe it to be the god Siva's). Consequently, Adam's Peak has been a place of pilgrimage by people of different faiths for over a thousand years, with all the special flavor of a sacred site.

As we saw earlier, Adam (A) was immensely tall.[47] Thus, it is said that when God sent him down from Paradise, his feet were upon the mountain while his head was in Paradise, and he heard the speech and glorification of the angels.[1] In his sorrow, he did not eat or drink for forty days, and for two hundred years he mourned bitterly for all he had lost because of his sin.

The angels were so in awe of the huge, suffering creature that they complained to God, and consequently He reduced Adam's size.[49] Ibn 'Abbas (R) reports a moving dialogue between Adam (A) and his Creator:

"My Lord," Adam said, when God decreased his height, "I was Your neighbor in Your House [that is, Paradise]. I have no Lord but You and no one to watch over me but You. There, I ate whatever I wished and dwelt wherever I desired, but then You set me down on this sacred mountain. And I used to hear

---

[46]'Ali ibn Abi Talib said, "The land with the sweetest smell on earth is the land of India. When Adam was cast down there, some of the smell of Paradise clung to India's trees." Consequently, says Ibn 'Abbas, the perfumes found in India originate from what Adam brought from Paradise (Tabari/*H*, I:291, 296).

[47]The Prophet (S) said, "Everyone who enters Paradise will be of the form of Adam, but the stature [of people] has not stopped decreasing up to now" (*Bukhari*, 4:543, 8:246). He also said that the people of Paradise would be in the form of their father Adam, sixty cubits tall (*Bukhari*, 4:544) — that is, about forty-one meters or 126 feet.

[48]This mountain is described as "a marvelous cone of polished gneiss. . . .Viewed from a ship at sea, the solitary situation of the mountain presents such a striking appearance that early Western travelers greatly overestimated its altitude. One of the first Europeans to see Adam's Peak was so impressed that he wrote:

> It hath a pinnacle of surpassing height, which on account of clouds can rarely be seen. . . . It is the highest mountain on the face of the earth. (Bernbaum, *Sacred Mountains*, p. 76)

[49]This corresponds to the Prophet's *ahadith*, cited above, stating that the stature of people continues to be reduced with the passing of time.

the voices of the angels and see them surrounding Your Throne and experienced the scent of Paradise and its beauty. Then you set me down on earth and reduced my height, so the sight and sound was cut off from me and the scent of Paradise went from me."

Then God the Mighty and Glorious replied to him, "Because of your sin, O Adam, I have done that to you" (Tabari/*Q*, "Adam").

As for Eve, some commentators assert that she came down on Mount Budh with Adam (A). Others say that she came down at Jiddah near Mecca in Arabia. Later, Adam went in search of her and eventually they were united at 'Arafat (whose three-letter root, *"'a-r-f,"* means to recognize or know), in the vicinity of Mecca.[50]

Thus it was. Strangers upon this planet and unaccustomed to any form of labor, how did Adam and Eve survive? How did they knew what to do?

To this we have no clear answer. Perhaps it was through a mixture of divine inspiration, common sense, and trial-and-error. Or perhaps, as has been suggested by Ibn 'Abbas (R) and other commentators, certain tools and implements were sent down with Adam (A) from Paradise. And he was taught how to use them, learning to plow and sow, water and harvest and thresh and winnow and grind flour and bake bread and work with iron, while Eve spun wool and wove cloth with his help.

The first husband and wife then established the first family. Perhaps Eve bore her children with difficulty and distress, as women have since her time, according to God's words,

> **His mother carried him in weakness upon weakness, and his weaning is in two years.** (31:14)
>
> **His mother carried him with hardship and gave birth to him with hardship, and his gestation and weaning is thirty months.**[51] (46:15)

Adam and Eve would toil until they were weary to eke out their livelihood from the earth, for now nothing would come to them without effort, as it had in Paradise. They and their descendants would have to struggle and labor within the framework of the natural forces on the planet: the endless cycle of building-up, maturation, dissolution, decay and renewal; of days and nights and seasons;

---

[50]This is the name of the vast plain near Mecca where pilgrims gather on the principal day of the *Hajj* (pilgrimage), spending the afternoon in solemn supplication for God's mercy and forgiveness.

[51]Ibn 'Abbas and other scholars understand this "thirty months" as referring to the very shortest period of pregnancy that can produce a living child, together with the maximum permissible period of twenty-four months for breast-feeding (Maududi/*Q*, 46:fn. 23).

amidst fertile lands, deserts, jungles, plains, vast frozen regions, mountains and oceans; during times of plenty and scarcity. Every sort of calamity would come upon them from the earth and sky — volcanic eruptions and floods, fires and fierce storms and earthquakes, droughts and famines — as well as every sort of benefit and blessing. All this was implied in their Lord's earlier warning:

> **O Adam, indeed, this is an enemy to you and your wife. Therefore, do not let him oust the two of you from Paradise so that you become miserable. It is surely granted to you not be hungry therein or unclothed, or to be thirsty therein or affected by heat.** (20:117-119)

And they would have to share the earth with countless other creatures. Some of these would be tameable and ready to work for them, while others would be fierce and dangerous; some would be useful and a means of ease and pleasure, and others would be nuisances or sources of trouble. And while the race of Adam would share many physical characteristics with animals, including the power to kill, their inner reality and nature would be totally different from that of any animal.

For unlike any animal species, we humans have been granted an existence that does not begin simply with the birth of the physical body or end with its death. We remain in this life as long as our Lord decrees, willing, acting, striving, and working out our eternal destiny. Then, once we have completed our term in this world, our body, devoid of soul, becomes a piece of decaying flesh which must be disposed of, like the body of any animal. At the same time, our freed soul returns to the spiritual world from which it came, awaiting its Lord's judgment.

Thus was the home of Adam and Eve (A) established on this earth. On this green, living planet, they and all the human beings who would come from them would live and strive and carry on the struggle between good and evil until the end of the world. On it they would die. Their mortal bodies would be buried in its soil and from it they would be raised on the Last Day. May God's mercy, blessings and peace be upon them, our first parents!

REFERENCES: Tabari/*Q*, "Adam"; Tabari/*H*, I:282-303, 334; Ibn Kathir/*Q*, "Adam"; Bernbaum, *Sacred Mountains*, p. 76; Wheeler, *Sri Lanka*, pp. 9, 115-117.

22. THE K'ABAH AND THE BLACK STONE

The first House [of God's worship] established for mankind was that at Bakkah [Mecca], blessed and a [source of] guidance for all mankind. In it are clear signs — the standing- place of Abraham — and whoever enters it shall be secure. (3:96)

THE SACRED HOUSE

In His infinite wisdom, the Lord of creation, the Bestower of attributes, the Knower of the most subtle mysteries of His creation, has invested certain spots on this planet with special spiritual qualities. And to Muslims, the place of greatest radiance, blessing and mercy is Mecca, the site of the Sacred House, the Holy K'abah.[52]

The Holy Prophet (S) is reported to have said that the earth was spread out from Mecca and that Mecca is the **"earth"** which God Most High mentioned in His saying, **"Indeed, I am going to appoint a *khalifah* on the earth"** [2:30].

There, the angels used to make ***tawaf***[53] around the Sacred House. And whenever a prophet's people were destroyed and he and the righteous believers with him were saved, they would come to the Sacred House, worshipping God there until they died. Thus, it is said, the graves of the prophets Noah, Hud, Saleh and Shu'ayb are between Zamzam, the Corner, and the Standing-Place or Station of Abraham.[54]

REFERENCE: Tabari/*C*, I:208.

---

[52]The two other places of special honor and blessing in Islam are Medina, the city of the Prophet (S), which to this day reflects his light, and Jerusalem, the site of the Temple of Solomon, **whose surroundings We have blessed** (17:1), from whence the Holy Prophet (S) ascended to the seven heavens and the Divine Presence during his Night Journey and Ascension (***al-Isra' wal-Me'raj***).

[53]***Tawaf*** refers to the Islamic practice of making seven circuits around the K'abah, while supplicating and praising God. ***Tawaf*** is part of the rites of both the annual pilgrimage to Mecca (***Hajj***), which falls during the lunar month of Dhul-Hijjah, and the lesser pilgrimage (***'Umrah***), which may be performed at any time.

[54]Hud, Saleh and Shu'ayb are three Arabian prophets. Zamzam is an ancient well adjacent to the K'abah, dating back to the time of Abraham. "The Corner" refers to the corner of the K'abah in which the Black Stone is fixed (see the next section), while the Station of Abraham (***Maqam Ibrahim***) is the spot where Abraham once stood in prayer. For more concerning the K'abah, please see the story of Abraham in this volume, pages 311-313, 318-321.

Just what is the K'abah? In physical terms, it is a plain, cube-shaped structure, hollow and empty inside, made of the black lava rock characteristic of the jagged volcanic peaks surrounding the city of Mecca.[55] But in spiritual terms, only God Most High knows its tremendous significance, for it is said that the K'abah is the earthly counterpart of a heavenly prototype known as ***al-Bait al-Ma'mur***, the Inhabited House in the fourth heaven, so called because hosts of angels make *tawaf* around it, glorifying their Lord without end.

The K'abah has been a place of pilgrimage since the time of Abraham (A), who left his wife and son, Hagar and Ishmael, at its site, upon which Abraham (A) later built the Sacred House at God's command, together with Ishmael (A). All Muslims worldwide, wherever they may be, take the K'abah as the ***qiblah*** (direction) which they face during their *salat* or formal prayers. Thus, the K'abah has been called "a spiritual center, a support for the concentration of consciousness upon the Divine Presence" (Glasse/*E*, "K'abah," p. 214).

According to some traditions, God Most High sent down a jewel from Paradise upon the site of the Sacred House, and Adam (A) was ordered to circumambulate it as he had seen the angels circle around the divine Throne. However, Ibn 'Abbas (R) states that God Most High revealed to Adam,

> "I have a scared precinct [upon the earth] in front of My Throne, so go there and build a house for Me in it, and come close to it as you have seen My angels closing around My Throne. There I shall respond to you and your children — to whomever among them is obedient to Me."
>
> Adam said, "Yes, my Lord, but how can I do that? I am not strong enough to do that, nor do I know how." God then appointed an angel for him and he accompanied him toward Mecca. Whenever Adam passed by a place with vegetation or a place which appealed to him, he would say to the angel, "Let us stop here," and the angel would reply to him, "As you wish," until they reached Mecca. Every place at which he stopped [later] became inhabited and every place he by-passed became a desert and a wasteland.
>
> He constructed the House with [materials from] five mountains: Mount Sinai, the Mount of Olives, Mount Lebanon, and Mount Judi, and built its foundations with [material from] Mount Hira'.[56] When he had finished building it, the angel took him toward 'Arafat and showed him all

---

[55]In our time, the K'abah is protected from the elements by a black cover (***kiswah***), embroidered in gold thread with Qur'anic verses, which is provided and replaced annually by the government of Saudi Arabia.

[56]Judi is the mountain or hill upon which Noah's Ark came to rest (see the story of Noah in this volume). Hira' is the mountain close to Mecca at whose summit is the cave in which Prophet Muhammad (S) received the first revelation of the Qur'an from the angel Gabriel.

the rites [of *Hajj*] that people perform today. He then proceeded with him [Adam] to Mecca, and he made *tawaf* of the House for an entire week. (Ibn Kathir/*Q*, "Adam").

REFERENCES: Tabari/*Q*, "Adam"; Tabari/*H*, I:293-295, 301-302; Ibn Kathir/*Q*, "Adam"; Ayoub/*Q*, I:158-159.

THE BLACK STONE

Among the black lava rocks that make up the walls of the K'abah, one stone is absolutely unique — **the Black Stone** (*al-Hajar al-Aswad*), a shiny, metallic-looking rock set into what is known as "the Corner [of the Stone]," surrounded by a silver sheath. This stone has been worn concave by the lips and hands of all the Muslims who have kissed or touched it throughout the centuries, in keeping with the Holy Prophet's practice of kissing, touching, or (when mounted) pointing to it, as reported in a number of *ahadith* (*Bukhari*, 2:673, 2:676- 677, 2:679- 682, 2:697).

Why would Muhammad (S), the greatest of all prophets, show such love and respect for a mere stone? This question was in the mind of one of the Prophet's closest Companions, 'Umar ibn al-Khattab (R), when he addressed the Black Stone, saying, "Indeed, I know that you are [nothing but] a stone, neither giving harm nor benefit, and if I had not seen the Messenger of God, God's peace and blessings be upon him, kissing you, I would not have kissed you" (*Bukhari*, 2:667, 2:675; *Muwatta*, 20.36.116).

As if in answer to our question, out of his immense reservoir of spiritual knowledge, the blessed Prophet (S) spoke of the Black Stone and its heavenly qualities, saying:

The Black Stone is the right hand of God on earth.[57]

The Black Stone is a jewel from among the jewels of Paradise. It will be raised on the Day of Resurrection having two eyes and a tongue with which it will speak, and it will bear witness for everyone who kissed it and testified to its truth. (*Tirmidhi*)

The Black Stone descended from Paradise whiter than milk, but in time the sins of the children of Adam made it black. (*Mishkat*, 2577)

The Black Stone is one of the stones of Paradise and there is no other from Paradise besides it, and it was as white as water; and if it were not for the abomination that touched it during the [pre-Islamic period of] Ignorance

---

[57]Cited in Abu Hamid al-Ghazali's work, *"Faysal al-Tafriqa bayn al-Islam wa l-Zandaq,"* in *Freedom and Fulfillment*, translated by Richard Joseph McCarthy, p. 156.

> [of God's guidance], every handicapped person who touches it would be healed. (Al-Houry, *Hadiths,* #537)
>
> The Corner [of the Black Stone] and the Station [of Abraham] are two jewels from among the jewels of Paradise whose light God has effaced, and if their light had not been effaced, it would have illuminated whatever is between the East and the West. (*Mishkat,* 2579)

Upon this entire planet, therefore, the Black Stone is unique — the one thing we possess from Paradise, and thus the most sacred thing on earth. When we are in its presence, it is as if we are the presence of a precious souvenir of home. This, it has been said, is the secret of the special attraction which Muslims feel at the K'abah, for the Black Stone is related to our soul's relationship to Paradise, our original homeland and place of final return.

REFERENCES: Tabari/*Q*, "Adam"; Tabari/*H*, I:293-295, 301, 303; Ibn Kathir/*Q*, "Adam"; Ayoub/*Q*, I:157-159.

23. THE TRUST AND THE PLEDGE

It is He who has revealed to you [Muhammad] the Book; in it are firm verses[58] — they are the foundation of the Book — and others that are allegorical. As for those in whose hearts is deviation, they pursue what is allegorical therein, seeking discord and seeking an interpretation [agreeable to themselves]. And no one knows its [ultimate] interpretation except God. But those firm in knowledge say, "We believe in it; all of it is from our Lord." And no one bears this in mind except people of understanding. (3:7)

Here it is appropriate to report two very important matters relating to Adam (A). While they are not part of his actual life-story, perhaps they are among the matters indicated in the verse cited above.

THE TRUST

At some point in the timelessness of the spiritual world, God Most High informs us,

> **We offered the Trust to the heavens and the earth and the mountains, but they declined to bear it and were afraid of it, but the human being took it up. He was surely unjust and ignorant.** (33:72)

Here, **"the Trust"** is mentioned as if it were a thing commonly understood by the generality of mankind. According to the interpretation of Ibn 'Abbas, **"the Trust"** refers to obedience to God's commands and the obligations of the religion, while **"the human being"** refers to Adam (A), who represents the entire human race. The meaning of this verse is that the human being is unjust toward himself and his Lord, as well as ignorant of the tremendous benefit and blessings he is giving up, by not being careful to observe the rights that he owes to God, which constitute this Trust.

Now, when God offered the Trust, first to the heavens with all the spiritual beings in them, then to the earth in its great physical strength, and then to the mountains, standing firm and high, it was not as a command. Rather, it was as a matter which they had the option to accept or decline, and if they declined it, it would not be a sin for them.

Out of awe of their Lord, they declined, knowing that they did not have the strength to bear such a burden and that if they did not fulfill this commitment

---

[58]That is, verses whose meaning is clear and decisive, which cannot have more than one interpretation, and which are secured from change, abrogation and interpretation other than what is obvious. A lengthy discussion concerning this verse is found in Ayoub/*Q*, II:20-46.

once they had made it, it would then become a sin for which they would be punished.

God then offered the Trust to Adam. "What does it involve?" he asked.

"If you obey, you will be rewarded, and if you disobey, you will be punished," God said.

At that, Adam, being naive, accepted it. And, says Ibn 'Abbas (R), although this acceptance took place at '*asr* time — that is, in the later part of the afternoon — before the time of *maghrib* or sunset, Adam had disobeyed His Lord.

The Trust, which can be understood as meaning commitment, responsibility and obedience to God's commands, was something that could only have been assumed by conscious beings having wills which would enable them to carry it out. As the Original Man, the father and representative of humankind, Adam (A) accepted this Trust on behalf of all his descendants up to the end of this world. And, by revealing this information about something that took place in the spiritual world, God Most High makes us aware of Adam's commitment on behalf of each one of us to live our lives in obedience and surrender to Him — that is, to use whatever He has granted us in keeping with His Will rather than our own often erring desires.

REFERENCES: Ibn Kathir/*T*, 7:172-173, 33:72; Maududi/*Q*, 33:fn. 120; Asad/*Q*, 3: fn. 5, 3780; Ayoub/*Q*, 11:20-46.

THE PLEDGE OF THE DAY OF PROMISES

The second all-important matter related to Adam (A) is the witnessing of what is known as the Day of Promises, referred to in the following verses:

> **[Mention, O Muhammad,] when your Lord took from the children of Adam, from their loins, their descendants, and had them testify concerning themselves, [asking,] "Am I not your Lord?" They said, "Yes, we bear witness [to it]"; lest you should say on the Day of Resurrection, "Indeed, we were unaware of this," or [lest] you should say, "It was only that our fathers previously took others as partners with God, and we were [merely their] descendants after them. Would You then destroy us for what the perpetrators of falsehood did?" Thus do We detail Our signs, and perhaps they will return.** (7:172-174)

Concerning this "event" in the world of souls, the Holy Prophet (S) said:

> God took the covenant from Adam's back at Na'man, which is 'Arafat, and He brought forth from his loins all his offspring, whom he multiplied and scattered before Him like tiny specks. He then spoke to them face to face, saying, **"Am I not your Lord?"** They said, **"Yes, we bear witness**

> **[to it]," [lest] you should say, "It was only that our fathers previously took others as partners with God, and we were [merely their] descendants after them. Would You then destroy us for what the perpetrators of falsehood did?"**[59] (*Mishkat*, 0121)

The meaning of **"testify concerning themselves"** in this verse is that since all human beings had borne witness on the Day of Promises to God's being their Lord, they would have no justification for claiming, on the Day of Judgment, that they did not know — firstly, that God was their Lord, and secondly, that they themselves had pledged to accept Him as their Lord.

Moreover, they would not be able to justify having taken other deities as objects of worship or allegiance, as their forefathers had done, with the excuse that **"we were** merely their **descendants after them."** Nor would they be able to reproach God for punishing them for their worship of false deities by saying, **"Would You then destroy us for what the perpetrators of falsehood did?"** as if to claim that it was their ancestors' fault, not their own, that they had been devoted to objects of worship other than Him, of whatever kind they might have been.

Finally, God's words at the end of these two verses, **Thus do We detail Our signs, and perhaps they will return,** leave open the possibility that, after knowing about this covenant with Him, those who did not understand correctly or who had deviated might turn to the pure, pristine faith ordained by God, known from the beginning of the history of mankind as *islam*.

REFERENCES: Tabari/*H*, I:304-307, 327-330; Ibn Kathir/*T*, 2:172-173, 33:72; Maududi/*Q*, 7:fn. 134.

---

[59]In another version of this *hadith*, when asked about the verse, **"When your Lord took from the children of Adam, from their loins, their descendants,"** the Holy Prophet (S) replied:

> God created Adam, and He passed His right Hand over his back and brought forth from it his descendants, saying, "I have created these for Paradise, and these will do the deeds of those who go to Paradise." Then He passed His Hand over his back [again] and brought forth from it his descendants, saying, "I have created these for Hell, and they will do the deeds of those who go to Hell.'"

A man then asked, "Then what is the good of doing anything, O Messenger of God?" The Prophet (S) replied:

> When God creates a slave [of His] for Paradise, He uses him to do the deeds of the people of Paradise until he dies according to the deeds of the people of Paradise, whereupon He causes him to enter Paradise thereby; and when He creates a slave [of His] for the Fire, He uses him to do the deeds of the people of the Fire until he dies according to the deeds of the people of the Fire, whereupon He causes him to enter the Fire thereby. (*Abu Dawud*, 4686; also *Mishkat*; *Muwatta*, 46.1.2)

Recognizing the Connection

Even though we are unable to remember it, this committment of our souls in the pre-earthly existence to take no one as Lord but God Most High remains deeply embedded within the human psyche. This is made clear by the Prophet's saying,

> God Most High will say to the person among the people of Hell who will have the least punishment on the Day of Resurrection, "If you had everything on the earth, would you ransom yourself [from punishment] with it?" whereupon he will say, "Yes!" Then He will say, "I desired less than that from you while you were in the loins of Adam — that you not associate any partner with Me — but you went on associating partners with Me" (*Bukhari*, 8:562; also 8:546),

meaning that, although you knew what was expected of you, you did not remain true to what you had acknowledged and accepted in the spiritual world.

Now, it is only natural to wonder why, if we made such a comittment with God, we are unaware of it. The reason is that our minds are formatted to deal with and recall only what relates to this present life, so that whatever we experienced in the spiritual world of souls is lost to our consciousness. Nonetheless, because we are inherently spiritual beings, connectedness to our Creator is part of the *fitrah* or innate nature with which He created us, and hence the tie of our souls to Him remains intact and unbreakable.

This may explain why we feel an intuitive connection with some Power higher than ourselves, even if we do not choose to call it "God". It may also be why we feel a sense of holiness, awe, mystery and majesty toward the unfathomable universe around us. And that is doubtless why, almost reflexively, we instinctively call upon God when we are in trouble or need. ***For our souls know***; because they belong to the unseen, spiritual realm, they know without any doubt or question.

Still other evidences exist of their knowing. One of these is the surprising feeling of familiarity we sometimes experience upon meeting someone for the first time. "It seems as if I've always known you," we may say. And perhaps we have, for the blessed Prophet (S) said,

> Souls are assembled troops, so those of them who recognize each other [from the spiritual world] will be in harmony, but those of them who do not know each other will differ. (*Muslim*, 6376, 6377; *Bukhari*, 4:552A)

But perhaps by far the most noteworthy and obvious sign of our connection to the spiritual world is dreams. During sleep, our souls are set free temporarily from the limitations of time, space and the material world, according to God's words,

> **God takes the souls at the time of their death, and those which do not die [He takes temporarily] during their sleep. Then He**

retains those for whom He has decreed death and releases the others until an appointed term. In that are surely signs for a people who reflect. (39:42)

Accordingly, when the Prophet (S) went to sleep, he would say, "O God, in Your name I live and in Your Name I die." And when he got up he would say, "Praise be to God Who gave us life after our death [during sleep], and to You is the resurrection" (*Muslim*, 6549).

In our dreams, we often see, hear and experience things in such extraordinary and vivid detail that it may almost seem as if we have two lives — the physical life of our waking state and the life we experience while sleeping, during which the soul may be in touch with the spiritual realm. This is why many people experience spiritual openings in the form of true dreams.[60] For although the line of prophets ended with the Last Messenger, Muhammad (S), this element of prophethood still remains. This is stated in a number of ***ahadith***, such as the Prophet's saying, "Nothing is left of prophethood except ***mubashshirat***," and when those around him asked, "What are ***mubashshirat***?" he replied, "Sound dreams"[61] (*Bukhari*, 9:119; *Muwatta*, 52.1.3; *Abu Dawud*, 4999). He also said:

> The good dream of a righteous man is one of the forty-six parts of prophethood. (*Bukhari*, 9:112, 9:116-118; *Muwatta*, 52.2.1)
>
> When the [End-]Time nears, the dreams of a believer will hardly be false, and a dream of a believer is one part among the forty-six parts of prophethood. Therefore, indeed it is not false. (*Bukhari*, 9:144; *Abu Dawud*, 5000)
>
> Whoever sees me while sleeping has certainly seen me because indeed Satan is unable to take my shape, and the dreams of the believer are one part of the forty-six parts of prophethood. (*Bukhari*, 9:123, 9:125, 9:126; *Muslim*, 5639)
>
> A true dream is from God and a bad dream is from Satan. Therefore, whenever one of you has a bad dream, he should seek refuge with God from it and spit on his left,[62] and then it will not harm him. (*Bukhari*, 9:113-115, 9:124, 9:133, 7:643; also 9:168-169; *Muslim*, 5620; *Muwatta*, 52.1.4; *Abu Dawud*, 5003)

---

[60]Thus it was that the Prophet's wife 'A'ishah was to say, "The first of what was manifested to the Messenger of God, God's peace and blessings be upon him, of the revelation was the good dream during sleep, and he did not see any dream without its coming like the breaking of dawn" (*Bukhari*, 1:3). And once he said to her, "O 'A'ishah, my eyes sleep but my heart remains awake" (*Bukhari*, 2:248; *Muwatta*, 7.2.9; also *Mishkat*, 161).

[61]One should, however, be extremely careful in interpreting dreams. Dream interpretation should only be done by a Muslim shaykh who is known for his soundness in this regard. Otherwise, grave errors may result.

All this constitutes a strong evidence that our souls are still in vital connection with the spiritual world, offering a clear proof that there is infinitely more to life than the material realm, according to the words of God the Exalted:

> **We will show them Our signs in the horizons and within themselves until it becomes clear to them that it is the truth.** (41:53)

> **And on the earth are signs for the certain, and within yourselves. Do you not then perceive?** (51:20-21)

*62 To spit without saliva toward one's left shoulder is mentioned in numerous ***ahadith*** as a means of freeing oneself from Satan's influence or suggestions.

24. Further *Ahadith* Concerning Adam

All of you are from Adam, and Adam was [created] from earth. (The Prophet's Farewell Sermon).

In addition to those already cited, Adam (A) is mentioned in a number of *ahadith* referring to the spiritual world. Among these are several that refer to his eating of the Tree in connection with the terrible trials of the Day of Judgment. We here combine these *ahadith* into the following narrative:

On the Day of Resurrection, the believers will be detained until they become distressed. Then they will say, "If only we could ask someone to intercede with our Lord to relieve us from our situation!"

They will then go to Adam (A) and say, "You are Adam, the father of mankind. God created you with His Hand, breathed into you from His Spirit, settled you in Paradise, had the angels prostrate to you, and taught you the names of all things. Will you intercede for us with your Lord until He relieves us of our situation?"

Adam (A) will say, "This day my Lord is angry as He never was before nor will ever be again. That is not for me,"[63] and he will recall the mistake he made: that he ate from the Tree, although he had been prohibited from it. He will then say, "Myself! Myself! Myself! Go to Noah, the first prophet sent by God to the people of the earth."[64]

The believers will go to Noah, who in turn will tell them to go to Abraham, who will tell them to go to Moses, who will tell them to go to Jesus, God's peace and blessings be upon them all. One after the other, all these, the greatest among prophets, will declare that they are not fit for this undertaking. The believers will then go to Muhammad (S), to whom God will grant the highest honor and privilege — to intercede for mankind — and he will continue interceding until everyone comes out of Hell except those for whom it is decreed for eternity — or, as is mentioned in some versions, whoever proclaims the oneness of God and has the smallest particle of faith in his heart.

We will refer to these *ahadith* again in subsequent prophets' stories.

REFERENCES: *Bukhari*, 9.532[C], 6:3, 6:236, 9:507; *Muslim*, 373, 377-378, 380.

---

[63]In another version, he will say, "What turned you out of Paradise was the sin of your father Adam. I am not in a position to do that" (*Muslim*, 380).

[64]In other versions (*Muslim*, 377, 380), Adam will send the believers to Abraham rather than to Noah.

A number of *ahadith* also report the blessed Prophet's meeting with Adam (A) during his *Me'raj* or Ascension to the Divine Presence. Again, we combine and summarize these *ahadith* as follows:

Muhammad (S), guided by Gabriel (S), was brought to the lowest heaven. There he saw a man sitting with a crowd of people at his right and at his left. When he looked toward his right he laughed and when he looked toward his left he wept.

When Muhammad (S) asked Gabriel (A) who he was, Gabriel (A) said, "He is Adam, and the people at his right and left are his offspring. Among the people on his right are the people of Paradise, and the crowd that is on his left are the people of Hell, so when he looks toward the right he laughs and when he looks toward the left he weeps." And he instructed him, "This is your father, so greet him."

Muhammad (S) greeted him and Adam (A) returned his greeting and said, "Welcome, O my son! What a good son you are!" and, "Welcome, righteous prophet and righteous son!"

REFERENCES: *Bukhari*, 1:345, 5:227, 9:608.

In a number of other related *ahadith*, the Prophet (S) said that on the Day of Resurrection, God will command Adam to separate out a portion of his descendants for Hell. Adam will then ask his Lord how many he is to separate out or who those are to be separated. In one version of this *hadith*, Adam is told to select 999 out of a thousand; in another, it is ninety-nine out of a hundred.

Those of the Prophet's Companions who were present became terribly distressed at hearing this, wondering which of them, among such a great number, would remain out of Hell. When they voiced their concern to the Prophet (S), he told them that the vast numbers selected for Hell would be non-believers, while the few who escaped Hell would be Muslims. He then said that the number of Muslims compared to that of others would be like a white hair on a black ox, meaning that the number of Muslims, beside that of all the unbelievers who had ever lived, would be minute. But he added that he hoped that Muslims would comprise from one-fourth to one-half of the people of Paradise.

REFERENCES: *Bukhari*, 8:536-537, 6:265, 4:567; also 9:575.

PART FIVE: THE DESCENDANTS OF ADAM

25. THE FIRST HUMANS

And among His signs is that He created you from dust, whereupon you are human beings, scattered about. And among His signs is that He created spouses for you from among yourselves in order that you might find tranquility in them, and He put love and mercy between you; surely in that are signs for people who reflect. And among His signs is the creation of the heavens and the earth, and the diversity of your languages and colors; surely in that are signs for the knowing. (30:20-22)

O mankind, be mindful of your Lord, who created you from a single soul and from it created its mate, and from the two of them scattered about many men and women. (4:1)

God has created spouses for you from among yourselves, and has created for you, from your spouses, children and grandchildren, and has provided you with good things. (16:72)

After Adam and Eve, may God's peace and blessings be upon them, began their life on earth, they began to populate it with their children.

Since this happened ages before the existence of any recorded history, we do not know clearly what those first human beings looked like. However, one thing is absolutely certain: *Adam and Eve and their children were fully conscious, spiritually-developed men and women, aware of God and of themselves,* not some kind of creatures who were half-human, half-ape — so-called "prehistoric man".

Obviously this statement conflicts with current scientific thinking about the origin of the human species. However, that thinking remains at the theoretical stage, and we may need to remind ourselves that a theory is a theory and evidence does not constitute fact. The difference between the information provided by the Creator and Knower of all things in comparison to so-called scientific evidence is like the difference between a living animal which we can observe and study, and the tracks left by its unknown prehistoric ancestor upon rock.

In the story of Adam (A), God Himself testifies unequivocally to the fact that He created man *as man*, with completely human qualities, not as a more highly evolved species of animal.[65] This is borne out by the fact that monkeys, from whom mankind is supposed to have evolved, still exist and are still monkeys. Moreover, while humans can master and train monkeys, monkeys cannot master or train human beings, nor can even the most advanced of them do the minutest fraction of what human beings are able to do. Furthermore, a human cannot reproduce any form of life in tandem with an animal.

But more importantly, while our bodies certainly resemble and function like the bodies of primates, a human being is not a mere body. Rather, we are immortal souls housed in physical bodies, and just as a house is not its inhabitant, neither is our body "us". Consequently, we are a distinctly different order of creation from any animal, possessing consciousness of ourselves (that is, the ability to observe, analyze and understand ourselves), the faculty of reason, and the ability to act on reason rather than instinct. Hence, there is no crossover between the worlds of humans and animals. An animal is an animal and a human is a human, not simply a higher form of animal life.

The theory of evolution, which holds that higher life forms 'evolved' from lower ones, is a useful tool for explaining certain things that we observe. However, it is not a proven or provable fact or truth. It should be understood for what it is: a scientific guess, based on certain observations, concerning what cannot be positively known or proved because none of us was present to witness or record it. But, as far as mankind is concerned, it is an incorrect guess which we should not confuse with fact, since the true facts about the origin of mankind can only come from the Creator of mankind.

There can be no question that an order of creatures which we term 'prehistoric man' did exist. But the Qur'anic account of Adam (A) makes it clear that whatever these earlier forms may have been, they did not belong to the same species as Adam and Eve, with their fully-matured human understanding and consciousness.

What were those prehistoric creatures, then? At this stage of our knowledge, we do not know clearly. All that we can say without any doubt whatsoever, based on the testimony of the Creator Himself, is that the very first totally conscious human beings on earth were the pair known as Adam and Eve, and that they and their descendants were a distinctly different species from any other — ***our kind, as we exist today.***

The evidence concerning prehistoric man is actually quite fragmentary, consisting mainly of various unconnected bones gathered from different parts of the globe. From the evidence presented by these fragments, scientists have put

---

[65]Adam's creation as a conscious human being is borne out by the Prophet's saying, "God created Adam in his [finished] form" (***Bukhari***, 8:246), which perhaps may also be understood as meaning that he possessed complete mental and spiritual faculties.

together a supposed profile of what the possessors of these bones looked like, their mental and physical abilities, and how they lived — but, again, this is all guesswork. Regardless of what these early creatures may have been, the Qur'anic account obliges us to conclude that Adam and Eve were sent to the earth after the period of the pre-humans had ended. In other words, our first grandparents were put on earth when God, in His infinite wisdom, decreed that fully developed, conscious humans should dwell upon it.

We now return to their story.

26. CAIN AND ABEL

Relate to them the story of the sons of Adam with truth. (5:27/30)

It has often been asked how the earth became populated through one man and one woman. And the answer to this question was given by the Holy Prophet (S) himself.

When the well-known Companion, Abu Dharr al-Ghiffari (R), asked God's Messenger (S) whether Adam was a prophet sent by God, the Prophet (S) replied that he was a messenger to his children, who were forty in number, consisting of pairs of male and female twins. He then recited the verse, **"[It is He] who created you from a single soul and from it created its mate, and from the two of them scattered about many men and women"** [4:1] (Ayoub/*Q*, I:76).

From this, it is evident that in the beginning God permitted marriage between brothers and sisters in order to populate the world. Ibn 'Abbas (R) states that each boy born to Adam was born together with a girl twin. Adam would marry the boy of one pregnancy to the girl of another, and vice versa. However, his children were forbidden to marry their own twins.

Among all these children of Adam and Eve, only two are mentioned in the Qur'an, although not by name. Islamic tradition gives them the names Qabil and Habil, or Cain and Abel, whose story is told in the Old Testament Book of Genesis.

Cain was the elder of the two, Ibn 'Abbas (R) informs us. He was a farmer, while Abel was a shepherd. Now, Cain's twin sister was more beautiful than Abel's twin. When Abel wanted to marry Cain's twin, Cain claimed that he was more deserving to marry her because she was his sister who had been born with him, because she was more beautiful than Abel's sister, and because he was the elder of the two and his father's executor. And although Adam ordered Cain to marry her to Abel, Cain refused.

The two brothers then offered a sacrifice to God. According to the majority of early commentators, its purpose was to determine which of the two brothers had more right to Cain's sister. Abel sacrificed a plump young sheep, while Cain offered a sheaf of ears of corn. Fire then came down from Heaven, consuming Abel's offering but leaving Cain's, according to God's words, **They each offered a sacrifice and it was accepted from one of them but was not accepted from the other** (5:27/30).[66]

---

[66]According to some interpretations, this was the sign that the girl was to be for Abel. According to others, it was the sign that Abel was an acceptable servant to his Lord, while Cain was not.

This infuriated Cain. **"I will certainly kill you!"** (5:27/30), he threatened, impelled by envy and hatred that had been kindled by his brother's desire to marry his twin or by the rejection of his sacrifice, or both.

"Indeed, God accepts only from those who are mindful of Him," Abel replied. And to make it clear that he did not intend to be provoked into killing his brother, he added, **"Even if you should stretch out your hand against me to kill me, I will not stretch out my hand against you to kill you. I surely fear God, Lord of the worlds** (5:27-28/30-32).

"Indeed, I want you take on my sin and your own sin, so you will be among the companions of the Fire,"[67] Abel continued, reminding Cain that if he killed him wrongfully, he would assume the burden of all of Abel's sins. **"And that is the recompense of the wrong-doers"** (5:29/32).

Then Cain pursued Abel while he was trying to escape from him. It is said that one day, as Abel was herding his flock on the mountains, Cain came upon him while he was alseep. **Then his lower self permitted to him the murder of his brother**. Picking up a big rock with which he crushed Abel's skull, **he killed him and thus became of the losers** (5:30/33) — that is, among those who have lost all good in this world and the Hereafter.

Not knowing what to do with Abel's bloody, mangled corspse, Cain let it lie there naked. **Then God sent a crow, digging in the ground, to show him how to hide the disgrace of his brother.** It is said that this crow was one of two brother crows. The two fought, and when one killed the other, it dug a hole for its body and covered it with earth. Seeing this, Cain cried out, **"Oh, woe be to me! Am I incapable of being like this crow and thus hiding the disgrace of my brother?" And he became of the regretful** (5:31/34).

Following the telling of this story, God Most High adds:

> **Because of that, We decreed for the Children of Israel that whoever slays a person, except for [retaliation for the life of] a person or corruption in the land, it would be as if he had slain all mankind, and whoever saves a life, it would be as if he had saved all mankind.**[68] **(5:32/35)**

Thus, the first blood was spilled on earth by one of its second generation of human inhabitants, bearing out the angels' prediction and setting the precedent for all future bloodshed. Concerning this, the Holy Prophet (S) said,

> "No one is killed wrongfully without the first responsibility for it [or,

---

[67]That is, in case of an unprovoked murder, the victim's sins, which are wiped out of his account by his being innocently killed, are transferred to his murderer's account.

[68]While this statement is not found in the Old Testament, it is reportedly found in the Talmud.

according to another wording, "for its blood"] being upon the son of Adam because he introduced the first murder." (*Bukhari*, 9:423)

According to Ibn 'Abbas (R), Eve later gave birth to a son and his twin sister. The angel Gabriel (A) informed Eve that the boy was God's gift to replace Abel. Consequently, he was named Seth (Shith), meaning "gift of God," a name derived from "Abel".

REFERENCES: Qur'an: 5:27-32/5:30-35 in some translations. Commentaries: Tabari/*H*, I:307-317, 324; Ibn Kathir/*Q*, "Adam"; Ayoub/*Q*, I:76; Asad/*Q*, 5:fn. 36.

27. PROPHETHOOD AND ITS BEGINNING

Indeed, God chose Adam and Noah and the family of Abraham and the family of 'Imran[69] above all mankind, descendants of one another. And God is Hearing and Knowing. (3:33-34)

Then We sent Our messengers in succession. (23:44)

ADAM, THE FIRST PROPHET

In addition to granting Adam (A) rule and authority on the earth, God Most High made him His first prophet and messenger.

The fact of Adam's prophethood is referred to in a number of *ahadith*. We have already mentioned Abu Dharr al-Ghiffari's asking the Prophet (S) whether Adam was a prophet sent by God and noted the Prophet's reply that he was a messenger to his children, who were forty in number (Ayoub/*Q*, I:76).

Abu Dharr (R) also reported asking the Prophet (S) which of the prophets was first, to which he replied, "Adam." Abu Dharr (R) then asked him, "Was he a prophet?" to which he replied, "Yes, a prophet who was addressed [that is, through divine revelation]." Abu Dharr (R) then asked how many messengers there had been. The Prophet (S) said, "Three hundred and some tens, a large number" In another version of the same *hadith*, Abu Dharr (R) asked, "O Messenger of God, what is the total number of prophets?" and the Prophet (S) replied, "One hundred and twenty thousand, the messengers among those being 315, a large number" (*Mishkat*, Book XXVI, Chapter XVII).

The Prophet (S) also said that God granted the rank of prophet to Adam when Adam's soul had not yet been joined to his body (*Mishkat*, 5758).[70]

It is said that God revealed twenty-one pages of scripture to Adam (A), who was taught their contents by the angel Gabriel (A) and then put them in writing. It is also said that the letters of the alphabet were revealed on these twenty-one pages, and that the prohibition of eating the flesh of dead animals, blood and pork was revealed to Adam (A).

Thus, Adam (A) was the first in a great, unbroken chain of prophets and messengers which continued up to the last and greatest of them, Muhammad, may God's peace and blessings be upon him and upon them all. And while some details certainly differed, each of these prophets and messengers brought

---

[69]The family of 'Imran includes Mary and the prophets Zechariah, John the Baptist and Jesus, peace be upon them all.

[70]Similar versions of the above *ahadith* are cited in Tabari/*H*, I:323.

the same original, pristine faith — that religion which God Most High perfected for mankind, with which He is pleased, and to which He gives the name of *islam*,[71] meaning "peace through submission and surrender": —

> **Assuredly, the religion in the sight of God is Islam.** (3:19)
>
> **This day[72] I have perfected your religion for you and completed My favor upon you and have been pleased with Islam for you as your religion.** (5:3/4)

And, derived from the word *"islam,"* God calls its followers *"muslims"*, meaning those who have voluntarily surrendered to Him: —

> **He [God] named you *muslims* earlier, and in this [Qur'an].** (22:78)

As will be seen in the stories that follow, all the prophets called their people to give their worship and service to their Creator alone, shunning all other objects of worship. Through divine revelation, they informed their communities about mankind's origin in Paradise, their accountability to God, the inevitability of the Day of Judgment, and the chance to return their heavenly homeland. The prophets were also given revealed guidance and laws by which they might lead their people to the clean, honorable, upright way of life God Most High desires for His servants, of which the prophets themselves were living examples.

REFERENCES: Tabari/*H*, I:322-324; Ayoub/*Q*, I:76; Akili/*B*, p. 155.

PROPHETS AND THEIR CHARACTERISTICS

Understanding the terminology of a religion in its own language is essential to understanding its concepts. Accordingly, we introduce here some key Arabic/Islamic terms related to prophets and prophethood. These terms — terms which are generally learned by Muslim children from an early age, shaping their world view and understanding of reality as they mature — actually convey concepts of very broad meaning and depth, which are critical for a correct understanding of Islam.

The Arabic word for "prophet," ***nabi*** (plural, ***anbiya'*** or ***nabiyin***), means "one who brings news, tidings or information." Thus, a prophet is one who, by means of divine revelation and inspiration, has access to information (***naba***)

---

[71]For purposes of clarity, we have used the words *"islam"/"muslims"* to denote the true faith and believers before the time of Muhammad (S) and "Islam"/"Muslims" for the faith and believers from the Prophet's time onward.

[72]This refers to the day, shortly before the death of the Prophet (S), on which God completed the revelation of the Qur'an to him.

that others do not have. This may be either information about the Unseen — that is, the divine realm of God and His attributes, His Will and plan for His creation; the inhabitants of the spiritual world, angels and jinn; the tidings of prophets and communities before or after their time; or about God's commands and guidance for His servants. However, in contrast to the Old Testament understanding, although God Most High certainly granted knowledge of future events to some of His prophets, especially to the Last Prophet, peace be upon him and upon them all, the Islamic understanding of prophethood (***nubuwwah***, derived from ***nabi***) is not based upon propheseying the future.

The revelation granted to a prophet may be for himself alone or for others. If he is commanded to convey it others, he is also a messenger (***rasul***, plural, ***rusul*** or ***mursalin***, sometimes translated as "apostle"), meaning "one who is sent." The message revealed to a ***rasul*** to be communicated to people is called a ***risalah***.

We have noted the Prophet's saying that, of the 120,000 or 124,000 prophets sent by God, some 315 were messengers. Among all these, twenty-six, who are both prophets and messengers, are mentioned by name in the Qur'an.[73] As for others not mentioned by name, Muslims believe in their collective existence, according to God's words:

> **[We sent] messengers about whom We have told to you [Muhammad] previously and messengers about whom We have not told to you. (4:164)**

Many of the prophets mentioned in the Qur'an had a dual role. On the one hand, they were bringers of good tidings (***mubashirin***) of God's mercy and forgiveness for those who turned to Him. At the same time, they were also warners (***mundhirin***) of His impending judgment and punishment for those who rejected His prophets and revelations, and who persisted in evil: —

[73] Out of these, eighteen are mentioned in the following passage:

> **We granted him [Abraham] Isaac and Jacob; each [of them] We guided. And Noah We guided previously, and among his descendants, David and Solomon and Job and Joseph and Moses and Aaron; and thus do We reward the doers of good. And Zechariah and John and Jesus and Elijah; all were among the righteous. And Ishmael and Elisha and Jonah and Lot, and all [of them] We preferred over [all] mankind, and some from among their fathers and descendants and brothers; and We chose them and guided them to a straight path. (6:84-87)**

> **Mankind was one community,[74] and then God sent the prophets as bringers of good tidings and warners, and sent down with them the scripture with truth to judge among people concerning that about which they differed.** (2:213)

From all this, it is evident that the prophets and messengers were very extraordinary individuals.[75] Among all the people living on earth, God Most High **chose them and guided them upon a straight path** (6:87, 19:58), making them His representatives and deputies, the connecting link between the spiritual realm and humankind. That is, God the Exalted trained and prepared each of these chosen ones until he had grown so near to Him that, like the angels, he surrendered his human will, manifesting only his Lord's divine Will and His exalted attributes. God then revealed to him whatever He willed to reveal, and ordered him to convey His guidance and act as an example to his people. This the messenger would do, steadfastly carrying on his mission against all odds until it was accomplished and God relieved him of it — in some cases through the destruction of his disbelieving and rebellious people, and in others through his own martyrdom.

The prophets and messengers were characterized by certain special attributes, among which are the following:

First: They were completely sincere to their Lord, worshipping and serving Him for His divine sake alone, and not out of the desire for any worldly gain or even heavenly reward. They loved Him beyond everything and did not consider anything too much to do for His sake. At the same time, they regarded Him with the utmost awe and were always conscious of their own utter insignificance in the face of His infinite greatness.

Second: Their character and morals were so perfect that they were free of evil and major sins. While they might make mistakes, they never committed acts of rebellion or deliberate disobedience, manifesting the highest standard of truthfulness, honesty and integrity in all their words, deeds and dealings

Third: The hearts of prophets were so clean and their intentions so pure that they were free of the attributes of selfhood and ego (*nafs*). Thus, each

---

[74]Meaning that the first dwellers on earth were worshippers of their Creator until they deviated to the worship of false gods, as we shall see shortly.

[75]This constitutes a major difference between Islam and its sister faiths, Judaism and Christianity, for the Bible depicts prophets as quite ordinary and indeed extremely fallible men. In fact, several Old Testament prophets are described as having committed such major sins as would disgrace any decent ordinary human being — for example, Noah's getting so drunk that he lay around naked (Gen. 9:21); Lot's becoming so drunk that his daughters were able to have intercourse with him on two consecutive nights (Gen. 19:31-36); and Aaron's fabricating the Golden Calf for the Israelites to worship (Gen. 32:1-6). These are tales which Muslims consider blatant fabrications and slanders against the noblest of God's servants.

prophet represented his Lord and not his own ego — even with himself. Because God's chosen ones were able to reject the desires and passions of their egoes, Satan's promptings, and everything related to the love of this world, they were perfect mediums for receiving their Lord's revelations and inspirations. Consequently, they were also able to convey what they received from God to their people with complete trustworthiness and faithfulness.

Fourth: They were the most scrupulous among mankind in carrying out God's rules and commands, setting a faithful example for others and never considering themselves exempt from any of the rules of religion because of their prophetic rank. For example, cleanliness of body and purity of heart are basic orders in every true religion, an essential part of correct servanthood to the holy Lord. As the most perfect servants of God, prophets were also the cleanest and purest among people: clean in their bodies and outward aspects, clean in their behavior and actions, and pure in heart, which is the seat of God's Presence in the human being.

Fifth: Among mankind, prophets were given the most difficult trials. Numbers of them were harrassed, persecuted, tortured, ridiculed, threatened, and some were even killed. However, one of the most outstanding charactersitics of prophets was their extraordinary patience, perseverance and steadfastness under all kinds of trials and difficulties, continuing on their appointed missions with unshakable trust in the wisdom and rightness of whatever their Lord might decree.

Sixth: The appearance, manners and behavior of God's messengers was so lovely, luminous and awe-inspiring that good-hearted, sound-minded people were instinctively drawn to them. Seeing the light of God in their faces, people would love them and want to follow their way. Thus, they were the living example of the Prophet's words, "The best of you are those who, when they are seen, are a means of God's being brought to mind" (*Mishkat, 5023*).

Seventh: In addition to superb intelligence, the men whom God chose as prophets were also granted extraordinary wisdom (***hikmah***). Because of this, they were able to look at everything with the broad, eternal perspective of spiritual understanding instead of the limited view of time- and locality-bound humans, governed by their erratic feelings and desires. They understood with God-given clarity the state of the hearts and minds of all kinds of people, and how to reach out to them and call them to their Lord.

Perhaps it may seem as if such people sound too good to be real; it may be difficult even to imagine someone of this sort. But this is how the prophets actually were. Without such distinguishing characteristics, they would have been ordinary men. As you read on, you may have occasion to note such qualities manifesting in the personalities and deeds of these noblest of human beings. And although prophethood ended with the Seal of the Prophets,

Muhammad (S), perhaps you may even be fortunate enough to actually meet a saintly, luminous believer who radiates such goodness, light and love that it becomes easy for you to believe in the reality of prophets and prophethood.

28. The Death of Adam

Every soul will taste of death. Then unto Us you will be returned.
(29:57)

Earlier, we cited a ***hadith*** in which the Prophet (S) stated that after his creation, Adam sneezed and praised God, and then he exchanged greetings with the angels. The continuation of this ***hadith*** is as follows:

God then showed Adam his closed Hands and said, "Choose whichever of them you wish."

Adam said, "I choose my Lord's right Hand, and both of my Lord's Hands are right and blessed."

Then God opened His Hand, and it contained Adam and his descendants. Adam asked, "My Lord, what are these?"

He said, "These are your descendants."

Now, every person's term of life was written on his forehead, and among them there was a man who was the brightest of them (or, according to another wording, one with a bright gleam of light upon his forehead). So Adam asked, "My Lord, who is this?"

God said, "This is your descendant David, and I have written his period of life for him as forty years."

Adam said, "My Lord, increase his life."

God said, "That is what I have written for him."

Adam said, "My Lord, I have given him sixty years of my life."[76]

God said, "That is as you wish."

Adam then lived in Paradise as long as God wished, the Prophet (S) continued, after which he was sent down from it. Now, Adam was reckoning the passing of time for himself, and when the Angel of Death came to him, Adam said to him, "You have come before your time. A thousand years has been written for me."

The Angel of Death replied, "Certainly, but you gave sixty years to your son David."

The Prophet (S) added, "Adam denied it and so did his descendants, and he forgot and likewise his descendants forgot." And the Prophet (S) said that, from that day, orders were given that a document be drawn up and witnesses be produced for any legal transaction or agreement. (*Mishkat*, 4662)

---

[76]In another version of this ***hadith***, Adam gives David forty years of his life (*Mishkat*, 118).

In spite of the years he had given away, Adam (A) lived for a full thousand years. Before dying, he made his son Seth his heir. According to ***ahadith***, Adam (A) died on a Friday (***Mishkat***, 1363; ***Abu Dawud***, 1041, 1042). The Prophet (S) is reported to have said that when Adam was near death, God sent down from Paradise embalming materials and a shroud. Angels washed Adam several times with extract of lote tree and water, and wrapped him in layers of shrouds. Then they prepared a grave and buried him, saying, "This (shall be) the custom of the children of Adam after him" (Tabari/*H*, I:333). Accordingly, the Muslim dead are always buried, never cremated.

The Qur'anic commentators differed concerning Adam's burial place. Some said that he was buried in the cave of Mount Abu Qubays, one of the mountains of Mecca. According to others, he died upon Mount Nudh, the mountain upon which he was sent down from Paradise. Eve, it is said, lived only a year after his death, and she was buried with him in the cave.

It is further said that during the Flood, Noah (A) took the bodies of Adam and Eve and placed them in a coffin in the Ark. When the earth had soaked up the water, he re-buried them.[77] Ibn 'Abbas (R) says that Noah re-buried Adam in Jerusalem, but another opinion is that he returned them to their previous burial place — either on Mount Qubays near Mecca or Mount Nudh. May God's best blessings and peace be upon our father Adam and our mother Eve for all eternity!

REFERENCES: Tabari/*Q*, "Adam"; Tabari/*H*, I:324, 327-334, 362; Ibn Kathir/*Q*, "Adam".

---

[77]See "Noah," page 159.

29. Seth (A) and His Successors

Those were some of the prophets upon whom God bestowed favor from among the descendants of Adam. (19:58)

Adam's son Seth (A) succeeded his father as a prophet and a messenger, and he continued in his father's righteous path.

Once when the Holy Prophet (S) was asked how many books God had revealed, he replied, "One hundred and four. God revealed fifty scrolls to Seth" (Tabari/*H*, I:325, II:130). It is said that Seth (A) added these scrolls to those that God had revealed to his father Adam, and he acted according to what they contained. However, in time both sets of scrolls disappeared without a trace.

It is reported that Seth (A) built the Kaʿbah with stones and clay, and that he stayed in Mecca, making pilgrimage to it until he died at the age of 912 years. He was buried with his parents in the cave of Abu Qubays. Every person on earth traces his or her ancestry back to Seth (A) because, among all of Adam's sons, only his line has continued — for, as we shall see, the remainder, coming from the line of Cain, were all eventually destroyed.

When Seth (A) fell ill before his death, he appointed one of his sons, Enosh (Yanish), as his successor. Enosh continued in his father's righteous ways and lived, it is said, for 905 years.

Enosh was succeeded by his son Kenan, who lived to be 910. Kenan in turn was succeeded by his son Mahalel (Mahalayil), who lived 895 years. Mahalel was succeeded by his son Jared (Yarid), who lived 962 years. And Jared was succeeded by Enoch, who is believed to have been the prophet Idris, peace be upon him and upon them all.

REFERENCES: Tabari/*H*, I:324-325, 335, 338, 342-344; Tabari/*H*, II:130; Ibn Kathir/*Q*, "Adam"; Akili/*B*, pp. 155-156.

30. THE BEGINNING OF CORRUPTION ON EARTH

Corruption has appeared on land and sea because of what people's hands have earned, that He may let them taste something [of the consequences] of what they have done, in order that they may turn back. (30:41)

What happened after the time of Seth (A) is shrouded in myth. However, Ibn 'Abbas (R) says that there were two tribes among Adam's descendants. One tribe, the descendants of Cain, lived in the plain, and the other, Seth's descendants, lived on a mountain. The mountain men were handsome but their women were ugly, while the plainswomen were beautiful but their men were ugly.

The mountain men started to go down and live with the Cainite women, and as a result wickedness appeared among the women. This, says Ibn 'Abbas (R), is what is meant by God's words, enjoining modesty upon Muslim women, **Do not display yourselves like the display of the former [period of] ignorance** (33:33).

It is said that the Cainites were godless tyrants, who were very tall in stature. They knew how to work copper and iron, and were the first to live in tents. They were occupied with worldliness and forbidden pleasures, and it is said that Satan inspired them to invent musical instruments, which they used for evil purposes.

Eventually, when Adam's righteous descendant Jared noticed adultery, drinking and corruption among the Cainites, he advised Seth's descendants not to go down among them or intermarry with them. But this advice was not heeded. As more men from among the descendants of Seth went down to the valley and began to live with the plainswomen, the numbers of Cain's descendants gradually spread out and filled the land. Consequently, there were presently two communities living on the earth: the community of believers who were true to their Lord and the teachings of their godly ancestors, and the community of the followers of Satan.

REFERENCES: Tabari/*H*, I:324, 338-341, 343.

31. Idris (A)

And [mention] Ishmael and Idris and Dhul-Kifl; all of them were among the patient. And We admitted them to Our mercy. Indeed, they were among the righteous. (21:85-86)

And mention Idris in the Book [the Qur'an]. Indeed, he was a truthful one and a prophet, and We raised him to a high station. Those were some of the prophets upon whom God bestowed favor from among the descendants of Adam and among those whom We carried [in the Ark] with Noah, and among the descendants of Abraham and Israel [Jacob], and among those whom We guided and chose. (19:56-58)

Who was the prophet Idris (A)? No one knows with certainty, for since the two passages above are the only references to Idris (A) in the entire Qur'an, he has not been positively identified. However, based on the following evidence and reasoning among early Qur'anic scholars, it has been suggested that he was the Biblical Enoch.

In 19:56 above, **those whom We carried with Noah** is said to refer to the prophets who came after Noah but before Abraham — prophets such as Hud and Saleh, peace be upon them all. Those **among the descendants of Abraham and Israel** refers to Abraham (A) and the prophets descended from him through the line of Jacob (A). **Those whom We guided and chose** refers to Prophet Muhammad (S), whom God chose from a people among whom His guidance had been lost, the pagan Arabs. Therefore, **the descendants of Adam** in the above verse was understood by early commentators to refer to those prophets who came between Adam and Noah, resulting in their identifying the prophet Idris with Enoch, who is mentioned very briefly in the following passage in the Book of Genesis:

> When Jared had lived 162 years, he became the father of Enoch. And after he became the father of Enoch, Jared lived 800 years and had other sons and daughters. Altogether, Jared lived 962 years, and then he died.
>
> When Enoch had lived 65 years, he became the father of Methusaleh. And after he became the father of Methusaleh, Enoch walked with God 300 years and had others sons and daughters. Altogether, Enoch lived 365 years. Enoch walked with God; then he was no more, because God took him away. (Gen. 5:18-24)

As modern Biblical scholarship has demonstrated, rather than being a revelation from the Creator, the Old Testament is primarily a history of the descendants of Adam through Abraham, written by numbers of human authors. The statement that Enoch "walked with God" is therefore not to be taken literally but rather indicates Enoch's closeness to his Lord. His being "no more" suggests that he reached such a high spiritual station that he ceased to be among the living on this planet because God raised him to Himself.

Muslim commentators, taking their information from Old Testament sources, state that Enoch or Idris (A) was the successor of his father Jared or Yarid. It is said that Idris (A) was deeply devoted to his Lord's worship and law; in fact, his name means "one who studies or teaches." It is also said that **the former scriptures,** mentioned in the verse, **Indeed, this is in the former scriptures, the scriptures of Abraham and Moses** (87:18-19), refer to the earliest scriptures revealed to the prophets Seth and Idris (A), so that this verse actually means, "Indeed, this is in the former scriptures [of Seth and Idris, and in] the scriptures of Abraham and Moses."

Although nothing is mentioned in the Qur'an concerning the life of Idris (A), the Prophet (S) spoke of him to his Companion, Abu Dharr al-Ghifari (R), saying, "Four — that is, messengers — were Syrians: Adam, Seth, Noah, and Enoch [Idris], who was the first to write with a pen. God revealed thirty scrolls to him" (Tabari/*H*, I:344, II:130). Ibn Kathir adds that Idris (A) was constantly occupied with the remembrance of God (***dhikr***) and that the number of his good deeds was equal to the number of good deeds of all the people on earth during his time. Ibn Kathir also mentions that Idris (A) worked as a tailor, and that with each stitch he would say, "***Subhanallah*** —glory be to God!" (Ibn Kathir/*Q*, "Idris").

According to some traditions, the words, **We raised him to a high station** (19:57), cited in the verses at the beginning of this section, imply that God raised Idris (A) to Himself without his experiencing death, but only God knows the truth. However, it is mentioned in ***ahadith*** that when the Holy Prophet (S) ascended to the seven heavens during his blessed ***Me'raj*** or Ascension, he met all the earlier prophets face-to-face, and Idris (A) was among them (***Bukhari***, 1:345, 5:227, 4:429, 9:608). May God's peace and blessings be upon Idris (A) and upon all the prophets!

After Enoch, his son and successor Methusaleh continued in God's path, calling His servants to Him; his lifespan is said to have been 919 years. Methusaleh's son Lamech succeeded him and he lived 780 years.

It is said that although all these righteous descendants of Adam (A) forbade their people to go among the corrupted descendants of Cain, their advice was not heeded. As time passed, almost all the people on the mountain went down and began to live among the Cainites, adopting their evil ways and forgetting the honorable, upright way of their grandfather Adam (A) and his righteous successors.

Then a son was born to Lamech who was named Noah. As the first major prophet after Adam (A), he was to have a grave impact on the future of mankind.

The following is the genealogy from Adam to Noah (A), given in the Bible and accepted by the early scholars of Islam:

1. Adam
2. Seth (the prophet Shith)
3. Enosh (Yanish)
4. Kenan
5. Mahalel (Mahalayil)
6. Jared (Yarid)
7. Enoch (the prophet Idris ?)
8. Methuselah
9. Lamech (Lamaq)
10. Noah (the prophet Nuh), peace be upon him and upon his righteous ancestors.

REFERENCES: Tabari/*H*, I:325, 336-337, 342-348, 353-354; Tabari/*H*, II:130; Ibn Kathir/*T*, 19:56-57; Ibn Kathir/*Q*, "Idris"; Akili/*B*, p. 155; Maududi/*Q*, 19:fns. 33-34; Asad/*Q*, 19: fns. 41-42; Ali/*Q*, fn. 2508.

32. Summing It Up

There is certainly, in their stories, a lesson for those of understanding.
(12:111)

As mentioned earlier, in addition to providing information about the beginning of our species, the story of Adam (A) is also an allegory concerning the human condition. Consequently, some of the meanings and lessons it contains are simple and obvious, while others are extremely deep and require much reflection to grasp. We therefore now turn our attention to the three primary matters addressed in this story.

Avoiding Heedlessness

One extremely important lesson this story teaches us is the importance of not being heedless, even for the briefest span of time.

When we let down our guard, Satan and our lower self or *nafs* are able to push us into doing things that we might never do if we were mindful and carefully attentive. And, as was the case with our first parents, the consequence of one single moment's heedlessness may be the loss of everything we value, both here and Hereafter. The first message of this story is, therefore, that we must try at all times to be as mindful, conscious and connected as possible.

Repenting and Turning to God

Another vital lesson is that when we do wrong, we must try to be like Adam (A), not like the arrogant, rebellious Iblis. Although both disobeyed their Lord's order, one did so deliberately and calculatedly, while the other did so out of forgetfulness and inattention — and herein lies the difference between a sin and an error. One persisted in his sin, attempted to justify it, and demanded to be allowed to go on sinning, while the other immediately repented, sincerely asked forgiveness, and was devastated by the consequences of his action. As a result, one was cursed and condemned for all eternity, while the other was not only forgiven but also honored and blessed by his Lord.

Guarding Against Satan

Another important aspect of the story of Adam (A) is the information it provides us, his descendants, about the eternal enemy of mankind, Satan.

In the Qur'an, God makes it clear beyond the shadow of any doubt that Satan exists. He is not simply a metaphor or an abstract principle but an actual, living being. And because he is evil and exemplifies evil, God's warnings against him are strong, direct and numerous. Among them are the following:

> **Do not follow the footsteps of Satan. Indeed, he is a clear enemy to you.** (2:168, 208; 6:142; 7:22; 43:62)
>
> **Indeed, he is a clear, misleading enemy!** (28:15)
>
> **Will you then take him [Satan] and his race as allies instead of Me, while they are enemies to you? — a wretched exchange for the wrong-doers!** (18:50; also 7:27)
>
> **O mankind, assuredly God's promise is true, so do not let the life of this world delude you, nor let the Deceiver deceive you about God. Indeed, Satan is an enemy to you, so take him as an enemy. He only calls to his party to be among the companions of the blazing fire.** (35:5-6)
>
> **Whoever takes Satan as an ally instead of God has certainly incurred a clear loss.** (4:119)
>
> **He to whom Satan is a companion, evil is he as a companion.** (4:38)

Now, having thus been repeatedly warned against this sworn enemy of our species, the question may well be asked, *How do we protect ourselves from his harm?*

Seeking Refuge with God

The first measure is to take refuge against this enemy of ours with God, our Protector and Defender, who says:

> **If an evil instigation from Satan incites you, then seek refuge in God. Assuredly, He is Hearing and Knowing. Indeed, those who are mindful of God — whenever an evil suggestion touches them from Satan, they remember [Him], whereupon at once they have insight.** (7:200-201, 41:36)
>
> **And say, "My Lord, I seek refuge with You from the urgings of the evil ones, and I seek refuge with you, my Lord, lest they be present with me."** (23:97-98)
>
> **Then, when you read the Qur'an, seek refuge in God from Satan the accursed.** (16:98)

Therefore, the Prophet (S) advised, any time we want to be safe from Satan's prompting or interference, we should say, "***A'udhu bil-Lahi min ash-Shaytani-r-Rajim*** — I seek refuge in God from Satan, the accursed."

He also said, "Do not say, 'May Satan perish,' because when you do, Satan becomes larger and says, 'By my power I have defeated him.' But if you say, '*Bismillah*' [In the name of God], Satan diminishes until he is like a fly" (Abu Dawud, Ahmad). This indicates that when we remember God in our hearts, Satan's power over us is weakened, while if we forget to mention Him, Satan becomes stronger and is able to overpower us.

The Prophet (S) also repeatedly advised reciting the last two *surahs* of the Qur'an, known as the *Surahs* of Seeking Refuge, especially before sleeping. They are as follows:

> **Say: "I seek refuge in the Lord of the dawn from the evil of what He created, and from the evil of darkness when it approaches, and from the evil of the blowers upon knots[78] and from the evil of an envier when he envies."** (113:1-5)
>
> **Say: "I seek refuge in the Lord of mankind, the King of mankind, the God of mankind, from the evil of the hidden whisperer, who whispers into the breasts of mankind, from among jinn and humankind."** (114:1-6)

REFERENCES: *Bukhari,* 4:496, 4:522, 7:643, 8:74, 9:124, 9:168-169; *Muslim*, 1106, 5463; Abu Dawud, 4703-4704; *Mishkat*, 0074.

Awareness

Another step is awareness of Satan's characteristics and how he operates. Interestingly, much of the information concerning this has been conveyed to us in the story of Adam (A) by the tongue of Satan himself through the devious arguments that he used to justify his disobedience to the divine command, and by what his Lord said concerning him in response, which may be described as follows:

1. Since unbelief is the opening to all evils, Satan's chief aim is to cause people to disbelieve and deny God and His manifold favors, as he himself did. And God warns:

> **Satan was ever ungrateful to his Lord.** (17:27)
>
> **Do not be deceived by the Deceiver about God.** (31:33, 35:5; also 57:14)
>
> **. . . Like the example of Satan, when he says to the human being, "Disbelieve!"** (59:16)

---

[78]That is, from magic and black arts, which are strictly prohibited in Islam as a form of unbelief.

2. Likewise, forgetfulness of God and the obligations of servanthood are of Satan's work, for

> **Satan only desires to . . . keep you from the remembrance of God and from prayer.** (5:91/94)
>
> **If Satan causes you to forget . . .** (6:68; also 12:42; 18:63)
>
> **Satan has overcome them and made them forget the remembrance of God.** (58:19)

3. Then, as we saw in the story of Adam (A), defiance, rebelliousness and disobedience are among Satan's chief characteristics, as well as pride, arrogance, conceit and self-importance (2:34; 7:12; 15:31, 33; 17:61-62; 18:50; 38:74, 76). Since these are among the attributes that empower our lower self or *nafs*, which always calls attention to itself and claims to be a partner to its Lord, it is critically important that we be aware of them and oppose them unremittingly, since they are displeasing to God and the means by which we, like Iblis, may lose everything of value.

4. Another of Satan's primary goals is to corrupt and mislead the children of Adam by arousing their base desires, making evil attractive to them, encouraging vice, injustice, immorality and wrong-doing, and tempting them to sin, as mentioned in the following verses of the Qur'an:

> **Satan desires to cause them to stray far away.** (4:60)
>
> **O you believe, do not follow the footsteps of Satan. And whoever follows the footsteps of Satan, indeed, he enjoins immorality and wrong-doing.** (24:21)
>
> **O children of Adam, do not let Satan seduce you [in the same way] as he removed your parents from Paradise, stripping them of their [heavenly] garments in order to show them their private parts. He certainly sees you, he and his tribe, from whence you do not see them. We have surely made the evil ones allies of those who do not believe.** (7:27)
>
> **Satan whispered evil suggestions to them/him.** (7:20, 20:120)
>
> **He . . . arouses desires in them.** (4:120)
>
> **Satan made what they were doing attractive to them.** (6:43, 8:48, 16:63, 27:24, 29:38)

Knowing this, we may be better able to identify the source of evil promptings within ourselves and to fight against them, on the side of God.

5. To achieve his evil aims, Satan makes false promises and threats, playing on people's hopes and fears. As we saw in the story of Adam (A), the Evil One

is also an expert in dealing in lies, trickery, cunning and deceit. Thus, God warns us against his tricks and traps, saying:

That is only Satan, arousing [in you] fear of his supporters. (3:175)

He makes promises to them and arouses desires in them, but Satan does not promise them anything but delusion. (4:120)

And Satan will say, when the matter has been concluded [on the Day of Judgment], "God surely promised you a promise of truth and I promised you, and then I failed you in keeping it. But I had no authority over you except that I called you and you responded to me. Therefore, do not blame me but blame yourselves. I cannot be called to your aid, nor can you be called to my aid. Indeed, I deny your previously taking me as a partner [with God]. Indeed, for the wrong-doers there is a painful punishment." (14:22)

Satan is ever a deserter of the human being. (25:29)

Satan enticed them and raised their hopes. (47:25)

Then, when he [the human being] disbelieves, he [Satan] says, "Indeed, I am dissociated from you." (59:16)

6. One of Satan's most sinister aspects is his inciting enmity, envy and hatred among the children of Adam, due to his own envy and hatred of them. Thus, God warns,

Satan only desires to cause enmity and hatred among you. (5:91/94)

Satan surely incites [enmity] among them. Indeed, Satan is an open enemy to the human being. (17:53)

Truly, all enmity, malice, ill-will and hatred among the family of mankind, and the prejudice, aggression, violence and oppression that follow from it, is the work of Satan. To allow ourselves to be party to any of the above is to ally ourselves with him, while to resist is to strike a blow against him.

Further information about the workings of Satan is provided by the Holy Prophet (S), with his intimate knowledge of the spiritual realm and the characteristics of angels, jinn and Satan. He said:

Indeed, Satan affects the human being with the effect of blood. (*Bukhari*, 3:251; also *Muslim*, 5404-5405)

"Satan exercises his influence upon the son of Adam, and likewise the angel exercises his influence [upon him]. The influence of Satan is that he holds the promise of evil and denial of truth, and the influence of the angel is that he holds the promise of good and the affirmation of truth. Therefore, the one who sees this [fulfillment of the good promise] should praise God, and the one who finds what is contrary to it should seek refuge with God from Satan the accursed." He then recited the verse, **"Satan threatens**

you with poverty and orders you to immorality" [2:268]. (*Mishkat*, 0074)

> Iblis sets up his throne upon the water. He then he sends out his detachments. Then the closest to him in status among them are the greatest among them in causing dissension. One of them comes [to Iblis] and says, "I did such-and-such," whereupon he says, "You did nothing at all!" One of them then comes and says, "I did not leave him [his prey] until I had made division between him and his wife." He [Satan] then comes close to him and says, "All right, you!" (*Muslim*, 6755, 6754)

Once the Holy Prophet (S) drew a line for his listeners and said, "That is the path shown by God." Then he drew several other lines on his right and left sides, and said, "These are the paths on every side of which there is a devil calling toward it."[79] He then recited the verse, **"And this is My path which is straight, so follow it"** [6:15] (*Mishkat*, 0166).

REFERENCES: Qur'an: 2:208, 268; 3:175; 4:60, 117-120; 5:90-91/93-94; 6:43, 68, 142; 7:16-17, 27, 200-201; 8:48; 12:42; 14:22; 15:39-40; 16:63, 98-100; 17:53, 61-62; 18:50, 63; 20:120; 23:97-98; 24:21; 27:24; 29:38; 35:5-6; 38:82-83; 41:36; 43:62; 47:25, 59:16; 113:1-5; 114:1-6.

Allying Ourselves with God

All this information about the characteristics of Satan, the enemy of our grandfather Adam (A) and of ourselves, is provided to us by our Creator not as abstract or academic knowledge. Rather, it is communicated to us so that we may recognize Satan as our enemy and learn how to deal with him, rather than mistakenly taking him as a friend.

---

[79]In Arabic, Satan is *ash-Shaytan*, literally meaning one who is far away or remote from the truth or from God's mercy. The same word is also used generically to mean anyone, whether a jinn or a human, who is a bad influence or plays an evil role, as when one says, "He is a devil." And while evil promptings and evil energies can come from human sources as well from jinn, in both cases they are related to Satan's work, as is clear from the following verses:

> **The word of your Lord will be fulfilled: "I will surely fill Hell with [the evil ones from among] jinn and humankind, all together." (11:119)**
>
> **Those are the ones upon whom the word [of God's judgment] has taken effect among the communities of jinn and humankind which passed on before them. They were indeed losers. (46:18)**
>
> **And thus have We appointed for each prophet an enemy — evil ones from mankind and jinn. (6:112)**

The final *surah* of the Qur'an (114), cited earlier, also refers to the evil ones from among jinn and humankind.

Now, Satan's method of working is of two kinds, direct and indirect. As for his direct workings, they are known to all of us. Which of us can truthfully claim not to have experienced his whispering in our hearts, which makes bad seem good, wrong seem right, and evil things seem desirable, or to never have felt an impelling urge, prompted by Satan, acting in cooperation with our lower selves, to do something we recognize as wrong?

Satan's indirect attacks, however, are a different matter. They consist of arousing and encouraging evil and destructive emotions and negativity among the family of mankind. And when we harbor negative feelings, thoughts and attitudes, or act in negative ways, the door is opened for harmful, destructive energies — energies related to doubt, disbelief, confusion, despair, darkness, coldness, enmity, anger, hate, lust, pride, envy, selfishness and greed — to dominate us and be projected onto the world. Although the effect of such negativity may not be immediately apparent, it invariably harms ourselves and others; even speaking negatively about things or people does. Even though it may seem to us that there are plenty of things to speak negatively about, the very act of speaking negatively contributes to the total pool of negativity inspired by Satan, eating away at our well-being and that of others.

As the latest research documents, positive inner attitudes create positive energy patterns within ourselves, enhancing spiritual and emotional soundness and physical health. And when we manifest positive attitudes and behaviors, we also funnel positive energy into the world around us, which, in some small, subtle way, *must* have a positive impact. Therefore, even if we cannot see the effects of being positive, we must know that the refusal to be negative is a positive thing in itself. Being positive benefits and heals. It is related to God, to belief and certainty, hope, goodness, love, light and spirituality.

While we may not always be able to choose our circumstances, nonetheless, one choice always remains to us: whether to allow ourselves to be positive or negative. This involves a conscious, voluntary decision to either cultivate positive, beneficent feelings, thoughts and behaviors, or negative, undermining ones and the actions which stem from them. We can either view things as lacking, bad and hopeless, and, by thus aligning ourselves with the forces of darkness and despair, add our personal contribution to the sum total of destructive energies in the world. Or we can look for the divine wisdoms and lessons in all things, trusting that God will ultimately bring all matters to the best conclusion, appreciating His abundant favors and mercies, and viewing others with love, compassion and concern, thereby lighting the universe with the bright energy of faith and goodness.

In this effort to defeat Satan within and around ourselves, God Himself is our Helper and Supporter. Indeed, He declares,

He [Satan] has no authority over those who believe and rely upon their Lord. His authority is only over those who take him as an ally and those who, through him, set up partners with God. (16:99-100)

God's promises of assistance and support are repeated again and again in the Qur'an, assuring us of His unvarying protection when we ally ourselves with Him and try to keep to His path: —

God is the supporter of those who believe. He brings them out of [multiple] darknesses into the light. (2:257)

Hold fast to God. He is your Protector, and excellent is the Protector and excellent is the Helper. (22:78)

When My servants ask you [Muhammad] about me, indeed, I am near. I respond to the supplication of the supplicant when he calls upon Me. So let them respond to Me and believe in Me, that they may be [rightly] guided. (2:186)

Whoever is mindful of God, He will make a way out for him and will provide for him from whence he does not expect. And whoever relies upon God, then He is sufficient for him. (65:2-3)

As we have seen, God Most High has granted us freedom of choice within the limits of His Will. Perhaps the most basic choice we are called upon to make is whether we will be of the allies and supporters of Satan or of God. Restated, this is nothing less than the issue of whether to be part of the problem or part of the solution. The problem is related to being allied with Satan, the enemy of mankind, and his workers and deeds, while the solution is related to being allied with God, our beneficent Creator, Friend and Protector, who calls us to Himself, to His light and love and His eternal Paradise, and with all people of goodwill and compassion who are allied with Him.

What we have presented here is both the story of Adam (A), the first man and first prophet, and the most profound of all allegories concerning the human condition. For as Adam (A) had his forbidden Tree, so does each of us have ours, forests of them. The Forbidden Tree is sin[80] — that is, whatever God Most High has prohibited that separates us from Him, following the promptings of Satan and our lower selves.

As Adam (A) was commanded by his Lord not to come near that Tree in Paradise, so are we also ordered to stay away from our trees. But as Adam (A) was tempted and seduced by Satan, so are we also tempted and succumb to temptation; as Adam (A) forgot and was heedless, so too are we forgetfulful and heedless concerning what God has forbidden. As he sinned, we sin, and as

[80]Metaphorically, the Tree presents the symbolism of a trunk which may be thought to represent sin in general, with many branches representing the various kinds of sins and misdeeds.

he repented we repent. And the Most Merciful Lord forgives us all, for **indeed, God forgives all sins. Indeed, it is He who is the Forgiving, the Merciful** (39:53).

This has been our life since the time of our earliest ancestors, and so it will continue to be until the Last Day. We are traveling through this life to God's Divine Presence, and everything that befalls us on this journey is part of our soul's experience as well as our test, preparing and leading us to us to our final destination. We pray that we and all the people we love may pass this test in such a way that our Lord will be pleased with us, and that we may return to the blessed abode of our first parents, which is our soul's true home.

Appendix A
Concerning 'Abdullah ibn 'Abbas (R)

Without doubt, the most illustrious among the early Qur'anic commentators was 'Abdullah ibn 'Abbas, known as Ibn 'Abbas,[281] a tower of piety, spirituality, and astonishing depth of knowledge of Islam.

Such an extraordinary ability to give interpretations of the Qur'an like those reported in these stories with absolute confidence and certainty can only be understood as a special gift and grant from God to one of His chosen servants. No other explanation is adequate. Therefore, for our readers' interest, we here offer a brief review of the life of this great Companion of the Prophet (S).

'Abdullah ibn 'Abbas (R) was the Prophet's first cousin. His father, 'Abbas bin Abu Muttalib (R), was the Prophet's beloved uncle — the brother of the Prophet's father, 'Abdullah, who had died before Muhammad's birth. Whether or not 'Abbas (R) was a Muslim before the emigration of the Prophet (S) is not clear, for he kept his acceptance of Islam a secret until the opening of Mecca. However that may be, he loved the Prophet (S) dearly and was very supportive of him and of the Muslims.

'Abdullah's mother was Umm al-Fadl (R), who had the honor of being the second woman to accept Islam, the first being the Prophet's wife Khadijah (R).[82] 'Abdullah (R) was born in Mecca in the year 619 C.E., three years before the Prophet's emigration to Medina, during the period of the boycott of the Prophet's clan, the Bani Hashim, by the pagan Quraysh, a time of severe hunger and other hardships. At the time of 'Abdullah's birth, the Prophet (S) was forty-eight years old.

'Abbas (R) brought the newborn 'Abdullah to the Holy Prophet (S), who put a drop of his blessed saliva in the baby's mouth and prayed for God's blessings upon him. This sharing of his saliva — a part of the Prophet's body, like the blood which runs in the veins of his family members and descendants — was undoubtedly a means of bringing 'Abdullah (R) into a deep spiritual connection with the Prophet (S).

Several years later, shortly before the opening of Mecca, 'Abbas (R) declared his Islam openly. He then left Mecca together with his wife and children

---

[81]Since there were several famous 'Abdullahs among the Companions of the Prophet (S), 'Abdullah ibn 'Abbas is generally referred to simply as "Ibn 'Abbas," meaning "the son of 'Abbas".

[82]Umm al-Fadl is mentioned in several *ahadith*, among which it is reported that she saw a dream indicating the birth of the Prophet's grandson, Husain (*Mishkat*, 6171).

to join the Prophet (S) and the Muslim community in Medina. At the time of his family's migration to Medina, 'Abdullah (R) was eleven years old.

The young 'Abdullah (R) loved his cousin Muhammad (S) with the deepest love. 'Abbas (R) encouraged his young son to spend as much time as possible with his noble kinsman, and this was made possible and easy due to the fact that 'Abdullah's aunt, his mother's sister Maimuna (R), was a wife of the Prophet (S).

Several reports document the special attention the Prophet (S) showed to his young cousin. Ibn 'Abbas (R) later related that once, while he was spending the night at his aunt Maimuna's house, the Prophet (S) got up to pray. 'Abdullah (R) also got up, and he stood and prayed behind the Prophet. The Prophet (S) then brought him forward and made him stand at his right side. Out of modesty, 'Abdullah (R) returned to his place behind the Prophet (S), and after finishing the prayer, the Prophet (S) asked him why he had done this. The boy replied that his reverence for him was such that he would never dare to stand next to him. The Prophet (S) then prayed for him, saying, "O God, grant him wisdom" (Akili/*B*, #877, p. 344). In another report of the same matter, the Prophet (S) prayed that God would expand 'Abdullah's knowledge and understanding[83] (ibid, #876, p. 343).

Ibn 'Abbas (R) reported that on another occasion, he placed a container of water for the Prophet's ***wudu'*** (washing for prayers). When the Prophet (S) asked who had done this and was told that it was 'Abdullah, he prayed for the boy, saying, "O God, give him understanding of the faith" (***Bukhari***, 1:145). Ibn 'Abbas (R) also reported that the Prophet (S) once folded 'Abdullah to his chest and said, "O God, teach him wisdom" (***Bukhari***, 5:100), and, either on the same or another occasion, "O God, teach him the Book [the Qur'an]" (***Bukhari***, 5:101, 1:75).

It is also reported that once the Prophet (S) put his hand on the young 'Abdullah's head and prayed for him with the words, "My Lord, grant him wisdom and teach him the explanation [of the Qur'an]." The Prophet then placed his hand on the chest of the boy, who felt its coolness in his spine, saying, "O God, fill him with wisdom and knowledge" (Akili/*B*, p. viii; #883, p. 345).

The Prophet (S) also prayed, "O God, bless him and further increase Your blessings upon him through his progeny" (ibid, #879, p. 344). On another occasion, he prayed, "My Lord, strengthen him with the holy spirit [the angel Gabriel]" (ibid, pp. viii-ix). Perhaps it was in answer to this prayer that Ibn 'Abbas (R),

---

[83]The original reports of 'Abdullah's praying the night prayer with the Holy Prophet (S) are found in ***Bukhari***, 1:140; ***Muslim***, 1671-1677, 1683-1684; and ***Abu Dawud***, 1352, 1359, 1362.

according to his own report, saw Gabriel (A) on two occasions.[84] The Prophet (S) further said to Ibn ʻAbbas (R), "Indeed, you are a blessed man, and an excellent interpreter of the Qur'an" (ibid, #884, p. 345).

These were experiences of the utmost importance in young ʻAbdullah's life. The fact that he was graced by the Holy Prophet's approval and prayers on his behalf gives us an idea of how highly God's Messenger (S) regarded him and the brightness of the future he saw for him as the inspired interpreter of the Qur'an in years to come.

From an early age, ʻAbdullah was totally immersed in Islam and in the Qur'an, while the later parts of it were being revealed to the Prophet (S). Because of his close relationship to the Prophet's family, ʻAbdullah had the tremendous privilege of spending time in the company of God's Messenger (S), and he was very keenly motivated to take whatever he could from the tongue and the heart of his blessed cousin. By the time the Prophet (S) left this life, ʻAbdullah (R), then thirteen or fourteen, had already drunk deeply from the spring of his knowledge and light. It was to remain his chief preoccupation and contribution throughout his life.

After the Prophet's death, ʻAbdullah (R) spent his time with the senior Companions of the Prophet, benefitting from their knowledge. Possessing a superb memory, he became well-known both for his eagerness to learn and his high intelligence. Among those who recognized ʻAbdullah's special gifts was ʻUmar ibn al-Khattab (R). And perceiving the depth of ʻAbdullah's understanding of Islam, ʻUmar (R) accepted it unquestioningly as accurate and reliable.

When ʻUmar (R) became the second caliph, he gave ʻAbdullah (R) a good deal of public encouragement. For example, he would invite him to his gatherings, attended by the senior Companions. At times, some of them would voice objections, saying, "We also have young sons but we do not bring them to such gatherings, whereas you invite this young boy." At that, ʻUmar (R) would reply that while ʻAbdullah might be young, his knowledge was equal to that of many of the senior Companions. And on occasions when ʻAbdullah (R) would hesitate to give his opinion out of deference to the elders, ʻUmar (R) would encourage him, saying, "Ibn ʻAbbas, knowledge does not depend on length of age. Do not consider yourself inferior but express whatever comes to your heart."

---

[84] *Mishkat*, 6150. In this report, Ibn ʻAbbas mentions that the Prophet (S) prayed for him twice. This may be understood to mean ***at least*** twice, for perhaps some of the above prayers were uttered on the same occasion. In another report, Ibn ʻAbbas states that the Prophet (S) prayed for his benefit ***many*** times (Al-Akili/*B*, #884, p. 345).

Indeed, 'Umar (R) had such confidence in in 'Abdullah's understanding that he would call upon him when he was unable to reach a decision concerning some legal issue. "This and the likes of it are what you are for," he would say, accepting 'Abdullah's judgment concerning the matter without consulting anyone else. And when 'Umar (R) wanted to understand the meaning of a Qur'anic verse but was not satisfied with the interpretations of other Companions, he would turn to 'Abdullah (R) and would accept his explanation.

Many instances of Ibn 'Abbas's keen understanding of the Qur'an have been recorded. It is reported that once 'Umar (R) asked some Muslims for their interpretation of ***Surah an-Nasr*** (*Surah* 110). After they had given it, he turned to Ibn 'Abbas (R). In marked contrast to the understandings of the others, Ibn 'Abbas (R) stated that the ***surah*** was an indirect reference to the Prophet's approaching death. At that, 'Umar (R) said, "I know only the explanation which you have just offered." On another occasion, 'Umar (R) was discussing the date of the Night of Power with some of the elder emigrant Muslims from Mecca, and he asked Ibn 'Abbas (R) for his view of the matter. When 'Abdullah, out of his deep insight and inspired wisdom, said that he believed it to be one of the last seven nights of Ramadan, 'Umar (R) expressed his astonishment that a young person should have such profound understanding.

Later Ibn 'Abbas (R) was to become a consultant to the caliph 'Uthman (R) and, after him, to 'Ali (R). During 'Uthman's caliphate, Ibn 'Abbas (R) participated in battles in Africa. It is reported that when 'Uthman (R) sent him as his ambassador to Gregory, an African ruler, Ibn 'Abbas spoke with such fluency, knowledge and courage that Gregory was astonished and said, "You are the scholar [***hibr***] of Arabia." Afterwards, when 'Ali (R) became the caliph, he appointed Ibn 'Abbas (R) as governor of Basra in Iraq.

The great Companions of the Prophet (S) and the generations following theirs all bore witness to Ibn 'Abbas' superior intelligence and the depth of his knowledge and insight. 'Abdullah ibn Mas'ud (R), another great Companion, stated that Ibn 'Abbas (R) was the best interpreter of the Qur'an. It was also said that when Ibn 'Abbas (R) explained the Qur'an, it was as though he was seeing the Unseen — as perhaps he was, due to the light of understanding that God had opened to his heart. 'Abdullah ibn 'Umar (R) said that Ibn 'Abbas (R) was the most knowledgeable about what had been revealed to the Prophet (S). A second generation scholar, Tawous (R), reported that several times he had witnessed discussions between Ibn 'Abbas (R) and seventy other Companions of the Prophet (S), and whenever there was a difference of opinion, in the end Ibn 'Abbas' opinion prevailed. Indeed, he was called "***al-Bahr***" (the Ocean) because of the excellence of his understanding.

Because of his amazing memory, Ibn 'Abbas (R) was a storehouse of knowledge of *ahadith*, for although he was quite young during the Prophet's final years, he remembered whatever he had heard from him. Following the Prophet's death, he heard and memorized numerous *ahadith* from senior Companions. He would also go out in search of new *ahadith*. Concerning this, he said, "If I heard that such-and-such a person knew a *hadith*, I would go to his house to ask about it, although if I had wished I could have called him to my house." Thus, Ibn 'Abbas (R) reported a surprising number of *ahadith*,[85] and all of them are considered sound. At the same time, he was very conservative and cautious in his reporting of *ahadith*, until a time came when he stopped reporting them altogether.

In addition to the religous sciences such as Qur'an, interpretation, *hadith* and *fiqh* (jurisprudence), Ibn 'Abbas (R) was also a master of literature and poetry, linguistics and vocabulary, biography, genealogy and mathematics. Due to his extraordinary memory, he memorized almost the entire vocabulary of the Arabic language and the body of Arabic literature. It is reported that once he memorized eighty couplets of a poem by hearing it recited a single time. As the chief scholar among Muslims in his time, he was sought out and visited by many people seeking knowledge of the permissible and prohibited (*halal* and *haram*), poetry, the Arabic language, and genealogy. And in addition to his vast knowledge, he was also renowned for his abundant hospitality.

But even more importantly, Ibn 'Abbas (R) was also known for his deep piety and spirituality. His deeds and his speech reflected constant mindfulness of his Lord. It is reported that his cheeks were marked by two deep lines made by the flow of his tears, and that his honoring of God's limits and prohibitions was so profound that it could cause one to weep.

In his later years, Ibn 'Abbas (R) became blind. He passed the closing years of his life in Taif near Mecca, where he died in 687 CE at the age of sixty-eight. An eyewitness reported that when his bier was set down for the funeral prayer, a white bird flew in, alighted upon his body, and then went in between the layers of his shroud. Those who were present searched for the bird to let it out but were unable to find it. When the funeral prayer was over and the body of Ibn 'Abbas had been laid in its grave, the congregation heard a clear voice,

[85]In *Reliance of the Traveler*, their number is reported as 1,660. In the principal collections of *ahadith*, namely, *Bukhari*, *Muslim*, *Abu Dawud*, *Mishkat al-Masabih* and *al-Muwatta*, we find a total of 742 *ahadith* and reports connected with 'Abdullah ibn 'Abbas, most of them reported by him and a small number about him. Ibn 'Abbas is second only to the great Companion of the Prophet, Abu Hurayrah, in the number of *ahadith* he reported.

although no one was to be seen, saying, **"O you serene soul, return to your Lord, pleased and well-pleasing. Enter then among My slaves, and enter My Paradise!"** (89:27-30).

May God's eternal blessings and exalted pleasure be upon His sincere servant, 'Abdullah ibn 'Abbas, to whose inspired interpretation of His Book we owe the understanding of so many of its complex and fascinating details.

REFERENCES: Akili/*B*, pp. viii-ix, 341-366; Ibn Kathir/*Juz' 'Amma*, p. 144; Ayoub/*Q*, I: 27-28; Keller/*R*, x149, p. 1052.

APPENDIX B
THE DIVINE NAMES

The Divine Names, or *Asma' al-Husna*, describe God Most High and His exalted attributes. Most of these Names are the names by which God calls Himself in the Qur'an, while others are derived from certain Qur'anic passages.

The holy Names are divided into two categories: the Names of the Divine Essence (*adh-Dhat*), such as ***ar-Rahman*** (the Most Merciful) or ***al-'Aliy*** (the Most High), and the Names of the Divine Attributes or Qualities (*as-Sifat*). As mentioned previously, these Divine Qualities can be expressed as Names of Mercy or Beauty (***Jamali***) and Names of Majesty or Severity (***Jalali***).

Some of the Divine Names are specific to God Most High alone — for example, His proper name, Allah, and descriptive names such as ***al-Khaliq*** (the Creator), ***al-Hayy*** (the Ever-Living), and ***al-Qayum*** (the Eternal). These are known as the Attributes of Transcendence (*Siffat Tanzihi*).

Such names are never used for naming a person. However, it is common for Muslims to name their sons after other, generalized attributes of God, preceded by the suffix ***'abd*** (the slave of...), as in 'Abdullah ('the slave of Allah), 'Abdur-Rahim (the slave of the Merciful), 'Abdul-Wahid (the slave of the Unique One), 'Abdul-Majid (the slave of the Glorious), 'Abdul-Wudud (the slave of the Loving One), and many others. In addition, other attributes that are not restricted to the Creator can be used as names without the prefix ***'abd*** — for example, Hakim (Wise), Jamal (Beautiful), Nur (Light), Matin (Firm), and the like.

The following are the ninety-nine Beautiful or Excellent Names of God, the Praised and Exalted, together with their pronunciation and meaning:

He is *Allah*, besides whom there is no deity,

1 ***al-Rahman*** (***ar-Rah-maan***) — the Most-Merciful

2 ***al-Rahim*** (***ar-Ra-heem***) — the Mercy-Giving

3 ***al-Malik*** (***al-Ma-lik***) — the King

4 ***al-Quddus*** (***al-Qud-doos***) — the Holy One

5 ***al-Salam*** (***as-Sa-laam***) — the Source of Peace

6 ***al-Mu'min*** (***al-Mu'-min***) — the Giver of Security

7 ***al-Muhaimin*** (***al-Mu-hai-min***) — the Guardian

8 ***al-'Aziz*** (***al-'A-zeez***) — the Mighty

9 *al-Jabbar* (*al-Jab-**baar***) —the Irresistible

10 *al-Mutakabbir* (*al-Mu-ta-**kab**-bir*) —the Superb

11 *al-Khaliq* (*al-**Khaa**-liq*) —the Creator

12 *al-Bari'* (*al-**Baa**-ri'*) —the Maker

13 *al-Musawwir* (*al-Mu-**saw**-wir*) —the Fashioner

14 *al-Ghaffar* (*al-Ghaf-**faa**r*) —the Forgiving

15 *al-Qahhar* (*al-Qah-**haar***) —the Dominant

16 *al-Wahhab* (*al-Wah-**haab***) — the Bestower

17 *al-Razzaq* (*ar-Raz-**zaaq***) —the Provider

18 *al-Fattah* (*al-Fat-**taah***) — the Opener

19 *al-'Alim* (*al-'A-**leem***) —the All-Knowing

20 *al-Qabid* (*al-**Qaa**-bid*) —the Withholder

21 *al-Basit* (*al-**Baa**-sit*) —the Bountiful

22 *al-Khafid* (*al-**Khaa**-fid*) —the Abaser.

23 *al-Raf'i* (*ar-**Raa**-f'i*) —the Exalter

24 *al-Mu'izz* (*al-Mu-**'izz***) —the Bestower of Honor

25 *al-Mudhil* (*al-Mu-**dhil***) —the Humiliator

26 *al-Sami'* (*as-Sa-**mi'***) — the All-Hearing

27 *al-Basir* (*al-Ba-**seer***) —the All-Seeing

28 *al-Hakam* (*al-**Ha**-kam*) —the Judge

29 *al-'Adal* (*al-**'Adal***) —the Just

30 *al-Latif* (*al-La-**teef***) —the Subtle

31 *al-Khabir* (*al-Kha-**beer***) — the Informed

32 *al-Halim* (*al-Ha-**leem***) — the Forbearing

33 *al-'Adhim* (*al-'A-**dheem***) —the Almighty

34 *al-Ghafur* (*al-Ghaf-**foor***) —the Forgiver

35 *al-Shakur* (*ash-Sha-**koor***) —the Rewarder

36 *al-'Aliy* (*al-'A-**lee***) —the Most High

37 *al-Kabir* (*al-Ka-**beer***) —the Great

38 *al-Hafidh* (*al-Ha-**feedh***) — the Preserver

39 *al-Muqit* (*al-Mu-**qeet***) —the Maintainer

40 *al-Hasib* (*al-Ha-**seeb***) —the Reckoner

41 *al-Jalil* (*al-Ja-**leel***) —the Majestic

42 *al-Karim* (*al-Ka-**reem***) —the Generous

43 *al-Raqib* (*ar-Ra-**qeeb***) —the Watchful

44 *al-Mujib* (*al-Mu-**jeeb***) —the Answerer

45 *al-Wasi'* (*al-**Waa**-si'*) —the Liberal

46 *al-Hakim* (*al-Ha-**keem***) —the All-Wise

47 *al-Wadud* (*al-Wa-**dood***) —the Loving

48 *al-Majid* (*al-Ma-**jeed***) —the Glorious

49 *al-Ba'ith* (*al-**Baa'**-ith*) —the Raiser

50 *al-Shahid* (*ash-Sha-**heed***) —the Witness

51 *al-Haqq* (*al-**Haqq***) —the Real

52 *al-Wakil* (*al-Wa-**keel***) —the Trustee

53 *al-Qawi* (*al-Qa-**wee***) —the Strong

54 *al-Matin* (*al-Ma-**teen***) —the Firm

55 *al-Waliy* (*al-Wa-**lee***) —the Patron

56 *al-Hamid* (*al-Ha-**meed***) —the Praiseworthy

57 *al-Muhsi* (*al-**Muh**-see*) —the Enumerator

58 *al-Mubdi* (*al-**Mub**-dee*) —the Originator

59 *al-Mu'id* (*al-Mu'-**id***) —the Restorer

60 *al-Muhyi* (*al-**Muh**-yee*) —the Giver of Life

61 *al-Mumit* (*al-Mu-**meet***) —the Causer of Death

62 *al-Hayy* (*al-**Hayy***) —the Ever-Living

63 *al-Qayyum* (*al-Qay-**yoom***) —the Eternal

64 *al-Wajid* (*al-**Waa**-jid*) —the Self-Sufficient

65 *al-Majid* (*al-**Maa**-jid*) — the Grand

66 *al-Wahid* (*al-**Waa**-hid*) — the One

67 *al-Ahad* (*al-A-**had***) — the Single

68 *al-Samad* (*as-Sa-**mad***) — the Self-Sufficient

69 *al-Qadir* (*al-**Qaa**-dir*) — the All-Powerful

70 *al-Muqtadir* (*al-**Muq**-ta-dir*) — the Prevailing

71 *al-Muqaddim* (*al-Mu-**qad**-dim*) — the Advancer

72 *al-Mu'akhkhir* (*al-Mu-**'akh**-khir*) — the Delayer

73 *al-Awwal* (*al-**Aw**-wal*) — the First

74 *al-Akhir* (*al-**Aa**-khir*) — the Last

75 *adh-Dhahir* (*adh-**Dhaa**-hir*) — the Outward

76 *al-Batin* (*al-**Baa**-tin*) — the Inward

77 *al-Wali* (*al-Waa-**lee***) — the Governor

78 *al-Muta'ali* (*al-Mu-ta-**'ali***) — the Exalted

79 *al-Barr* (*al-**Barr***) — the Kind

80 *al-Tawwab* (*at-Taw-**waab***) — the Relenting

81 *al-Muntaqim* (*al-Mun-ta-**qim***) — the Avenger (of Wrongs)

82 *al-'Afuw* (*al-'A-**foow***) — the Pardoner

83 *al-Ra'uf* (*ar-Ra'**oof***) — the Kindly

84 *Malik al-Mulk* (***Maa**-lik al-Mulk*) — Possessor of the Dominion

85 *Dhu-l-Jalali wal-Ikram* (*Dhu-l-Ja-**laa**-li wal-Ik-**raam***) — the Possessor of Majesty and Splendor

86 *al-Muqsit* (*al-**Muq**-sit*) — the Equitable

87 *al-Jami'* (*al-**Jaa**-mi'*) — the Gatherer

88 *al-Ghani* (*al-Gha-**nee***) — the Independent

89 *al-Mugni* (*al-**Mug**-nee*) — the Enricher

90 *al-Mani'* (*al-**Maa**-ni'*) — the Preventer

91 *al-Darr* (*ad-**Daarr***) — the Afflictor

92 al-Nafi' (***an-Naa-fi'***) —the Benefitter

93 al-Nur (***an-Noor***) —the Light

94 al-Hadi (*al-**Haa**-dee*) —the Guide

95 al-Badi' (*al-Ba-**di'***) —the Originator

96 al-Baqi (***al-Baa**-qee*) —the Everlasting

97 al-Warith (*al-**Waa**-rith*) —the Inheritor

98 al-Rashid (*ar-Ra-**sheed***) —the Director

99 al-Sabur (*as-Sa-**boor***) —the Patient

That is God, our Lord, may His glory be exalted!

REFERENCES: *Mishkat*, 2285; Glasse/*E*, "Divine Names," pp. 99-100; Bayrak, *The Most Beautiful Names.*

APPENDIX C

THE RECORDING AND GUARDIAN ANGELS

Among all mankind, God's Messenger, Muhammad (S), possessed the most profound knowledge of the unseen, spiritual world. Consequently, from his own knowledge and experience, as well as by divine inspiration, he was able to provide us with much detail about angels, including the angels who record deeds and guard each human being, according to God's words, **There is no soul but that it has a protector over it** (86:4).

Through divine inspiration, the Prophet (S) spoke about the manner in which our deeds are recorded, saying,

> Indeed, God the Honored and Glorious records the good and the bad deeds; then He made that [good and bad] clear. So whoever intends to do a good deed but does not do it, God records it for him with Himself as a completed good deed. Then, if he intends to do it and [actually] does it, God records for him with Himself ten good deeds to seven hundred to many more [than that]. And whoever intends to do a bad deed but does not [actually] do it, God records it for him with Himself as a completed good deed. Then, if he intends to do it and does it, God records it for him as a single bad deed. (*Bukhari*, 8:498; also 1:39A, 1:40, 4:629, 9:592; *Muslim*, 233, 235)

Concerning the recording angels, the Holy Prophet (S) said:

> There come to you in succession angels by night and angels by day, and they join together at the time of the *Fajr* and *'Asr* prayers.[86] Then those [angels] who have spent the night with you ascend, and then He [God] asks them, although He knows [everything] about them, "How did you leave My slaves?" They say, "We left them while they were praying and we came to them while they were praying." (*Bukhari*, 1.530; *Muwatta*, 9.24.25)

This is further clarified in another ***hadith***. It is reported that once the Prophet's Companion, 'Uthman bin Affan (R), asked the Prophet (S) how many angels there are with each human being. The Prophet (S) replied:

> There is one on the right who writes the good deeds, and he is superior to the one on the left. When you do a good deed, he writes ten [good deeds] instead of one, but when you do a bad deed, the angel on the left asks the angel on the right whether or not to record it. The angel on the right says, "Wait a minute. Perhaps he will repent and ask

---

[86]That is, at dawn and in the latter part of the afternoon.

for forgiveness." Then he waits and asks three times, and if during that period the person does not repent, the angel of the good deeds says to him, "Yes, record it. May God protect us from this person! He is a bad companion who has no fear of God or shame in front of Him"

God says, **For him [the human being] are successive [angels] in front of him and behind him; they protect him by God's command** [13:11]. There is an angel who is in front and holding your forelock. When you are humble before God, he raises your rank, and when you become rebellious and proud before God, he humbles you. And there are two angels beside your lips. When you invoke blessings upon me, they protect them. There is an angel at your mouth who does not let insects and the like fall into it, and there are two angels at your eyes. So there are in all ten angels with each person, and they are separate for the day and for the night, and thus there are twenty angels who have been appointed for each human being. Then, to tempt him, during the day there is Iblis and at night his offspring." (Ibn Kathir/*T*, 13:11)

The Prophet (S) also taught us the proper manners (***adab***) and respect that should be observed in front of our unseen companions, saying:

Let one of you be as shy of the two angels who are with him as he would be shy of two righteous men among his neighbors who are with him by night and day. (Al-Houry, ***Hadiths***, #985)

Avoid being naked, for there are those with you who never leave you except when you are relieving yourselves and when a man has intercourse with his wife. Therefore, observe modesty before them and honor them. (***Mishkat***, 3115)

QUR'ANIC REFERENCES — ADAM

2:30-39

[Mention, O Muhammad,] when God said to the angels, "Indeed, I am going to appoint a *khalifah* on the earth."

They said, "Are You going to place on it one who will cause corruption on it and shed blood, while we exalt Your glory with praise and sanctify You?"

He said, "Indeed, I know what you do not know." (30)

And He taught Adam the names, all of them. Then He presented them to the angels and said, "Inform me of the names of these, if you are truthful." (31)

They said, "Glory be to You! We have no knowledge except what You have taught us. Indeed, it is You who are the Knowing, the Wise." (32)

He said, "O Adam, inform them of their names." Then, when he had informed them of their names, He said, "Did I not tell you that indeed I know the Unseen of the heavens and the earth, and I know what you disclose and what you conceal?" (33)

And when We said to the angels, "Prostrate to Adam," then they prostrated, except Iblis. He refused and was arrogant, and became of the deniers. (34)

And We said,"O Adam, dwell, you and your wife, in Paradise, and eat from it in abudance, as you will. But do not come near this Tree, lest you be among the wrong-doers." (35)

Then Satan caused them to slip out of it and removed them from that in which they had been. And We said, "Go down, enemies to one another, and on the earth will be a dwelling-place and [means of] enjoyment for you for a time." (36)

Then Adam received words from his Lord and He accepted his repentance. Indeed, He is the Acceptor of Repentance, the Merciful. (37)

We said, "Go down from it, all. However, if there comes to you guidance from Me, then whoever follows My guidance, no fear will be upon them nor will they grieve. (38) And the ones who rejected and falsely denied Our signs, those will be the people of the Fire; they will remain therein." (39)

4:117-120

They call upon none but a rebellious Satan, (117) who is cursed by God. And he [Satan] said, "I will surely take an appointed share of Your servants, (118) and I will mislead them and will arouse desires in them, and I will command them so they will slit the ears of cattle and will command them so they will alter God's creation." And whoever takes Satan as an ally instead of God has certainly incurred a clear loss. (119) He makes promises to them and arouses desires in them, but Satan does not promise them [anything] but delusion. (120)

5:27-31/30-34

And relate to them the story of the sons of Adam with truth, when they each offered a sacrifice and it was accepted from one of them but was not accepted from the other.

He [the latter] said, "I will certainly kill you."

He [the former] said, "Indeed, God accepts only from those who are mindful of Him. (27/30) Even if you should stretch out your hand against me to kill me, I will not stretch out my hand against you to kill you. I surely fear God, Lord of the worlds. (28/31) Indeed, I want you take on my my sin and your [own] sin, so you will be among the companions of the Fire. And that is the recompense of the wrong-doers." (29/32)

Then his lower self permitted to him the murder of his brother, and he killed him and thus became of the losers. (30/33) Then God sent a crow, digging in the ground, to show him how to hide the disgrace of his brother. He said, "Oh, woe be to me! Am I incapable of being like this crow and thus hiding the disgrace of my brother?" and he became of the regretful. (31/34)

7:11-27

We certainly created you, then formed you. Then We said to the angels, "Prostrate to Adam," whereupon they prostrated, except Iblis. He was not among those who prostrated. (11)

He [God] said, "What prevented you from prostrating when I commanded you?"

He [Iblis] said, "I am better than he! You created me from fire, while You created him from clay." (12)

He [God] said, "Then go down from it, for it is not for you to be arrogant in it. Then go forth! Indeed, you are of the debased." (13)

He [Iblis] said, "Defer me until the day they [mankind] are resurrected." (14)

He [God] said, "Indeed, you are of those deferred." (15)

He [Iblis] said, "Because you have let me fall in error, I will certainly lie in wait for them on Your straight path. (16) Then I will come upon them from the front of them and from behind them, and at their right and at their left. And You will not find most of them thankful." (17)

He [God] said, "Go out of it, blameworthy and cast out! Whoever follows you among them, I shall fill Hell with you, all together! (18) And O Adam, dwell, you and your wife, in Paradise and eat from wherever you will, but do not come near this Tree, lest you be among the wrong-doers." (19)

Then Satan whispered to them to make apparent to them what was concealed from them of their private parts, and he said, "Your Lord only prohibited you from this tree lest you become angels or become of the immortal." (20) And he swore to them, "I am surely among the sincere advisors to you." (21)

Thus, he caused them to fall by deceit. And when they tasted of the Tree, their private parts became apparent to them, and they began to fasten together [something] of the leaves of Paradise upon themselves. And their Lord called to them, [saying,] "Did I not prohibit you from that Tree and tell you that Satan is a clear enemy to you?" (22)

They said, "Our Lord, we have wronged ourselves, and if You do not forgive us and have mercy upon us, we will surely be among the lost." (23)

He [God] said, "Go down, enemies to one another, and on the earth will be a dwelling-place and [means of] enjoyment for you for a time." (24) He said, "On it you will live and on it you will die, and from it you will be brought forth." (25)

O children of Adam, We have bestowed upon you [the use of] clothing to conceal your private parts and as adornment. But the clothing of mindfulness of God — that is best. That is among the signs of God, that perhaps they may remember. (26) O children of Adam, do not let Satan seduce you as he ousted your parents from Paradise, stripping them of their garments in order to show them their private parts. Indeed, he sees you, he and his tribe, from whence you do not see them. We have surely made the evil ones allies of those who do not believe. (27)

15:26-43

We certainly created the human being from ringing [potters's] clay [coming] from altered mud, (26) and We created the jinn previously from scorching fire. (27)

And [mention, O Muhammad,] when your Lord said to the angels, "I am surely going to create a human being out of ringing clay [derived] from altered mud. (28) Then, when I have formed him and breathed into him of My Spirit, fall down in prostration to him." (29) Then the angels prostrated, all of them together, (30) except Iblis. He refused to be among those who prostrated. (31)

He [God] said, "O Iblis, what is with you that you were not among those who prostrated?" (32)

He [Iblis] said, "It is not for me to prostrate to a human being whom you created out of ringing clay [derived] from altered mud!" (33)

He [God] said, "Then go out of it, for indeed you are damned, (34) and the curse will surely be upon you until the Day of Recompense!" (35)

He [Iblis] said, "My Lord, then defer me until the Day they are resurrected." (36)

He [God] said, "Then indeed you are among those deferred (37) until the Day of the well-known time." (38)

He [Iblis] said, "My Lord, because you have let me fall into error, I will surely make [evil and disobedience] attractive for them on the earth, and I will mislead them all, (39) except Your sincere servants among them." (40)

He [God] said, "This is a straight path to Me. (41) Indeed, My servants — no authority will you have over them, except those who follow you among the misguided. (42) And Hell is surely the promised place for them all!" (43)

17:61-65

And when We said to the angels, "Prostrate to Adam," they prostrated, except Iblis.

He said, "Am I to prostrate to one whom You created out of clay?" (61) He said, "Do You see this one whom You have honored above me? If You defer me until the Day of Resurrection, I will surely destroy his descendants, except a few." (62)

He [God] said, "Go, and whoever follows you among them, indeed, Hell will be your recompense, an ample recompense! (63) And incite whomever you can among them with your voice, and assault them with your cavalry and your foot-soldiers, and become their partner in wealth and children, and make promises to them. But Satan promises them nothing but delusion. (64) Indeed, you will have no authority over My servants. And your Lord is sufficient as Guardian." (65)

18:50

And when We said to the angels, "Prostrate to Adam," then they prostrated, except Iblis. He was of the jinn, and he deviated from the command of his Lord. Then will you take him and his race as allies instead of Me, while they are enemies to you — an evil exchange for the wrong-doers?

19:56-57

And mention Idris in the Book. Indeed, he was a truthful one and a prophet, (56) and We raised him to a high station. (57)

20:115-126

And We had previously enjoined [an obligation] on Adam, but he forgot and We did not find firmness in him. (115)

And when We said to the angels, "Prostrate to Adam," they prostrated, except Iblis. He refused. (116)

Then We said, "O Adam, indeed, this is an enemy to you and your wife. Therefore, do not let him oust the two of you from Paradise so that you become miserable. (117) It is surely granted to you not be hungry therein or unclothed, (118) or to be thirsty therein or affected by heat." (119)

Then Satan whispered to him, saying, "O Adam, shall I direct you to a tree of immortality and a dominion that will never decay?" (120)

Then they ate from it, and then their private parts became apparent to them and they began to fasten together [something] of the leaves of Paradise upon themselves. And Adam disobeyed his Lord and erred. (121) Then his Lord chose him and turned to him in forgiveness and guided [him]. (122)

He [God] said, "Go down from it, all, enemies to one another. But if there comes to you guidance from Me, then whoever follows My guidance will neither go astray nor be miserable. (123) And whoever turns away from My remembrance — he will surely have a narrowed-down life, and We will raise him up blind on the Day of Resurrection." (124) He will say, "My Lord, why have You raised me up blind, whereas before I used to see?" (125) He will say, "Thus did Our revelations come to you but you forgot them, and thus will you be forgotten this Day." (126)

21:85-86

And [mention] Ishmael and Idris and Dhul-Kifl; all of them were among the patient. And We admitted them to Our mercy. Indeed, they were among the righteous.

38:71-85

[Mention, O Muhammad,] when your Lord said to the angels, "I am surely going to create a human being out of clay. (71) Then, when I have formed him and breathed into him [something] of My Spirit, fall down in prostration to him." (72) Then the angels prostrated, all of them together, (73) except Iblis. He was arrogant and became of the deniers. (74)

He [God] said, "O Iblis, what prevented you from prostrating to what I created with My hands? Were you arrogant or were you of the self-exalted?" (75)

He [Iblis] said, "I am better than he! You created me from fire, while You created him from clay." (76)

He [God] said, "Then go out of it, for indeed you are damned, (77) and My curse will surely be upon you until the Day of Recompense." (78)

He [Iblis] said, "My Lord, then defer me until the Day they are resurrected." (79)

He [God] said, "Then indeed you are among those deferred (80) until the Day of the well-known time." (81)

He [Iblis] said, "Then, by Your might, I will surely mislead them all, (82) except Your sincere servants among them." (83)

He [God] said, "Then this is the truth, and the truth I do speak: (84) [that] I will surely fill Hell with you and those of them who follow you, all together." (85)

55:14-15

He created the human being from clay like pottery, (14) and He created the jinn from a smokeless flame of fire. (15)

The Story of Noah (Nuh)

peace be upon him

Then We sent Our messengers in succession. Each time there came to a nation its messenger they denied him, whereupon We made them follow one another [in destruction], and We made them [mere] tales. (23:44)

Those communities — We relate to you [Muhammad] some of their tidings. And their messengers certainly came to them with clear proofs, but they would not believe in what they had previously denied. Thus does God seal up the hearts of the unbelievers. (7:101)

Before them, the people of Noah and the factions after them denied, and each nation intended [a plot] for its messenger, to seize him and to argue with falsehood in order to refute the truth thereby.
Then I seized them, and how [terrible] was My punishment! (40:5)

1. The Importance of Noah Among the Prophets

Indeed, God chose Adam and Noah and the family of Abraham and the family of 'Imran[1] above all mankind, descendants of one another. And God is Hearing and Knowing. (3:33)

And We certainly sent Noah and Abraham, and established prophethood and scripture among their descendants; and among them are the guided, but many of them are defiantly disobedient. (57:26)

As we saw earlier, among the 124,000 prophets who have lived upon the earth since the time of Adam (A), twenty-six are mentioned by name in the Qur'an. Among these, the greatest — known as ***'ulu-l-'azm*** or Possessors of Determination — are Noah, Abraham, Moses, Jesus and Muhammad, God's peace and blessings be upon them all. These five most illustrious leaders of mankind are mentioned together in the following verses:

> **He has ordained for you [mankind], of the religion, what He enjoined upon Noah and that which We have revealed to you [Muhammad], and what We enjoined upon Abraham and Moses and Jesus: to establish the [true] religion and not be divided concerning it.** (42:13)
>
> **[Mention, O Muhammad,] when We took from the prophets their covenant,[2] and from you [Muhammad], and from Noah and Abraham and Moses and Jesus son of Mary — and We took from them a solemn covenant.** (33:7)

Noah or Nuh, may God's peace and blessings be upon him, is so important that he is mentioned by name forty-two times in the Qur'an, and a total of 115 verses relate to him and his people. In addition, the seventy-first *surah* or chapter of the Qur'an, "*Nuh*," is named for him.

The classic commentators suggest a number of reasons for Noah's greatness among the prophets, among which are the following: It is said that he was the first prophet to be sent after his grandfather Enoch or Idris (A). He was the first prophet to warn people against ***shirk*** —that is, setting up partners or associating others with God[3] — and the first to bring a ***shari'ah***— a divinely-revealed law or path. He was also the first prophet to be persecuted by his nation, as well as the first prophet whose people were punished for rejecting his

---

[1]See "Adam," footnote 69.

[2]That is, in the spiritual world of souls.

[3]*Shirk* may take the form of ascribing godhood to false deities, as in polytheism or idol-worship; ascribing divine attributes or powers to others than God; or giving the devotion which is the exclusive right of the Creator to someone other than Him.

message. And among all the prophets and messengers, he was the only one who prayed for the destruction of his people, as we shall presently see.

It is reported that God granted Noah (A) various miracles, all relating to him personally. Among these were that he lived to a great age without loss of strength, his hair turning gray, or losing a tooth. This is all the more noteworthy because he fasted continually and because, it is said, no prophet ever bore such torment and abuse, both physical and verbal, from his people as Noah (A) did throughout his life. Nonetheless, in spite of it, he remained a faithful, **thankful slave** (17:3) to his Lord.

REFERENCE: Keller/*R*, x290, p. 1087.

2. Paganism and Prophethood

They worship, in place of God, that which neither harms them nor benefits them, and they say, "These are our intercessors with God."
(10:18)

They [their false gods] have surely led astray many among mankind.
(14:35)

The Origins of Idol-Worship

With the story of Noah (A), we leave the realm of eternity and enter the realm of pre-history. For although there is no historical record of Noah (A) as such, the gods worshipped by his people are mentioned in the Qur'an through the mouth of Noah (A) himself: —

> **And they [Noah's people] have devised a great conspiracy and said, "Never abandon your gods, and never abandon Wadd or Suwa' or Yaghuth or Ya'uq or Nasr!" and they have led many astray.** (71:23)

Our distinguished guide to the Holy Qur'an, 'Abdullah ibn 'Abbas (R), states that idols were made in the time of Adam's descendant Jared, due to which some were turned away from *islam*, the original faith of mankind. Ibn 'Abbas (R) also says: "All the idols which were worshipped by the people of Noah were worshipped later by the Arabs." He then named the Arabian tribes in which four of these gods, Wadd, Suwa', Ya'uq and Nasr,[4] were worshipped, adding:

> They [those for whom the idols were named] were the names of righteous men among Noah's people. Then when they died, Satan inspired their people to set up images at the places where they used to sit and call them by their names. So they did this, but they were not worshipped until, when those [who made them] had died and the knowledge [of the origin of the statues] was altered, they were worshipped. (*Bukhari*, 6:442)

This should not surprise us, knowing what we do about the godly men who preceded Noah (A). Possibly some or all of them had come to the Cainites and tried to call them back to their Lord. And although the Cainites had rejected the message of these righteous ones, their extraordinary qualities had not gone unnoticed. But, as has happened in various other communities throughout history, people began to ascribe divine qualities to them, and after that it was an

---

[4]Wadd was believed to be the god of manly strength; his idol was made in the form of a huge man. Suwa', the goddess of beauty, was given the form of a female figure, and the idols of Yaghuth, the god of physical strength, were in the shape of lions or bulls. Ya'uq was the god of swiftness, whose idols were in the shape of a horse, while the idols of Nasr, the god of sharp sight, were in the form of vultures, eagles or falcons.

easy step to making idols of them and worshipping them. In fact, the shrines of these gods were found all over the Arabian peninsula and they were still worshipped by the Arabs when Islam was revealed to Muhammad (S).

Earlier, we pointed out that God's saying, **I did not create jinn and human beings except to worship Me** (51:56), indicates that it is an instinctive part of human nature to worship. And when people's connection to the unseen God becomes weak, paganism tends to flourish. At such times, groups of people, inspired by Satan, often invent other objects of worship in the place of or in addition to the Creator, and pagan themes become dominant in their religion, culture and way of life.

But it would be incorrect to suppose that the people of such communities denied the *existence* of the Creator or His power, for the fact that this was not the case is attested to repeatedly in the Qur'an.[5] Indeed, they clearly believed in God's existence and repeatedly referred to Him. However, they regarded Him as too high and too remote to have any interest in human affairs. Thus, in order to bring divinity down to a familiar, tangible level, they invented various deities whom they believed to be partners, associates or intermediaries to the Creator, ascribing to them godlike powers and worshipping them instead of Him. This is known in Arabic as ***shirk***, and one who practices it is a ***mushrik***, plural, ***mushrikin.***

Among various peoples, *shirk* would take various forms. In some communities, the ruler would establish himself as a god and people would worship him. In others, the sun, moon and stars, fire, a mountain, a particular tree or

---

[5]This is clear from such verses as the following:

> **Say, [O Muhammad:] "Who provides for you from the sky and the earth, or who controls hearing and sight, and who brings forth the living from the dead and brings forth the dead from the living, and who arranges the affair [of all creation]?" They [the unbelievers] will then say, "God," so say: "Will you not then be mindful of Him?" (10:31)**
>
> **Say, [O Muhammad:] "Whose is the earth and whoever is in it, if you know?" They will say, "They are God's." Say: "Will you not then remember?" Say: "Who is Lord of the seven heavens and Lord of the mighty Throne?" They will say, "They are God's." Say: "Will you not then be mindful of Him?" Say: "In whose hands is the dominion of all things, and He protects, while none can protect against Him, if you know?" They will say, "They are God's." Say: "How then are you deluded?" (23:84-89)**

Indeed, some pagan communities, including those of Arabia in the time of the Prophet (S), referred to God as "the Most Merciful" (*al-Rahman*), as mentioned in the following verses:

> **And they say, "The Most Merciful has taken a son." (19:88, 21:26)**
>
> **[The pagans said to their messengers,] "You are nothing but mortals like ourselves, and the Most Merciful has not revealed anything. You are only lying!" (36:15)**

rock, certain people or animals, and various other natural phenomena were regarded as gods or spirits. Or statues would be fabricated out of various materials, according to the imaginations of their makers, and worshipped.[6] As a result, the people would set God aside altogether — not as the Creator, but as the Ruler of creation and the Law-Giver for mankind, who alone is entitled to be worshipped and obeyed, according to His words, **While you have thrust Him behind your backs, disregarded** (11:92).

REFERENCES: Tabari/*H*, I:344, 354; Ibn Ishaq/*M*, p. 36; Maududi/*Q*, 71:fn. 17; Ali/*Q*, Appen. XIII, 2 and 3.

The Characteristics of Pagan Societies

Now, the values of any society are obviously governed by the beliefs it holds about the ultimate source of authority for its people and man's place in the scheme of things. History attests to the fact that in earlier pagan societies, the values of freedom, equality and basic human rights which we take forgranted today were often lacking or non-existent. Instead, the people were usually governed by the 'rules' of false deities, communicated through their spokesmen, the priests, oracles and soothsayers, and were a prey to superstitions of all kinds, fabricated upon whim, as is expressed in the words:

> **Or do they have partners [in divinity] who have prescribed for them a religion to which God has not consented? (42:21)**

Such societies were often dominated by a rigid class system in which special privileges were reserved for the priests, the wealthy and the powerful, and the poor and weak were oppressed and misused. Accordingly, slavery or serfdom was the order of the day, and masters had the right to determine the life and death of those whom they owned. Anyone who questioned authority was threatened or severely punished — or, at best, ostracized and left to stand alone, one against the ruling elite and his people, with no position, no protection, no voice, and in constant danger of being harmed or annihilated, as was the case with many of the prophets.

It is well-known that in such societies, a state of idleness, decadence and unhealthy luxury prevailed among the upper classes. Sexual immorality, obscenity, shamelessness and perversions of various kinds flourished. Entertainments that inflamed people's passions and lower natures, leading to immorality and debauchery, were the order of the day. Various kinds of unclean, impure food were consumed, and the use of intoxicants of various kinds was com-

---

[6]These various objects of worship are discussed in Appendix B at the end of the story of Abraham in this volume.

mon. Squeezing money from the needy through usury was an accepted practice. Occult practices were prevalent, and sorcery and black magic were conveniently used to intimidate or destroy one's enemies.

Consequently, wherever paganism prevailed, it was not merely religious beliefs that were in error. Rather, the misguidance produced by false beliefs affected every aspect of life, fostering unwholesome conditions and destroying the innate connection of people's hearts to their Creator.

THE SENDING OF PROPHETS

Because all things are included in God's knowledge, such unbelief and error are obviously part of His divine plan, the test of the human's faculty of discernment. However, the majority of mankind has not fared well in this test, as is evident from their taking false objects of worship. Nevertheless, there have always been certain men of clear spiritual insight who possessed an understanding of truth, through whom God Most High conveyed His guidance to humanity. Thus, He says:

> **Mankind was [originally] one community, and then God sent the prophets as bringers of good tidings and warners, and sent down through them the scripture with truth, in order to judge between people concerning that about which they differed.** (2:213)

Earlier, we saw that a prophet or messenger (*nabi* or *rasul*) is a special, spiritually-gifted person whom God chooses as His personal ambassador to people. Little by little, before the actual call to prophethood came to any prophet, God Most High would prepare him to receive His revelations and holy commands. The prophet's heart would be connected very strongly to God, while, at the same time, his inclination to follow Satan, his lower self and its passions, and the attractions of this world would become weaker and weaker. And when his certainty was perfect, his will totally surrendered to his Lord's divine Will, and his heart purified and emptied of everything except Him, prophethood would be granted to him.

Thus, from the time of Adam (A) up to the Last Prophet, Muhammad (A), when the people of a community ceased to follow the divine guidance and became corrupt, God Most High would appoint for them a prophet from among themselves. This prophet would be both a warner (*nadhir*) of the awful consequences of ignoring God's call and a bringer of good tidings (*bashir*) of God's forgiveness, mercy and eternal reward for those who turn to Him. When the people had heard the message repeatedly and refused to heed it, the divine punishment would come upon them as promised, and they would be removed, as an entire community, from the face of the earth.[7] But regardless of what might happen to the unbelievers, their prophet and those who believed with him would remain safe and unharmed, under the protection of their Most Merciful Lord.

[7]It is stated in the Qur'an that among the communities of the warner-prophets, the only one **that believed so that its faith benefitted it** was that of Jonah (10:98).

3. The Commencement of Noah's Mission

And previously We guided Noah. (6:84)

And indeed, We sent Noah to his people, and he remained among them one thousand years minus fifty. (29:14)

According to Ibn 'Abbas (R), between Adam and Noah (A) there were ten generations, all of which followed a true religious law. After that, disagreements arose among them. Thus, God says, **Mankind was nothing but one community, but then they differed** (10:19), whereupon **God sent the prophets as bringers of good tidings and warners** (2:213).

It is said that ultimately only Lamech and his son Noah (A) remained on the mountain. All the rest of their people had gone down into the plains and joined the ungodly descendants of Cain, who had now spread widely. They were given over to corruption and wickedness, and idol-worship had replaced the worship of the Creator.

Then God **sent Noah to his people** (7:59, 11:26, 23:23) to call them to repent, return to their Lord, and live according to His revealed guidance. Ibn 'Abbas (R) says that Noah was appointed as a prophet when he was 480 years of age. After 120 years of his prophethood had passed, God commanded him to build the Ark. He did so, embarking in it at the age of 600 years. He lived 350 years more, thus equalling the **one thousand years minus fifty** mentioned in 29:14. It is said that Noah was a carpenter.

REFERENCES: Tabari/*H*, I:344, 347-348, 353-355, 366.

Noah Calls to His People

Indeed, We sent Noah to his people, saying, **"Warn your people, before a painful punishment comes to them"** (71:1) — this how this great prophet's story opens in the Qur'an. And when this order came to Noah (A) from his Lord, he called together the chiefs of his people and addressed them in the words which are reported in the Qur'an.

Here it is important to note that the stories of the prophets in the Qur'an do not read like conventional stories, with events and dialogues presented in clear chronological order. Rather, since God's purpose in narrating these stories is to teach, warn and guide, the main message is repeated again and again, with variations. Hence, it must be understood that the words exchanged between the prophets and their people were not uttered on one or two or ten occasions, but (especially in the case of Noah, with his immensely long period of prophethood) perhaps hundreds or even thousands of times over the course of many years.

"O my people, worship God!"[8] Noah (A) said. **"You have no deity but Him, so will you not be mindful of Him?"** (7:59, 23:23). That is, leave off your worship of false deities, your adherence to their fabricated rules and the corrupt way of life in which you delight, and come to the worship of the One who created you and grants you endless divine favors and mercies. And, deeply concerned about his people's well-being, he added, **"Indeed, I fear for you the punishment of an awful day!"** (7:59).

When it became clear to the chiefs of his people that Noah (A) was calling them to the worship and obedience to the unseen Creator alone and demanding that they give up their false gods, they reacted with anger and contempt. **"We certainly see you in clear error"** (7:60), they mocked.

"O my people," Noah (A) replied earnestly, **"there is no error in me, but rather I am a messenger from the Lord of the worlds. I convey to you the message of my Lord and advise you, and I know from God what you do not know** (7:61-62).

"Do you then wonder that a reminder from your Lord has come to you through a man from among yourselves," he continued, **"in order that he may warn you and that you may be mindful of God, and that you may be shown mercy?"** (7:63). In this manner did Noah (A) gently reprimand his people, and especially their leaders, for responding negatively to a reminder that was intended to be a source of good and mercy for them, simply because it was brought by a familiar person from among themselves.

HOSTILITY AND REJECTION

Thus began God's call to one of the earliest communities of disbelievers. And from this beginning up to the ending of prophethood with Muhammad (S), no prophet who came with such a message was ever welcomed and listened to with respect by the majority of his people. Quite the contrary, anyone bringing something so radical was met with rejection and ill-treatment or worse, for this is the natural reaction of the uncontrolled human ego to everything that threatens its enjoyment, power and status, as the following verse attests:

> **Has there not reached you the news of those before you — the people of Noah and 'Aad and Thamud and those after them. None knows them but God. Their messengers brought them clear proofs, but they put their hands on their mouths and said, "We surely dis-**

[8]As pointed out in the story of Adam, the same Arabic root word "*'a-b-d*" denotes both "worship" and "service".

believe in what you have been sent with and we are certainly in uneasy doubt about that to which you are calling us." (14:9)

A similar reaction was very clearly evident thousands of years later when prophethood was bestowed upon Muhammad, may God's peace and blessings be upon him. In one of the most awesome spiritual encounters ever to take place between a heavenly being and a mortal, the angel Gabriel (A) came to Muhammad (S) during the Night of Power ***(Lailat al-Qadr)*** while he was in seclusion in a cave on a mountaintop outside Mecca. After imparting to him the verses that formed the first revelation of the Qur'an, Gabriel (A) made known to him that he was the Messenger of God.

Being untaught and illiterate, Muhammad (S) knew nothing about prophethood or the true histories of earlier prophets. Terrified, he rushed out into the darkness and made his way down the steep mountainside to his home. There he poured out to his beloved wife Khadijah (R) the story of what he had seen and heard.

After comforting her husband and caring for his immediate needs, Khadijah (R), a wise, mature woman, went to consult her aged relative, Waraqah bin Naufal, a Christian who was deeply learned in scripture, about Muhammad's experience.

When Waraqah had asked Muhammad (S) about what he had seen and received his account of the matter, he said, "This is the same spirit" — meaning the angel Gabriel — "whom God sent to Moses. Oh, I wish I were young during it" – that is, the time of your prophethood. "I wish I could be alive when your people drive you out!"

"Will they drive me out?" Muhammad (S) asked innocently.

"Yes," Waraqah replied. "No man has come with anything like what you have brought without arousing hostility, and if I should last to your day, I would support you strongly" (*Bukhari*, 1:3).

From this incident alone, we can understand the enmity that people whose highest values are power, wealth, worldly pleasures, position and maintaining the status quo feel toward the truth and moral correctness. And it was this enmity that was now unleashed against Noah (A), once the chiefs of his people realized that his message threatened not only their corrrupt way of life but also their personal rank and power. Consequently, they began a campaign to humiliate and undermine him in the eyes of the people, calling him a liar and a cheat, and claiming that he only wanted to make himself important and great among them.

Answering their arguments as God inspired him, Noah (A) continued to admonish and warn. As well as trying to make his people realize that there is no Lord except the Creator of all things and the consequent falsity of all other objects of worship, he also tried to make them understand his own role as God's prophet.

"O my people, indeed, I am a clear warner to you, saying to you, 'Worship God and be mindful of Him, and obey me' (71:2-3). **Indeed, I am a trustworthy messenger to you,"** he assured them, **"so fear God and obey me"** (26:107-108).

Noah (A) would reiterate his message over and over with different words. **"Indeed,"** he would say, **"I am a clear warner to you that you worship no one but God"** (11:25-26). He would also inform them, as God had informed *him*, that if they did not respond to his call and turn back to Him, a serious punishment would come upon them, saying, **"Indeed, I fear for you the punishment of a painful day"** (11:26, 7:59). And he promised, on his Lord's behalf, that if they heeded his call and turned back to God, **"He will forgive you of your sins and delay you for a specified time"** (71:4), meaning up to the time of their natural death, for **"indeed, the term set by God, when it comes, will not be delayed, if you but knew"** (71:4).

But as before, Noah's words were met with disbelief, scorn, insults, threats, and perhaps even physical violence. The leaders of his people thought up one argument, one tactic, after the other to discredit and defeat the man who was undermining their religion and their authority. And thus matters continued for a great period of time. Not deterred or intimidated by their mockery or harsh words, Noah (A) continued, with extraordinary patience, to preach and warn. Yet the reaction of his people, especially of their leaders, remained the same: arrogance, pride, anger, defiance, mockery, and relentless harrassment of their prophet himself.

"This is nothing but a mortal like yourselves who wants to make himself superior to you," the chiefs of the disbelievers among his people would say. **"And if God had willed to send a messenger among us, He would have sent down angels. We did not hear of this among our ancestors of former times,"** they would add, shamelessly belying the heritage of their righteous ancestors. **"He is nothing but a man possessed by a jinn,[9] so wait for a while concerning him!"** (23:24-25).

If we should need further proof of the fact that the concept of God was not a new one to Noah's people, despite their claim that they had not heard of such a thing among their ancestors, it is contained in their words, **"If God had willed, He would have sent down angels."** But while Noah's people certainly did not deny God's existence, they were unwilling to acknowledge Him

---

[9]This may also be understood as being insane.

as the only Lord, much less to obey the guidance conveyed by Him through one of their own community. Jealousy of their prophet and the desire to retain their power and customary way of life prevented them from admitting the truth, even though it might have been absolutely clear to them.

Against their enmity, Noah (A) had no defense except the unshakeable certainty that God the All-Knowing is in control of all things. Patiently he bore all the humiliations his people heaped upon him, taking refuge in His Lord's remembrance and calling upon Him for help.

"My Lord," he prayed, **"support me because they have denied me!"** (23:26). And, as he had been commanded, he continued faithfully and steadfastly to convey the Message.

REFERENCES: Qur'an: 7:59-63; 11:25-26; 14:9; 23:23-26; 26:105-110; 29:14; 71:1-4. Commentaries: Tabari/*H*, I:347-348, 353-355; Ibn Kathir/*T*, 29:14.

4. Believers and Unbelievers

It is He who created you, and among you is the disbeliever and among you is the believer. And God is Seeing of whatever you do. (64:2)

After listening to Noah (A) for some time, a few individuals among his people accepted his way. These were weak and lowly members of the society, whom the unbelievers regarded with contempt. Apart from the believers in Noah's own family, only these poor, humble, despised ones acknowledged the truth which the others were too proud and arrogant to admit.

Seeing that Noah (A) was gathering followers, the leaders of his people began to take the threat he presented more seriously. Obviously, if this trend continued, the lower classes might begin to assert themselves, and their own authority and power would be weakened.

Within Noah's own household, too, there were unbelievers, even enemies. One of these was his wife, according to God's words:

> **God sets forth an example of those who disbelieved: the wife of Noah and the wife of Lot. They were under [the charge of] two servants among His righteous servants but they betrayed them, and they [their prophet-husbands] did not benefit them at all before God. And it was said to them, "Enter the Fire with those who enter [it]!"** (66:10)

The betrayal mentioned in this verse was not due unfaithfulness, for, according to the statement of Ibn 'Abbas (R), no wife of a prophet was ever unfaithful to her husband. But, it is reported, Noah's wife rejected her husband's prophethood and told the people that he was crazy. She also carried news about Noah (A) and his followers' movements and plans to the unbelievers.

The other unbeliever in Noah's family was his son Kenan, otherwise known as Yam. According to traditions, Noah and his wife had four sons, the other three being Shem (Sam), Ham and Japeth. The first three sons and their wives were believers, as was Kenan's wife. But, disobedient and rebellious toward his prophet-father, Kenan had joined the unbelievers.

In spite of all these trials and difficulties, Noah (A) continued steadfastly to preach. **"Will you not be mindful of God?"** he would ask. **"Indeed, I am a trustworthy messenger to you, so fear God and obey me."** And he would make it clear that he was advising them purely for the sake of God, without desiring any gain or advantage for himself, saying, **"And I do not ask of you any recompense for it. My recompense rests only upon the Lord of the worlds. Then be mindful of God and obey me!"** (26:106-110)

To such admonitions as these, the chiefs of Noah's people always had a stock of ready responses. And now that their self-proclaimed had gathered some followers, they attacked him from another direction. **"Are *we* to believe in you, while you are followed by the lowest?"** (26:111), they would demand.

But Noah (A) immediately challenged this new line of argument, which turned the lowly status of the believers and their past deeds into an excuse for denying the truth of God's Message. **"And what is my knowledge of what they used to do?"** he would reply. **"Their accounting rests only upon my Lord, if you could but perceive, and I am not one to drive away the believers. I am but a clear warner"** (26:112-115).

"We do not see you as anything except a human being like ourselves, nor do we see you followed by any except those who are lowest among us, without thought,"[10] the chiefs would retort. **"And we do not see in you all any superiority over ourselves. Rather, we regard you as liars!"** (11:27).

"O my people," Noah (A) would reply earnestly, **"have you considered: If I should be taking my stand upon clear evidence from my Lord, while He has granted me mercy from Himself which is not apparent to you, would we be able to force it upon you, while you are averse to it?"** (11:28). That is, although I am bringing you clear evidence from God, who has granted me favors and mercies that you cannot perceive, even then it would not be possible for me to force you to accept His guidance if you did not wish to be guided.

"And, O my people," he would repeat, **"I do not ask of you any wealth for it; my recompense rests only upon God. But I am not one to drive away those who have believed. They will surely meet their Lord, whereas I see that you are a people behaving ignorantly,"** meaning that while the believers are certain of the meeting with God, *you* are displaying total ignorance by denying the inevitable Day of Accounting and the necessity of preparing for it. **"And, O my people, who would protect me from God if I drove them away? Will you not then be reminded?** (11:29-30).

"And I do not say to you, 'God's treasuries are with me,' nor, 'I know the Unseen,' nor do I say, 'I am an angel,'" Noah (A) would add. **"Nor do I say of those whom your eyes despise that God will not grant them any**

---

[10]According to Ibn Kathir, **"without thought"** here refers to the fact that the believers accepted Noah's message without question, for the truth is sometimes so obvious that it does not need much reflection. In the same way, thousands of years later, Abu Bakr as-Siddiq was to accept Islam without questioning as soon as he heard about it from his distant relative Muhammad (S), thus becoming the first adult male Muslim. The Prophet (S) was later to say about him, "I did not invite anyone to Islam without his hesitating except Abu Bakr. Indeed, he did not hesitate." Consequently, Ibn Kathir continues, when the Prophet (S) died, his Companions pledged their allegiance to Abu Bakr without a great deal of thought or consideration because his superiority was so evident to them. That is why the Prophet (S) said, "I intended to write a document appointing Abu Bakr as the successor after me, but then I did not feel the need to do so because God and the believers would not accept anyone except Abu Bakr" (Ibn Kathir/*T,* 11:25-49).

good, for God is most knowing of what is within them. Indeed, if I did so, I would be among the unjust" (11:31). That is, I refuse, for the sake of making you believe in me, to discourage or turn away the poor, humble ones who believe with me.

Little by little, the arguments given to Noah (A) by his Lord tore to shreds the unbelievers' lies and excuses, now centered around their unwillingness to believe as the 'lowest' people among them believed. Bit by bit, they were being made to understand that rank and wealth and external appearance have nothing to do with how God Most High looks at His servants — at how He looked at the lowly and weak among them, and how He looked at *them*, the important and powerful. But they would have none of it.

"O Noah," the leaders exclaimed in disgust, **"you have disputed with us and have prolonged your dispute with us"** — that is, you have gone on preaching at us until we have had absolutely enough of you. And they threw out a impudent challenge to him, saying, **"Then bring us what you are threatening us with, if you are among the truthful!"** (11:32).

"Only God can bring you it, if He wills, and you will not be able to escape," Noah (A) replied firmly. **"Nor will my advice benefit you, although I desired to advise you, if God intends that you err. He is your Lord, and to Him you will be returned** (11:33-35).

"O my people," Noah (A) said, with deep sincerity, **"if my residing among you and my reminding you of God's signs is burdensome for you, then I have relied upon God"** (10:71). And so deep was the prophet's certainty of God's help and support that he now threw back at them a bold challenge:

"Therefore, resolve upon your plan and summon your partners. Furthermore, let not your plan be unclear to you. Then carry it out upon me and do not give me respite" (10:71). That is, decide what you want to do about me and call upon the false 'partners' you have set up with God. Afterwards, have no doubts about your plan and implement it against me as you will. **"And if you turn away,"** he added, **"I have asked no recompense from you. My recompense rests only upon God, and I have been commanded to be of the *muslims*. Then be mindful of God and obey me!"** (10:71-72).

However, the deniers of God had shut their hearts and their ears. **Indeed,** God says of them, **they were a blind people** (7:64). The result of that faithful prophet's preaching and calling to his people throughout all those long, long, difficult years was that only a very few people listened to him and believed in him. The rest, guided by their chiefs and notables, were all dead-set against him and his divine Message.

REFERENCES: Qur'an: 7:64; 10:71-72; 11:17-35; 26:111-115; 66:10. Commentaries: Tabari/*H*, I:360; Ibn Kathir/*T*, 66:10, 11:25-35; Ibn Kathir/*Q*, "Nuh"; Maududi/*Q*, 66:fn. 24; Asad/*Q*, 11:fn. 56.

5. Noah's Last Supplication

And Noah, when he called [to his Lord] previously, then We responded to him and saved him and his family from the great affliction, and We supported him against the people who denied Our revelations. Indeed, they were an evil people, so We drowned them all together. (21:76-77)

Noah certainly called Us, and [We are] the Best of Responders. (37:75)

Finally the time came when Noah's people had had enough of him. He had become too annoying, with his constant insistence that they give up their idols and turn to the worship of the Creator alone. What was worse, since some people were now following him, he had become a clear threat to the structure and stability of their class-based society.

They then menaced Noah (A) openly, saying, **"If you do not leave off, O Noah, you will surely be of those who are stoned** to death!" (26:116). And God Most High, the Witness of all things, says of this:

> **The people of Noah denied, and they rejected Our servant and said, "A madman!" and he was threatened.** (54:9)

Then that faithful, steadfast, persecuted prophet called to his Lord from the depths of his helplessness and need, saying, **"Indeed, I am overpowered, so help!"** (54:9-10). And, as He has promised all His true servants, the Most Merciful responded to His prophet's call.

You may recall that it was said about Noah (A) that he bore more trouble from his people than any other prophet. He had now been among them for several hundred years, calling them to repentance and reform perhaps thousands of times. But the only thing that had changed was that their hearts had become even more hardened, and their hostility and persecution of him had intensified to its climax.

Now, when his people threatened to kill him, the patient prophet understood that the matter had reached its final stage. Since he had now been prevented, under the threat of death, from continuing to call his people to their Lord, all hope that others might yet believe had been cut off. No matter how troubled he might be about the fate of his disbelieving people, there was nothing more to be done for them. Their stubbornness and rebellion had passed all bounds, and, as he had warned them, God's punishment *must* come upon them.

"My Lord," he said, **"indeed, my people have denied me. Then judge between me and them with decisive judgment, and save me and whomever is with me of the believers!"** (26:117-118).

Then, as reported in the seventy-first ***surah***, "*Nuh*," the prophet summarized the entire story of his mission to his people and put it before his Maker.

"My Lord," he said humbly **"indeed, I called my people night and day, but my calling increased them in nothing except fleeing"** — that is, from the truth and from me, as its representative. **"And indeed, each time I called to them, that You might forgive them, they put their fingers in their ears and covered themselves with their garments, and persisted and became still more arrogant** (71:5-7).

"Indeed, I invited them openly," Noah (A) continued, recalling the history of the countless decades he had spent among his people. **"Then I proclaimed to them publicly and confided to them privately, and I said, 'Seek forgiveness from your Lord. Indeed, He is Ever-Forgiving. He will pour out the sky upon you in plenty with rain and will increase you in wealth and children, and will provide for you gardens and provide for you rivers'** (71:8-12).

"'What is amiss with you that you do not attribute to due **grandeur to God, while He created you in stages?'"** Noah (A) went on, recalling how he had tried to make his people grasp the obvious and abundant signs of God's power. **"'Do you not consider how God has created seven heavens one above the other, and made the moon a light therein and made the sun a lighted lamp?'"** (71:13-16).

He then recalled how he had reminded them of their creation from the earth and their growth through the various phases of life, saying, **"'And God has caused you to grow from the earth with gradual growth. Then He will return you to it and bring you forth again.'"** He further recalled how he had spoken to them of God's wisdom and beneficence in making the earth suitable for their journeying across its face as they liked: **"'And God has made the earth an expanse for you, that you may travel in its broad pathways'"** (71:17-20).

By such decisive arguments and evidences, Noah (A) had tried repeatedly to reach his people's minds and hearts. But their hearts were closed against him and there was no response from their side except denial, rejection and more intense hostility. Even though they could not fail to recognize the truth of everything he had said to them, they refused to accept his way because accepting it would cost them their power, prestige and the unsavory way of life they loved.

"My Lord," Noah (A) continued, **"indeed, they have disobeyed me and followed those whose wealth and children are increasing them in nothing but loss"** — that is, their corrupt, greedy leaders, and no doubt the priests of their false religion. **"And they have devised a great conspiracy"** — that of deluding the people through the false gods — **"saying, 'Never**

abandon your gods, and never abandon Wadd or Suwa' or Yaghuth or Ya'uq or Nasr!' And they" — the leaders, rich in wealth and children — **"have led many astray. And,** my Lord," he prayed, **"do not increase the wrong-doers in anything but error!"** (71:21-24).

Noah's people had now gone so far that he could no longer hope or ask for mercy for them. Apart from a few believers, throughout the long, difficult years of his prophethood, the rest of his people had consistently refused to listen and heed God's Message. Instead of obeying the prophet whom God had sent as their guide, they had insulted, persecuted and finally uttered a threat against his life. Not only that, they had taken the worst men in their community — the men of power, wealth, importance and influence — as their leaders and models. Thus, there was no hope left, either for the present generation or for future ones, guided and trained by such evil examples.

Now, according to a *hadith*, each prophet was granted a supplication for his people which was always answered.[11] Understanding that the last possibilty of reform for his people had been cut off, Noah (A) now used the supplication he had been granted for his people to pray for their destruction. This he did not due to anger or ill-will toward them, but because he realized that their wickedness had gone so far that nothing good could ever be hoped from them or their descendants.

"My Lord," he prayed, **"do not leave any inhabitant from among the unbelievers upon the earth.[12] Indeed, if You leave them, they will mislead Your servants and will not give birth to any except wicked ones and unbelievers. My Lord, forgive me and my parents and whomever enters my house as a believer, and the believing men and women. And do not increase the unbelievers in anything except destruction!"** (71:26-28).

The divine inspiration then came to Noah's heart: **"None of your people will believe except those who have believed already. Therefore, do not be distressed about what they have been doing"** (11:36).

Thus it was made clear to Noah (A) that the matter was closed and his people's doom was sealed. The few who had believed up to that point would be safe, but all the others would suffer the collective fate of the community. They had violated God's limits so long and so gravely that sorrow concerning them was no longer appropriate, even for their compassionate prophet.

REFERENCES: Qur'an: 11:36; 21:76-77; 26:116-118; 37:75; 54:9-10; 71:5-28. Commentaries: Tabari/*H*, I:355; Ibn Kathir/*T*, 71:1-28.

[11]For more concerning a prophet's supplication, please see Appendix A at the end of this story.

[12]This can also be understood as meaning **"in the land"**.

6. The Building of the Ark

And he built the Ark. (11:38)

There then came to Noah (A) an intimation of what was to come, together with instructions about the means of delivering the believers to safety, detailing to him the stages of what he was to do.

"Build the Ark under Our Eyes and Our inspiration,"[13] came the divine order. **"Then when Our command comes and the water pours forth, load into it two mates of every species and your family — except those of them against whom the sentence has gone forth. And do not address Me concerning those who have done wrong. Indeed, they are to be drowned!**[14]

"Then, when you have boarded the Ark, you and those with you, say, 'Praise be to God, who has saved us from the wrong-doing people,'" Noah (A) was instructed further. **"And say, 'My Lord, cause me to land at a blessed landing-place, for You are the best of those who cause to land'"** (23:28-29).

In this manner did God the All-Knowing give His prophet the tidings of what was to come, even informing him that the faithless members of his own family were among those who had been condemned by the divine justice. At the same time, He forbade Noah (A) to plead for the evil-doers, again including his family members, for the sentence that had justly been passed upon them by his Lord was not to be changed.

---

[13]The command to build the Ark is introduced very suddently, even abruptly, in the twice-repeated identical words of 11:37 and 23:27 above. However, the fact that Noah is instructed to build *the* Ark rather than to build *an* ark suggests that he might have had previous tidings concerning the building of such a ship from his Lord.

[14]This is a combination of two passages in which the same instructions are given, although with different sentence order:

> **"And build the Ark under Our Eyes and Our inspiration, and do not address Me concerning those who have done wrong. Indeed, they are to be drowned!". . . [So it was,] until, when Our comand came and the water gushed forth, We said, "Load into it two mates of each [species] and your family, except those against whom the sentence has gone forth, and whomever has believed."** (11:37-40)

> **"Build the Ark under Our Eyes and Our inspiration. Then, when Our command comes and the water pours forth, load into it two mates of each [species] and your family, except those of them against whom the sentence has gone forth. And do not address Me concerning those who have done wrong. Indeed, they are to be drowned!"** (23:27)

As God had ordered, Noah (A) and the believers set about constructing the Ark. The Qur'an contains no hint of a doubt, question or objection voiced by any of them, although we may suppose that the construction of a vessel large enough to hold such a cargo was a mind-boggling prospect, requiring an enormous amount of effort, patience, and boundless trust in God's wisdom and beneficence on their part.

How they did it, with what materials, and how long it took — these are questions that have puzzled scholars throughout the centuries. If, as is reported, Noah (A) was indeed a carpenter, building with wood would have been the most familiar work to him. And because the entire task was to be carried out under God's guidance and direction, he would hardly have been concerned about technicalities. As his Lord had ordered, so he would do, relying entirely upon His divine support.

Since we have no information about the place where Noah (A) lived, we do not know whether or not there were forests and wood in the area.[15] However, the source of the Ark's wood has been mentioned in a part of a *hadith* which states that

> Noah had stayed among his people for 950 years calling them to God. Then at the end of this time, he planted a tree which grew and spread in all directions. He then cut it down and began to build an ark. (Tabari/*H*, I:356)

Salman al-Farisi (R) reported that Noah (A) let this tree grow for forty years, and that he worked on the Ark for four hundred years (Tabari/*H*, I:356). Perhaps this may not be as unbelievable as it sounds, given the fact that the lifespan of people in that time was several hundred years.

At a spot which may possibly have been hundreds of miles distant from any body of water, the little group of believers, guided by the divine inspiration conveyed to their prophet, cut the wood, dried it, forged iron and made pitch. Working dilligently over a great period of time, they constructed the skeleton of a huge vessel from the wood of the miraculous tree, very probably unlike anything ever built before or since.

And he built the Ark, and whenever the chiefs of his people passed by him, they mocked at him. Noah (A) would respond to their sarcasm by saying, **"If you are mocking at us, we shall mock at you just as you are mocking. Then you will know who will receive a punishment that will disgrace him and upon whom an everlasting punishment will fall!"** (11:38-39).

---

[15]Ibn 'Abbas states that the Ark was built on Mount Nudh — that is, in India — where the Flood appeared (Tabari/*H*, I:358, 364).

What the unbelievers saw taking shape was probably a long, rectangular, flat-bottomed vessel of three stories. There are widely differing reports concerning its size. For example, one account attributed to Ibn 'Abbas (R) states that it was 1200 cubits long x 600 cubits wide (640 x 320 meters, or 2000 x 1000 feet), while another account from the same source states that it was 300 cubits long x 50 cubits wide x 30 cubits high (160 x 26 x 16 meters, or 500 x 83 x 50 feet) (Tabari/*H*, I:357-358). But God alone knows the truth.

The unbelievers of course could have had no inkling of its future purpose. Never could they have imagined that its vast bulk was intended to hold great numbers of animals and birds, as well as their prophet, the members of his family and the other believers, and perhaps (although we have no information concerning this) a great supply of provisions for them all. Consequently, it was probably not only the fact of a boat's being built on dry land that stirred the pagans to mockery, but also its huge size.

But to Noah (A) and the believers, there was nothing strange about it whatsoever. They knew beyond any doubt that God, their Creator and Sustainer, is able to do anything He pleases. As He likes, He causes things to happen; as He wishes, He prevents their happening. As He pleases, He destroys; as He sees fit, He saves. And He had informed His prophet that all the unbelievers were going to be drowned.

When and how was not their concern. Noah (A) and his followers were simply following divine orders by building the Ark, hoping to somehow be safe from the punishment that would come upon the deniers of God. And since the pure, sinless heart of the prophet was always receiving his Lord's inspirations, nothing could shake his confidence, for he knew with total certainty that God was with him, guiding and directing all his actions. And so the little group of believers worked, and the unbelievers mocked and threatened.

REFERENCES: Qur'an: 11:37-40; 23:27. Commentaries: Tabari/*H*, I:355-359, 364; Ibn Kathir/*T*, 11:25-44.

7. The Embarkation

And a sign for them is that We carried their ancestors in the loaded Ark.[16] (36:41)

At length the Ark was complete. And the punishment of the unbelievers was at hand, waiting only for the order of the Lord whom they had denied.

Then the divine command went forth. What occurred was probably a deluge of tremendous proportions, as God **opened the gates of the sky with water pouring forth.** At the same time, God caused the earth to gush forth with springs, as water from underground sources surged up to meet the water streaming down from the clouds. Thus, **the waters** from the sky and from within the earth **met for a matter already pre-ordained**[2] (54:11-12). Perhaps there has never been such a sight before or since. The cleansing of the earth from evil had begun!

Then, **when the face of the earth overflowed,**[3] God said to Noah (A), **"Load into it** — the Ark — **two mates of each species and your family, except those against whom the sentence has gone forth, and whomever has believed"** (11:40). But the fact was that, among all of Noah's people, only **a few believed with him** (11:40).

16**"Their ancestors"** refers to the ancestors of all mankind, who are descended from the believers who were carried in the Ark and who afterwards repopulated the earth.

17The **"matter already pre-ordained"** may mean either the Flood itself or the amount of water that would cover the earth, or both.

18This is a free translation of the Arabic idiom, ***"fara at-tannur"*** (11:40, 23:27), which literally means "the oven (***at-tannur***) gushed forth, overflowed, shot up or boiled over (***fara***)." Now, a ***tannur*** is an outdoor oven for baking flat bread; fire is made in the bottom and the top is open. Some commentators are of the opinion that these words refer to a specific oven and that the overflowing of water from it was the signal for the beginning of the Flood. However, ***tannur*** also denotes the surface of the ground, the highest part of the earth or ground, any place from which water pours forth, a place where the water of a valley collects, or the rise of dawn (Lane/*L*, I:319). In keeping with these meanings, Muhammad Asad says that ***"fara at-tannur"*** literally means "the face of the earth boiled over." He cites the explanation given by such commentators as al-Tabari and Ibn Kathir, on the authority of Ibn 'Abbas and Ikrimah, that "a***t-tannur*** [lit. "oven"] denotes the face of the earth," adding Razi's comment: "[T]he Arabs call the face of the earth ***tannur***" (Asad/*Q*, 11: fn. 62). Ibn Kathir states that the only plausible interpretation is that of Ibn 'Abbas: that the springs of the earth burst forth to such an extent that water poured forth even out of these ovens in the place of fire (Ibn Kathir/*T*, 11:40). The words suggest still another possibility: that because the presumed area of the Flood (or, more precisely, the area where the Ark rested when the Flood ended) is one of intense vulcanism, geothermal and seismic activity, the water of hot springs and geysers gushed forth to meet the torrents of water falling from above, together with the outpouring of the water of springs. For more concerning this, please see Appendix C at the end of this story.

"Embark in it," Noah (A) then ordered the believers. **"In God's name be its passage and its anchorage. Indeed,"** he remined them, **"my Lord is Forgiving and Merciful"** (11:41).

The believers went on board. According to a *hadith*, the embarkation occurred on the first day of the lunar month of Rajab, and Noah (A) and all the believers were fasting (Tabari/H, I:367). And they praised and glorified God with the words He had revealed to their prophet, saying, **"Praise be to God, who has saved us from the wrong-doing people. My Lord, cause me to land at a blessed landing-place, for You are the best of those who cause to land"** (23:28-29). And God Most High adds,

> **Indeed, in that are signs, and indeed, We are ever testing [Our servants] (23:30).**

There were eighty people in the Ark, Ibn 'Abbas (R) informs us: Noah (A); his three believing sons, Shem, Ham and Japeth; their wives; and seventy-three children of Seth (A) who believed in Noah (A). Without doubt, their hearts were full of dread at the calamity that was to come, of which the unbelievers were completely unaware. But at the same time, they must have had deep certainty of their Lord's mercy and beneficence.

Ibn 'Abbas (R) also tells us that when the rain came, the wild animals, domesticated animals and birds all went to Noah (A) and became subjected to him. As God had commanded him, he put into the Ark a male and female pair of each species. The bottom floor was for the animals, the middle for the humans, and the top for the birds. The Ark had three entrances, one under the other, as well as windows. It is reported that Noah (A) also carried in the Ark the body of Adam (A), which he placed as a barrier between the men and the women. Later, when the Ark landed, Noah (A) reburied it in Jerusalem.[19]

REFERENCES: Qur'an: 11:40-41; 23:28-30; 36:41; 54:11-12; 69:10-12. Commentaries: Tabari/*H*, I:334, 357-365, 367; Ibn Kathir/*T*, 11:36-40.

---

[19]According to other accounts, Noah carried the bodies of both Adam and Eve with him, and when the flood waters dried, he returned them to their original burial place.

8. The Flood

But they denied him, so We saved him and those with him in the Ark, and We drowned those who denied Our signs. Indeed, they were a blind people! (7:64; also 10:73)

And [We destroyed] the people of Noah previously; indeed, they were a defiantly disobedient people. (51:46)

As for what happened next, imagination must supply the details.

We can assume that at first the ground would have became saturated with water like a soaked sponge until all the land was awash. The buildings would have been flooded, in a state of collapse. Presently there would have been no place in the area that offered safety, nor any boats to escape in — except *that* one! And it floated, sound and tight, by God's command, a safe haven for the believers and their prophet.

As for the unbelievers, we can easily imagine their confused, frightened state. When their houses became flooded, they would have become seriously concerned about what was happening. But outdoors was no better. Perhaps the water rose so fast that no one had time to think or to take care of others, and the very young, the weak and the old would have drowned then and there. As for the strong and able, they would have raced for higher ground at the foot of nearby mountains. No longer was there any other place of safety left, even for their most prominent, powerful leaders.

Perhaps, among those fleeing, was Noah's unbelieving, faithless wife. Although there are no authoritative reports concerning her end, certain hints are given. The first is God's instructing Noah (A) to load into the Ark a pair of each kind of animal, the believers, **"and your family, *except those of them against whom the sentence has gone forth*"** (11:40, 23:27). The second is Noah's prayer that God would **not leave any of the unbelievers** — and his wife was one of them — **upon the earth** (76:26). And the third is God's mentioning Noah's wife in 66:10, cited earlier, as **an example of those who disbelieved**, together with the wife of Lot.

Meanwhile, Noah (A) and the believers were safe in the Ark, which **floated with them upon waves like mountains** (11:42). And from his place aboard the ship, Noah (A) caught sight of his disobedient son Kenan, **who was apart** from him and the believers (11:42), and was now struggling in the rising waters.

"O my son," Noah (A) called out with a father's love, despite the fact that his son had joined himself with the deniers of God, **"come aboard with us and do not be with the disbelievers!"** (11:42).

But even when death threatened him from every side, Kenan remained stubborn in his refusal to accept faith. **"I will take shelter on a mountain to save myself from the water"** (11:43), he shouted back at his father.

But Noah (A) knew better. **"There is no protector this day from God's decree but for him to whom He shows mercy,"** he cried. But then **the waves came between them,** and Kenan, an unbeliever to the end, was carried away in the flood and **was among the drowned** (11:43).

Again, we may try to imagine the scene. Steadily the thundering waves grew higher and more menacing. Now the slopes of the mountains were dotted with frantically climbing figures, clawing their way upward, in a state of terror as they understood that the judgment of God whom they had denied had in truth come upon them, as their prophet had warned.

Now the flood waters thundered against the sides of the mountains, rising higher and yet higher. As the water rose, it plucked the fleeing people off its slopes one by one. And by God's command, the flood carried away the very last one of those rebellious, defiant unbelievers.

> **Because of their sins they were drowned and made to enter the Fire, and they did not find for themselves any helpers apart from God.** (71:25)

Thus, the entire population, the descendants of Cain, perished, including Noah's son and presumably his faithless wife. At the same time, God protected Noah (A) and those with him from two calamities: the harm threatened by their people and the calamity of the Flood, carrying them to safety in **the loaded Ark** (26:120; 36:41). And God says:

> **And indeed, We sent Noah to his people, and he remained among them one thousand years minus fifty. Then the Flood took them away while they were wrong-doers. But We saved him and the people of the ship, and We made them a sign for all the worlds.**[20] (29:14-15)

> **And the people of Noah — when they denied the messengers,**[21] **We drowned them and made them a sign for mankind. And We have made ready a painful punishment for the wrong-doers.** (25:37)

REFERENCES: Qur'an: 7:64; 11:42-43; 25:37; 26:120; 29:14-15; 36:41; 71:25. Commentaries: Tabari/*H*, I:356, 361-362; Ibn Kathir/*T*, 11:42-43.

---

[20]See "Adam," footnote 13, for the meaning of **"worlds"** in this context.

[21]That is, Noah and the prophets before him.

The consequences of Noah's people's denial of the messengers — both Noah (A) and his righteous ancestors — did not end with their death. According to a *hadith*, Noah will be called on the Day of Resurrection, and he will say, "*Labbayk wa sa'dayk* —responding and at Your pleasure, O my Lord!"

Then God will ask, "Did you convey the Message?".

Noah will say, "Yes."

It will then be asked of Noah's *ummah* [community], "Did he convey the Message to you?"

They will say, "No warner came to us."

God will then ask Noah, "Who will testify for you?"

Noah will say, "Muhammad and his *ummah*."

Muhammad (S) and his *ummah* will then testify that Noah did convey the Message, for that is the saying of the Mighty and Glorious, **And thus have We made you [Muslims] a median *ummah*,[22] that you may be witnesses over mankind, and the Messenger will be a witness over you** [2:143] (*Bukhari*, 6:14).

The meaning here is that although Noah's people, in a futile attempt to justify and exonerate themselves, may try to deny the fact that their prophet delivered God's Message to them, Noah (A) will depend upon the veracity of the truthful prophet, Muhammad (S), and his followers to testify to the truth.

[22]That is, a just and balanced faith community, keeping to a middle course between extremes.

9. The Ending of the Flood

So We saved him and those who with him in the loaded Ark; then We drowned the others thereafter. Indeed, in that is a sign, yet most of them are not believers. (26:119-121)

They disobeyed their Lord's messenger, so He seized them with an exceedingly strong grip. Indeed, when the water overflowed, We carried you [mankind] in the ship, that We might make it a reminder for you and an attentive ear might retain it. (69:10-12)

Months passed. The Ark continued to float on the angry flood waters that covered the land, a tiny speck tossed about on the face of a tremendous ocean. The only creatures left alive were the people and animals within it, preserved in safety by their Most Merciful Lord under the command of their inspired prophet.

And We carried him upon a thing of planks and nails, floating under Our Eyes, a recompense for him who had been denied. (54:13-14)

A ship full of all kinds of animals and birds, with eighty human passengers — how they lived one can only guess.[23] That lone ship must have been a mini eco-system in itself. One thing mentioned in traditions concerning this is that the pigs kept the ship clean of human and animal wastes. As for the humans, without doubt Noah (A) and his people spent much of their time in prayer and worship, beseeching their Lord for help and deliverance.

Ibn 'Abbas (R) states that it rained for forty days and nights, and that the water rose fifteen meters above the highest mountain. The Ark floated upon the flood waters for six months, traversing the entire earth. Eventually it reached the sacred territory of Mecca, the site of God's holy House, the K'abah, built by Adam (A).

Ibn 'Abbas (R) reports that God had caused the Sacred House to be lifted up on Mount Abu Qubays, one of the mountains around Mecca, so that it would not be submerged. For a week the Ark floated in circles around the sacred territory, making *tawaf* around the House. After that, the Ark continued to float across the face of the earth until it reached the area of Judi in what is is now northeastern Turkey:[24]

---

[23]Had Noah stowed enough provisions in the Ark prior to the Flood to feed all the people and animals on board? Or were they fed by divine Providence, or is there some other explanation? Scientists have speculated that the animals may have been in a state of hibernation due to the darkness inside the Ark, a possibility made plausible by the report that the animals lived in the lower story, which would have been below the water.

And it was said, "O earth, swallow your water, and, O sky, cease," and the water subsided and the matter was accomplished. And it [the Ark] settled on Judi, and it was said, "Away with the wrong-doing people!" (11:44)

Ibn 'Abbas (R) mentions that presently Noah (A) sent out a crow to see if there was dry land below, but it got involved in eating carrion and did not return. The prophet then sent out a pigeon, which returned with an olive leaf in its beak and clay on its feet. From this, Noah (A) understood that the flood water had receded and the earth was drying out.

All this time the tender-hearted prophet had not been able to forget his son Kenan. It was true that Kenan had been rebellious and disobedient and had joined himself with the unbelievers, even to the last. Nevertheless, he *was* his son, and although Noah had seen him drown before his eyes, he hoped that God might somehow miraculously restore him to life — or, if not, that He would have mercy upon his soul.

"My Lord," he said, speaking from a father's heart, **"indeed, my son was of my family and indeed, Your promise is true, and You are the Most Just of Judges"** (11:45).

An important lesson is contained in Noah's prayer. Out of good manners toward his Lord, he did not ask directly that his son be restored to him. Instead, he simply voiced his hope that God's promise to save the members of his family (contained in His words, **"Load into it two mates of each species and your family"** [11:40, 23:27]), would not exclude Kenan, for in spite of Kenan's rejection of God and his own prophethood, he *was* his son. At the same time, he had not forgotten that God's promise of safety for the members of his family was followed by the words, **"Except those of them against whom the sentence has gone forth. *And do not address me concerning those who have done wrong. Indeed, they are to be drowned*"** (11:40, 23:27). Therefore, Noah's saying, **"And You are the Most Just of Judges"** (11:45), indicates his complete, unqualified acceptance of whatever judgment God, in His absolutely perfect divine justice, might see fit to decree.

"O Noah," the All-Knowing Lord replied, gently chiding Noah, **"indeed, he was not of your family!"** (11:46). By this indirect rebuke, God reminded his faithful prophet that for a spiritually conscious person, kinship is not a matter of birth or blood but of common belief and direction. Hence, the people who belonged to Noah, who formed his spiritual family, could only be believers.

---

[24]For further, fascinating information concerning this resting place of the Ark, see Appendix C at the end of this story.

"Indeed, he acted unrighteously,"[25] God Almighty continued, **"so do not ask Me for that about which you have no knowledge"** — that is, knowledge of the divine wisdoms underlying God's dealings with His servants and their destinies. **"I do admonish you, lest you be among the ignorant!"** (11:46), meaning lest you be so unwise as to desire to change God's perfect decree for personal reasons which are outside the pale of divine justice.

Then the prophet's heart became clear. Had not he himself prayed to his Lord to leave no **inhabitant from among the unbelievers upon the earth** (71:26), and had not his son been one of them? Even to the last, when death and destruction had threatened him from every side, Kenan had refused to come aboard the Ark of Safety with his father, relying upon physical supports for protection from God's decree. Consequently, it was perhaps this last act of his that determined his destiny, for by dying unrepentant and an unbeliever, he lost all claim on the mercy of his Creator.

"My Lord," Noah (A) said, deeply regretful for his error, **"indeed, I take refuge with You from asking something about which I have no knowledge. And unless You forgive me and have mercy upon me, I will be among the lost!"** (11:47).

"O Noah," the gracious Lord responded, passing over the matter as it it had never been, **"go down out of the Ark in peace from Us, and blessings upon you and upon nations to come from those with you. But,"** God Almighty added, both warning and giving a hint of what was to come in the future, **"other nations — We shall grant them enjoyment, but afterwards a painful punishment from Us will befall them"** (11:48). That is, future nations would be tested by an ample taste of the pleasures of this life for a time, until, like Noah's people, they turned their backs upon accountability to their Lord, as a result of which His punishment would come upon them as well.

The divine Author of the Qur'an then brings Noah's story to a conclusion with the words,

> **That is of the news of the Unseen which We reveal to you [Muhammad]. You did not know it, neither you nor your people, before this. Therefore, be patient; indeed, the [best] outcome is for the righteous.** (11:49)

The Ark had been afloat for six months — according to a *hadith*, from the first day of the month of Rajab, when all the believers were fasting, until the tenth day of the month of Muharram, the day known in Islamic tradition as 'Ashurah Day.[26] On that blessed day of the Ark's landing, Noah (and, accord-

[25] Although these words literally mean "He was a worthless act," it is reported that the Prophet (S) read them with the meaning given above (*Abu Dawud*, 3971-3972).

ing to the report of Ibn 'Abbas and other classical commentators, the believers who were with him) fasted, and Noah (A) ordered all the animals with him likewise to fast in thankfulness to God.

REFERENCES: Qur'an: 11:44-49; 26:119-121; 54:13-14; 69:11-12. Commentaries: Tabari/*H*, I:357, 362-367; Ibn Kathir/*Q*, "Nuh"; Ibn Kathir/*T*, 11:44-46, 23:27.

---

[26] "*'Ashurah*" means "ten". In some parts of the Muslim world, a dish known as *'ashurah* or Noah's Ark Pudding, made of whole wheat grains, chickpeas, walnuts, raisins and apricots, cooked together for many hours, is prepared for the day of 'Ashurah and sent to relatives, neighbbors and friends. The tenth of Muharram is also the day of the exodus of Moses and the Israelites from Egypt, and it is a well-known *sunnah* (practice) of the Prophet (S) to observe a voluntary fast on the ninth and tenth of Muharram in commemoration of this event.

10. The New Beginning

But they denied him, so We saved him and those with him in the Ark, and We made them successors and drowned those who denied Our revelations. Then see what was the end of those who were warned! (10:73)

Noah certainly called Us, and [We are] the Best of Responders, and We saved him and his family from the great affliction, and We made his descendants those remaining [on earth]. (37:75-77)

When Noah (A) and the eighty believers left the Ark, Ibn 'Abbas (R) tells us, they settled at a place which came to be called Suq Thamanin, meaning "Eighty". Here they all built houses and life began anew.

All the descendants of Cain had been drowned in the Flood, and during the period the believers had been in the Ark no new children had been born to them. Afterwards, the earth was re-populated by the descendants of Noah (A), as stated in the verses cited above.

Commenting on the word **"descendants"** in 37:77 above, the Holy Prophet (S) said that these descendants were Shem, Ham and Japheth, Noah's three believing sons, who became the ancestors of all mankind (Tabari/*H*, I:369). The Prophet (S) also stated that Shem was the father of the Arabs, Japheth the father of the Byzantines, and Ham the father of the Abyssinians (Tabari/*H*, II:20-21) — that is, the ancestors of Semites, Europeans and Africans, respectively. Consequently, all the known succeeding prophets were also descendants of Noah (A), in keeping with God's words,

> **We sent Noah and Abraham, and established prophethood and scripture among their descendants; and among them is he who is rightly-guided, but many of them are defiantly disobedient.** (57:26)

Thus we conclude the story of one of the greatest of prophets, about whom God says,

> **We left [this invocation] for him among the later peoples: "Peace be upon Noah, among all mankind!" Thus do We reward the doers of good; indeed, he was among Our believing servants. Then We drowned the others.** (37:75-82)

Highest honor be to Noah, the patient prophet who was the grandfather of us all! May God's choicest blessings and peace be upon him!

REFERENCES: Tabari/*H*, I:364-366, 368-370; Tabari/*H*, II:10, 12, 20-21.

Appendix A

The Importance of a Prophet's Supplication

Earlier, we referred to the special supplication or ***du'a'*** granted to each prophet for his community or ***ummah***, as mentioned in the following ***ahadith:***

> For each prophet there is a supplication by which he supplicates, and I wish to keep my supplication as intercession for my ***ummah*** in the Hereafter. (*Bukhari*, 8:317; *Muwatta*, 15.8.26)
>
> For each prophet there is a supplication which is granted, but each prophet was hasty in his supplication. But I have reserved my supplication to intercede for my ***ummah*** on the Day of Resurrection, and it will be granted, God willing, for anyone among my ***ummah*** who dies without ascribing any partner to God. (*Muslim*, 389; 385-388, 390-392, 396)

As we have seen, when Noah (A) felt that his people were beyond all possibility of reform, he used his supplication to pray for their destruction. It is said that among all the prophets, he was the only one who used his supplication to pray that his people be removed from the face of the earth. And although his prayer was accepted, he wept bitterly afterwards because of it. In fact, it is said that although his name was actually 'Abdul-Ghaffar (meaning the "Slave of the Forgiving One"), he was called Nuh or Noah (from the Arabic verb ***naha***, meaning "to weep") because of his copious weeping.

Noah's regret at the supplication he made against his people is mentioned in a number of ***ahadith*** concerning the distressed state of the believers on the Day of Resurrection, which we summarized previously in connection with Adam (A). As noted earlier, the Prophet (S) said that the believers will first ask Adam for his intercession but Adam will say that he is not fit to intercede because he was forbidden to eat from the Tree but disobeyed, and he will send them to Noah.

The believers will then go to Noah and say, "O Noah, you are the first messenger to the people of the earth, and God called you **'a thankful slave'** [17:3]. Intercede for us with your Lord! Do you not see what a state we are in?"

Noah will reply, "Today God the Honored and Glorious is angry as He has never been before nor will ever be afterwards. And indeed I had a supplication with which I supplicated against my people. Myself! Myself! Myself! Go to someone else; go to Abraham."

This request for interecession will be made to each of the major prophets in turn, ending with the Seal of the Prophets, Muhammad (S), whose intercession will be liberally accepted by his Lord.

REFERENCES: *Bukhari*, 9.532[C], 6:3, 6:236, 9:507; *Muslim*, 373, 377-378, 380.

APPENDIX B

THE FLOOD — REGIONAL OR GLOBAL?

The story of Noah (A) leaves us with two unanswered questions. The first of these is whether the Flood covered the entire earth or affected only the region where Noah (A) lived, which is commonly supposed to have been the Middle East.

The Qur'an and *ahadith* are silent concerning the locus and extent of the Flood, and the early Islamic traditionists also differed concerning it. As for Noah's supplication, **"My Lord, do not leave any inhabitant from among the unbelievers upon the earth [*al-ard*]"** (71:26), we have already pointed out that the word ***"ard"*** can also mean "land".

It is true that geological evidence points to the occurrence of a flood over much of the earth in remote antiquity. Moreover, Flood traditions are found in many different cultures. But if the Flood covered the entire earth, we are left with an unanswerable issue related to the divine justice, for God Most High declares:

> **Your Lord would not destroy communities for wrong-doing while their people were unaware.** (6:131)
>
> **We did not destroy any community but that it had warners as a reminder, and never have We been unjust.** (26:208-209)
>
> **Never would your Lord have destroyed the cities [which He destroyed] until He had sent a messenger to their mother-cities, reciting to them Our revelations. And never would We destroy the communities except while their people were wrong-doers.** (28:59)

Consequently, it is clear that God would never destroy a people as long as they were unaware of the divine guidance. In other words, destruction was only sent upon a people when they had consistently, over a period of time, rejected the warners who were sent to them and were all evil-doers, like the peoples of Noah (A) and the warner prophets who succeeded him.

However, the Qur'anic text suggests that Noah (A) was the first major prophet to be sent as a warner to any community. Consequently, if we accept the possibility that the Flood covered the entire earth, we are left with only three possible explanations:

1. All humanity at that time was hopelessly corrupt and deserved to be destroyed.

2. More than one flood occurred in antiquity in various parts of the earth, following various unknown communities' rejection of prophets other than Noah (A), about whom we have not been informed.

3. In Noah's time, the only inhabited part of the earth was the area where he lived, which was populated by the corrupted descendants of Cain. Thus, the destruction of his people meant the destruction of the entire population of the earth.

Otherwise, we are left with the probability that the Flood covered only a particular part of the earth, including the area of Mecca and India.[27] Recent research by William Ryan and Walter Pitman of Columbia University, documented in their book, *Noah's Flood* (1997), points to the Black Sea as the locus of the Flood, as does the research of Robert Ballard (see NationalGeographic.com, "Proof of Noah's Flood"). This, however, should not be taken to mean that the Flood was confined to the area now covered by the Black Sea, but merely that it was of limited rather than global scope. As in the stories of other prophets whose people who were destroyed for their sins, this does seem the more likely case, but only God knows the truth. Perhaps this is one question whose answer we will never know with certainty.

[27]Al-Tabari mentions two reports (one by Ibn 'Abbas) indicating that the Flood began in India (Tabari/*H*, I:363-364).

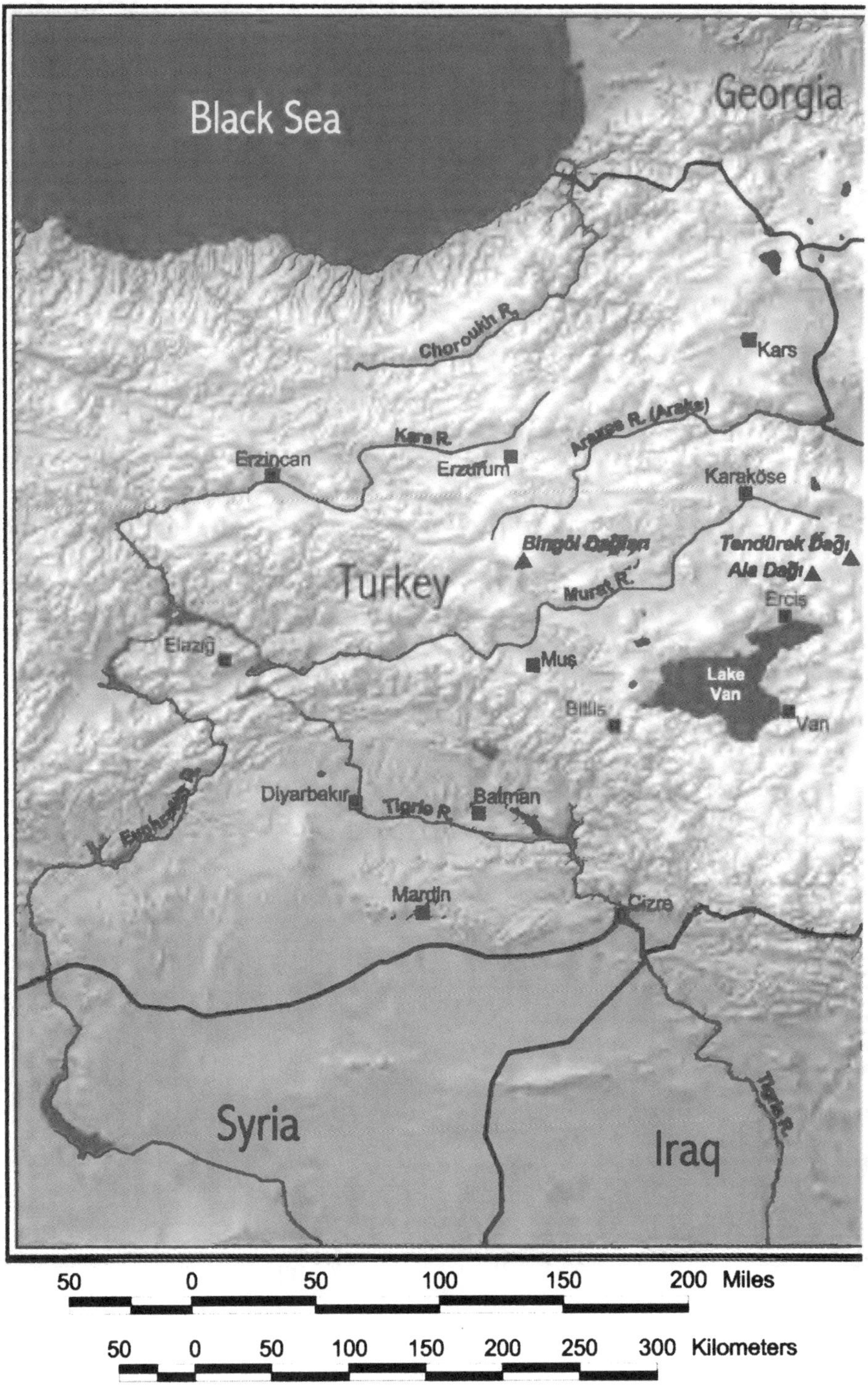
Black Sea
Georgia
Kars
Kara R.
Erzincan
Erzurum
Karaköse
Turkey
Erciş
Elaziğ
Muş
Lake Van
Van
Bitlis
Diyarbakır
Batman
Mardin
Cizre
Syria
Iraq
50 0 50 100 150 200 Miles
50 0 50 100 150 200 250 300 Kilometers

Map 4. The region of the Flood

APPENDIX C
THE LANDING PLACE OF THE ARK

The second unanswered question connected with the story of Noah (A) concerns the landing place of the Ark, which continues to puzzle and intrigue people today, as it did in the past.

The suggestion that the remains of the Ark may still exist somewhere on the earth is contained in God's words:

> **We carried him upon a thing of planks and nails, floating under Our Eyes, a recompense for him who had been denied. And We left it as a sign, so is there anyone who will remember?** (54:13-15)

> **Indeed, when the water overflowed, We carried you [mankind] in the ship, that We might make it a reminder for you and a retentive ear might retain it [Noah's story].** (69:11-12)

We may therefore justifiably ask, *If this "sign" and "reminder" was left, where is it now?* And while this question has no absolutely certain answer, perhaps we can offer some clues.

ARARAT VERSUS JUDI

The story of Noah (A) is found in two revealed scriptures, the Qu'ran and the Bible. Concerning the resting-place of the Ark, the Bible states:

> On the seventeenth of the seventh month the ark came to rest on the mountains of Ararat. (Gen. 8:4)

For reasons that are unclear, the words, "mountains of Ararat," have been widely understood as referring to the specific peak known as Mount Ararat (Turkish, "Agrı Dağ"), an extinct volcano which is the highest peak (16,946 feet) in the Ararat range in northeastern Turkey, a mountainous volcanic region with many peaks of 8,000-10,000 foot elevation. But, as we have seen, God Himself informs us in the Qur'an that **the Ark settled on Judi** (11:44).[28] Consequently, the discrepancy between these two statements gives rise to some very interesting questions: *What is actually meant by "the mountains of Ararat"? What is "Judi"? And what is the relationship between the two?*

---

[28]Interestingly, it is after the mention of the Ark's settling on Judi in 11:44 that God says, addressing Muhammad (S) and, through him, all mankind, **That is of the news of the Unseen which We reveal to you [Muhammad]. You did not know it, neither you nor your people, before this** (11:49).

In trying to sort out the matter, we consulted two Biblical concordances. Clow's *Bible Reader's Encyclopaedia and Concordance*, an old work lacking a date of publication, states simply that Ararat is a "mountainous region in Armenia, resting place of the ark" (p. 29). Our second source, *Smith's Bible Dictionary*, describes Ararat as "a mountainous district of Asia mentioned in the Bible . . . the resting-place of the Ark after the Deluge. . . ." This entry continues:

> In its Biblical sense it [Ararat] is descriptive generally of the Armenian highlands — the lofty plateau which overlooks the plain of the Araxes [River] on the N., and of Mesopotamia on the S.[29] Various opinons have been put forth as to the spot where the Ark rested, as described in Gen. viii. 4; but Berosus the Chaldean, contemporary with Alexander the Great, fixes the spot on the mountains of *Kurdistan.* Tradition still points to the *Jebel Judi* as the scene of the event. Europeans have given the name Ararat exclusively to the mountain which is called *Massis* by the Armenians, *Agri-Dagh*, i.e., *Steep Mountain*, by the Turks, and *Kuh-i Nuh*, i.e. *Noah's Mountain*, by the Persians. . . . Lower down, in the plain of Araxes, is *Nachdjevan* [Nakhichevan], where the patriarch [Noah] is reputed to have been buried. (*Smith's Bible Dictionary*, p. 4)

Among Islamic sources, the eminent Qur'anic commentator and historian al-Tabari states:

> The boat settled on Mount al-Jūdī in Qardā on the seventeenth day of the sixth month. Upon leaving the ark, Noah chose a place in the region of Qardā in the Jazīrah [Ibn Umar] and built himself a village there which he called Thamānīn ("Eighty") because he had built a house there for each of the men who were with him; they were eighty. To this day, the village is called Sūq Thamānīn. (Tabari/*H*, I:366)

This is confirmed in some early commentaries which state that at the time the Muslims conquered Iraq, ***the Ark was present on a mountain named Judi and some early Muslims actually saw it.*** Thus, Ibn Kathir, referring to the opinions of various classic commentators, states:

> Mujahid says this is a mountain in Jazirah [Ibn 'Umar]. All other mountains were under water except this, and Noah's Ark settled there. Qatadah says that the Ark remained there [on Judi] for a month and all the people [who had been in it] descended, and this Ark is still there in its whole condition, so that even the people of this *ummah* of earlier times saw it, although many well-built ships that came after it are extinct. Ad-Dhahak says that Mount Judi is in Mosul. (Ibn Kathir/*T*, 11:44)

---

[29]Although various sources we have quoted here identify Mount Ararat as being in Armenia, it is actually in the northwestern corner of Turkey. While in antiquity this was the region of the Urartu empire, extending from Caucasia in the north to northern Iraq in the south, it later became known as Azerbaijan. The Armenian highlands mentioned in Smith's entry are actually to the north of the Araxes River rather than the south.

The modern commentators of the Qur'an also agree in principle with the above descriptions. Writes Yusuf Ali:

> Let us get a little idea of the geography of the place. The letters J, B, and K are philologically interchangeable, and Jūdī, Gūdī, Kūtī are sounds that can pass into each other. There is no doubt that the name is connected with the name "Kurd", in which the letter *r* is a later interpolation, for the oldest Sumerian records name a people called Kūtī or Gūdū as holding the middle Tigris region not later than 200 B.C..... That region comprises the modern Turkish district of Bohtan, in which Jebel Jūdī, is situated (near the frontiers of modern Turkey, modern 'Irāq, and modern Syria), and the town of Jazīrat ibn 'Umar (on the present Turco-Syrian frontier), and it extends into 'Irāq and Persia. The great mountain mass of the Ararat plateau dominates this district. This mountain system "is unique in the Old World in containing great sheets of water that are bitter lakes without outlets, Lake Van and Lake Urumiya being the chief"..... The region has many local traditions connected with Noah and the Flood. The Biblical legend of Mount Ararat being the resting place of Noah's Ark is hardly plausible, seeing that the highest peak of Ararat is over 16,000 feet high. If it means one of the lower peaks of the Ararat system, it agrees with the Muslim tradition about Mount Jūdī (or Gūdī,), and this is in accordance with the oldest and best local traditions. These traditions are accepted by [the historian] Josephus, the Nestorian Christans, and indeed by all the Eastern Christians and Jews, and they are the best in touch with local traditions. (Ali/*Q*, fn. 1539)

Abul-A'la Maududi writes:

> According to the Qurān, the Ark rested upon Mount Jūdī, which is situated North-east of Jazīrah Ibn 'Umar in Kurdistan.[30] But according to the Bible its resting place was Mount Ararat in Armenia, which is one of the ranges of mountains of the same name that extends from Armenia to southern Kurdistan. Mount Jūdī is one of the mountains of the Ararat range, and is known by the same name even today. The ancient histories confirm that the resting place of the Ark was Mount Jūdī. For instance, Berasus, a religious leader of Babylonia, who lived about 250 years before Christ, says in his history of the Chaldeans that Noah's Ark rested upon Mount Jūdī. Abydenus, a pupil of Aristotle, not only confirms the same but also says that many people of 'Irāq of his time possessed pieces of the Ark, which they ground in water and gave to the sick as a medicine. (Maududi/*Q*, 11:fn. 46)

But perhaps the most convincing account of all comes from Muhammad Asad, who says:

---

[30]This is located on Maududi's map (Vol. 5, p. 86 [1972]) as being east of Mardin in Turkey, due north of Mosul and Nineveh in Iraq.

This mountain [Judi], known in ancient Syriac as Qardū, is situated in the region of Lake Van, almost twenty-five miles north-east of the town Jazīrat Ibn 'Umar, capital of the modern Syrian district of Al-Jazīrah. It "owes its fame to the Mesopotamian tradition which identifies it, and not Mount Ararat, with the mountain on which Noah's ark rested .... This localization of the ark's resting-place ... is certainly based on Babylonian tradition" (*Encyclopedia of Islam* I, 1059). We should, however, remember that the designation Ararat (the Assyrian Urartu) at one time included the *whole area* to the south of Lake Van, in which Jabal Jūdī is situated: This might explain the Biblical statement that "the ark rested ... upon the mountains of Ararat" (Genesis viii, 4). (Asad/Q, 11:fn. 66)

REFERENCES: Tabari/*H*, I:362-363; 366:fn. 1137; Ibn Kathir/*T*, 11:44; Ibn Kathir/*Q*, "Nuh"; Ali/*Q*, fn. 1539; Asad/*Q*, 11:fn. 66; Maududi/*Q*, 11:fn. 46.

During the past century or more, many attempts have been made to find the Ark on Mount Ararat's rugged, glacier-covered slopes. Some explorers have returned with claims of having seen an enormous rectangular wooden structure, broken in half by avalanches, embedded in glacial ice on the slopes of the mountain. However, due to the extremely severe weather and permanent ice on this peak, it has been very difficult for anyone to get at this object.

A documentary entitled "The Incredible Discovery of Noah's Ark" was aired on CBS television on February 20, 1993. After the program was shown, however, the accounts of certain explorers who claimed to have gone inside the supposed Ark on the slopes of Mount Ararat were exposed as fabrications.

At the same time, recent research in Turkey has provided some interesting and perhaps more definitive clues concerning the Ark's resting place. An article entitled, "Scientists say boat buried high on mountain is Noah's Ark," originally written by Martin Wroe for *The London Observer* in 1994, reads as follows:

LONDON — Noah's Ark has been found on the Turkish-Iranian border, 30 kilometers from Mount Ararat, according to the leader of a team of scientists who have been investigating the site for six years.

The Turkish government is so convinced by the team's findings that, after years of intransigence, it has designated the site one of special archeological interest and agreed to its excavation next summer.

The remote site contains a buried, ship-like object, resting — oddly, for a ship — at an altitude of 2,300 meters [6900 feet]. At 170 meters long and 45 meters wide, it conforms almost exactly to the 300 cubits by 50 cubits specified by G-d in building instructions to Noah, according to chapter six of the Bible's Book of Genesis.

On the surrounding terrain, the American and Middle Eastern scientists have identified huge stones with holes carved at one end which they believe are "drogue-stones", dragged behind ships in the ancient world to stabilize them.

Salih Bayraktutan, head of geology at Turkey's Atatürk University, estimates the age of the "vessel" at more than 100,000 years.[31] The site is immediately below the mountain of Al-Judi, named in the Koran as the resting place of the Ark.[32]

David Fasold, an American ship-wreck specialist with no religious affiliations, says sub-surface radar surveys of the site have produced very good pictures. "The radar imagery about 25 meters down from the stern is so clear you can count the floorboards between the walls."

He believes the team has found the fossilized remains of the upper deck and that the original reed sub-structure has disappeared.

During the course of writing of this work, I contacted Dr. Bayraktutan. Understanding my keen interest in this subject and my desire to share information concerning it with my readers, he graciously agreed to make available to me the following outline of his investigations.

The Research on the Ark in Northeastern Turkey

Dr. M. Salih Bayraktutan, Director of the Earthquake Research Center at Atatürk University in Erzurum in eastern Turkey, works in various earth science disciplines related to eastern Anatolia, and since 1984 has been carrying out field investigations in southern Caucasia and northwestern Iran. He also heads a large-scale project related to the Flood and Noah's Ark known as "The study of the pre-Sumerian inscriptions and remains of civilizations in the Ararat region (SEPAC)."

Atatürk University was selected and authorized by the Turkish High Educational Council and Ministry of Cultural Affairs as the Turkish scientific body designated to conduct all research related to the Flood, Mount Ararat and the Ark. Since 1985, Dr. Bayraktutan has been working as the leader of some joint projects, primarily with American groups, concerned with evidence of the Flood, all possible Ark sites, and the first post-Flood settlements in the region of Mount Ararat and the surrounding area of about 200 km diameter.

---

[31]Dr. Bayraktutan notes that this figure is not correct because no dating has yet been done.

[32]Possibly this hill, the crest south of the Ark, may be one of the Judi mountains, says Dr. Bayraktutan.

The objective of this project is to collect and interpret material evidence related to these matters, utilizing sophisticated geophysical, geochemical, isotopic, electronic and remote sensing technologies. Four different kinds of data are being collected for evaluation: (1) data procured through applications of remote sensing technology, radar imagery and space photography for interpretation of recent movements of continental blocks along fault planes; (2) geologic data, obtained through ground and remote sensing technology; (3) archaelogic data; and (4) religious texts and traditions.

The geological aspects of the study include the sedimentological, volcanic, seismic and morphological evolution of the region under investigation. Its geothermal, volcanic and seismic activities, and their chronological correlation, are being extensively studied in association with analysis of sedimentation products found at altitudes approaching 3000 m, in order to determine the time of deposition of clastic detritus and the paleo-geographic environment before and after the presumed period of the Flood. As a result of these studies, chronological changes in geomorphology, climate, seismicity, sedimentation, the development of the volcanic cones of Ararat, Tendürek and others in the region, lava flows, and vertical movements of the region (uplift/subsidence) will be determined. Such changes over the last 50,000 years will be evaluated in the light of data from the other sources mentioned above.

Finally, all sites claimed as resting places of the Ark will be sampled, drilled and analyzed chemically and physically, thereby eliminating all but one site. The final conclusions will be discussed at an international conference. The ultimate aim of this project is to put an end to speculation by collecting and analyzing scientific evidence of the Flood — its extent, time, duration and effects — and by locating the actual remains of the Ark, if indeed it exists in the area.

Geological Overview of the Area

The region under study, comprising eastern Turkey, southern Caucasia and northwestern Iran, is a high volcanic plateau (average altitude 2000 m), which has acted as a ceiling — the second highest in the world after Tibet — in the Alpine-Himalaya Orogenic Zone. Known as the Turk-Iran High Volcanic Plateau (TIHVP), this triangular-shaped region is surrounded by three bodies of water: the Black Sea to the northwest, the Caspian Sea to the northeast, and the Eastern Mediterranean and Persian Gulf to the south.

This region has experienced flooding several times during the last five million years. There is clear evidence of a flood, preceding Noah's Flood, which caused sea water from the eastern Mediterranean (at that time connected to the Persian Gulf) to pour over eastern Anatolia into the Caspian Basin through the Euphrates' channels.[33] It is likely that more recent floods have occurred as well.

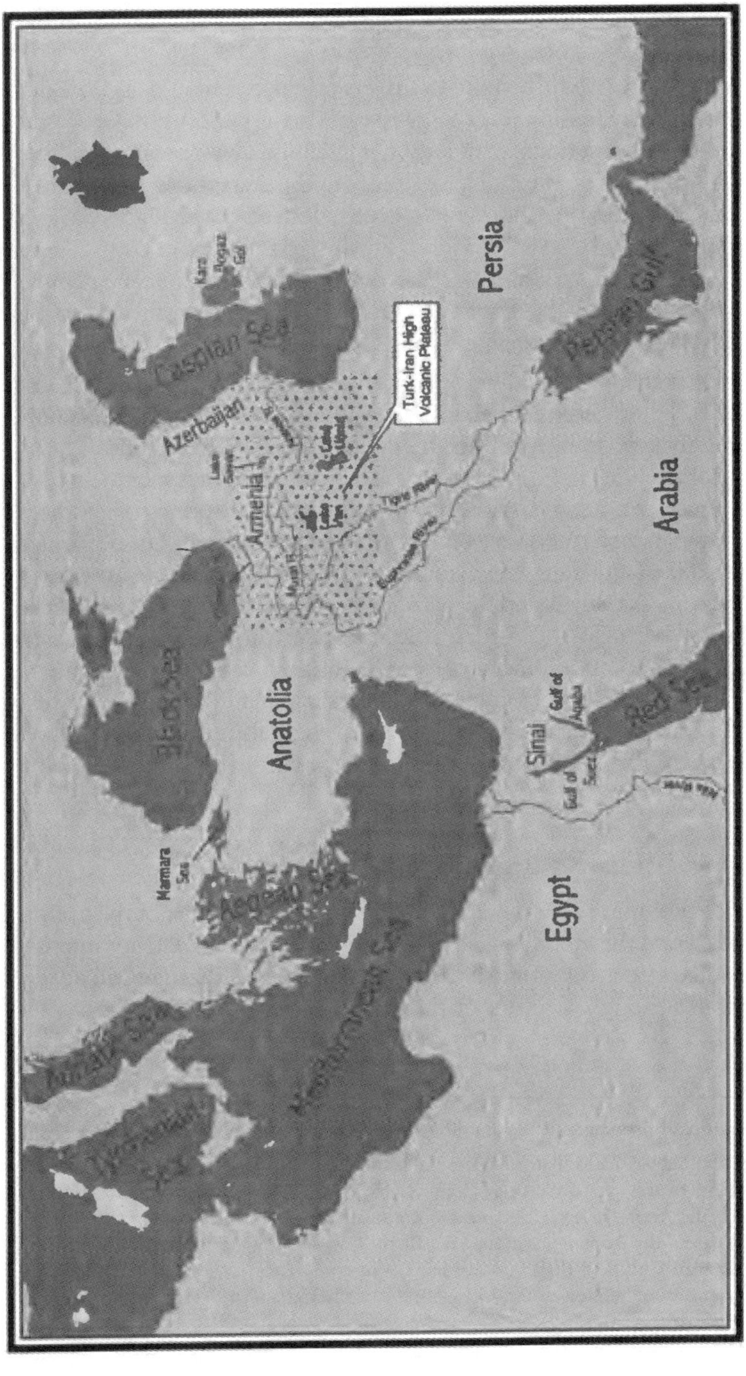

Map 5. The seas, lakes and rivers of the region of the Flood

It is hoped that these events can be corroborated through examination of the evidence.

This is a region from which numerous rivers originate and radially flow out in all directions, finally joining three large rivers which pour into three seas as parts of an ancient ocean; hence, this region is traditionally known as the "the area where the rivers originate." These rivers are the Araxes (Araks or Aras), flowing to Lake Caspian; the Choroukh (Çoruh), flowing to the Black Sea; and the Euphrates and its tributary, the Murat, flowing to the Persian Gulf. There are also three large lakes in the area — Lake Van in Turkey, Lake Gokçe (Ozero Sevan) in Armenia, and Lake Urmia in Iran — which are postulated to be remnants of Noah's Flood or previous floods.[34]

This region is characterized by very concentrated volcanic, geothermal and seismic activity. These geological phenomena are manifestations of a collision between the Arabian plate and the Turk-Iran microplates along the Bitlis-Zagros suture zone some eight million years ago. This compressional regime is still active in the region, resulting in the escape of volcanic gases, springs of geothermal fluids (water and gas), and very high seismic activity, which causes marked deformations of the earth's surface. Hundreds of large volcanic cones, the best-known of which are the Büyük and Küçük Ağri (Big and Little Ararat), Tendürek, Nemrut, Bingöl, Meydan and Aladağ volcanoes, dot the area, and hot gases escape at numerous points. Remains of rapid deposition (catastrophic sedimentation products), such as poorly-graded sediments and deformation structures, are also evident at various altitudes (in places, even at altitudes of 3000 m or more). This means that at the time of the Flood, the altitude of any given point was lower than it is now.

Religious Traditions Relating to the Area

This brief geological overview supports the Qur'anic report of the events that occurred during the Flood, possibly describing geothermal activity, intense vulcanism and strong ground movements — mechanisms that are still active over the region, although their rate of occurrence is now extremely slow.

---

[33]This is discussed and documented in a publication by Bayraktutan and Tchepalyga, 1995.

[34]Interestingly, Ibn 'Abbas states that the water that came down from the sky during the Flood became the oceans (or seas) that are on earth today (Tabari/*H*, I:363). A look at the map seems to confirm this, for the Ararat-Judi region consists of a relatively small land mass surrounded by large bodies of water: the Adriatic, Aegean, Aral, Black, Caspian, Mediterranean and Red Seas, as well as the Persian Gulf, and the two large lakes, Van and Urmia. The area is also honeycombed with rivers, as mentioned above, including the headwaters of the Tigris and Euphrates, two of the world's largest rivers.

The statement in Qur'an, 11:44, that the Ark **"settled on Judi"** (spelled "Cudi" in Turkish) has been understood by most Muslims as referring to Mount Judi, a mountain near Cizre, a small town on the Turkish side of the Turko-Syrian border near the northwestern corner of Iraq. However, there are two errors in this assumption. The first is that the word "Mount" is not found in the Qur'anic text, a critically important point, suggesting that the "Judi" on whch the Ark landed is not a point but a region. Second, there are several mountains and hills called Judi in the same region. It is obviously unwarranted to poinpoint one of these as *the* Judi without sufficient evidence, basing the entire speculation on one particular mountain to the exclusion of all others.

Hence, the Judi mentioned in the Qur'an may be understood as referring either to an undetermined, specific mountain named Judi or to the Judi region, which is synonymous with the Turk-Iran High Volcanic Plateau, in which there are a number of mountains or hills named Judi. The latter possibility is parallel with the statement of Genesis 8:4, that "the ark came to rest on the mountains of Ararat,"[35] in which "Ararat" refers to ***an entire region, not*** a ***specific point.*** And since the Judi region and the mountains of Ararat in fact comprise one single area, there is no conflict on the basis of religion concerning the resting-place of the Ark. Writes Dr. Bayraktutan:

> The region of Urartu is comprised of northern Iraq at the southern end up to the Araxes River in the north. Historically, this entire region was Azerbaijan, but today it is divided among four countries and includes northern Iraq, eastern Turkey, northwestern Iran, and southern ex-Soviet Armenia. Geologically, the region is known as the Turk-Iran High Volcanic Plateau (TIHVP).
>
> The hints and clues given by the geology of the area and by scriptures all point to this region, each confirming the other. My own interpretation of the mechanism of the occurrence of the Flood and the location of the landing place of the Ark, from a religious, archaelogical and geological standpoint, is that when the Flood occurred, water flowed northward from the south to the area of Urartu, which coincides with the area of Judi, and that the Ark rested in this area.

Possible Sites of the Ark

Based on various evidences, two possible sites for the landing place of the Ark have been considered and studied. These are the following:

---

[35]Again, as noted in Asad's comment (Asad/Q, 11:fn. 56), this is the region that comprised the ancient Urartu empire, from which the word Ararat is derived.

1. The Üzengili Site

Up to the present, only the Üzengili site in northeastern Turkey shows evidence of an ark-shaped object whose dimensions closely correspond to those given in Genesis 6:15-16. This object is located at an altitude of 2000 m in an enormous, highly active mud flow, whose debris flows northward down to the Doğubayazıt plain. This site is 25 km east of the town Doğubayazıt and 40 km south of the summit of the Büyük Ağrı volcano — that is, Mount Ararat. However, this site has no relation to Mount Ararat itself. Rather, it is on the mountainous slopes forming the south margin of the Doğubayazıt Basin.

This object was photographed for the first time in 1949 by Ilhan Durupınar, a Turkish pilot. As mentioned in a book by David Fasold, at that time the side walls of the object were about 1-2 m high. As the material surrounding the object has flowed and subsided downslope, the object itself has slowly lifted, so much so that at present the side-wall height is 8-10 m.

This object possesses perfect symmetry and some kind of regular internal structure. Ground penetration radar scanning, carried out during 1985-87, shows approximately nine longitudinal and thirteen transversal elements having equal intervals in most places. The reason for these signals has not yet been understood.[36] The ark-shaped body is made up of pebbles, sand, mud and soil. Rock fragments plus muddy matrix form the surrounding area.

However, the existing location is not the place of origin of the supposed Ark. Another site, consisting of a depression with the same dimensions but at a higher altitude (2300 m), is observed from space images, aerial photographs and ground observation. This means that the supposed Ark slid down to its present location. The long axis of the original ark-shaped depression is oriented approximately east-west, whereas the long axis of the ark-shaped object observed at the present location is oriented at N15°E to the direction of flow around the site.

The vicinity in which the supposed Ark rests is called the Üzengili Mud Flow (UMF). This mud flow was formed and later reactivated in three successive stages (the last of which is still active) by earthquakes in the area, as a result of which the ark-shaped mass was also uplifted and became more visible over time. However, the Üzengili site is experiencing very slow deformation due to an environment marked by flowing mud and seismic activity.

There are numerous graves and remains of primitive structures around this site. It is claimed that this place was the location of the first human settlement called Nakhuan. Various artefacts (tools, decorated bones) and fossil soils are

---

[36]Details are given in a publication by Bayraktutan and Baumgartner, 1987.

found in this area. These need to be analyzed and dated in order to demonstrate a relationship to the Flood.

Nakhuan was completely destroyed by earthquakes, probably several times. The people of the area moved further eastward to the area in Azerbaijan which is called Nakhichevan today. This Nakhichevan is located in the valley floor of the Araxes River, about 160 km east of Mount Ararat. The surrounding area contains an abundance of inscriptions related to the Flood, supporting the possiblity that this settlement was established by the prophet Noah.

2. The Büyük Ağrı Volcano (Mount Ararat)

The Büyük Ağrı Volcano (Mount Ararat) is the focus of Biblical research on the Ark. Both in the past and present, there have been very intense speculations about the location and properties of Noah's ship on this mountain. Coming to it with the conviction that the Ark landed at the summit of this mountain, some investigators claimed to have found remains of the Ark at several points near its summit at altitudes of 3500-4500 m (9,100-9,700 ft.).

One such supposed location, about 1.5 km northwest of the summit, is on a high plateau near the northern margin, under glacial ice. A second location, on the same high plateau but near the western margin, is also buried under a glacier at about 4500 m. A third location is in Cehennem Valley on the southwestern slope at about 3800 m to the north of the summit, in an area of very steep, steplike slopes. A fourth location is in the same valley but at a relatively lower altitude. Here, it is claimed, the Ark split into two or even three parts, some of which rested on the opposite, eastern side of the valley.

However, at none of these locations have any physical remains of the supposed Ark been found to date, despite the production of so-called evidence by some investigators, including what they claimed were pieces of wood from the Ark, whose falsity was quickly unmasked. Almost all the information concerning the site of the Ark on Mount Ararat is fictitious, the product of oral tradition or false evidence. Up to the present, no tangible physical evidence of an ark-shaped body has been found on Mount Ararat, nor does there exist any authentic written testimony concerning it.

Other matters of interest related to Mount Ararat are caves with inscriptions on nearby rock surfaces, found at Korhan on the northwestern slope of Mount Ararat and at low altitudes in nearby Cehennem Valley. These have been deciphered and dated as belonging to the pre-Sumerian period.

Rectangular, plate-shaped black stones, of 0.30 x 1.00 x 2.50 or 0.40 x 1.00 x 3.00 m dimension, have been found around Mount Ararat, about twenty of them at the villages of Kazan and Sağliksu, 25 km northwest of Doğubayazit. These stones have holes at one end, presumably for hanging or pulling; one surface or side has a cross and inscriptions. One authority has identified the crosses as being from the time of David, predating Christianity; hence, it may be assumed that local Christians later changed the shape and added other figures and crosses, something quite common in many ancient structures in northeastern Turkey. Similar stones are found in the northern part of the Igdir-Erivan plain in Armenia. Some investigators, including David Fasold and others, assumed these stones to have been anchor- or drogue-stones, used by Noah for balancing the Ark, and later used as grave stones by the local inhabitants.

Dr. Bayraktutan summarizes the investigations on Mount Ararat by saying:

> My conclusion concerning the sites on Mount Ararat is that there would have been an extremely remote chance for a floating object to land on a volcanic cone which was active or even erupting at the time. However, even if the Ark had landed on the slopes of Mount Ararat, the eruptions which are known to have occurred after the time of the Flood would almost certainly have destroyed it by tremors, lava flows and ejected pyroclclastic materials, barring some unknown means of its preservation. However, all possible sites of the resting place of the Ark are included in the US-Turkey Joint Project and are being considered with equal weight.

Unquestionably, the eyes of all those interested in this subject from the three monotheistic faith traditions will be focused on this very promising investigation as it unfolds over the course of the years. We extend our deep appreciation to Dr. Bayraktutan for making this information available, and wish him and his team every success in the carrying out of this most valuable and fascinating research.

Qur'anic References — Noah and His People

4:163

Indeed, We have revealed to you [Muhammad] as We revealed to Noah and the prophets after him.

6:84

And previously We guided Noah.

7:59-64

We certainly sent Noah to his people, and he said, "O my people, worship God; you have no deity but Him. Indeed, I fear for you the punishment of an awful day." (59)

The chiefs from among his people said, "We certainly see you in clear error." (60)

He said, "O my people, there is no error in me, but I am a messenger from the Lord of the worlds. (61) I convey to you the message of my Lord and advise you, and I know from God what you do not know. (62) Do you then wonder that a reminder from your Lord has come to you through a man from among yourselves, in order that he may warn you and that you may be mindful of God, and that you may be shown mercy?" (63) But they denied him, so We saved him and those with him in the Ark, and We drowned those who denied Our signs. Indeed, they were a blind people! (64)

9:70

Has there not reached them the new of those before them — the people of Noah and 'Aad and Thamud, and the people of Abraham and the dwellers in Midian and the Overturned Cities? Their messengers came to them with clear proofs. And never would God have wronged them, but [rather] they wronged themselves.

10:71-73

Relate to them the story of Noah, when he said to his people, "O my people, if my residing among you and my reminding you of God's signs is burdensome for you, then on God have I relied. Therefore, resolve upon your plan and [summon] your partners. Furthermore, let not your plan be unclear to you. Then carry it out upon me and do not give me respite. (71) And if you turn away, I have asked no recompense from you. My recompense rests only upon God, and I have been commanded to be of the *muslims*." (72)

But they denied him, and We saved him and those with him in the Ark, and We made them successors and drowned those who denied our revelations. Then see what was the end of those who were warned! (73)

11:25-34, 37-48

We certainly sent Noah to his people, [saying], "Indeed, I am a clear warner to you that you worship no one except God. Indeed, I fear for you the punishment of a painful day." (26)

Then the chiefs among those who disbelieved from among his people said, "We do not see you as anything except a human being like ourselves, nor do we see you followed by any except those who are lowest among us, without thought. And we do not see in you all any superiority in you over ourselves. Rather, we regard you as liars!" (27)

He said, "O my people, have you considered: If I should be [taking my stand] upon clear evidence from my Lord, while He has granted me mercy from Himself which is not apparent to you, would we be able to force it upon you while you are averse to it? (28) And, O my people, I do not ask of you any wealth for it; my recompense rests only upon God. But I am not one to drive away those who have believed. They will surely meet their Lord, whereas I see that you are a people behaving igorantly. (29) And, O my people, who would protect me from God if I drove them away? Will you not then be reminded? (30) And I do not say to you, 'God's treasuries are with me,' nor, 'I know the Unseen,' nor do I say, 'I am an angel,' nor do I say of those whom your eyes despise that God will not grant them any good. God is most knowing of what is within them. Indeed, if I did so, I would be among the unjust."(31)

They said, "O Noah, you have disputed with us and have prolonged your dispute with us. Then bring us what you are threatening us with, if you are among the truthful!" (32)

He said, "Only God can bring you it, if He wills, and you will not be able to escape. (33) Nor will my advice benefit you, although I desired to advise you, if God intends that you err. He is your Lord, and to Him you will be returned." (34)

. . . It was revealed to Noah, "None of your people will believe except those who have believed already; therefore, do not be distressed about what they have been doing. (36) And build the Ark under Our Eyes and Our inspiration, and do not address Me concerning those who have done wrong. Indeed, they are to be drowned!" (37)

And he built the Ark, and whenever the chiefs of his people passed by him, they mocked at him. He said, "If you are mocking at us, we shall mock at you just as you are mocking. (38) Then you will know who will receive a punishment that will disgrace him and upon whom an everlasting punishment will fall!" (39)

[So it was,] until, when Our comand came and the face of the earth overflowed, We said, "Load into it two mates of each [species] and your family, except those against whom the sentence has gone forth, and whomever has believed."

But only a few believed with him. (40) And he said, "Embark in it; in God's name be its passage and its anchorage! Indeed, my Lord is Forgiving and Merciful." (41)

It floated with them upon waves like mountains. And Noah called to his son, who was apart [from him], "O my son, come aboard with us and do not be with the disbelievers." (42)

He said, "I will take shelter on a mountain to save myself from the water."

He [Noah] said, "There is no protector this day from God's decree but for him to whom He shows mercy." And the waves came between them, and thus he was among the drowned. (43)

And it was said, "O earth, swallow your water, and, O sky, cease," and the water subsided and the matter was accomplished. And it [the Ark] settled on Judi, and it was said, "Away with the wrong-doing people!" (44)

And Noah supplicated his Lord and said, "My Lord, indeed, my son was of my family and indeed, Your promise is true, and You are the Most Just of Judges." (45)

He said, "O Noah, indeed, he was not of your family. Indeed, he acted unrighteously, so do not ask Me for that about which you have no knowledge. I do admonish you, lest you be among the ignorant!" (46)

He said, "My Lord, indeed, I take refuge with You from asking something about which I have no knowledge. And unless You forgive me and have mercy upon me, I will be among the lost!" (47)

It was said, "O Noah, go down in peace from from Us, and blessings upon you and upon nations to come from those with you. But [other] nations — We shall grant them enjoyment, but afterwards a painful punishment from Us will befall them." (48)

11:89

[Shu'ayb said,] "And, O my people, do not let dissension with me cause you to sin, lest there befall you something like what befell the people of Noah."

14:9-15

Has there not reached you the news of those before you — the people of Noah and 'Aad and Thamud and those after them. None knows them but God. Their messengers brought them clear proofs, but they put their hands on their mouths and said, "Indeed, we disbelieve in what you have been sent with, and indeed, we are in uneasy doubt about that to which you are calling us." (9)

Their messengers said, "Can there be doubt about God, Creator of the heavens and the earth. He calls you that He may forgive you of your sins and delay you to a specified term. "

They said, "You are nothing but mortals like ourselves who want to turn us away from what our fathers worshipped. So bring us a clear authority!" (10)

Their messengers said to them, "We are only mortals like yourselves, yet God confers favor upon whomever He wills of His servants. And it is not for us to bring you an authority except by God's permission, and let the believers rely upon God. (11) And why should we not rely upon God when He has guided us to our paths? And we will surely be patient regarding whatever harm you may you do us. And let the relying rely upon God." (12)

And those who disbelieved said to their messengers, "We will surely drive you out of our land, or [otherwise] you must return to our religion."

Then their Lord inspired to them, "We will surely destroy the wrong-doers (13) and We will surely settle you in the land after them. This for the one who fears standing before Me [on the Day of Judgment] and fears My threat." (14) And they asked for judgment, and every obstinate oppressor was thwarted. (15)

17:3

And We gave Moses the scripture and made it a guidance for the Children of Israel, [saying:] "Take no other than Me as Disposer of affairs, (2) O descendants of those We carried [in the Ark] with Noah. Indeed, he was a thankful slave." (3)

21:76-77

And Noah, when he called [to his Lord] previously, then We responded to him and saved him and his family from the great affliction, (76) and We supported him against the people who denied Our revelations. Indeed, they were an evil people, so We drowned them all together. (77)

22:42

And if they deny you [Muhammad], thus did the people of Noah and 'Aad and Thamud deny [their prophets] before them.

23:23-29

We certainly sent Noah to his people, and he said, "O my people, worship God. You have no deity but Him, so will you not be mindful of Him?" (23)

But the chiefs of those who disbelieved from among his people said, "This is nothing but a mortal like yourselves who wants to make himself superior to you. And if God had willed, He would have sent down angels. We did not hear of this among our ancestors of former times. (24) He is nothing but a man possessed by a jinn, so wait for a while concerning him." (25)

He said, "My Lord, support me because they have denied me!" (26)

Then We revealed to him, "Build the Ark under Our Eyes and Our inspiration. Then, when Our command comes and the water overflows, load into it two mates of each [species] and your family, except those of them against whom the sentence has gone forth. And do not address Me concerning those who have done wrong. Indeed, they are to be drowned! (27) Then, when you have boarded the Ark, you and those with you, say, 'Praise be to God, who has saved us from the wrong-doing people,' (28) and say, 'My Lord, cause me to land at a blessed landing-place, for You are the best of those who cause to land.'" (29)

Indeed, in that are signs, and indeed, We are ever testing [Our servants]. (30)

25:37

And the people of Noah — when they denied the messengers, We drowned them and made them a sign for mankind. And We have made ready a painful punishment for the wrong-doers.

26:105-120

The people of Noah denied the messengers, (105) when their brother Noah said to them, "Will you not be mindful of God? (106) Indeed, I am a trustworthy messenger to you, (107) so fear God and obey me. (108) And I do not ask of you any recompense for it. My recompense rests only upon the Lord of the worlds (109) Then be mindful of God and obey me!" (110)

They said, "Are we to believe in you, while you are followed by lowest?" (111)

He said, "And what is my knowledge concerning what they used to do? (112) Their accounting rests only upon my Lord, if you could but perceive, (113) and I am not one to drive away the believers. (114) I am but a clear warner." (115)

They said, "If you do not leave off, O Noah, you will surely be of those who are stoned!" (116)

He said, "My Lord, indeed, my people have denied me. (117) Then judge between me and them with decisive judgment, and save me and whomever is with me of the believers!" (118)

So We saved him and those with him in the loaded Ark; (119) then We drowned the others thereafter. (120) Indeed, in that is a sign, yet most of them are not believers. (121)

29:14-15

And indeed, We sent Noah to his people, and he remained among them one thousand years minus fifty. Then the Flood took them away while they were wrong-doers. (14) But We saved him and the people of the ship, and We made them a sign for mankind. (15)

33:7

And when We took from the prophets their covenant, and from you [Muhammad], and from Noah and Abraham and Moses and Jesus the son of Mary — and We took from them a solemn covenant.

36:41

And a sign for them is that We carried their ancestors in the loaded Ark.

37:75-82

And Noah certainly called Us, and [We are] the best of responders, (75) and We saved him and his family from the great affliction, (76) and We made his descendants those remaining [on earth]. (77) And We left [this invocation] upon him among the later peoples: (78) "Peace be upon Noah, among all mankind!" (80) Thus do We reward the doers of good; (81) indeed, he was among Our believing servants. Then We drowned the others. (82)

38:12-14

Before them, the people of Noah and 'Aad and Pharaoh, possessor of the stakes, (12) denied, and Thamud and the people of Lot and the dwellers in the thorn bush. Those were the factions. (13) Each denied the messengers, wherefore My punishment was justified. (14)

40:5

Before them, the people of Noah and the factions after them denied, and each nation intended [a plot] for its messenger, to seize him and to argue with falsehood in order to refute the truth thereby. Then I seized them, and how [terrible] was My punishment!

40:30-31

[The Secret Believer among Pharaoh's people said,] "O my people, indeed, I fear for you the like of the Day of the Confederates — (30) like the case of Noah's people and 'Aad and Thamud and those after them. And God desires no injustice for [His] servants." (31)

42:13

He [God] has ordained for you [mankind], of the religion [Islam], what He enjoined upon Noah and that which We have revealed to you [Muhammad], and what We enjoined upon Abraham and Moses and Jesus: to establish the religion and not be divided concerning it.

50:12-14

Before them, the people of Noah denied, and the dwellers in al-Rass and Thamud denied, (12) and 'Aad and Pharaoh and the brethren of Lot, (13) and the dwellers in the thorn bush and the people of Tubba'. All denied the messengers, wherefore My threat was justly carried out. (14)

51:46

And [We destroyed] the people of Noah previously; indeed, they were a defiantly disobedient people.

53:50-52

And that He destroyed the first 'Aad (50) and Thamud, and He did not spare [them], (51) and the people of Noah previously. Indeed, it was they who were most unjust and oppressive. (52)

54:9-16

Before them, the people of Noah denied, and they rejected Our servant and said, "A madman!" and he was threatened. (9)

Then he called to his Lord, "Indeed, I am overpowered, so help!" (10) Then We opened the gates of the sky with water pouring forth, (11) and We caused the earth to gush forth with springs, and the waters met for a matter already preordained. (12) And We carried him upon a thing of planks and nails, (13) floating under Our Eyes, a recompense for him who had been denied. (14) And We left it as a sign, so is there anyone who will remember? (15) Then how [severe] were My punishment and warnings! (16)

57:26

And We certainly sent Noah and Abraham, and established prophethood and scripture among their descendants; and among them are the guided, but many of them are defiantly disobedient.

66:10

God sets forth an example of those who disbelieved: the wife of Noah and the wife of Lot. They were under [the charge of] two servants among His righteous servants but they betrayed them, and they [their prophet-husbands] did not benefit them at all before God. And it was said to them, "Enter the Fire with those who enter [it]!"

69:10-12

They disobeyed their Lord's messenger, so He seized them with an exceedingly strong grip. (10) Indeed, when the water overflowed, We carried you [mankind] in the ship, (11) that We might make it a reminder for you and an attentive ear might retain it. (12)

71:1-28

Indeed, We sent Noah to his people, [saying], "Warn your people, before there comes to them a painful punishment." (1)

He said, "O my people, indeed, I am a clear warner to you, (2) [saying], 'Worship God and be mindful of Him, and obey me. (3) He will forgive you of your sins and delay you for a specified term. Indeed, the term set by God, when it comes, cannot be delayed, if you but knew.'" (4)

He said, "My Lord, indeed, I have called my people night and day, (5) but my calling increased them in nothing except fleeing. (6) And indeed, each time I called to them, that You might forgive them, they put their fingers in their ears and covered themselves with their garments, and persisted and became still more arrogant. (7)

"Indeed, I invited them openly. (8) Then I proclaimed to them publicly and confided to them privately, (9) and I said, 'Seek forgiveness from your Lord. Indeed, He is Ever-Forgiving. (10) He will pour out the sky upon you in plenty (11) and will increase you in wealth and children, and will provide for you gardens and will provide for you rivers. (12)

"'What is amiss with you that you do not attribute [due] grandeur to God, (13) while He created you in stages? (14) Do you not consider how God has created seven heavens one above the other, (15) and made the moon a light therein and made the sun a lighted lamp? (16) And God has caused you to grow from the earth with gradual growth. (17) Then He will return you to it and bring you forth again. (18) And God has made the earth spread out for you, (19) that you may travel in its broad pathways.'" (20)

Noah said, "My Lord, indeed, they have disobeyed me and followed those whose wealth and children are increasing them in nothing but loss. (21) And they have devised a great conspiracy (22) and said, 'Never abandon your gods, and never abandon Wadd or Suwa or Yaghuth or Ya'uq or Nasr!' (23) and they have led many astray. And do not increase the wrong-doers in anything except error!" (24)

Because of their sins they were drowned and made to enter the Fire, and they did not find for themselves any helpers apart from God. (25) And Noah said, "My Lord, do not leave any inhabitant from among the unbelievers upon the earth. (26) Indeed, if You leave them, they will mislead Your servants and will not give birth to any except wicked ones and unbelievers. (27) My Lord, forgive me and my parents and whomever enters my house as a believer, and the believing men and women. And do not increase the unbelievers [in anything] but destruction!" (28)

THE STORY OF HUD

peace be upon him

Thamud and 'Aad denied the striking calamity.[1] . . . And as for 'Aad, they were destroyed by a howling, furious wind, which He imposed upon them for seven successive nights and eight days, so you [Muhammad] could see the people therein overthrown, as if they were hollow palm tree trunks. Do you then see any remnant of them? (69:4-8)

As for 'Aad, they were arrogant in the land without right and they said, "Who is stronger in power than we?" Did they not see that God who created them was stronger in power than they? And they strove against Our revelations. Then We sent upon them a howling wind during days of calamity in order to make them taste the disgraceful punishment in the life of this world. But the punishment of the Hereafter is more disgraceful and they will not be helped. . . . And We saved those believed and were mindful of God. (41:14-16, 18)

---

[1]Referring to the Day of Judgment.

1. The Arabian Prophets

Then, after him [Noah] We sent messengers to their peoples and they brought them clear proofs, but they would not believe in what they had previously treated as false. Thus do We seal the hearts of the transgressors! (10:74)

For a time, the descendants of Noah (A) continued to worship God Most High and to live by His injunctions. But gradually things changed.

Little by little, people lost sight of the clear guidance brought to them by Noah (A). As before, idol-worship replaced the worship of the Creator, and man-made rules, alleged to have been revealed by the 'gods' through their priests and oracles, replaced the God-centered way of life of the preceding generations.

Throughout the Arabian peninsula (and perhaps far more widely than that), traditions concerning Noah (A) and the Flood remained very much alive among the people, who traced their descent from Noah. And it was to the people of this region that God sent the next two known prophets, Hud and Saleh; then centuries later, Shu'ayb, and still later, Muhammad, may His peace and blessings be upon them all. Thus, the Holy Prophet (S) was to say to Abu Dharr al-Ghifari (R), "Four [prophets] were from Arabia: Hud and Saleh and Shu'ayb and your prophet, O Abu Dharr"[2] (Ibn Hibban).

Like Noah (A), these prophets were sent as warners to their corrupt people, who, after consistently rejecting God's guidance and denying their prophets, were eventually wiped out, destroyed by divine punishment. But even though these peoples became extinct, their stories left a lasting mark upon the minds of their descendants in the area. In fact, up to the time of Prophet Muhammad (S) some 2500 or so years after Shu'ayb, the people of Arabia were quite familiar with the stories Noah and his successors, as is evident from the following verses of the Qur'an:

> **Has there not reached them [the pagan Meccans of Muhammad's time] the news of those before them — the people of Noah and 'Aad and Thamud, and the people of Abraham and the dwellers in Midian and the Overturned Cities?[3] Their messengers came to them with clear proofs. And never would God have wronged them, but [rather] they wronged themselves.** (9:70)

---

[2]Saleh's story follows Hud's, and Shu'ayb's is the last story in this volume.

[3]In this single verse, the Meccan unbelievers were reminded of not less than six prophets with whose stories they were familiar: Noah, Hud (the prophet of the 'Aad), Saleh (the prophet of the Thamud), Abraham, Shu'ayb (the prophet of Midian), and Lot (the prophet of the Overturned Cities).

Has there not reached you the news of those before you — the people of Noah and 'Aad and Thamud and those after them. None knows them but God. (14:9)

If they deny you [Muhammad], the people of Noah and 'Aad and Thamud denied [their prophets] before them. (22:42)

And [We destroyed] 'Aad and Thamud, and it [their fate] has been made clear to you from [the ruins of] their dwellings. And Satan made their deeds attractive to them and thus kept them back from the path, although they were granted perception. (29:38)

But if they turn away, then say, [O Muhammad:] "I have warned you of a blast like the blast of 'Aad and Thamud." (41:13)

Have you [Muhammad] not considered how your Lord dealt with 'Aad, Iram of the lofty columns, the like of which had never been created in the lands; and [with] Thamud, who hewed out the rocks in the valley; and [with] Pharaoh, possessor of the stakes — those who committed excesses in the lands and increased the corruption therein? So then your Lord poured upon them a scourge of punishment. Indeed, your Lord is on the watch! (89:6-14)

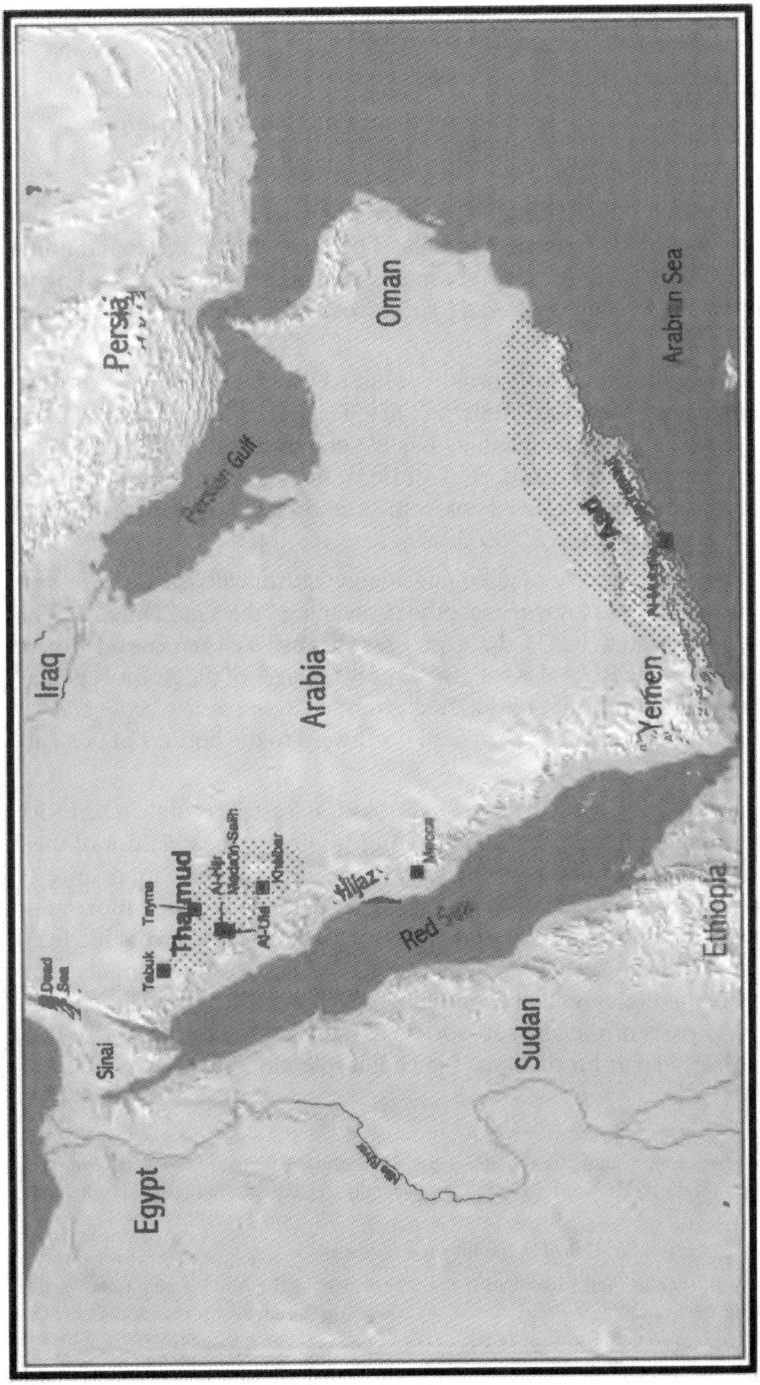

Map 6. The territories of the 'Aad and Thamud

2. The 'Aad

Then, after them [the people of Noah], We brought forth another generation. And We sent among them a messenger from among themselves.[4] (23:31-32)

Many centuries after Noah (A), a tribe known as the 'Aad lived in the southeastern part of the Arabian peninsula. The 'Aad were an ancient community, the first after Noah's people to be mentioned in the Qur'an, according to God's words, **He made you ['Aad] successors after the people of Noah** (7:69).

The 'Aad of the time of the prophet Hud (A) are referred to as "the first 'Aad." They were the original Arabs and Semites, tracing their ancestry from 'Aad, the son of Aus (or Uz), son of Noah's grandson Iram,[5] son of Shem. Iram's descendants were known as 'Aadi Iram, or simply as 'Aad. The time period during which the 'Aad lived was from around 2200 B.C. to around 1500 B.C., or between 4,200 and 3,700 years ago.

The 'Aad were a people of great power and wealth, who ruled over a vast area. Their territory was known as al-Ahqaf, meaning "the Sand Dunes". The center of their civilization was Hadramaut, which lies between Yemen and Oman, and extends up to the Rub' al-Khali, the Empty Quarter of the Arabian peninsula. However, the authority of the 'Aad extended over a much larger area — that is, from the coast of the Persian Gulf northward to the borders of present-day Iraq.

It is believed that during the time of the 'Aad, at least parts of their territory were well-watered, green, fertile and beautiful, adding to the splendor of their civilization.[6] This is confirmed in the Qur'an's mention of their abundance of **cattle and children, and gardens and springs** (26:132-134). Their most valuable crop was frankincense, a precious and costly aromatic resin extracted from rare trees that grew in their area. The 'Aadites' major role as producers and distributors of this highly-valued commodity, which was widely used in religious ceremonies in parts of the ancient world such as Egypt, Babylon and Judea, accounts at least in part for their prosperity and splendor.

---

[4]Since these verses follow immediately after a passage narrating the story of Noah, they may either refer specifically to Hud and his people, or generally to all the warner prophets who came after Noah.

[5]In Gen. 10:22, Aram is mentioned as the fifth son of Shem.

[6]Classical writers, such as Pliny, described the southern part of the Arabian peninsula (Arabia Felix) as being mist-covered and very fertile, with wooded mountains, rivers and unbroken forest tracts.

During their own time, the fame of the 'Aad spread far and wide because of their power and wealth — and afterwards, because of their sudden destruction. They were often mentioned in Arabic poetry. In fact, it is reported that a man once came to Prophet Muhammad (S) and related to him certain details of the story of the 'Aad that had evidently been passed down through oral tradition over the centuries (Tabari/*H*, II:29-31; Ibn Kathir/*T*, 7:70-72).

The people of this tribe were also well-known for their physical strength, which is reflected in Hud's words, **"And recall when He made you successors after the people of Noah and increased you greatly in stature"** (7:69). The 'Aad were, moreover, famed for their great skill in stone masonry and building. With this highly-developed craft, they built grand stone houses, palaces and temples with pillars. The splendor of their civilization and architecture is reflected in God's referring to them as **'Aad, Iram of the high columns, the like of which had never been created in the lands**[7] (89:7-8).

It may be hard for us to imagine such a highly-developed civilization flourishing in what is now a bleak region of sand and dunes, but thus it was. The 'Aadites were so powerful that it has been said that they were the super power of their time. At the same time, however, they were extremely proud of their power and used it oppressively and unjustly: —

> **As for 'Aad, they were arrogant in the land without right and they said, "Who is stronger in power than we?" Did they not see that God who created them was stronger in power than they? And they strove against Our signs. (41:15)**

During the long interval that had passed since the time of Noah (A), the memory of the Flood had remained keenly alive among the people of the area, for their own forefathers had been the chief actors in that drama. Nevertheless, despite this, its people had lost all traces of the God-centered faith of their predecessors. The beliefs and practices that Noah (A) had taught had been all but forgotten.

---

[7]The 'Aadites' architectural skill is also reflected in Hud's words, **"Do you construct tokens upon every high place, amusing yourselves, and do you prepare structures for yourselves, that you may remain eternally?"** (26:128-129). The Roman historians, Pliny and Strabo, mention the cities of this region as being adorned with beautiful temples and palaces. The tenth century Arab historian, al-Hamdani, speaks of ruins having extraordinarily beautiful columns in the territory formerly inhabited by the 'Aad, and earlier reports mention columns of silver or gold-covered silver (reported in Dr. Mikal Rahman's webpage, http://www.alislam.org/~sultan/review/09_94/ ad0994.html, "The Extinct Arabian People of 'Ad and Their Famous Pillars of the Iram). While such descriptions cannot be localized to any one city or place in southern Arabia, they give an idea of its people's affluence and skill. Ibn Kathir, however, rejects such reports as blatant fabrications. Rather, he suggests, these words indicate that the 'Aad were a nomadic people whose tents were supported by high poles (Ibn Kathir/*Juz' 'Amma*, p. 137).

To the 'Aad, like Noah's people before them, Allah or God was unquestionably the Creator. However, they conceived of Him as a impersonal deity, too remote to have anything to do with the affairs of human beings. Consequently, in His place, they had set up and worshipped various other deities, especially three chief gods, each of whom had a special role or function.[8] The fabricated religion of these gods encouraged the 'Aad to be proud, cruel, unjust and tyrannical.

Then, in keeping with His eternal divine plan, God Most High appointed Hud, son of 'Abdullah, son of Rabah al-Jarud, son of 'Aad, son of 'Aus, son of Iram, son of Shem, son of Noah, to call his people to Him and to warn them of His punishment.

Because he was an Arabian prophet, Hud (A) is one of the few Qur'anic prophets not mentioned in Bible. Consequently, there is no English equivalent of his name. The eleventh *surah* of the Qur'an, *"Hud,"* is named for him, and the forty-sixth *surah*, *"Al-Ahqaf,"* in which part of his story is told, is named for the sand dunes which were the most prominent feature of his area. Hud (A) himself is mentioned by name seven times in the Qur'an, and his people, the 'Aad, are mentioned sixteen additional times as an example of a community that doomed itself by its refusal to turn back to God.

REFERENCES: Tabari/*H*, II:28-29; Ibn Kathir/*T*, 7:65-72, 89:7-8; Maududi/*Q*, 7:fns. 51, 53, 26:fn. 89, 46:fn. 25, 89:fns. 3-4; Asad/*Q*, 7:fn. 48; Ali/*Q*, fn. 1040; Nadvi/*G*, pp. 42, 76-77, 92-93.

---

[8]One of these was the moon god Sin, who was also later worshipped by the people of Abraham.

3. Hud Calls to His People

And to 'Aad, [God sent] their brother Hud. (7:65, 11:50)

And mention [O Muhammad,] the brother of 'Aad, when he warned his people in al-Ahqaf — and warners had passed on before and after him — [saying,] "Do not worship anyone but God. Indeed, I fear for you the punishment of a terrible day!" (46:21)

As with Noah (S) and several other prophets, Hud's story opens when he begins to call his people, who were so gravely abusing the power and wealth they had been granted, to their Lord. And as in the stories of other prophets, several detailed dialogues between Hud (A) and his people, doubtless occurring over a period of many years, are reported in the Qur'an.

"O my people, worship God!" Hud (A) said. **"You have no deity but Him, so will you not be mindful of Him?"** (11:50, 7:65).

Like Noah's people before them, the 'Aadite chiefs reacted contemptuously to this challenge to their gods and their own authority, and put Hud (A) down with a variety of insults and taunts. **"Indeed, we see you as weak-minded,"** they proclaimed, **"and indeed, we consider you among the liars"** (7:66).

"O my people," Hud (A) replied, **"there is no weak-mindedness in me, but I am a messenger from the Lord of the worlds. I convey to you the messages of my Lord and I am a trustworthy advisor to you"** (7:67-68).

Again and again Hud (A) would plead with his people to the turn to their Maker, saying, **"Will you not be mindful of God? Indeed, I am a trustworthy messenger to you, so be mindful of God and obey me"** (26:124-126). And in precisely the same words Noah (A) had spoken before him, he would ask, **"Do you then wonder that there has come to you a reminder from your Lord through a man from among yourselves, that he may warn you?"** Then, referring to matters which were common themes in the 'Aad's oral traditions, poetry and songs, he would say: **"And recall when He made you successors after Noah's people and increased you in physical strength. Therefore,"** he would urge, **"remember God's favors, that you may prosper"** (7:69).

In response to Hud's call, the chiefs of the 'Aad initiated a course of opposition and enmity against him that was designed to undermine any influence he might have in their society. For in spite of being thoroughly familiar with the account of the Flood, they were unwilling to acknowledge the similarities between their situation and that of Noah's people. At the same time, they refused to consider giving up their false religion, with all the advantages it gave them, in exchange for worshipping the remote, unseen Creator. And in keeping with this outlook, they regarded anyone who spoke out against their gods and their abuses of power as an enemy rather than a well-intentioned advisor.

Thus, they put Hud (A) down and brought up every argument, logical or illogical, they could think of to defeat and humilate him. But in spite of their opposition and enmity, their prophet continued to proclaim his Lord's Message as the inspirations came to his pure, receptive heart.

As for the false gods, religion, rules and way of life that his people and their ancestors had invented and adopted, Hud (A) did not hesitate to proclaim boldly, **"You are nothing but fabricators of lies"** (11:50). Then, to remind them that he was acting solely on behalf of God Most High, who had appointed him to prophethood, and that he desired no worldly benefit for himself, he would add: **"And I do not ask of you any recompense for it. My recompense rests only upon the One who created me, the Lord of the worlds. Will you not then use reason?** (11:51, 26:127).

"And, O my people," he would urge, **"ask forgiveness of your Lord and then repent to Him."** And, as Noah (A) had said before him, he would add: **"He will pour out the sky upon you in plenty** with rain **and will add strength to your strength. Then do not turn away as sinners!"** (11:52).

"O Hud," the leaders would reply scornfully, putting forward one excuse after another, **"you have not brought us any clear evidence, and we are not ones to leave our gods on your word, nor are we believers in you. We merely say that some of our gods may have touched you with evil"** (11:53-54) — that is, with madness or demonic possession.

Appalled at the suggestion that their imaginary deities might have power to affect his mind, or indeed anything else in existence, Hud (A) took a decisive stand. **"Indeed, I call upon God to witness, and you bear witness, that I am free of that to which you ascribe divinity apart from Him"** (11:55-56), he declared. He then threw out a bold challenge to his people:

"Then plot against me, all together, and do not give me respite! I have surely relied upon God, my Lord and your Lord. There is no creature but that He holds its forelock" — meaning no creature that He does not control and direct. **"Indeed, My Lord is on a straight way,"** the way of absolute truth and justice.

"Then," he added, **"if you turn away, I have conveyed to you that with which I was sent to you. And my Lord will grant succession to a people other than you and you will not harm Him in the least. Indeed, my Lord is Guardian over all things"** (11:56-57).

REFERENCES: 7:65-69; 11:50-57; 26:123-127.

4. The Warning

But if they turn away, then say, [O Muhammad:] "I have warned you of a blast like the blast of 'Aad and Thamud." When their messengers came to them before them and after them,[9] [saying,] "Worship no one but God," they said, "If our Lord had willed, He would have sent down angels, so indeed we are disbelievers in that with which you have been sent." (41:13-14)

The 'Aad continued to deny and oppose their prophet, out of envy and arrogance rejecting the guidance that God was sending them through one of themselves. Nevertheless, despite all the unbelievers' opposition, insults and threats, Hud (A) kept on patiently preaching. According to his Lord's inspirations, he tried every approach, every possible way of reaching his people's hearts.

Sometimes he would remind them of God's favors and blessings to them. At other times he would reproach them for the sinfulness of their conduct and warn them of the punishment that was certain to come upon them if they continued to deny their Creator, while giving them the good tidings of His mercy if they repented and turned to Him.

"Do you construct tokens upon every high place, amusing yourselves,[10] and do you make ready fortresses for yourselves, that you may remain eternally, and when you strike, you strike as tyrants?" he would ask. **"Then be mindful God and obey me! And do be mindful of the One who provided you with what you know — provided you with cattle and children, and gardens and springs."** And he would remind them again and again that rejecting God's revelations and guidance was bound to have the most dreadful consequences, saying, **"Indeed, I fear for you the punishment of a terrible day!"** (26:128-135).

"It is all the same to us whether you advise or are not among the advisors," the unbelievers would respond coldly. **"This is nothing but a custom of the former peoples, and we are not to be punished!"** (26:136-138). And, full of pride and glory in their civilization and accomplishments, they challenged God Himself by saying, **"Who is stronger in power than we?"** (41:15).

---

[9]Meaning from every direction and point of view. The messengers reminded their people of what had happened to the corrupt, unbelieving communities of earlier prophets, and also warned them of what was would inevitably befall them if they persisted in their denial of God and their erroneous beliefs, worship and way of life.

[10]This may refer to an ancient Semitic custom of worshipping tribal gods at hilltop altars or shrines.

> **Did they not see that God who created them was stronger in power than they? And they strove against Our signs.** (41:15)

In spite of the enmity of the majority, however, a few thinking, feeling individuals among Hud's people eventually accepted their prophet's Message and joined him. How many and who these were, we have not been told. Unlike the believers in Noah's time, their accepting faith evidently did not create much of a stir, for their existence is mentioned briefly only in three verses: **We saved Hud and those who believed with him by mercy from Ourselves** (11:58, 7:72), and, **We saved those believed and were mindful of God** (41:18).

REFERENCES: 7:72; 11:58; 26:128-138; 41:13-15, 18.

5. Drought

Before them [the Meccan pagans], the people of Noah and 'Aad and Pharaoh, possessor of the stakes, denied, and Thamud and the people of Lot and the dwellers in the thorn bush.[11] Those were the factions. Each [group] denied the messengers, wherefore My punishment was justified. (38:12-14)

After a time, God sent a severe drought upon the 'Aad to arouse them from their indifference to His warnings.

It is said that when God had withheld rain from them for three years, they began to suffer because of it. Their green, fertile land, well-watered with canals, was becoming dead and dry, turning gradually into a wasteland. Perhaps their precious frankincense crop had also begun to fail.

All the while, Hud (A) had continued to preach and warn, hoping that his people might accept guidance. But when he spoke to them, they continued to refute him by all kinds of arguments and excuses. **"Have you come to us that we should worship God alone and leave what our fathers used to worship?"** they would demand. **"Then bring us what you promise us, if you are among the truthful!"** (7:70).

"Disgrace and wrath have already fallen upon you from your Lord," Hud (A) would retort, referring to the drought. **"Do you dispute with me about** mere **names by which you have named them"** — your gods — **"you and your fathers, for which God has not sent down any authority? Then wait! Indeed, I am among those waiting with you"** (7:71).

On another occasion, Hud (A) said to them, **"Do not worship anyone except God. Indeed, I fear for you the punishment of a terrible day"** (46:21).

"Have you come to us to turn us away from our gods?" his people demanded. And they repeated their previous challenge: **"Then bring us what you are promise us, if you are among the truthful!"** (46:22).

To this, Hud (A) replied simply, **"The knowledge of it is only with God, and I** simply **convey to you that with which I was sent"** — that is, to call you to your Lord and to warn you. **"But I see that you are a people behaving ignorantly"** (46:21-24), meaning, "You people are not intelligent or wise enough to understand that the command is for God, who can send punishment upon you if, when and how He wills, nor to read the obvious signs of His anger in the terrible drought which is draining the life out of your previously fertile and productive land."

---

[11]The people of the prophet Shu'ayb.

As the drought continued, the suffering of the 'Aad increased. At length, they decided to send a delegation to Mecca, the site of the House of God, to pray for rain. One of their chiefs, Qayl bin 'Anz, was appointed as the leader of the delegation, which consisted of seventy men.

The journey of these 'Aadites took one month. When the members of the delegation approached Mecca, they stopped at the outskirts of the city at a house belonging to one Mu'awiyah bin Bakr. Mu'awiyah's mother was an 'Aadite woman, and Mu'awiyah himself was related to some members of the delegation. Accordingly, Mu'awiyah offered them his hospitality and treated them with honor.

The 'Aadites stayed in Mu'awiyah's home for a month, pleasantly whiling away the time in drinking wine and listening to the delightful singing of two slave girls known as "the Two Locusts". Eventually two months passed in this manner, during which their people continued to suffer in their drought-stricken land.

The host, Mu'awiyah, well-aware that his people had sent the delegation to pray for rain, was deeply distressed by the situation, imagining that his kinsfolk might have died during this interval. However, since the members of the delegation were his relatives and guests, he could not even hint to them that they should go and carry out the mission on which they had been sent.

Mu'awiyah voiced his concerns to the Two Locusts. They cleverly suggested that he write a poem referring to the matter indirectly. They would then sing it to the members of the delegation, who would have no idea who had written it. Accordingly, Mu'awiyah wrote a number of couplets, speaking in subtle metaphors about the sufferings of the drought-striken 'Aad, while their relatives enjoyed themselves in luxury in Mecca.

When the Two Locusts recited this poem to the gathered delegation, its members looked at one another in shame, recalling the pupose for which their people had sent them on this journey. Then, led by Qayl, they went to Mecca to pray to God for rain for their people.

If we reflect on this, we will see that by it the 'Aad added a final and ultimate wrong to the list of their sins — namely, that, as many people do in times of trouble, they acknowledged God and called upon Him for help when they needed Him. But when all was going well they denied Him, replaced Him with their false gods, and rejected the prophet whom He had sent for their guidance.

REFERENCES: Qur'an: 7:70-71; 46:21-23. Commentaries: Tabari/*H*, II:29-39; Ibn Kathir/*T*, 7:65-72; Ibn Kathir/*Q*, "Hud"; Maududi/*Q*, 7:fns. 52, 54.

6. The Cloud

Then they denied him [Hud], so We destroyed them. In that is surely a sign, but most of them are not believers. And indeed your Lord, He is the Almighty, the Most Merciful. (26:139-140)

God Most High then sent three clouds, one white, one red and one black. And a voice spoke to Qayl from the clouds, telling him to chose one among those clouds for himself and his people. Assuming that the black cloud was the one most full of water, Qayl chose it, thereby unknowingly sealing his people's fate.

By the decree of the All-Knowing Lord, the black cloud that Qayl had chosen traveled to the 'Aad territories, carrying within it the arms of divine retribution.[12] Seeing the approaching cloud, the 'Aadites rejoiced, saying, **"This is a cloud bringing us rain!"**[13] (46:24). Little did they imagine that it contained the doom that they had earlier challenged their prophet to hasten by their taunting words, **"Then bring us what you promise us, if you are among the truthful!"** (7:70, 46:22).

Then, from that cloud, God Most High sent against the 'Aad a violent, deadly wind, described in words that strike a chord of fear in our hearts:

> **And when they perceived it [their doom] as a cloud approaching their valleys, they said, "This is a cloud bringing us rain!" No, rather it is that which you wished to hasten — a wind wherein is a painful punishment, destroying everything by command of its Lord. Then they became such that nothing was seen [of them] except their dwellings. Thus do We recompense the sinful people!** (46:24-25)

---

[12]Possibly this cloud was a dense layer of dust stirred up by the fierce wind. The fact that the people did not recognize it as a dust cloud but expected it to bring them rain suggests that rain was common in the 'Aadite territories and that its people were unused to dust storms.

[13]Concerning this, 'A'ishah, the wife of the Holy Prophet (S), said:

> I did not see the Messenger of God, God's peace and blessings be upon him, laugh so that I saw the back of his throat; he only used to smile. And whenever he perceived cloudiness or windiness, it could be recognized on his face. I said, "O Messenger of God, surely people, when they see clouds, are happy, hoping that there is rain in them, whereas I notice that when you see them, aversion to them can be discerned on your face." Then he said, "O 'A'ishah, what will safeguard me if there is punishment in it? A people were punished by the wind. And people certainly saw the punishment [approaching] but they said, **'This is a cloud bringing us rain.'**" (*Bukhari*, 6:353)

He also said, "It [the wind] is God's mercy. It brings blessing and it brings punishment. So when you notice it, do not revile it, but ask God for the good of it and seek refuge in God from the evil of it (*Abu Dawud*, 5078).

Then We sent upon them a howling wind during days of calamity in order to make them taste the disgraceful punishment in the life of this world. But the punishment of the Hereafter is more disgraceful, and they will not be helped. . . . And We saved those believed and were mindful of God. (41:14-16, 18)

'Aad denied; then how [severe] were My punishment and warnings! Indeed, We sent upon them a howling wind on a day of continuous calamity, tearing out the people as if they were uprooted palm tree trunks. Then how [severe] were My punishment and warnings! (54:18-21)

As for 'Aad, then they were destroyed by a howling, furious wind, which He imposed upon them for seven successive nights and eight days, so you [Muhammad] could see the people therein overthrown, as if they were hollow palm tree trunks. Do you then see any remnant of them? (69:4-8)

Throughout those terrible days and nights, the wind howled and hammered at the 'Aadite communities, snatching the people out of their well-constructed dwellings and smashing everything in its path.[14] Perhaps the only thing we might be able to compare it to would be a violent tornado lashing a wide area with full fury for a week.

The wind produced such complete destruction that it left nothing **that it came upon but that it made it like a thing decayed** (51:42). The 'Aad had been so completely destroyed **that nothing was seen** of them **except their dwellings** (46:25), those fine homes and magnificent columned palaces and temples that had been their pride and delight. But those strong, well-constructed buildings had not been able to shelter them when God's punishment came upon them — not at all; nor, of course, had their false, made-up 'gods'. For the 'Aadites had acted like blind, deaf people, denying the Giver of these manifold favors and using them to oppress others, striving against their Lord's signs and revelations, rejecting His prophet, and refusing to accept guidance, according to God's words:

[We destroyed] 'Aad and Thamud, and it [their fate] has been made clear to you from [the ruins of] their dwellings. And Satan had made their deeds attractive to them and kept them back from the path, although they were granted perception. (29:38)

And We had certainly established them in that which We have not established you [the Meccan idolaters], and We had granted

---

[14]Ibn Kathir states that the wind was so strong that it lifted people up into the air and then smashed them onto the ground with such force that their heads were severed from their bodies, leaving them **overthrown, as if they were hollow palm tree trunks** (Ibn Kathir/*T*, 7:65-72).

> **them hearing and vision and hearts. But neither their hearing nor their vision nor their hearts availed them in the least when they strove against God's revelations, and they were engulfed by that at which they used to mock. (46:26)**

But what of the prophet Hud (A) and the believers? It is said that they went into an enclosed space, where nothing of the wind reached them except what was gentle to their bodies and pleasing to their souls. And God says:

> **Then We saved him and those with him by mercy from Ourselves, and We cut off the last remnant of those who denied Our signs, and they were not believers. (7:70-72)**
>
> **Then, when Our command came, We saved Hud and those who believed with him by mercy from Ourselves — and We saved them from a harsh punishment! And that was 'Aad. They strove against their Lord's signs and disobeyed His messengers and followed the command of every powerful oppressor. And they were pursued by a curse in this world and on the Day of Resurrection. Indeed, 'Aad disbelieved in their Lord. Then away with 'Aad, the people of Hud! (11:58-60)**

May God's best peace and blessings be upon Hud, the prophet of the 'Aad!

REFERENCES: Qur'an: 7:72; 11:58-60; 26:139-140; 29:38; 38:12-14; 41:13-16, 18; 46:24-26; 51:41-42; 54:18-21; 69:4, 6-8. Commentaries: Tabari/*H*, II:35-36, 39-40; Ibn Kathir/*T*, 7:65-72.

7. The Second 'Aad

He destroyed the first 'Aad. (53:50)

Arab historians considered the 'Aad to be among the extinct tribes, for none of its people survived except the prophet Hud (A), the believers who were with him, and the 'Aadites living in Mecca. The territory which they once inhabited has been an empty desert for thousands of years, abounding in the ruins of bygone peoples, buried beneath the wind-blown, shifting desert sands

It is said that Hud (A) lived for 150 years. Ancient historical records suggest that after their people's destruction, his followers formed a community of righteous believers. Syed Muzaffar-ud-din Nadvi and Maulana Maududi report that an explorer, searching the area where the 'Aad had lived, found an inscription in their language, written some 1800 years before Christ.[15] The translation of a section of it reads:

> We lived for a long period in this fort in great prosperity. Our canals were always full of water. . . and our rulers were noble kings who were free from evil. They were, however, hard on those who disturbed the peace. They ruled over us according to the Law of Hud and used to enter all important decisions in a book. We believe in miracles and life after death. (Maududi/*Q*, 7:fn. 56; also Nadvi/*History*, p. 105)

It is reported that up to this day, the grave of the prophet Hud (A) can be found in a place called Mukalla in southern Arabia, the site of ancient ruins and inscriptions.[16] Mukalla is in the region which has been known for centuries as Hadramaut, a name which, it is said, refers to the terrible end which came to those who once dwelt there. For a European exploring Hadramaut in the 1890s reported the people of the area as saying that Hadramaut got its name from the last words Hud (A) uttered concerning his people, namely, "*Hadara-l-maut*," meaning "Death has come." This local tradition still connects this region with the prophet Hud (A) and, by association, with his people, the 'Aad.

REFERENCES: Tabari/*H*, II:35; Ibn Kathir/*T*, 7:65-72; Maududi/*Q*, 7:fns. 51, 56, 46:fn. 25; Ali/*Q*, fn. 1040; Nadvi/*History*, pp. 76-77, 98-99, 106-108.

---

[15]It is reported that some of the believing 'Aad continued to live until the beginning of the Christian Era. In their accounts of the inhabitants of Yemen and Hadramaut, the Greeks referred to them as "Oditai" ("'Aad") or "Adramitai" ("'Aadi 'Imran").

[16]However, the people of Hadramaut say that Hud lived in Hadramaut after the destruction of the 'Aad until he died and that he was buried two stages from the city of Tahrim near the valley of Barhut. 'Ali ibn Abi Talib is reported to have said that his grave is upon a red mound. At the same time, the Palestinian people say that Hud is buried in Palestine and each year they visit his grave. However, the Hadramauti's claim seems to be more reasonable because Hadramaut, or al-Ahqaf in southern Arabia, was the territory of the 'Aad (An-Najjar/*Q*, "Hud").

Qur'anic References — Hud and His People

7:65-72

And to 'Aad, [God sent] their brother Hud. He said, "O my people, worship God; you have no deity but Him, so will you not be mindful of Him?" (65)

The chiefs of those who disbelieved among his people said, "Indeed, we see you as weak-minded, and indeed, we consider you among the liars." (66)

He said, "O my people, there is no weak-mindedness in me, but I am a messenger from the Lord of the worlds. (67) I convey to you the messages of my Lord and I am a trustworthy advisor to you. (68) Do you then wonder that there has come to you a reminder from your Lord through a man from among yourselves, that he may warn you? And recall when He made you successors after Noah's people and increased you greatly in stature. Therefore, remember God's favors, that you may prosper." (69)

They said, "Have you come to us that we should worship God alone and leave what our fathers used to worship? Then bring us what you promise us, if you are among the truthful!" (70)

He said, "Disgrace and wrath have already fallen upon you from your Lord. Do you dispute with me about [mere] names by which you have named them, you and your fathers, for which God has not sent down any authority? Then wait! Indeed, I am among those waiting with you." (71)

Then We saved him and those with him by mercy from Ourselves, and We cut off the last remnant of those who denied Our signs, and they were not believers. (72)

9:70

Has there not reached them the news of those before them — the people of Noah and 'Aad and Thamud, and the people of Abraham and the dwellers in Midian and the Overturned Cities? Their messengers came to them with clear proofs. And never would God have wronged them, but [rather] they wronged themselves.

10:74

Then, after him [Noah] We sent messengers to their peoples and they brought them clear proofs, but they would not believe in what they had previously treated as false. Thus do We seal the hearts of the transgressors!

11:50-60

And to 'Aad, [God sent] their brother Hud. He said, "O my people, worship God; you have no deity but Him. You are nothing but fabricators [of falsehood]. (50) O my people, I do not ask of you any recompense for it. My recompense rests only upon the One who created me. Will you not then use reason? (51) And, O my people, ask forgiveness of your Lord and then repent to Him. He will pour out upon you the sky in plenty and add strength to your strength. Then do not turn away as sinners!" (52)

They said, "O Hud, you have not brought us any clear evidence, and we are not ones to leave our gods on your word, nor are we believers in you. (53) We merely say that some of our gods may have touched you with evil." (54)

He said, "Indeed, I call upon God to witness, and you bear witness, that I am free of that to which you ascribe divinity apart from Him (55). Then plot against me, all together, and do not give me respite. I have surely relied upon God, my Lord and your Lord. There is no creature but that He holds its forelock. Indeed, my Lord is on a straight way. (56) Then, if you turn away, I have conveyed to you that with which I was sent to you. And my Lord will grant succession to a people other than you and you will not harm Him in the least. Indeed, my Lord is Guardian over all things." (57)

Then, when Our command came, We saved Hud and those who believed with him by mercy from Ourselves — and We saved them from a harsh punishment! (58) And that was 'Aad. They strove against their Lord's signs and disobeyed His messengers, and followed the command of every powerful oppressor. (59) And they were pursued by a curse in this world and on the Day of Resurrection. Indeed, 'Aad disbelieved in their Lord. Then away with 'Aad, the people of Hud! (60)

11:89-90

[Shu'ayb said,] "And, O my people, do not let dissension with me cause you to sin, lest there befall you something like what befell the people of Noah or the people of Hud or the people of Saleh, nor are the people of Lot far removed from you. (89) And seek forgiveness from your Lord and then repent to Him. Indeed, my Lord is Merciful and Loving!" (90)

14:9-14

These verses are cited in "Qur'anic References — Noah."

22:42

And if they deny you [Muhammad], thus did the people of Noah and 'Aad and Thamud deny [their prophets] before them.

25:38

And [We destroyed] 'Aad and Thamud and the dwellers in al-Rass, and many generations between them.

26:123-139

'Aad denied the messengers, (123) when their brother Hud said to them, "Will you not be mindful of God? (124) I am surely a trustworthy messenger to you, (125) so be mindful of God and obey me. (126) And I do not ask of you any recompense. My recompense rests only upon the Lord of the worlds. (127)

"Do you construct tokens upon every high place, amusing yourselves, (128) and do you make ready fortresses for yourselves, that you may remain eternally, (129) and when you strike, you strike as tyrants? (130) Then be mindful God and obey me! (131) And do be mindful of the One who provided you with what you know (132) — provided you with cattle and children, (133) and gardens and springs. (134) Indeed, I fear for you the punishment of a terrible day!" (135)

They said, "It is all the same to us whether you advise or are not among the advisors. (136) This is nothing but a custom of the former peoples, (137) and we are not to be punished!" (138)

Then they denied him, so We destroyed them. In that is surely a sign, but most of them are not believers. (139) And indeed your Lord, He is the Almighty, the Most Merciful. (140)

29:38

And [We destroyed] 'Aad and Thamud, and it has been made clear to you from [the ruins of] their dwellings. And Satan had made their deeds attractive to them and kept them back from the path, although they were granted perception.

38:12-14

Before them, the people of Noah and 'Aad and Pharaoh, possessor of the stakes, (12) denied, and Thamud and the people of Lot and the dwellers in the thorn bush. Those were the factions. (13) Each [group] denied the messengers, wherefore My punishment was justified. (14)

40:5

Before them, the people of Noah and the factions after them denied, and each nation intended [a plot] for its messenger, to seize him and to argue with falsehood in order to refute the truth thereby. Then I seized them, and how [terrible] was My punishment!

40:30-31

[The Secret Believer among Pharaoh's people said,] "O my people, indeed, I fear for you the like of the Day of the Confederates — (30) like the case of Noah's people and 'Aad and Thamud and those after them. And God desires no injustice for servants." (31)

41:13-16, 18

But if they turn away, then say, [O Muhammad:] "I have warned you of a blast like the blast of 'Aad and Thamud." (13) When their messengers came to them before them and after them, [saying,] "Worship no one but God," they said, "If our Lord had willed, He would have sent down angels, so indeed we are disbelievers in that with which you have been sent." (14)

As for 'Aad, they were arrogant in the land without right and they said, "Who is stronger in power than we?" Did they not see that God who created them was stronger in power than they? And they strove against Our signs. (15) Then We sent upon them a howling wind during days of calamity in order to make them taste the disgraceful punishment in the life of this world. But the punishment of the Hereafter is more disgraceful, and they will not be helped. (16) . . . And We saved those believed and were mindful of God. (18)

46:21-26

And mention [O Muhammad,] the brother of 'Aad, when he warned his people in al-Ahqaf — and warners had passed on before and after him — [saying,] "Do not worship anyone but God. Indeed, I fear for you the punishment of a terrible day!" (21)

They said, "Have you come to us to turn us away from our gods? Then bring us what you are promising us, if you are among the truthful!" (22)

He said, "The knowledge [of it] is only with God and I [simply] convey to you that with which I was sent; but I see that you are a people behaving ignorantly." (23)

And when they perceived it as a cloud approaching their valleys, they said, "This is a cloud bringing us rain!" No, rather it is that which you wished to hasten — a wind wherein is a painful punishment, (24) destroying everything by command of its Lord. Then they became such that nothing was seen [of them] except their dwellings. Thus do We recompense the sinful people! (25) And We had certainly established them in that which We have not established you, and We had granted them hearing and vision and hearts. But neither their hearing nor their vision nor their hearts availed them in the least when they strove against God's revelations, and they were engulfed by that at which they used to mock. (26)

50:12-14

Before them, the people of Noah and the dwellers in al-Rass and Thamud denied, (12) and 'Aad and Pharaoh and the brethren of Lot, (13) and the dwellers in the thorn bush and the people of Tubba'. All denied the messengers, wherefore My threat was justly carried out. (14)

51:41-42

And in 'Aad [is a sign], when We sent against them the barren wind. (41) It left nothing that it came upon but that it made it like a thing decayed. (42)

53:50

. . . And that He destroyed the first 'Aad.

54:18-21

'Aad denied; then how [severe] were My punishment and warnings! (18) Indeed, We sent upon them a howling wind on a day of continuous calamity, (19) tearing out the people as if they were uprooted palm tree trunks. (20) Then how [severe] were My punishment and warnings! (21)

69:4-8

Thamud and 'Aad denied the striking calamity. (4) . . . And as for 'Aad, then they were destroyed by a howling, furious wind, (6) which He imposed upon them for seven successive nights and eight days, so you [Muhammad] could see the people therein overthrown, as if they were hollow palm tree trunks. (7) Do you then see any remnant of them? (8)

89:6-14

Have you [Muhammad] not considered how your Lord dealt with 'Aad, (6) Iram of the lofty columns, (7) the like of which had never been created in the lands, (8) and [with] Thamud, who hewed out the rocks in the valley; (9) and [with] Pharaoh, possessor of the stakes (10) — those who committed oppression in the lands (11) and increased the corruption therein? (12) Then your Lord poured upon them a scourge of punishment. (13) Indeed, your Lord is in observation! (14)

The Story of Saleh

peace be upon him

Before them, the people of Noah and 'Aad and Pharaoh, possessor of the stakes, denied, and Thamud and the people of Lot and the dwellers in the thorn bush. Those were the factions; each denied the messengers, wherefore My punishment was justified! (38:12-14)

1. The Thamud

The dwellers in al-Hijr certainly denied the messengers, and We granted them Our signs but they turned away from them; and they used to hew dwellings out of the mountains, secure. (15:80-82)

Time passed over the generations of the children of Adam upon the earth. And on the opposite side of the Arabian peninsula from the home of the 'Aad, probably during the period 1800 and 1600 B.C., there lived a tribe called the Thamud.

After the 'Aad, the Thamud were the best-known of the ancient Arabian tribes, a powerful people with a well-developed civilization. The Thamud are mentioned in the stories, poetry and speeches of the Arabs prior to Islam and on tablets found in Assyria. The ancient geographers and historians of Greece, Alexandria and Rome also mentioned them. Indeed, al-Tabari says that among the Arabs both before and during the time of Islam, the repute of Hud and Saleh and their people was like that of Abraham and his people (Tabari/*H*, II:46).

The territory of the Thamud was in northwestern Arabia and what is now southern Jordan — a region of high rock cliffs in which they made their dwellings, skillfully hollowing out the rock to create rooms and tombs, and decorating the outside with columns and statues. This area is known as al-Hijr, meaning "the Rock". The fifteenth *surah* of the Qur'an, *"al-Hijr,"* which contains the verses cited above, is named for it. Consequently, the people of the prophet Saleh (A) who inhabited this area are known as ***as-hab al-Hijr*, the People of the Rocky Tract** (15:80) — that is, **Thamud, who hewed out the rocks in the valley** (89:9).

Up to this day, the dwellings that the Thamud carved out of rocky cliffs are to be found scattered over thousands of acres in a bleak, deserted region that shows signs of a devastating earthquake in the remote past. But at the time of the Thamud, it was full of **gardens and springs, and fields of crops and date palms with mellow fruit** (26:147-148). And, as water is very important for any people who practice agriculture, God made water a test for the Thamud, as we shall soon see.

It is estimated that during the time of the prophet Saleh (A), the population of the Hijr area may have been about 500,000. Its capital city, al-Hijr or Mada'in Saleh, was an important station on the ancient gold and frankincense route between Yemen, Egypt and Syria. Mada'in Saleh is in northwestern Saudi Arabia, about 180 miles northwest of Medina, 170 miles northeast of Tabuk, on the

Hijaz railway line. To the west and northwest of the site of the city lie three vast lava flows, known as ***harrats,*** stretching as far as Tabuk.[1]

The strong-bodied Thamud possessed a very high standard of living. But like the 'Aad before them, they were idol-worshippers, devoted to six false gods. Interestingly, these included three deities, al-Lat, Manat and Hubal, that were still worshipped many centuries later by the Arabs in the time of Prophet Muhammad (S), as mentioned in 53:19-20. This false religion in turn gave rise to false values and a society in which the weak were scorned and oppressed, and power was held securely in the hands of a few. And among these few, the very worst of men were the most powerful and respected.

REFERENCES: Qur'an: 15:80-82; 26:147-148; 89:9. Commentaries: Maududi/*Q*, 7:fn. 57, 15:fn. 45, 26:fns. 95, 99, 29:fn. 65; Asad/*Q*, 7:fn. 56; Ali/*Q*, App. IX; Nadvi/*History*, pp. 109-110.

---

[1]The rocky cliffs and ***harrat*** of this area are described by the historian, C. M. Doughty, in his book *Arabia Deserta*, published in 1888, as "mighty sand-rock precipices (which here resemble ranges of city walls, fantastic towers, and castle buildings), and upon them lie high shouldering sand drifts. The bottom is sand, with much growth of desert bushes; and I perceived some thin sprinkled volcanic drift. Westward is seen the immense mountain blackness, terrible and lowering, of the Harrat" (Ali/*Q*, Appendix to *Surah* 26).

2. Saleh (A)

But if they turn away, then say, [O Muhammad:] "I have warned you of a blast like the blast of 'Aad and Thamud." When their messengers came to them before them and after them, [saying,] "Worship no one but God," they said, "If our Lord had willed, He would have sent down angels, so indeed we are disbelievers in that with which you have been sent." (41:13-14)

In the due course of time, God Most High bestowed prophethood upon a man of the Thamud — **their brother Saleh** (7:73, 26:141, 27:45). Saleh (A) is mentioned in the Qur'an by name nine times, while his people, the Thamud, are mentioned twenty-five times. It is reported that, like Hud (A) before him, Saleh (A) was a descendant of Noah (A) through his son Shem or Sam, but in the tenth generation.

Nothing is known of Saleh's life before prophethood was granted to him. However, like Noah and Hud (A) before him, Saleh (A) began his mission by calling his people to faith.

"O my people, worship God," he said. **"You have no deity but Him** (7:73, 11:61). **He produced you from the earth and caused you to dwell in it, so ask His forgiveness and then repent to Him. My Lord is surely near and responsive"** (11:61).

As was to be expected, these words, which challenged the Thamud's false belief system, were received with the same sort of hostility as was shown by the peoples of the earlier prophets. But not to be deterred from carrying out the mission with he had been entrusted, Saleh (A) continued to address his people, using the arguments and evidences granted to him by his Lord.

"O my people," he would say, in the very same words spoken by the prophets who had preceded him, **"will you not be mindful of God? Indeed, I am a trustworthy messenger to you, so be mindful of God and obey me"** (26:142-146). And to assure them that he had no interest in acquiring any material benefit for himself, he would add: **"And I do not ask of you recompense for it. My recompense rests only upon the Lord of the worlds"** (26:142-146).

Like the chiefs of the earlier communities of unbelievers, the leaders of the Thamud began to undermine Saleh (A) and his Message by discrediting him and fabricating arguments against him. **"O Saleh,"** they would taunt, **"you were a man of promise among us before this"** — that is, of outstanding intelligence and character. **"Do you forbid us to worship what our fathers worshipped? And indeed, we are in uneasy doubt about that to which you call us"** (11:62).

"O my people, have you considered?" Saleh (S) would reply earnestly. **"If I am taking my stand upon clear evidence from my Lord, while He has granted mercy from Himself, who would help me against God if I disobeyed Him. Therefore, you would not increase me but in loss"** (11:63). That is, since God has granted me both clear evidence and special favors from Himself, no one would be able to save me from Him if I obeyed your wishes instead of His. Rather, I would lose everything.

Then, fearing the punishment that would befall his people if they failed to heed his advice, Saleh (A) began to warn them that they were courting disaster by rejecting their Lord's guidance.

"Will you be left in what is here, secure — in gardens and springs, and fields of crops and date-palms with mellow fruit, and you skillfully hew dwellings out of the mountains?"[2] (26:146-149), he would ask. By this, he called his people's attention to the fact that well-being and prosperity were not something to take forgranted, nor the fact that their Lord had provided them with both the rocky cliffs in which they lived and the skill to shape them into dwelling places. Did they have no fear of the One who created them, and could they not understand that these favors might be snatched away from them at any moment as a recompense for their sins and disobedience? **"Then be mindful of God and obey me,"** Saleh (A) would add, **"and do not obey the command of the transgressors — those who make corruption in the land and never reform!"** (26:150-152).

But the leaders of the unbelievers had ready answers for anything Saleh (A) might say, and they entertained themselves by putting him down by mockery and taunts.

"Are we to follow a single man from among ourselves?" they would demand. **"If so, we would indeed be in error and madness! Has the Message been sent down upon him alone amongst us? No, rather he is an insolent liar!"** (54:25).

God the All-Knowing then revealed to His faithful prophet a hint of what was to come, saying, **"Tomorrow they will know who is the insolent liar!**

---

[2]Commenting on this verse, Muhammad Asad writes:

> A reference ot the elaborate rock-dwellings or tombs — to be seen to this day — which the Thamud carved out of the cliffs west of Al-Hijr, in northern Hijaz, and embellished with sculptures of animals as well as many inscriptions attesting to the comparatively high degree of their civilization and power. In popular Arabian parlance, these rock-dwellings are nowadays called *Mada'in Salih* ("the Towns of Salih"). (Asad/Q, 7:fn. 59)

Indeed, We are sending the She-Camel as a trial for them, so watch them and be patient" (54:26-27).

REFERENCES: 7:73; 11:61-63; 26:141-152; 27:45; 41:13-14; 54:25-27.

3. The She-Camel

We granted Thamud the She-Camel, a visible sign, but they wronged her. (17:59)

As we noted in the story of Hud (A), the life-stories of the Arabian prophets and their people were passed down by word of mouth from generation to generation. They were transmitted from elders to children, from story-tellers and poets to their audiences, and by the tongues of the prophets who succeeded them to their communities.

These stories were still current and alive among the Arabs of the Arabian peninsula at the time of Prophet Muhammad (S). Consequently, their details, as narrated by the Holy Prophet (S) and his Companions, have reached our time via the early Islamic commentators and historians, with well-preserved names, genealogies and other information.

No indication exists of how many months or years Saleh (A) spent preaching to his people. But whether it was a long or a short time, suddenly an unprecedented event occurred, the report of which we take from the eminent classical commentator, Ibn Kathir.

According to his narrative, one day while the unbelievers were gathered in a meeting place of theirs, Saleh (A) came in among them. At that, they began to fling their stock-in-trade of accusations and taunts at him.

"You are merely one of those under a magic spell," they mocked. **"You are nothing but a mortal like ourselves, so bring a sign, if you are among the truthful!"** (26:153-154).

The notion of a sign appealed to all of them. For a while, they talked among themselves about what this sign should be. Then they put forward their demand: Saleh should call upon his Lord to produce before them a she-camel with unique characteristics. According to their description, she should be tall and pregnant. Only if Saleh could bring them such a sign would they believe in him.

Now, the prophets were the most compassionate of mankind. Fearing God's just punishment, they grieved over their peoples' sins and wrong-doings, and longed to have them turn to their Creator and be saved. So, impertinent and brazen as the unbelievers' demand was, Saleh (A) earnestly hoped that its fulfillment might be the means of their salvation. And he prayed for it to his Lord.

All at once a pregnant camel matching his people's description emerged out of a rock on a hill. Saleh (A) called her ***"Naqat-Allah,"*** God's She-Camel (7:73,

11:64, 91:13), adding *"Allah"* to the word *"naqah"* (She-Camel) to give her respect and honor.

What was this she-camel? We have no absolutely definitive answer to this question, but it is obvious that she was no ordinary camel.

The Holy Prophet's words, "There was no prophet among the prophets but that he was given such signs that people believed in him" (*Bukhari*, 6:504), make it clear that each prophet was granted certain miracles by his Lord. The fact that God Himself speaks of the She-Camel as **a sign for you** (7:73, 11:64), **a visible sign** (17:59), and **a clear evidence from your Lord** (7:73), suggests that she was His miracle to Saleh (A). So does the fact that the She-Camel appeared suddenly as a result of Saleh's prayer, according to specifications of the unbelievers. Clearly, if the She-Camel had been some ordinary camel that happened to come strolling into town, she would not have been the conclusive sign and evidence mentioned in the Qur'an. Indeed, she was such a decisive sign and proof that, as a result of her appearance, a number of people accepted faith.

The special nature of the She-Camel is also clear, as we shall soon see, from the fact that the lives of an entire tribe were connected with her life. Moreover, according to the Qur'anic commentators, the She-Camel produced such an enormous quantity of milk as could not have come from an ordinary animal. And a final evidence of her miraculousness is the fact that the ringleaders of the unbelievers hatched complicated plots for getting rid of her, which would hardly have been necessary if she had been an ordinary camel.

The Thamud had had the affrontery to demand that the Lord God send them a sign as a proof of Saleh's truthfulness, and the sign had been sent. Moreover, this "sign," for all its miraculousness, was a living, feeling creature. How they would react to and treat God's living sign would soon determine their fate.

Saleh (A) then addressed his people on behalf of God Most High. **"There has surely come to you a clear evidence from your Lord"** (7:73), he declared. **"O my people, this is God's She-Camel, a sign for you. So let her feed upon God's earth"** (7:73, 11:64).

This order did not pose a problem, since the camel's grazing would not lessen his people's own food supply. But her drinking was a different matter, for, due to the She-Camel's large size, she would consume a great quantity of water from their wells. However, the divine order now came to Saleh (A) concerning her unequivocal right to drink: **"Inform them that the water is to be shared between them"** — that is, the herds they owned and the ownerless She-Camel — **"each drinking attended by turn"** (54:28).

Saleh (A) conveyed his Lord's instructions to his people. **"This is God's She-Camel,"** he said, **"so let her drink** (91:13). **She has her share of water and you have your share of water, each on a fixed day"** (26:155). And to safeguard the camel from the malice and enmity which the unbelievers would certainly feel toward a creature that would consume a large share of the water which they had up to now regarded as solely their own, he added, **"And do not touch her with harm, lest you be seized by the punishment of a terrible day."**[3]

These words suggest that Saleh (A) anticipated trouble from the ringleaders of the unbelievers. Nevertheless, hoping that they might take heed, he reminded them of God's abundant favors and blessings, saying, **"And recall when He made you successors after the 'Aad and settled you in the land. You make castles upon its plains and hew the mountains into dwellings. Then remember God's favors and do not act wickedly in the land, causing corruption!"** (7:74).

For a time, the She-Camel enjoyed complete freedom of movement among the people, grazing freely at will. And as they had been ordered, they also allowed her access to their water supply.

She would drink one day, using one particular well among several, and the people and their animals would drink on other days from the other wells. On the camel's day, no one else used the water. And while her drinking had reduced the people's use of the water, she gave a huge amount of milk. Thus it was, in effect, her milk in exchange for the water, for Ibn Kathir cites a ***hadith*** stating, "They used to drink their water one day and her milk the alternate day" (Ibn Kathir/Q, "Saleh"). And presently she gave birth to a male calf, who trailed along at her side on long, unsteady legs.

Doubtless, during this period Saleh (A) continued to preach and warn. But the majority of the unbelievers remained unmoved. In spite of the age-old traditions concerning God and His prophets, Noah and Hud, regardless of any messenger or sign He might send them, they had no intention of ever abandoning their many fabricated gods or submitting to Saleh's instructions. And, like all the unbelievers both before and after their time, they made all kinds of excuses for their refusal to accept guidance. God's sign, the She-Camel, had made no difference to them at all!

---

[3]This command occurs in three different passages: **"This is God's She-Camel, a sign for you, so let her feed upon God's earth and do not do her any harm, lest a painful punishment seize you"** (7:73); **"And, O my people, this is God's She-Camel, a sign for you, so let her feed upon God's earth and do not do her any harm, lest a punishment near [at hand] seize you"** (11:64); and, **"This is a she-camel. She has her share of water and you have your share of water, [each] on a fixed day, and do not do her any harm, lest you be seized by the punishment of a terrible day!"** (26:155-156).

But to others among the Thamud, it had, for after witnessing the miracle of the She-Camel, a number of people accepted faith, as is indicated by the words,

> **We certainly sent to Thamud their brother Saleh, [saying,] "Worship God," whereupon they became two disputing groups.** (27:45)

One group followed the righteous, inspired prophet, while the other followed the lead of the worst people in their society.

Some of the believers were from the weak, oppressed classes. And now, in an attempt to sow doubt and confusion among them, **the chiefs of those who were arrogant among his people said to those who were oppressed** — that is, **to those who believed among them — "Do you really know that Saleh is sent by his Lord?"** (7:75).

"Indeed, we are believers in that with which he has been sent" (7:75), Saleh's followers replied firmly.

"Indeed, we are disbelievers in that which you believe" (7:76), the arrogant ones retorted contemptuously. Thus, the war of words went on, underscoring the eternal conflict between truth and falsehood, good and evil.

Still Saleh (A) continued to try to reach the unbelievers' hearts. **"O my people,"** he would say, **"why do you seek to hasten the evil in advance of the good?"** — that is, why do you challenge God to send down a punishment upon you? **"Why do you not** rather **seek forgiveness from God, that you may be shown mercy?"** (27:46).

"We attribute an evil omen to you and to those with you" (27:47), the unbelievers would counter, invoking their pagan superstitions as a fresh excuse for not accepting faith.

"Your 'evil omen' is with God," Saleh (A) would reply firmly. **"Rather, you are a people being tested"** (27:47). But, as before, his people's only response was rejection.

REFERENCES: Qur'an: 7:73-74; 11:64; 17:59; 26:153-154; 27:45-47; 91:13. Commentaries: Tabari/*H*, II:41-42; Ibn Kathir/*Q*, "Saleh"; Maududi/*Q*, 7:fn. 58, 26:fns. 103-104; 27:fn. 60, 54:fn. 19; Asad/*Q*, 7:fn. 95.

4. MURDER!

Then they hamstrung the She-Camel and were insolent toward the command of their Lord. (7:77)

Burning with anger at having to follow the despised Saleh's orders which restricted their access to their wells to alternate days, the leaders of the Thamud now met to resolve the issue of the She-Camel once and for all.

If they killed the camel, they decided, they would again have all their water for themselves. At the same time, everyone would see that Saleh's warnings and threats had come to nothing. As a result, he would lose all his followers and there would then be no one to dispute their power.

In their evil plotting against an innocent creature, the chiefs chose to ignore the fact that the She-Camel had been sent to them by God in response to their own demand for a sign. They also disregarded the fact that the water, their Lord's free grant, did not belong to them or to anyone else. Finally, they overlooked the fact that, from the water which the camel drank, she gave them plentiful milk — and, milk being more valuable than water, she gave more than she took of 'their' resources. Disregarding their prophet's warning not to harm God's sign, out of malice and hatred toward the She-Camel and the detested Saleh, the chiefs of the unbelievers decided to strike.

Now, **there were in the city nine heads of families, causing corruption in the land and not amending** (27:48) themselves or the affairs of their community. In Ibn Kathir's commentary on this verse, the nine are mentioned by name — the ringleaders and bad, tough bully-boys of the Thamud. But one among them, a ruddy man whose name was Qidar bin Salif, stands out as more vicious than the rest, according to God's words:

> **Thamud denied [their prophet] in their excessiveness, when the greatest wretch among them was sent forth. And the messenger of God said to them, "[This is] God's She-Camel, so let her drink!" But they denied him and hamstrung her, whereupon their Lord brought down upon them destruction for their sin and made it equal [upon them all]. And He does not fear the consequences thereof.**[4] (91:11-15)

---

[4]This is interpreted by Ibn 'Abbas and other classic commentators as meaning that God Almighty fears no one with regard to His destruction of Thamud. That is, He answers to none but all will answer to Him, for **He is not questioned about what He does, but they will be questioned** (21:23).

Perhaps it may be difficult for us to imagine people so hardened and vicious as to conspire to cruelly kill a creature that had done them no harm — that had, on the contrary, supplied them with their fill of milk. It may be even more difficult to imagine people who were so bold and fearless before the Lord of the heavens and the earth that they would dare to attack the sign He had sent them at their own demand. Nevertheless, this is precisely what happened.

The gang of nine went out as a body and stalked the She-Camel. Although they were hesitant, nonetheless they urged each other on. **Then they called their comrade,** Qidar bin Salif, who caught up with the innocent animal, **and he took and hamstrung her**[5] (54:29).

It is said that he drew his sword and slashed the tendons of one of her legs, and then killed her. As the camel fell to the ground, mortally wounded, a terrible cry came from her throat — a cry of anguish and also of warning to her young calf. Seeing his mother's dreadful fate, the calf ran toward a nearby mountain, uttering three loud cries, and disappeared inside the rock. The cruel murderer then finished his job by slitting his mother's throat. And so the She-Camel, God's sign to the Thamud, died a terrible, painful death — and that by the hand of one who had most likely been nourished on her abundant milk.

The fact that this was a crime of unimaginable viciousness is reflected in a comment of the Holy Prophet (S) concerning the killer. It is reported that once the Prophet (S) asked 'Ali ibn Abi Talib (R) — one of the noblest among Muslims, who later, during his rule as the fourth caliph of Islam, died at the hands of an assassin — "Shall I not tell you about the most wicked of people? When 'Ali replied, "Yes," the Prophet (S) said, "The ruddy Thamudite, who hamstrung the She-Camel, and the one who will strike you, O 'Ali, here," and he pointed to his head, "until it reaches here," indicating his beard (Ibn Kathir/ Q, "Saleh").

The Prophet (S) also mentioned the one who hamstrung the She-Camel as being a man of honor and invincibility among his people (*Bukhari*, 4:560). On another occasion, he spoke of the She-Camel and the one who hamstrung her in a sermon, reciting the words, **"When the greatest wretch among them was sent forth"** (91:12). He then said, "A powerful, vicious man, invincible among his tribe, like [a man named] Abi Zam'a, set out against her"' (*Bukhari*, 6:466).

All this makes it clear that the one who did the deed was the very worst among bad ones. But, as the above *ahadith* make clear, **the greatest wretch**

---

5 **"He took"** is understood as meaning either that the killer took a sword in his hand or that he took hold of the camel. Hamstringing refers to the act of cutting the tendons of an animal prior to slaughtering it. This barbarous custom was so common in pre-Islamic Arabia that the verb *'aqr*, to hamstring, gradually became synonymous with slaughtering in a cruel manner.

among them was also one who enjoyed power, rank and protection among his people.

REFERENCES: Qur'an: 7:77; 27:48; 54:29; 91:11-15. Commentaries: Tabari/*H*, II:4; Ibn Kathir/*T*, 54:29, 91:12; Ibn Kathir/*Juz' 'Amma*, pp. 161-162; Ibn Kathir/*Q*, "Saleh"; Maududi/*Q*, 27:fn. 62; Asad/*Q*, 7:fn. 61.

5. The Plot

And they devised a plot and We devised a plot, and they did not perceive. Then see what was the end of their plot: that We destroyed them and their people, all together! (27:50-51)

After insolently rebelling against the command of their Lord and brutally murdering the She-Camel, the unbelievers came back to confront their prophet. **"O Saleh,"** they taunted, **"bring us what you promise us, if you are among the messengers!"** (7:77).

Now, this atrocious deed and the plotting that preceded it had been done with the encouragement and active participation of the entire Thamudite population. According to Ibn Kathir, all of them, young and old, male and female, had taken a vow of allegiance to the killer, and as he had killed the She-Camel with the support and agreement of all his people, they all shared in the collective guilt.

No longer could Saleh's great, wide prophet's heart hold any compassion for his people, nor could he hope for God's mercy upon them: they were as good as dead. Out of envy, spite and malice, they had deliberately, calculatedly defied God's command and committed an act of unimaginable viciousness. And as directed by divine inspiration, Saleh (A) said to them, **"Enjoy yourselves in your homes for three days,"** underscoring the inevitability of what was to befall them by adding: **"That is a promise not to be belied!"** (11:65).

But, unconcerned about divine retribution, the nine ringleaders deliberated among themselves as to their next move. And they reached a decision: that they would make Saleh follow his She-Camel in death. They had had more than enough of him!

"Swear by God that we will attack him and his family by night," they said to one another, planning a sneak attack on his home, where they would murder him, together with his wife and children. **"Then,"** they agreed, **"we will say to his executor"** — that is, the one responsible for executing his will and avenging his blood — **"'We did not witness the destruction of his family, and indeed, we are truthful!'"** (27:49).

But as they slipped silently through the night, headed for Saleh's house, the divine retribution overtook them. It is reported that a huge boulder, carried by angels, fell upon them from the sky, smashing their skulls, and they all died together, their punishment preceding that of their people.

We can imagine the frightful mood of the remainder of Saleh's people after this catastrophe. Overwhelmed by guilt over the vicious murder of the She-Camel, they were now stunned by the sudden, terrible fate of the nine conspirators. Even worse, they were in a state of absolute terror concerning the nameless calamity which they now knew would descend upon them. And they waited in blank, resigned despair for God's vengeance to fall.

The She-Camel had been murdered on a Wednesday. And now, for each of the three cries uttered by her suffering, bereaved calf, God Almighty, the Lord of Retribution, sent the Thamud one day of waiting for the calamity to fall.

It is reported that when they awoke and looked at one another on the morning of Thursday, they saw with horror that all the faces had turned dark yellow. When they awoke on the second day, Friday, the faces had turned deep, blood red. Then on the third day, Saturday, all the faces had become black. And although they were beside themselves with terror, they knew that God's just sentence would not be revoked. Thus, they remained, utterly, abjectly hopeless, waiting for the end.

REFERENCES: Qur'an: 7:77; 11:65; 27:49-50. Commentary: Tabari/*H*, II:43-45; Ibn Kathir/*T*, 91:11-15, 27:48-50; Ibn Kathir/*Juz' 'Amma*, pp. 161-162; Ibn Kathir/*Q*, "Saleh"; Maududi/*Q*, 7:fn. 63.

6. The Blast

But they hamstrung her and so became regretful, and the punishment overtook them. Indeed, in that is a sign, but most of them are not believers. And indeed, your Lord — He is the Almighty, the Merciful.[6] (26:157-159)

As day dawned on Sunday, the Thamud still waited in numb, dumb terror for the punishment to strike. From whence it would come — from the sky above them or from the ground beneath their feet — they did not know. Then suddenly it descended.

What was that punishment? The sudden devastating catastrophe that came upon the Thamud is described in the Qur'an in several different ways, all of which give an impression of a tremendous, overwhelming calamity.

God Most High refers to it as ***al-sayhah***, meaning a sound, noise, cry, shout or clamor.[7] Regarding the ***sayhah*** that struck the Thamud, He says:

> **The clamor overtook those who did wrong, so they became prostrate in their homes, as if they had never dwelt there.** (11:67-68)

> **The clamor overtook them in the early morning, so nothing availed them of what they used to earn.** (15:83-84)

> **Then how [severe] were My punishment and warnings! Indeed, We sent upon them a single sound, and they became like the dry twig fragments of a [cattle] pen.** (54:30-31)

God also speaks of it as ***al-rajfah***, a quaking, shaking, trembling, rocking or convulsion, mentioned in the verse:

> **Then the quaking overtook them and they became prostrate in their homes.**[8] (7:78)

---

[6]That is, while God's might was manifested in the power and severity with which He justly dealt with the guilty Thamud, at the same time He is merciful to all His creation. Here, because of the context, His might is mentioned before His mercy.

[7]This kind of a sound is well-known during earthquakes. For example, during the Turkish earthquake of August 1, 1999, an eyewitness reported: "A crying sound first emanated from the earth. Thereafter a terrifying roar was heard from the depths of the earth." Another said, "The sound was so frightening that it gripped our hearts. We thought it was the Day of Judgment and we thought we were finished." A musician who was present said that if the sound had lasted for a minute longer, people would have died from it.

[8]In his commentary on this verse, Muhammad Asad, says:

> The term ***rajfah*** which occurs at the beginning of this sentence signifies any violent commotion or trembling, and is often, though not always, applied to an earthquake (***rajfat al-ard***). It is possible that the earthquake mentioned here was accompanied by

Again, God refers it as ***al-taghiyah***, the outburst, saying,

> **Thamud and 'Aad denied the sudden calamity [i.e., the Day of Resurrection]. Then, as for Thamud, they were destroyed by the outburst. . . . Do you then see any remains of them?** (69:4-5, 8)

Finally, He speaks of it as ***al-sa'iqah***, a strike that stuns, causes unconsciousness or destroys, a blast resembling a thunderbolt or a lightning strike, mentioned in the verses:

> **But if they turn away, then say, [O Muhammad:] "I have warned you of a blast like the blast of 'Aad and Thamud."** (41:13)

> **As for Thamud, We guided them, but they preferred blindness over guidance, so the blast of the humiliating punishment overtook them because of what they used to earn.** (41:17)

> **And in Thamud [was a sign], when it was said to them, "Enjoy yourselves for a time." But they were insolent toward the command of their Lord, so the blast overtook them while they were looking on, and they were not able to rise up nor could they help themselves.** (51:44-45)

From all this, it is clear that a single word is not sufficient to describe the terrible calamity that came upon the Thamud. Evidently it consisted of a tremendous, shattering roar from the depths of the earth, accompanied by a frightful, devastating quaking. And the Thamud were destroyed inside their own cliff homes, in which they had felt so invincible and secure.

But what of the prophet Saleh (A) and the believers? Although no details are given, their fate is mentioned in the following verses:

> **And We saved those who believed and were mindful of God.** (27:53; 41:18)

> **Then, when Our command came, We saved Saleh and those who believed with him by mercy from Ourselves, and [We saved them] from the disgrace of that day. Indeed, it is your Lord who is the Powerful, the Almighty.** (11:66)

And, in safety and in peace among his believing companions, Saleh (A) turned away from the remains of the formerly proud and prosperous Thamud. **"O my people,"** he said, **"I surely conveyed my Lord's Message to you and gave you sincere advice, but you do not like sincere advisors"** (7:79).

---

the volcanic eruption which at some time overtook the historical dwelling-places of the Thamud tribe, and to which the extensive black lava-fields (***harrah***) of northern Hijaz, and particularly near Mada'in Salih, . . . bear eloquent witness to this day. (Asad/Q, 7:fn. 62)

Nothing is known with certainty about the remainder of Saleh's life. But local traditions around the holy mountain, Sinai, suggest that Saleh (A), together with the believers, fled to it and that he ended his days there as a recluse. It is said that his grave is in a valley called "al-Sheikh" or "al-Sheikh Nabi Saleh" at the foot of Mount Sinai, where, each year on the birthday of Prophet Muhammad (A), the Sinai tribesmen gather to honor the one who is buried there.

It is also reported that the imprint of a camel's foot, known as *athar nakat al-nabi,* meaning "the Hoofprint of the Prophet's Camel," can be seen in a rock near the summit of Mount Sinai. But whose camel it was — whether that of the prophet Saleh or of Moses (A), who was to come to the holy mountain many centuries later — only God knows. May the best blessings be upon Saleh from his Lord!

REFERENCES: Qur'an: 7:78-79; 11:66-68; 15:83-84; 26:158-159; 27:51-53; 41:13, 17-18; 51:44-45; 54:30-31; 69:4-5. Commentaries: Tabari/*H*, II:45; Ibn Kathir/*Q*, "Saleh"; Maududi/*Q*, 7:fn. 57, 51:fn. 41; Asad/*Q*, 7:fn. 62; Golding, *In the Steps of Moses*, pp. 186-187; Taher, *Sinai*, p. 34.

7. The Relics of the Thamud

These are their homes, desolate because they did wrong. In that is surely a sign for a people who know. (27:52)

Up to this day, the broken cliff dwellings of the Thamud remain, eerily empty of all life, the architectural legacy of a talented but spiritually blind people, testifying to the truth of God's words:

> **And [We destroyed] 'Aad and Thamud, and it has been made clear to you from [the ruins of] their dwellings. And Satan had made their deeds attractive to them and kept them back from the path, although they were granted perception.** (29:38)

In this verse, the words, **It has been made clear to you from [the ruins of] their dwellings**, refer to the fact that the former territory of the Thamud lies on what used to be a major caravan route from Hijaz to Syria, even during the time of Prophet Muhammad (S). Abul 'Ala Maududi writes:

> Every Arab [of pre-Islamic times] was acquainted with the lands where these two nations ['Aad and Thamud] had lived. The whole of southern Arabia now known as Ahqāf, Yaman [Yemen] and Hadramaut, was the land of 'Ād in the ancient times, and the Arabs knew it. The whole area in the north of the Hijāz, from Rābigh to 'Aqābah and from Madinah and Khaiber to Taimā' and Tabūk, still abounds with Thamūdic monuments, which must have been more prominent than they are today in the time when the Qur'ān was being revealed. (Maududi/*Q*, 29:fn. 65)

It is reported that when the Prophet (S) passed by the Thamudite territory, al-Hijr, he said, "Do not enter the dwellings of those who wronged themselves unless you are weeping, lest there come upon you what came upon them." He then covered his face with his cloak while he was on the camel saddle (*Bukhari*, 4:563, 4:564).

However, during the campaign of Tabuk, he halted in al-Hijr with his army, but ordered his Companions not to drink water from its well or store water from it. When they said to him, "We have already kneaded [dough for bread] from it and drawn water," he ordered them to throw away that dough and pour out that water (*Bukhari* 4:561). In another version of this ***hadith***, it is reported the Prophet (S) ordered them to pour out the water they had taken from the wells and to feed the camels the dough they had made with it, taking water for their own use only from the well that the She-Camel had used[9] (*Bukhari*, 4:562). It is further

---

[9]In addition to the well of the She-Camel, the pass over a hill by which she came to the Thamud and her kneeling-place are still identified.

reported that when the Prophet (S) camped at al-Hijr during the Tabuk campaigh, he said to his Companions,

> "O people, do not ask your prophet for signs! Saleh's people asked of their prophet that a sign be sent to them, so God Most High sent them [a sign], mentioning that in the She-Camel there was a sign. On the day of her turn, she would come to them from this pass and would drink their water, while on the day of their turn, they would be supplied with it and would then milk her in an amount similar to what they taken of water before this milking. She would then depart from that pass.
>
> "Then they disobeyed the command of their Lord and hamstrung her, whereupon God promised them punishment after three days, and a promise from God is never false. God then destroyed whomever was of them in the east and the west of the earth, but for one man who was in God's sanctuary [*haram*], and God's sanctuary was prohibited to [be touched by] God's punishment." They asked, "Who was that man, O Messenger of God?" He said, "Abu Righal."[10] (Tabari/Q, "Saleh")

These *ahadith*, with their detailed descriptions, again demonstrate the clarity and vividness of the Holy Prophet's knowledge of earlier messengers and their communities through the divine inspirations coming to his heart. They also serve as proof that the story of the Thamud as told in the Qur'an represents the true history of this people.

The Thamud's former dwellings were later visited by Muslim geographers. Among them was Ibn Battutah, who passed through the valley of al-Hijr in the eighth century after *Hijrah* (the fifteenth century C.E.) on his way to Mecca. He wrote of having seen the Thamud's structures, hewn out of red mountains, their paintings as bright as if they had been of recent origin, and that decayed human bones could be found in their rock homes up to that time (Maududi/Q, 15:fn. 45).

The late Islamic scholar, Maulana Maududi, visited the territory of the Thamud in 1959. He wrote the following description of the area:

---

[10]Abu Righal is mentioned in other *ahadith*, in which it is reported that once, when the Prophet (S) went with some Companions toward Ta'if, they passed a grave. The Prophet (S) said, "This is the grave of Abu Righal, and he was [called] Abu Thaqif and was of the Thamud. He was in this sacred mosque [*haram*], which was averting it [the punishment] from him. When he came out of it, the same calamity befell him as had befallen his nation at this place, and so he is buried here. The sign of it is that a golden branch was buried with him. If you exhume him, you will find it with him." The people then did so and took out the golden branch (*Abu Dawud*, 3082). The meaning here is that as long as Abu Righal remained in the sacred sanctuary he was protected, but, being of the people upon whom the divine retribution had been decreed, as soon as he left it, the protection ceased and the punishment that had fallen upon his people befell him as well.

This place is situated between Al-Madīnah and Tabūk, a few miles to the north of Al-'Ulā (Wād-il-Qurā of the Holy Prophet's time) in Hejāz. The local inhabitants call it Al-Hijr and Madā'in Sālih even today. Al-'Ulā is still a green and fertile valley abounding in water springs and gardens, but Al-Hijr appears to be an abandoned place. It has thin population, little greenery and a few wells, one of which is said to be the one at which Prophet Sālih's she-camel used to drink water. This well is now dry and located within a deserted military post of the time of the [Ottoman] Turks. When we entered this territory and approached Al-'Ulā, we found hills which seemed to have been shattered to pieces from top to bottom as if by a violent earthquake. We saw the same kind of hills while traveling to the east, from Al-'Ulā to Khaibar [in Saudi Arabia], for about 50 miles, and towards the north inside Jordan, for about 30 to 40 miles. This indicated that an area, stretching well over 300 to 400 miles in length and 100 miles in width, had been devastated by the terrible earthquake. (Maududi/*Q*, 26:fn. 99)

REFERENCES: Tabari/*H*, II:45-46; Tabari/*Q*, "Saleh"; Maududi/*Q*, 7:fn. 57, 15:fn. 45, 26:fn. 99, 29:fn. 65; Ali/*Q*, Appen. IX after *Surah* 26.

Qur'anic References — Saleh

7:73-79

And to Thamud [We sent] their brother Saleh. He said, "O my people, worship God; you have no deity but Him. There has surely come to you a clear evidence from your Lord. This is God's She-Camel, a sign for you, so let her feed upon God's earth and do not do her any harm, lest a painful punishment seize you. (73) And recall when He made you successors after the 'Aad and settled you in the land. You make castles upon its plains and hew the mountains into dwellings. Then remember God's favors and do not act wickedly in the land, causing corruption!" (74)

The chiefs of those who were arrogant among his people said to those who were oppressed — to those who believed among them — "Do you [really] know that Saleh is sent by his Lord?"

They said, "Indeed, we are believers in that with which he has been sent." (75)

Those who were arrogant said, "Indeed, we are disbelievers in that which you believe." (76)

Then they hamstrung the She-Camel and were insolent toward the command of their Lord, and they said, "O Saleh, bring us what you promise us, if you are among the messengers!" (77)

Then the quaking overtook them and they became prostrate in their homes. And he turned away from them and said, "O my people, I surely conveyed my Lord's Message to you and gave you sincere advice, but you do not like sincere advisors." (78)

9:70

Has there not reached them [the pagan Meccans of Muhammad's time] the news of those before them — the people of Noah and 'Aad and Thamud, and the people of Abraham and the dwellers in Midian and the Overturned Cities? Their messengers came to them with clear proofs. And never would God have wronged them, but [rather] they wronged themselves.

11:61-68

And to Thamud [was sent] their brother Saleh. He said, "O my people, worship God; you have no deity but Him. He produced you from the earth and caused you to dwell in it, so ask His forgiveness and then repent to Him. My Lord is surely near and responsive." (61)

They said, "O Saleh, you were a man of promise among us before this. Do you forbid us to worship what our fathers worshipped? And indeed, we are in uneasy doubt about that to which you call us." (62)

He said, "O my people, have you considered: if I am [taking my stand] upon clear evidence from my Lord, while He has granted me mercy from Himself, who would help me against God if I disobeyed Him? Therefore, you would not increase me but in loss." (63)

"And, O my people, this is God's She-Camel, a sign for you, so let her feed upon God's earth and do not do her any harm, lest a punishment near [at hand] seize you." (64) But they hamstrung her, whereupon he said, "Enjoy yourselves in your homes for three days. That is a promise not to be belied!" (65)

Then, when Our command came, We saved Saleh and those who believed with him by mercy from Ourselves, and [We saved them] from the disgrace of that day. Indeed, it is your Lord who is the Powerful, the Almighty. (66) And the clamor overtook those who did wrong, so they became prostrate in their homes, (67) as if they had never dwelt there. Unquestionably, Thamud disbelieved in their Lord. Then away with Thamud! (68)

11:89-90

[Shu'ayb said,] "And, O my people, do not let dissension with me cause you to sin, lest there befall you something like what befell the people of Noah or the people of Hud or the people of Saleh, nor are the people of Lot far removed from you. (89) And seek forgiveness from your Lord and then repent to Him. Indeed, my Lord is Merciful and Loving!" (90)

14:9-15

These verses are cited in "Qur'anic References — Noah"

15:80-84

And the dwellers in al-Hijr certainly denied the messengers, (80) and We granted them Our revelations but they turned away from them; (81) and they used to hew dwellings out of the mountains, secure. (82) Then the clamor overtook them in the early morning, (83) so nothing availed them of what they used to earn. (84)

17:59

We granted Thamud the She-Camel as a visible sign, but they wronged her.

22:42

And if they deny you [Muhammad], the people of Noah and 'Aad and Thamud denied [their [prophets] before them.

25:38

And [We destroyed] 'Aad and Thamud and the dwellers in al-Rass, and many generations between them.

26:141-159

Thamud denied the messengers, (141) when their brother Saleh said to them, "Will you not be mindful of God? (142) Indeed, I am a trustworthy messenger to you, (143) so be mindful of God and obey me. (144) And I do not ask of you any recompense for it. My recompense rests only on the Lord of the worlds. (145)

"Will you be left in what is here, secure (146) — in gardens and springs, (147) and fields of crops and date palms with mellow fruit, (148) and you skillfully hew dwellings out of the mountains? (149) Then be mindful of God and obey me, (150) and do not obey the command of the transgressors — (151) those who make corruption in the land and never reform!" (152)

They said, "You are merely one of those under a magic spell. (153) You are nothing but a mortal like ourselves, so bring a sign, if you are among the truthful!" (154)

He said, "This is a she-camel. She has her share of water and you have your share of water, [each] on a fixed day. (155) And do touch her with harm, lest you be seized by the punishment of a terrible day!" (156) But they hamstrung her and so became regretful, (157) and the punishment overtook them. Indeed, in that is a sign, but most of them are not believers. (158) And indeed, your Lord — He is the Almighty, the Merciful. (159)

27:45-53

And We certainly sent to Thamud their brother Saleh, [saying,] "Worship God," whereupon they became two disputing groups. (45)

He said, "O my people, why do you seek to hasten the evil in advance of the good? Why do you not seek forgiveness from God, that you may be shown mercy?" (46)

They said, "We attribute an evil omen to you and to those with you."

He said, "Your 'evil omen' is with God. Rather, you are a people being tested!" (47)

And there were in the city nine heads of families causing corruption in the land and not amending. (48) They said, "Swear by God that we will attack him and his family by night. Then we will say to his executor, 'We did not witness the destruction of his family, and indeed we are truthful!'" (49)

And they devised a plot and We devised a plot, and they did not perceive. (50) Then see what was the end of their plot — that We destroyed all of them and their people together! (51) And these are their homes, desolate because they did wrong. In that is surely a sign for a people who know. And We saved those who believed and were mindful of God. (52)

29:38

And [We destroyed] 'Aad and Thamud, and it has been made clear to you from [the ruins of] their dwellings. Satan had made their deeds attractive to them and kept them back from the path, although they were granted perception.

38:12-14

Before them, the people of Noah and 'Aad and Pharaoh, possessor of the stakes, (12) denied, and Thamud and the people of Lot and the dwellers in the thorn bush. Those were the factions; (13) each denied the messengers, wherefore My punishment was justified. (14)

40:30-31

[The Secret Believer among Pharaoh's people said,] "O my people, indeed, I fear for you the like of the Day of the Confederates — (30) like the case of Noah's people and 'Aad and Thamud and those after them. And God desires no injustice for servants." (31)

41:13-14, 17-18

But if they turn away, then say, [O Muhammad:] "I have warned you of a blast like the blast of 'Aad and Thamud." (13) When their messengers came to them before them and after them, [saying,] "Worship no one but God," they said, "If our Lord had willed, He would have sent down angels, so indeed we are disbelievers in that with which you have been sent." (14)

. . . And as for Thamud, We guided them, but they preferred blindness over guidance, so the blast of the humiliating punishment overtook them because of what they used to earn. (17) And We saved those who believed and were mindful of God. (18)

50:12-14

Before them, the people of Noah and the dwellers in al-Rass and Thamud denied; (12) and 'Aad and Pharaoh and the brethren of Lot, (13) and the dwellers in the thorn bush and the people of Tubba' — all denied the messengers, wherefore My threat was justly carried out. (14)

51:43-45

And in Thamud [was a sign], when it was said to them, "Enjoy yourselves for a time." (43) But they were insolent toward the command of their Lord, so the blast overtook them while they were looking on, (44) and they were not able to rise up nor could they help themselves. (45)

53:50-51

And that He destroyed the first 'Aad (50) and Thamud, and did not spare [them]. (51)

54:23-31

Thamud denied the warnings (23) and said, "Are we to follow a single man from among ourselves? If so, we would indeed be in error and madness! (24)

Has the Message been sent down upon him [alone] amongst us? No, rather he is an insolent liar!" (25)

[God said,] "Tomorrow they will know who is the insolent liar! (26) Indeed, We are sending the She-Camel as a trial for them, so watch them and be patient. (27) And inform them that the water is to be shared between them, each drinking attended by turn." (28)

Then they called their comrade, and he took and hamstrung her. (29) Then how [severe] were My punishment and warnings! (30) Indeed, We sent upon them a single sound, and they became like the dry twig fragments of a [cattle] pen. (31)

69:4-5

Thamud and 'Aad denied the sudden calamity. (4) Then, as for Thamud, they were destroyed by the outburst. (5)

85:17-18

Has there come to you [Muhammad] the story of the troops (17) — of Pharaoh and Thamud? (18)

89:6-14

Have you [Muhammad] not considered how your Lord dealt with 'Aad, (6) Iram of the lofty columns, (7) the like of which had never been created in the lands, (8) and [with] Thamud, who hewed out the rocks in the valley, (9) and [with] Pharaoh, possessor of the stakes — those who committed oppression in the lands (10) and increased the corruption therein? (11) Then your Lord poured upon them a scourge of punishment. (13) Indeed, your Lord is in observation! (14)

91:11-15

Thamud denied [their prophet] in their transgression, (11) when the greatest wretch among them was sent forth. (12) And the messenger of God [Saleh] said to them, "[This is] God's She-Camel, so let her drink!" (13) But they denied him and hamstrung her, whereupon their Lord brought down upon them destruction for their sin and made it equal [upon them all], (14) and He does not fear the consequences thereof. (15)

The Stories of Abraham, Ishmael, Isaac and Jacob

peace be upon them

Indeed, God chose Adam and Noah and the family of Abraham and the family of 'Imran above all mankind, descendants of one another. (3:33-34)

Indeed, We have revealed to you [Muhammad] as We revealed to Noah and the prophets after him; and We revealed to Abraham and Ishmael and Isaac and Jacob and the descendants [of Israel]. (4:163)

PART ONE

1. The Importance of Abraham (A) Among the Prophets

And they say: "Be Jews or Christians [so] you will be guided." Say, [O Muhammad:] "No, but [we follow] the religion of Abraham, inclining toward truth, and he was not of the *mushrikin*."[1] Say, [O believers:] "We believe in God and what was revealed to us, and what was revealed to Abraham and Ishmael and Isaac and Jacob and the descendants [of Israel], and what was given to Moses and Jesus, and what was given to the prophets by their Lord. We make no distinction between any of them, and we surrender to Him [in Islam]." (2:135-136; also 3:84-85)

Abraham's Illustrious Rank

In one brief statement, the above verse summarizes the Islamic teachings concerning God's messengers: that all of them were equally chosen, guided and granted revelation by their Lord, and that what each of them brought was the true, original religion, to which God gives the name "Islam". At the same time, God also says:

> **Those messengers — We caused some of them to excel others. Among them are those to whom God spoke, and He exalted some of them in rank.** (2:253; also 17:55)

We now come to one of the most honored of all the prophets, Abraham or Ibrahim, may God's best blessings and peace be upon him. Testifying to his high rank, God says:

> **Abraham was indeed an *ummah*,[2] devoutly obedient to God, inclining toward truth [*hanifa*], and he was not among the *mushrikin*, [and he was] grateful for His favors. He chose him and guided him to a straight path. And We gave him good in this world, and indeed, in the Hereafter he will be among the righteous. Then We revealed to you [Muhammad] to follow the faith of Abraham, inclining toward truth [*Ibrahima hanifa*], and he was not among the *mushrikin*.** (16:120-123)

---

[1]Those who associate other deities with God, polytheists.

[2]Nation or community. This verse has been interpreted both as meaning that Abraham (A) had the faith and carried on the work of an entire nation by himself, and that he was an example and model for all mankind.

What is the reason for Abraham's outstanding importance and high rank among the prophets? The many Qur'anic verses revealed concerning him suggest that it was because of the purity and sincerity of his relationship with his beloved Lord, to whom he totally surrendered his will. Thus, God says:

> **Who would be averse to the faith of Abraham except one who makes a fool of himself? And We chose him in this world, and indeed, in the Hereafter he will be among the righteous. When his Lord said to him, "Surrender!" he said, "I have surrendered to the Lord of the worlds."** (2:130-131)

The greatness of Abraham's standing with God is confirmed in a number of ***ahadith***. The Holy Prophet (S) referred to him as "the best of creation" (*Muslim*, 5841-5843) and mentioned him as one of the prophets whose intercession the believers would seek on the Day of Judgment (*Bukhari*, 6.236, 6.3, 9.507, 9.532[C], 9:507; *Muslim*, 373, 377-378, 380). The Prophet (S) also reported meeting Abraham (A) in one of the heavens during his ***Me'raj*** or Ascension to the Divine Presence, saying that he had found Abraham (A) seated in ***al-Bait al-Ma'mur***,[3] the Populated House, in which 70,000 angels pray in successive groups, never to return to it again (*Bukhari*, 4:429; also 1:345, 4:647, 5:227; *Mishkat*, 2311).

The Prophet (S) also related that once, when he was granted a vision of Paradise, he saw in the midst of it "a man so tall that I could almost not see his head because of his height in the sky, and around the man were more children than I had ever seen." Later, in response to his asking the two beings who escorted him who all these were, he was told, "As for the tall man who was in Paradise, he is Abraham, God's peace and blessings be upon him. And as for the children who were around him, they are all children who died in a state of natural purity [***fitrah***]." Some of his Companions then asked, "O Messenger of God, and the children of ***mushrikin***?" to which the Prophet, God's peace and blessings replied, "And the children of ***mushrikin***" (*Bukhari*, 9:171). Because of this, the classic Qur'anic commentator al-Qurtubi wrote:

> Do you not see that the meaning of Ibrahim is ***ab rahim*** [a merciful father], because of his mercy toward children? For this reason he and his wife Sarah were made guardians of the children of the people of faith who die young, until the Day of Resurrection. (Ayoub/Q, I:152)

REFERENCES: Qur'an: 2:124-138; 16:120-123. Commentaries: Ibn Kathir/Q, "Ibrahim"; Maududi/Q, 16:fn. 119, 52:fn. 3; Ayoub/Q, I:151-152; Ali/Q, fn. 2156; Saheeh/Q, fn. 664.

---

[3]The spiritual prototype of the Holy K'abah in the fourth heaven, mentioned in the story of Adam, p. 76.

ABRAHAM, THE *HANIF*

The word *"hanif,"* which occurs again and again in the Qur'an, means inclining toward the truth with pure faith, keeping to the straight, correct God-centered monotheistic religion and avoiding all objects of worship other than God Most High.[4] Thus, God says of Jews and Christians:

> **They were not commanded but to worship God, being sincere to Him in the religion, inclining to truth, and to establish *salat* and to give *zakat*.[5] And that is the correct religion.** (98:5)

> **And, [O Muhammad,] direct your face toward the religion, inclining to truth, and do not be among the *mushrikin*; and do not invoke, apart from God, that which neither benefits you nor harms you, for if you did, you would indeed be among the wrong-doers.** (10:105-106)

This pure, sound religion corresponds to *fitrah* — that is, the original nature, constitution, disposition and innate character with which God (who is *al-Fatir*, the Originator) created each thing in existence, including mankind, according to His words,

> **Then set your face toward the religion, inclining to truth — the God-given nature [*fitrat-Allah*] with which He endowed mankind. No change shall there be in God's creation. That is the correct religion, but most people do not know — turning to Him; and be mindful of Him and establish *salat*, and do not be among the *mushrikin*.** (30:30-31)

---

[4]The contemporary Qur'anic translator and commentator, Muhammad Asad, writes:

> The expression *hanif* is derived from the verb *hanafa*, which literally means "he inclined [towards a right state or tendency]". . . . Already in pre-Islamic times, this term had a definitely monotheistic connotation, and was used to describe a man who turned away from sin and worldliness and from all dubious beliefs, especially idol-worship; and *tahannuf* denoted the ardent devotions, mainly consisting of long vigils and prayers, of the Unitarian God-seekers of pre-Islamic times. Many instances of this use of the terms *hanif* and *tahannuf* occur in the verses of pre-Islamic poets. (Asad/*Q*, 2:fn. 110)

Cyril Glasse connects the word *"hanif"* with Abraham, saying that it is

> used in the Koran to describe one who adheres to pristine monotheism (pl. *hunafa*). A descriptive name in the Koran for Abraham, and for those before Islam who by the purity and uprightness of their nature did not succumb to paganism and polytheism. The *hunafa'* between Abraham and the time of the Prophet were thus the faithful representatives of the Abrahamic-Ishmaelite tradition during the period called the *Jahiliyyah* ("Age of Ignorance") which saw a descent into paganism. (Glasse/*E*, p. 148)

[5]As basic obligations of their faith, the followers of Moses and Jesus, and other prophets such as Ishmael, Isaac and Jacob, were commanded to establish and observe regular, ritual prayer (*salat*) and to give the prescribed charity known as *zakat* (see, for example, 2:83, 5:12/13; 19:31, 55; 21:73).

From this we can understand that the human being's connection to the Creator pertains to the inherent, unchangeable nature with which every soul comes into the world. It is this nature or *fitrah* that causes a child to be intuitively open to God and to pure religion unless its mind has been bent in some other direction by the influences surrounding it,[6] according to the saying of the Holy Prophet (S) reported by the eminent Companion, Abu Hurayrah (R):

> "No baby is born without being born in *fitrah*, but then his parents Juda-ize or Christian-ize or Magian-ize him,[7] as an animal brings forth a whole animal. Do you notice anything mutilated in it?" Abu Hurayrah then recited: **"The religion, inclining to truth — the God-given nature with which He endowed mankind. No change shall there be in God's creation. That is the correct religion"** [30:30]. (*Bukhari*, 2:440, 2:441; *Muwatta*, 16.16.53)

It is the prophet Abraham (A), of whom God says,

> **Abraham was neither a Jew nor a Christian, but he was one inclining toward truth [*hanifa*], a *muslim*, and he was not among the *mushrikin*** (3:67),

who is singled out as the prototype and exemplar of ***al-dina hanifa*** — that is, the path of belief and worship of God the Praised and Glorious, the Lord of exalted divine attributes, in His absolute uniqueness and endless glory, not associating any partners with Him nor ascribing to Him any of the attributes of any created being. Thus, the well-known Companion of the Prophet (S), 'Abdullah ibn 'Umar (R), reports that when when a Jewish and a Christian scholar of his time were asked, "What is *hanif*?" both gave the same reply: "*Hanif* is the faith of Abraham, who was neither a Jew nor a Christian, and he worshipped no one but God"[8] (*Bukhari*, 5:169).

This pure faith was the religion (***din***) of all the true monotheists prior to Islam — that is, of the prophets and their communities: the religion of absolute, uncompromising belief in God the Exalted as the only Lord, and of sincerity to Him in worship and all the affairs of life, according to God's instructions to His Last Prophet (S):

> **Say, [O Muhammad:] "Indeed, my Lord has guided me to a straight path, a correct religion: the faith of Abraham, inclining toward truth, and he was not among the *mushrikin*." Say: "Indeed, my *salat* and my rites of sacrifice and my living and my dying**

---

[6]*Fitrah* has been defined as "the natural inborn inclination of man to worship his Creator prior to the corruption of this nature by external influences. Thus, Islamic monotheism is described as the religion of *fitrah* — that of the inherent nature of mankind" (Saheeh/*Q*, fn. 1070).

[7]This refers to the Zoroastrian religion.

[8]Cf., 10:104-106, 22:31, 98:5.

are for God, Lord of the worlds, who has no partner. And this I have been commanded, and I am the first [among you] of the Muslims." (6:161-163)

REFERENCES: Qur'an: 3:67-68; 6:161-163; 10:105-106; 30:30-31; 98:5. Commentaries: Ayoub/*Q*, I:164-165, Ayoub/*Q*: II:208-21; Maududi/*Q*, 10:fn. 108, 30:fns. 43-45, 3:fn. 59, 6:fn. 143; Asad/*Q*, 2: fn. 110; Lane/*L*, Part 2, 658.

Abraham, the Friend of God

One of the most impressive indications of Abraham's high rank is the fact that God chose him to be His close friend, according to His saying:

> **And who is better in religion than one who surrenders himself to God, while being a doer of good and follows the religion of Abraham, inclining toward truth? And God took Abraham as a close friend [*khalil*].** (4:125)

Now, this may well be a cause for wonder to us. It is almost beyond imagination that God the Exalted and Glorious, the Creator of all things, the Lord of the universes and all they contain, should chose a finite, insignificant mortal, regardless of how 'good' he may be, as His close, dear friend. Nonetheless, this is what God Himself says about Abraham (A) and what His Last Prophet (S) confirmed in a number of *ahadith*, such as the following.[19]

The Prophet (S) said, "Each prophet has a close friend among the prophets, and my close friend [*wali*] among the prophets is my father and the close friend [*khalil*] of my Lord, Abraham." He then recited the verse, **"Indeed, the foremost people with respect to Abraham are those who followed him, and this prophet [Muhammad] and those who believe. And God is Protector of the believers"** [3:68] (Tirmidhi).

It is reported that once the Holy Prophet (S) came upon some of his Companions who were speaking together. One of them said that God had taken Abraham as a friend; another said that He had spoken directly to Moses; another said that Jesus was God's word and spirit; and another said that God had chosen Adam. The Prophet (S) then said to them,

> I have heard what you said, and you are wondering that Abraham was God's friend, as indeed he was; that Moses was God's confidant, as indeed he was; that Jesus was His spirit and word, as indeed he was; and that Adam was chosen by God, as indeed he was.[10] (*Mishkat*, 5762)

On another occasion, the Prophet (S) stood up among the Muslims and addressed them, saying,

---

[9]Abraham's being the friend of God is also mentioned in the Old Testament (II Ch. 20:7 and Isa. 41:8).

> You will be gathered barefoot, naked and uncircumcised, [according to God's saying,] **As We began the first creation, We shall repeat it** [21:104]. And the first to be clothed on the Day of Resurrection will be Abraham, the Friend [of God]." (*Bukhari*, 4:568, 8:533)

Again, the Prophet referred Abraham (A) as the Friend of God in connection with his great-grandson, the prophet Joseph, saying,

> The noblest [among people] is Joseph, the son of a prophet of God [Jacob], the son of a prophet of God [Isaac], the son of the Friend of God.[11] (*Bukhari*, 4.593, 4.597, 6.211)

REFERENCES: Qur'an: 3:68; 4:125. Commentaries: Ibn Kathir/*T*, 3:68; Ayoub/*Q*, II:213.

Other Honors and Favors Granted to Abraham

All this makes clear to us the wonderfully intimate, trusting relationship that existed between Abraham (A) and his beloved Lord. And because Abraham (A) was so close and so dear to Him, God granted him very special honors and divine favors, among which are the following:

1. Abraham (A) ranks among the five greatest prophets (*'ulu-l-'azm*), the others being Noah, Moses, Jesus and Muhammad, God's peace and blessings be upon them all, as mentioned in the following verses:

> **He has ordained for you [mankind], as the religion, what He enjoined upon Noah and that which We have revealed to you [Muhammad], and what We enjoined upon Abraham and Moses and Jesus: to establish the religion and not be divided concerning it.** (42:13)

> **[Mention, O Muhammad,] when We took from the prophets their covenant, and from you [Muhammad], and from Noah and Abraham and Moses and Jesus son of Mary — and We took from them a solemn covenant.**[12] (33:7)

---

[10]The Prophet (S) went on to say, not to praise himself but as a simple statement of fact, "I am the one whom God loves, and this is no boast. On the Day of Resurrection I shall be the bearer of the banner of praise under which will be Adam and the others, and this is no boast. I shall be the first intercessor and the first whose intercession is accepted on the Day of Resurrection, and this is no boast. I shall be the first to rattle the knocker of Paradise, and God will open for me and bring me into it, accompanied by the poor ones among the believers, and this is no boast. I shall be the most honorable in God's estimation among those of the earlier and later times, and this is no boast" (*Mishkat*, 5762).

[11]In another version of this *hadith*, the Prophet (S) referred to the prophet Joseph as "the noble [*al-karim*], son of the noble, son of the noble, son of the noble — Joseph, son of Jacob, son of Isaac, son of Abraham, the friend of the Most Merciful" (*Bukhari*, 4:596, 4:603).

2. Because of the depth of his faith, God Most High made Abraham (A) one of the greatest religious figures of all times, according to His promise, **"Indeed, I will make you a leader of mankind"** (2:124). And truly, Abraham's profound faith and noble deeds have been an example for believers throughout the ages, the gold standard by which all religion is measured: —

> **And who is better in religion than the one who surrenders himself to God, while being a doer of good, and follows the religion of Abraham, inclining toward truth?** (4:125)
>
> **Strive for God with the striving due to Him. He has chosen you and has not placed upon you any difficulty in the religion: the faith of your father Abraham. He [God] named you "*muslims*" beforehand and in this [revelation].** (22:78)

3. God answered Abraham's prayer, **"My Lord, grant me [sound] judgment and join me with the righteous, and grant me a mention of honor among later generations"** (26:83-84), by granting him the highest honor and repute among all the generations of believers who came after him.

Thus it is that the followers of the three monotheistic faiths, Judaism, Christianity and Islam, all deeply revere Abraham (A), mentioning his name with respect and invoking God's blessings upon him. In particular, Muslims throughout the world mention Abraham (A) with the highest honor each time they complete their *salat*, following the instructions and example of the Holy Prophet (S), for when he was asked by his people, "O Messenger of God, how shall we invoke blessings upon you?" he replied:

> Say: "O God, bestow Your grace upon Muhammad and upon the people of Muhammad, as You bestowed Your grace upon Abraham and upon the people of Abraham. Indeed, You are Praised and Glorious. And bless Muhammad and the people of Muhammad, as You blessed Abraham and the people of Abraham. Indeed, You are Praised and Glorious." (*Salat al-Ibrahimiyah*, the Prayer of Abraham; *Bukhari*, 4:588, 4:589)

4. God answered Abraham's prayer for a son from among the righteous (37:100) by granting him Isaac as well as Ishmael (A), also a prophet, from whose line of descent came the last and greatest of the prophets, Muhammad, God's peace and blessings be upon him and upon them all. More than this, Abraham's prayer for the people of Mecca, **"Our Lord, and send among them a messenger from among themselves, who will recite to them Your verses, and teach them the scripture and wisdom and purify them"** (2:129), was also fulfilled through Muhammad (S). Abraham's other prayers for Mecca and its inhabitants, contained in 14:35-41, were also similarly answered.

---

[12]Referring to what occurred in the spiritual world of souls.

5. God revealed to Abraham (A) a sacred scripture, about which we are told in the following verses:

Or has he not had been informed of what was in the scriptures of Moses and Abraham, who fulfilled [his obligations]? (53:36-37)

Indeed, this is in the former scriptures, the scriptures of Abraham and Moses. (87:18-19)

No known trace of this book remains. However, it is mentioned in a *hadith*, in which the eminent Companion of the Prophet (S), Abu Dharr al-Ghifari (R), asked the Prophet (S) what Abraham's scripture or scrolls dealt with. The Prophet (S) replied that they contained parables and admonitions, such as God's addressing a king and informing him that He had not placed him in his position to amass wealth or tyrannize over people, but rather to help the oppressed and deal justly with them on His behalf (Akili/*B*, p. 156).

On another occasion, Abu Dharr (R) asked the Prophet (S) if anything remained in this world of the texts of the ancient scriptures such as those revealed to Abraham and Moses (A). In reply, the Prophet (S) instructed him to read the verses, **He who purifies himself and mentions the name of his Lord and prays has certainly succeeded. But you prefer the life of this world, while the Hereafter is better and more lasting. Indeed, this is in the former scriptures, the scriptures of Abraham and Moses** [87:18-19] (Akili/B, p. 156).

6. Abraham (A) was granted the honor of establishing many of the basic practices of the *islam* of the believers prior to Muhammad's time, which were later followed by Prophet Muhammad (S) and which continue to be followed by the community of Muslims up to this day. We shall speak of these further in Chapter 22.

7. God further honored Abraham (A) by ordaining that Muslims recall him and important events in his life in the rites of the major and minor pilgrimage (*Hajj* and *'Umrah*). Connected with this is also the commemoration of Abraham's sacrifice of his son during the Festival of Sacrifice, *'Eid al-Adha*, all of which we will discuss later in detail.

8. As we shall see, all the prophets mentioned in the Qur'an who lived after Abraham's time were his descendants. Thus, the three God-centered faiths that originate in divine revelation — Judaism, Christianity and Islam — are connected with Abraham (A) and claim him as their spiritual ancestor.

REFERENCES: Qur'an: 2:124, 129; 4:125; 22:78; 26:83-84; 33:7; 53:36-37; 87:18-19. Commentaries: Ibn Kathir/*T*, 26:83-25; Ibn Kathir/*Q*, "Ibrahim"; Ayoub/*Q*, I:164-165; Akili/*B*, p. 156.

Special Matters Concerning Abraham

Abraham, may God's peace and blessings be upon him, was certainly one of the most special individuals who ever lived, and from special people special things are expected. The following are some other aspects relating to Abraham's extraordinary rank and personality:

A *hadith* that does not originate with the Prophet (S) is reported in Imam Malik's *Al-Muwatta*. It mentions the following matters concerning Abraham (A).

First, Abraham (A) was the first to show hospitality to guests, initiating the traditional Muslim practice of honoring one's visitors.[13] Second, Abraham (A) was the first person to be circumcised. Third, he was the first person to trim his moustache.[14] Fourth, Abraham (A) was the first person to notice his grey hair. When he saw it, he said, "O Lord, what is this?" And God the Blessed and Exalted replied, "It is dignity, Abraham." To this Abraham (A) responded, "Lord, increase me in dignity!" (*Muwatta* 49.3.4).

Abraham (A) has the distinction of being mentioned by name in the Qur'an sixty-nine times, fifteen times in the second chapter, *Surah al-Baqarah*, alone. The fourteenth *surah*, *"Ibrahim,"* which contains one of Abraham's incomparable prayers, is named for him. Some of the verses in which he is mentioned cite his greatness as a prophet and an example for mankind, while in others, parts of his life-story — a life full of miracles — are reported.

We are now ready to begin the exciting and eventful history of the Friend of the Most Merciful, followed by the interrelated stories of his sons, Ishmael and Isaac, and his grandson Jacob, may God's peace and blessings be upon them all.

---

[13]This may be understood as meaning that Abraham was the first to understand that showing hospitality is an obligation to God.

[14]This relates both to appearance and hygiene. We will speak further about it on pages 339-340.

PART TWO

2. The People of Abraham

Indeed, among his [Noah's] followers was Abraham, when he came to his Lord with a sound heart. (37:83-84)

About 4000 years ago,[15] a community of idol-worshippers lived in Ur, the capital of Sumer, in what is now the southern part of Iraq.

The site of Ur is located on the Euphrates River just west of a spot known as Ur Junction, a stop for the train from Baghdad. Nothing now remains of a place which in ancient times teemed with the life of a complex, highly-developed society — neither buildings nor agriculture, but only a vast, empty plain, punctuated by the topless hulk of its ziggurat tower, built when Ur was at the height of its glory. Its tall spiral, in Abraham's time the temple of Ur's god, Sin or Nannar, still thrusts upward toward the sky.

This, according to tradition, is the place where Abraham (A) began his mission as a prophet. In his time, the city of Ur was a flourishing industrial and business center, with a population of probably a quarter to half a million. Trade with other areas was well-developed, and the people were mostly craftsmen and merchants.[16]

Archeological records show that the Sumerians, who governed a vast empire, possessed a very highly developed civilization. Indeed, their language, Sumerian, which has no known roots or descendants, was the language of the first known writing.

Like all pagan societies, the social life of the Sumerians was built on a rigid class structure. Within its three classes — the class of priests, state officials and military officers; the class of merchants, craftsmen and farmers; and the class of slaves — there was ample scope for the strong to oppress the weak. Many

[15]The time period of Abraham's life remains approximate, ranging from 1800 to 2100 B.C.

[16]A *National Geographic* article reads:

> Ur was old when Abram [the name originally given to him in the Book of Genesis] was young, a bustling, prosperous commercial center somewhat past its prime. Priest-ruled and merchant-ridden, it offered luxury to the privileged and subsistence to its slaves and peasants. Artisans plied their crafts with skills unequalled in all the world save Egypt. Astrologists applied the mathematics invented here by their ancestors. In temple rooms scribes practiced another art which Sumer had created: writing.
>
> . . . The city was encircled by a wall. Ships with the goods of India and the East crowded the quays, and canals transported smaller vessels to other centers. They also carried water to the fields, since without irrigation nothing would grow in such a dry area where rain fell only in winter. (Kenneth MacLeish, "Abraham, the Friend of God," *Nat. Geo. Mag.*, Dec. 1966, pp. 743-745)

other evils may also have flourished: bribery, usury, lying, cheating, sexual immorality, tryanny and injustice, to name only a few. These would have been encouraged, as in any pagan society, by the false religion and its leaders.

The well-preserved tablets that have been excavated at Ur mention the names of about five thousand gods that were worshipped by the Sumerians. In addition, each Sumerian city had its own special patron god, who was entitled to greater reverence than any of the others. As we have mentioned, the patron god of Ur was Sin or Nannar, the moon god; similarly, the sun was the god of another city in the area. Under these chief gods were many minor ones, most of which were related to the stars or planets, and a few to earthly objects. These lesser gods were believed to grant prayers for less important matters.

A great amount of wealth was given over to the god Nannar/Sin and his worship. His shrines occupied many tracts of land, gardens and buildings, and taxes were collected for these in the name of the god. His statue was kept in a grand temple — the ziggurat, with its spiral staircase leading up to the top, built on the highest peak in the city.

The highest court of justice was also located in Nannar's temple. The priests, who enjoyed many special privileges, were among its judges, and their decisions were considered to be those of the god himself. Thus, it will be seen that the pagan religion was not merely a belief system but a way of life, affecting every part of the people's existence.

The Sumerians at the time of Abraham (A) were ruled by a proud, tyrannical king named Nimrod. It said that he was one of the four greatest kings of ancient times, the others being the prophet-king Solomon (A), Dhu-l-Qarnain,[17] and Nebuchadnezzar. In addition to being the supreme ruler, Nimrod had established himself as a god who was worshipped by his people, together with their other gods.

REFERENCES: Tabari/*H*, II:48-50; Maududi/*Q*, 6:fn. 52, 18:fn. 62; Asad/*Q*, 18:fn. 81; MacLeish, "Abraham, the Friend of God," *National Geographic Magazine*, Dec. 1966, pp. 742-789.

[17]Mentioned in the Qur'anic passage 18:83-98, Dhul-Qarnain is sometimes identified with Alexander the Great. However, this appears to be an error since Alexander was not a believer. Others have identified him with Cyrus the Great.

3. The Beginning of Abraham's Life

And mention Abraham in the Book. Indeed, he was a man of truth and a prophet. (19:41)

The early Qur'anic commentators trace the genealogy of Abraham (A) back to Shem, the son of Noah (A). The name of Abraham's father, Azar, is preserved in the Qur'an.[18] It is reported that Abraham (A) had two brothers, Nahor and Haran.

Now, the tyrant king Nimrod lived in Babylon near Kufah. A number of Qur'anic commentators, including Ibn 'Abbas and Ibn Mas'ud (R), report that before Abraham's birth, a star appeared, of such brightness that it outshone the sun and moon. This so frightened the king that he called his magicians, astrologers, diviners and the like to ask them what it could mean.

They replied that a man would arise in his territory who was destined to destroy him and his rule. Hearing this, Nimrod left Babylon and moved to another town, compelling all the men to leave with him, while leaving the women behind. At the same time, he ordered the killing of any boy who would be born to them.

At this time, the account continues, a matter came up in Babylon for which Nimrod could only trust Azar, the future father of Abraham. Accordingly, Nimrod sent him to take care of his business but ordered him not to have relations with his wife, which Azar replied that he was too firm in his religion to do.

However, when he went to Babylon and visited his wife, he was unable to restain himself. He then fled with her to the town of Ur, between Kufah and Basrah. There he placed her in a cave, promising to bring her whatever supplies she needed.

After a time, when the astrologers' and soothsayers' prophecies were not fulfilled, Nimrod decided that they had been merely the lies of magicians. He then ordered his people to return home and soon forgot about the matter.

Meanwhile, Abraham (A) was born in the cave, where he spent his early years. "He grew so fast," the account continues, "that each day that passed was like a week, and each week like a month, and each month like a year" (Tabari/*H*, II:53). And he grew up without seeing any human beings besides his parents.

After some time, Azar consulted his companions about the matter of the son whom he had hidden, asking them if they thought there was anything to be feared from the king if he brought him out. When he was assured to the

[18] 6:74. In the Bible Azar is called Terah (Gen. 11:24-32, Josh.24:2).

contrary, he went to the cave and took the boy out. It is said that Abraham (A) was then about ten.

As he looked at the things around him, which were all new to him, Abraham (A) asked his father what they were. Azar then told him the names of things, saying that such-and-such was a camel, a cow, a horse or a sheep. Then Abraham (A), with the pure *fitrah* of one whose soundness of mind has been uncontaminated by his environment, said, "These things must have a Lord."

REFERENCES: Tabari/*Q*, "Ibrahim"; Tabari/*H*, II:53-54.

4. Enlightenment and Prophethood

And thus did We show Abraham the realm of the heavens and the earth, that he might be among the certain. (6:74)

It is only reasonable to suppose that during the time the boy was growing up in the cave, his father would have taught him about the religion of his people. Abraham (A) would thus have known about their various deities: the moon god, Sin or Nannar, whose statue was housed in a grand temple that he had never seen, and their worship of the sun, stars and various other gods. We can imagine him as an intensely serious lad, pondering precociously over the deepest of matters.

Indeed, it seems that, at a time of life when other children are occupied with childish pursuits, Abraham (A) had already come to his own conclusions about the idols his people worshipped. It is also possible that, impelled by an urgent passion for truth, he had already begun to discuss and debate the matter with his father, for the Qur'anic narrative suggests that at an early stage in his spiritual development, he said to his father Azar, **"Do you take idols[19] as gods? Indeed, I consider you and your people to be in clear error"** (6:74).

Yet it may be that, while the young Abraham (A) had realized the foolishness of worshipping objects made by human hands, he had not yet come to any conclusions about the worship of the heavenly bodies. Then, we are told, **when night fell upon him, he saw a star[21]** (6:76).

"This is my Lord!" (6:76) Abraham (A) exclaimed. Ibn 'Abbas (R) explains these words as meaning that the boy came out of the cave for the first time after sundown, and because this occurred at the end of the month, he saw the star before seeing the moon (Tabari/*H*, II:54). **But when it set, he said, "I do not like those that set"** (6:76), meaning, "I do not like a Lord who disappears."

---

[19]The word used here, ***"asnam,"*** means anything having a form that is worshipped. In this sense, perhaps it may be understood as including the heavenly bodies worshipped by Abraham's people.

[20]The word ***"kaukab"*** used here refers generally to stars and constellations, and specifically to the planet Venus. Perhaps Azar had told Abraham that the heavenly bodies were the gods of his people, but then, with his extraordinary clarity of heart and independence of mind, the future prophet, guided by his Lord, came to his own conclusions.

[21]The story of Abraham in the cave is also mentioned by Imam al-Ghazali (1058-1111 C.E.), one of the greatest thinkers and mystics the Muslim world has produced, who says:

> It has been said that he [Abraham] was a child when that happened to him. It is not farfetched that such a thought might occur, in his childhood, to one who was to be a Prophet. . . . As for seeing the star first, why it has been reported that Abraham, in his childhood, was kept in a cave and emerged from it only at night." (Al-Ghazali, ***Freedom and***

Then, when he saw the moon rising,[21] **he said, "This is my Lord!"** But when it too set, Abraham (A) reconsidered the matter. This disappearing object could not be his Lord or the Lord of anything else any more than the first. And with the innate understanding of his pure *fitrah*, he turned to the true Lord for enlightenment, saying, **"Unless my Lord guides me, I will surely be among the straying people"** (6:77).

These words are remarkable for two things. First, they reveal Abraham's absolute certainty of the existence of a supreme Lord — and not only that, but of a very personal Lord, **"*my* Lord."** Second, they show his clear awareness of the fact that those whom this Lord does not guide are astray, and that, without his Lord's guidance, he would be among them.

Presently day dawned. Then, when he saw the sun rising, he said, **"This is my Lord! This is greater!"** — meaning greater than anything else. But by the end of the day, **when it** too **set** (6:78), his understanding had resolved itself into an unshakeable conviction: that the disappearing objects which his people considered gods and worshipped were themselves finite, created things, appearing and disappearing, without stability and permanence.

Thus did Abraham (A) conclude that his people, with their worship of heavenly bodies and images made by their own hands, were in the gravest error and confusion.[22] There could be no God except the Creator of all things, *including* those heavenly bodies which were the greatest of all material objects and which his people unthinkingly worshipped in place of the One who had created them.

Abraham's pure heart was now firmly fixed upon his Lord with deep certainty. **"O my people,"** he said, **"indeed, I am clear of whatever you associate with God. I have surely turned my being toward the One who created the heavens and the earth, as one inclining toward truth, and I am not among the *mushrikin*"** (6:78-79).

And the heart of the young prophet-to-be, guided and illuminated by his Lord, expanded and deepened, as God revealed to him the secrets of His divine Essence, the mysteries of creation, and the great, all-wise workings of His Will, according to His words:

Fulfillment, p. 159)

However, another interpretation of Abraham's words, which does not mention the cave episode, has been given by classic commentators such as Ibn Kathir — namely, that Abraham uttered these words merely to show his people the fallacy of their belief in the divinity of heavenly bodies (Ibn Kathir/*T*, 6:78-79).

[22]It is evident that since Abraham had rejected the divinity of idols — including that of the chief god of his people, Sin or Nannar, the god of the moon — he would also reject the lordship of the entity that the idol was supposed to represent, the moon itself.

Thus did We show Abraham the realm of the heavens and the earth, that he might be among the certain.[23] (6:75)

Consequently, **he came to his Lord with a sound heart** (37:83-84), free of any trace of doubt or questioning. So deep and absolute was Abraham's faith **that when his Lord said to him, "Surrender!" he said, "I have surrendered to the Lord of the worlds"** (2:131).

Then, at some point during his spiritual growth, in order that his certainty might be quite complete and perfect, Abraham (A) made a request of his Lord. The deeply loving familiarity and intimacy that existed between him and his Maker is shown in his manner of making the request.

"My Lord," Abraham (A) said humbly, **"show me how You give life to the dead"** (2:260).

"Do you not have faith?" (2:260), came the divine response.

"Yes," Abraham (A) replied firmly, **"but that my heart may be satisfied"**[24] (2:260), meaning, "That is why I am asking this."

Then the most gracious Lord gave Abraham (A) the answer, but not in a direct fashion. Rather, He put forth a subtle metaphor concerning the process by which the dead will be recalled to life on the Last Day.

"Then take four birds and make them attached to you," God Most High instructed the young prophet. **"Then put part of them on each hill**

---

[23]This relates to what Imam al-Ghazali refers to as "the science of illuminations, which is the science of the inner aspects. . . . This knowledge is possessed by the Sincere and the Intimates of God." He continues:

> The science of illuminations is actually a light that appears in the heart when it is cleansed and purified of all reprehensible qualities. This light shines upon realities whose names have been heard before but which were never clearly understood, or only vaguely imagined.
>
> By this light a person aquires the true understanding, [first,] of the reality of the Person of Allah Most High; of His eternal and perfect attributes; of His works; of His purpose in creating this world and the next; and of His reason for preferring the next world over this.

Al-Ghazali then lists sixteen other aspects of Reality which are opened to the purified heart by illumination. Among them are the significance of prophethood and prophets; the meaning of divine revelation; the realm of the heavens and earth (relating to what is mentioned in 6:75); and the Hereafter, which includes everything pertaining to the Day of Judgment and Heaven and Hell, and the meeting and Presence of God Most High (Al-Ghazali, *Ihya 'Ulum a-Din, Kitab al 'Ilm* [*Revival of the Religious Sciences, Book One: The Book of Knowledge*]).

[24]The explanation of this verse puzzled Qur'anic commentators greatly, so much so that Ibn 'Abbas remarked, "There is no other verse in the Qur'an more puzzling to me than this one" (Ayoub/*Q*, I:265). Some commentators have suggested that Satan planted a trace of doubt in Abraham's heart, perhaps based on the Prophet's saying, "We are more entitled to be in doubt than Abraham when he said, '**My Lord, show me how You give life to the dead**'" (*Bukhari*,

and call them. They will come to you quickly. And know that God is Almighty and Wise" (2:260).

Some Qur'anic commentators have said that the four birds referred to were a peacock, a raven, a rooster and an eagle. Abraham (A) was commanded to cut these birds into pieces, mix together their flesh and feathers, and divide the mixture into four parts. These parts were to be put on four separate hills.

It is reported that Abraham (A) carried out the order, keeping the birds' heads with him, and then he called the birds to him. The parts of the four birds, including their feathers, then came together, and when he reattached their heads, they became as they had been before.

Through this deep parable, Abraham (A) was shown the limitless power of the One who creates and recreates as He wills. And through Abraham's question and the divine response, God Most High informs all mankind that, just as trained birds are attached to their master by invisible bonds, so, when He calls us on the Day of Resurrection, regardless of how long we may have been dead and the condition of our earthly remains, we will respond to Him and return to life, for

> **He who produced them the first time will give them life, and He is Knowing of all creation** (36:79) —

infinitely Powerful, unimaginably Aware, Informed and Wise.

REFERENCES: Qur'an: 2:131, 260; 6:74-79; 21:51; 37:83-84. Commentaries: Tabari/*Q*, "Ibrahim"; Tabari/*H*, II:54; Ibn Kathir/*T*, 2:260, 6:76-79; Ibn Kathir/*Q*, "Ibrahim"; Ayoub/*Q*, I:163-164, 264-265; Maududi/*Q*, 6:fn. 50; Asad/*Q*, 2:fn. 257.

4:591). But others have denied this as a possibility because doubt is related to disbelief, whereas prophets are protected from both greater and lesser sins.

Al-Tabari suggests that Abraham asked to see how God revives the dead, not because he doubted God's power but because he simply desired to know ***how*** He does so in order that he might have a clear understanding of the matter. Similarly, Ibn Kathir says that, although Abraham knew with certainty that God has the power to raise the dead, he desired to observe the process with his own eyes so that his certainty of knowledge might become the certainty of observation (***'ain al-yaqin***), and so God responded to his request and granted him this high privilege (Ibn Kathir/*Q*, "Ibrahim").

Another interpretation is that of al-Wahidi, who says, on the authority of Ibn 'Abbas, Sa'id ibn Jubayr and al-Suddi, that when God made Abraham His friend, the Angel of Death asked His permission to bring this good news to Abraham. The angel then came to Abraham and said, "I come to bring you glad tidings: God has made you His Friend!" At that, Abraham thanked God and asked the angel what the sign of this would be. The angel replied that it would be God's answering his prayers and raising the dead by his supplication. Abraham then said, **"My Lord, show me how You give life to the dead."** And when God answered, **"Do you not have faith?"** Abraham said," Yes, but only that my heart may rest at ease in the knowledge that You shall answer me when I pray to You and grant me what I ask for, and that You have taken me as a Friend" (Ayoub/*Q*, I:264-265).

5. Abraham Speaks to His People

And that was Our argument which We gave Abraham against his people. We raise in ranks whomever We will. Indeed, your Lord is Wise and Knowing. (6:83)

From Ibn 'Abbas (R), we learn that Azar earned his living by making idols, which he gave to his sons to sell for him. While selling them, however, the young Abraham (A) would say, "Who will buy something that will neither harm nor benefit him?" Consequently, while his brothers would go home after having sold their idols, Abraham (A) would return with all of his unsold. And he challenged not only his father but also his people concerning their worship of false gods.

In the Qur'an, God Most High reports a number of dialogues between Abraham (A) and his people. In what order and under what circumstances these dialogues took place, we do not know. However, they were all to lead up to the eventual climactic confrontation between the young prophet and the forces of falsehood.

"What do you worship?" (26:70, 37:86), Abraham (A) asked his father and his people on one occasion.

"We worship idols and remain devoted to them" (26:71), was the reply.

"Do they hear you when you call, or do they benefit you or do harm?" (26:72-73), the young prophet asked, trying to make his people reflect.

"No," they replied. **"But we found our fathers doing so"** (26:74), meaning that since they had inherited their religion from their forefathers, they were not prepared to question it.

"Then do you see what you have been worshipping, you and your fathers of old?" (26:75-76), Abraham (A) demanded. Then, in an eloquent statement, he made clear his position with regard to their gods, saying:

"Indeed, they are all enemies to me, except the Lord of the worlds, who created me. And it is He who guides me, and who gives me food and drink. And when I am ill, it is He who cures me, and who will cause me to die and then bring me to life, and who, I hope, will forgive me my faults on the Day of Recompense" (26:75-82).

Abraham (A) then addressed his Lord in one of the most beautiful prayers of all time:

"My Lord, grant me authority and join me with the righteous, and grant me a mention of honor among later generations, and make me among the inheritors of the Garden of bliss" (26:83-85). And, with a son's love, he pleaded for the misguided Azar, saying, **"And forgive my father. Indeed, he has been among the straying."**

Then, thinking of the Last Day and the two things on which people depend most in this life, wealth and children, he prayed, **"And do not disgrace me on the Day they are resurrected, the Day when neither wealth nor sons will avail, but only he who comes to God with a sound heart"** (26:86-89).

And Abraham (A) went among his people, calling them to their Lord and attempting to convince them of the foolishness of ascribing divinity to anything other than Him.

"Worship God and be mindful of Him," he would urge. **"That is best for you, if you but knew. In place of God, you worship mere idols and you fabricate falsehood. Indeed, those whom you worship besides God do not have power to provide for you. So seek provision from God and worship Him and be thankful to Him. To Him you will be returned. And if you deny** the Message, **nations have denied before you. And the duty of the messenger is only clear communication** of the Message"[25] (29:16-18).

On another occasion, when his people argued with him, Abraham (A) replied, **"Do you argue with me concerning God, while He has guided me? And I do not fear what you set up as partners with Him,"** he added, **"unless my Lord should will something"** (6:80). That is, no harm can possibly come to me from your false gods unless God wills to test me by them, and even in such a case, whatever happens to me will be from God, not from the lifeless, powerless statues or heavenly bodies that you worship.

"My Lord includes all things in His knowledge," he continued, meaning that God knows all about you and your idols, and about me and my situation. **"Will you not then bear this in mind? And how should I fear what you associate** with God," he continued, **"while you do not fear that you have associated with God that for which He has not revealed to you any authority?"** Then, with one final thrust at their false gods and false religion, he drove home his point: **"Then which of the two groups has more right to security, if you should know?"** (6:81).

Thus did God answer the arguments of those who worshipped false deities by the tongue of His young prophet, who spoke so passionately and fearlessly on behalf of his Lord.

REFERENCES: Qur'an: 6:80-81, 83; 26:70-89; 29:16-18. Commentary: Tabari/*H*, II:54-55.

---

[25]Commentators differ as to whether the last two sentences are part of Abraham's speech or words of support from God to the Holy Prophet (S).

6. The Destruction of the Idols

And previously We had certainly given Abraham his correctness [of understanding and conduct,] and We were well-acquainted with him.
(21:51)

A time came when, according to the account of Ibn 'Abbas (R), Azar informed Abraham (A) that his people would soon observe a festival. And he invited his son to attend the celebration so that he might learn to like their religion.

An idea then presented itself to Abraham (A) for dealing with the idols, and so he agreed to go along. His plan was an extraordinarily bold and clever one, calculated to show the idol-worshippers the error of their beliefs so conclusively that they could no longer deny the truth. It was also such a daring plan that it might well cost him his life. Nevertheless, he resolved upon it as the most powerful argument he could devise against their false gods.

In order to carry out his plan, Abraham (A) would have to have an excuse for staying behind while the rest of his people went off to attend the celebration. Initially, however, on the day of the festival, Abraham (A) set off with some companions as if to attend the ceremonies.

On the way, he challenged them concerning their worship of idols. **"What do you worship?"** he asked. **"Is it false deities other than God you desire?"** meaning, "You know very well that the Creator is God, the Lord of all things, so why do you ascribe divinity to others?" He then asked, **"Then what then is your thought about the Lord of the worlds?"** (37:85-87).

At the same time, he attacked the foolish notion of worshipping something made by human hands, asking, **"What are these statues to which you are so devoted?"** (21:51-52).

"We found our fathers worshippers of them" (21:53), his companions replied lamely.

"You have certainly been in obvious error, you and your fathers" (21:54), Abraham (A) proclaimed forthrightly.

"Have you brought us the truth, or are you among the jokers?" (21:55), his companions demanded, meaning that his suggestion that they and their fathers were misguided and in error was too far-fetched to be taken seriously.

"No," Abraham (A) replied, **"but rather your Lord is the Lord of the heavens and the earth, who created them, and I am among those who testify to that"** (21:56).

And he cast a glance at the stars. Then, according to the account of Ibn 'Abbas (R), he flung himself down, saying to his companions, **"Indeed, I am ill"** (37:88-89), meaning, "My foot is in pain."

His companions remained with him for a while as he lay there, sitting by his feet, but presently **they turned away from him, departing** (37:90). And as the last two left, he said audibly, **"And by God, I will surely plot against your idols after you have turned and gone away!"** (21:57).

Ibn 'Abbas' account continues:

> Abraham went back to the house of the gods, which was in a great hall. Opposite the entrance to the hall was a great idol, and at his side a smaller one, and next to him a smaller one, and so on down to the entrance to the hall. The people had prepared food and placed it before the gods, saying, "When we come back the gods will have blessed our food, and we will eat." (Tabari/*H*, II:55)

"Do you not eat?" Abraham (A) mocked, observing the food in front of the idols. Naturally, there was no response. **"What is it with you that you do not speak?"** (37:91-92), he demanded.

And he turned upon them a blow with his **right hand** (37:93), meaning with all his strength, hacking at them with an axe. **Then he made them into fragments, excepting a big one among them, that**, when the people came back, **they would return to it** (21:58). It is reported that he cut the hands off some, the feet off others, and the heads off still others. When he was done, he hung the axe around the neck of the largest idol and left.

Later, when the people came to take back their food, they found their idols smashed and broken upon the ground. **"Who has done this to our gods?"** they asked one another in horror. **"Indeed, he is among the wrong-doers!"** (21:59).

"We heard a youth mention them who is called Abraham" (21:60), reported those who had heard the last words Abraham had spoken as they departed for the celebration.

"Then bring him in front of the eyes of the people," came the demand, **"that they may testify"** (21:61) — either meaning so that they might testify that he was the one who had done this deed, or that they might testify as to what should be done to the destroyer of their idols.

Then they came toward him, hastening (37:94). **"Have you done this to our gods, O Abraham?"** (21:62), they clamored.

We have seen how extremely daring and courageous the young prophet was. At the same time, he was also brilliantly intelligent, a match for anyone. This is shown not only by the extraordinarily clever plan he had just carried out but also by the reply he now gave to his accusers, by which he neither denied or admitted his guilt. Instead, to shock them into the realization of the falsity of their position, he replied, **"Rather, this, the biggest of them, did it, so ask *them*, if they are able to speak!"** (21:63).

Abraham's words hit home. The unbelievers now **turned back to themselves** (21:64) in confusion and embarrassment, unable to find words with which to reply to him. **"Indeed, you yourselves are the wrong-doers"** (21:64), they admitted shamefacedly. But when they had time to consider the matter further, they reversed themselves,[26] saying to Abraham, **"You already knew that these idols do not speak"** (21:64-65).

"Do you worship that which you yourselves carve," Abraham (A) demanded, **"while God created you and whatever you do?"** (37:95-96). And he hammered home his point, saying, **"Do you worship, besides God, that which neither benefits you in the least nor harms you? Shame on you and on what you worship instead of God! Will you not then use reason?"** (21:66-67).

But the response of his people was only that they said, **"Kill him or burn him!"** (29:24). And the outcry resounded among them: **"Burn him and support your gods, if you are to act!"** (21:68).

REFERENCES: Qur'an: 21:51-68; 29:24; 37:85-96. Commentaries: Tabari/*Q*, "Ibrahim"; Tabari/*H*, II:55-57; Ibn Kathir/*T*, 37:91-93, 21:64-67; Ibn Kathir/*Q*, "Ibrahim"; Maududi/*Q*, 37:fn. 48; Asad/*Q*, 21:fn. 63; Ali/*Q*, fn. 2722.

---

[26]The literal meaning of the Qur'anic wording is, "They were turned upside down upon their heads," an Arabic idiom denoting reversal of position.

7. Nimrod Disputes with Abraham

Have you not considered the one who disputed with Abraham about his Lord because God had granted him kingship? (2:258)

Perhaps it was at this time that Abraham (A) came face to face with the powerful tyrant king, Nimrod or Namrud, whose name is often used in Arabic to mean a tyrant or oppressor.

Over the years, since there was no one above him and everyone was under him, Nimrod's unchallenged ego had grown to such monstrous proportions that he imagined himself to be God on earth. The god-king now called into his presence the young citizen of his domain, accused of destroying the idols of his people, and began to question him about God. The inspired prophet replied to the proud, invincible ruler on behalf of his Lord, fearlessly pointing out the contrast between the infinite glory and majesty of the Creator and Sustainer of the universes and Nimrod's minute, temporal bit of earthly power and pomp.

In response, the Nimrod began to dispute with Abraham (A), imagining himself to be equal to the Creator **because God had granted him kingship**. Thus it was that when Abraham (A) said, **"My Lord is the One who gives life and causes death"** (2:258), Nimrod retorted,

"I give life and cause death" (2:258).

At that, it is said, he had two men brought forward whom he had condemned to death. One of them he spared, while the other he had executed as a proof of his words, as if to say that God may be the Lord in the heavens, but *my* law and authority rules in this land.

Then God, the Lord of Majesty and Honor, granted His prophet a decisive argument with which to defeat the earthly king who had set himself up as His rival in power and authority. **"Indeed, God brings up the sun from the East,"** Abraham (A) said simply. **"So bring it up from the West!"** (2:258).

At these words, the proud ruler was nonplussed and speechless, unable to contend with the powerful logic of truth. He could not dispute the fact that anyone claiming to be God must have power and control over creation equal to that of the Creator. Thus, God says,

Then the one who disbelieved was confounded. And God does not guide the wrong-doing people. (2:258)

It is related by the Prophet's Companion, Salman al-Farisi (R), that Nimrod starved two lions so that they might devour the Friend of God, Abraham. However, when the lions came to him, they stood before him in reverence, then licked him and prostrated at his feet (Akili/*B*, p. 204).

REFERENCES: Qur'an: 2:258. Commentaries: Tabari/*Q*, "Ibrahim"; Tabari/*H*, II:57-58, 106; Ibn Kathir/*Q*, "Ibrahim"; Ayoub/*Q*, I:258; Maududi/*Q*, 2:fn. 291; Akili/*B*, p. 204.

8. The Burning of Abraham

But the response of his people was only that they said, "Kill him or burn him," but God saved him from the fire. Indeed, in that are signs for a people who believe. (29:24)

Abraham's people had had enough of the man who had rebelled against their gods. **"Build a structure for him and throw him into the blaze!"** (37:97), they clamored. For although some among them certainly recognized the truth of his words, they struck at the very foundations of their false beliefs and established way of life. And since the truth was unbearable to them, the one who proclaimed it would have to go!

Accordingly, Abraham (A) was imprisoned and the people went out to gather fuel for the fire. It is said that an enormous pile of wood was collected and then set ablaze, although for burning a person only a small amount of wood is needed. But through that fire, its makers intended to burn not merely the man called Abraham, but the truth, which they refused to accept — to get rid of it once and for all, or so they imagined.

It is reported that as Abraham (A) was being bound and shackled before being thrown into the fire, the angel Gabriel (A) came to him. "O Abraham, do you have any need?" he asked.

"Yes, but not from you," was the steadfast reply (Ibn Kathir/*Q*, "Ibrahim").

It is said that an especially wicked unbeliever devised a catapault by which the noble prophet was hurled into the midst of the roaring fire. Ibn 'Abbas (R) states that the last words Abraham (A) spoke before he was flung into the blaze were, "*Hasbuna-Llah wa ni'am-l-Wakil* — God is sufficient for us, and how excellent a Protector!" (*Bukhari*, 6:86, 6:87). And all the gathered people watched, waiting for the fire to consume him to ashes.

But the Lord of creation, the Guardian and Protector of believers, commanded, **"O fire, be coolness and peace for Abraham"** (21:69). Concerning this, Ibn 'Abbas and Abu 'Aliyah said, "If God had not said, **'Be coolness and peace for Abraham,'** Abraham would have been harmed by its cold" (Ibn Kathir/*Q*, "Ibrahim). That is, says Ibn 'Abbas, "If its cold had not been followed by peace, Abraham would have died of the cold. Every fire on earth that day went out, thinking that it was the one that was meant" (Tabari/*H*, II:59:-60).

And Abraham (A) sat, in the midst of the inferno, in a heavenly garden provided by his beloved Lord for whose sake he was enduring this awesome trial, in safety and peace and total satisfaction with Him. It is said that the angel of shade sat at his side, comforting him, and indeed, the Prophet (S) mentioned that the fire burned nothing on Abraham (A) except the ropes that bound him (Al-Houry/*H*, #959).

Thus it was that, by one of the greatest miracles of all time, Abraham the Friend of God (A) emerged from the fire safe and unharmed. Ibn Kathir summarizes the story thus:

> Then they dug a deep pit and collected wood for several days and put it in the pit and set fire to it, and when it became very hot and flames reached the sky, they caught hold of Abraham (A) and put him in a catapult and threw him into the fire. But God turned it into a beautiful garden. He remained there and after several days he came out of it as whole as he had gone in.
>
> Because of this and similar sacrifices, he was granted the position of leadership [of mankind], and all the religions of the world honor, respect and love him. (Ibn Kathir/ *T*, 29:24)

And Abraham(A) stood before his people and once again confronted them with the truth, neither frightened nor intimidated by their attempt to destroy him.

"You have adopted idols in place of God only out of liking among yourselves during the life of this world," he charged. He then warned them that although their false religion might seem to be to their advantage for the moment, **"On the Day of Resurrection, you will deny each other and curse each other, and your dwelling-place will be the Fire and you will not have any helpers"** (29:25).

REFERENCES: Qur'an: 21:68-69; 29:24-25; 37:97. Commentaries: Tabari/*H*, II:58-61; Ibn Kathir/*Q*, "Ibrahim"; Akili/*B*, pp. 20-21.

9. ABRAHAM'S EMIGRATION

He [Abraham] said, "Indeed, I shall go to my Lord; He will guide me. (37:99)

Perhaps it may have been at this time that Abraham (A) tried one last time to reach his father's heart.

"O my father, why do you worship that which does not hear or does not see and does not benefit you in the least?" he asked, out of a son's deep love and concern. **"O my father, there has surely come to me something of knowledge that has not come to you, so follow me. I will guide you to a correct path** (19:42-43).

"O my father," Abraham (A) continued earnestly, **"do not worship Satan"** — that is, by making idols and rendering other services to the cause of evil. **"Indeed, Satan is a rebel to the Most Merciful. O my father, indeed, I fear that a punishment from the Most Merciful will touch you, so you become a companion to Satan"** (19:43-45) both in this world and in Hell.

"Do you detest my gods, O Abraham?" Azar retorted angrily. **"If you do not leave off, I will surely stone you, so avoid me for a long time!"** — or, according to the interpretation of some commentators, **"forever"** (19:46).

The parting of their ways had come. After such absolute, final rejection, there was nothing more Abraham (A) could do. ***"Salamun 'alaika*** **— peace be upon you,"** he said. Nonetheless, out of respect for his father, he added: **"I shall ask forgiveness for you from My Lord. Indeed, He is ever gracious to me. And I will withdraw from you and whatever you call upon apart from God, and I will call upon my Lord. I hope that I will not be unfortunate** — that is, unblessed and unresponded to — **in my supplication to my Lord"** (19:47-48).

According to Ibn 'Abbas and other commentators, the one who had argued with Abraham (A) about his Lord — that is, Nimrod — now gave orders that he be exiled from the city. Thus, by the decree of the Best of Planners, Abraham's mission in Ur came to an end.

"Indeed, I shall go to my Lord," he announced. **"He will guide me"** (37:99). He then cut himself off forever from everything that his people stood for and worshipped by declaring to his father and his people, **"Indeed, I am clear of that which you worship"** — meaning acquitted of any blame or association with your gods — **"apart from Him who created me, and He will surely guide me"** (43:26-27). And Abraham made his witnessing to the Oneness of the partnerless Creator and the falsity of all deities but Him **a word remaining among his descendants, that they might return to it** (43:28).

But Abraham (A) was not destined to leave his birthplace alone, for God says, as a preface to the speech that follows,

> **There has already been an excellent example for you in Abraham and those with him, when they said to their people . . .** (60:4).

The early Qur'anic commentators differ as to the identity of **those with him**. Some say that the only believers alive on the face of the earth at that time were Abraham (A), his wife Sarah (Sara), and Lot, the son of his brother Haran, about whom God says, **And Lot believed in him** (29:26). According to another opinion, some of Abraham's people became his followers after seeing what God had done for him, although they were still afraid of Nimrod and the people of their community.[27]

And what was it these believers said that God Most High praises so highly? It was the following declaration to their unbelieving people, which has been memorialized in the Book of God:

"Indeed, we are clear of you and of whatever you worship apart from God. We have rejected you" — this is said to refer to their idols — **"and there has arisen eternal enmity and hatred between us and you"** — the worshippers of those idols — **"until you believe in God alone"** (60:4). The sole exception to this was Abraham's saying to his father, **"I will certainly ask forgiveness for you."** But, ever truthful, he added: **"But I have no power to do anything for you against God"**[28] (60:4).

---

[27]This seems more probable because the words, **There has already been an excellent example for you in Abraham and those with him . . . There has certainly been an excellent example for you in them** (60:4, 6), suggests that there were several or even many believers, who were united in making a public statement of their dissociation from their people and their false gods.

[28]Although it is not permissible for a Muslim to ask for God's forgiveness for one who is a polytheist or a declared unbeliever (9:113), the Qur'an contains several references to Abraham's praying for forgiveness for his father, an idol-worshipper, an enemy of God, and a champion of the false religion. These are contained in the words of Abraham above, after his father threatened to stone him, **"I shall ask forgiveness for you from My Lord. Indeed, He is ever gracious to me"** (19:47); the prayer of Abraham, cited earlier, **"And forgive my father. He is surely among the straying"** (26:87); Abraham's promise above, **"I will certainly ask forgiveness for you, but I have no power to do anything for you against God"** (60:4); and God's saying, **And Abraham's asking forgiveness for his father was only because of a promise he had made him** (9:114).

From the last of these verses, it is evident that Abraham continued to pray for his father because of the promise he had made him, until, **when it became clear to him that he [his father] was an enemy to God, he dissociated himself from him** (9:114) and stopped praying for him, despite being extremely tender-hearted and forbearing. As for Abraham's prayer which we will report later, **"Our Lord, forgive me and my parents and the believers on the Day when the Accounting is established"** (14:41), it is reported that he uttered it prior to realizing that his praying for his father was unacceptable.

Thus did Abraham (A) and the believers surrender their wills to God, the Guide and Protector, resting all their affairs upon Him. **"Our Lord,"** they said, **"upon You we rely and to You we turn, and to You is the destination. Our Lord, do not make a test for those who disbelieve, and forgive us, our Lord. Indeed, it is You who are the Almighty, the Wise"** (60:5). And God Most High concludes this chapter in the life of Abraham (A) and his fellow-believers by reiterating,

> **There has certainly been an excellent example for you in them, for anyone whose hope is in God and the Last Day. And whoever turns away, then indeed God is the Free of all need, the Praiseworthy. (60:6)**

And putting all his trust in his beneficent Lord who was directing his every word and every step, Abraham (A) departed from his birthplace, saying, **"I will surely emigrate to my Lord. Indeed, He is the Almighty, the Wise"** (29:26).

The idol-worshippers had wickedly plotted to kill their prophet by the most awful death imaginable, but God had saved him and brought their plot to nothing. As for Nimrod, his arrogance and rebellion against God the Exalted was to continue for a long time — for four hundred years, it is said — in spite of God's leniency to him. The examples and proofs of His Lordship that God had shown him had only made him more obstinate in wrong-doing.[29]

Eventually the tyrant king built a high tower to heaven, the Tower of Babel, so that he might look at the God of Abraham, but the One who arranges all affairs in the earth and the heavens destroyed it. Many hundreds of years later, God Most High was to reveal through His Last Prophet (S) a verse that is said by al-Tabari to refer to Nimrod's tower:

> **But God came at their structure from the foundations, so the roof fell upon them from above them, and the punishment came upon them from whence they did not perceive. (16:26)**

---

[29]Both al-Tabari and Ibn Kathir mention a report that once, when Nimrod assembled his armies at dawn, God sent upon them swarms of mosquitoes. The mosquitoes ate the flesh of the soldiers and drank their blood, so that nothing was left except bones. And although Nimrod was spared this, a mosquito (obviously no ordinary one) flew into his nostril and it remained inside his skull for four hundred years. It is said that it gnawed at his brain, causing him such anguish that he could get relief only when people hit him on the head with hammers, and the most compassionate person in his sight was one who beat him over the head with his clasped hands (Tabari/*H*, II:106-108; Ibn Kathir/*T*, 16:26; Ayoub/*Q*, I:257-258). The moral of this story is that God Almighty has at His disposal every means of harm or benefit, both ordinary and extraordinary, for His servants. He can even create new, unheard-of means. Consequently, we must fear His anger and His punishment for wrong-doing.

Historical records bear out the fact that after the emigration of Abraham (A) and the believers, Nimrod's kingdom was afflicted by continuous disasters, according to God's words, **And they intended to frame a plot for him** [Abraham] **but We made them the greatest losers** (21:70) and **We made them the most debased** (37:98). The capital city, Ur, fell and Nimrod was captured, along with the idol of the chief god, Nannar, as a result of which the people of Ur completely lost faith in the false gods that had failed to protect them from ruin.

REFERENCES: Qur'an: 9:114; 14:41; 16:26; 19:42-48; 21:70; 26:87; 29:26; 37:98-99; 43:26-28; 60:4-6. Commentaries: Tabari/*Q*, "Ibrahim"; Tabari/*H*, II:61-62, 105-108; Ibn Kathir/*T*, 16:261, 29:26, 9:114; Ayoub/*Q*, I:257-258; Maududi/*Q*, 6:fn. 52.

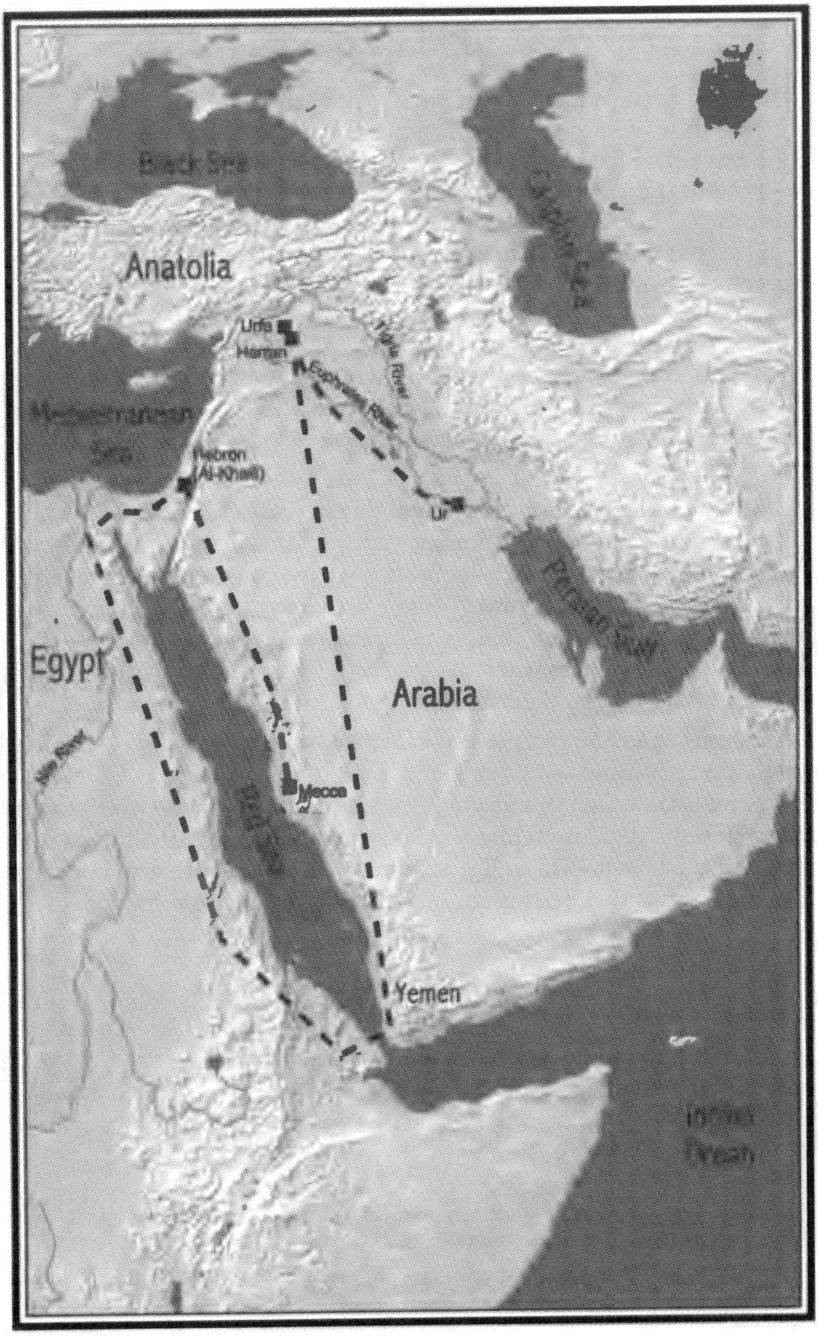

Map 7. The travels of Abraham

10. SARAH

Abraham migrated with Sarah. With her, he entered a city in which there was a king among kings or a tyrant among tyrants. Then he sent to him [Abraham, saying,] "Send her to me," and he sent her. He then started up toward her her, whereupon she arose and made ***wudu'***[30] and prayed, and she said, "O God, if I have believed in You and in Your messenger [Abraham], then do not give the tyrant mastery over me!" Then he made a sound that caused him to thrash about with his legs. (*Bukhari*, 9:82)

It reported that after journeying for a time, Abraham (A) and the small group who accompanied him reached Harran, according to God's saying, **And We delivered him and Lot to the land which We had blessed for all mankind** (21:71).

This land is what was known in earlier times as ***Bilad ash-Sham,*** the land of Syria. Not to be confused with present-day Syria, the Sham of old comprised the territory that was known as Palestine prior to the partitioning of the former Ottoman Empire by the Allies after World War I into present-day states of Syria, Lebanon, Jordan and Israel. This is an area especially blessed by and dear to God — the land of Abraham and the prophets descended from him, peace be upon them all, a land of unique spiritual significance and sanctity.

Abraham (A) and his party settled in Harran, which to this day is connected through local traditions with the Friend of God,[31] for as long as God willed. Then, at some later time, Abraham (A), accompanied by Sarah, went toward Yemen. However, because Yemen was in the grip of famine, they did not settle there but turned northward to Egypt. And it was in Egypt that an important incident in Abraham's life occurred, an incident involving his wife Sarah — and a lie.

Now, Abraham's nature was so totally upright nature that he was ready to give his life for the pleasure of His beloved Lord. From this, it might be expected that he would never lie under any circumstances — or, if he did, it would be purely for the sake of God and therefore excusable. But a lie is a lie, regardless. Thus it was that the Prophet (S) was to say, many centuries later,

---

[30]The ablution for prayers (*salat*), which was practiced and taught by the prophets both before and after the time of Prophet Muhammad (S).

[31]The Turkish city of Urfa and a mountain in its vicinity called Namrud Dağ (Nimrod Mountain) are both strongly connected by local tradition to Abraham. While most commentators assert that Nimrod was the king of Ur, others believe him to have been the king of Harran, which is also suggested by local traditions.

"Abraham did not lie except three times" (*Bukhari*, 4:577), and he also mentioned the matter indirectly in several *ahadith* which we will report shortly.

The incidents involving these lies are reported by the Prophet's Companion, Abu Hurayrah (R), in the following narrative:

> Abraham, peace and blessings be upon him, did not tell but three lies. Two of them were for the sake of God, the Possessor of Honor and Glory: his saying, **"Indeed, I am ill"** [39:89], and his saying [after destroying the idols], **"Rather, this, the biggest of them, did it, so ask them, if they are able to speak!"** [21:63].
>
> The third occurred one day when, while he was with Sarah, they came upon one of the greatest of tyrants, [namely, the Egyptian king of that time]. Then it was said to him, "This man is accompanied by a woman who is one of the most beautiful of people."
>
> Then he sent to him [Abraham] and asked him about her, saying, "Who is she?"
>
> He said, "My sister."
>
> He [Abraham] then went to Sarah and said, "O Sarah, there are no believers on the face of the earth but me and you, and this person asked me [about you] and I told him that you are my sister, so do not contradict me."
>
> He [the king] then sent for Sarah, and when she went in to him, he was about to take hold of her with his hand but he was hindered from moving. Thereupon he said, "Pray to God for me and I will not harm you," and she prayed to God and he was released.
>
> He then tried to take hold of her a second time but his hand was hindered from moving as before, or more strongly. He then said to Sarah, "Pray to God for me and I will not harm you," and she prayed and he was released.
>
> Afterwards he called one of his guards and said, "Indeed, you have not brought me a human, you have brought me but a devil!" Then he gave her Hagar as a servant.
>
> Sarah then went to him [Abraham] while he was standing in prayer, and he gestured with his hand [as if asking] what had happened. She said, "God has thrown back the scheme of the unbeliever or immoral one upon his own neck and has given Hagar for service." (*Bukhari*, 4:578)

We may wonder why Abraham (A) found it necessary to say that Sarah was his sister instead of his wife. The primary reason may be that, since the prophets acted and spoke according to divine inspiration, he was directed to do so by his Lord. And indeed, in one respect his words were true, for as a believing woman, Sarah was his sister-in-faith, as mentioned in the Prophet's saying,

"Abraham said of his wife, 'This is my sister,' and that was [his sister] in God" (*Bukhari*, 9:82). Moreover, besides being his wife, Sarah was also his cousin, the daughter of his father's brother Haran, which in some cultures is considered similar to a sister.[332] But still another possible reason is suggested by the early commentators.

According to the rules prevailing in the ancient world, a man (even a ruler) would not take the wife of a man while her husband was alive. Instead, he would first kill the husband and then take possession of his widow. Consequently, if the king had known that Abraham was Sarah's husband, he might easily have had him killed in order to possess her, whereas if he believed Sarah to be his sister, he would not have needed to eliminate Abraham in order to take her.

Yet it is not imaginable that Abraham (A), who had felt no fear in the face of death by burning, would have lied in order to save his life,[33] for to one so near to God, truth and honor are dearer than life itself. Moreover, his implicit reliance upon God precludes such a possibility. The matter must therefore have another explanation.

It has been suggested that, although Abraham (A) never doubted the fact that God, the Guardian and Protector of all things, was able to protect Sarah as He had protected himself, nevertheless, as her husband and brother-in-faith, he was responsible for doing everything he could to save her. And although Abraham (A) was utterly powerless against the lustful king, still, as long as God permitted him to live, he could do one thing for his wife: support her spiritually and pray for her. Thus it was that when Sarah returned to him after having been released by the king, he was standing in prayer, prepared, as before this ordeal, to be fully repsonsible for her.

---

[32]In Urdu, for example, this relationship would be termed "cousin-sister".

[33]This account differs markedly from what is reported in the Book of Genesis, which states that Abraham (Abram) took Sarah (Sarai) to live in Egypt because of famine in Palestine. Knowing that Sarah would be seized by Egypt's pharaoh, Abraham said to her, "I know what a beautiful woman you are. When the Egyptians see you, they will say, 'This is his wife.' Then they will kill me but will let you live. Say you are my sister, so that I will be treated well for your sake and my life will be spared because of you." Sarah was then taken into the king's harem with her husband's blessing and permission, and Pharaoh "treated Abram well for her sake, and Abram acquired sheep and cattle, male and female donkeys, menservants and maidservants, and camels." Afterwards, when "the Lord inflicted serious diseases on Pharoah and his household" because of his sinful relationship with Sarah, the king reproached Abraham for having said that she was his sister, sending him away with her and with all the property he had acquired due to Sarah's relationship with Pharaoh (Gen. 12:10-17). This is but one example of the striking contrast between the Biblical and Qur'anic understandings of the character and exalted rank of those whom God Most High honored with divine revelation and prophethood.

Thus the matter ended. But since Abraham (A), the Friend of God, was one of the most truthful and sincere human beings of all times, he considered himself to have been forever tarnished by the lie he had told, in addition to the two previous lies, even though the first two were strategems in the war between truth and falsehood, and the third was to save his pure, believing wife from abandonment on the face of the earth.

Abraham's deep shame at these lies is made clear in the *ahadith* of intercession which we mentioned earlier in connection with Adam and Noah (A), in which the distressed believers will ask the greatest of all the prophets to intercede for them with God on the Day of Resurrection. You may recall the Prophet's saying that they will first go to Adam, who will decline because of his mistake and advise them to go to Noah, who will likewise decline because of his mistake and advise them to go to Abraham.

> Then they will go to Abraham and say, "O Abraham, you are God's prophet and His Friend from the earth. Intercede for us with your Lord! Do you not see what state we are in?"
>
> Then he will say to them, "Indeed, my Lord is angry today as He has never been angry before nor will ever be angry afterwards. And indeed, I told three lies" (and here the sub-narrator, Abu Hayan, mentioned them). "Myself! Myself! Myself! Go to someone else; go to Moses."[34]

Moses will advise them to go to Jesus, who will advise them to go to Muhammad (S), who will accept their plea and make fervent intercession for them, which will be accepted liberally by his Lord (*Bukhari*, 6:236).

What was the divine wisdom of God's sending Abraham (A) and Sarah to Egypt and subjecting the two of them to such an awesome trial? Only He knows. But a clue lies in the fact that, because of what occurred in Egypt, the Egyptian Hagar (Arabic, Hajar) became part of Abraham's household, with all that was to follow from that fact.[35]

This incident again reflects Abraham's total trust and reliance upon his Lord, while at the same time doing whatever a powerless human being can do in

---

[34]The same theme is repeated in a number of other *ahadith* (*Bukhari*, 4:581, 9:507, 9:532C; *Muslim*, 373, 377-378, 380), with the following variations: In *Bukhari*, 9:507, Noah says, "But go to Abraham, the Friend of the Most Merciful." When the believers go to Abraham, he says, "That is not for me," and mentions to them the mistakes he made; in *Bukhari*, 9:532C, it is "the three false statements [that he made]." In *Muslim*, 373, it is, "He will recall the mistake he made and will feel ashamed of his Lord because of it." In *Muslim*, 380, Adam says, "Go to my son Abraham, the Friend of God," without mentioning Noah, and Abraham says, "I am not the person for that. I was only the Friend from the past. Go to Moses." The remaining parts of these *ahadith* will be cited later in connection with Moses and Jesus, peace be upon them.

in the face of evil and tyranny. And while Abraham's resistance involved telling a lie or a partial truth, this lie was told for the protection of his wife and the carrying out of his responsibility toward her, while harming no one.

This makes clear to us what the twin strategies of a believer should be: first, relying upon God with absolute trust for the outcome of all affairs, and second, doing whatever is in our power, especially through prayer, to help ourselves or others. And in the story of Sarah and the king of Egypt, we witness another miracle in the life of Abraham, may God's best blessings and peace be upon him.

REFERENCES: *Bukhari*, 4:578, 3:803, 4:578, 6:236, 7:21, 9:82; Tabari/*H*, II:62-65; Ibn Kathir/*Q*, "Ibrahim".

---

[35]The fact that Hagar was an Egyptian is clear from the following ***hadith:*** A Companion of the Prophet named al-Zuhri reported that the Prophet (S) once said, "When you conquer Egypt" (as he knew by divine inspiration would happen in the near future), "treat its people well, for they can claim our protection and kinship." And when al-Zuhri was asked what the Prophet (S) meant by this "kinship," he replied that Hagar, the mother of Ishmael, was of their stock (Ibn Ishaq/*M*, p. 4). This is confirmed by the fact that at the end of the narrative of Abu Hurayrah cited earlier concerning Sarah and the king of Egypt, Abu Hurayrah referred to the descent of the Arabs from Hagar by saying, "That [Hagar] was your mother, O Bani Ma'i-s-Sama' [meaning the Arabs] (*Bukhari*, 4:578, 7:21).

PART THREE

11. Hagar and Ishmael

[Abraham prayed,] "My Lord, grant me [a son] from among the righteous," so We gave him the good tidings of a forbearing boy.
(37:100-101)

After leaving Egypt, Abraham (A), accompanied by Sarah and her Egyptian maid-servant Hagar, returned to Syria and settled there permanently.

Years passed, no one knows how many. Still no child was born to the prophet and his wife, who had by then both become elderly. And eventually, at Sarah's suggestion, Abraham (A) married Hagar, perhaps in the hope that she would be able to bear him a successor in prophethood.

"My Lord, grant me a son **from among the righteous"** (37:100), Abraham (A) prayed. And in response, the Most Gracious Lord gave Abraham (A) the good tidings of a son, informing him, even before that son's birth, that he would be **a forbearing boy** (37:101). And thus, by the working of the divine Will, Hagar, the younger, newer wife became the mother of a son, Ishmael (Arabic, Isma'il), while the elderly Sarah remained painfully barren and childless.

Echoing the account contained in Gen. 16:4-5, 21:10, some Qur'anic commentators have asserted that Sarah then became so jealous of Hagar and her son that she made Hagar's life miserable, and that for this reason Abraham (A) removed them both from his house. However, Ibn 'Abbas, the most authoritative of the commentators, refrained from making such judgmental statements.

All that can be stated with authority is that, while Ishmael was still a nursing baby, Abraham (A) left home with him and his mother. And while it has been claimed that he did this because of Sarah's jealousy, we must be careful about accepting such a simplistic explanation for Abraham's action, for it is unimaginable that a prophet, especially one of Abraham's distinguished rank, would be under the domination of his wife or make such a grave decision due to her insistence. Therefore, while Sarah's feelings may have been something of a factor (as the report which we will cite shortly from Ibn 'Abbas suggests), it cannot have been the real reason for Abraham's action.

It is clear from what follows that Abraham (A) did what he did, as he did everything else, by the command of his Lord. Perhaps this may have been one of the divine **"words"** that are meant by God's saying,

And when Abraham was tried by his Lord through words [of command] and he carried them out (2:124).

These **"words"** or commands in turn constituted that part of the divine plan, which embraces all things visible and hidden, material and spiritual, which Abraham (A) had been destined to carry out. Within this plan, all things are so inseparably interwoven that each depends on whatever precedes and follows and surrounds it. Thus, while we may be able to discern something of the obvious reasons, material causes, or external factors at work in Abraham's story, at the same time, unseen, secret causes were likewise at work, as will become clear from what follows.

REFERENCE: Tabari/*H*, II:65, 69, 71-72.

12. The Settling of Abraham's Family in Mecca

"Our Lord, I have settled some of my descendants in a valley without vegetation near Your Sacred House." (14:37)

The account of what then occurred has come to us in two well-known narratives reported by Ibn 'Abbas (R),[36] which follow one another in one of the two most authoritative of all the collections of *ahadith*, *Sahih al-Bukhari*. In order to form the most complete, detailed narrative possible, we have alternated or interwoven these two narratives here.

Ibn 'Abbas (R) begins his first account by saying:

> The first among women to use a belt was Umm Ishmael [Ishmael's mother]. She used a belt to wipe out her tracks from Sarah (*Bukhari*, 4.583),

while his second account begins:

> After what happened between Abraham and his wife, he left with Ishmael and Umm Ishmael. They had with them a waterskin containing water. Umm Ishmael would drink water from the waterskin so that her milk would increase for her child. (*Bukhari*, 4:584)

What was the destination of this tiny group of travelers? By the order of their Lord, it was a barren spot several hundred miles distant, which was later to become the city of Mecca. To reach this destination, Abraham, Hagar and their infant son would have traveled for many days, journeying southward to a site that God Most High would make known to Abraham (A).

Now, anyone who has been in Mecca can testify to the fact that it is an extraordinarily bleak, barren place. The city sits in a bowl-shaped depression ringed around by high, black, jagged lava peaks. Unlike some other parts of the Arabian peninsula where vegetation is found, Mecca is a place where nothing grows naturally except the most meager sorts of desert plants. In summer, the sun blazes fiercely a sky resembling bright blue steel, as the daytime temperatures soar up to 120° F (49° C). There is very little rainfall, and when the wind blows, the sky is overcast with haze, the air full of swirling dust. And it was at this inhospitable, terrifyingly lonely and uninhabited spot, with no shelter but an overspreading tree, no source of water nor any defense against predators, that God commanded Abraham (A) to leave his wife and long-desired infant son.

---

[36]These two accounts are contained in *Bukhari*, 4.583 and 4:584. Narratives such as these are known as ***mursal ahadith*** — that is, they go back to a Companion of the Prophet rather than to the Prophet (S) himself. However, in the two reports cited here, Ibn 'Abbas often breaks into his own narrative and quotes directly from the Prophet's tongue, as indicated in our text.

But appearances may often mask realities. Despite its being outwardly a terribly bleak, desolate spot where no life flourished, the spiritual reality of the place was entirely different, for the divine wisdom had ordained it to be nothing less than the spiritual center of this planet.

This was the same spot to which Adam (A) had come thousands of years earlier and upon which God Most High had sent down His Sacred House, with its jewel from Paradise, and around which the Ark of Noah (A) had floated in circumambulation. It was the place where Abraham (A) would, in years to come, construct the Holy K'abah, a place of sacred pilgrimage, around which the city of Mecca would arise. It was, moreover, the place where, many centuries later, the most perfect of all creation, God's Messenger Muhammad, may His peace and blessings be upon him, would be born and pass the first fifty-three years of his life.

> Then Abraham arrived [at this spot] with her and her son Ishmael, [Ibn 'Abbas continues,] while she was suckling him, and placed the two of them near the [site of the Sacred] House by a tree with many branches above Zamzam,[37] in the highest part of the [site of the] mosque. And there was no one in Mecca at that time nor was there water in it. And he set them up there and placed a sack containing dates and a waterskin containing water beside them. Then he retraced his steps, departing. (*Bukhari*, 4.583)

Who can imagine what Abraham, the tender-hearted and forbearing, must have felt at separating from his nearest ones and leaving them alone in such an empty, inhospitable desert, especially as Ishmael had been born to him so late in life and was, at that time, his only son?[38] And since Hagar was no less his wife than Sarah, no doubt he loved her as any man loves his wife. But God's command had come to him, and Abraham (A) did not will otherwise than as his

---

[37]Zamzam is the name of the famed well in Mecca, located inside the Sacred Mosque near the Holy K'abah. However, in the above narrative Zamzam refers to the original site from which the spring was to flow, which was unknown at the time of Abraham's settling his family beside it.

[38]Some commentators assert that Isaac had been born by this time. However, this does not seem accurate in view of the fact that Ishmael was still a nursling when these events occurred — that is, under the age of two. Moreover, if Isaac had been born, there would have been no occasion for Sarah's jealousy. It would also mean that only a few months separated Ishmael and Isaac, whereas it seems more likely that they were years apart, since Sarah had been childless at least up to the time of Ishmael's birth. Indeed, Ibn Kathir states in connection with the sacrifice of Ishmael, which occurred when Ishmael was in his late childhood or early young manhood, that Ishmael was at that time Abraham's only son.

The first mention of Isaac in connection with Abraham is contained in Abraham's saying, **"Praise be to God, who has granted to me Ishmael and Isaac in my old age. Indeed, my Lord is the Hearer of prayer"** (14:39), which, according to most interpretations was spoken at the time when Abraham built the K'abah — that is, several years later, when Ishmael was a

Lord willed. Moreover, he possessed unshakable certainty of the rightness and perfection of whatever He willed.

Since Ishmael's birth had been announced to him by divine revelation, Abraham (A) had the clear assurance that the child would not only survive in these bleak surroundings but also become distinguished in God's sight.[39] Consequently, Abraham (A) understood clearly that he had been ordered to leave his wife and child here for a purpose — perhaps a most important purpose — and that purpose involved their living, not dying.[40] Just as his Lord had preserved and sustained him in the fire, so would He take care of Hagar and Ishmael, and bring His divine plan for them to fruition.

But what of Hagar, who was, together with her child, the principal person concerned in the matter? The continuation of Ibn 'Abbas' narrative supplies the answer:

> Then Umm Ishmael followed him and said, "O Abraham, where are you going, leaving us in this valley in which there is no companionship nor anything [else]?" She said that to him repeatedly but he did not look back at her, so she asked him, "Is it God who has ordered you to do this?"
>
> He said, "Yes."
>
> She said, "Then He will not let us perish." She then returned [to the spot where Abraham had placed her]. (*Bukhari*, 4:583)

The second report of Ibn 'Abbas (R) reads as follows:

> Umm Ishmael followed him and when they reached [a spot called] Kada', she called out to him from behind, "O Abraham, to whom are you leaving us?"
>
> He said, "To God."
>
> She said, "I am pleased with God." (*Bukhari*, 4:584)

Yet another narrative of Ibn 'Abbas (R) reports the matter as follows:

> The prophet of God, Abraham, brought Ishmael and Hagar and set them up in Mecca at the site of Zamzam. Then when he was leaving, Hagar called, "O Abraham, I ask you three times: Who commanded you

---

young man.

[39]That is, the divine announcement to Abraham of the birth of **a forbearing son** (37:101) was, in effect, God's guarantee to him of Ishmael's survival, for forearance is one of the qualities of a mature individual, not of a nursling destined to die in infancy.

[40]Abraham's understanding of this is suggested by his words, **"Our Lord, I have settled some of my descendants in a valley without vegetation near Your Sacred House, our Lord, that they may establish *salat*"** (14:37) — in other words, so that they may establish God's religion and its practices among the people of the area.

to put me in a land in which there are no crops or cattle, and no people or water or provision?"

He said, "My Lord commanded me."

She said, "Then indeed, He will not let us perish."

Then, as Abraham retraced his steps, he said, **"Our Lord, indeed, You know what we conceal and what we disclose,"** because of the sadness [he felt]. **"And nothing is hidden from God on the earth or in the heavens"** [14:38]. (Tabari/*Q*, "Ibrahim")

How amazingly steadfast Hagar's faith was! Her accepting Abraham's decision without a protest makes it clear that she too had absolute confidence both in the rightness of God's decree, as well as the correctness of whatever her husband, God's prophet, would decide. Her words show that, like Abraham (A), she was empowered by the complete, unwavering certainty that God would take care of her and her child, for He would not have ordered them to come here merely to die.

We are moved by the poignancy of this scene: the steadfast prophet turning his back, at his Lord's command, on his beloved family and setting out for home alone. Perhaps he did not look back at Hagar lest he be moved by love and pity to disobey the order that had come to him, or lest his heart be torn in two. And Hagar, as surrendered as her husband, returning to the spot where he had placed her, awaiting whatever her Lord would send to her and her infant son.

Then, [continues Ibn 'Abbas,] Abraham went on until, when he was at Thaniyah, where they could not see him, he turned his face toward the [site of the Sacred] House, and raising his hands, he prayed to God with this supplication:

"Our Lord, I have settled some of my offspring in a valley without vegetation near Your Sacred House, our Lord, that they may establish *salat.* Then make hearts of people be drawn to them, and provide them from the fruits [of the earth], that they may be grateful"[41] [14:37]. (*Bukhari,* 4:583)

The words, **"near Your Sacred House,"** uttered at a time when the Sacred House was but a site without any physical structure, make it quite clear that Abraham (A) was fully aware of the spiritual reality of the place where he was leaving his family, and of his and their future role in calling the people of that region to God. Indeed, because of his nearness to his Lord, perhaps he was aware of much more than that — including the fact that the most perfect among

[41]According to other accounts, Abraham uttered this prayer in Mecca many years later.

all mankind, his descendant Muhammad (S) through Ishmael, would be born and dwell on this sacred soil.

REFERENCES: Qur'an: 14:37-39. Commentaries: Tabari/*Q*, "Ibrahim"; Tabari/*H*, II:74, 76; Ibn Kathir/*T*, 14:35-36; Ayoub/*Q*, I:160-161.

13. Hagar's Search for Water

Or has he not been informed of what was in the scriptures of Moses and Abraham, who fulfilled [his obligations]: that no bearer of burdens shall bear the burden of another; and that man shall have nothing except what he strives for; and that his effort will be seen, and then he will be recompensed for it with the fullest recompense; and that to your Lord is the final end? (53:36-42)

We now return to the two accounts of Ibn 'Abbas (R), here interwoven. The material from *Bukhari*, 4:583, is given in italics.

Then she [Umm Ishmael] returned and began to drink from the waterskin, and her milk flowed for her boy. And Umm Ishmael set about suckling Ishmael and she drank from that water until, when what was in the waterskin had been used up, she became thirsty and her son became thirsty. She started to look at him writhing and kicking, and then she left him because she could not bear to look at him. And she said [to herself], "If I go and look, perhaps I will see someone."

She then found that [what came to be known as] Safa was the hill nearest to her on that land, and she stood on it. Then she faced the valley, looking whether she could see someone, but she did not see anyone.

Then she descended from Safa until, when she reached the valley, she tucked up the bottom of her dress and then hastened with the hastening of a person striving with great effort until she crossed the valley. She then came to [the hill of] Marwah and stood on it and looked whether she could see someone, but she did not see anyone. And she did that seven times.

Then she said [to herself], "Maybe I should go and check on the boy," so she went and looked, and he was in a state of wheezing near death. Thus, her soul could not find rest, so she said [to herself], "If I go and look, perhaps I will see someone."

Then she went and climbed on Safa and looked and looked, but she could not see anyone until she had completed seven [rounds]. *Said Ibn 'Abbas: The Prophet (S) said, "And that was the hastening* [sa'i] *of the people between the two [hills]."*[42]

Then, when she came in sight of Marwa, she heard a voice and said, "Sh-h!" meaning herself. Then she listened and heard it again, and she said, "You who have made hear your voice — do you have any help [to offer me]?"[43]

---

[42]That is, the rite of *sa'i*, which will be discussed in the next section.

[43]Or, "Help, if there is [any] good with you!" (*Bukhari*, 4.854).

Then she saw the angel [Gabriel] at the site of Zamzam. And he dug with his heel (or with his wing) until the water gushed forth.[44] *And she began to make a trough around it, using her hands, like this, and began scooping up the water into her waterskin. Each time, after she scooped up the water with her hand, the water would gush out. Said Ibn 'Abbas: The Prophet (S) said, "May God have mercy upon Umm Ishmael! If she had left it [without trying to control it], or if she had not scooped up [the water of] Zamzam, Zamzam would have been a spring flowing above ground."*

Then she drank and suckled her son. Then the angel said to her, "Do not be afraid of perishing, for indeed this is the [site of the] House of God, which will be built by this boy and his father, and indeed God does not let His people perish." And the [site] of the House was on a high part of the ground like a hill, so that when the torrents [of rain] came, they flowed to its right and its left. (*Bukhari*, 4:583, 4:584)

REFERENCES: Tabari/*H*, II:73-77; Ayoub/*Q*, I:161.

The Rite of *Sa'i*

Some years after his settling his family in Mecca, Abraham (A) was to build the House of God, the K'abah, near the spring of Zamzam. Long afterwards, a structure which came to be known as *al-Masjid al-Haram*, the Sacred Mosque, was built to enclose the Sacred House.

The hillocks of Safa and Marwah, located just beside the Sacred Mosque, are about a quarter of a mile apart. In recent years, they have been enclosed in a long corridor from which the K'abah may be glimpsed. And since the time of Prophet Muhammad, they have been the site of one of the rites of pilgrimage known as *sa'i* — that is, hastening seven times between these two hills in commemoration of Hagar's anguished search for help, as mentioned in the words,

Indeed, Safa and Marwah are among God's signs. Therefore, whoever makes *Hajj* to the House or performs *'Umrah*, there is no blame on him for going between them.[45] **(2:158)**

[44]The word "*zamzam*" means "copious" or "abundant".

[45]What is the meaning of there being **"no blame"** on those who carry out a prescribed rite? Ibn 'Abbas answers this question by stating that during *Jahiliyah* (the period of Ignorance of the divine guidance before the revelation of Islam), there were satans who spent the night between Safa and Marwah, and between them there were idols. Consequently, when Islam was revealed, the first Muslims said "O Messenger of God, we will not hasten between Safa and Marwah because they are [associated with] *shirk*." The above verse was then revealed. It is also reported that during *Jahiliyah* there were idols on Safa and Marwah, which people used to touch when they made *sa'i* between the two hills. Because of this, the Muslims considered it incorrect to perform *sa'i*, whereupon God revealed this verse (Ayoub/*Q*, I:177; also *Bukhari*, 6:384).

and the Holy Prophet's order, "O people, hasten! God has made *sa'i* incumbent upon you" (Ahmad).

Each pilgrim who clambers up onto these two low outcroppings of lava rock, whose stones are worn smooth by the feet of countless pilgrims throughout the centuries, treads on the very same stones on which Hagar trod several thousand years in the course of her tremendous test of faith. The rite of *sa'i* is God's lasting honor for that patient, surrendered woman — the wife of one prophet, the mother of another, and the ancestress of the Seal of the Prophets, Muhammad, God's peace and blessings be upon him and upon them — for the depth of her obedience and trust in Him. And in the inclusion of *sa'i* in the rites of pilgrimage there is a lesson for all mankind, and it is this:

Although Hagar obeyed God's order and trusted in His mercy, she did not merely sit passively, waiting for a miracle. Rather, she did her best to find help. Thus, the rite of *sa'i* is meant to teach us the importance of striving, of making an effort, of doing whatever is in our power, even if it may seem totally useless, to help ourselves or to change a difficult situation. For although God Most High is *al-Wahhab*, the Granter of help and support, the Bestower of mercy, at the same time He wants us to do our part, for, indeed, **There is nothing for man but what he strives for** (53:39).

Besides this, Hagar's story teaches us, once again, that God Almighty can do anything, for to the Creator of all things in existence, the possessor of all command and control, nothing whatsoever is impossible. He is able to create something out of nothing, to keep His servants safe in the midst of the deadliest dangers, and to provide for their needs under any and every condition. Therefore, nothing in our lives is as important as believing and trusting in Him, knowing that, regardless of how things may appear, He will never send us but what is best for us.

"Something out of nothing. . . " From under the dry, totally barren soil of Mecca, where rain seldom falls, the water of that miraculous spring, Zamzam, has been flowing ever since it first began to pour forth under the angel's touch.[46] Where its water was prior to that, only God knows.[47] Today the outlets of the spring are under the floor of the Sacred Mosque beneath the Holy K'abah, pouring out of modern-day faucets. Its water is believed to have miraculous properties, according to the Prophet's saying:

---

[46]Although it is incorrectly placed at Beer Lahai Roi in the northern Sinai peninsula, the well is mentioned in Gen. 16:7, 14 and 21:19.

[47]In view of Ibn 'Abbas' statement that the Flood covered the area of Mecca (see "Noah," page 163), we may speculate on the possibility that the spring of Zamzam originated from or was fed by underground Flood water. Ibn 'Abbas also mentions that the remnant of the Flood's water was at Hisma, which is believed to be in the northernmost part of Arabia or even further north in Harran (Tabari/*H*, I:362).

> The water of Zamzam is effective for the purpose for which it is drunk: the one who drinks it for an illness, God will cure him; for hunger, God will fill him up; for a certain need, God will fulfill it for him. The water of Zamzam is a cure for every ailment. (Al-Houry/*H*, #1014)

If we need a proof of miracles, this is surely one — one of the greatest. This miracle is known to everyone who visits Mecca, drinking or washing with Zamzam's water, and bringing home bottles of it as the most precious memento of their visit to the Sacred House — a clear, visible proof of God's power and beneficence that no sane human being can possibly deny.

REFERENCES: Ayoub/*Q*, I:176-179; Maududi/*Q*, 2:fn. 158; Asad/*Q*, 2:fns. 127-128.

14. The Populating of Mecca

[Abraham prayed,] "Then make hearts of people be drawn to them, and provide them from the fruits [of the earth], that they may be grateful." (14:37)

In his account, Ibn 'Abbas (R) next informs us of what happened subsequently to Hajar and her son, saying:

And thus it was until some people of the [bedouin tribe of] Jurhum or a family of the Jurhum passed by them, approaching by way of Kada'. They halted in the lower part of Mecca and saw a bird circling, whereupon they said, "Surely this bird only circles over water, although we know this valley and there is no water in it."

So they sent a messenger or two, and they came to the water. Then they returned and told them about the water, and they [the Jurhumites] approached. And Umm Ishmael was near the water, so they said, "Will you allow us to camp near you?"

She said, "Yes, but you will have no rights over the water."

They said, "Certainly."

Ibn 'Abbas said: The Prophet (S) said, "And Umm Ishmael felt in harmony with that, for she liked companionship. So they stayed and sent for their families, and remained with them until some of them became settlers in it.

And the boy grew up and learned Arabic from them. And he was valued by them and pleased them when he became a young man, and when he reached the age of maturity they married him to one of their women. (*Bukhari*, 4.583)

REFERENCE: Ayoub/*Q*, I:162.

15. Abraham's Vision

So We gave him the good tidings of a forbearing boy. Then, when he reached [the age of] working with him, he [Abraham] said, "O my son, indeed, I have seen in a vision that I am sacrifcing you, so see what you think." He said, "O my father, do what you are commanded. You will find me, God willing, among the patient."
(37:101-102)

As we have seen, the life of Abraham (A) was marked by extraordinary events, and by tests and trials that would easily have destroyed a person of lesser faith. But perhaps the most difficult of his trials was now to come.

When Ishmael (A) had reached the age of doing a man's work side-by-side with his father, which is understood as being the age of fully developed consciousness and the ability to reason clearly,[48] a vision came to Abraham (A). Concerning it, Ibn Kathir says:

> God mentions that His Friend, when he migrated, asked for [a son] **from among the righteous** [37:100], whereupon God gave him tidings of a **forbearing boy** [37:101], and that is Ishmael. He was the first child to be born [to Abraham,] at the age of eighty-six. There is no dispute about his being the first. And there is God's saying, **When he [Ishmael] reached [the age of] working with him** [37:102], meaning that he became mature and was capable of working with his father, of doing what his father did.
>
> And while it was thus, one night Abraham saw in a vision that he had been ordered to cut the throat of this, his son[49] — and prophets' visions [or dreams] are revelations.
>
> This, then, was a trial from God Most High to his Friend: to slaughter his beloved son who had come [to him] at an advanced age, after ordering him to take him and his mother to a distant land, to a place where there was no companionship, no vegetation, nothing of any kind. And he obeyed this command without hesitation and left them there, relying upon Him alone, and God opened ways for them and fed the two of them from sources which they could not have imagined. And after all

---

[48]In Islam, puberty is recognized as the time when an individual is sufficiently conscious and mature to be accountable for his or her own actions.

[49]There is a minor difference of opinion among the early Qur'anic commentators about whether the object of sacrifice was Isaac, as stated in Gen. 22, which contains many other discrepancies with the Qu'ranic account, or Ishmael. However, the generally accepted understanding — indeed, the only understanding that fits what is known of the matter — is that it was Ishmael. For a detailed discussion of this point, please see Appendix A at the end of this story.

this, he was to sacrifice his son, who was [at that time] the only son! (Ibn Kathir/Q, "Ibrahim")

It may be that Abraham (A) tried to understand the vision with his extraordinarily keen mind, turning it over and over in an effort to make sense out of it. With his pure understanding of truth, he knew that his Lord, who is endlessly merciful and compassionate, has no need or desire for blood — not only human blood but *any* blood — to be sacrificed and offered up to Him. Indeed, the very association of such a notion with his loving Lord would surely have been totally abhorrent to him. As a prophet, he also knew better than anyone else that taking an innocent life is among the most terrible of crimes — and what could be a graver evil or more horrible crime than the killing of a child by his own father?

At the same time, there was the assurance he had been granted when he left Hagar and Ishmael in the barren desert of the child's living, not dying. Therefore, was it now imaginable that **the forbearing son**, of whom he had been given tidings even before his birth, was really to die in his youth — and that by his father's hand?

However, it may be that Abraham's inner state was such that he did not try to approach the matter with his mind at all, for the visions of prophets pertain to Reality, and their knowledge of this Reality comes through direct experience. The veils have been lifted between their purified hearts and the spiritual world, so that they see and experience with the eye of absolute certainty.

Whatever the case may have been, Abraham (A) did not question God's order nor dispute with His Will. Rather, he understood his sacrifice of his son as something that *must* happen — that indeed had already happened in the spiritual dimension outside of time and space. Thus it was that, once again, **when his Lord said to him, "Surrender!" he said, "I have surrendered to the Lord of the worlds"** (2:131). As he had seen himself doing in the vision, he would now do in the physical plane.

But the vision concerned Ishmael even more than himself. Abraham had not been ordered to murder his son without his knowledge or consent; rather, Ishmael too must surrender his will. And thus it was that he consulted with the boy to determine his reaction to his vision.[50] Ibn Kathir continues:

> Yet he [Abraham] responded to the order willingly and hastened to implement it. He then asked his son to see how he responded to this order, saying, **"O my son, indeed, I have seen in a vision that I am sacrificing you, so see what you think"** [37:102].

[50]Whether Abraham was in Mecca at time time of this vision or traveled to Mecca after having the vision is not known.

And the answer of his son was, **"O my father, do what you are commanded. You will find me, God willing, among the patient"** [37:102]. And this was the utmost a son could do in obedience to his father and in obedience to his Lord. (Ibn Kathir/*Q*, "Ibrahim")

Ishmael's words make it clear that he did not question the meaning of what his father had seen or seek to find a way out for himself. Young as he was, he was trained in perfect obedience — firstly, to his Lord and secondly, to his father, a prophet of tremendous spiritual stature. If this was what his father understood as an order, it must be carried out, regardless of how it would affect him personally. For Ishmael, as for Abraham, peace be upon them both, the possibility of deciding otherwise did not exist. Perhaps it is for this reason that God speaks of Ishmael (A) as **a forbearing boy** (37:101) and mentions him as being **among the patient** and **among the righteous** (21:85-86).

Ishmael (A) is mentioned by name twelve times in the Qur'an. The remaining verses in which he is mentioned will be cited in their place.

REFERENCES: Qur'an: 2:131; 6:84-87; 19:54-55; 21:85-86; 37:101-102; 38:45-48. Commentaries: Ibn Kathir/*T*, 37:100-107; Ibn Kathir/*Q*, "Ibrahim".

The Sacrifice

Thus it was that Abraham (A) and his young son set out to materialize the vision, carrying a length of rope and a sharp knife. Perhaps the heart of the son trembled more for the suffering of his father, and the father for his son, than each did for himself in the carrying out of this most difficult of commands.

Ibn 'Abbas (R) reports that when the two of them passed the place where Hagar had hastened between Safa and Marwah, Satan appeared to Abraham (A) and ran after him. But Abraham (A) outran him and continued on his way, accompanied by the angel Gabriel (A).

When Abraham (A) reached the site at which the stone pillar of 'Aqabah stands in Mina,[51] Satan came to him again. Abraham (A) then threw seven pebbles at him to drive him away and continued toward his destination. At the site of the middle stone pillar, Satan reappeared, and again Abraham (A) threw

[51]The pillar of 'Aqabah is one of three stone pillars in Mina, a small town near Mecca, marking the spots where Satan appeared to Abraham to deflect him from carrying out God's order. Here, to this day, Abraham's tradition of stoning Satan is observed as a rite of the *Hajj*. On the 11th of Dhul-Hijjah, while the pilgrims are encamped in Mina, they go to the pillar of 'Aqabah (the pillar closest to Mecca) and throw seven pebbles at this symbolic representation of the Tempter. On each of the following two days, they throw seven more pebbles at the 'Aqabah pillar and at each of two other pillars, symbolizing their rejection of Satan and his evil promptings.

seven pebbles at him. Finally, when Satan realized that Abraham (A) was firm and intent upon carrying out God's command, he left him alone.

At length, the father and son reached the place for carrying out the sacrifice, which is believed to be on Mount Thabir near Mecca. It is reported that Ishmael was wearing a white shirt. "O my father," he said, "I have no garment to be buried in except this, so take it off me and bury me in it."

What that much-tried father and his son, may God's endless peace and blessings be upon them, felt as they both surrendered their wills to God and Abraham (A) put Ishmael (A) in place for the sacrifice, is a secret that will forever be between them and their Lord. As for the events that followed, Ibn Kathir supplies the details:

> God says, **Then, when they had both surrendered and he had put him down on his forehead** [37:103]. It is said that he [was about to] cut his throat in such a way as not to see his face. Al-Suddi and others say that he started cutting with the knife at his throat but it would not cut at all. It is said that God inserted a layer of brass between the knife and his throat.
>
> Then God Most High called out to Abraham (A), **"O Abraham, you have fulfilled the vision"** [37:104-105], meaning that the objective of his testing and obedience, and his willingness to carry out his Lord's command, had been achieved. That is why God says, **Indeed, this was a clear trial.** And He **ransomed him with a great sacrifical victim** [37:106-107] and replaced him with a victim which was easy for him to sacrifice in the place of his son. The majority of the commentators say that it was a white ram, wide-eyed and with big horns, which he saw stuck in the bushes. (Ibn Kathir/*Q*, "Ibrahim")

Says Ibn 'Abbas (R):

> It was a ram from Paradise that had been grazing there for forty years. When Abraham (A) saw the ram, he left his son and started to chase it. At the site of the first stoning-place [in Mina], he threw seven pebbles [at the ram to disable it]. The ram then ran to the middle stoning-place. There Abraham (A) threw another seven pebbles. Then he chased it to the largest stoning-place, where he threw another seven pebbles, and finally he brought it to the place of sacrifice [in Mina, where animals are sacrificed during the *Hajj*] and slaughtered it. Up to the beginning of Islam, its head, together with its horns, were still hanging by the door of the K'abah in a dried-up state. (Ibn Kathir/*T*, 37:102-107)

Why does God speak of the ram substituted for Ishmael as **"a great sacrifical victim"** (37:107)? Here, the word **"great"** obviously refers to much more than the specific animal that was provided as a ransom for the life of Ishmael (A). Rather, it relates to the fact that God ordained the offering of animal sacrifices (about which we will speak more in the next section) on the same day throughout the world to be an established *sunnah* (practice) up to the Day of Resurrection, thereby keeping alive the memory of Abraham's unparalleled faithfulness and devotion to His command.

Thus did God Most High try His Friend with another almost unimaginable trial. Finding him surrendered, He relieved him and restored his son to him, to become his successor in prophethood and the ancestor of the Seal of the Prophets, Muhammad, may God's peace and blessings be upon him and upon them. And God praises Abraham (A) with the highest praise and honor, saying:

> **Thus do We surely reward the doers of good. Indeed, this was a clear trial. And We ransomed him with a great sacrifice, and We left [this invocation] for him among the later generations: "Peace be upon Abraham!" Thus do We reward the doers of good. Indeed, he was among Our believing servants.** (37:105-111)

In the story of Abraham's sacrifice, we learn the way of those who are nearest to God — the prophets (*anbiya'*), messengers (*rusul*), and holy people (*salehin* or *awliya'*). It is the way of perfection: the total surrender of their own personal wills and unswerving commitment to carrying out the Will of their Lord, which is communicated to their innermost being — without questions asked, without reasons given, even if it goes against logic and common sense, against all they cherish, against everything that is accepted as reasonable and right. Such are the people who say, from their hearts, what God commanded Prophet Muhammad (S) to say:

> **Indeed, my Lord has guided me to a straight path, the correct religion: the faith of Abraham, inclining toward truth, and he was not of the *mushrikin*. Say: "Indeed, my *salat* and my rites of sacrifice and my living and my dying are for God, Lord of the worlds; He has no partner. And this I have been commanded, and I am the first [among you] of the Muslims."** (6:162-163)

One who adheres to such a standard for himself cannot even imagine exercising his own will in place of God's Will when it becomes clear to him, for he lives by an unshakable conviction of the wisdom and goodness of whatever God may decree. Often the good is hidden and secret to the point of being quite undiscernable, especially when what happens seems, by any human standard of judging, anything *but* good. But in spite of outward appearances and circumstances, such a person possesses absolute certainty of the divine wisdom — indeed, in the perfection — of whatever God Most High may will for him, knowing that

We will surely test you with something of fear and hunger and loss of wealth and lives and fruits; but give good tidings to the patient, who, when a calamity afflicts them, say, "Indeed, to God we belong and indeed, to Him we will return." Those are the ones upon whom are blessings from their Lord and mercy. And it is those who are the guided. (2:156-157)

REFERENCES: Qur'an: 37:103-111. Commentaries: Tabari/*H*, II:91-97; Ibn Kathir/*T*, 37:102-107; Ibn Kathir/*Q*, "Ibrahim"; Maududi/*Q*, 37:fn. 66; Asad/*Q*, 37:fn. 43.

Dahiya (Charitable Sacrifice)

In earlier times, the offering of sacrifices of grain, food or animals to God or to idols was an established practice in many religions. In some, human sacrifice was even common.

Through the lesson of Abraham's intended sacrifice of his son, God Most High made it clear for all time to come that He, the Most Merciful and Perfectly Just, who strictly prohibits taking any human life except for a capital crime or in battle, would never accept having a human being, the best of His creation, sacrificed to Him. Such a "sacrifice" would be monstrous — indeed, nothing but deliberate murder. Likewise, the notion that He "needs" or "likes" the flesh and blood or odor of animal sacrifices is not only revolting but blasphemous, and so degrading to His divinity and sanctity that it amounts to a denial of His transcendent reality.

Nonetheless, as in Judaism in earlier times, animal sacrifice is an important practice in Islam, established by both Abraham and Muhammad (S), according to God's words:

For every [faith] community We have appointed a rite [of sacrifice], that they may mention the name of God over what He has provided them of [sacrifical] animals. (22:34)

What, then, does the Islamic sacrifice of animals consist of and what is it all about?

Animal sacrifice is a part of the observances of *Hajj*, following the example of the Friend of God (A), according to God's words:

And the sacrifical animals[52] — We have appointed them for you as among God's symbols; in them there is good for you. (22:36)

Simultaneously, during the days of *'Eid al-Adha*, the Festival of Sacrifice which occurs concurrently with *Hajj*, Muslims throughout the world who are

[52]Referring to the animals that are brought to Mina each year for sacrifice during *Hajj*.

able to afford it sacrifice animals in their home communities in commemoration of Abraham's dual sacrifice: the total sacrifice of his will to his Lord and his sacrifice of the ram in the place of his son.

Islamic sacrifice (*dahiya*) is nothing more nor less than the slaughtering of an animal for the purpose of eating its meat and sharing it with others.[53] This is a common practice not only during *Hajj* and *'Eid al-Adha*, but also after a baby is born, in thankfulness for some special favor, and the like. Thus, in Islam there is absolutely no notion sacrificing animals *to God* in the sense of offering of their flesh and blood to Him, a completely pagan and revolting notion. Rather, they are slaughtered as food. However, the difference between the slaughtering of a "sacrificed" animal and any other animal lies in ***the intention of sharing its meat with others as an act of charity;*** hence the term, "charitable sacrifice". This is expressed in God's saying,

> **Their meat does not reach God nor their blood, but rather it is piety from you that reaches Him.** (22:37)

Now, Islam has two festivals. These are, as mentioned above, *'Eid al-Adha*, the Festival of Sacrifice at the time of *Hajj*, and *'Eid al-Fitr*, the Festival of Fast-Breaking at the end of Ramadan, the month of fasting. The distinctive religious features of these two festivals are, first, the special morning congregational prayer, with its sermon, and second, the charity specified for each occasion.

The charity of *'Eid al-Fitr* consists of a specific quantity of the staple food of the area (such as wheat or rice) or, as is now common in the Western world, its equivalent in money, given to a needy person on behalf of each member of one's household before the commencement of the *'Eid* prayer. And the charity of *'Eid al-Adha* consists of a portion of the meat of the animals slaughtered during the four days of the festival.[54]

However, the charity of *'Eid al-Adha* extends not only to the poor (as on *'Eid al-Fitr*) but to others as well, for it is recommended to divide the meat of the slaughtered animal into three parts. Customarily, one-third is kept for the use of one's own household, one-third is given to relatives and friends (who may

---

[53]Muslims are permitted and encouraged to eat of whatever God provides them for food (with the exception of the two prohibited foods, pork and alcohol), including domesticated grazing animals such as camels, beef cattle, sheep and goats, as mentioned in 6:142, 16:5, 23:21-22 and 36:71-73. Islamic slaughter is preceded by the words, "***Bismillah, Allahu akbar*** — In the name of God, God is Most Great," indicating that the life of this creature is taken with its Lord's permission. The throat of the animal is then cut and its carcass hung to bleed.

[54]While the charity of *'Eid al-Fitr* is obligatory upon all who can afford it, the charity of *'Eid al-Adha*, is *sunnah* (recommended but not obligatory).

return the favor from their own supply of meat), and one-third is given to the poor, according to God's order,

> **Mention the name of God, on appointed days, over what He has provided for them of cattle [for sacrifice]. Then eat of them and feed the distressed and poor.** (22:28)
>
> **And when they are [lifeless] on their sides, then eat of them and feed the needy one who does not ask and the beggar. Thus have We subjected them to you, that you may be thankful.** (22:36)

Due to this large-scale sharing of meat, in Third World countries where meat is very expensive, *'Eid al-Adha* may be the one time in the entire year when poor people are able to taste it. Consequently, the charities of the two *'Eids* consist of a great, world-wide sharing of God's bounties, and of goodwill and kindness, among the community of Muslims.

But, it may be asked, if money can be given in the place of the staple grain for *'Eid al-Fitr*, why not for *'Eid al-Adha*? The reason is that the sacrifice of *'Eid al-Adha* is carried out in commemoration of Abraham's sacrifice and following his example. Thus, when some of the Prophet's Companions asked him about the significance of these sacrifices, he replied, "It is a custom which has come down from your father Abraham." They asked what reward they would receive for them and he replied, "For every hair, you will receive a blessing." Then they asked about the wool and he replied, "For every strand of wool, you will receive a blessing" (*Mishkat*, 1476).

This makes it clear that the reward of carrying out a charitable sacrifice is not merely on account of the expense incurred in purchasing the animal (or, if one is the owner, of decreasing one's herd), but also for adhering to the practice of Abraham (A), the Friend of the Most Merciful. However, at this time when meat is plentiful and inexpensive in many parts of the world, Muslims in affluent countries often send money to areas where meat is scarce or expensive so that a sacrifice can be carried out in their name, thereby fulfilling God's injunction to **feed the distressed and poor** (22:28).

REFERENCES: Qur'an: 22:28, 33-34, 36-37.

16. Abraham Visits Ishmael

And mention Ishmael in the Book. Indeed, he was true to his promise, and he was a messenger and a prophet. And he used to enjoin *salat* and *zakat* on his family, and he was pleasing to his Lord. (19:54-55)

Years passed, and Ishmael (A) was married to a woman of the tribe who had settled in Mecca, the Jurhum. As reported in the continuation of Ibn 'Abbas' narrative, Abraham (A) then paid a visit to his firstborn son.

> Umm Ishmael died, and after Ishmael's marriage, Abraham came to [Mecca to] look for what he had left [there]. But he did not find Ishmael, so he asked his wife about him and she said, "He has gone out to seek [provision] for us."[55]
>
> He then asked her about their means of sustenance and their way of life, and she said, "We are in an evil state, we are in destitution and hardship," complaining to him.
>
> He said, "When your husband returns, greet him and tell him to change his threshold."
>
> When Ishmael came, he sensed something and asked, "Did anyone come to you?"
>
> She said, "Yes. An elderly shaykh[56] of such-and-such description came, and he asked us about you and I told him. And he asked how our living is, and I told him that we are under strain and hardship."
>
> He asked, "Did he give you any advice?"
>
> She said, "Yes. He told me to greet you and says to change the threshold of your door."
>
> He said, "That was my father, and he instructed me to separate from you. Go and be with your family," and he divorced her. And he married another woman from among them [the Jurhum].[57] (*Bukhari*, 4.583)

From this account, we note that Ishmael's remarkably obedient and respectful relationship with his father had continued into his adult life, despite the

---

[55]That is, by hunting, as is clear from what follows.

[56]The word "shaykh" has many meanings: the leader of a group, the head of a tribe or holder of an office, or any respected male Muslim, especially an elder. In a religious sense, a shaykh may be either an Islamic scholar, teacher or spiritual guide. According to the classic commentator as-Suddi, Abraham used to come to visit Ishmael, his successor in prophethood, mounted upon Buraq, the heavenly steed on which the Holy Prophet (S) rode during his Night Journey and Ascension (*al-Isra' wal Me'raj*) (Tabari/*H*, II:126).

[57]The wording of Ibn 'Abbas' second narrative is:

> Then it seemed good to Abraham [to visit his son], so he said to his wife [Sarah], "I am going to look for the one I have left." Then he came and greeted [Ishmael's wife] and asked, "Where is Ishmael?" His wife said, "He has gone hunting." He said, "When he comes, tell him, 'Change the threshold of your house.'" (*Bukhari*, 4:584)

physical distance that separated father and son. And we can readily understand why this was the case.

The verses cited at the beginning of this section inform us that God Most High had chosen Ishmael (A) as a prophet, following in his father's footsteps. Ishmael's earlier response to his father's vision demonstrated that Abraham (A) had trained his son from an early age in the total surrender of his will — first, to his Lord and second, to himself, both as his father, prophet, teacher and spiritual guide.

Through this training, Ishmael (A) had undoubtedly learned to be extremely attentive to subtle cues. He therefore immediately understood the "coded" advice Abraham (A) had left for him and acted on it. For if his father, whom God Himself describes as **tender-hearted and forbearing** (9:114, 11:75), considered it necessary that he separate from his wife, it could only be because he perceived that she was a source of harm to him, perhaps because of her unappreciative, complaining nature.

> He then married another woman from among them, [continues Ibn 'Abbas,] and Abraham stayed away from them as long as God willed. Afterwards he came to them but did not find him [Ishmael], so he went to his wife and asked her about him.
>
> She said, "He has gone out to seek [provision] for us."
>
> He asked, "How are you doing?" and questioned her about their means of sustenance and their way of life.
>
> She said, "We are very well-off," and she praised God, the Mighty and Glorious.
>
> Then he asked, "What is your food?"
>
> She said, "Meat."
>
> He asked, "And what is your drink?"
>
> She said, "Water."
>
> He said, "O God, bless them in their meat and their water."
>
> [Ibn 'Abbas said:] The Prophet said, "They did not have grain at that time, but if they had had it, he would have prayed for them con-

[58]Ibn 'Abbas' second narrative reads:

> Then it seemed good to Abraham [to visit his son,] so he said to his wife [Sarah], "I am going to look for the one I have left." So he came and asked, "Where is Ishmael?" His wife said, "He has gone hunting," and then she asked, "Will you come in and eat and drink?" Then he asked, "And what is your food and what is your drink?" She said, "Our food is meat and our drink is water." He said, "O God, bless them in their food and drink." [Ibn 'Abbas then said:] Abu-l-Qasim [that is, the Prophet] said, "There is blessing because of Abraham's supplication." (*Bukhari*, 4:584)

cerning it.[58] If anyone outside of Mecca had only these two things to depend on, they would not agree with him."

He [Abraham] said, "When your husband comes, greet him and tell him to make firm the threshold of his door."

When Ishmael returned, he asked, "Did anyone come to you?"

She said, "Yes. An elderly shaykh of handsome appearance came to me," and she praised him. "He asked me about you and I told him, and he asked me about our livelihood and I told him that we are in a good state."

He asked, "Did he give you any advice?"

She said, "Yes. He greeted you and instructed you to make your threshold firm."

He said, "That was my father and you are the threshold. He instructed me to hold fast to you." (*Bukhari*, 4:583)

By means of his advice, the wise and understanding prophet Abraham (A) is giving an important message to mankind. This message concerns the vital importance of having a life-partner who is thankful to God, positive and cheerful, who looks at the bright side of things, and who is appreciative of her spouse's efforts. The love, trust, support and approval of a caring partner strengthens a man's self-confidence and gives him an incentive for doing his best, helping him to reach his potential both materially and spiritually, according to the Prophet's saying:

> The best property is a tongue that mentions God, a grateful heart, and a believing wife who helps a man with his faith. (*Mishkat*, 2275)

Conversely, a wife who is negative, always looking at the dark side of things, who is unappreciative of what her husband does for her and her children, and who whines, complains, nags or puts down her husband, not only robs him of his self-esteem and motivation but drags him down — and herself with him.

However, this obviously applies just as much to men as as to women, for God says:

> **Among His signs is that He created spouses for you from among yourselves, that you might find tranquility in them, and He put love and mercy between you. Surely in that are signs for people who reflect.** (30:21)

> **They [wives] are garments for you and you are garments for them.** (2:187)

Thus, a man who is negative, pessimistic and self-centered, who gives his wife little attention, appreciation or praise, who vents anger and frustration on her, or who complains, puts her down or finds fault with her, not only deprives her of happiness, but breaks her spirit and hurts her heart as well. And these are serious sins in the sight of God, which will be a source of grief to him on the Day of Judgment, just as he caused his wife grief during this life.

Being positive, thankful, and turning to God in both difficulty and ease — these are qualities that promote the health of a marriage and spiritual and emotional well-being. Where there is no appreciation, either of God's favors or of the good qualities and efforts of one's spouse, marriage can easily become a source of injury and pain instead of the benefit and pleasure it was intended by God to be.

REFERENCES: Tabari/*H*, II:77-78, 126; Ayoub/*Q*, I:163.

17. The Building of the K'abah

And [mention, O Muhammad,] when We designated the site of the House for Abraham. (22:26)

At some time after the birth of his second son Isaac,[59] which we will report in the next section, Abraham (A), now very old and somewhat weak, visited Ishmael (A) again. Ibn 'Abbas (R) continues:

> So he [Abraham] stayed away from them as long as God willed. Then afterwards he came while Ishmael was sharpening his arrows under a spreading tree near Zamzam.[60] And when he saw him, he stood up to greet him, and they did as a father does to his son and a son does to his father.
>
> He [Abraham] said, "O Ishmael, God has given me a command."
>
> He [Ishmael] said, "Then do what your Lord has commanded you."
>
> He asked, "And will you help me?"
>
> He said, "And I will help you." (*Bukhari*, 4:583)

Now, this may seem at a first glance like a very casual conversation, but indeed it was not, for when Ishmael (A) promised to help his father carry out his Lord's order, he had no idea what that order might be. You may recall that previously, when Abraham (A) had told him about his vision of the sacrifice, Ishmael (A) had responded to God's command with very similar words: **"O my father, do what you are commanded"** (37:102). And now his submission to his Lord was being tested again with respect to a totally unknown order. Nevertheless, his response shows that regardless of what that order might be, he was ready, as before, to help his father carry it out.

> He [Abraham] said, "Then indeed, God has commanded me to build a House here," and he pointed to a hillock which was higher than the land surrounding it.[61] (*Bukhari*, 4:583)

---

[59]The fact that Isaac had been born by this time is clear from Abraham's saying, while he was building the K'abah, **"Praise be to God, who has granted to me in my old age Ishmael and Isaac"** (14:39). Gen. 17:25 gives Ishmael's age shortly before Isaac's birth as thirteen. However, this is contradicted by the account of Gen. 21:15-18, in which he is depicted as a baby or a very young child at the time.

[60]Related to this is the report that the Prophet (S) once passed by some people who were competing in archery and said to them, "Shoot, sons of Ishmael, for indeed your father [Ishmael] was an archer" (*Bukhari*, 4:148, 4:592).

[61]The second account of Ibn 'Abbas (R) reads:

> He [Abraham] said, "Indeed, your Lord has commanded me to build a House for Him." He [Ishmael] said, "Obey your Lord." He [Abraham] said, "He has also commanded me that you should help me with it." He [Ishmael] said, "So I shall," or similar words. (*Bukhari*, 4:584)

This hillock was the same mound or earthern dome where Abraham (A) had left Hagar and the infant Ishmael (A) many years earlier. It was also the same spot where, in antiquity, Adam (A) built the original House of God.

Let us go back in time for a moment. You may recall that when Adam (A) was sent down to the earth from Paradise, he complained to his Lord that he no longer heard the voices and the praises of the angels. God Most High then instructed him to build a House for His worship in His sacred territory, and to circle around it as the angels circle around His divine Throne. Adam (A) then built the House and was shown the rites of *Hajj* by the angel who accompanied him.[62] However, nothing now remained of the House except its sacred site, which is referred to in God's words, **And [mention, O Muhammad,] when We designated the site of the House for Abraham** (22:26).

> Then, [continues Ibn 'Abbas,] they built the foundation of the House. And Ishmael brought the stones and Abraham built, until, when they had made the building taller,[63] he brought this stone and placed it for him. And he [Abraham] stood on it and built, and Ishmael handed him the stones, while both of them were saying, **"Our Lord, accept** this **from us. Indeed, You are the Hearing, the Knowing"** [2:127]. Then they went on building until they had made *tawaf* around it, while both of them were saying, **"Our Lord, accept** this **from us. Indeed, You are the Hearing, the Knowing."** (*Bukhari*, 4:583)

Then, it is said, when Abraham (A) had completed the building of the House except for the last stone, Gabriel (A) brought him the Black Stone (*al-Hajar al-Aswad*) and he set it in its place.

You may recall that this was the sacred stone that had come down from Paradise at the time of Adam (A), which to this day remains fixed in one of the corners of the Sacred K'abah. Several *ahadith* speak of the singular love and respect that Prophet Muhammad (S) showed for this relic of Paradise, kissing, touching, or (if mounted) pointing to it whenever he made *tawaf* around the K'abah, as Muslims do to this day, following his blessed *sunnah* or practice.

God Most High then gave His Friend His orders concerning His sacred House. **"Do not associate anyone with Me"** (22:26), He commanded, meaning, "Do not ascribe divinity to anything other than Me. **"And purify My House for those who make *tawaf* and those who remain** beside it **in worship, and those who stand** in prayer **and bow and prostrate** in *salat*." (22:26,

---

[62]"Adam," pages 75-76.

[63]Here the second account reads:

> . . .Until the building became tall and the shaykh [Abraham] became too weak to carry the stones. So he stood upon a stone of the standing-place [the Station of Abraham], and he [Ishmael] went on handing the stones to him, while both of them were saying, **"Our Lord, accept** this **from us. Indeed, You are the Hearing, the Knowing."** (*Bukhari*, 4.584)

2:125). For the Sacred House was to be kept clean of everything impure and foul — above all else, of the pollution of idols, which are considered filthy and abominable in Judaism and Christianity as well as Islam.[64]

REFERENCES: Qur'an: 2:125, 127; 14:39; 22:26. Commentaries: Tabari/*H*, II:70, 79, 102; Ayoub/*Q*, 158-159.

THE PRAYERS OF ABRAHAM

As we have seen, from the time of leaving Hagar and Ishmael in the desert, over the course of years Abraham (A) made a number of trips to Mecca, perhaps including others that are not mentioned. During these trips, he prayed for his descendants who would dwell in the city that would arise in that spot, which was later to become known as Bakkah, as Umm al-Qura; (the Mother of Cities), and then as Makkah al-Mukarramah (Mecca the Noble). These prayers of Abraham (A) are among the most beautiful of all recorded supplications, poured out of the devoted prophet's faithful heart.[65]

The security of this sacred city and the faith of his descendants who would dwell in it was foremost in Abraham's heart as he addressed his beloved Lord. **"My Lord, make this city secure, and keep me and my sons from worshipping idols,"** he prayed. **"My Lord, indeed, they have led astray many among mankind"** (14:35). Truly, who knew better than he the evils caused by idol-worship, after his trials in Ur?

"Therefore," he continued, **"whoever follows me, indeed, he is of me."** As for the others, he left their fate to their Maker, saying, **"And whoever disobeys me, indeed, You are Forgiving and Merciful"**[66] (14:36).

And Abraham (A) poured out his gratitude for the blessing of the two sons who had been granted to him so late in life in response to his supplication.

---

[64]This is emphasized in the following verses: **Then avoid the filth of idols and avoid false speech, inclining [only] to God, not associating anything with Him** (22:30), and, **O you who believe, indeed, intoxicants and gambling and [sacrificing to false deities on] stone altars and divining the future are only filth from among the work of Satan, so avoid it, that you may be successful** (5:90/93).

[65]Just when these prayers were uttered, in what sequence, and on how many occasions is not known.

[66]Meaning, "Whatever You decide to do with them depends on Your mercy." It is reported that once the Prophet (S) mentioned this saying of the Friend of God and the saying of the spirit of God, Jesus, **"If You should punish them, indeed, they are Your slaves"** [5:118/121], and he wept copiously, mentioning his own followers. God Most High then sent Gabriel to enquire why he was weeping (although of course He knew why), and he told Gabriel the reason. Then

"Praise be to God, who has granted me, in my old age, Ishmael and Isaac," he said humbly. **"Indeed, my Lord is the Hearer of prayer."** He then prayed for himself, his progeny, his parents and all believers, saying, **"My Lord, make me an establisher of *salat*, and also of my descendants. Our Lord, and accept my supplication. Our Lord, forgive me and my parents and the believers on the Day the Accounting is established"**[67] (14:39-41).

While he was building the house, Abraham (A) again prayed for the safety of Mecca and the provisioning of its people, saying, **"My Lord, make this a secure city and provide its people with fruits** of the earth — **whoever among them believes in God and the Last Day** (2:126).

But God the All-Aware knew that despite the purity and sanctity of this city, idolatry, with all its attendant evils, would flourish here in the future. Indeed, in time to come, idols would even be set up inside and around the Sacred K'abah,[68] consecrated by His Friend to His exclusive worship. Consequently, God responded to Abraham's prayer for the provisioning of the believers dwelling in Mecca by saying, **"And whoever disbelieves, I shall grant him enjoyment for a while; then I shall drive him to the punishment of the Fire, and wretched is the destination!"** (2:126). That is, what Abraham (A) had requested exclusively for believers had been granted to both unbelievers and believers in the life of this world, while on the Day of Judgment the unbelievers' destination would be Hell.

"Our Lord, accept the building of this Sacred House **from us,"** Abraham (A) continued. **"Indeed, You are the Hearing, the Knowing. Our Lord, and make us surrenderers to You, and of our descendants, a nation surrendered to You. And show us our rites and accept our repentance. Indeed, You are the Acceptor of Repentance, the Merciful"** (2:127-128).

Then, thinking of his descendants who would dwell in this city in the future, Abraham (A) besought God for their guidance and spiritual well-being.

"Our Lord," he prayed, **"and send among them a messenger from among themselves, who will recite to them Your verses, and teach them the scripture and wisdom and purify them. Indeed, You are the Almighty, the Wise"** (2:129).

God said, "We will make you happy concerning your followers, and you will not be displeased" (Ibn Kathir/*T*, 5:116-118/119-121).

[67]Meaning the Day of Judgment. Ibn Kathir comments that Abraham uttered this prayer for his parents before God revealed to him that he was not to do so (Ibn Kathir/*T*, 14:41).

[68]Idol-worship among the descendants of Ishmael is discussed in Appendix B at the end of this story.

God Most High was to grant His Friend's prayer for the security of Mecca. The entire territory of Mecca was to be — and is to this day — a sanctuary, a safe haven, where all living things (except those that are harmful or dangerous) are secure from harm, as mentioned in 2:125 and 3:97 above. At the same time, God declared, **Whoever intends deviation or wrongdoing therein, We shall cause him to taste of a painful punishment** (22:25).

God also granted Abraham's prayer for the provision of his descendants. In time to come, Mecca was to become a center of trade whose commerce flourished through the journeys of merchant caravans to the neighboring lands in the north and south. This is memorialized in the well-known *Surah Quraysh*:

> **For the uniting of the Quraysh, their uniting in the winter and summer journey, let them worship the Lord of this House, who has fed them against hunger and made them safe from fear.** [69] **(106:1-5)**

Abraham's prayers for the purity of faith of his descendants who would live in Mecca and for their being shown the rites of their faith and the practice of *salat* — all these were answered in time to come. And most important of all, the Most Merciful Lord granted His Friend's supplication that He would send among his descendants in the sacred territory **a messenger from among themselves,** who would **recite to them** His **verses, and teach them the scripture and wisdom and purify them** (2:129).

Some 2500 years later, the last and greatest of all the prophets, Muhammad, God's peace and blessings be upon him, was to become the fulfillment of Abraham's prayer — a messenger from among the inhabitants of Mecca who brought God's final revelation and guidance, not only to the people of his city and region, but to the entire world.

REFERENCES: Qur'an: 2:126-129; 14:35-36, 39-41; 22:26; 106:1-5. Commentaries: Tabari/*H*, II:79; Ayoub/*Q*, I:162; Ayoub/*Q*, II:261-262; Maududi/*Q*, 22:fn. 44; Asad/*Q*, 3:fn. 75; Lane/*L*, Part One, p. 79.

---

[69] The Quraysh, the Prophet's tribe, were the keepers of the K'abah, which prior to Islam was venerated throughout Arabia as a sacred, although pagan, shrine. Because of its importance, the Quraysh were also given respect outside the borders of their land. Consequently, their caravans were able to travel the long distances to Syria in the north and Yemen in the south during both winter and summer in security and peace, returning laden with goods. The **"uniting"** mentioned in this ***surah*** refers to the mutual respect of the Qurayshite clans for each other, as well as to the respect accorded to the Quraysh throughout the region as the keepers of the K'abah.

The Station of Abraham

God Most High honored His Friend by referring to the place where he stood in prayer (known as *Maqam Ibrahim,* the Station of Abraham) as one of His **"signs,"** as mentioned in the following passage:

> **Indeed, the first House [of God] established for mankind was that at Bakkah,[70] a blessed place and a guidance for the worlds. Therein are clear signs — the standing-place of Abraham.[71] And whoever enters it shall be safe.** (3:96-97)

God further honored Abraham by making the praying of two *rak'ats* at his standing-place a part of the rites of *Hajj* and '*Umrah*, saying:

> **And [mention, O Muhammad,] when We made the House a place of return for people and of security. And take the standing-place of Abraham as a place of prayer.** (2:125)

Concerning Abraham's standing-place, the Holy Prophet (S) said:

> The Corner [of the Black Stone] and the Station of Abraham are two sapphires from among the sapphires of Paradise, whose light God dimmed. If their light had not been dimmed, it would have illuminated the earth from East to West. (*Mishkat*, 2579)

It is reported that once the Prophet (S) kissed the Black Stone. Then he ran during three rounds of *tawaf* and walked during four. At the conclusion of this, he prayed two *rak'ats* at the Station of Abraham, reciting, **"And take the standing-place of Abraham as a place of prayer"** [2:125] (*Muslim*, 2803).

The stone upon which Abraham (A) stood remains up to this day. Encased in a small glass kiosk which stands near the Black Stone corner of the K'abah, it is familiar to those who have visited the Sacred Mosque — a natural stone slab imprinted with a footprint, believed to be the footprint of the original builder of the Sacred K'abah, God's Friend Abraham, may His best blessings and peace be upon him.

REFERENCES: Qur'an: 2:125; 3:96-97. Commentaries: Ayoub/*Q*, I:157-158; Ayoub/*Q*, II:257-260, 263, 266.

---

[70]An ancient name for Mecca.

[71]According to the opinion of some commentators, Abraham's footprint in the stone is itself among the **"clear signs"**. However, others add other matters to it.

18. THE SACRED CITY AND THE HOLY K'ABAH

Have We not established a safe sanctuary for them, to which are brought the fruits of all things, as provision from Us? (28:57)

THE SACREDNESS OF MECCA

We have already spoken of the desolate, barren surroundings of the city of Mecca, which lies in the harshest of settings — a burningly hot **valley without vegetation** (14:37), encircled by dark, steep, naked lava peaks. But since nothing happens without a divine reason and purpose, it is clear that the establishment of the most sacred city on earth in this bleak site was ordained by the special knowledge of the Lord of creation. Concerning it, the classical Qur'anic commentator, Fakhruddin al-Razi, commented:

> There is in this choice of location great divine wisdom. First: By this God placed the trust of the people of His sanctuary and guardians of His house in Himself alone. Secondly, no tyrants or oppressors would ever live in Makka, for such men seek the good things of this world. Thus God has exalted this spot over the impurities of the people of this world. Thirdly, God did this in order that no people would travel to the Kaaba for material benefits, but only for pilgrimage and worship. Fourthly, God has by this act manifested the high honor of poverty, for He placed the most excellent of all houses in one of the poorest spots on earth. It is as though He said, 'I have made the poor of this world the denizens of the secure town, and thus will I make them in the world to come the people of the secure station.' (Ayoub/*Q*, II:259-260)

Emphasizing the sanctity of the sacred territory, God ordered His Messenger, Muhammad (S), to say:

> **I have only been ordered to worship the Lord of this city, who made it sacred and to whom all things belong.** (27:91)

And the blessed Prophet (S) said:

> Indeed, God made this place sacred on day He created the heavens and the earth, and it is sacred with God's sacredness until the Day of Resurrection. (*Bukhari*, 3:60)

> Indeed, God made Mecca sacred; people did not make it sacred. Therefore, one who believes in God and the Last Day should neither shed blood in it nor cut down its trees. (*Bukhari*, 1:104)

And addressing the holy city, the Prophet (S) said:

> By God, you are the most excellent spot of God's earth and the dearest spot to Him. If I had not been driven out, I would never have left you. (*Mishkat*, 2724)

REFERENCE: Ayoub/*Q*, II:257-263.

The Sacred House

It is only fiitting that Mecca, the most sacred city on earth, should be the site of the most sacred of all structures, the Holy K'abah, about which God says:

> **God has made the K'abah, the Sacred House, a support for mankind.**[72] (5:97/100)

> **And [mention, O Muhammad,] when We made the House a place of return for people and of security.** (2:125)

Says Fakhruddin al-Razi:

> There is no edifice in the world more honored than the K'abah, for it was built by order of the Lord of Majesty. Its engineer was Gabriel, its builder the intimate friend (*khalil*) and the apprentice Ishmael. (Ayoub/*Q*, II:259)

The Holy K'abah is also known as *al-Bait*, the House (2:125, 127, 158; 396-97; 8:35; 22:26; 106:3), and as *Bait-Allah*, the House of God. It is referred to in the Qur'an as *al-Bait al-'Atiq*, the Ancient House or the Ransomed House (22:29, 33), because it was saved from destruction during the Flood. It is also called *al-Bait al-Haram*, the Sacred or Prohibited House (5:2/3, 97/100; 14:37), and *al-Masjid al-Haram*, the Sacred or Prohibited Mosque (22:25), because idol-worshippers were forbidden to enter it. And it is called the K'abah (5:97/100), meaning "cube," because it is square.

It has been said that the K'abah is square because it was modeled on *al-Bait al-Ma'mur*, the Populated House in the fourth heaven (52:4), so named because great numbers of angels circle around it. It is further said that the Populated House was made square because it was modeled on the divine Throne, which is square because the words on which Islam is founded are four: *Subhanallah* (Glory be to God), *Alhamdulillah* (Praise be to God), *La ilaha illa-Llah* (There is no deity except God), and *Allahu akbar* (God is Most Great).

---

[72] That is, "a standard by which [men's] affairs are made sound or improved" (Asad/*Q*, 5:fn. 117).

The sacredness, blessedness and importance of the K'abah is clear from the fact that God Most High made pilgrimage to it, about which we will speak shortly, one of the five obligatory acts of worship in Islam.

REFERENCES: Qur'an: 2:125; 5:97/100. Commentaries: Ayoub/*Q*, I:157, Ayoub/*Q*, II:257-261; Asad/*Q*, 5:fn. 117.

The Change of the *Qiblah*

Still another evidence of the K'abah's tremendous importance and honor is the fact that God made it the *qiblah* — the direction faced during *salat* and other worship — for Muslims for all time to come.

The first *qiblah* which the Messenger of God (S) and the earliest Muslims faced for prayer was *al-Bait al-Maqdis*, the Sacred House in Jerusalem — that is, the site of Solomon's Temple. It is reported that they continued to face it for several months after the Prophet's emigration to Medina.

During this period, the Prophet (S) expressed the wish that he could pray facing the K'abah, and he turned his face toward Heaven, hoping for a response to this request (*Bukhari*, 1.39; *Muwatta*, 14.4.7). God Most High then revealed to him the first order to change the *qiblah*, saying,

> **We have certainly seen the turning of your face toward Heaven, so We will surely turn you toward a *qiblah* that will please you. Therefore, turn your face toward the Sacred Mosque. And wherever you all are, turn your faces toward it [for worship]. And indeed, those who have been given the scripture know well that it is the truth from their Lord.[73] And God is not unmindful of what they do. (2:144)**

This order was repeated a second time:

> **For each [faith community] is a direction toward which it faces. . . . And from wherever you [Muhammad] go forth, turn your face toward the Sacred Mosque, and indeed, it is the truth from your Lord. And God is not unmindful of what you do. And from wherever you [Muhammad] go forth, turn your face toward the Sacred Mosque. And wherever you [all] may be, turn your faces toward it. (2:148-150)**

---

[73]According to al-Tabari, this refers to Jewish rabbis and learned Christians of the Prophet's time, who knew with certain knowledge that the K'abah was their rightful *qiblah*, as well as the *qiblah* of Abraham and all the prophets preceding Muhammad (S). But out of reasons of self-interest, they concealed this fact, the Christians facing east in their prayers and Jews facing the Sacred House in Jerusalem (Ayoub/*Q*, I:174; Maududi/*Q*, 2:fn. 148).

The change of the *qiblah* naturally caused controversy, especially among the Jews of Medina, who disparaged Muhammad's prophethood and upheld the previous *qiblah*, Jerusalem. The change, moreover, proved difficult for many Muslims.

Prior to this time, taking Jerusalem as the *qiblah* had been a problem for the new Muslims who were Arabs. But the order to change it from Jerusalem to Mecca now became a serious test of faith for some other Muslims, especially the converts from Judaism and Christianity, for whom facing Jerusalem in prayer was but natural and obvious. What made it even more difficult was the fact that during this period the K'abah was a still pagan shrine given over to the worship of idols. The Muslims of course could not know that within a very short time its idols would be destroyed and banished forever, and it would be re-consecrated to the Lord of Glory and Honor, who had ordained its sancitity and made it the focus of His worship for all time to come.

In spite of these difficulties, however, the response of the Muslims to the emphatic and repeated divine command to take the K'abah as their *qiblah* was immediate. In fact, it is reported that when various groups of Muslims heard about the order, they turned to face Mecca while they were in the very act of praying (*Bukhari*, 1:39; *Muslim*, 1071-1075; *Abu Dawud*, 507). All this was in keeping with the divine purpose stated in the verse,

> **And We did not appoint the *qiblah* which you used to face but that We might distinguish those who followed the Messenger from those who would turn back on their heels. And indeed, it is difficult except for those whom God has guided.** (2:143)

REFERENCES: Qur'an: 2:142-150. Commentaries: Ayoub/Q, I:146-148, 167-175, 259; Ayoub/Q, II:257-261; Maududi/Q, 2:fns. 142, 145-146, 148; Asad/Q, 2:fns. 116, 120, 123, Ali/Q, fn. 141.

The Excellence of the Holy K'abah

God the Praised and Exalted confirmed the superiority of the K'abah over the Sacred House in Jerusalem and His appointing it as the *qiblah* by revealing,

> **Indeed, the first House [of God] established for mankind was that at Bakkah, a blessed place and a guidance for the worlds.** (3:96)

The meaning of **"the first House"** in the above verse is that the K'abah was the first structure for the worship of God on earth, almost equal in antiquity to the first man, Adam (A). When 'Ali ibn Abi Talib (R) was asked if the K'abah was the first house built on earth, he said, "No, . . . rather it was the first to be established with great blessing, for it is Abraham's station, and whoever enters it shall be safe" (Ayoub/Q, II:257). Thus, one reason for the K'abah's excellence and superiority is its connection with both the prophets Adam and Abraham, God's peace and blessings be upon them.

It has been said that one reason the K'abah has been called **"a blessed place"** in the verse above is because acts of worship performed at it will be so highly rewarded. For example, the Holy Prophet (S) said that making *'Umrah* — the minor pilgrimage, during which one visits the Sacred House and performs *tawaf* and *sa'i* — atones for the sins committed between it and the next *'Umrah*, and that the reward of a *Hajj* which is accepted by God is nothing but Paradise (*Bukhari*, 3:1; *Muwatta*, 20.21.6). The Prophet (S) also said that *salat* performed in his mosque — that is, the Prophet's Mosque in Medina — is better than a thousand prayers performed in any other mosque except the Sacred Mosque in Mecca, giving the Sacred Mosque superiority over every other place of worship (*Bukhari*, 2:282; *Muslim*, 3213; *Muwatta*, 14.5.9). And if this were not enough, he also said that *salat* in the Sacred Mosque is equivalent to 100,000 prayers.[74]

Another reason for the K'abah's blessedness is that at all times of the day and night, people in some part of the globe are facing it in *salat*. This prayer circle remains ever unbroken and constant, for there is never a moment when some Muslims somewhere are not engaged in prayer. And around the K'abah itself, there is likewise an unbroken, constant stream of worshippers, standing, bowing and prostrating in *salat*, making *tawaf* of the House, and occupied with glorification and supplication to God, the Praised and Exalted.

The K'abah is thus the spiritual center of this planet, illumined by the light of the Lord of the worlds, the focus of the highest spiritual energy and blessing, with which Muslims connect each time they turn toward in worship or in their actual visits to the Sacred House.

REEFERENCES: Ayoub/*Q*, II:257-271; Maududi/*Q*, 3:fns. 79-80; Asad/*Q*, 3:fns. 75-77.

---

[74]This is mentioned in the following *hadith*, reported by Anas bin Malik:

> The *salat* of a man in his house is [equal to] one prayer; and his *salat* in the mosque of his tribe is [equal to] to twenty-five prayers; and his *salat* in a large congregational mosque is [equal to] five hundred prayers; and his *salat* in the Farthest Mosque [*Masjid al-Aqsa* in Jerusalem] is [equal to] 50,000 prayers; and his *salat* in my mosque [*al-Masjid al-Nabawi* in Medina] is [equal to] 50,000 prayers; and his *salat* in the Sacred Mosque in Mecca is [equal to] 100,000 prayers. (*Mishkat*, 0752)

19. The Pilgrimage

Complete the *Hajj* and *'Umrah* for God. (2:196)

And pilgrimage to the House is [an obligation] toward God for people, [for] whomever is able to find a way to it.[75] (3:97)

The Establishment of *Hajj*

Returning to the story of Abraham (A), Ibn Kathir and others report that when he had completed the building of the Sacred House, his Lord gave him a further command: **"And proclaim the *Hajj* to mankind"** (22:27), that pilgrimage to the house might be an obligation on all who follow in his path up to the Last Day.

"O Lord, how will my voice reach them?" Abraham (A) asked.

"The calling is your task," God replied. "Making it reach is *My* responsibility."

Then Abraham (A) stood, either upon the stone known as the Station of Abraham or on top of the hill of Safa or the summit of Mount Abu Qubays, and called, "O people, there is a house of your Lord here, so come for *Hajj*." And, it is said, his voice reached the whole world, to the extent that the unborn children in their fathers' loins or mothers' wombs heard the sound, and all the people who were destined to make *Hajj* in the future called out, "*Labbayk!* Here I am, O God!" (Ibn Kathir/*T*, 22:27).

Abraham (A) was then taught the rites of *Hajj* by the angel Gabriel (A).[76] These rites were the same as those that, centuries later, the Last Messenger, Muhammad (S), would teach the first community of Muslims, in obedience to God's order:

---

[75]**"To find a way to it"** is understood as meaning safe conditions of travel and sufficient health, strength and financial means to be able to undertake the journey to Mecca.

[76]The Prophet (S) is reported to have said:

> Gabriel came to Abraham on the day of Tarwiyah [the eighth day of Dhul-Hijjah, preceding the Day of 'Arafat, which constitutes the central event of *Hajj*] and went with him to Mina, praying the midday, afternoon, sunset, late evening, and dawn prayers in Mina. Then in the morning he took Abraham to Arafat and set him down at the thorn bush where people stay [during the afternoon of the Day of 'Arafat,] and prayed with him the midday and afternoon prayers together. He stood with Abraham until he had prayed the sunset prayer very quickly, then rushed him into a crowd and prayed with him the sunset and evening prayers together. Then they remained and together they prayed the dawn prayer very quickly and then very slowly. After that he rushed Abraham to Mina, threw the stones, performed the sacrifice, shaved his head, and finally hurried to the House. (Tabari/*H*, II:82)

Thus, We revealed to you [Muhammad] to follow the faith of Abraham, inclining toward truth, and he was not among the *mushrikin*. (16:123)

Those rites have not changed up to the present day, nor will they change as long as the world continues. Thus, each Muslim who takes part in the *Hajj* is following the *sunnah* of two of the greatest prophets of all time — Abraham, the Friend of God, and the Seal of the Prophets, Muhammad, may God's best blessings and peace be upon them both.

REFERENCES: Tabari/*H*, II:79-82; Ibn Kathir/*T*, 22:27; Ayoub/*Q*, II:261-268.

Hajj Throughout the Centuries

In time to come, in response to their Lord's call, countless pilgrims would travel to the the Sacred House by various means of transport, according to God's words:

They will come to you on foot and and on every kind of lean mount, they will come from every far-distant pass,[77] that they may witness things beneficial to themselves, and mention the name of God, on appointed days, over what He has provided for them of cattle for sacrifice. Therefore, eat of them and feed the distressed and poor. Then let them complete their rites and fulfill their vows and make *tawaf* of the Ancient House. (22:27-29)

For centuries, pilgrims would come mounted on camels or by sea in crowded pilgrim ships. Some would even make the journey on foot. In order to reach the House, they would brave all kinds of hardships and dangers, the journey often taking months or even years. Indeed, for countless pilgrims, the journey to *Hajj* would be the final act of their lives. Despite all these difficulties, how-

[77]These verses memorialize those pilgrims who would make the long, difficult journey to Mecca on foot and on the backs of camels, lean from weeks or months of travel to the sacred territory. **"Every far distant pass"** refers to the far-off places, remote from Mecca, from which pilgrims would come to *Hajj*. **"That they may witness things beneficial to themselves"** relates to the tremendous spiritual benefits, as well as the extradordinary sense of the brotherhood of all Muslims, which pilgrims experience during *Hajj*. It is also interpreted as referring to the permissibility of engaging in business during *Hajj*. **"That they may . . . mention the name of God, on appointed days, over what He has provided for them of cattle for sacrifice"** refers to mentioning God's name prior to slaughtering the sacrifical animals during *Hajj*. The **"appointed days"** are the fixed days of *Hajj* during which the charitable sacrifice of animals is carried out. The pilgrims are then commanded to **complete their** well-known *Hajj* **rites and fulfill their vows** — that is, any vows they may have made for the occasion. For further details concerning the rites of *Hajj*, please refer to any authoritative book on the subject, such as Keller's *Reliance of the Traveler* [j9.4 -j9.13]).

ever, the lifelong dream of every faithful Muslim was, and is, to be present in worship at the House of the Lord, in preparation for the meeting with the Lord of the House on the Last Day.

Early in the nineteenth century, as new modes of transportation came into being, pilgrims started coming to the House in automobile caravans crawling across the land, traveling in rickety vehicles which often broke down along the way, in slow-moving trains from points in the Middle East, or in heavily-laden ships from even more distant places.[78] Later, thousands came in crowded buses or private automobiles from areas within driving distance, such as Turkey, Syria, Jordan, Iraq, Iran and the Gulf states, and, still more recently, by air from more distant areas. And the number of pilgrims has steadily increased up to this day.

During the first ten days of Dhul-Hijjah, the month of pilgrimage, Mecca and the area around it hums with the sound of thousands and thousands of voices repeating *talbiyah*, the age-old pilgrims' response to God's call to them to be present at the *Hajj*:

Labbayk, Allahumma, labbayk!	Here I am, O God, here I am!
Labbayk, la sharika laka, labbayk.	Here I am. No partner have You! Here I am.
Inna-l-hamda wa-ni'mata laka wal-mulk.	Indeed, all the praise and the grace are Yours, and the dominion.
La sharika laka!	No partner have You!

In this, again, the pilgrims are following the instructions of the angel Gabriel (A) and the *sunnah* of the two prophets, Abraham and Muhammad, may God's peace and blessings be upon them. The Prophet (S) said:

> Gabriel came to me and told me to tell my Companions, or whoever was with me, to raise their voices while saying *talbiyah*. (*Muwatta*, 20.10.34; Abu Dawud, 1810)

His saying,

> No Muslim raises his voice in *talbiyah* without everything on his right and left, stones or trees or clods, doing the same until the earth is traversed on both sides (*Mishkat*, 2550),

hints at the tremendous spiritual energy that fills the place during the first days of Dhul-Hijjah.

---

[78]The video, "The Guests of God," is an excellent commentary on *Hajj*, both past and present. Also of interest is "The Hajj, One American's Pilgrimage," featuring Michael Wolfe, aired on ABC "Nightline," April 18, 1997.

In our time, the conditions of *Hajj* have improved dramatically. Nonetheless, the pilgrimage remains physically taxing and full of hardships without the expectation of any material benefit. But the difficulties — the expense, the strain of travel and the physical discomforts — cannot keep away God's worshippers. The pilgrimage to the Sacred House continues to draw Muslims like a magnet, for they come, out of love and desire for their Lord, to fulfill a major obligation of their faith, with thirsty, longing hearts eager for a taste of His divine mercy. And He, their Lord, grants them the highest of rewards, according to His Prophet's words:

> '*Umrah* is an expiation for the sins committed [between it and the previous *'Umrah*], and the reward of a *Hajj* which is accepted by God is nothing but Paradise. (*Bukhari*, 3:1; *Muwatta*, 20.21.66)
>
> Those who make *Hajj* and those who make *'Umrah* are people who have come to visit God. If they supplicate Him, He will respond to them, and if they ask Him for forgiveness, He will forgive them. (*Mishkat*, 2536)
>
> When it is the day of 'Arafat,[79] God descends to the lowest heaven. Then He expresses pride in them [the pilgrims] to the angels and says, "Look at My servants, coming to Me unkempt, covered with dust, and calling out from every direction. I call you to witness that indeed I have forgiven them." Then they [the angels] say, "My Lord, such-and-such did evil, and such-and-such, and such-and-such a woman." Then God, the Honored and Glorious, replies, "I have forgiven them." And the Prophet (S) added: "Therefore, there is no day when God frees more people from Hellfire than the Day of 'Arafat." (*Mishkat*, 2601)

REFERENCES: Qur'an: 22:27-29. Commentaries: Ibn Kathir/*T*, 22:26-30.

---

[79]The principal day of *Hajj*, during which, from noon up to sunset, the entire throng of pilgrims, gathers on the vast plain of 'Arafat near Mecca, occupied with supplication for God's forgiveness and mercy.

PART FOUR

20. Isaac and Jacob

And We gave him [Abraham] the good tidings of Isaac, a prophet from among the righteous. And We blessed him and Isaac. But among their descendants is the doer of good and the one who clearly wrongs himself. (37:112-113)

Then We gave her [Sarah] good tidings of Isaac, and after Isaac, Jacob. (11:71)

Isaac (A)

We now go back in time to pick up the thread of the story of Abraham's second son, Isaac (Arabic, Ishaq, pronounced Is-*haq*), God's peace and blessings be upon them both.

After leaving Hagar and the infant Ishmael (A) in the desert of Mecca, Abraham (A) returned home to his wife Sarah. However, Sarah remained barren, and the years passed until she and Abraham (A) were very aged.[80]

It is said that Abraham (A) lived in Beersheba in the land of Palestine, which is the desert portion of Syria. There he dug a well and built a house of prayer, but when some of its people did him harm, he left them and went to live between Ramlah and Jerusalem.

There again he dug a well and settled. Eventually he became prosperous, blessed with plentiful provision, wealth and servants. And he was very fond of showing hospitality to guests.

One day three handsome strangers, whom Abraham (A) naturally enough took to be travelers, appeared at his door. **They entered upon him and said "*Salam*"** (15:51, 11:69, 51:25), the greeting of peace of believers.

Surprised by their presence, Abraham (A) responded, **"*Salam*"** (15:51, 11:69, 15:51, 51:25), while saying to himself, **"Unknown people!"** (51:25).

Then, desiring to give his guests, although strangers, his best hospitality, **he did not delay** but **turned to his household and came with a plump calf, and placed it near them**[81] (11:69, 51:26-27).

---

[80]Ibn Kathir states that Abraham's age at the time of Isaac's birth was about one hundred, while Sarah was ninety, as stated in Gen. 17:17 and 21:5 (Ibn Kathir/*Q*, "Ibrahim").

[81]In 11:69, it is, **He did not delay in bringing a roasted calf.** Ibn Kathir comments that this is the manner in which a host should care for his guests, preparing food for them unobtrusively without asking or announcing it, and then putting it in front of them so they may eat (Ibn Kathir/*T*, 51:26-27).

He said, "Will you not eat?" (51:26-27). **But when he saw their hands not reaching toward it, he mistrusted them and felt apprehensive of them** (11:70, 51:28). And he expressed his feelings frankly to his visitors, saying, **"We feel afraid of you"** (15:52).

But they reassured him, saying, **"Do not fear"** (11:70, 15:53, 51:28). And they made known to him that they were angels — Gabriel, Michael and Israfil — who had been sent by their Lord on a two-fold errand.

"Indeed," they told Abraham (A), **"we have been sent to the people of Lot,"** who lived at some distance among a depraved, perverted people. **And his wife was standing by and she laughed** (11:70-71).

The commentators have given various interpetations of Sarah's laughter. One is that she laughed with relief at knowing that there was nothing to fear from the strangers. Another is that she laughed because of the strangeness of their not partaking of the food, despite the honor and lavish hospitality shown to them by Abraham, while she herself stood by to serve them. And yet another is because of what she knew of the vices of Lot's people.

The subject then changed abruptly, for the angels had a second errand which concerned Abraham (A) personally — and equally his wife. And they now made it known.

"Indeed," they announced, **"we give you good tidings of a boy possessing knowledge"** (15:53, also 51:28).

Abraham (A) reacted with natural disbelief. **"Do you give me such good tidings although old age has come upon me?"** he asked in amazement. **"Of what, then, do you give tidings?"** (15:54), as if to say, "What sort of tidings are these when the thing you are telling me is obviously impossible?"

"We have given you the good tidings in truth," the angels assured him, **"so do not be among the hopeless"** (15:55).

"And who is hopeless of the mercy of his Lord except the straying?" (15:56), Abraham (A) rejoined, as it became clear to him that this announcement had in truth come from none other than God Himself. Impossible though it might be according to human experience, it was evident that he was now destined to become the father of a second son — this time from the barren, aged Sarah.

However, Sarah herself reacted to the angels' announcement with profound disbelief and unbearable sadness. And she **came forward with a cry and hit her face and said, "A barren old woman!"** (51:29).

"Thus has your Lord said," the angels replied, gently reassuring her. **"Indeed, He is the Wise, the Knowing!"** (51:30).

But the seeming impossibility of the thing kept Sarah from trusting the news she had been given. **"Woe be to me!"** she cried in the bitter agony of an aged woman who has remained barren througout her life. **"Am I to bear a child when I am an old woman and this, my husband, is an old man? This is surely an amazing thing!"** (11:72).

"Do you wonder at God's decree?" the angels responded. **"God's mercy and His blessings be upon you, people of the house. Indeed, He is the Praiseworthy and Glorious!"** (11:73).

In this manner did God give Abraham (A) and Sarah the **good tidings of Isaac, a prophet from among the righteous** (37:112). Then, as if that were not enough, they were also informed of a grandson to come, according to God's words:

> **Then We gave her good tidings of Isaac, and after Isaac, Jacob.** (11:71)

Through the birth of Isaac (A), God Most Gracious once again wrought a miracle for His Friend, contravening all known natural laws. And according to His endlessly wise, all-embracing divine plan, the second son thus granted to Abraham (A) and Sarah in their advanced old age was, like his half-brother Ishmael, destined to become a vital link in the future of revealed religion

Although Isaac (A) is mentioned by name in the Qur'an sixteen times (three times by himself and thirteen coupled with the names of other prophets), nothing is reported concerning his life-story.[82] Whatever has been said about him by the Qur'anic commentators has been taken, due to lack of authentic Islamic material, from the Book of Genesis, and hence we will not repeat it here.

REFERENCES: Qur'an: 11:69-72; 15:51-53; 21:72; 37:112-113; 51:24-29. Commentaries: Tabari/*Q*, "Ibrahim"; Tabari/*H*, II:65-69, 88-89, 127-129; Ibn Kathir/*T*, 51:25-27, 11:71; Ibn Kathir/*Q*, "Ibrahim"; Asad/*Q*, 11:fn. 103.

---

[82]Isaac is mentioned in two well-known ***ahadith,*** one of which we mentioned earlier on page 256. In the second, it is reported that the Prophet (S) used to seek refuge with God for his grandsons, Hasan and Husain, saying, "Your father [Abraham] used to seek refuge for Ishmael and Isaac by this: 'I seek refuge with the perfect words of God from every satan and harmful reptile [or insect] and from every evil [or envious] eye'" (***Bukhari***, 4:590).

Jacob (A)

After Isaac, the prophetic line continued with Jacob (Arabic, Ya'qub), who was to become known as Israel (Isra'il), as mentioned in the following verses:

> **We granted him [Abraham] Isaac and Jacob; We guided each of them.** (6:84)
>
> **Then, when he [Abraham] had left them [his people] and what they worshipped apart from God, We granted him Isaac and Jacob, and We made each of them a prophet. And We granted them of Our mercy and ordained for them a mention of high honor.** (19:49-50)
>
> **And We granted him Isaac, and Jacob in addition, and We made each upright. And We made them leaders, guiding by Our command. And We inspired to them the doing of good deeds and the establishment of *salat* and the giving of *zakat*, and they were worshippers of Us [alone].** (21:71-73)
>
> **And We granted him [Abraham] Isaac and Jacob, and appointed prophethood and scripture among his descendants.** (29:27)
>
> **And mention Our servants, Abraham and Isaac and Jacob, those of strength and vision. Indeed, We chose them for a special purpose: the remembrance of the [Eternal] Home, and indeed, with Us, they are among the chosen and the excellent.** (38:45-47)

Jacob (A) is mentioned in the Qur'an twenty times, twice by his adopted name, "Israel". However, nothing of his life-story is reported except in connection with his illustrious son, the prophet Joseph (A), which will be told in its place. However, the following passage which relates to Jacob (A) requires clarification:

> **All food was lawful to the Children of Israel except what Israel [Jacob] had prohibited to himself before the *Taurat* was revealed.[83] Say, [O Muhammad:] "Then bring the *Taurat* and recite it, if you are truthful. And whoever invents a falsehood about God after that, then those are the wrong-doers."** (3:93-94)

In explanation of these verses, Ibn 'Abbas (R) reports that once some Jews of Medina came to the Prophet (S), saying that they wished to ask him certain questions whose answer only a prophet would know. He told them to ask whatever they pleased on the condition that if he replied to them correctly, they would accept Islam and follow him.

---

[83] *Taurat* is the Arabic name of the original scripture revealed to Moses, prior to the interpolations and innovations that later found their way into it.

Promising to accept his condition, they asked him four questions, the first of which was, "What food did Israel prohibit to himself?"

"When Jacob or Israel became ill," the Prophet (S) replied, "he vowed that if God cured him, he would forego eating the food he liked most. Therefore, when he became well, he left off camel meat and milk"[84] (Ibn Kathir/*T*, 3:87-98).

From this, it may be inferred that, over time, these purely personal prohibitions of Jacob's assumed a sort of religious sanctity and thus came to be regarded as equivalent to sacred laws.

REFERENCES: Qur'an: 3:93-94; 6:84; 11:71; 19:49-50; 21:71-73; 29:27; 38:45-47. Commentaries: Tabari/*C*, I:269; Ibn Kathir/*T*, 3:87-98; Ayoub/*Q*, II:250-257; Maududi/*Q*, 3:fn.77; Asad/*Q*, 3:fns. 73-74.

[84]Ibn 'Abbas and other early Qur'anic commentators state that Jacob fled from Harran, the dwelling-place of his grandfather Abraham, when he was pursued by his brother Esau. During his journey, he encountered an angel, whom he took to be a highway robber. When Jacob tried to wrestle him to the ground, the angel injured Jacob's leg, resulting in extremely painful sciatica. In consequence of this, Jacob vowed never again to eat sinews and camel meat (Ayoub/*Q*, II:251-252). Thus, in Gen. 32:32, we read, "Therefore to this day the Israelites do not eat the tendon attached to the socket of the hip, because the socket of Jacob's hip was touched near the tendon."

21. The Death of Abraham

And We granted him [Abraham] his reward in this world, and indeed, in the Hereafter he will be among the righteous. (29:27)

There is no mention in the Qur'an of Abraham's remaining years. But some classical commentators confirm the report in Gen. 23:1, 19, that Sarah preceded him in death and that she was buried in a field which Abraham (A) bought in Hebron in Palestine.

The commentators also confirm the statement in Gen. 25:1-2 that after Sarah's death Abraham (A) married a Canaanite woman named Keturah (Qaturah or Qanturah) and that she bore him six sons (the prophet Shu'ayb, whose story we will narrate later in this volume, is said to have been Abraham's descendant through this marriage). Thus, Abraham (A) was ultimately the father of eight sons, including Ishmael and Isaac, God's peace and blessings be upon them all.

Earlier, we mentioned Abraham's love of showing hospitality to guests and having people eat with him. It is reported in a ***hadith*** that one day he set out to find someone to invite but found no one. When he returned home, he found a stranger inside his house.

"O servant of God, how is it that you entered my house without my permission?" Abraham (A) asked.

"I entered by permission of its Lord," the stranger replied.

"Who are you, then?" Abraham (A) asked.

"I am the Angel of Death," he replied, "and my Lord has sent me to one of His servants to give him the good news that He has chosen him as His friend."

"And who is he?" Abraham (A) asked. "For, by God, if you tell me about him, I will go and visit him even if he is in the most remote place, and I will become his neighbor until death separates us."

"That servant is *you*," the angel replied.

"Me?"

"Yes."

"For what reason has my Lord chosen me as His friend?" Abraham (A) asked.

"Because you give to people and do not ask anything of them," was the reply. (Ibn Kathir/Q, "Ibrahim")

Imam al-Ghazali, may God's blessings be upon him, cites a report originating with Ibn 'Abbas (R), stating that Abraham (A) was a conscientious man. He had a house that he used for his worship, which he would lock when he left.

One day, when he went to this house, he saw that there was a man inside. When he asked the man who had let him in, he replied, "I was admitted to it by its Master."

"But I am its master," Abraham (A) replied.

"I was admitted to it by One who has mastery over it more than you or I," the man said.

"Then which of the angels might you be?" Abraham (A) asked, immediately understanding the nature of his visitor.

"I am the Angel of Death."

"Are you able to show me the form in which you take the soul of a believer?"

"Yes," the angel replied, and he instructed Abraham (A) to turn away from him.

Abraham (A) did, and when he turned back, a young man with a handsome face, perfumed and beautifully attired, stood before him. "O Angel of Death," Abraham (A) exclaimed, "were the believer to encounter only your form upon his death it would quite suffice him!" (Al-Ghazali, *The Remembrance of Death*, pp. 44-45)

Such was Abraham, the true, the faithful, who was so completely at one with the divine Will that **when his Lord said to him, "Surrender," he said, I have surrendered to the Lord of the worlds.**" And he charged his sons to firmly keep to the pure faith appointed for them by their Lord, and so did Jacob (A) after him, saying,

> **"O my sons, indeed, God has chosen the religion for you, so do not die except that you be *muslims*."** (2:132)

If you should ever go to the West Bank of Palestine, which is now in the state of Israel, you may visit the burial place of this illustrious prophet. His mortal remains are buried in a cave under the floor of the Mosque of Abraham in Hebron, a city known in Arabic as "al-Khalil" after *Khalil ar-Rahman*, the Friend of the Most Merciful, upon whom people of faith perpetually invoke God's highest blessings and peace.

> **And We left [this invocation] for him among the later generations: "Peace be upon Abraham!" Thus do We surely reward the doers of good. Indeed, he was among Our believing servants.** (37:108-111)

REFERENCES: Tabari/*H*, II:125, 127, 129-130; Ibn Kathir/*Q*, "Ibrahim"; al-Ghazali, *The Remembrance of Death*, pp. 44-45.

22. Prophethood After Abraham

Indeed, We have revealed to you [Muhammad] as We revealed to Noah and the prophets after him; and We revealed to Abraham and Ishmael and Isaac and Jacob. (4:163)

We had already granted the family of Abraham the scripture and wisdom, and granted them a great kingdom. (4:54)

After Abraham's passing from this life, his pure faith was continued and carried on by his two prophet-sons, Ishmael and Isaac (A), from whom two lines of prophethood were to descend, and after them, by Jacob or Israel (A).

Jacob (A) was destined to become the father of twelve sons. These sons in turn became the fathers of the twelve tribes of Israel, who kept alive the faith of their ancestors. And from this line of descent came all the Israelite prophets, as indicated by the following verses:

Say, [O Muhammad:] "We believe in God and what was revealed to us, and what was revealed to Abraham and Ishmael and Isaac and Jacob and the descendants [of Israel], and what was given to Moses and Jesus and the prophets by their Lord. We make no distinction between any of them, and we surrender to Him [in Islam]." (3:84; also 23:36)

And We granted him [Abraham] Isaac and Jacob; each [of them] We guided. And previously We guided Noah, and among his descendants, David and Solomon and Job and Joseph and Moses and Aaron. And thus do We reward the doers of good. And Zechariah and John and Jesus and Elijah — all were among the righteous; and Ishmael and Elisha and Jonah and Lot — and all [of them] We preferred over mankind, and some from among their fathers and descendants and brothers; and We chose them and guided them to a straight path. (6:84-87; also 2:136)

Those were the ones upon whom God bestowed favor of the prophets among the descendants of Adam and among those whom We carried [in the Ark] with Noah, and among the descendants of Abraham and Israel, and among those whom We guided and chose. When the signs of the Most Merciful were recited to them, they fell down prostrating and weeping. (19:58)

At the same time, Abraham's line of descent through Ishmael (A) was preserved through the Arabs of the Arabian peninsula. And it was from this line that the last and greatest of all the prophets, God's beloved, Muhammad (S), was to come in the sixth century of the Christian era.

In time, upon the foundation built by Moses (A) and the prophets who followed him, the faith known as Judaism came into being. Still later, Christianity, with its Jewish roots, emerged out of Palestine. Then, in the sixth century, the final revelation from the Lord of the universes was bestowed upon the Seal of the Prophets, God's peace and blessings be upon him, completing and perfecting the faith of all the prophets who had preceded him.

While Abraham (A) is equally the spiritual ancestor of Jews, Christians and Muslims, God Most High declares emphatically that the faith of His Friend was neither Judaism nor Christianity, but rather the original, unadulterated religion ordained by God for mankind, which has been the faith of all the prophets and rightly-guided believers since the time of Adam (A), *islam*.[85] Concerning this, He says,

> **O People of the Scripture,[86] why do you dispute about Abraham while the *Taurat* and the *Injil*[87] were not revealed until after him? Will you not then use reason? . . . Abraham was neither a Jew nor a Christian, but he was one inclining toward truth, a *muslim*, and he was not among the *mushrikin*. Indeed, the most worthy people in relation to Abraham are those who followed him and this prophet [Muhammad] and those who believe [in Muhammad]. And God is the Protector of the believers.** (3:65, 67-68)
>
> **They say, "Be Jews or Christians [so] you will be guided." Say, [O Muhammad:] "No, but [we follow] the religion of Abraham, inclining toward truth, and he was not among the *mushrikin*." Say: "We believe in God and what was revealed to us, and what was revealed to Abraham and Ishmael and Isaac and Jacob and the descendants [of Israel], and what was given to Moses and Jesus, and what was given to the prophets by their Lord. We make no distinction between any of them and we surrender to Him [in Islam]." . . . Or do you say that Abraham and Ishmael and Isaac and Jacob and the descendants [of Israel] were Jews or Christians? Say: "Do you know, or does God?" And who is more unjust than one who hides**

---

[85]Ibn 'Abbas reports that once some Christians of Najran (a Christian city in southern Arabia near Yemen) and some Jewish rabbis came together to dispute with the Prophet (S), the rabbis claiming that Abraham was a Jew and the Christians that he was a Christian. God then revealed the verse, **O People of the Scripture, why do you dispute about Abraham while the *Taurat* and the *Injil* were not revealed until after him? Will you not then use reason?** (3:65), nullifying the claims of both groups. The classical commentator Mujahid says that God dissociated Abraham from both the Jews and Christians when they claimed that he belonged to them, associating him instead with those who follow the *hanifiyyah*, — that is, the pure, pristine, original faith, *islam* (Ayoub/Q, II:208-210).

[86]That is, Jews and Christians.

[87]The Arabic name of the original scripture revealed to Jesus.

the testimony that he has from God? And God is not unmindful of what you do. (2:135-136, 140)

May God's best blessings and peace be upon the noble prophet Abraham, his sons Ishmael and Isaac, his grandson Jacob, his great-grandson Joseph, his later descendants Moses and Jesus, and upon all the prophets in his line, up to the last of them all, God's illustrious Messenger, Muhammad (S).

23. The Legacy of Abraham, the Friend of God

Say, [O Muhammad:] "Indeed, my Lord has guided me to a straight path, a correct religion: the faith of Abraham, inclining toward truth, and he was not among the *mushrikin*." (6:161)

The Practices of Abraham

Many of the Qur'anic verses we have cited concerning Abraham (A) demonstrate his Lord's great regard for him. What could possibly be higher praise than His words,

> **Who would be averse to the way of Abraham except one who makes a fool of himself? And We chose him in this world, and indeed, in the Hereafter he will be among the righteous. When his Lord said to him, "Surrender," he said, "I have surrendered to the Lord of the worlds" (2:130-131);**
>
> **Who is better in religion than the one who surrenders himself to God, while being a doer of good, and follows the faith of Abraham, inclining toward truth? And God took Abraham as an intimate friend (4:125);**
>
> **Abraham was indeed an *ummah*, devoutly obedient to God, inclining toward truth, and he was not among the *mushrikin*, [and he was] grateful for His favors. He [God] chose him and guided him to a straight path. And We gave him good in this world, and indeed, in the Hereafter he will be among the righteous. Then We revealed to you, [Muhammad], to follow the faith of Abraham, inclining toward truth, and he was not among the *mushrikin* (16:120-123)?**

From these verses, it is evident that Abraham's high standing with God was due to his pure and perfected faith and his total surrender to the divine Will, which is further referred to in God's saying,

> **And [mention, O Muhammad,] when Abraham was tried by his Lord through words [of command] and he carried them out. He said, "Indeed, I will make you a leader of mankind." He [Abraham] said, "And of my descendants?" He said, "My covenant does not include the wrong-doers." (2:124)**

Throughout this story, we have been witness to the several ways in which Abraham (A) was **tried by his Lord.** However, since the above verse does not specify the **"words"** by which God tried His Friend, the classical commentators have given various interpretations of them, among which are the following:

1. Ibn 'Abbas (R) says that Islam consists of thirty parts,[88] and no one was ever tried with the obligation represented by these **"words"** or commands and fulfilled it completely except Abraham (A). Consequently, God ordained for him immunity from disobedience to Him, saying, **And Abraham, who fulfilled [*waffa*] [his obligations]** [53:37] (Ibn Kathir/*T*, 2:124).

Concerning the meaning of "***waffa***"[89] in the above verse, the Holy Prophet (S) said:

> The word "***waffa***" is said of Abraham because each morning and evening he used to say, **"Then glorified be God when when you reach the evening and when you reach the morning, and to Him is [due all] praise throughout the heavens and the earth, and at night and when you reach noon. He brings forth the living from the dead and brings forth the dead from the living, and He brings the earth to life after its death. And thus will you be brought forth"** [30:17-19]. (Ibn Kathir/*T*, 2:124; 53:36)
>
> Each day at daybreak, he [Abraham] would pray four *rak'ats* without fail, and that was his "fulfilling," in keeping with the divine command contained in the ***hadith qudsi:*** "Son of Adam, if you pray four *rak'ats* for me at the beginning of the day, I shall supply what you need until the end of it." [Tirmidhi]

2. Al-Tabari's interpretation of the **"words"** of command mentioned in 2:124 is as follows:

> When God Most High recognized Abraham's steadfastness concerning everything with which He tried him, his carrying out all the obligations He laid upon him, and his preferring obedience to Him above all things, He took him as a friend, made him a leader of those who came after him among his people, and choose him as a messenger to his people. And He appointed prophethood and scripture and messengership among his descendants, and favored them with revealed books and deep wisdoms, and appointed among them scholars and leaders and rulers and chiefs. Whenever a noble personage among them passed away, another chief of high degree succeeded him, and He caused the mention of them to remain among those who came afterwards.
>
> All the nations make him their patron and praise him, and speak of this excellence as an honor from God to him in this world. But the honor

---

[88]Among these, ten of its commands are contained in *Surah Taubah* (9:112), ten in *Surah al-Ahzab* (33:35), and ten in *Sarah al-Ma'arij* (70:22-34).

[89]The verb "***waffa***" means to meet, keep, live up to, fulfill or be faithful to an obligation, agreement, covenant or promise. In this context, it refers to Abraham's faithfulness in adhering to whatever God Most High had commanded or prohibited to him, and fulfilling all the obligations of his perfected faith.

that is stored up for him in the Hereafter is too glorious and great to be fully described by any speech. (Tabari/Q, "Ibrahim")

3. Ibn Kathir says that the "trying" mentioned in 2:124 consisted of words of command and prohibition with which God charged Abraham (A), all of which he carried out faithfully. As a result of his steadfastness, God made him **a leader of mankind**. But, like his descendant Muhammad (S), who always appealed to his Lord on behalf of his ***ummah***, Abraham (A), the humble and sincere, had no desire to accept honors and leadership for himself alone. Rather, he thought of all his descendants-to-come throughout the ages, and by his words, **"And of my descendants?"** requested that they might share the favors and honors he had been granted.

But God knew with perfect knowledge that among Abraham's descendants there would not only be the best among mankind, the prophets and their believing followers, but also great numbers who would turn away from the faith of their prophet-ancestors and engage in every kind of wrong-doing, as is stated in the following verses:

> **We certainly sent Noah and Abraham, and established prophethood and scripture among their descendants; and among them are the guided, but many of them are defiantly disobedient. (57:26)**
>
> **We blessed him [Abraham] and Isaac. But among their descendants is the doer of good and the one who clearly wrongs himself.**[90] **(37:113)**

Thus, God replied to Abraham's request for his descendants indirectly, neither accepting nor denying it. Rather, by declaring that **My covenant does not include the wrong-doers** (2:124),[91] He made clear for all time to come that prophethood and spiritual leadership are not granted on the basis of family connection or descent but are conferred purely by His choosing.

4. When asked about the **"words"** by which Abraham (A) was tested, the well-known classical commentator al-Hasan al-Basri said, "When God tested Abraham with a command, he was steadfast in obeying it. He tested him with the star, the sun, and the moon, and he did well with those and knew that his Lord is eternal and He will not cease." Abraham (A) then turned his **being toward the One who created the heavens and the earth, as one inclining**

---

[90]See "Adam," page 58, for a discussion of the concept of wronging or being unjust to one's own self.

[91]This is also indirectly stated in God's response to Abraham's supplication to provide the future people of Mecca, his descendants, **whoever among them believes in God and the Last Day,** with the fruits of the earth for their sustenance — namely, **"And whoever disbelieves, I shall grant him enjoyment a while, but then I shall drive him to the punishment of the Fire, and wretched is the destination!"** (2:126).

toward truth, and he was **not among the *mushrikin*** [6:79]. Al-Hasan continues:

> He then tested him with the emigration, and he left his land and took his people to Syria, journeying to God. Before the emigration He tested him with the fire and he was steadfast, and He tested him with the sacrifice of his son and with circumcision, and he was steadfast (Tabari/*H*, II:103-104).

5. Yet another interpretation of these **"words"** or commands is that they refer to the basic measures of hygiene — that is, to the removal of whatever is contrary to the highest standards of personal cleanliness. Thus, Ibn 'Abbas (R) says, God tried Abraham (A) with purification (*taharah*) in five matters pertaining to the head and five to the body. Those pertaining the head were trimming the mustache,[92] rinsing the mouth, rinsing the nostrils,[93] cleaning the teeth with a twig toothbrush (*miswak*),[94] and parting the hair. And those pertaining to the body were trimming the nails, shaving the pubic hair,[95] circumcision,[96] depilating the hair of the armpits, and washing away traces of urine and feces with water[97] (Ibn Kathir/*Q*, "Ibrahim"; Tabari/*H*, II:99-100, Ayoub/*Q*, I:152).

---

[92]Centuries later, Prophet Muhammad (S) was to order Muslim males to trim their mustaches, while allowing their beards to grow (*Bukhari*, 7:776-781; *Muslim*, 498-503; *Mishkat*, 4437; *Muwatta*, 51.1.1). Ibn 'Abbas reported, "The Prophet (S) used to clip or take something off his moustache, and Abraham, the Friend of the Merciful, [also] used to do so" (*Mishkat*, 4437; also *Muwatta*, 49:3.4). The Holy Prophet emphasized this practice by saying, "He who does not take something off his moustache is not one of us" (*Mishkat*, 4438), meaning that it is inconsistent with dignity and cleanliness for a man to permit his moustache to grow untidily, its hairs trailing over his mouth. Rather, it is to be trimmed until the rim of the lip appears (*Muwatta*, 49.3.4).

[93]The mouth and nostrils are routinely rinsed during *wudu'*, the washing preceding *salat*.

[94]This natural toothbrush is the twig of a tree which grows in the Arabian peninsula. The Prophet (S) used the *miswak* very regularly and stressed its importance to the point of saying, "If it were not burdensome upon my community, I would have ordered them to use the *miswak* at each prayer" (*Mishkat*, 390). This suggests that the benefit of using a *miswak* extends far beyond the physical act of brushing the teeth. Modern research has demonstrated that dental hygiene plays a role in cardiac and other aspects of health, and that the *miswak* has significant hygienic and therapeutic properties.

[95]Making for much greater ease of cleaning the genital area, eliminating odors and infections, and reducing the possibility of body lice.

[96]The Prophet (S) said that Abraham fulfilled the order of circumcision at the age of eighty with an adze (*Bukhari*, 4:575). The order to circumcise is not found in the Qur'an but rather in the *ahadith* quoted in footnote 98. In Islam, circumcision is practiced purely as a hygienic measure, observed by Abraham and the prophets after his time. The notion that circumcision constitues a covenant between God and men, as mentioned in Gen. 17:9-14, is not found in Islam.

[97]In Islam, urine and feces are regarded as filthy and defiling; therefore, no trace of them should be left on the body or clothing. Hence, the practice of cleaning with water after using the toilet is universal among Muslims. The left hand is used for such cleaning, and washing the hands well afterwards is a matter of common decency.

Ibn 'Abbas (R) also states that of the ten commands given to Abraham (A), six are related to the body and four to the rites of *Hajj*. Those related to the body are shaving the pubic hair, circumcision, depilating the hair of the armpits, cutting the nails, trimming the mustache, and showering on Friday (the day of congregational worship for Muslims). The four related to *Hajj* are making *tawaf* of the K'abah, doing *sa'i* between Safa and Marwah, stoning the pillars, and hastening out of 'Arafat on the ninth of Dhul-Hijjah, the month of pilgrimage (Tabari/*H*, II:100, 102, Ayoub/*Q*, I:152).

Which of these practices of purification were meant by the **"words"** of command referred to in 2:124, it is impossible to say. Perhaps all of them were, for all of them were carried out not only by Abraham (A) but also by his descendant Muhammad (S), who taught them to his ***ummah***. The Holy Prophet (S) mentioned them as pertaining to the basic ***fitrah*** or innate nature and disposition of the human being.[98] And since his time, Muslims have continued to observe them in keeping with his example, out of conviction that following the ***sunnah*** of the last and greatest of God's messengers, the most perfect of mankind, strengthens their faith, supports their well-being, and brings them honor, blessings and reward.

REFERENCES: Tabari/*H*, II:98-105; Ibn Kathir/*T*, 2:124, 53:36; Ibn Kathir/*Q*, "Ibrahim"; Ayoub/*Q*, I:151-157.

---

[98]The Prophet (S) said:

> Five things pertain to the ***fitrah***: circumcision, shaving the pubic hair, clipping the mustache, cutting the nails, and depilating the armpits (***Bukhari***, 7:777, 7:779; ***Muslim***, 495-496; ***Muwatta***, 49.3.3). The last four should be not be neglected for more than forty nights (***Muslim***, 497).

> There are four characteristics [which constitute] the ***sunnahs*** of the messengers of God: modesty, but some say circumcision, the use of perfume, the ***miswak***, and marriage. (***Mishkat***, 382)

> Pertaining to the ***fitrah*** are shaving the pubic hair, cutting the nails and clipping the mustache. (***Bukhari***, 4:778)

> Ten things pertain to the ***fitrah***: clipping the mustache, letting the beard grow, using the ***miswak***, sniffing water up the nose [in ***wudu'***], cutting the nails, washing the finger joints, depilating the hair of the armpits, shaving the pubic hair, and cleaning the genitals with water [after elimination]. [These are nine, for the narrator of this ***hadith*** forgot the tenth but said that it may have been rinsing the mouth]. (***Muslim***, 502; also ***Muwatta***, 52)

The Wisdom of Abraham

One of the outstanding gifts which God Most High bestowed upon Abraham (A), and after him upon his descendants, was the attribute of wisdom, as mentioned in the verse,

> **We had already granted the family of Abraham the scripture and wisdom, and granted them a great kingdom.**[99] (4:54)

"The scripture" (***al-kitab***) mentioned in these verses refers to the holy books revealed to certain prophets in the Abrahamic line: to Abraham himself, to Moses, David, Jesus and Muhammad, God's peace and blessings be upon them all. And **"wisdom"** (***al-hikmah***) is a special attribute of those with spiritual vision, mentioned again and again in the Qur'an as the property of the prophets.[100]

What is wisdom? It is that inner understanding granted to some servants' hearts by God Most Gracious, an understanding different from that of any secular knowledge or knowledge found in books — the ability to look beyond the seeming observed "facts" and recognize the deeper meanings and realities underlying the apparent and obvious, seeing with something of the limitless vision of the Creator. Concerning it, God says:

> **He grants wisdom to whomever He wills, and the one who has been granted wisdom has surely been granted great good. And none will bear this in mind except those of understanding.** (2:269)

As we have seen, Abraham (A) originated in a pagan society, and one characteristic of pagan societies is preoccupation with material things and forms. But one who possesses wisdom looks beyond forms and objects and appearances, beyond immediate physical explanations, to the spiritual realities behind things and events.

Abraham's keen spiritual insight is made clear by God's saying, **Thus did We show Abraham the realm of the heavens and the earth** (6:75). And throughout his long life, we see this theme repeated.

At a young age, when Abraham (A) renounced the stars, moon and sun as objects of worship, he turned away from the realm of created, material objects to the realm beyond all forms, outside of time and space and change. It was there he sought and found His Lord, for his pure, uncontaminated *fitrah* instinctively recognized and acknowledged the divine Reality.

---

[99]The **great kingdom** referred to here relates to the spiritual leadership and guidance of mankind granted to Abraham and his prophet-descendants, including the Last Prophet (S).

[100]See 2:151, 231, 247, 251; 3:48, 58, 79, 81, 164; 4:54, 113; 5:110/113; 12:22; 15:33; 17:39; 19:12; 28:14; 38:20; 46:63.

The same theme of seeing beyond physical "facts" to spiritual realities is repeated in Abraham's understanding of the metaphor of the four birds by which God, the All-Wise, showed him how He will recall the dead to life on the Last Day. It recurs again in Abraham's certainty that his fate would be determined not by the raging fire into which he was destined to be thrown, but by the Lord of the fire, who has power over all things in creation.

This understanding is again clearly evident in Abraham's awareness that the outwardly desolate, barren spot where he was commanded to leave his wife and child was, in reality, vital to the future of true faith, and that nothing was appropriate on his part except total surrender to the divine Will. It was demonstrated again in his faithfulness to his inner vision in the sacrifice of his son, contrary to all reason, logic, common sense, and accepted laws of conscience and conduct. Later, it was evident in his quick perception of the inner nature of Ishmael's two wives. It was manifested once again in his understanding of the immense spiritual significance of the crude stone building which he and Ishmael (A) constructed in the barren emptiness of Mecca. And finally, it was demonstrated in his calling all pilgrims-to-come in the future, outside of time and space, to pilgrimage at his Lord's Sacred House.

All these incidents suggest that, by means of the wisdom that God Most Gracious had poured into his heart, Abraham (A) recognized the interconnectedness of all things in existence and the divine perfection underlying them through the working of the one divine Will. His life was lived so completely in accordance with this understanding that **when his Lord said to him, "Surrender!" he said, "I have surrendered to the Lord of the worlds"** (2:131). Having turned his being away from all finite, transitory objects and interests **toward the One who created the heavens and the earth, as one inclining toward truth** (6:79), **he came to his Lord with a sound heart** (37:84) — a heart in which there was no questioning, doubt or confusion, no preoccupation with forms or material causes, no room for anything but his beloved Lord, who had taken him as His friend, firmly grounded in the certainty that

> **Everyone on it [the earth] will perish, yet there will remain the Face of your Lord, Possessor of Majesty and Honor.** (55:26-27)

APPENDIX A

WHICH SON — ISAAC OR ISHMAEL?

In Genesis 22:2, Isaac (A) is mentioned as the object of sacrifice, and Jewish tradition gives this fact considerable importance.[101] Indeed, even among the early Islamic scholars and Qur'anic commentators, there was some difference of opinion about which of Abraham's two sons was to be sacrificed, for nowhere does the Qur'an mention the name of this son. And while the consensus of Muslim scholars strongly holds that it was Ishmael (A), we present here both opinions, for each of which support is drawn from the following passage in *Surah as-Saffat*, 37:99-112:

> **And he [Abraham] said, "Indeed, I shall go to my Lord; He will guide me.** (99)
>
> **"My Lord, grant me [a son] from among the righteous!"** (100) **so We gave him the good tidings of a forbearing boy.** (101)
>
> **Then, when he reached [the age of] working with him, he [Abraham] said, "O my son, I have indeed seen in a vision that I am sacrificing you, so see what you think."**
>
> **He said, "O my father, do what you are commanded. You will find me, God willing, among the patient."** (102)
>
> **Then, when they had both surrendered [themselves] and he had put him down on his forehead,** (103) **We called to him, "O Abraham,** (104) **you have fulfilled the vision!" Thus do We surely reward the doers of good.** (105) **Indeed, this was a clear trial,** (106) **and We ransomed him with a great sacrifice,** (107) **and We left [this**

---

[101]The Biblical account may be summarized as follows:

In Gen. 16:6, Hagar flees from Sarah while she is pregnant with Ishmael. An angel finds her beside a spring or well called Beer Lahai Roi (situated in the north of the Sinai peninsula near Kadesh Barnea) (Gen. 16:7, 14). The angel instructs her to go back to her mistress and submit to her (Gen. 16:9). The same story is repeated, with different details, in Gen. 21:9-21. Here, Sarah forces Abraham to send away Hagar and Ishmael *after* the birth of Isaac (Gen. 21:10-14). Hagar wanders about in the wilderness of Beersheba (east of the southern end of the Dead Sea, north-west of the previously-mentioned Beer Lahai Roi) where she is comforted by an angel and is shown a well (Gen. 21:14, 19). Ishmael grows up in the Desert of Paran (the central part of the Sinai peninsula), and his mother gets him a wife from Egypt (Gen. 21:20-21). As for the sacrifice of Abraham's son, in Gen. 22:2 and 22:16 Isaac is mentioned as his "only son" in spite of the references to Ishmael in Gen. 16:15-16, 17:23-24 and 21:5, 9-13 which make it clear that he, not Isaac, was Abraham's firstborn son. In Gen. 22:2, God commands Abraham to carry out the sacrifice of Isaac in the "region of Moriah," a place whose whereabouts is uncertain. Isaac is not consulted in the matter of his being sacrificed. On the contrary, he asks his father, "Where is the lamb for the burnt offering?" (Gen. 22:7).

invocation] for him among the later generations: (108) **"Peace be upon Abraham!"** (109) **Thus do We reward the doers of good.** (110) **Indeed, he was among Our believing servants.** (111)

And We gave him the good tidings of Isaac, a prophet from among the righteous. (112)

ISAAC:

Al-Tabari cites a number of reports from the early Islamic commentators, prominent among whom was Ka'b al-Ahbar, a Jewish convert to Islam who was very knowledgable concerning the Torah, stating that Isaac (A) was the object of sacrifice. In fact, al-Tabari even reports a ***hadith*** to this effect. He explains this position by referring to the foregoing passage, 37:99-112, as follows:

Abraham's prayer for a son was made at his leaving Ur, when he and Sarah were young and had every expectation of having children, and when Hagar had not even been heard of. According to this interpretation, the son **from among the righteous** for whom Abraham (A) prayed in verse 100 and **the forbearing boy** mentioned in verse 101 both refer to Isaac.

It is thus Isaac (A) who is spoken of in verse 102 as having reached the age of working with his father, and hence it is he who is the intended sacrificial victim. At the end of this passage, in verse 112, God refers to the annunciation of Isaac's birth a second time, saying, **"And We gave him the good tidings of Isaac, a prophet from among the righteous,"** thus answering — and echoing — Abraham's earlier prayer in verse 100: **"My Lord, grant me [a son] from among the righteous."**

REFERENCE: Tabari/*H*, II:83-86, 89-92.

ISHMAEL:

The commentators who claim that the object of sacrifice was Ishmael (A) base their arguments on the following evidence:

1. The same passage, 37:99-112 cited above in connection with Isaac (A), suggests the following:

While Abraham's prayer for a son in 37:99 may have been uttered at the time he left Ur, **the forbearing boy** (37:101), his firstborn, announced in verse 101, was not born until many years later — and there is no question about the fact that Abraham's firstborn son was Ishmael (A). It is he who is meant in verse 102 as having reached the age of working with his father and who was the intended victim of the sacrifice. We may add to this that since there is no break in the continuity of the passage, which reads, **So We gave him the good tidings of a forbearing boy. Then, when he reached [the age of] working with him . . .** (37:101-102), it is logically impossible that the "**he**" spoken of in this verse should be anyone but the **forbearing boy** — that is, the firstborn, Ishmael.

Isaac (A), who is positively identified only in the last verse of this passage, 37:112, in the words, **And We gave him the good tidings of Isaac, a prophet from among the righteous,** is obviously a different son from the one whose birth was announced previously in verse 101. Thus, reasoning backwards, we are led to conclude that **the forbearing boy** referred to in verse 101 was the only son of Abraham who was alive at the time of the sacrifice — namely, Ishmael (A).

As for Abraham's prayer for a son **from among the righteous** (37:100), it was answered in both his sons, for God Most High speaks of Isaac (A) as **a prophet from among the righteous** (37:112). At the same time, He says,

> **And Ishmael and Idris and Dhu-l-Kifl — all were among the patient, and We admitted them them to Our mercy. Indeed, they were among the righteous. (21:85-86)**

2. God says, **Then We gave her [Sarah] good tidings of Isaac, and after Isaac, Jacob** (11:71). Now, if the intended object of sacrifice had been Isaac — while God had already informed his parents about Isaac's son Jacob, prior to his birth — Abraham's vision would have been meaningless and unclear to him. From this one point alone, Ibn Kathir argues that the object of sacrifice

> has to be Ishmael and cannot be Isaac because God says, **We gave her good tidings of Isaac, and after Isaac, Jacob** — and how could God give the tidings of Isaac, and that he would have a son, Jacob, and then order Abraham to sacrifice Isaac while he was young before Jacob had [even] been born to him? This is impossible and would contradict the earlier tidings. But God knows best. (Ibn Kathir/*Q*, "Ibrahim")

3. The birth of Abraham's two prophet-sons was announced to him by divine revelations in which the special characteristics of each was mentioned.

In the case of Ishmael, Abraham (A) was given the tidings of a "***ghulamin halim***"(37:101), meaning a forbearing, gentle, long-suffering, patient boy, while in the case of Isaac (A), the announcement was of a "***ghulamin 'alim***"(15:53, 51:28) — that is, a wise, learned, knowing boy.

It is reasonable to assume that anyone, perhaps especially a child or youth, who is asked to agree to sacrifice his life for God needs to have the qualities of patience, forbearance and the ability to deal with suffering, rather than wisdom, knowledge and learning. And this is in keeping with Ishmael's words when Abraham (A) informed him about his vision, namely, **"You will find me, God willing, among the patient"** (37:102), as well as with God's mentioning Ishmael (A) as being **among the patient** (21:85).

4. While the fact that Abraham and Isaac (A) lived in Palestine (that is, Syria) has never been disputed, no one has ever claimed that Isaac (A) had the remotest connection with the region of Mecca or with the K'abah. However, the connection of Abraham and Ishmael (A) to Mecca and its Sacred House was well preserved in the oral and written traditions of their descendants, the Arabs of the area, prior to Islam. Indeed, even up to the time of Prophet Muhammad (S), people used to carry out animal sacrifices at Mina, the place at which Abraham's intended sacrifice is said to have taken place. Moreover, Hagar and Ishmael (A) are buried close to the K'abah.

This connection is amply confirmed in Ibn 'Abbas' lengthy narrative about Abraham's leaving Hagar and Ishmael (A) in Mecca at the site of the Sacred House, and in both the Qur'an and ***ahadith*** in relation to the building of the K'abah by Abraham and Ishmael (A) some years later. Moreover, the rites of *Hajj* and *'Umrah*, taught to Abraham (A) by the angel Gabriel, commemorate events in the lives of Abraham, Hajar and Ishmael (A), without any mention of Isaac (A) whatsoever. This, above all, makes it clear that the object of sacrifice was Ishmael and not Isaac (A), and that the site of the sacrifice was the area of Mecca, not Palestine.[102]

Centuries later, the Messenger of God (S) followed the same rites of *Hajj* and *'Umrah* as Abraham (A) had done before him, recalling the same events from the lives of Abraham, Hagar and Ishmael (A), again without any mention of Isaac (A). It is hardly possible to question the fact that Muhammad (S), God's last and greatest prophet, knew with certain knowledge which of Abraham's two sons was the object of sacrifice, and this is reflected in the practices which he passed on to his ***ummah***, as well in the following ***hadith:***

A Companion of the Prophet (S) named al-Sunabihi reported being with the Prophet (S) when a man came to him, saying, "O Messenger of God! Repeat to me the knowledge God has given you, O son of the two victims!" The Messenger of God laughed and they said to him, "Who are the two victims, O Messenger of God?" He said, "When 'Abd al-Mutallib [the Prophet's grandfather] was ordered to dig Zamzam, he vowed that if God would make it easy for him, he would sacrifice one of his sons. The choice fell upon 'Abdullah [the Prophet's father], but his maternal uncles prevented it, saying, 'Ransom

---

[102]It is notewothy that while al-Tabari cites two reports purportedly from Ibn 'Abbas stating that the sacrificial victim was Isaac, he cites ten others from Ibn 'Abbas stating that it was Ishmael (Tabari/*H*, II:83-84, 86-87). As for a ***hadith*** reported by al-Tabari stating that Isaac was the intended victim, it is so clearly against all evidence and common understanding that it must be questioned (Tabari/*H*, II:83).

your son with one hundred camels.' So he did that, and Ishmael was the other victim" (Tabari/*H*, II:83).

4. A related, although non-conclusive piece of evidence is that the horns of the ram sacrificed by Abraham (A) hung at the K'abah up to the year 692 A.C. — that is, about sixty years after the death of the Prophet, when the K'abah was destroyed by Hajjaj ibn Yusuf.[105] This is mentioned by Ibn 'Abbas (R), as well as by another Companion of the Prophet, 'Uthman bin Talha (R), who said:

> The Prophet (S) sent for me and said to me, "I used to see the ram's horns when I came to the [Sacred] House. Did you forget that I ordered you to cover them? Then go and cover them, for it is not appropriate that anything which distracts the worshippers should be in the House." (Ibn Kathir/*Q*, "Ibrahim")

From all this, it is clear that the Islamic understanding that Ishmael (A) was the object of sacrifice rests on solid and conclusive evidence.

REFERENCES: Tabari/*H*, II:82-90; Ibn Kathir/*Q*, "Ibrahim"; Maududi/*Q*, 37:fn. 67.

---

[103]Abraham and Ishmael lived in about 2000 B.C. Consequently the ram's horns would have been about 2600 years old when Islam was revealed to the Prophet (S) in the sixth century A.C. To verify the possibility that ram's horns could last such a long time, I asked a taxidermist. "Sure!" he said. "They could last forever."

APPENDIX B

IDOL-WORSHIP AMONG THE DESCENDANTS OF ISHMAEL

After Ishmael's time, idol-worship gained a foothold in the sacred territory of Mecca and mingled with the pure God-centered faith passed on by Abraham and his prophet-son to their descendants in the region.

Says the early biographer of the Prophet, Ibn Ishaq, in his classic work, *The Life of Muhammad*:

> They say that the beginning of stone worship among the sons of Ishmael was when Mecca became too small for them and they wanted more room in the country. Everyone who left the town took with him a stone from the sacred area to do honour to it. Wherever they settled they set it up and walked round it as they went round the Ka'ba. This led them to worship what stones they pleased and those which made an impression on them. (Ibn Ishaq/*M*, pp. 35)

And an eye-witness who later accepted Islam reports:

> We used to worship a stone and when we found a stone that was better than it, we would throw it away and take the other. But if we did not find stones, we would collect a pile of earth, then bring a sheep and milk it upon it, then make *tawaf* at it. . . . (*Bukhari*, 5:661)

It is also reported that when a traveler halted at a place, he would collect four stones, using three to support his cooking pot and worshipping the best-looking among them. When he left the place, he would leave the stones behind.

> Thus [Ibn Ishaq continues,] as generations passed they forgot their primitive faith and adopted another religion for that of Abraham and Ishmael. They worshipped idols and adopted the same errors as the peoples before them. Yet they retained and held fast practices going back to the time of Abraham, such as honouring the temple [the K'abah] and going round it, the great and little pilgrimage [*Hajj and 'Umrah*], and the standing on 'Arafa and Muzdalifah, sacrificing the [animal] victims, and the pilgrim cry at the great and little pilgrimage, while introducing elements which had no place in the religion of Islam. (Ibn Ishaq/*M*, pp. 35-36)

The result of this was a mind-boggling paganism mingled with pathetic remnants of the faith of Abraham and Ishmael (A). Ibn 'Abbas (R) reports, for example, that when the idol-worshippers of the Prophet's time gave the traditional pilgrims' call (*talbiyah*), they would begin with the correct words, "*Labbayk, la sharika laka* — Here I am, [O God]; You have no partner," but would add, while making *tawaf* of the K'abah, ". . . Except the [one] partner You have.

You have mastery over him but he does not have mastery [over You] (*Muslim*, 2671; Ibn Ishaq/*M*, p. 36). Moreover, apart from the Hums (that is, the Quraysh and their descendants), they would perform *tawaf* of the K'abah naked (*Bukhari*, 2:726). Thus, God Most High revealed to the Prophet (S) concerning their false religion,

> **Most of them do not believe in God except while they associate others with Him (12:106),**

and, concerning the pagan pilgrimage that was sacriligeously carried out at His Sacred House,

> **Their *salat* at the House was nothing but whistling and hand-clapping (8:35).**

As mentioned previously, among the gods worshipped in Arabia were the same deities as were worshipped by the people of Noah (A), mentioned in 71:23, and many more besides. Sayyid Qutb, a well-known modern scholar, writes:

> Idol worship proliferated among them, some of the idols representing angels, others their ancestors, and yet others imaginary deities. The Ka'bah, which had been built solely for the worship of Allah, was filled with idols, their number reaching three hundred and sixty. In addition, there were major idols of other kinds. Among them were Al-Lat, Al-'Uzza, and Manat, which are mentioned in the Qur'an [63:19-28], and Hubal, on whose behalf Abu Sufyan [one of the chief enemies of Islam], on the day of [the Battle of] Uhud, shouted "May Hubal be exalted!" (Qutb/*Concept*, pp. 30-31)

Each tribe had its favorite god or godesses. To cite but one example, an idol known as al-Khalasa was set up in the lower part of Mecca. Its worshipers "used to put necklaces on it, and bring gifts of barley and wheat. They poured milk on it, sacrificed to it, and hung ostrich eggs on it" (Ibn Ishaq/*M*, p. 39). False rites were observed at the shrines of these idols, and the imposition of various taboos and omen-seeking was common. People also worshipped planets and stars, one tribe worshipping the sun, another the moon, and others worshipping Jupiter, the Dog-Star, Sirius and Mercury.

But it did not stop here. Each household kept an idol indoors which they used to worship. The last thing a man would do when setting off on a journey was to rub himself against this idol, and when he returned the first thing he did, even before going in to his family, was again to rub himself against it. Consequently, when God appointed Muhammad (S) to convey the Message of His Oneness, his tribe, the Quraysh, said, **"Has he made [all] the gods one God? Indeed, this is an amazing thing!'** [38:5].

> Now along with the Ka'ba the Arabs had adopted Tawaghit, [continues Ibn Ishaq,] which were temples which they venerated as they vener-

ated the Ka'ba. They had their guardians and overseers and they used to make offerings to them as they did to the Ka'ba and to circumambulate them and sacrifice at them. Yet they recognized the superiority of the Ka'ba because it was the temple and mosque of Abraham the friend (of God). (Ibn Ishaq/*M*, p. 38)

The result of all this was that, in spite of the heritage of pure faith that had come down to them from Abraham and Ishmael (A), the made-up rules, rituals and social order based on the false claims of polytheism shaped and dominated Arab society after the decline of monotheism until the coming of Islam. Consequently, when God Most High ordered His Last Messenger, Muhammad (S), to call his people to belief in His Oneness and he began to attack their idolatrous practices, the Quraysh turned against him with great vehemence. It was not until the twentieth year of his prophethood in 630 C.E., ten years after his emigration to Medina, when he returned to Mecca victorious and its people accepted Islam as a body, that idolatry was abandoned.

Concerning the Prophet's return to Mecca, the Companion, 'Abdullah ibn Mas'ud (R), reports:

> The Messenger of God (S) entered Mecca, and there were 360 statues [or images] around the K'abah. Then he began to thrust at them with a cane in his hand, saying, **"The truth has come and falsehood has passed away. Indeed, falsehood is ever bound to pass away** [17:81]. **The truth has come, and falsehood can neither originate nor repeat [anything]"** [34:49]. (*Bukhari*, 6:244)

The Quraysh had put pictures inside the K'abah, including those of Jesus and Mary, God's peace and blessings be upon them. The Prophet (S) ordered that these pictures be erased, excepting those of Jesus and Mary (Ibn Ishaq/*M*, p. 552, 774). He then ordered 'Umar ibn al-Khattab to destroy all the images in the K'abah, and he himself did not enter it until all the images were destroyed (*Abu Dawud*, 4144). Thus was the prayer of Abraham (A),

> **Our Lord, and send among them a messenger from among themselves who will recite to them Your verses and teach them the scripture and wisdom and purify them** (2:129),

fulfilled through the noblest of his descendants, who cleansed the Sacred House from the abomination of idol-worship and brought his people to the worship of God, the Praised and Exalted, alone.

REFERENCES: Ibn Ishaq/*M*, pp. 35-39; Lings/*M*, p. 300; Sayyid Qutb/*Concept*, pp. 30-31.

Qur'anic References — Abraham, Ishmael, Isaac, Jacob

2:124-133

And [mention, O Muhammad,] when Abraham was tried by his Lord by words [of command] and he carried them out. He said, "Indeed, I will make you a leader of mankind."

He [Abraham] said, "And of my descendants?"

He said, "My covenant does not include the wrong-doers." (124)

And [mention] when We made the House a place of return for people and of security. And take the standing-place of Abraham as a place of prayer. And We enjoined on Abraham and Ishmael, "Purify My House for those who make *tawaf* and who remain [beside it] in worship, and those who bow and prostrate [in *salat*]."

And [mention] when Abraham said, "My Lord, make this a secure city and provide its people with fruits — whoever among them believes in God and the Last Day."

He [God] said, "And whoever disbelieves, I shall grant him enjoyment for a while, but then I shall drive him to the punishment of the Fire, and wretched is the destination!" (126)

And [mention] when Abraham was raising the foundations of the House, and Ishmael, [saying,] "Our Lord, accept [this] from us. Indeed, You are the Hearing, the Knowing. (127) Our Lord, and make us surrenderers to You, and of our desendants, a nation surrendering to You, and show us our rites and accept our repentance. Indeed, You are the Acceptor of Repentance, the Merciful. (128) Our Lord, and send among them a messenger from among themselves who will recite to them Your verses, and teach them the scripture and wisdom and purify them. Indeed, You are the Almighty, the Wise." (129)

And who would be averse to the way of Abraham except one who has made a fool of himself? And We chose him in this world, and indeed, in the Hereafter he will be among the righteous. (130) When his Lord said to him, "Surrender!" he said, "I have surrendered to the Lord of the worlds." (131)

And this Abraham enjoined [on his sons,] and so did Jacob: "O my sons, indeed, God has chosen the religion for you, so do not die except that you be *muslims*." (132)

2:135-136

And they say: "Be Jews or Christians [so] you will be guided."

Say, [O Muhammad:] "No, but [we follow] the religion of Abraham, inclining toward truth, and he was not of the *mushrikin*." (135)

Say, [O Muslims:] "We believe in God and what was revealed to us, and what was revealed to Abraham and Ishmael and Isaac and Jacob and the descendants [of Israel], and what was given to Moses and Jesus, and what was given to the prophets by their Lord. We make no distinction between any of them, and we surrender to Him [in Islam]." (136)

2:140

Or do you say that Abraham and Ishmael and Isaac and Jacob and the descendants [of Israel] were Jews or Christians? Say: "Do you know, or does God?" And who is more unjust than one who hides the testimony that he has from God? And God is not unmindful of what you do. (140)

2:258

Have you not considered the one who disputed with Abraham about his Lord because God had granted him kingship? When Abraham said, "My Lord is the One who gives life and causes death," he said, "I give life and cause death."

Abraham said, "Indeed, God brings up the sun from the East, so bring it up from the West!"

Then the one who disbelieved was confounded. And God does not guide the wrong-doing people.

2:260

And mention, [O Muhammad,] when Abraham said, "My Lord, show me how You give life to the dead."

He [God] said, "Do you not believe?"

He said, "Yes, but that my heart may be satisfied."

He said, "Then take four birds and make them attached to you. Then put part of them on each hill and call them. They will come to you quickly. And know that God is Almighty and Wise."

3:33-34

Indeed, God chose Adam and Noah and the family of Abraham and the family of 'Imran over all mankind, (33) descendants of one another. And God is Hearing and Knowing. (34)

3:65, 67-68

O People of the Scripture, why do you dispute about Abraham while the *Taurat* and the *Injil* were not revealed until after him? Will you not then use reason? (65)

. . . Abraham was neither a Jew nor a Christian, but he was one inclining toward truth, a ***muslim***, and he was not among the ***mushrikin***. (67) Indeed, the most worthy people in relation to Abraham are those who followed him, and this prophet [Muhammad] and those who believe [in his message]. And God is the Protector of the believers. (68)

3:83-85

Is it then other than the religion of God they desire, while whoever is in the heavens and the earth has submitted to Him, willingly or unwillingly, and to Him they will be returned? (83)

Say, [O Muhammad:] "We believe in God and what was revealed to us, and what was revealed to Abraham and Ishmael and Isaac and Jacob and the descendants [of Israel], and what was given to Moses and Jesus and the prophets by their Lord. We make no distinction between any of them, and we surrender to Him [in Islam]." (84) And whoever desires other than Islam as a religion, never will it be accepted from him, and in the Hereafter he will be among the losers. (85)

3:96-97

Indeed, the first House [of God's worship] established for mankind was that at Bakkah, a blessed place and a guidance for the worlds. Therein are clear signs — the standing-place of Abraham. And whoever enters it shall be safe. (96) And pilgrimage to the House is [an obligation] toward God for people, for whomever is able to find a way to it. But whoever disbelieves, then indeed, God is free from need of all the worlds. (97)

4:54

But We had already granted the family of Abraham the scripture and wisdom, and granted them a great kingdom.

4:125

And who is better in religion than the one who surrenders himself to God, while being a doer of good, and follows the faith of Abraham, inclining toward truth? And God took Abraham as a close friend.

4:163

Indeed, We have revealed to you [Muhammad] as We revealed to Noah and the prophets after him; and We revealed to Abraham and Ishmael and Isaac and Jacob and the descendants [of Israel]. . . .

6:74-83

And [mention, O Muhammad,] when Abraham said to his father Azar, "Do you take idols as gods? Indeed, I consider you and your people to be in clear error." (74) And thus did We show Abraham the realm of the heavens and the earth, that he might be among the certain. (75)

Then, when night fell upon him, he saw a star. He said, "This is my Lord." But when it set, he said, "I do not like those that set." (76)

Then, when he saw the moon rising, he said, "This is my Lord!" But when it set, he said, "Unless my Lord guides me, I will surely be among the straying people." (77)

Then, when he saw the sun rising, he said, "This is my Lord; this is greater [than anything]." But when it set, he said, "O my people, indeed I am clear of whatever you associate with God. (78) I have surely turned my being toward the One who created the heavens and the earth, as one inclining toward truth, and I am not among the *mushrikin.* (79)

And his people argued with him. He said, "Do you argue with me concerning God, while He has guided me? And I do not fear what you set up as partners to Him, unless my Lord should will something. My Lord includes all things in His knowledge; will you not then bear this in mind? (80) And how should I fear what you associate [with God] while you do not fear that you have associated with God that for which He has not revealed to you any authority? Then which of the two groups has more right to security, if you should know?" (81)

Those who believe and do not obscure their belief with wrong-doing — for them is security and they are [rightly]-guided. (82) And that was Our argument which We gave Abraham against his people. We raise in ranks whomever We will. Indeed, your Lord is Wise and Knowing. (83)

6:84-87

And We granted him [Abraham] Isaac and Jacob; each [of them] We guided. And previously We guided Noah, and among his descendants, David and Solomon and Job and Joseph and Moses and Aaron. And thus do We reward the doers of good. (84) And Zechariah and John and Jesus and Elijah — all were among the righteous; (85) and Ishmael and Elisha and Jonah and Lot — and all [of them] We preferred over mankind, (86) and some from among their fathers and descendants and brothers; and We chose them and guided them to a straight path. (87)

6:161

Say, [O Muhammad:] "Indeed, my Lord has guided me to a straight path, a correct religion: the faith of Abraham, inclining toward truth, and he was not among the *mushrikin.*" Say: "Indeed, my *salat* and my rites of sacrifice and my living and my dying are for God, Lord of the worlds, who has no partner. And this I have been commanded, and I am the first [among you] of the Muslims."

9:70

Has there not reached them the news of those before them — the people of Noah and 'Aad and Thamud, and the people of Abraham and the dwellers in Midian and the Overturned Cities? Their messengers came to them with clear proofs. And never would God have wronged them, but [rather] they wronged themselves.

9:114

And Abraham's asking forgiveness for his father was only because of a promise he had made him. But when it became clear to him that he was an enemy to God, he dissociated himself from him. Indeed, Abraham was tender-hearted and forbearing.

11:69-73

And Our messengers certainly came to Abraham with the good tidings. They said, "*Salam.*"

He said, "*Salam,*" and did not delay in bringing a roasted calf. (69) But when he saw their hands not reaching toward it, he mistrusted them and felt apprehensive of them.

They said, "Do not be afraid. Indeed, we have been sent to the people of Lot." (70)

And his wife was standing by and she laughed. Then We gave her good tidings of Isaac, and after Isaac, Jacob. (71) She said, "Woe be to me! Am I to bear a child when I am an old woman and this, my husband, is an old man? This is surely an amazing thing!" (72)

They said, "Do you wonder at God's decree? God's mercy and His blessings be upon you, people of the house. Indeed, He is the Praiseworthy and Glorious!" (73)

11:75

Indeed, Abraham was forbearing, tender-hearted, turning [to God].

14:35-41

And [mention, O Muhammad,] when Abraham said, "My Lord, make this city secure, and keep me and my sons from worshipping idols. (35) My Lord, indeed, they have led astray many among mankind. Therefore, whoever follows me, indeed, he is of me, and whoever disobeys me, indeed, You are the Forgiving and Merciful. (36)

"Our Lord, I have settled some of my offspring in a valley without vegetation near Your Sacred House, our Lord, that they may establish *salat.* Then make the hearts of people be drawn to them and provide them from the fruits [of the earth], that they may be thankful. (37) Our Lord, indeed, You know what we conceal and what we disclose, and nothing is hidden from God on the earth or in the heavens. (38)

"Praise be to God, who has granted to me, in my old age, Ishmael and Isaac. Indeed, my Lord is the Hearer of supplication. (39) My Lord, make me an establisher of ***salat***, and [also] among my descendants. Our Lord, and accept my supplication. (40) Our Lord, forgive me and my parents and the believers on the Day when the Accounting is established." (41)

15:51-57

And inform them about the guests of Abraham, (51) when they went in to him and said, ***"Salam."***

He said, "We feel afraid of you." (52)

They said, "Do not fear. Indeed, we give you good tidings of a boy possessing knowledge." (53)

He said, "Do you give me [this] good tidings although old age has come upon me? Of what, then, do you give tidings?" (54)

They said, "We have given you the good tidings in truth, so do not be among the hopeless." (55)

He said, "And who is hopeless of the mercy of his Lord except the straying?" (56)

16:120-123

Abraham was indeed an ***ummah***, devoutly obedient to God, inclining toward truth, and he was not among the ***mushrikin***, (120) [and he was] grateful for His favors. He chose him and guided him to a straight path. (121) And We gave him good in this world, and indeed, in the Hereafter he will be among the righteous. (122)

Then We revealed to you [Muhammad] to follow the faith of Abraham, inclining toward truth, and he was not among the ***mushrikin***. (123)

19:41-50

And mention Abraham in the Book. Indeed, he was a man of truth and a prophet. (41)

[Mention, O Muhammad,] when he said to his father, "O my father, why do you worship that which does not hear or see and does not benefit you in the least? (42) O my father, there has surely come to me [something] of knowledge that has not come to you, so follow me; I will guide you to a correct path. (43) O my father, do not worship Satan. Indeed, Satan is a rebel to the Most Merciful. (44) O my father, indeed, I fear that a punishment from the Most Merciful will touch you, so you become a companion to Satan." (45)

He said, "Do you detest my gods, O Abraham? If you do not leave off, I will surely stone you, so avoid me for a long time!" (46)

He [Abraham] said, "Peace be upon you. I shall ask forgiveness for you from My Lord. Indeed, He is ever gracious to Me. (47) And I will withdraw from you and whatever you call upon apart from God, and I will call upon my Lord. I hope that I will not be unfortunate in my supplication to my Lord." (48)

Then, when he had withdrawn from them and what they worshipped apart from God, We granted him Isaac and Jacob, and We made each of them a prophet. (49) And We granted them of Our mercy and ordained for them a mention of high honor (50).

19:54-55

And mention Ishmael in the Book. Indeed, he was true to his promise, and he was a messenger and a prophet. (54) And he used to enjoin *salat* and *zakat* on his family, and he was pleasing to his Lord. (55)

19:58

Those were some of the prophets upon whom God bestowed favor from among the descendants of Adam and among those whom We carried [in the Ark] with Noah, and among the descendants of Abraham and Israel [Jacob], and among those whom We guided and chose. When the signs of the Most Merciful were recited to them, they fell down prostrating and weeping.

21:51-73

And previously, We had certainly given Abraham his correctness [of understanding and conduct,] and We were well-acquainted with him. (51) When he said to his father and his people, "What are these statues to which you are so devoted?" (52) they said, "We found our fathers worshippers of them." (53)

He said, "You have certainly been in obvious error, you and your fathers." (54)

They said, "Have you brought us the truth, or are you among the jokers?" (55)

He said, "No, but rather, your Lord is the Lord of the heavens and the earth, who created them, and I am among those who testify to that. (56) And by God, I will surely plot against your idols after you have turned and gone away!" (57) Then he made them into fragments, excepting a big one among them, that they would return to it. (58)

They said, "Who has done this to our gods? Indeed, he is among the wrong-doers!" (59)

They said, "We heard a youth mention them who is called Abraham." (60)

They said, "Then bring him in front of the eyes of the people, that they may testify." (61) They said, "Have you done this to our gods, O Abraham?" (62)

He said, "Rather this, the biggest of them, did it, so ask them, if they are able to speak!" (63)

Then they turned back to themselves and said, "Indeed, you are the wrong-doers." (64) Then they reversed themselves, [saying,] "You already knew that these [idols] do not speak." (65)

He said, "Then do you worship, besides God, that which neither benefits you in the least nor harms you? (66) Shame on you and on what you worship apart from God! Will you not then use reason?" (67)

They said, "Burn him and support your gods, if you are to act!" (68)

We said, "O fire, be coolness and safety for Abraham." (69) And they intended to frame a plot for him, but We made them the greatest losers. (70)

And We delivered him and Lot to the land that We had blessed for [all] mankind. (71) And We granted him Isaac, and Jacob in addition, and We made each upright. (72) And We made them leaders, guiding by Our command. And We inspired to them the doing of good deeds and the establishment of *salat* and the giving of *zakat*, and they were worshippers of Us [alone]. (73)

21:85-86

And Ishmael and Idris and Dhu-l-Kifl — all were among the patient, (85) and We admitted them them to Our mercy. Indeed, they were among the righteous. (86)

22:26-29

And [mention, O Muhammad,] when We designated the site of the House for Abraham, [saying,] "Do not associate anything with Me, and purify My House for those who make *tawaf* and those who stand and bow and prostrate [in *salat*]. (26)

"And proclaim the *Hajj* to mankind. They will come to you on foot and and on every [kind of] lean mount, they will come to you from every far-distant pass, (27) that they may witness things beneficial themselves and mention the name of God, on appointed days, over what He has provided for them of cattle [for sacrifice]. Then eat of them and feed the distressed and poor. (28) Then let them complete their rites and fulfill their vows and make *tawaf* of the Ancient House." (29)

22:42-44

And if they deny you [Muhammad], thus did the people of Noah and 'Aad and Thamud deny [their prophets] before them, (42) and the people of Abraham and the people of Lot (43) and the dwellers in Midian.

22:78

And strive for God with the striving due to Him. He has chosen you and has not placed upon you any difficulty in the religion: the faith of your father Abraham. He [God Most High] named you "Muslims" beforehand and in this [Qur'an].

26:69-89

And recite to them the tidings of Abraham (69), when he said to his father and his people, "What do you worship?" (70)

They said, "We worship idols and remain devoted to them." (71)

He said, "Do they hear you when you call (72), or do they benefit you or do harm?" (73)

They said, "No, but we found our fathers doing so." (74)

He said, "Then do you see what you have been worshipping, (75) you and your fathers of old? (76) Indeed, they are enemies to me, except the Lord of the worlds, (77) who created me. And it is He who guides me, (78) and who gives me food and drink. (79) And when I am ill, it is He who cures me, (80) and who will cause me to die and then bring me to life, (81) and who, I hope, will forgive me my faults on the Day of Recompense. (82) My Lord, grant me authority and join me with the righteous, (83) and grant me a mention of honor among later generations, (84) and make me among the inheritors of the Paradise of bliss (85). And forgive my father; indeed, he has been among the straying. (86) And do not disgrace me on the Day they are resurrected, (87) the Day when neither wealth nor sons will avail, (88) but only he who comes to God with a sound heart." (89)

29:16-18

And [mention] Abraham, when he said to his people, "Worship God and be mindful of Him. That is best for you, if you but knew. (16) In place of God, you worship mere idols and you fabricate falsehood. Indeed, those you worship besides God do not have power to provide for you. So seek provision from God and worship Him and be thankful to Him. To Him you will be returned. (17) And if you deny [me or my Message], nations have already denied before you. And the duty of the messenger is only clear communication [of the Message]." (18)

29:24-28

But the reply of his people was only that they said, "Kill him or burn him!" but God saved him from the fire. Indeed, in that are signs a sign for a people who believe. (24)

And he said, "You have adopted idols in place of God only out of liking among yourselves during the life of this world. But on the Day of Resurrection, you will deny each other and curse each other, and your dwelling-place will be the Fire and you will not have any helpers." (25)

And Lot believed in him. And he [Abraham] said, "I will surely emigrate to my Lord. Indeed, He is the Almighty, the Wise." (26) And We granted him Isaac and Jacob, and appointed prophethood and scripture among his descendants. And We granted him his reward in this world, and indeed, in the Hereafter he will be among the righteous. (27)

33:7

And [mention, O Muhammad,] when We took from the prophets their covenant, and from you [Muhammad], and from Noah and Abraham and Moses and Jesus son of Mary — and We took from them a solemn covenant.

37:83-113

And indeed, among his [Noah's] followers was Abraham, (83) when he came to his Lord with a sound heart. (84)

[Mention, O Muhammad,] when he said to his father and his people, "What do you worship? (85) Is it false deities other than God you desire? (86) Then what is your thought about the Lord of the worlds?" (87)

And he cast a glance at the stars (88) and said, "Indeed, I am ill." (89) Then they turned away from him, departing. (90)

Then he advanced toward their gods and said, "Do you not eat? (91) What is it with you that you do not speak?" (92) And he turned upon them a blow with [his] right hand. (93)

Then they came toward him, hastening. (94) He said, "Do you worship that which you [yourselves] carve, (95) while God created you and whatever you do?" (96)

They said, "Build a structure for him and throw him into the blaze!" (97) And they intended [to frame] a plot against him but We made them the most debased. (98) And he said, "Indeed, I shall go to my Lord; He will guide me. (99)

"My Lord, grant me [a son] from among the righteous!" (100) so We gave him the good tidings of a forbearing boy. (101)

Then, when he reached [the age of] working with him, he said, "O my son, indeed, I have seen in a vision that I am sacrificing you, so see what you think."

He said, "O my father, do what you are commanded. You will find me, God willing, among the patient." (102)

Then, when they had both surrendered [themselves] and he had put him down on his forehead, (103) We called to him, "O Abraham, (104) you have fulfilled the vision!" Thus do We surely reward the doers of good. (105) Indeed, this was a clear trial, (106) and We ransomed him with a great sacrifice, (107) and We left [this invocation] for him among the later generations: (108) "Peace be upon Abraham!" (109) Thus do We reward the doers of good. (110) Indeed, he was among Our believing servants. (111)

And We gave him good tidings of Isaac, a prophet from among the righteous. (112) And We blessed him and Isaac. But among their descendants is the doer of good and the one who clearly wrongs himself. (113)

38:45-48

And mention Our servants, Abraham and Isaac and Jacob, those of strength and vision. (45) Indeed, We chose them for a special purpose: the remembrance of the [Eternal] Home, (46) and indeed, with Us, they are among the chosen and the excellent. (47) And mention Ishmael and Elisha and Dhu-l-Kifl — and all are among the excellent. (48)

42:13

He has ordained for you, as the religion, what He enjoined upon Noah and that which We have revealed to you [Muhammad], and what We enjoined upon Abraham and Moses and Jesus: to establish the [true] religion and not be divided concerning it. (13)

43:26-28

And [mention, O Muhammad,] when Abraham said to his father and his people, "Indeed, I clear of that which you worship (26) apart from Him who created me, and He will surely guide me." (27) And he made it a word remaining among his descendants, that they might return. (28)

51:24-30

Has the story reached you [Muhammad] of Abraham's honored guests, (24) when they went in to him and said, "*Salam.*"

He said, "*Salam,*" [and thought,] "Unknown people." (25) Then he turned to his household and came with a plump calf (26) and placed it near them. He said, "Will you not eat?" (27) and felt apprehensive of them.

They said, "Do not fear," and gave him good tidings of a boy possessing knowledge. (28) Then his wife came forward with a cry and hit her face and said, "A barren old woman!" (29)

They said, "Thus has your Lord said. Indeed, He is the Wise, the Knowing!" (30)

53:36-37

Or has he not had been informed of what was in the scriptures of Moses (36) and Abraham, who fulfilled [his obligations]? (37).

57:26

And We certainly sent Noah and Abraham, and established prophethood and scripture among their descendants; and among them are the guided, but many of them are defiantly disobedient.

60:4-6

There has already been an excellent example for you in Abraham and those with him, when they said to their people, "Indeed, we are clear of you and of whatever you worship apart from God. We have rejected you, and there has arisen eternal enmity and hatred between us and you until you believe in God alone" — except for Abraham's saying to his father, "I will certainly ask forgiveness for you, but I have no power to do anything for you against God.

"Our Lord, upon You we rely and to You we turn, and to You is the destination. (4) Our Lord, do not make a test for those who disbelieve, and forgive us, our Lord. Indeed, it is You who are the Almighty, the Wise." (5)

There has certainly been an excellent example for you in them, for anyone whose hope is in God and the Last Day. And whoever turns away, then indeed God is the Free of all need, the Praiseworthy. (6)

87:18-19

Indeed, this is in the former scriptures, (18) the scriptures of Abraham and Moses. (19)

The Story of Lot (Lut)

peace be upon him

And We granted him [Abraham] Isaac and Jacob; each [of them] We guided . . . and Ishmael and Elisha and Jonah and Lot. And We preferred all [of them] over all mankind.
(6:84, 86)

To Lot We granted judgment and knowledge. (21:74)

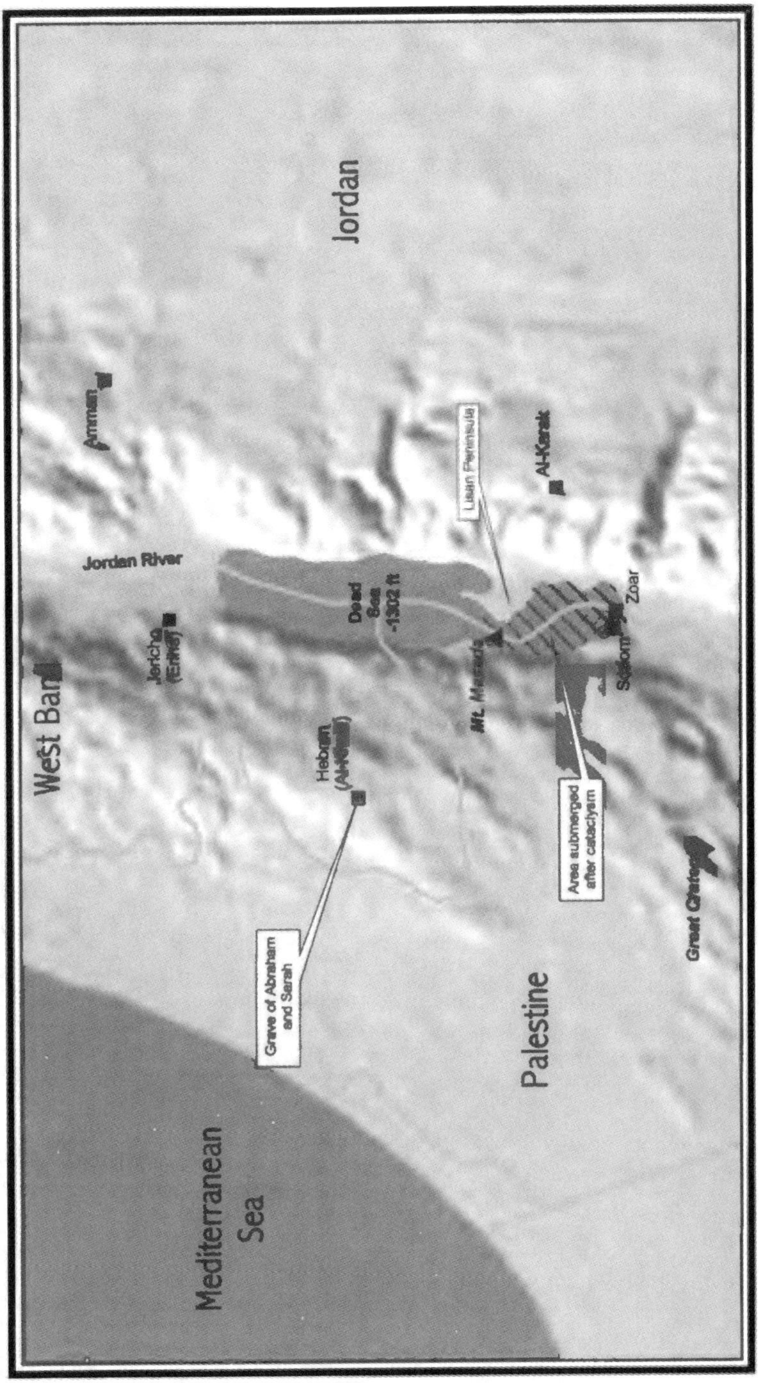

Map 8. The Overturned Cities

1. The People of Lot (A)

And the Overturned Cities committed sin. (69:9)

Indeed, Lot was among the messengers. (37:133)

Lot (Arabic, Lut), you may recall, was the nephew of Abraham (A), who left Ur with him and settled in Palestine. It is supposed that Lot (A) lived between 2300 and 1900 B.C.

Lot's name is mentioned in the Qur'an twenty-seven times, both by itself, in conjunction with the names of other prophets, and in connection with his transgressing people.

Nothing authoritative is known of Lot's earlier life. What is evident is that at some point after his settling, God appointed him as prophet to communities on the shore of what is now the Dead Sea, at a distance of twenty-four hours' journey from Abraham's home.

In the region where Lot (A) settled, there were five cities, referred to in the Qur'an as ***al-Mu'tafikat*** (9:70, 53:53, 69:9), meaning **"the Overturned Cities."** The largest of these, in which Lot (A) lived, was Sodom (Arabic, Sudum).

Archeological traces indicate that this was a prosperous, well-populated area during Lot's time. However, from what is reported in the Qur'an concerning the people of the region, it is clear that they were exceedingly corrupt and depraved. Indeed, the Qur'anic commentators depict them as a people who lacked even a trace of ordinary decency and whose morals and behavior were of the lowest kind.

Although they were guilty of several vices, one stands out glaringly among all the rest. In the Arabic language, the word ***luwwat*** (derived from *Lut*) refers to the most serious of their trangsressions: homosexuality or sodomy.

It is reported that the people of this region would commit perverted deeds openly in their gatherings, and that they cut the access of travelers to their roadways, robbing and killing them, after perhaps first forcing them to engage in unnatural acts. And it was not only some or even a majority of Lot's people who engaged in such practice. Rather, the entire population was involved.

But in the scale of divine justice, even these most depraved of all people were entitled to a prophet to warn them. Therefore, God in His mercy caused Lot (A) to settle among them so that they might perhaps be guided.

REFERENCES: Tabari/*H*, II:111-112; Maududi/*Q*, 26:fn.114.

2. Lot Warns His People

Lot's people denied the messengers. (26:160)

When God's command came to Lot (A) to warn his people, he began his mission, in the manner of the prophets who had preceded him, by calling them to fear their Lord and to obey him, the prophet whom He had appointed for their guidance.

"Will you not be mindful of God?" he said, appealing to them to reflect on their accountability to their Creator. And assuring his people of his absolute reliability, he added: **"Indeed, I am a trustworthy messenger to you, so be mindful of God and obey me. And I do not ask you for any recompense for it. My recompense rests only upon the Lord of the worlds"** (26:161-164).

Then, at some point he brought up the issue of their besetting sins. As if holding up a mirror in front of his people, Lot (A) tried to make them look at the awfulness of their perverted habits and criminal behaviors. Four dialogues between him and his people — possibly with the inhabitants of the different cities in the region — which no doubt occurred, with variations, on dozens or even hundreds of different occasions over a period of time, are reported in the Qur'an.

"Do you commit vileness, while you observing?" (27:54), Lot (A) would ask. These words have been have been interpreted as referring to the Sodomites' awareness that their actions were sinful and constituted rebellion against the natural order established by the Creator, or to the fact that they committed unnatural acts openly in their assemblies without shame while others looked on. **"Do you indeed approach men with desire to the exclusion of women? No, but you are a people behaving ignorantly!"** (27:55), Lot (A) would say, meaning, "Are you really so ignorant and bold as to go against the normal way of life that your Lord, in His endless knowledge and wisdom, has ordained for His servants?"

But the response of his people, already extraordinarily hardened and callous, was only that they said, **"Drive Lot's family out of your city,"** adding sarcastically: **"Indeed, they are people who keep themselves pure!"** (27:54-56).

Lot's admonition then became a little stronger: **"Would you perpetrate such vileness as no one among mankind has done before you?"** (7:80), he asked. Some commentators say that these words indicate that Lot's people were the first on earth to engage in homosexuality, for while earlier peoples had followed the way of unbelief, denial of the prophets, or disobedience to God's commandments, no one before them had done this. **"Indeed,"** Lot (A) continued, **"you approach men with desire to the exclusion of women. No, but you are a transgressing people!"** (7:81).

But to this, his people only replied with the same words as previously: **"Drive them out of your city! Indeed, they are people who keep themselves pure!"** (7:82)

But ignoring their enmity and threats, Lot (A) faithfully continued to preach and warn, reiterating his message. **"Among all mankind, do you approach males and leave what your Lord has created for you as mates?"** (26:165-166), he would ask, emphasizing the error and ingratitude of turning away from the spouses whom God had granted them for the natural fulfillment of their needs. **"No, but you are a transgressing people!"** (26:166).

But as before, his admonition was met with threats: **"If you do not leave off, O Lot, you will surely be of those driven out!"** (26:167).

"Indeed, I am of those who detest your doings" (26:168), Lot (A) exclaimed. **"My Lord, save me and my family from what they do!"** (26:165-169).

Continuing to preach despite his people's hostility and threats, he then enumerated the entire catalogue of their misdeeds, saying, **"You surely perpetrate such vileness as no one among mankind has done before you! Indeed, you approach men and menace the road and commit abomination in your meetings!"** (29:28-29).

These words refer first to their major sin and then to others: their practice of accosting travelers, robbing and killing them — according to some accounts, after forcing them to engage in their favorite pasttime. It is said that they would openly engage in homosexual acts in their assemblies without anyone's objecting to it, as it was a generally accepted practice. They would spout obscenities in their gatherings, and pass wind and laugh at it. They relished cock, pigeon and goat fights. It is also said that they used to mock passersby, throwing rocks and whistling at them, and that they walked about naked.[1]

---

[1]The reports of the disgusting and perverted habits of Lot's people fill several pages of al-Tabari's *History*. The Prophet (S) is reported as saying that they would sit by the road, cutting off travelers and mocking them. It has also been said that they committed depravity with anyone who came into their city (Tabari/*H*, II:112-115). Ibn 'Abbas says that they would expose their private parts in front of people of the same sex, whistle with their fingers, open their shirts to display their chests, and wear long trousers which trailed on the ground. It is also said that they played backgammon and cheated with regard to weights and measures (Adh-Dhahabi/*MajorSins*, pp. 58-59).

Steeped in sin, they were deaf to all of Lot's admonitions. Thus, **the answer of his people was only that they said, "Bring us God's punishment, if you are among the truthful!"** (29:29).

"My Lord," Lot (A) prayed, **"support me against the corrupt people!"** (29:30).

In fact, in the entire region, there was only one household of righteous people and that was his own, according to God's words, **"But We did not find among them other than a single house of *muslims*"** (51:36). And although Lot's two daughters were believers, his wife, who is said to have been a Sodomite, was connected to the people of the area and her loyalty was with them.

REFERENCES: Qur'an: 7:80-82; 26:160-169; 27:54-56; 29:28-30; 51:36. Commentaries: Tabari/*H*, II:66-68, 112-115; Ibn Kathir/*T*, 27:54-55, 29:28-30, 37:54-55; Ibn Kathir/*Q*, "Lut"; Adh-Dhahabi/*Major Sins*, pp. 58-59; Maududi/*Q*, 27:fn. 68; Asad/*Q*, 27:fn. 50.

3. The Angels' Visit to Abraham

Then, when the fear had left Abraham and the good tidings had reached him, he disputed with Us concerning Lot's people. Indeed, Abraham was forbearing, tender-hearted, [constantly] returning [to God]. (11:74-75)

As the above verses indicate, Lot's story is inextricably interwoven with Abraham's. We therefore now return to the Qur'anic narrative concerning the angels' visit to Abraham (A).

You may recall the mistrust Abraham (A) felt when he saw that his visitors did not touch the food he had set before them and his saying to them openly, **"We feel afraid of you"** (15:52).

They then reassured him, saying, **"Do not be afraid. Indeed, we have been sent to Lot's people"** (11:70). And they made known to him that they were angels, sent by God.

The angels' errand to Lot's people was then temporarily put aside while they gave Abraham (A) and Sarah the tidings of the son who was to be born to them, Isaac. But once that matter had been addressed, Abraham (A), who knew well that angels do not visit human beings except for some very serious purpose, returned to the subject of Lot's people.

"Then what is your business, O messengers?" (15:57; 51:31), the aged prophet asked them, meaning, "Then what else is the reason for your visit besides giving us the tidings of a son?"

The angels then made their errand clear to Abraham (A).

"Indeed," they said, **"we have been sent to a criminal people** (15:58, 51:32), **to send down upon them stones of clay, marked by your Lord for the transgressors** (15:18, 51:33-34) — **excepting Lot's family,"** they added. **"We will surely save them all, except his wife; We have decreed that she be among those who remain behind**[2] (15:59-60). **We will surely destroy the**

---

[2]Here, **"We"** may either be understood as the angels speaking of God's decree or as God Himself speaking of His decree. It may therefore be asked, If God Himself decreed that Lot's wife remain behind, how could she be blamed for something she was destined to do?

No less than seven passages relate to this matter, emphasizing its importance: (1) The angels' saying to Lot, **"And let not any of you look back — except your wife; she will surely be struck by whatever strikes them"** (11:81); (2) their saying to Abraham above, **"We will surely save them all, except his wife. We have decreed that she be among those who remain behind"** (15:59-60); (3 and 4) **Then We saved him and his family, all, except an old woman among those who remained behind** (26:170-171, 37:134-135); (5) **Then We saved him and his family, except his wife; We destined her to be among those who remain behind** (27:57); (6)

people of that city," they reiterated. **"Indeed, its people have been evil-doers"** (29:31).

"But Lot is surely in it!" (29:32), Abraham (A) exclaimed in alarm.

"We are more knowing of who is in it" (29:32), the angels assured him, repeating, **"Indeed, we will save him and his family, except his wife. She is to be among those who remain behind"** (29:32).

But even then Abraham (A) did not remain silent, for God says,

> **When the fear had left Abraham and the good tidings had reached him, he argued with Us concerning Lot's people. (11:74)**

The divine Author of the Holy Book then adds, almost as if Abraham's appealing for such sinful and criminal people required an explanation, **"Indeed, Abraham was forbearing, tender-hearted,** constantly **returning** to God" (11:74-75), and thus unable to bear the thought that any righteous person should be punished along with the evil-doers.

However, when Abraham (A) pleaded with them thus, the angels rebuked him gently. **"O Abraham, give up this!"** they said. **"Your Lord's decree has surely gone forth, and there will indeed come to them a punishment which cannot be turned back"** (11:76).

Nevertheless, Ibn 'Abbas (R) and other commentators report, Abraham (A) continued to plead until the angel told him that if there were five people in Lot's city who prayed, the punishment would be averted from them.

REFERENCES: Qur'an: 11:70, 74-76; 15:57-60; 29:31-32; 51:31-34. Commentary: Tabari/ *H*, II:116-117.

---

the angels' saying to Abraham, **"We will surely save you and your family, except your wife. She is to be among those who remain behind"** (29:33); and (7) **"We will surely save him and his family, except his wife. She is to be among those remain behind"** (29:32).

The words, **All, except an old woman among those who remained behind** (26:170-171, 37:134-135), suggest that when Lot asked his wife to leave with him, she chose to stay back with her people. The words, **She will surely be struck by whatever strikes them** (11:81) further suggests that because she had cast her lot with her evil-doing community rather than with her prophet-husband (especially by informing her people about the arrival of the strangers, with all the consequences that she certainly knew would follow from it), it was inevitable that she be stricken by the same punishment that befell her people. This is confirmed by God's saying about her and the wife of Noah, **They were under [the charge of] two servants among His righteous servants but they betrayed them, and they [their prophet-husbands] did not benefit them at all before God** (66:10).

4. The Angels' Arrival in Sodom

And when Our messengers came to Lot, he was grieved for them and felt straitened concerning them. (11:77)

The three angels — said to have been Gabriel, Michael and Israfil (A) — then arrived at the outskirts of Lot's town. Ibn 'Abbas (R) supplies the details of what happened next:

When the angels reached the river of Sodom, they met Lot's daughter, drawing water for her family. "O lass," they said to her, "is there any house near here?"

"Yes," she replied. Then, thinking of what might happen to them if her people knew of their presence, she added: "But stay where you are and do not come into the town until I return to you."

She then went to her father and said, "O my father, some young men want you at the gate of the city. Never have I seen more handsome faces than theirs! Do not let your people take hold of them and violate them." For Lot's people had previously forbidden him to show hospitality to anyone, saying to him, "Leave them to us. *We* will give hospitality to the men."

Lot (A) then went out to the strangers and brought them to his house secretly, so that no one but his family knew that they were there. However, his wife went out to inform her people, saying, "In Lot's house there men whose like I have never seen, nor have I ever seen such handsome faces."

"You are surely unknown people" (15:62), Lot (A) said to his visitors in the very same words words Abraham (A) had used previously (51:25), thus giving them an indirect hint of what they might expect in his town.

However, his guests showed no trace of fear or concern. **"No, but we have come to you with that which they were disputing, and we bring you the truth and indeed, we are truthful. Therefore,"** they instructed Lot, **"set out with your family during a portion of the night and follow behind them, and let not any of you look back and continue on to wherever you are commanded"** (15:63-65).

Despite this reassurance, Lot (A) remained greatly troubled about the strangers' safety. Although, as his guests, they were under his protection, he knew well enough that as soon as their presence became known, the men of the town would be at his door. God Most High describes his disturbed state of mind, saying,

> **And when Our messengers came to Lot, he was grieved for them and felt straitened concerning them, and he said, "This is a distressing day!"** (11:77; also 29:33)

As Lot (A) had anticipated, the news of incredibly handsome strangers visiting the city brought the townsmen to his house in haste. The Qur'anic descriptions are quite graphic: **And his people came hurrying toward him, and before this they had been doing evil deeds** (11:78), and, **And the people of the city came, rejoicing** (15:67) at the prospect of the male visitors.

"Indeed, these are my guests, so do not shame me," Lot (A) exclaimed when they arrived at his door. **"And fear God and do not disgrace me!"** (15:68-69).

"And have we not prohibited you from everyone?" (15:70), the men demanded sarcastically, referring to their having previously forbidden him to show hospitality to anyone.

"O my people, these are my daughters, if you would do anything," Lot (A) pleaded. **"They are purer for you"** (11:78, 15:69-71). **"So fear God and do not disgrace me concerning my guests! Is there not a right-minded man among you?"** (11:78).

How are we to understand Lot's reference to his **"daughters"**? According to the majority of classic commentators, it relates to the fact that prophets are the fathers of their nations, in keeping with God's words, **"The Prophet is closer to the believers than themselves, and his wives are their mothers"** [33:6; *Bukhari*, 3:584], and to the saying of some of the Companions and predecessors in Islam, "He [the Prophet] is a father to them." Accordingly, Lot's words concerning his **"daughters"** have been understood as a means of calling his people's attention to their surpression and abandonment of their women, who were his daughters-in-God. This interpretation is related to his saying, **"Among** all **mankind, do you approach males and leave what your Lord has created for you as mates?"** [26:165-166], says Ibn Kathir, adding that this is the opinion of a number of early commentators, such as Mujahid, Sa'id ibn Jubayr, Rabi' bin Anas, Qatadah, al-Suddi, Muhammad ibn Ishaq, and that it is correct. Ibn Kathir says further:

> The other saying [namely, that **"my daughters"** refers to Lot's biological daughters] is incorrect and is taken from the People of the Scripture [i.e., Jews and Christians]. Their description is [also] incorrect in their saying that there were two angels [Gen. 19:1] and that they ate with him [Abraham] [Gen. 19:3]. In this story, the People of the Scripture have deviated greatly.[3] (Ibn Kathir/*T*, 11:78-79)

---

[3]The statement attributed to Lot in Gen. 19:8, "Look, I have two daughters who have never slept with a man. Let me bring them out to you, and you can do what you like with them. But don't do anything to these men, for they have come under the protection of my roof," is regarded by the Qur'anic interpreters as blatantly false, disgusting and outrageous. This is also true of the other, equally disgraceful things alleged about Lot in Gen. 19:30-36, and in several

"You certainly know that we have no claim on your 'daughters'," the intruders flung back at their prophet, **"and indeed you know what we want!"** (11:79), meaning, "O Lot, you know that we have no interest in women, and you know exactly what our desire and intention is."

"If only I had power against you or I could take refuge in a strong support!" (11:80),[4] Lot (A) cried out in anguish, feeling totally powerless to save the guests to whom he had given the protection of his house.

"Your support *is* strong!" the strangers reassured him. **"O Lot, indeed, we are messengers of your Lord. They will never reach you!"** (11:81).

These last words suggest that the attackers intended to eliminate Lot (A) to get at his guests. But as the men approached in the heat of their unnatural lust, or perhaps tried to force their way in, the angels took away their their sight, according to God's words, **And they had desired of him his guests, but We obliterated their eyes** (54:37). The aggressors were then so distracted in their blindness that God says of them, addressing His Last Prophet (S), **By your life,** O Muhammad, **indeed, they were groping about blindly in their bewilderment** (15:72).

"Do not fear nor grieve," the angels said to Lot (A). **"Indeed, We will save you and your family, except your wife; she will be of those who remain behind. We will surely bring down a punishment from the sky upon the people of this community because they have been defiantly disobedient!"** (29:33-34).

They then repeated their instructions to the harried prophet: **"Therefore, set out with your family during a portion of the night and let not any of you look back — except your wife; she will surely be struck by whatever strikes them. Indeed, their appointed time is morning. Is not the morning near?"** (11:81).

Even today as we read the words, ***"Is not the morning near?"*** a chill passes over us at the awesome divine threat which they convey. Yes, truly, the morning was near — very, very near! And God **conveyed to him that decree: that the [very] last of those would be cut off by early morning** (15:66).

---

other places in the Old Testament about other prophets, suggesting that either God Almighty was incompetent to choose good men as prophets or that the men so chosen were incapable of fulfilling their role.

[4]Referring to this verse, the Prophet (S) said, "May God have mercy upon Lot! He desired to take refuge in a powerful support" (*Bukhari,* 4:591). The meaning here is that, powerless as Lot was to protect his guests, he groped for some physical means to deal with them, momentarily forgetting that God, the Almighty and All-Powerful, is sufficient as the Guardian and Protector of His servants.

Summarizing this segment of the story, Ibn 'Abbas (R) says:

When Lot said, **"If only I had power against you or I could take refuge in a strong support!"** [11:80], Gabriel spread his wings and knocked out their eyes, and they came out, treading in each other's steps, blinded, saying, "Save me, save me, for in Lot's house there are the most powerful magicians on earth!" according to the saying of the Most High, **And they had demanded of him his guests, but We obliterated their eyes** [54:37].

And they said to Lot, **"O Lot, indeed, we are messengers of your Lord. They will never reach you! Therefore, set out with your family during a portion of the night, and let not any of you look back"** [11:81]. He [Gabriel] said, "Travel with them by night and go wherever you are instructed," and God Most High directed them to go toward Syria. And Lot asked, "Are you going to destroy them now?" but they said, "We have not been ordered to do it except in the morning. **Is not the morning near?"** [11:81].

Then, when it was early dawn, Lot departed with his family, except his wife, according to the saying of the Most High, **Excepting Lot's family; We saved them before dawn** [54:34]. (Tabari/*Q*, "Lut")

REFERENCES: Qur'an: 11:77-81; 15:62-72; 29:33-34; 54:37. Commentaries: Tabari/*Q*, "Lut"; Tabari/*H*, II:115, 117-123; Ibn Kathir/*T*, 11:78-79; Ibn Kathir/*Q*, "Lut".

5. Retribution!

Lot's people denied the warnings. Indeed, We sent against them a storm of stones, excepting Lot's family; We saved them before dawn, a favor from Ourselves. Thus do We reward one who is grateful. And he had already warned them of Our assault but they disputed the warnings. And they had demanded of him his guests, but We obliterated their eyes. Then taste My punishment and warnings! And there came upon them by morning a lasting punishment. Then taste My punishment and warnings! (54:33-39)

As he had been directed, Lot (A) set out with his family. Who its members were, other than his two believing daughters, and whether there was anyone else with them, is not known. What is clear is that, among all the people of the area, there was only one household of believers — that of Lot (A) himself,[5] for God Most High says:

> **Then We brought out whomever was in them of the believers, but We did not find in them more than a [single] house of *muslims.*** (51:35-36)

Then, when Lot (A) and his party had cleared the area, the divine command went forth: —

> **And the clamor[6] seized them at sunrise. Then God made its highest part its lowest and rained upon them stones of hard clay** (15:73-74);
>
> **And We rained upon them a rain. Then see what was the end of the criminals!** (7: 84);
>
> **And He toppled the Overturned Cities, so there covered them that which covered** (53:53-54);

perhaps referring either to the the ejecta from the volcanic eruption that overwhelmed them or to the waters of the Dead Sea that engulfed them.

In explanation of the words, **"We made its highest part its lowest"** (11:82, 15:73), various commentators have said that the angel Gabriel (A) lifted up all the sinful towns into the sky, together with their inhabitants, and turned them over; hence the name *al-Mu'tafikat*, the Overturned Cities. Then God **rained upon them a rain, and evil was the rain of those who were warned** (26:173,

---

[5]This demonstrates that the truthfulness or value of a true man of God is not necessarily reflected by the number of people following him.

[6]For the meaning of ***"al-sayah,"*** please see "Saleh," page 237.

27:58), as He sent upon them **a storm of stones** (54:34) **of hard clay in succession, marked by your Lord for the transgressors** (11:82-83, 51:33-34). It is said that each stone was inscribed with the name of the person for whom it was intended, and that the heavenly missiles struck the heads of their human targets, smashing their brains.

Thus were the flourishing cities of Sodom and the four other towns in the vicinity obliterated with all their people, including the wife of their prophet, as a recompense for the wickedness and perverse lusts of its inhabitants — and, God says, such punishment **is not** ever **far from the wrong-doers** (11:83). But the handful of believers, led by their prophet, were in safety and peace, protected their Guardian Lord: —

> **And to Lot We granted judgment and knowledge, and We saved him from the community that was doing wicked deeds. They were surely an evil people, defiantly disobedient. And We admitted him to Our mercy. Indeed, he was among the righteous.** (21:74-75)

May God's best blessings be upon Lot, the much-tried prophet of the Overturned Cities!

REFERENCES: Qur'an: 11:82-83; 15:73-75; 21:74-75; 51:35-37; 53:53-54; 54:33-39. Commentaries: Tabari/*H*, II:123-125; Ibn Kathir/*Q*, "Lut".

6. The Signs of the Overturned Cities

And they have already come upon the town that was rained upon with an evil rain. Have they then not seen it? But they are not anticipating resurrection.[7] (25:40)

Now, did any of this really happen or is it simply an ancient legend or a morality tale — a story or history?

Historical and physical evidence and clues exist for the stories of virtually all the prophets mentioned in the Qur'an. We therefore now present what seems to be physical confirmation of Lot's story, as told by the Knower of all things.

In a number of verses, God Most High refers to a **"sign"** related to the destruction of Lot's people and their civilization, saying,

> **And We certainly left a sign of it as clear evidence for a people who use reason.** (29:35)
>
> **And We rained upon them a rain, and evil was the rain of those who were warned! Indeed, in that is a sign, but most of them are not believers.** (26:173-174)
>
> **Then We made its highest part its lowest and rained upon them stones of hard clay. In that are surely signs for the attentive. And indeed, they are upon an established road. In that is surely a sign for the believers.** (15:74-77)
>
> **Then We brought out whomever was in them of the believers, but We did not find in them more than a single *muslim* family. And We left therein a sign for those who fear the painful punishment.** (51:35-37)

Now, if God Almighty says that something has been left as a sign, we would expect that sign to be visible. What, then, is the sign of the punishment that came upon Lot's people?

Various scholars have commented upon this point. The late Muhammad Asad states:

> This is an allusion to the Dead Sea — known to this day as *Bahr Lūt* ("The Sea of Lot") — which covers most of the region in which Sodom and Gomorrah were once situated. Its waters contain so high a percentage of sulphur and potash that no fish or plants can live in them. (Asad/*Q*, 29:fn. 29)

---

[7]Here, **"they"** here refers to the unbelievers of the Prophet's time, who frequently passed by the evidences of the destruction of the Overturned Cities but derived no lesson or warning from them.

Maulana Maududi confirms this, saying:

"A clear sign": the Dead Sea, which is also called Sea of Lot. . . . Today it is being admitted with near certainty that the southern end of the Dead Sea came into being as a result of a violent earthquake when the area in which Sodom, the central city of the people of Lot, was located sank underground. In this part there are still signs of some submerged habitations. Exploratory attempts are being made with the modern diving apparatus but the results are still awaited. (Maududi/*Q*, 29:fn. 59)

Elsewhere, Maududi says:

The hundreds of ruins found in the waste and uninhabited land lying to the south and east of the Dead Sea indicate that this must have been a prosperous and thickly populated area in the past. The archaeologists have estimated that the age of prosperity of this land lasted between 2300 and 1900 B.C. According to historians, Prophet Abraham lived about 2000 B.C. Thus the archaeological evidence confirms that this land was destroyed in the time of Prophet Abraham and his nephew Prophet Lot.

The most populous and fertile part of the area was "the vale of Siddim" as mentioned in the Bible [Gen. 14:3, 8, 10]. . . .The present-day scholars are of the opinion that that valley is now under the Dead Sea and this opinion is supported by firm archaelogical evidence. In the ancient times the Dead Sea did not so much extend to the south as it does today. Opposite and to the west of the present Jordanian city of Al-Karak, there is a small peninsula called Al-Lisan. This was the end of the sea in ancient days. The area to the south of it, which is now under sea water (the shaded portion in the map) was a fertile valley, "the vale of Siddīm," in which were situated Sodom, Gomorrah, Admah, Zeboin, Zoar,[8] the famous cities of the people of Lot. In about 2000 B.C. this valley sank as a result of a violent earthquake and was submerged in sea water. Even today this is the most shallow part of the Sea . . .

According to the Bible and the ancient Greek and Latin writings, the region abounded in pits of petroleum and asphalt and at places inflammable gas also existed.[9] It appears from the geological observations that with the violent earthquake shocks, petroleum, gases and asphalt were thrown up and ignited, and the whole region exploded like a bomb. The Bible says that when Prophet Abraham got the news [of the destruction of Lot's people] and went up from Hebron to see the affected valley, he saw

---

[8]In Arabic, Sudum, ʻAmarah, Duma, Sabʻah and Saʻrah.

[9]The tar pits in the Vale of Siddim prior to the catastrophe are mentioned in Gen. 14:10.

that "the smoke of the country went up as the smoke of a furnace" [Gen. 19:28].[10] (ibid, 26:fn. 114)

And Yusuf Ali writes:

> The whole tract on the east side of the Dead Sea (where the Cities were situated) is covered with sulphureous salts and is deadly to animal and plant life. The Dead Sea itself is called in Arabic the Bahr Lūt (the sea of Lot). It is a scene of utter desolation. . . . (Ali/Q, fn. 3457)

Other geological evidence supports all of the above. For example, in Jordan, not far from the Dead Sea, there is a terraced hot spring, the popular resort of Wadi Zarqa Ma'in, which resembles Mammoth Hot Springs in Yellowstone National Park. What do these two places, Ma'in and Yellowstone, have in common? Simply that both are the products of intense vulcanism and geothermal activity.

Amman, Jordan's capital, is situated on a high plateau with moderate temperatures. But when one takes the steep, winding road westward to the Dead Sea, a dramatic (and in summer, very uncomfortable) increase in temperature is encountered due to the marked decrease in altitude. For the Dead Sea lies 392 meters below sea level, with the maximum depth of its sea bottom going down to 793 meters below sea level.

From the western shore of this small sea on the Jordanian side, one can look over at the high plateau of Israel; in fact, the lights of the city of Jerusalem are visible from it by night. From the distance the high plateau of Israel looks very similar to the high plateau of Jordan. It may be that the wide valley in which the Jordan River and the Dead Sea lie, known as the Jordan Rift or the Great Rift, which extends from Syria into Africa, was formed by a cataclysm that sliced a clear-cut north-south rift into what was formerly a single upland. The fact that the Dead Sea is cut by two major faults adds weight to this possibility. The occurrence of a mighty earthquake as the cause is a sound scientific guess.

When one combines this with the abundant signs of volcanic activity in the area, earthquake plus volcanic eruption becomes the most likely explanation of the nature of the divine cataclysm that came upon the Overturned Cities, emphasizing the fact that the All-Wise Creator uses whatever means He chooses to carry out His decree.

---

[10] Gen. 19:23 reads:

> By the time Lot reached Zoar, the sun had risen over the land. Then the Lord rained down burning sulfur on Sodom and Gomorrah — from the Lord out of the heavens. Thus he overthrew those cities and the entire plain, including all those living in the cities — and also the vegetation in the land. But Lot's wife looked back, and she became a pillar of salt,

which may be presumed to have some relationship with the extreme salinity of the Dead Sea.

Another **"sign"** of the Overturned Cities is referred to in following verses:

> **And you surely pass by them [the Overturned Cities] in the morning and at night. Will you not then use reason?** (37:137-138)
>
> **Indeed, they [the Overturned Cities] are upon an established road. Indeed, in that is a sign for the believers. And the dwellers in the thorn bush**[11] **were wrong-doers, so We took retribution from them, and indeed, both [Midian and the Overturned Cities] are on a clear road.** (15:76-79)

These verses refer to the fact that the obliterated cities lay on a major trade route and hence were very well known to the Meccan merchants of Prophet Muhammad's time, who used to **pass by them in the morning and at night** (37:137-138) during their northbound trading journeys to Syria, Palestine and Egypt. The reference to their being on **an established road, . . . a clear road** (15:76, 79) which was visible to all, points to the continued existence of this road as another **"sign"** for anyone who is willing to read the record of God's workings from the earth's surface. It was thus a reminder to the Quraysh that a similar fate could overtake them if they did not heed the warning issued by their own prophet, Muhammad (S), to whose truthfulness and integrity they had themselves testified by calling him, prior to the arousal of their enmity toward him on account of his Message, *al-Amin*, the Trustworthy.

The existence of this road is confirmed by Ibn Kathir, whose comment on 15:76-79 above states that where the the Overturned Cities once stood, there is now a great body of salt water, and beside this water is a roadway on which people come and go (Ibn Kathir/T, 15:75-77). It is also corroborated by the two contemporary commentators, Muhammad Asad and Maulana Maududi, who write

> The existence of that road, which led from northern Hijāz to Syria, skirting the Dead Sea — to the north-east of which Sodom and Gomorrah were situated — has received startling confirmation through aerial photographs recently published by the American School of Oriental Research (New Haven, Connecticut). These photographs clearly show the ancient road as a dark streak winding northwards, more or less parallel with the eastern shores of the Dead Sea. (Asad/Q, 15:fn. 55)
>
> That is, "The smitten territory lies on the high road from Hijāz (Arabia) to Syria and Egypt". Travellers come across these Signs of destruction which are very prominent in the territory that lies to the south-east of the Dead Sea. The geographers are of the opinion that there is no other land

---

[11]That is, the Midianites, the people of the prophet Shu'ayb.

on the surface of the Earth which looks desolate as this territory, especially its southern part. (Maududi/*Q*, 15:fn. 42)

REFERENCES: Qur'an: 15:75-79; 25:40; 26:173-174; 29:35; 37:137-138; 51:35-37. Commentaries: Tabari/*H*, II:125; Ibn Kathir/*T*, 15:75-77; Maududi/*Q*, 25:fn. 54, 15:fn. 42; Asad/*Q*, 15:fn. 55. Other works: Burdon, ***Handbook of the Geology of Jordan***, pp. 13, 49, 52-53, 62, 65; Bender, ***Geology of the Arabian Peninsula: Jordan***, p. 17.

7. Time Out for Reflection

And if they deny you [Muhammad], so did the people of Noah and 'Aad and Thamud deny before them, and the people of Abraham and the people of Lot and the dwellers in Midian, and Moses was denied. So I gave respite to the unbelievers for a time and then I seized them, and how [terrible] was My rejection [of them]! Then how many a township did We destroy while it was engaged in wrong-doing, so it has fallen into ruin, and [how many] an abandoned well and lofty castle! Then have they not traveled through the earth, and do they have hearts with which to feel and ears with which to hear? For indeed, it is not the sight which is blinded, but blinded are the hearts which are within the breasts! (22:42-46)

For those who are interested in discerning the workings of God's will in historical events, the **"signs"** of Lot's people may provide a valuable and fascinating lesson.[12]

As we have seen, earlier communities were destroyed for denying God and ascribing partners to Him, together with various social evils. Both before and after Lot (A), the prophets Noah, Hud, Saleh, Abraham, Shu'ayb (whose story we will tell later in this volume), and Moses, peace be upon them all, spent countless years calling their various peoples to belief, repentance and reform.

Lot's people seem to have differed from the earlier destroyed communities in the extensiveness and pervasiveness of their misdeeds. Indeed, it would seem that among the inhabitants of the five cities, there were not even five righteous individuals, since, according to the report of Ibn 'Abbas (R), if there had been only five among them who prayed, God would have spared them (Tabari/H, II:116), for **never would God destroy the communities except while their people were wrong-doers** (28:59). Moreover, the descriptions of the early commentators suggest that Lot's people had rejected the most basic standards of decency that are common to civilized people. Lot's preaching, therefore, focused mainly on his people's glaring social sins.

It may be useful to review the catalogue of their misdeeds here. First, they denied their Creator, rejected the guidance conveyed to them by their prophet, and treated that prophet with harshness and hostility. Second, they were given

---

[12]God the All-Knowing places great emphasis on the **"signs"** by which He grants mankind knowledge, wisdom and insight, saying, **We have detailed the signs for a people who know. . . . We have detailed the signs for a people who understand** (6:97-98; also 7:32, 9:11, 10:6); **Thus do We detail the signs for a people who reflect** (10:24) and **who use reason** (30:28); **Thus do We detail the signs, and perhaps they will return** (7:174); and, **Thus do We detail the signs, and the way of the criminals will become evident** (6:55).

over to unnatural sexual lusts and perversions, as a result of which they also committed the sin of abandoning the women of their community as partners.[13] Third, they menaced the roads in their area, assaulting, robbing, killing and raping travelers. And fourth, they publicly engaged in other behaviors which are generally regarded as indecent, disgusting and obnoxious. So brazen were Lot's people about their conduct that they even went as far as to challenge the Lord of the heavens and earth, telling their prophet, **"Bring us God's punishment, if you are among the truthful!"**[14] (29:29).

All this suggests that it was perhaps not one sin but the total collection of their sins and crimes, culminating in their assault upon the strangers who were under their prophet's protection, that brought down upon Lot's people the divine punishment, which they had actually gone so far as to demand.

---

[13]Please see Appendix A on page 389 ff. for a discussion of the Islamic position on homosexuality.

[14]We noted this challenge previously in the stories of earlier prophets — for example, the saying of Noah's and Hud's people: **"Then bring us what you are threatening us with, if you are among the truthful!"** (11:32, 7:70, 46:22), and of Saleh's people: **"Bring us what you are threatening us with, if you are [really] among the messengers!"** (7:77). And after their time, Shu'ayb's people would similarly say, **"So cause pieces of the sky to fall upon us, if you are among the truthful!"** (26:187).

APPENDIX A

THE ISLAMIC POSITION REGARDING SEX

Due to its focus on a very contemporary issue, the story of Lot (A) has special relevance to us today. Living in this time, each of us is called upon to clarify our personal attitude toward homosexuality, which has gone from being a crime punishable by law less than a century ago to an open life-style which in some places may even include legally-sanctioned marriage, and for which not only acceptance but also special rights are sought.

We present here the Islamic position regarding both heterosexuality and homosexuality, which is based on the eternal perspective of the Maker of all things and His relationship with His creation. This position may be understood as follows:

First, maleness or femaleness is an integral part of an individual's identity, assigned by the Creator. **God knows what every female carries** (13:8), and **He creates whatever He wills: He grants females to whomever He wills and grants males to whomever He wills, or he makes them [both] males and females, and He renders whomever He wills barren. Indeed, He is Knowing and Able [to do everything]** (42:49-50). And the Holy Prophet (S) said:

> God assigns an angel to the womb, and he says, "O my Lord, a sperm drop! O my Lord, a clot! O my Lord, a lump!" Then, if God wishes to complete its creation, he says, "O my Lord, a male or a female? Wretched or happy? What will its provision be? What will its term of life be?" so that is written [while it is] in its mother's womb. (*Bukhari*, 8:594; also *Muslim*, 6392)

Thus, the gender with which we are born is not simply the result of blind chance or some quirk of fate, nor is it a matter of choice or option. Rather, it is knowingly and purposefully determined by very specific command and decree of the Creator. "It's a girl!" we say when a female is born, or, "It's a boy!" In short, there is no "me" without my gender being an integral part of the total "package" out of which I am formed.

Second, the human sexual drive is so powerful that unless it is regulated and channelized into a socially beneficial outlet, it can be tremendously destructive. In Islam, as in every religion, marriage between a man and a woman is that outlet, ordained by the Creator as the basic institution of human society, as expressed in His words:

> **It is He who created man from water and appointed for him relationships by blood and relationships by marriage. And your Lord is ever Able [to do all things].** (25:54)

Thus, God designed and created men and women to be complementary partners in a binding, permanent, responsible relationship, fitting together like the two halves of a whole, not merely biologically but in all aspects of their common life together: —

> **God created you from dust, then from a sperm-drop; then He made you mates.** (35:11)

> **O mankind, be mindful of your Lord, who created you from a single soul and from it created its mate.** (4:1)

This paired, shared life has three primary purposes and functions. One is to foster love, mercy and tranquility between the two spouses, and provide them both with satisfaction, stability and pleasure: —

> **It is He who created you from a single soul and from it made its mate, that he might find tranquility in her.** (7:189)

> **And among His signs is that He created mates for you from among yourselves, that you might find tranquility in them, and He put love and mercy between you. Surely in that are signs for people who reflect.** (30:21)

> **They [wives] are garments for you and you are garments for them.** (2:187)

The second purpose of marriage is to provide a clean, safe, beneficial, publicly recognized and sanctioned sexual outlet for the two partners, according to God's order:

> **Marry the unmarried among you. . . . And let them who do not find [the means for] marriage abstain [from sex] until God enriches them out of His bounty.** (24:32, 33)

And because marriage is a pemanent, binding commitment or contract, God Most High has ordained that the relationship between husband and wife be safeguarded against anything that could harm or encroach upon it.

The third purpose of marriage is obviously to bring forth children, to be reared, within the family unit that marriage initiates,[15] through the complementary, supporting roles and interaction of the two partners. Thus, God says:

> **He has made for you mates from among yourselves, and from among cattle, by which He multiplies you.** (42:11)

> **God has created spouses for you from among yourselves, and has created for you, from your spouses, children and grandchildren.** (16:72)

---

[15]Even the prophets, who were the most spiritual and pious among mankind, married and had children, according to God's words, **We certainly sent messengers before you, and appointed for them wives and descendants** (13:38).

It is noteworthy that the Arabic word ***rahmah***, "mercy," with its various derivatives denoting mercy, compassion and beneficence, is related to the word ***rahm***, meaning "womb". Thus, even linguistically, the divinely-ordained marriage relationship has an intrinsic connection to the love, mercy and compassion inherent in familial ties.[16] And, speaking by divine inspiration, the Holy Prophet (S) said,

> [The word] "*al-rahm*" [the womb] is closely connected to "*al-Rahman*" [the Most Merciful], so God said, "I will keep good relations with the one keeps good relations with you [the womb], and I will cut off relations with the one who cuts off relations with you." (*Bukhari*, 8:17, 8:18; also 8:16)

Because a sound family is the nurturing ground of security, stability, love, compassion, empathy, tolerance, understanding and every good quality, the strength of any society is inextricably bound to the strength of its families. If the institution of the family becomes weak, society reflects this weakness, begins to decline, and may eventually disintegrate altogether. And because the family is the source of emotional well-being, sound personality, good character, correct values and morals, God has protected it by the strongest possible safeguards.

Third, the Creator has prescribed rules governing the uses of whatever He has granted us. These rules have been conveyed to mankind by His prophets throughout the ages. Simply put, obeying these divine rules brings success and happiness, while disobeying them brings chaos, misery, and the destruction of individuals and society.

While the One who created all things is All-Knowing, absolutely Wise, Informed and Aware, we human beings, by comparison, possess only a tiny iota of information, knowledge, wisdom and understanding, even concerning our own selves. And since we are able to judge only by what is immediate and apparent, we are often unable to distinguish what is harmful from what is beneficial. Consequently, there is no definitive way for us to clearly assess what may harm the most vital element of our being, our immortal souls — or even our bodies or minds or societies, for only God possesses such complete knowledge. Therefore, He alone is able to prescribe the correct, wholesome, sound uses of what He has created, including the parts of the bodies that have been entrusted to us,

---

[16]In Islam, the meaning of family embraces the whole spectrum of blood relationships (parents, children, siblings, grandparents, aunts, uncles, cousins), relationships through marriage (spouse and in-laws), foster relationships (relationships formed through the previous marriage of a parent or spouse, or by breast-feeding from the same mother) in a circle of mutual love, interaction and benefit. Good treatment of relatives, especially parents, is very strongly stressed, and unless they advocate joining partners with God or disobedience to His laws, breaking relations with them is considered a serious sin.

in a manner that will benefit and not harm us in any aspect of our personal or collective life.

Out of His perfect awareness of all things, God Most High permits and indeed encourages sexual relations between man and wife as not only ***halal*** (permissible) but also as wholesome and beneficial. At the same time, He designates as ***haram*** (prohibited) whatever can damage the harmonious interaction between husband and wife that forms the basis of sound family life, or whatever is unsound, harmful or dangeous to the body, mind or heart — that is, every form of sexual expression other than what is within the framework of marriage,[17] saying:

> **Do not come near immoralities, whatever is apparent of them and what is concealed.** (6:151)
>
> **Indeed, God . . . forbids immorality and bad conduct and oppression.** (16:90)
>
> **My Lord has only forbidden immoralities — what is apparent of them and what is concealed.** (7:33)
>
> **Do not come near prohibited sexual relations. Indeed, it is ever an immorality and an evil way.** (17:32)

Fourth, breaking God's rules inevitably results in serious and lasting consequences in this world and in the Hereafter.

Because of our limited, time-bound perspective, it is often difficult or even impossible for us to grasp the long-term consequences of our actions, individually or collectively, or even the fact that there will *be* consequences. However, it is an unalterable divine law that we get what we give, that what goes around comes around. Or, in God's words:

> **That is because of what your hands have put forth, and because God is not ever unjust to [His] servants.** (3:182, 8:51, 22:10)

---

[17]This includes all forms of pre- and extra-marital heterosexual activity; anal and oral intercourse; and intercourse during menstruation or post-partum bleeding. Anything outside these limits falls under the heading of sinful or unnatural sexual behavior. As for homosexuality, the Prophet (S) said, "Lesbianism is ***zina*** [adultery or fornication] between women," and, "God will not look at a man who has anal intercourse with a man or with a woman," including his wife. He also said, "Four types of people awaken under God's anger and go to bed under His displeasure." When he was asked who those were, he replied, "Men who imitate women, women who imitate men, those who approach animals, and those [men] who approach men — that is, like Lot's people." Among those at whom God will not look on the Day of Resurrection and to whom He will say, **"Enter the Fire with those who enter [it]"** [66:10], the Prophet (S) counted the following: the active and passive partners in homosexuality, the one who has sex with animals, the one who is married to a woman and her daughter at the same time, and the one who masturbates regularly, unless they repent and reform (Adh-Dhahabi, ***Major Sins***, pp. 58-59). This is similar to the Jewish and Christian position, in which homosexuality and sodomy are strictly prohibited (Lev. 18 and Rom. 1:24-27).

Whatever befalls you of disaster, it is because of what your hands have earned; but He pardons much. (42:30)

Corruption has appeared on land and sea because of what people's hands have earned, and so He will let them taste something [of the consequences] of what they have done, that they may turn back. (30:41)

Now, the correct use of human sexuality proclaimed by all religions is inseparably related to procreation. The fact that the world's population would die out in two or three generations if non-reproductive sex were universally practiced makes it patently obvious that homosexuality is against the divinely-ordained natural order. Homosexuality is therefore prohibited both because it is a perversion of this natural order and because it constitutes a violation the divinely-ordained rules of sexual conduct. The very fact that of its being prohibited indicates that it is a harmful behavior, and harmful behaviors inevitably have harmful consequences, both for individuals who engage in them and for society.

Another factor in the prohibition of homosexuality is that it suppresses or artifically alters the God-given sexual identity of one of the two partners who engage in it, denying his or her intrinsic, God-given nature, while at the same time perverting the inherent parental instinct. One consequence of this is the devastating personal conflict that is experienced by many who practice homosexuality, which cannot be totally rationalized away even by its most enthusiastic supporters. Since no one grows up in a moral vacuum, in their deepest hearts, many or even most homosexuals feel secretly uneasy and ashamed of following a path condemned by religion and mainstream society. Adding to their burden is awareness of the terrible suffering that their behavior may have caused their loved ones.

In addition, homosexuals often carry a sense of being pitted against the remainder of the population. Those who have not "come out" live double lives, haunted by the fear of discovery, while those who have gone public may feel constantly on the defensive, suspicious and hostile toward "straights," and fearful of being harmed, with a tremendous scarring of their psyches as a result. As we are seeing in our time, this eventually leads to a general polarization of homosexuals and their supporters against heterosexuals, resulting in a massive social rift.

Besides this, it is hardly necessary to mention the terrible toll that this deviant and prohibited use of sexuality takes on the health, productivity and lives of those who practice it. Each case of AIDS represents a shattered life, with repercussions spreading like ripples throughout the society and the world. But, as a wise man has said, this disease does not flourish in controlled bodies, and opting not to exercise that control carries with it its own punishment.

These are some of the consequences of breaking the divine rules in this world, and perhaps there will be even more devastating ones as time goes by. However, the consequences in the Hereafter will certainly be infinitely more serious and lasting, and this in itself should be a major deterrent from such prohibited behavior to any who **fear their Lord unseen, while they are apprehensive of the Hour** of Judgment (21:49).

Fifth, while there is no accountability for prohibited thoughts, feelings or urges, we are accountable for allowing ourselves to act on them.

As we have seen, Islam teaches that this life and everything in it is a test, including our hearts which feel, our minds which think and reason, weigh and judge, and our bodies which act. Therefore, once we have reached physical maturity, we are responsible for all our actions, including what our ears listen to, what our eyes look at, what our hands reach for, and what our feet walk toward, for, **indeed, hearing and sight and the heart — all those will be enquired into** (17:36) on **a Day when their tongues and their hands and their feet will bear witness against them because of what they used to do** (24:24; also 36:65) — **the Day when a person will see what his hands have sent forth, and the disbeliever will say, "Oh, if only I were dust!"** (78:40).

During childhood, we gradually learn to sort out our feelings and impulses, and how to control them. An essential aspect of this is the control of our sexuality, in keeping with the restraints imposed by religion and society. Nonetheless, the desires of our lower self (*nafs*), coupled with the incitations of Satan, often cause prohibited thoughts, desires or urges to surface within us, according to God's words:

> **Indeed, We have created the human being and We know what his *nafs* whispers to him, and We are closer to him than his jugular vein. (50:16)**
>
> **Indeed, the *nafs* is a persistent enjoiner of evil, except as my Lord shows mercy. Indeed, my Lord is Forgiving and Merciful. (12:53)**
>
> **[Satan said,] "I will surely take an appointed share of Your servants, and I will mislead them and will arouse desires in them." (4:119)**
>
> **Satan orders you to immorality. (2:268)**
>
> **And whoever follows the footsteps of Satan, indeed, he enjoins immorality and wrong-doing. (24:21)**
>
> **And who is more astray than one who follows his desire without guidance from God? (28:50)**

At the same time, the higher, **self-admonishing self** (*an-nafs al-lawwamah* or conscience) (75:2) constantly monitors these urges and restrains us from acting on them: —

> **[By] the soul and Him who balanced it, and inspired it [with discernment of] its wickedness and its righteousness, he has succeeded who purifies it and he has failed who buries it.** (91:7-10)

According to the Islamic teachings, feelings, thoughts or urges do not constitute sins as long as they are not acted upon or spoken about. The Holy Prophet (S) said:

> Indeed, God passes over what the lower selves of my *ummah* whisper or provoke them to as long as they does not act on it or speak [of it]. (*Bukhari*, 8:657)

A man once came to the Prophet (S) and said, "O Messenger of God, one of us has thoughts of such a nature that he would rather be reduced to charcoal than speak about them." The Prophet's response was to exclaim, "*Allahu akbar! Allahu akbar! Allahu akbar!* [God is Most Great]. Praise be to God who has reduced Satan's guile to evil prompting!" (Abu Dawud, 5093) — that is, rather than actualization in deeds.

Indeed, as we mentioned previously, the Messenger of God (S) informed us that refraining from doing a bad deed is counted as a good deed, saying that when a person thinks of doing a good deed but does not carry it out, God records it as a single good deed. If he carries it out, God records from ten to seven hundred or more goodnesses for him. At the same time, if he thinks of doing a bad deed but does not do it, God records it as a good deed (because of the evil he avoided), while if he does a bad deed, it is recorded only as one (*Bukhari*, 8:498, 9:592; also 1:40, 4:629; *Muslim*, 233, 235).

With regard to the subject at hand, mere feelings of attraction toward members of the same sex do not automatically "make" a person a homosexual. Like all other unacceptable feelings or urges, we are expected to fight against them and not act on them. This is but one aspect of the unending spiritual struggle that goes on throughout our conscious adult lives against our lower self and its passions; against the whisperings of Satan, who arouses desires within us and urges us to immorality and indecency (4:120, 2:268); and against the attractions of this world. Thus it was that once the Prophet (S), upon returning from battle (*jihad*), referred to this lifelong internal struggle as "the greater *jihad*" or struggle.

This emphasis on the ongoing spiritual struggle required of us as human beings contrasts sharply with the position of those who claim that homosexuality is the result of "genetic predisposition" rather than a choice of behavior — a claim whose truth has yet to be established. Ironically, those making this claim somehow ignore the fact that it conradicts another much-publicized claim — that of freely-chosen "sexual preference" or "sexual orientation".

Islam's position is that whether or not there is a genetic predisposition to homosexuality — or to any other type of undesirable behavior, for that matter — predisposition does not compel anyone to act in a certain way. Acting on this predisposition, if in fact it does exist, is therefore ultimately a matter of choice. Certainly great numbers of people, genetically predisposed or otherwise, experience urges to engage in various kinds of deviant, harmful and even criminal behaviors. And while people who have such urges may not be able to control the urges themselves, they are nevertheless expected to refrain from acting on them — and if they do not, the penalties for socially unacceptable behaviors are well-known.

Thus, religion and society alike insist that regardless of what we may happen to feel, our actions must be controlled — and homosexual urges are no different from the many other harmful, unacceptable urges or desires that human beings learn to control. Unquestionably, in the unpublicized privacy of their innermost selves, a great many people who experience homosexual feelings *do* control them rather than acting on them, out of respect for morality, religion, society, their families and their own selves. Therefore, while we may feel compassion for those who experience such feelings, this does not alter the fact that if they act on them, they may be judged as having chosen to engage in behavior which is harmful and which, from the standpoint of religion, is a violation of God's limits and a grave sin.

Finally, God invites all who have violated His limits to turn to Him, promising forgiveness to those who repent sincerely.

While Islam views homosexuality as a violation of the divinely-ordained natural order and God's clear command, and hence as a major sin and even as a crime against society, this is not to be construed as permission to hate or harm homosexuals, for the souls and personalities of each of the children of Adam is sacred. Rather, those who practice this behavior are to be looked upon with compassion as people who have given in to temptation and lost their way, perhaps out of ignorance of the divine guidance.

At the same time, God assures all who turn to Him, seeking His forgiveness, of His endless mercy, saying,

> **Your Lord has prescribed mercy upon Himself.** (6:54; also 6:12)
>
> **Inform My servants that it is I who am the Forgiving, the Merciful.** (15:49)
>
> **The one who does a wrong or wrongs himself but then seeks forgiveness of God will find God Forgiving and Merciful.** (4:110)

We mentioned previously that the most often mentioned of God's Beautiful Names or divine attributes is *al-Rahman*, the Most Merciful. He is also *al-Tawwab*, the Acceptor of Repentance; *al-Ghaffar*, the Forgiving; *al-Ghafur*, the Forgiver; and *al-'Afuw*, the Pardoner. Literally dozens of verses of the Qur'an speak of His mercy and forgiveness.[18]

However, repentance and reform must go hand in hand; merely asking for forgiveness while continuing on a prohibited path is unacceptable. True repentance must therefore be accompanied by the sincere intention to leave the wrong action and change one's behavior, and then to struggle without ceasing to materialize this intention.[19] Perhaps, in today's permissive society, in which the incentives for reform and change may not be sufficient to pull one out of a deeply-entrenched and cherished habit, the fear of our Maker and the desire for His mercy and pleasure may: —

> **But as for him who feared the standing before his Lord and kept back the *nafs* from [prohibited] inclinations, then indeed Paradise will be the refuge.** (79:40-41)

Now, as in the time of the prophet Lot (A), God calls us back to Himself. Although each of us has frailties, commits mistakes, misdeeds and sins, nevertheless His forgiveness and mercy is greater than all our sins, and it is extended to each one of us, His servants. No one should ever be hopeless of that mercy or feel beyond redemption, for He says:

> **O My servants who have transgressed against their souls, do not despair of God's mercy. Indeed, God forgives all sins. Indeed, it is He who is the Forgiving, the Merciful.** (39:53)
>
> **And hasten to forgiveness from your Lord and a Paradise as wide as the heavens and the earth, made ready for the God-conscious, who spend [on good works] in ease and hardship, and who restrain anger and pardon people — and God loves the doers of good; and those who, if they do something indecent or wrong themselves, remember God and seek forgiveness for their sins — and who can forgive sins except God? — and do not persist in that which they have done, while they know. Those — their reward is forgiveness from their Lord and gardens beneath which rivers flow, abiding in them forever. And excellent is the recompense of the workers!** (3:133-136; also 57:21)
>
> **But those who did evil deeds and then repented after them and believed — indeed, your Lord is, after that, Forgiving and Merciful.** (7:153)

---

[18]See, for example, 4:31, 106, 110; 5:74/77; 7:153; 11:90; 71:10; 85:14.

[19]This is expressed in the following verses, among others: 4:17; 16:119; 19:59; 20:82; 28:67.

> **But indeed, I am assuredly the Forgiver of the one who repents and believes and does righteous deeds and then continues in guidance.** (20:82)
>
> **The slaves of the Most Merciful are those who walk upon the earth mildly . . . those who do not invoke another deity with God, nor take a life that God has made sacred except by [legal] right, nor engage in prohibited sexual relations. And whoever does that will encounter a penalty. The punishment will be multiplied for him on the Day of Resurrection and he will remain therein, humiliated, except those who repent and believe and do righteous deeds. For them, God will replace their evil deeds with good. And God is ever Forgiving and Merciful.** (25:63, 68-70)

Indeed, even the Prophet (S), the best among mankind, used to seek God's forgiveness a hundred times a day (*Muslim*, 6522-6523). And speaking by divine inspiration, he said:

> God is more gladdened by the repentance of His servant when he repents to Him than one of you is over his mount's getting loose in a place and wandering away from him, while his food and his drink are upon it, whereupon he despairs concerning it. He then comes to a tree and lies down in its shade, having despaired concerning his mount [and likewise his life]. Then, while he is in this state, behold, there it is, standing before him! He then seizes it by its halter and says, in the intensity of his joy, "O God, You are my servant and I am Your Lord!" making this mistake out of the intensity of his joy. (*Muslim*, 6618; also *Muslim*, 6611-6617, 6619; *Bukhari*, 8:320-321)
>
> Whoever repents before the rising of the sun from the West [that is, at any time before the Day of Resurrection], God will turn to him in forgiveness. (*Muslim*, 6525)
>
> If you did not commit sins, God would have created creatures that would have sinned and He would have forgiven them. (*Muslim*, 6620-6222)

The Holy Prophet, God's peace and blessings be upon him, also said:

> God, the Mighty and Glorious, said, "I am to My servant as thinks of Me, and I am with him insamuch as he remembers Me." By God, God is more gladdened by the repentance of His servant than one of you is at finding his [camel] lost by by escaping [in the desert]. [And, speaking on behalf of his Lord, he added:] "Whoever draws near Me a span, I draw near him by a cubit, and whoever draws near Me a cubit, I draw near him by a fathom, and when he comes close to Me walking, I come close to him hastening." (*Muslim*, 6610)

Son of Adam, as long as you supplicate Me and hope in Me, I shall pardon you in spite of what you have done, and I do not care. Son of Adam, if your sins were as numerous as to reach the lofty regions of the sky and then you asked My forgiveness, I would forgive you, and I do not care. Son of Adam, if you were to meet Me with enough sins to fill the earth and then you met Me, not associating partners with Me, I would bring you as much pardon as would fill the earth. (*Mishkat*, 2332)

Qur'anic References — Lot and His People

6:84-87

And We granted him [Abraham] Isaac and Jacob; each [of them] We guided. And previously We guided Noah, and among his descendants, David and Solomon and Job and Joseph and Moses and Aaron. And thus do We reward the doers of good. (84) And Zechariah and John and Jesus and Elijah — all were among the righteous; (85) and Ishmael and Elisha and Jonah and Lot — and all [of them] We preferred over [all] mankind, (86) and some from among their fathers and descendants and brothers; and We chose them and guided them to a straight path. (87)

7:80-84

And [mention] Lot, when he said to his people, "Would you perpetrate such vileness as no one among mankind has done before you? (80) Indeed, you approach men with desire to the exclusion of women. No, but you are a transgressing people!" (81)

But the reply of his people was only that they said, "Drive them out of your city! Indeed, they are people who keep themselves pure!" (82)

Then We saved him and his family, except his wife; she was among those who stayed behind. (83) And We rained upon them a rain. Then see what was the end of the criminals! (84)

9:70

Has there not reached them the news of those before them — the people of Noah and 'Aad and Thamud, and the people of Abraham and the dwellers in Midian and the Overturned Cities? Their messengers came to them with clear proofs. And never would God have wronged them, but [rather] they wronged themselves.

11:69-70, 74-83

And Our messengers certainly came to Abraham with the good tidings. They said, "*Salam.*"

He said, "*Salam,*" and did not delay in bringing a roasted calf. (69) But when he saw their hands not reaching toward it, he mistrusted them and felt apprehensive of them.

They said, "Do not be afraid. Indeed, we have been sent to Lot's people." (70).

. . .Then, when the fear had left Abraham and the good tidings had reached him, he disputed with Us concerning Lot's people. (74) Indeed, Abraham was forbearing, tender-hearted, [constantly] returning [to God]. (75)

[They said,] "O Abraham, give up this! Your Lord's decree has surely gone forth, and there will indeed come to them a punishment which cannot be averted." (76)

And when Our messengers came to Lot, he was grieved for them and felt straitened concerning them, and he said, "This is a distressing day!" (77) And his people came hurrying toward him, and before this they had been doing evil deeds. He said, "O my people, these are my daughters; they are purer for you. So fear God and do not disgrace me concerning my guests. Is there not a right-minded man among you?" (78)

They said, "You certainly know that we have no claim on your 'daughters,' and indeed you know what we want!" (79)

He said, "If only I had power against you or I could take refuge in a strong support!" (80)

They said, "O Lot, indeed, we are messengers of your Lord. They will never reach you! Therefore, set out with your family during a portion of the night, and let not any of you look back — except your wife; she will surely be struck by whatever strikes them. Indeed, their appointed time is the morning. Is not the morning near?" (81)

Then, when Our command came, We made its highest part its lowest and rained upon them stones of hard clay in succession, (82) marked by your Lord. And it is not far from the wrong-doers. (83)

11:89-90

[Shu'ayb said,] "And, O my people, do not let dissension with me cause you to sin, lest there befall you something like what befell the people of Noah or the people of Hud or the people of Saleh. Nor are the people of Lot far removed from you. (89) And seek forgiveness from your Lord and then repent to Him. Indeed, my Lord is Merciful and Loving!" (90)

15:57-79

He [Abraham] said, "Then what is your business, O messengers?" (57)

They said, "Indeed, we have been sent to a criminal people, (58) excepting Lot's family. We will surely save them all, (59) except his wife; We have decreed that she be among those who remain behind. (60)

And when the messengers came to Lot's family, (61) he said, "You are surely unknown people." (62)

They said, "No, but we have come to you with that which they were disputing, (63) and we have come to you with the truth and indeed, we are truthful. (64) Therefore, set out with your family during a portion of the night and follow behind them, and let not any of you look back and continue on to wherever you are commanded." (65) And We conveyed to him that decree: that the [very] last of those would be cut off by early morning. (66)

And the people of the city came, rejoicing. (67) He said, "Indeed, these are my guests, so do not shame me. (68) And fear God and do not disgrace me!" (69)

They said, "And have we not forbidden you from everyone?" (70)

He said, "These are my daughters, if you would do [anything]." (71) By your life, [O Muhammad,] indeed, they were wandering blindly in their bewilderment. (72) Then the clamor seized them at sunrise, (73) and We made its higher part its lowest and rained upon them stones of hard clay. (74) In that are surely signs for the attentive. (75) And indeed, they are upon an established road. (76) In that is surely a sign for the believers. (77)

And the dwellers in the thorn bush were [also] wrong-doers, (78) so We took retribution from them, and indeed, both [Midian and the Overturned Cities] are on a clear road. (79)

21:71, 74-75

And We delivered him [Abraham] and Lot to the land which We had blessed for [all] mankind (71). . . . And to Lot We granted judgment and knowledge, and We saved him from the community that was doing wicked deeds. They were surely an evil people, defiantly disobedient. (74) And We admitted him to Our mercy. Indeed, he was among the righteous. (75)

22:42-46

And if they deny you [Muhammad], so did the people of Noah and 'Aad and Thamud deny [their prophets] before them, (42) and the people of Abraham and the people of Lot (43) and the dwellers in Midian, and Moses was denied. So I [gave respite] to the unbelievers for a time and then I seized them; then how [terrible] was My rejection [of them]! (44)

Then how many a community did We destroy while it was engaged in wrongdoing, so that its roofs caved in, and [how many] an abandoned well and lofty castle! (45) Then have they not traveled through the earth, so that they have hearts with which to feel and ears with which to hear? For indeed, it is not the sight which is blinded, but blinded are the hearts which are within the breasts! (46)

25:40

And they have already come upon the town that was rained upon with an evil rain. Have they then not seen it? But they are not anticipating resurrection.

26:160-174

Lot's people denied the messengers, (160) when their brother Lot said to them, "Will you not be mindful of God? (161) I am surely a trustworthy messenger to you, (162) so be mindful of God and obey me. (163) And I do not ask you for any recompense for it. My recompense rests only upon the Lord of the worlds. (164) Among [all] mankind, do you approach males (165) and leave what your Lord has created for you as mates? No, but you are a transgressing people!" (166)

They said, "If you do not leave off, O Lot, you will surely be of those driven out!" (167)

He said, "Indeed, I am of those who detest your doings. (168) My Lord, save me and my family from what they do!" (169)

Then We saved him and his family, all, (170) except an old woman among those who remained behind. (171) Then We destroyed the others, (172) and We rained upon them a rain, and evil was the rain of those who were warned! (173) Indeed, in that is a sign, but most of them are not believers. (174)

27:54-58

And Lot, when he said to his people, "Do you commit vileness, while you are observing? (54) Do you indeed approach men with desire to the exclusion of women? No, but you are a people behaving ignorantly!" (55)

But the answer of his people was only that they said, "Drive Lot's family out of your city. Indeed, they are people who keep themselves pure!" (56) Then We saved him and his family, except his wife; We destined her to be among those who remained behind. (57) And We rained upon them a rain, and evil was the rain of those who were warned! (58)

29:26

And Lot believed in him. And he [Abraham] said, "I will surely emigrate to my Lord. Indeed, He is the Almighty, the Wise."

29:28-35

And [mention] Lot, when he said to his people, "You surely perpetrate such vileness as no one among mankind has done before you! (28) Indeed, you approach men and menace the road and commit abomination in your meetings."

But the answer of his people was only that they said, "Bring us God's punishment, if you are among the truthful!" (29)

He said, "My Lord, support me against the corrupt people!" (30)

And when Our messengers came to Abraham with the good news, they said, "We will surely destroy the people of that city. Indeed, its people have been evildoers." (31)

He said, "But Lot is surely in it!"

They said, "We are more knowing of who is in it. Indeed, We will save him and his family, except his wife; she is to be among those who remain behind." (32)

And when Our messengers came to Lot, he was grieved for them and felt straitened concerning them. And they said, "Do not fear nor grieve. Indeed, we will save you and your family, except your wife. She is to be among those who stay behind. (33) We will surely bring down a punishment from the sky upon the people of this community because they have have been defiantly disobedient." (34) And We certainly left a sign of it as clear evidence for a people who use reason. (35)

37:133-138

And indeed, Lot was among the messengers. (133) [Mention, O Muhammad,] when We saved him and his family, all, (134) except an old woman among those who remained behind. (135) Then We destroyed the others. (136) And you surely pass by them [the Overturned Cities] in the morning (137) and at night. Will you not then use reason? (138)

38:12-14

Before them, the people of Noah and 'Aad and Pharaoh, possessor of the stakes, (12) denied, and Thamud and the people of Lot and the dwellers in the thorn bush. Those were the factions; (13) each denied the messengers, wherefore My punishment was justified. (14)

50:12-14

Before them, the people of Noah and the dwellers in al-Rass and Thamud denied, (12) and 'Aad and Pharaoh and the brethren of Lot, (13) and the dwellers in the thorn bush and the people of Tubba' — all denied the messengers, wherefore my threat was justly carried out. (14)

51:31-37

He [Abraham] said, "Then what is your business, O messengers?" (31)

They said, "Indeed, we have been sent to a criminal people, (32) to send down upon them stones of clay, (33) marked by your Lord for the transgressors." (34)

Then We brought out whomever was in them of the believers (35), but We did not find in them other than than a single house of *muslims.* (36) And We left therein a sign for those who fear the painful punishment. (37)

53:53-54

And He destroyed the Overturned Cities, (53) and covered them by that which He covered. (54)

54:33-39

Lot's people denied the warnings. (33) Indeed, We sent against them a storm of stones, excepting Lot's family; We saved them before dawn, (34) a favor from Ourselves. Thus do We reward one who is grateful. (35) And he had already warned them of Our assault, but they disputed the warnings. (36) And they had demanded of him his guests, but We obliterated their eyes. Then taste My punishment and warnings! (37) And there came upon them by morning a lasting punishment. (38) Then taste My punishment and warnings! (39)

66:10

God sets forth an example of those who disbelieved: the wife of Noah and the wife of Lot. They were under [the charge of] two servants among His righteous servants but they betrayed them, and they [their prophet-husbands] did not benefit them at all before God. And it was said to them, "Enter the Fire with those who enter [it]!"

69:9

And Pharaoh and those before him, and the Overturned Cities, committed sin.

THE STORY OF JOSEPH (YUSUF)

peace be upon him

We granted him [Abraham] Isaac and Jacob, and We appointed prophethood and scripture among his descendants.
(29:27)

1. The Family of Jacob

And We granted him [Abraham] Isaac and Jacob; each [of them] We guided. And previously We guided Noah, and among his descendants, David and Solomon and Job and Joseph and Moses and Aaron. And thus do We reward the doers of good. (6:84)

We now come to a story which is unique among the stories of prophets in the Qur'an — the story of Joseph (Yusuf), son of Jacob, the grandson of Isaac, and the great-grandson of Abraham, may God's peace and blessings be upon them all. Its uniqueness lies in the fact that it is the only story of a prophet that is told in entirety in a single *surah* or chapter of the Qur'an — that is, the twelfth *surah*, *Yusuf*,[1] of whose 111 verses, ninety-eight relate to Joseph (A).

It is in this story that the noble personality of Jacob (A) also comes alive. However, it is difficult to correctly understand the story of Jacob and Joseph, peace be upon them both, without some understanding of background material.

Ibn Kathir reports that the People of the Scripture — that is, Jews and Christians — say that when Isaac (A) was forty years of age, during the lifetime of his father Abraham (A), he married Rebecca, daughter of Bethuel. When no children were born to her, Isaac (A) prayed to his Lord and she bore twin sons, Esau and Jacob (Y'aqub).

Like his father and grandfather before him, Jacob (A) and his family lived in Hebron in Palestine. They were bedouin people, herders of sheep and goats, who were closely related by ties of kinship and culture to the Arabs of the Arabian peninsula.

It is said that Jacob (A) first married Leah, the daughter of his maternal uncle Laban, and she bore him six sons: Reuben, Simeon, Levi, Judah, Issachar, Zebulon, and a daughter named Dinah. Then Leah died and Jacob (A) married her sister Rachel,[2] who bore him Joseph and Benjamin (Binyamin). Another of Jacob's wives, Bilhah, bore him two more sons, Dan and Naphtali, and a fourth, Zilpah, bore him two others, Gad and Ashar, making a total of twelve. Biblical scholars give the date of Joseph's birth as around 1906 B.C.

---

[1]Apart from this *surah*, Joseph's name occurs only twice in the Qur'an, in 6:84 and 40:34. While 6:84 is cited above, 40:34 relates to the story of Moses and will be cited in his story in Volume Two.

[2]According to some sources (taken, as is the above material, from Genesis), Jacob was married to both sisters at once. However, this could have been the case only if such marriages had not been prohibited at that time by divine law, as they later were in Islam.

As we know, Jacob (A) succeeded Isaac (A) in prophethood. At some point in his life, Jacob (A) came to be called Israel (Isra'il), because of which, both in the Bible and in the Qur'an, his descendants are called the Children of Israel (*Bani Isra'il*) or, more simply, Israelites. Since there is no mention in the Qur'an of Jacob's "people" in the sense of "Noah's people" or "Lot's people," perhaps he was a prophet only to his own family members, who were quite numerous, as is suggested by God's saying,

> **And this Abraham enjoined [on his sons], and so did Jacob: "O my sons, indeed, God has chosen the religion for you, so do not die except that you be *muslims*" (2:131-132).**

The divine wisdom of appointing Jacob (A) as a prophet to his large family becomes apparent in the later history of the Children of Israel, for perhaps the descendants of Jacob (A) were the only people in the entire world at the time who worshipped the Creator, may His glory be exalted, and lived according to His guidance.

REFERENCES: Tabari/*H*, II:134-139; Ibn Kathir/*Q*, "Yusuf"; Maududi/*Q*, Intro. to ***Surah Yusuf*** [12]; Ali/*Q*, fn. 1632.

2. Joseph's Vision

These are the verses of the clear Book. Indeed, We have revealed it as an Arabic Qur'an, that you may understand.[3] We relate to you [Muhammad] the best of stories in what We have revealed to you of this Qur'an, although you were, before it, among the unaware. (12:1-3)

With these words, God Most High opens **"the best of stories"**[4] — the fascinating history of the prophet Joseph, may God's peace and blessings be upon him.

The opening of the story depicts Joseph (A) as a boy, living in his father's house together with his younger brother Benjamin and his ten step-brothers, who were all his elders. Various circumstances suggest that Joseph's age may have been about ten at the time.[5]

It is only natural that there should be friction, rivalry and jealousy among the twelve sons of four mothers. But in the case of Joseph (A), there was more to the matter than that. The Qur'anic account makes it clear that Joseph (A) excelled his brothers as the sun outshines the stars, as might indeed be expected, since he had been chosen by God for prophethood. However, it was his very excellence that gave his ten step-brothers cause for envy and enmity.

One cause of this envy was undoubtedly the fact that the young Joseph (A) was incredibly handsome, for the Prophet (S) said of him, "Joseph and his mother were given half of all the beauty in the world" (Tabari/*H*, II:148). And if

---

[3]**"You"** here refers to the Arabic-speaking people of Muhammad's time, among whom the Qur'an was originally revealed.

[4]**"*Ahsana-l qasas,*"** meaning the nicest, loveliest, most excellent or best of stories, or, alternatively, a narrative related in the best manner or with the most excellent explanation.

[5]While al-Tabari suggests (no doubt based on Gen. 37:2), that Joseph was seventeen at this time, the following details given in the Qur'anic narrative suggest that he may have been considerably younger:

First, Joseph's brothers ask their father if they can take him on an outing to **enjoy himself and play** (12:12), which suggests that he was still a boy. Afterwards they tell their father that they went racing and left Joseph behind to take care of their things (12:17), implying that he was not at their level in racing and could be treated like an underling. In addition, Jacob's fear that Joseph might be eaten by a wolf (12:13), and his brothers' subsequent claim that this had actually occurred (12:17), would not have made sense if he had been a full-grown youth of seventeen. The remaining clue to Joseph's age is contained in God's words, **When Joseph reached the age of full strength, We granted him wisdom and knowledge** (12:22), after he had lived in the home of his Egyptian master for some time, for according to the common understanding, **the age of full strength** denotes the age of physical maturity, manly strength, full consciousness and understanding — that is to say, the late teens.

this were not sufficient cause, it was clearly obvious to his brothers that he was more dear to their father than themselves.

This was not merely because of Joseph's beauty or (as claimed in Gen. 37:3) because he was born to Jacob (A) in his old age, but rather because of the loveliness of his spirit. As a prophet possessing deep wisdom and insight, Jacob (A) naturally recognized the excellence of Joseph's nature and his spiritual gifts, and hence he cherished him like a treasure among his other sons.

As the story opens, the young Joseph (A) is engaged in a private and intimate conversation with his father, during which he relates a dream or a vision he has just had.

"O my father," he said, **"indeed, I saw eleven stars and the sun and the moon — I saw them prostrating to me"** (12:4).

Jacob (A) immediately grasped the meaning of his son's vision. Being yet a boy, Joseph (A) did not realize its significance, but his father knew that his brothers would have no difficulty understanding it. Jacob (A) therefore cautioned the innocent lad to keep what he had seen to himself.

"O my son," he warned, **"do not tell your vision to your brothers, or they will make a plot against you. Indeed, Satan is a clear enemy to the human being"** (12:5). These words suggest that Jacob (A) had had sufficient evidence of his sons' enmity toward the young Joseph to make him concerned that they might scheme against him. Then, having said this, he informed Joseph (A) of the meaning of what he had seen.

"And thus will your Lord choose you and teach you the interpretation of events, and complete His favor upon you and upon the family of Jacob, as He completed it previously upon your fathers, Abraham and Isaac," Jacob (A) prophesied, clearly seeing the auspicious future that was in store for his beloved son. **"Indeed, your Lord is Knowing and Wise"** (12:6).

In the future, these words would serve as a reminder to Joseph (A) that, no matter what difficulties he might face, all things are in the hands of the All-Knowing, All-Wise Lord, who is indeed the Best of Planners. Reading them in Arabic, one experiences a sense of mystery — the understanding that the story of Joseph (A) and his brothers, as well as being a history, is also a parable concerning the subtle interplay between the divine Will and human knowledge and control over events.

REFERENCES: Qur'an: 12:4-6. Commentaries: Tabari/*H*, II:148, 183-184; Maududi/*Q*, 12:3; Asad/*Q*, 12:fn. 5.

3. Joseph and His Brothers

Indeed, in Joseph and his brothers are signs for the enquiring. (12:7)

After this, the narrative shifts from Jacob (A) to his sons, as Joseph's ten step-brothers complain to one another about Joseph's favored position. The brothers' speech and manner stand out in harsh contrast to Joseph's innocence and sincerity.

"Joseph and his brother" — that is, Benjamin, Joseph's full brother from his own mother — **"are more dear to our father than we, while we are a clan,"**[6] they grumbled among themselves. **"Indeed, our father is in clear aberration"** (12:8). They then began to exchange ideas about how to resolve this problem once and for all.

"Kill Joseph or banish him to a distant **land,"** one of them proposed. **"Your father's regard will** then **be accessible to you."** Then, as if to offer an excuse for the horrendous deed he had suggested, he added: **"And after that, you will be righteous people"** (12:9), as if to say, "Once we get rid of the external cause of our unrighteousness, we will automatically become good."

But one among the ten brothers was of a better nature.[7] **"Do not kill Joseph,"** he suggested, **"but, if you must do something, put him into the bottom of the well. Some travelers will pick him up"** (12:10).

The other nine agreed to this plan and the plot was laid. The brothers then approached Jacob (A).

"O our father," they said, **"why do you not entrust us with Joseph, while we are indeed his sincere well-wishers?"** (12:11).

This question, with its reference to trust, indicates that the brothers were well aware that Jacob (A) knew of their envy and hostility toward Joseph. It also suggests that they might previously have asked their father to let Joseph go out with them and have been refused.[8] But now, with their plot in mind, they pressed him to agree.

"Send him with us tomorrow to enjoy himself and play, and indeed we will be his guardians" (12:12), the deceitful brothers urged, pretending that they were only concerned with Joseph's well-being.

---

[6]The meaning here may be, "Although we are many, this single one is dearer to our father than all the rest of us put together."

[7]This brother is identified in Gen. 37:21 as Reuben, the eldest of Leah's sons.

[8]One possible explanation of this is that earlier Joseph might have been too young to go on an outing to the desert, where wolves prowled in broad daylight.

Perhaps something of this sort was precisely what Jacob (A) had meant when he cautioned Joseph against telling his brothers his vision. Knowing his sons' ill nature, he understood well enough that they had thought up some scheme against the brother who surpassed them all so greatly in character and disposition. But he was trapped. Refusing their request would only add fuel to their ill-will toward Joseph, with perhaps even worse consequences.

Nonetheless, Jacob (A) made one last attempt to protect the son whom he loved so dearly. **"Indeed, it saddens me that you should take him,"** he said, **"and I fear that a wolf may devour him while you are heedless of him"** (12:13).

"If a wolf were to devour him while we are a clan, we would then indeed be losers!" (12:14), the brothers protested falsely. And their father said no more. Although he realized that terrible events might be in store for his beloved son, he was powerless to protect him indefinitely from his brothers' evil — or indeed from anything else with which his Lord might see fit to test him.

At the same time, Joseph's vision had made it clear that a very special future lay ahead of him. Because of this, Jacob (A) possessed the assurance that no matter what troubles might befall Joseph during his life, he *must* reach the exalted rank that had been promised through his vision. Regardless of the trials and sufferings that might come to the dearest of his sons — and to himself, loving that son as he did — the final outcome, arranged by his Lord, would be for the best. Even though separation and sorrow would now come upon him and his beloved Joseph, nothing could destroy Jacob's certainty and trust in God's wisdom and mercy. And he surrendered himself inwardly to whatever the All-Wise Lord might decree.

The following day, the treacherous brothers took the unsuspecting Joseph on their "outing". Presently they seized him, stripped him of his shirt, and **put him into the bottom of the well** (12:15), where they left him to his fate. And they stained his shirt with the blood of an animal they had killed as evidence to their father that he was really dead.

And they came to their father at night, weeping false tears. "O our father," they cried, **"indeed, we went racing and left Joseph with our things, and a wolf devoured him."** Then, observing Jacob's disbelief, they added: **"But you would not believe us even if we were truthful!"** And to convince him that they were not lying, **they produced his shirt with false blood upon it** (12:16-18).

We can imagine Jacob's feelings at that point: his terrible anxiety over Joseph's unknown fate — had his brothers then killed him, so that this blood was really his? — and at the same time, his horror at the naked evil that he saw so clearly within his sons. And although he was their father and a prophet, he had no power to deal with them.[9] There were ten of them, acting as a body in their wickedness, entirely out of his control, impelled by the worst of all ill feelings, envy.

Jacob (A) had already understood and accepted the fact that some calamity would befall his beloved son. But the brothers' claim that a wolf had eaten him — after his saying to them the previous day, **"I fear that a wolf may devour him while you are heeldess of him,"** and their reply, **"If a wolf were to devour him while we are a strong clan, then we would indeed be losers"** — did not ring true. As for the shirt, obviously a wolf does not devour a person and leave his shirt behind. At the same time, there was Joseph's vision, like a bright beacon of hope, assuring him that his dearest son would live to see a distinguished future.

But whatever the case might be, something deep, devious and terribly wicked was afoot, although Jacob (A) could not know what. Something ***had*** happened to Joseph, but not *this*. And if not this, then *what*?

Yet Jacob's trust in his Lord did not waver. **"No, but your lower selves have enticed you to something,"** the noble prophet said to his sons, surrendering his will and purpose to his Lord. **"Therefore, patience is most befitting, and God is the One sought for help against that which you describe"** (12:18).

REFERENCE: Qur'an: 12:7-18. Commentary: Tabari/*H*, II:149-151.

[9]This again confirms what we observed in relation to Noah's son, Abraham's father, and Noah's and Lot's wives: that being related to a prophet or to any other good person in no way benefits his immediate relatives unless they keep to his way.

4. Joseph's First Ordeal

And they schemed and God schemed. And God is the Best of Schemers. (3:54)

Meanwhile, the young Joseph (A) remained in the bottom of the well. We can imagine his state of mind at his horrendous betrayal by his brothers. We can also imagine the pain he must have felt for his beloved father's grief.

Then, in that desperate and troubled state, the divine revelation came to his heart: **"You will surely inform them about this affair of theirs while they do not perceive"** (12:15). Thus did his Lord comfort Joseph in his sorrow and relieve him of his fear and dread at his unknown future, supported by the promise of a blessed outcome, shown to him in his vision.

It is reported that Joseph (A) stayed in the well for three days and three nights. Then, at a time decreed by God, **there came a company of travelers** in an Egyptian caravan.[10]

They sent their drawer of water to the well **and he let down his pail.** Catching hold of the rope, Joseph (A) was pulled out. **"Good news!"** exclaimed the drawer of water when he saw the extraordinarily handsome boy. **"Here is a lad!"** (12:19).

According to the interpretation of the classic commentators, the treacherous brothers now appeared and demanded payment for Joseph (A). **And they sold him** to the people of the caravan **for a low price, a few dirhams.** Here the divine Author of the Book adds parenthetically, **And they were of those satisfied with little regarding him** (12:20), either because they were so eager to get rid of him or because they held him in such low esteem. It is said that they followed behind him, saying to those who had bought him from them, "Make sure he does not escape" — that is, until they had safely reached Egypt with him.

The men who had bought Joseph (A) **concealed him as merchandise** (12:19), meaning as a treasure they had found, for they supposed that if the others in the caravan knew about him, they would demand a share in his price when he was sold as a slave once they reached Egypt. **And God was Knowing of what they did** (12:19), guiding and directing their every movement, and supporting the frightened, grieving Joseph (A) throughout his ordeal with His mercy and tender love.

---

[10]This well is identified as being near Dothan in the northern part of Palestine, and the caravan that picked up Joseph as coming from Gilead across the Jordan River.

Thus it was that, hidden from the others in the caravan, Joseph (A) entered Egypt. There he was bought by one who recognized his value, a man of power and prestige referred to in the Qur'an as ***al-'Aziz***, a title meaning "the Exalted One"[11] — the Potiphar of Gen. 37:36, 39. It is said that he was a high-ranking official in charge of the Egyptian treasury.

Joseph's master brought his newly-acquired slave boy to his home in Memphis, the capital city of Egypt.[12] **"Make his stay honorable,"** he said to his wife. **"Perhaps he may benefit us or we may adopt him as a son"** (12:21). And here God Most High adds:

> **And thus did We establish Joseph in the land, that We might teach him the interpretation of events.[13] And God is predominant over His affair, but most people do not know.** (12:21)

REFERENCES: Qur'an: 12:19-21. Commentaries: Tabari/*H*, II:151-153; Ibn Kathir/*T*, 12:19-20; Maududi/*H*, Intro. to *Surah Yusuf* (12), 12:fns. 15-16; Asad/*Q*, 12:fn. 19.

---

[11]Since Joseph himself was later addressed as *al-'Aziz* when he attained a high position, this appears to have been a generic title used for people of power and authority in ancient Egypt.

[12]The ruins of this city are still to be found on the Nile about four miles south of Cairo.

[13]Or dreams. These words relate, at least in part, to Joseph's future interpretation of the dreams of his two fellow-prisoners and all that was to follow from it.

5. Joseph's Second Ordeal

And she in whose house he was sought to seduce him. (12:23)

The next scene in the life of Joseph (A) opens an undetermined number of years later. During the period of his sojourn in Egypt, living in the house of his high-ranking master and patron, Joseph (A) had grown to adulthood both physically and spiritually, trained and guided by his Lord, who says of him,

> **And when he reached maturity, We granted him judgment and knowledge, and thus do We reward the doers of good** (12:22),

which is understood as indicating that prophethood had by then been bestowed upon him.

A few words need to be said here about the situation of Egypt during this period. We are accustomed to thinking of it as having always been ruled by pharaohs or god-kings. However, according to historians, in the year 1790 B.C., Egypt was invaded by a Semitic people known as the Hyksos or Aamu.

The Hyksos were of bedouin Arab stock, hailing from the Sinai peninsula, and their language and habits were very similar to that of the bedouin Hebrews, who, centuries earlier, had migrated from the Arabian peninsula to Mesopotamia and later to Syria. Having brought their religion with them, these newcomers to Egypt did not acknowledge the Egyptian gods, with the exception of the god Set, whom they adopted and to whom they erected a huge temple at Avaris.

The Hyksos gained control of a very important part of Egypt, the Nile Delta. They established their dynasty as kings (not pharaohs) of Egypt for a time, ruling from the ancient Egyptian capital of Memphis. Al-Tabari reports that the king of Egypt during the time of Joseph was a man of Amalekite descent — that is, related by race and tradition to Abraham (A) and his people. This is one possible explanation for the willingness of Joseph's master to take a Hebrew slave boy into his family and treat him as a son. On the other hand, the explanation may have nothing to do with this but rather with Joseph's personal outstanding nobility and beauty.

Joseph's master, it is said, was not only childless but may also have been impotent as well. Possibly he was a eunuch, as the highest ranking court officials in Egypt at that time were. Consequently, his wife, to whom tradition gives the name Zulaikha, although most beautiful and desirable, remained a virgin.

Disappointed in her husband, perhaps her eyes had been fixed for some time on the incredibly handsome youth who lived in her home. And one day, unable to contain herself any longer, she maneuvered Joseph (A) into an empty room. Quickly she closed the doors. **"Come, you!"** (12:23), she ordered him as one orders a slave.

"God be my refuge!" Joseph (A) exclaimed, horrified. His first thought was of Potiphar, who had taken him in and treated him with honor and kindness. **"Indeed, he is my master, who has made my stay good. Indeed, the wrongdoers will not prosper!"** (12:23).

Whether Joseph (A) was at this point a prophet or a prophet-in-training, he was nevertheless a man in the full prime of life, and Zulaikha was no doubt a most beautiful, desirable woman. Moreover, she was his mistress and he was, in truth, her slave, over whom she had full command and control. **And she certainly desired him, and he would have inclined toward her if he had not seen his Lord's proof. Thus it was,** God Most High adds, **that We might avert evil and immorality from him. Indeed, he was among Our chosen servants** (12:24).

The above words makes it clear that Zulaikha approached Joseph (A) in the full intensity of her desire and that he responded to her. The early Qur'anic commentators give two interpretations of his response. One is that he merely felt desire for her without acting on it. The other, reported by Ibn 'Abbas (R), is that he was on the verge of possessing her and might have done so if he had not at that moment seen something so decisive — **his Lord's proof** — that it averted **evil and immorality from him** (12:24).

What was that **"proof"**? Some commentators say that the figure of his father appeared to him standing inside the house, biting his fingers and cautioning him against giving in to his desire. Others say that he heard a voice, and still others that he saw writing on the wall. In any case, whatever the **"proof"** may have been, it caused Joseph (A) to turn and flee from Zulaikha.

The slave and his mistress **both raced to the door**, and as Zulaikha reached out for Joseph (A), **she tore his shirt from the back.** Then, without warning, **they found her husband at the door** (12:25).

Frantically Zulaikha tried to clear herself of blame. **"What is the recompense of one who intended evil to your wife except that he be imprisoned or a painful punishment?"** (12:25), she demanded of her husband.

But Joseph (A) boldly proclaimed his innocence. **"It was she who sought to seduce me!"** (12:26), he exclaimed.

The betrayed husband did not know whom to believe. Although Zulaikha was his wife, he knew her state of mind. Moreover, he knew well enough the plots and intrigues by which the high society women of the city were used to gaining their ends. At the same time, Joseph's integrity and noble character were also known to him. Which of the two was telling the truth?

Then **a witness from her household testified**, pointing to the evidence of Joseph's truthfulness. **"If his shirt is torn from the front, then she has told the truth and he is of the liars,"** he declared, in the manner of one experienced in understanding such matters. **"But if his shirt is torn from the back, then she has lied and he is of the truthful"**[14] (12:27).

Joseph's master was a wise, just man. He did not attempt to defend or exonerate Zulaikha simply because she his wife. Rather, his interest was in determining the truth. Therefore, **when he saw his shirt torn from the back, he said** to his wife, **"This is of your scheming"** — that is, of the wiles that women collectively use to seduce men. **"Terrible indeed is your scheming!"** (12:28)

Potiphar then turned to his young slave, whom he loved, saying, **"Joseph, turn away from this,"** meaning, "Do not mention this and pass over it as if it had not happened." And again addressing Zulaikha, he said,

"And ask forgiveness for your sin. Indeed, you were of the sinful" (12:29).

Thus did God Most High try His servant Joseph (A) and save him a second time. But, as we shall see, that was only the beginning rather than the end of the matter.

REFERENCES: Qur'an: 12:22-29. Commentaries: Tabari/*H*, II:153-158; Ali/*Q*, Appen. IV (V); Asad/*Q*, 12:fn. 44; Maududi/*Q*, Intro. to *Surah Yusuf.* Other works: Barnavi/*Atlas*, p. 3; Daiches/*Moses*, pp. 23-25, 28; Montet/*Pharaohs*, p. 69; Newby/*Pharaohs*, pp. 20-21.

[14]The Holy Prophet (S) said, "There were four people who spoke when they were small," and he mentioned among them this witness to Joseph's innocence (Tabari/*H*, II:157), thereby suggesting that the witness from among Potiphar's household was a keen, clever child.

6. The Women's Meeting with Joseph

And when they saw him, they extolled him greatly. (12:31)

Word of what had taken place between the beautiful, aristocratic wife of Potiphar and Joseph (A) soon leaked out and spread among the noblewomen of the city.

"The wife of al-'Aziz is seeking to seduce her slave," they whispered to one another. **"He has inflamed her with love."** And they passed judgment upon her, saying, **"Indeed, we see her in clear aberration!"** (12:30).

This talk reached Zulaikha's ears. Because she was an experienced woman, skilled in dealing with the politics of the capital city, she was not one to be put down by the gossip of her peers. However, she was also not one to submit to it in silence. Consequently, a subtle plan for teaching the women a lesson worked itself out in her mind.

So when she heard of their scheming, she sent for them, inviting them to her palace, **and prepared a banquet for them** of great luxury, with couches upon which to recline. And when the women were in their places, **she gave each of them a knife** (12:31) for cutting the variety of fruits she had set before them.

She then called Joseph (A), saying, **"Come out before them!"** (12:31), and, as her slave, he had no choice but to obey. And when the women saw him, they were so amazed at his almost superhuman beauty that they unknowingly cut their hands with the knives they were holding. And **they extolled him greatly,** saying, **"How perfect is God! This is not a mortal, this is nothing but a noble angel!"** (12:31).

Zulaikha's scheme had worked beautifully; her point had hit home. Although it was true that she had lost control of herself over Joseph, her sophisticated, high-born friends and companions had likewise not been proof against him.

"That, then, is the one concerning whom you blamed me," she announced triumphantly. **"And I certainly sought to seduce him but he firmly refused."** Then her tone changed and became menacing. **"And if he does not do what I order him, he will surely be imprisoned and will be among the debased!"** (12:32).

Joseph (A) stood before the wealthiest, most elegant ladies of the capitol in all the purity of his innocent young manhood, with a face more beautiful than any in this world. And he called upon his Creator.

"My Lord," he said, **"prison is more to my liking than that to which they are inviting me."** After what had happened, he could never return to the honorable position he had occupied in his master's house — and now other women besides his mistress were at his heels! **"And if You do not turn away their plot from me,"** he continued, **"I might incline toward them and thus be among the ignorant"** (12:33), meaning that without God's help against their scheming, he might gradually lose his sense of right and wrong and be seduced.

REFERENCES: Qur'an: 12:30-34. Commentary: Tabari/*H*, II:158-160.

7. Joseph's Third Ordeal

So his Lord responded to him and averted their plot from him. Indeed, He is the Hearing, the Knowing. (12:34)

After becoming aware of their wives' infatuation with Joseph (A), the aristocrats of the city became concerned.

It then occurred to them, after they had seen the signs of Joseph's obvious innocence, **that he** — Potiphar — **should certainly imprison him for a time** (12:35). In prison, Joseph would be out of the way of any woman who desired him — and now *all* their wives were involved! Perhaps they reasoned that it was better to let one innocent person suffer than to tolerate this kind of disturbance in their households. It was a case of Joseph's interests versus their own, and, because they did not want to prolong or expose the scandal that had now erupted among them, their interests prevailed over justice.

Various opinions have been put forward as to Joseph's age at the time he entered prison but none of them is authoritative. However, it is supposed that he may have been about twenty. It is evident from the Qur'anic account that he was by now a prophet, receiving revelations and inspirations from his Lord. Perhaps these, together with the knowledge that some high destiny awaited him, revealed in his childhood vision and the inspiration he had received in the well, sustained and supported him through this new ordeal. And he now began to carry out his divinely appointed mission inside the prison walls.

By the Will of the All-Seeing, the All-Knowing, **there entered the prison with him two young men** (12:36). According to some reports, both were servants of the king, one in charge of his drink and the other of his food, or one his cupbearer and the other his baker. The fact that both were Egyptians, worshippers of many gods, is apparent from what follows.

At some point, each of them had a dream which he felt to be of significance. Observing Joseph's uprightness and piety, they reported their dreams to him, certain that he would be able to interpret them correctly.

"Indeed, I have seen myself pressing wine" (12:36), said the cupbearer.

And the baker said, **"Indeed, I have seen myself carrying bread upon my head, from which birds were eating."** And speaking on behalf of himself

---

[15]This is in keeping with the statement in Gen. 39:20-23 that God was with Joseph in prison and granted him favor in the eyes of the warden, to the extent that the warden put him "in charge of all those held in the prison and he was made responsible for all that was done there. The warden paid no attention to anything under Joseph's care, because the Lord was with Joseph and gave him success in whatever he did."

and his companion, he said to Joseph (A), **"Inform us of the interpretion of it. We surely perceive you to be among the doers of good"**[15] (12:36).

Joseph's reply was addressed to both of them: **"You will not receive** any of the **food that is provided for you until I inform you of its interpretation before it comes to you."**[16] And, to assure his listeners that he would not give the interpretation from himself, he added: **"That is from what my Lord has taught me"** (12:37).

By his words, Joseph (A) assured his two listeners that he would do what they had requested of him within a given time frame. But before doing so, he put before them the outlines of the pure faith of his fathers in an attempt to make them examine their own beliefs.

He did this by explaining to them both what he believed and what he did not. **"Indeed,"** he said, **"I have left alone the religion of a people who do not believe in God and they are disbelievers in the Hereafter,**[17] **and I have followed the religion of my fathers, Abraham and Isaac and Jacob.**[18] **It was not for us to associate anything with God,"** he added, referring to the fact that he and his forefathers had steadfastly rejected the ascribing of any partner to God.

"That is from God's favor upon us and upon mankind, but most of mankind are not grateful" (12:37-38), Joseph (A) continued. That is, one of God's greatest favors is possessing the certainty that a single all-wise, all-knowing, compassionate Lord guides and controls all things, rather than fake, non-existent 'gods' of man's inventing.

---

[16]Why would Joseph have made the two men wait for the interpretation of their dreams? It has been suggested that he actually did not want to interpret their dreams at all because the second dream involved such a painful matter, and that he therefore began by speaking of something other than that what they had asked. Another possible explanation is that he began by speaking about himself in order to make the two men feel comfortable and familiar with him, since they knew him but did not know about his religion. This delay enabled him to convey his Lord's Message to them, focusing their minds on their Creator rather than on the particular events that were to befall them, especially in the case of the one who was destined to be executed. Thus, by the time Joseph told them the interpretation of their dreams, he had already called them to belief in their Lord. Yet another possible explanation is that he wanted to pray and ask for guidance before giving the dream interpretations.

[17]As is well-known, the ancient Egyptian religion placed great emphasis on the afterlife. But because this belief was based entirely on man-made notions rather than upon revealed truth, Joseph here discounts it completely, saying in effect that it represents no belief at all.

[18]The people of the caravan that had brought Joseph to Egypt were related to the family of Abraham, whose name was also known to the Egyptians. Although Joseph could have used his close relationship to his great-grandfather Abraham to his own advantage at the time of his rescue from the well, he did not do so. He mentioned it now only to bring home the truth of the Message to his two listeners, perhaps especially to the one who was soon to die.

"O two companions of the prison," Joseph (A) continued, **"are separate lords better or God, the One, the Dominant? You worship, besides Him, mere names** by which **you have named them"** — your so-called gods — **"you and your fathers, for which God has sent down no authority"** (12:39-40).

He then called their attention to the fact that it is for God alone to declare what is real and true, what is fake and false, saying, **"The authority is only for God. He has commanded that you worship no one but Him. That is the correct religion, but most of mankind do not know"** (12:40).

Thus did Joseph (A) convey to his two prisonmates the message of God's Oneness and omnipotence, trying, with the evidences and arguments granted him by his Lord, to turn them away from idolatry and ***shirk***. For while the two prisoners' dreams concerned their fate during this temporary life, what they had just heard from Joseph (A), perhaps for the very first time in their lives, was critical to their final destiny in the life-to-come.

Then, after having conveyed the most important principles of faith to his prison mates, Joseph (A) addressed the matter of their dreams.

"O two companions of the prison," he said to the first of the two, **"as for one of you, he will give drink to his master**, the king, **of wine."** He then turned to the second, saying, **"And as for the other, he will be crucified and birds will eat from his head."**[19] And to convince the man that his fate was unchangeable and sealed, and that he must now come to terms with it and prepare for the meeting with his Lord, he added, **"The matter about which you both enquire has been decreed"** (12:41).

And he said to the one whom he supposed would be saved, "Mention me before your master" (12:42). That is, once you are released from prison and are in a favorable position, please speak about me to your master, the king, who perhaps may already be familiar with my name due to the wide publicity of the affair of the women.

In due course, the man was released from prison, as Joseph (A) had foretold. **But,** as God willed, **Satan caused him to forget the mention** of Joseph (A) **to his master, and so he remained in the prison for a** few **more years** (12:42). It is said that Joseph's prison term lasted altogether seven years, so that by the time he was released he was around thirty years of age.[20]

REFERENCES: Qur'an: 12:35-42. Commentaries: Tabari/*H*, II:160-163; Maududi/*Q*, 12:fns. 30, 34[2]-[3]; Ali/Q, fn. 1696.

---

[20]Up to this day, flesh-eating vultures are to be found in Egypt. Thus, the **"bread"** which the prisoner saw birds eating from his head may have symbolized his own flesh.

[21]The Holy Prophet (S) mentioned the extended the length of Joseph's prison term, saying that if he had stayed in prison as long as Joseph stayed and then the summons came to him, he would have accepted it (*Bukhari*, 4:601, 9:121; also 6:216; 4:591).

8. The King's Dream

And thus did We establish Joseph in the land, that We might teach him the interpretation of events. (12:21)

By the working of the divine Will, in the due course of time Joseph (A) was delivered from prison — but under the most unexpected of circumstances.

The king of Egypt had a dream.[21] Perplexed as to its meaning, he related it to his chiefs and advisors.

"Indeed, I saw seven fat cows being eaten by seven lean ones, and seven green ears of grain, **and others dry,"** he said, adding: **"O nobles, explain my dream to me, if you are able to interpret dreams"** (12:43).

But the high ranking officials around the king were as puzzled as he was. **"A mixture of false dreams,"** they declared, adding, **"And we are not knowledgeable about the interpretation of dreams"** (12:44).

Now, Joseph's former prison mate — **the one of the two who was saved** — had for some time been the king's cupbearer. When he heard about his master's dream, he recalled the man who had correctly interpreted his own dream years earlier in prison. **"I shall inform you of its interpretation,"** he volunteered. **"Therefore, send me forth"** (12:45).

The cupbearer returned to his former prison. He found there the one he sought and addressed him with the respect that he realized was due to him.

"Joseph, O you truthful one," he said, **"inform us of the meaning of seven fat cows eaten by seven lean ones, and seven green ears and others**

---

[21]Concerning this ruler of Egypt, Muhammad Asad writes:

> This king seems to have been one of the six Hyksos rulers who dominated Egypt from about 1700 to 1580 B.C., after having invaded the country from the east by way of the Sinai Peninsula. The name of this dynasty, which was undoubtedly of foreign origin, is derived from the Egyptian . . . , meaning "rulers of nomad lands", or . . ."shepherd kings": all of which points to their having been Arabs who, despite the fact that before their invasion of Egypt they were already well-established in Syria, had to a large extent preserved their bedouin mode of life. This would explain the confidence which the king mentioned in this story was later to place in Joseph, the Hebrew, and the subsequent settlement of the latter's family (and, thus, of what in due course became the Israelite nation) in Egypt: for it must be borne in mind that the Hebrews, too, descended from one of the many bedouin tribes who some centuries earlier had migrated from the Arabian Peninsula to Mesopotamia and later to Syria . . . ; and that the language of the Hyksos must have been very akin to Hebrew, which, after all, is but an ancient Arabian dialect. (Asad/*Q*, 12:fn. 44)

Indeed, some of the Hyksos rulers of Egypt had Semitic names, prefixed with Jacob- (Breasted/*History*, p. 220; Daiches/*Moses*, p. 23).

dry, so that I may return to the people of the court, that they may know" (12:46). The last words are understood as meaning so that the king and others who were concerned in the matter might know Joseph's true worth and the error of keeping him unjustly imprisoned.

Then, from the springs of wisdom and knowledge that God Most High poured into Joseph's pure heart, he disclosed to the cupbearer the meaning of the king's dream.

"You will plant for seven years consecutively," he said, speaking as one who sees with the eye of certainty what lies ahead, **"and what you harvest, leave it in its sheaves, except a little, from which you will eat. Then after that will come seven hard** years **which will consume what you have set aside for them, except a little of that which you have stored.**[22] **Then after that will come a year in which the people will have rain and in which they will press** oil and wine" (12:47-49), as before.

REFERENCES: Qur'an: 43-49. Commentaries: Tabari/*H*, II:163-164; Maududi/*Q*, 12:fn. 40; Asad/*Q*, 12:fns. 44, 48; Saheeh/*Q*, 12:46. Other works: Breasted/*History*, p. 220; Daiches/*Moses*, p. 23.

[22]The **"little of that which you will have stored"** refers to what was to be put aside for planting when rain again became abundant.

9. Joseph's Rise to Power

Thus did We establish Joseph in the land, to settle therein wherever he willed. We touch with Our mercy whomever We will, and We do not permit the reward of the doers of good to be lost. And the reward of the Hereafter is better for those who believe and are mindful of God.
(12:56-57)

The cupbearer returned to the king with these tidings, and perhaps he added his own thoughts about the extraordinary man who had formerly been his prisonmate. In any case, the king was impressed with what he heard. **"Bring him to me"** (12:50), he ordered.

But Joseph's response, when the king's messenger came to release him from prison, was not at all what the king had expected. **"Return to your master,"** Joseph (A) instructed him, **"and ask him what is the case of the women who cut their hands,"** adding: **"Indeed, my Lord is Knowing of their scheme"** (12:50).

Now, why would Joseph (A) have responded in such a manner to the offer of freedom from the king of Egypt after such long, hard years in prison? The following reasons have been suggested:

To Joseph (A), the prophet of God, two considerations were far more important than freedom. The first was that his integrity and innocence should be established beyond any doubt by clearing him of guilt in the matter of Zulaikha and her companions. If this were not done, his former master and the husbands of the other women involved might continue to blame or doubt him, or undermine his credibility in the eyes of others. A public announcement of his innocence would be especially crucial if he were established in a position of influence, power and trust as a result of his interpretation of the dream, so that people might have unshakable confidence in him and in whatever he might order, and might follow the guidance that God would reveal through him.

Second, Joseph (A) needed an assurance that if he left prison he would not continue to be harrassed by the highly-placed women of the city, and by Zulaikha in particular. If one or both of these conditions were not met, he preferred remaining in prison, terrible though it was, to regaining his freedom.

Joseph's words, **"Ask him what is the case of the women who cut their hands,"** show his unwillingness, out of the nobility of his nature, to single out and implicate his former mistress. They also show his awareness that the king was thoroughly familiar with what had occurred years earlier.

The king's response to Joseph's request in turn makes it clear that he was aware of Joseph's story, for he summoned the high society ladies who had been involved in the matter and began to question them.

"What was your affair when you sought to seduce Joseph?" (12:51), he asked.

The women's response was immediate and spontaneous. **"How perfect is God!"** they exclaimed. **"We know nothing of evil concerning him"** (12:51).

Joseph's former mistress — **the wife of al-'Aziz** — then added her testimony to theirs. **"Now the truth has become evident,"** she said. And bearing eloquent witness to Joseph's truthfulness and innocence, she openly admitted her guilt, saying, **"It was I who sought to seduce him, and indeed, he is of the truthful"** (12:51).

For the aristocratic Zulaikha, this public confession of her blameworthiness was no doubt the ultimate act of penance and abasement. Earlier, she had defended herself in front of the other women, even going so far as to proclaim her desire for Joseph publicly, and to insist that he be humiliated and imprisoned if he did not yield to her demand. But during the intervening years, she had had ample time to reflect upon her own actions and upon the absolutely unwavering integrity and purity of the man whose life she had deliberately set out to ruin.

The king's messenger then returned to Joseph (A) in prison and informed him of the women's response. And Joseph (A) made a statement of his purpose in having brought up the matter after so many years.

"That" — his request that the king would clear the matter of the women — **"is so that he"** — his former master, Potiphar — **"will know that I did not betray him in secret and that God does not guide the scheming of the betrayers**[23] (12:52).

---

[23]The passage containing the verses cited above reads as follows:

> **Now the truth has become evident. It was I who sought to seduce him, and indeed, he is of the truthful. (51) This is so he will know that I did not betray him in secret and that God does not guide the plot of the betrayers. (52) Nor do I acquit myself. Indeed, *nafs* is a persistent enjoiner of evil, except as my Lord shows mercy. Indeed, my Lord is Forgiving and Merciful. (53)**

The Qur'anic commentators differ concerning the identity of the speakers of these words. While it is clear that verse 51 was spoken by Zulaikha, there is a difference of opinion as to whether verses 52 and 53 were spoken by Joseph or by Zulaikha, or 52 by Zulaikha and 53 by Joseph. Ibn Kathir maintains that both were spoken by Zulaikha; among modern commentators, Yusuf Ali holds the same view. Other classical commentators, such as Ibn 'Abbas, al-Tabari, Jalalayn, and Maududi and Asad among the moderns, hold both 52 and 53 to have been spoken by Joseph. Indeed, Ibn 'Abbas states that after Joseph said, **"God does not guide the**

"Nor do I absolve myself," he continued. **"Indeed, the *nafs* is a persistent enjoiner of evil,[24] except as my Lord shows mercy. Indeed, my Lord is Forgiving and Merciful"** (12:53).

These words reveal the tremendous purity and integrity of Joseph's character. Although he was a prophet, protected by God from Satan and his ***nafs***, he did not hesitate to admit publicly that he too could be subject to temptation. And he pointed out an essential fact for all mankind to take note of: that the ***nafs*** always, without exception, incites or urges or commands us to do evil, unless God's mercy intervenes. This is a very vital piece of information because, unless we are aware of this fact, we will not be able to understand, much less control, the desires and demands of our ***nafs*** or lower self. Armed with this knowledge, however, we can understand its tricks and traps, and take measures to control it, allying ourself with God against it, even though it is part of ourselves.

Joseph's honor and integrity had now been vindicated by the very person who had originally accused him and on whose account he had been imprisoned. Perhaps the king was now even more impressed with Joseph (A) and eager to have him by his side. Again he sent for him, instructing his messenger, **"Bring him to me. I shall appoint him exclusively for myself"**[25] (12:54).

---

scheming of the betrayers," the angel Gabriel said to him, "Did you not desire her for but a single day?" to which Joseph replied, **"Nor do I acquit myself . . ."** to the end of the verse. We have followed the latter view as being closest to the purport of the words (Tabari/*H*, II:165; Ibn Kathir/*T*, 12:52-53; Ali/*Q*, fn. 1712; Maududi, *Q*, 12:fn. 46; Asad/*Q*, 12:fn. 51; Saheeh/*Q*, fn. 551).

[24]The Arabic word ***nafs*** means self or soul. However, as explained earlier, it is also commonly used to mean the lower self or ego, a **persistent enjoiner of evil**. The ***nafs*** is that part of ourselves which impels us to action and achievement, and without which we would have no motivation or interest in anything related to this life. It is, at the same time, the element of our being which urges us to every sort of evil — greedy, grasping, amoral, intensely selfish and self-centered, preoccupied with the drive for power, wealth, possessions, fame, self-importance, rank and pleasure, and harboring passions such as hate, greed, lust, pride and anger. Because the ***nafs*** knows no limits for its desires, the more one gives in to its demands, the more it demands. In its innate greed for everything pertaining to this world's life, it is the antagonist of the soul and the higher self (***al-nafs al-lawwamah***, the self-reproaching self or conscience [75:2]), which yearns for God and the spiritual world. Control of the ***nafs*** is an essential part of Islamic training (***tarbiyah***), in which praying, fasting, ***zakat***, ***Hajj*** and other Islamic practices play a major role.

Like all other human beings, all the prophets had a ***nafs***, but with God's help and support, they were able to bring it completely under control. Because of this, they were able to act purely for the sake of their Lord without intermingling any of the desires of their lower selves with their worship and service, so that their every step and breath was for the divine Will alone.

[25]According to Ibn Kathir, the king accepted faith at the hand of Joseph. Al-Tabari reports that at about this time, Potiphar died and the king gave Zulaikha (also known as Ra'il) to Joseph in marriage, and she bore him two sons, Manasseh and Ephraim (Tabari/*H*, II:166).

This time the messenger returned with Joseph (A), newly freed. And when the king had spoken to him, he decided to appoint him to a high office,[26] saying, **"Assuredly, you are this day established and trusted in our presence"** (12:54).

Then, directed and guided by his Lord, Joseph (A) made a request of the king.

"Appoint me over the storehouses of the land," he said. **"Indeed, I will be a knowledgeable guardian"**[27] (12:55), meaning, it is said, one who knows how to gather, store and make the best use of the stocks of grain of the land.

The king granted his request. Thus it was that Joseph (A) became the chief minister of Egypt, bearing the title of *al-'Aziz*, the Exalted One.[28] It is said that he was the highest official in the land after the king himself. As such, Joseph (A) proclaimed his Lord's Message and established a just law based on God's com-

---

[26]It is mentioned in Gen. 41:38-41, 44 that when the king ("Pharaoh") had talked to Joseph, who told him of his plan for storing and distributing the stocks of grain in the land, the king said, "Can we find anyone like this man, one in whom is the spirit of God?" He then said to Joseph, "Since God has made all this known to you, there is no one so discerning and wise as you. You shall be in charge of my palace, and all my people are to submit to your orders. Only with respect to the throne will I be greater than you." He added: "I hereby put you in charge of the whole land of Egypt," and, "I am Pharoah, but without your word no one will lift hand or foot in all Egypt," hereby confirming God's words, **Thus did We establish Joseph in the land, to settle therein wherever he willed** (12:56), and 12:72, in which Joseph is referred to as **"the king"**.

[27]At this point, Joseph was aware that the king had singled him out for a high post in the administration of Egypt, possibly any that he himself might choose. The words, **"Indeed, I will be a knowledgeable guardian,"** cannot therefore be understood as boastfulness on his part. Rather, it is simply a statement, doubtless uttered under divine inspiration or command, that Joseph considered himself to be best suited for the position of guardian of the stores of grain, through which, during the coming famine, he would be able to benefit God's servants. It is also possible that he forsaw, either by divine revelation or logical deduction, that he would be dealing with his brothers when famine struck the neighboring land of Canaan in which they lived.

[28]Since *al-'Aziz* seems to have been a generic title for high-ranking officials, the suggestion that Joseph now replaced the recently-deceased Potiphar in his office and title does not seem to carry weight. In case we wonder at so much authority being to given to a single official, this was not unheard of in Egyptian history. For example, it appears that a Hyksos king named Khenzer entrusted the affairs of the country largely to his vizier or chief minister, Enkhu (Breasted/*History*, p. 221). This was also the case with a certain Arisu, a Syrian administrator in Egypt, mentioned in a papyrus dated 1215-1209 BC, whose case seems to have been similar to that of Joseph (Daiches/*Moses*, p. 24). Some scholars believe that Joseph may have been the chief minister of the monotheistic pharaoh Akhenaton, but this theory presents historical difficulties (Barnavi/*Atlas*, p. 4).

mands.[29] In addition to this, he stored up the country's grain during the first seven years of plenty, except that portion that the people ate.[30]

REFERENCES: Qur'an: 12:50-53. Commentaries: Ibn Kathir/T, 12:52-57; Tabari/H, II:140, 164-167; Ali/*Q*, fn. 1712; Maududi, *Q*, 12:fns. 45-46; Asad/*Q*, 12:fn. 51; Saheeh/*Q*, fn. 551. Other works: Barnavi/*Atlas*, p. 4; Breasted/*History*, p. 221; Daiches/*Moses*, p. 24; James/*Egypt*, pp. 60-61, 74-75.

[29]For evidence of this, see the interpretation of 40:34 in Volume Two, Chapter 22.

[30]Interestingly, one of the tributaries of the Nile River is called Bahr Yusuf (the River of Joseph). While the origin of this name not known, it is not impossible that it was named for the prophet Joseph. This river winds through a part of Egypt called al-Faiyum, which is noted for its abundance of water courses. There is evidence that in ancient times some hydrologic projects were carried out which made the river crucial to the high fertility of the region (James/*Egypt*, pp. 60-61, 74-75). Again, we may speculate whether it could have been Joseph, in his position of chief minister, who was responsible for such advanced developments.

10. Joseph's Meeting with His Brothers

And Joseph's brothers arrived and came to him, and he recognized them but he was unknown to them. (12:58)

During the first seven years of his administration — the years of plenty — Joseph (A) set aside abundant stocks of grain from what the people harvested as provision for the lean years that were ahead. Then came the drought and the barren years began. And when the people became became hungry, Joseph (A) distributed the stored-up grain to them.

The famine affected the neighboring lands as well. And to any person who came to him from surrounding areas, Joseph (A) would give one camel-load of grain. Thus, by the blessing of God, he was able to distribute his stocks of grain to any who were in need.

When the nearby land of Palestine was hit by the famine, hunger began to afflict Jacob's family. Presently reports reached them that the chief minister of Egypt was bartering food for goods.[31] Accordingly, Jacob (A), who was now advanced in years, dispatched ten of his sons, Joseph's half-brothers, to Egypt to buy food. But he kept home the son who was dearest to him among his remaining sons, Joseph's full brother Benjamin.

When the ten brothers arrived in Egypt and came into the presence of Joseph (A), **he recognized them**, but since had had been separated from them at a young age, **he was unknown to them** (12:58). Since they had no idea of what had happened to him after the caravan took him away, how could they possibly have imagined that the lad whom they had sold into slavery had become the chief minister of Egypt?

One can imagine Joseph's feelings when he saw them, and how eager he was for news of his beloved father, mother and Benjamin. It is said that he talked to the ten brothers in such a way that they would not recognize him, asking them for what purpose they had come.

They replied that they had heard that he sold grain. Then, using a strategem, he said, "But I wonder if you are not spies."

---

[31]Ibn Kathir says that while Joseph, the king and the entire army ate only once a day, at lunchtime, Joseph would feed other people as much as they wanted. Ibn Kathir also reports that during the first year of the famine, Joseph sold grain for money. Then, during the second, third and fourth years, he bartered grain for goods. After that, he bartered grain for the people and their children, so that they all became his property. He then fed them without payment and returned their property to them. However, Ibn Kathir points out, the sources of this information are questionable (Ibn Kathir/*T*, 12:55-56).

They denied this emphatically. Joseph (A) then asked them where they lived. "In Canaan," they replied, "and our father is a prophet of God. His name is Jacob."

Joseph (A) then asked whether their father had any other sons besides themselves. "We were originally twelve brothers," they replied, never suspecting to whom they were speaking. "But the younger, who was most loved by our father, was killed. He had another full brother, but our father did not send him with us, keeping him at home because he loves him so much."

In keeping with his strategem, Joseph (A) expressed suspicions as to the truth of their story. But within himself, he was deeply concerned about the condition of his father and his household. He issued orders that his brothers be treated as official guests and that when they were given grain, their bags should be filled completely, giving them as much as they could carry.

Then, before they left on the return trip home, Joseph (A) made clear to them his terms for dealing with them in the future.

"Bring me a brother of yours from your father," he ordered, meaning that son to whom their father was most attached after their brother who had perished. **"Do you not see that I give full measure and that I am the best of hosts? But if you do not bring him to me, no measure** of grain **shall you have from me, nor shall you** even **approach me"**[32] (12:59-60).

"We will try to dissuade his father from him" — that is, from preventing Benjamin from returning with them — **"and indeed we shall do so"** (12:61), they declared.

When they had departed, Joseph (A) sent certain of his servants to the place where his brothers' camels were tethered. **"Put their property into their saddlebags so they may recognize it when they have gone back to their people, that perhaps they will return"** (12:62), he instructed them. Accordingly, his servants secretly put back into the saddlebags whatever the brothers had traded for grain.

REFERENCES: Qur'an: 12-58-62. Commentaries: Tabari/*H*, II:167-169; Ibn Kathir/*T*, 12:55-60.

[32]Two reasons sugggest themselves for Joseph's demand that his brothers bring Benjamin to him before he would deal with them again. One is that God inspired him with a scheme for using Benjamin's coming to him as the basis of revealing his identity to his brothers, and of eventually bringing his father and the rest of his family to Egypt, where food was plentiful. Another is that he was deeply concerned for the suffering of his people and wanted to add an extra camel-load to their stores, which he could only do, according to his own rules, if there were an extra person in their party.

11. The Brothers' First Return to Jacob

And when they opened their baggage, they found their property returned to them. (12:65)

The brothers then set out on the long, arduous journey back to Canaan. Without doubt, they were very anxious about how their father would react to their demand that Benjamin return with them to Egypt. But they also knew that Jacob (A) had no choice. He must either send their half-brother with them or they and their families would starve.

When they reached home, they reported to their father all that had happened. It is said that they told him that the ruler of Egypt had showed them such honor that even if he had been another son of Jacob, he could not have honored them more. However, the great man had made it clear that unless they brought Benjamin along on their next trip to Egypt, they would get no grain nor even come near him.

"O our father," the brothers pleaded, "further **measure has been denied to us, so send our brother with us, that we may be given measure"** (12:63). They also pointed out to him that by taking Benjamin, they would return with eleven camel-loads instead of the present ten — and that was critical for their large families during the present famine. **"And we will surely be his guardians"** (12:63), they assured the aged prophet, in the very same words they had spoken to him years earlier in the matter of Joseph (12:12). But this time, they knew that their lives and those of their families depended on their keeping their word.

Jacob (A) was greatly troubled by their demand, for in truth he had never recovered from the pain of his sons' earlier betrayal of his trust. After their treachery in the matter of Joseph, his heart trembled at the thought of entrusting Benjamin to them. Indeed, for all he knew, this might be merely another plot of theirs for getting rid of their step-brother. **"Shall I entrust you with him except as,** due to your pressure, **I entrusted you with his brother previously?"** (12:64), he asked them, uneasy and saddened at the prospect.

But, as in the case of Joseph, Jacob (A) was powerless. His sons *must* return to Egypt to bring more grain to feed their families, since there was little or none to be had in Canaan — and if their story was true, they would not even be able to approach the ruler of Egypt unless Benjamin accompanied them. Thus, Jacob (A) again surrendered his will to whatever the All-Knowing Lord might decree for him and his sons. **"But God is the best guardian,"** he said resolutely, **"and He is the Most Merciful of the Merciful"** (12:64).

Then to the brothers' amazement, when they unpacked their saddlebags, they found that what they had bartered for grain had been returned to them.

"O our father," they exclaimed joyfully, **"what more could we desire? This is our property, restored to us."** And they now began to plan their next journey to Egypt, revelling at the thought of the extra grain they would get by taking Benjamin with them. **"And we will obtain supplies for our family and will guard our brother, and we will obtain an increase of a camel's load,"**[34] they said in eager anticipation. **"That is an easy measure!"** (12:65), meaning a measure of grain obtained with ease because of Benjamin's presence.

However, rather than reassuring Jacob (A), the strangeness of his sons' treatment by the Egyptian nobleman now became another source of uneasiness: the man's enquiring about their family until he learned that they had another brother at home; his declaring that he would not deal with them at all in the future unless they brought that brother with them; and, perhaps strangest of all, his returning the property they had exchanged for the grain, like a lure to ensure that they would return.

But the aged prophet's understanding was governed both by patience and by wisdom. Reading the signs, he readily understood that the matter had been decreed by his Lord and that his responsibility was to accept the destiny ordained for himself and his sons. However, for his own peace of mind, he now bound them by a solemn pledge.

"Never will I send him with you until you give me a promise by God that you will bring him back **to me,"** he said to the ten brothers, **"unless you should be surrounded"** — that is, hemmed in by enemies and killed. **And when they had given their promise, he said, "God is witness over what we say"** (12:66).

Nonetheless, Jacob (A) remained very disquieted in mind. What his sons had reported to him did not make sense, and the situation seemed full of strange, mysterious unknowns. The elderly prophet therefore advised the brothers to use a stratagem in approaching Egypt's capital city.

"O my sons," he said, **"do not enter by one gate, but enter by different gates.**[35] **Yet I cannot avail you against God in the least,"** he added.

---

[33]Here we note the ordering of the brothers' priorities in this crucial conversation with their father, whom they were about to deprive of his best beloved son. Their casual mention of guarding of their brother after their main objective of obtaining grain shows how little concern they had for Jacob's well-being.

[34]Al-Tabari states that Jacob imposed this caution upon his sons because they were a troop of handsome, well-built men, and thus he feared that they might attract people's envy if they entered the city together (Tabari/*H*, II:170). Perhaps it also occurred to him that if they all entered as a group, wearing foreign clothing and speaking a different language, they might more easily be taken as spies.

"The decision is only for God. Upon Him have I relied, and let the relying rely upon Him" (12:67).

By this, Jacob (A) meant to say that although logic and prudence supported the plan he had suggested to them, it could in no way alter God's decree. The advice he had given his sons was simply **a need within Jacob's soul, which he satisfied**[35] (12:68), for in spite of his uneasiness over the strange, unexplainable aspects of the situation, he nevertheless remained certain that the final outcome of the matter would, in some unforseen manner decreed by God, still turn out for the best. Thus God says of Jacob (A), **He was surely a possessor of knowledge** — that is, of the working of God's Will and all-wise plan — **because of what We had taught him. But most of mankind do not know** (12:68).

REFERENCES: Qur'an: 12:63-67. Commentaries: Tabari/*H*, II:168-170; Ali/*Q*, fn. 1730.

---

[35]This speech of Jacob's contains a lesson which may be summarized as "Do your utmost and then trust in God." In other words, when you have done all you can in practical terms to safeguard yourself or bring about the result that you feel is desirable, know that the outcome of all affairs rests with the Decider of all things and is governed by His infinite wisdom.

12. The Brothers' Second Journey to Egypt

And when they went in whence their father had ordered them, it did not avail them against God in the least. (12:68)

In due course of time, the brothers set out again for Egypt, taking Benjamin along. As their father had advised, they entered the city by different gates. And soon they were again in the presence of the Great One.

We can imagine Joseph's feelings when he saw his beloved younger brother again after a separation of so many years. It is reported that Joseph (A) then paired off the ten brothers two by two for eating and sleeping. Then, since Benjamin was without a partner, Joseph (A) paired him with himself.

"Indeed, I am your brother," Joseph (A) revealed to him secretly. **"So do not grieve over what they used to do** (12:69) — that is, over what his brothers had done to him in the past and what they might do in the future.

Then, in keeping with his custom, Joseph (A) ordered that one load of grain be given to each of the eleven men. Afterwards, **when he had furnished them with their supplies, he put the cup** — said to be a golden cup or bowl used for measuring grain, as well as for drinking — **into his brother's bag** (12:70).

The eleven brothers set out for home with their loads. Then all at once they heard someone calling out from behind them, saying, **"O you people of the caravan, indeed, you are thieves!"** (12:71). And looking around, they saw officials of the Great One, whose presence they had recently left, hastening toward them.

The eleven men halted in alarm and turned to face their pursuers. **"What is it you are missing?"** (12:72), they enquired anxiously. Perhaps at that moment they uneasily recalled their father's foreboding of trouble or danger.

"We are missing the king's measuring cup. And he who produces shall have a camel's load," the official said, adding: **"And I am responsible for it"** (12:73).

"By God," the brothers retorted, **"you certainly know that we did not come to make corruption in the land, nor are we thieves!"**[36] (12:73).

"Then what should its recompense be if you are liars?" (12:74), the official demanded, meaning, "What should the punishment be, according to your law, if theft is proved upon you?"

---

[36]Al-Tabari states that since the brothers had brought Joseph back the money which he had returned to them the first time, they now reminded him that they would not have done this if they were thieves (Tabari/*H*, II:173).

"Its recompense will be that he in whose bag it is found — he himself will be the recompense," the brothers replied, meaning that the thief would become the slave of the one whose property he had stolen. **"Thus do we,"** in our religion, the faith of our great-grandfather Abraham, **"recompense the wrong-doers!"** (12:75).

The eleven brothers were then taken back to Joseph (A), who started to search their saddlebags for the cup. And **he began with their bags before his brother's bag. Then he took it out of his brother's bag** (12:76).

Thus did God Most High **plan for Joseph,** for **he could not have taken his brother under the law of the king except that God willed** (12:76). That is, the king's law did not stipulate that a thief become the property of the one from whom he had stolen. However, because the brothers had themselves declared that in their faith the recompense of theft was the taking of the thief as a slave (which Joseph knew and had planned on), he was thereby empowered to arrest Benjamin and detain him.

No doubt the brothers were profoundly shocked and bewildered by the evidence before them. Yet although they did not have the means to disprove it, neither did they make the slightest attempt to defend Benjamin's honor or deny the accusation, which they certainly knew to be false. Instead, all their old grievances and envy of Joseph and his brother now found a vent, perhaps inflamed by jealousy over the fact that the Great One had paired Benjamin with himself.

Consequently, instead of coming to Benjamin's defense and proclaiming their conviction of his innocence despite appearances, they now joined in the accusation against him, possibly out of eagerness to clear themselves of suspicion. **"If he steals, a brother of his had stolen previously"**[37] (12:77), they said to Joseph (A). Thus did they fail both Benjamin and their father, with whom they had taken a sacred oath by God to do all in their power to protect their youngest brother and bring him safely home. As they had sold Joseph in

---

[37]What did the brothers mean by the words, **"A brother of his had stolen previously"**? Were they simply lying or were they referring to something that had happened in the past?

Various commentators have suggested possible explanations for these words. One is a report that in his early life, Joseph had taken an idol belonging to his maternal grandfather and broken it (Tabari/*H*, II. 139, 174; Ibn Kathir/*T*, 12:77). Another possible explanation is the following:

It is said that Joseph was raised during his early years by his aunt, Jacob's older sister, who loved him very dearly. Then when Joseph had grown up a little, Jacob asked his sister to return the boy to him. When the sister refused, Jacob insisted. Now, the aunt had inherited a belt from her father Isaac which was supposed to remain with the eldest person in the family. When Jacob insisted that Joseph be returned to him, the sister told Jacob that he could take Joseph back after a few days. She then put her father's belt on Joseph under his clothes. Afterwards she pretended

the past for a paltry price, they now sold Bejamin in exchange for a load of grain, thereby also failing God's testing of them to determine, by means of these strange circumstances, whether they would act as treacherously toward Benjamin as they had acted toward Joseph (A) in the past.

Hearing his brothers' accusation, **Joseph kept it** — the entire matter, including all that he had observed of their selfishness and greed — **within himself and did not disclose it to them** (12:77). He merely said within himself, **"You are worse in position, and God is most knowing of that which you describe"** (12:77) — that is, of your claim that I stole, whereas it was *you* who stole me from my father.

But now, recalling their solemn promise to their father, the brothers began to reflect on the difficulty of their situation. Although they did not value their father greatly or care about his well-being, they were nevertheless deeply troubled about how they would face him with such news, which would add so greatly to his grief over the loss of Joseph, whom he had never ceased to mourn, that it might kill him.

"O 'Aziz," they pleaded, **"indeed, he has a father, an old man."** It is reported they spoke to Joseph (A) about their father's advanced age and weakness, and the great love he had for Benjamin. They also repeated that Benjamin's full brother has been lost in the past, and since their father was already brokenhearted on that account, he would probably die when he heard this news. **"So take one of us in his place!"** they begged, adding, in the same words spoken by Joseph's prisonmates years earlier, **"We surely perceive you to be among the doers of good"** (12:78).

But the Great One remained adamant. **"God forbid that we should take** anyone **except him with whom we found our property,"** he replied firmly. **"We would then indeed be unjust"** (12:79).

The ten brothers then realized that they had reached dead end. There was nothing further to be hoped for from the Great One unless they complied with his demand.

---

to look for it, making a great fuss over the matter and insisting that everyone be searched. Naturally, when Joseph was searched, the belt was found on him and consequently he was accused of having stolen it. The matter was reported to Jacob, and according to the same law of Abraham to which the ten brothers had now referred, Joseph was obliged to remain with his aunt until she died. Nevertheless, while Joseph's brothers may have been referring to this incident when they said that a brother of Benjamin's had stolen in the past, this spiteful accusation was in itself an indication of their treachery toward Benjamin (Tabari/*H*, II:148-149; Ibn Kathir/*T*, 12:77).

We may well wonder why Joseph (A) would have resorted to such a ruse rather than directly announcing his identity to his brothers. And since prophets are the most kind, merciful and compassionate among mankind, why would he have taken a course of action that would cause his beloved father such tremendous pain, possibly even resulting in his death?

There can be only one possible answer to this question: that as God's prophet to whom He had granted **judgment and knowledge** (12:22), Joseph (A) did not act by his own will or desire but rather by divine inspiration and command. Indeed, this is made clear by God's saying, after the mention of his taking the cup out of Benjamin's bag, **Thus did We plan for Joseph** (12:76), linking Joseph's scheme and actions to the divine plan for his brothers and father, hinted at by his vision and by the revelation that had come to him in the bottom of the well as a boy (12:15).

As concerns the brothers, Joseph's primary objective was their repentance and reform. If he had revealed himself to them at once without determining how they would respond to subsequent events, thereby compelling them to look deeply at themselves and the evil of their deeds, there might have been no repentance but merely more envy and resentment. The desired lesson and effect was therefore to be produced through suspense, drama and mystery, letting the brothers feel the threat of being denied grain to feed their families and of encountering unknown troubles in Egypt.

As for his father, after mentioning Jacob's advising his sons not to all go in by the same gate, God Most High says, **He was surely a possessor of knowledge because of what We had taught him** (12:68). Jacob (A) was moreover later to say of himself, **"I know from God that which you do not know"** (12:86), and **"Did I not tell you that I know from God that which you do not know?"** (12:96).

From this, it is clear that Jacob (A) had been granted extraordinary knowledge by his Lord, due to which, despite his grief, he had the clear, unshakable certainty that all would somehow turn out well for Joseph. Indeed, due to Joseph's childhood vision, he possessed the assurance that some great destiny awaited his beloved son, whom he had never really believed to be dead. Thus, Joseph (A) may have been directed by divine inspiration to test his father's faith still further, in order that his Lord's plan for the sons of Jacob, the descendants of God's Friend Abraham, might be fulfilled, as we shall soon see.

When the ten brothers **despaired of him**, meaning when they realized that it was impossible to change the Great One's mind, **they gathered in private consultation** (12:80). Their sins were now coming back on their heads and they were in trouble — deep, terrible trouble! In spite of their lack of respect and love for Jacob (A), he was nevertheless their father; not only that, he was also their prophet, the inheritor of their grandfather Abraham (A). And they realized that if they now returned to him without the second of his best beloved sons, old and frail as he was, they might be responsible for his death.

The eldest of them then took charge.[38] **"Do you not know that your father has taken an oath from you by God, and previously you failed concerning Joseph?"** he said. **"Therefore, I will never leave the land until my father gives me permission or God decides for me** in some other manner. **And He is the Best of Judges** (12:80).

"Return to your father," he instructed the other nine, **"and say, 'O our father, indeed, your son has stolen, and we do not testify except to what we knew, nor were we guardians of the Unseen,'"** meaning that we could not have known what would happen when we promised you to guard him. **"'And enquire at the town where we were and of the caravan in which we came. And indeed, we are truthful'"** (12:82). And thus was the matter decided among the ten brothers.

REFERENCES: Tabari/*H*, II:139, 148-149, 170-176; Ibn Kathir/*T*, 12:70, 75-80; Asad/*Q*, 12:fns. 70, 80, 82; Ali/*Q*, fns. 1752-1753.

[38]In Gen. 44:18-34, this brother is identified as Judah.

13. The Brothers' Second Return to Jacob

Indeed, the one who fears God and is patient, then surely God does not permit the reward of the doers of good to be lost. (12:90)

Nine brothers now returned home with their loads of grain — and with heavy, troubled hearts.

But when they put the whole matter in front of their father, the aged, weakened prophet did not collapse or die in front of their eyes, as they had feared. On the contrary, Jacob (A) was totally the master of himself. Although he understood that his sons were in some unexplained way implicated in this loss of his second son, he did not show anger or heap reproaches upon them. Instead, he responded to their news with the same words he had spoken when they brought him the false tale of Joseph's death: **"No, but your lower selves have incited you to something. Therefore, patience is most befitting"** (12:83, 18).

These words suggest that Jacob (A) no more believed their report of what had occurred in Egypt, especially their assertion that Benjamin had committed theft, than the story they had told him previously about Joseph's death. But while he had no explanation for the events they reported, because of the inner knowledge God had granted him, which included Joseph's early vision, he did not lose hope or despair. Now, as before, it was clear that God's Will was working in some strange, mysterious fashion, and he had firm faith that it was toward some good end. **"Perhaps God will bring them to me, all together,"** he said wistfully. **"Indeed, it is He who is the Knowing, the Wise"** (12:83).

Nonetheless, the pain of separation and the strangeness of the situation in which he and his sons seemed to be caught worked upon the bereaved father's heart. This time, he had lost not one son, but two more.

And he turned away from them. "Oh, my sorrow over Joseph!"[39] he murmured. **And his eyes became white from grief** — meaning blind or dim from the tears that they shed — **for he was a suppressor** of his pain within himself (12:84).

---

[39]The statement that Jacob's anguish for Joseph was "as strong as the emotion of seventy bereaved mothers"; that the reward for his patient bearing of it was "the reward of one hundred martyrs"; and that he that he did not think ill of God for even a single moment by day or by night, has been attributed both to the Prophet (S) and to Hasan al-Basri. The latter also said, "From the time Joseph left Jacob's presence until he returned, eighty years passed, and for all that time grief did not leave his heart, nor did he cease weeping until his sight was gone. By God, there is no creature on earth nobler to God than Jacob" (Tabari/*H*, II:177-178, 183).

Now, the aged prophet had only recently parted with the second of his best beloved sons, who had subsequently been arrested as a criminal by the highest official in Egypt. Jacob had, moreover, also been deprived of the support of the kindest of the remaining ten, the son who had remained behind as a surety in Egypt. Yet, although such long years had passed, it was Joseph (A) about whom he still thought most.

Why was this so? First of all, on a simple human level, Joseph (A) was a child — a most extraordinary, lovely, spiritually-gifted child, with unusually promising and endearing characteristics — when he was torn away from his father, and thus Jacob (A) had missed spending with him the vital years of his development into maturity and manhood. Joseph (A) was also the son who was closest to and most devoted to his father. But perhaps there is a stronger reason still.

Subtle hints in the Qur'anic text suggest that Jacob (A) was not only Joseph's beloved father and prophet, but also his mentor, teacher, shaykh and spiritual guide.[40] Jacob's longing for Joseph was therefore not merely the ordinary longing of a father for his son. Rather, it was an urgent and deeply felt need for the being who was spiritually nearest to him, because of which Jacob (A) never ceased to think of Joseph, and to miss his beloved presence in the most acute manner.

Despite the fact that it was they who had brought this trouble upon their old father, his nine sons were anything but sympathetic as they listened to his broken-hearted murmuring. Although we may wonder how such a noble prophet could be surrounded by such hard, unfeeling children, at the same time, this only makes Jacob's longing for his best loved son the more understandable.

"By God," the sons reproached their father, **"you will not cease remembering Joseph until you become fatally ill or become of those who perish!"** (12:85).

"I only complain of my suffering and grief to God," the aged prophet replied with great dignity, meaning that his inner state was a matter between himself and his Lord, and that he looked for consolation to no one but Him. **"And,"** he added, **"I know from God what you do not know"** (12:86), referring to the secret inner knowledge that he possessed and to his certainty, based on Joseph's childhood vision, that some outstanding destiny awaited his son, whom he had never really believed to be dead.

---

[40]The strong spiritual connection between Jacob and Joseph is indicated, firstly, by Joseph's reportedly having had a vision of his father at the time of his temptation by Zulaikha; second, by the intimations Jacob had of Joseph's presence in what follows hereafter (12:94-96); and third, the manner in which Jacob subsequently regained his sight.

"O my sons," Jacob (A) then said, addressing them without the slightest trace of bitterness or anger, **"go and seek information about Joseph and his brother."** And overlooking their lack of sympathy and support, he tried, despite his own grief, to give them comfort in their uneasy and troubled state, saying, **"And do not despair of relief from God. Indeed, no one despairs of relief from God except the disbelieving people"** (12:87).

Perhaps, even now, some strange feelings were stirring in Jacob's heart — some incoherent, indefinable sensations of Joseph's dear presence. Or perhaps he was granted an intimation from his Lord that his long, painful separation from his best beloved son was soon to come to an end.

REFERENCES: Qur'an: 12:83-87. Commentaries: Tabari/*H*, II:176-178, 183; Asad/*Q*, 12:fns. 87, 91.

14. The Third Journey to Egypt

He said, "I am Joseph and this is my brother." (12:90)

The nine brothers now returned once more to Egypt. Again they stood before the Great One. But this time their pride was broken, their dignity stripped away.

Since the famine was severe in their country, they were now poor, having little to barter for grain. **"O 'Aziz,"** they said, **"adversity has touched us and our family, and we have come with scanty goods. But give us full measure and be charitable to us. Indeed, God rewards the charitable"** (12:88). At the same time, they begged him to release their brother Benjamin, who was by his side.

It is said that when the brothers thus appealed to Joseph (A) and described the sufferings of their family, he began to weep. And while God had ordered him not to reveal himself to his brothers the first two times they came to him, the command now came to make himself known to them, actualizing what had been revealed to him years earlier when they had abandoned him in the well: **"You will surely inform them about this affair of theirs while they do not perceive"** (12:15).

Joseph (A) now took off the coronet he wore upon his head and looked at his brothers. **"Do you know what you did to Joseph and his brother, when you were ignorant?"**[41] (12:89), he asked them.

The brothers fell back in astonishment at hearing Joseph mentioned by the virtual ruler of Egypt. Then, it is reported, they saw on his forehead, now that he had removed his coronet, a mark which they recognized as belonging to Joseph. Even then, they could hardly believe the evidence of their eyes. **"Are you indeed Joseph?"** (12:90), they asked in utter amazement.

"I am Joseph and this is my brother,"[42] Joseph (A) replied. **"God has certainly been gracious to us. Indeed, the one who is mindful of God and is patient, then surely God does not permit the reward of the doers of good to be lost"** (12:90).

---

[41]Al-Tabari suggests that Joseph's mentioning Benjamin with himself in this speech was an indirect reference to the brothers' having parted him and Benjamin (Tabari/*H*, II:179). Two other explanations have also been suggested: that of the brothers' having accepted so readily the accusation of theft against Benjamin, whom they knew to be innocent, thereby injuring him as they had injured Joseph himself, and their early envy and malice toward the two sons of Rachel.

[42]While the brothers assumed that, rightly or wrongly, Benjamin had been detained as a thief, and perhaps imprisoned or enslaved, Joseph now presented Benjamin to them as his beloved, respected and innocent brother.

We can imagine the deep shame and humiliation the brothers must have felt at that moment. When God had tested them, they had listened to Satan, allowing envy and enmity to dominate their lives. While they had tried to destroy Joseph when he was vulnerable and weak, even to the point of contemplating his murder, he had repaid their evil by unstinting generosity and kindness. While they had hated and envied him, he had shown them utter nobility of heart.

"By God, God has certainly preferred you over us, and indeed we have been sinners!" (12:91), were the only words they found to say. No excuses, no explanations could be offered in the face of the long, long, hard years of loss and suffering they had inflicted on their father, Joseph and Benjamin. Dumbfounded, they were now forced to acknowledge Joseph's superiority over themselves.

If Joseph (A) had been an ordinary man, he might well have reproached and shamed them, cursed them, or even punished them for their evil deeds, and he would certainly have been justified in doing so. At the very least, he would have held enmity and bitterness against them in his heart. However, his response to his brothers shows nothing but wisdom, forbearance and compassion.

As God's prophet, Joseph's first consideration was his brothers' relationship with their Lord. Understanding deeply the complexities of human nature, he knew well that, humbled and shamed by the evil of their inner state and deeds, they might now change the direction of their lives and become God-fearing men, the carriers of the faith of their fathers. Any word of anger or reproach from him at this point would not only have been mean-spirited and petty but destructive of the effect that he desired to produce in them. Gentle and forbearing, he had, moreover, no desire to take revenge on them by even so much as a hint of reproach. **"No blame is there upon you this day,"** were his only words. **"God will forgive you, and He is the Most Merciful of the Merciful"** (12:92).

We may suppose that there now occurred a grand reunion among the twelve brothers, half-joyful, half-grudging and deeply ashamed on the part of the ten. Willingly or not, they were now forced to admit the sinfulness of their deeds and the fact that God had indeed decreed an extraordinary destiny for Joseph, in spite of what they had done to destroy him.

From Joseph's side, the absolute certainty that all things are governed by the Will and plan of God, the All-Knowing, the All-Wise, affording a test and a trial for all involved, was vindicated. But while the test was now over for him and his brothers, his aged father remained uneasy and distressed at home in Canaan. And from the spiritual knowledge granted him by God, Joseph (A) told his brothers what they were now to do.

"Go with this, my shirt, and put it over my father's face," he instructed them. **"He will become seeing. And come to me with all your family"** (12:93). And so the brothers set out again for home.

REFERENCES: Qur'an: 12:88-93. Commentaries: Tabari/*H*, II.178-179; Ibn Kathir/*Q*, 12:88; Asad/*Q*, 12:fn.91.

15. The Reunion of Jacob and Joseph

And when they entered upon Joseph, he took his parents to himself and said, "Enter Egypt, God willing, in safety." And he raised his parents upon the throne, and they bowed to him in prostration. (12:98-99)

When the caravan departed from Egypt, Jacob's premonitions and intimations from God became very strong. **"Indeed, I feel the scent of Joseph,"** he said to those around him, adding, in the face of their silent contempt, **"if you do not think me weakened in mind"**[43] (12:94) due to grief or senility.

But the aged prophet's family members showed him no pity or sympathy. **"By God,"** they said unfeelingly, **"indeed, you are in your old aberration!"** (12:95) — that is, the deranged mental state brought about by your perpetual recollection of Joseph.

Thus the matter rested until the caravan reached home. Then, **when the bearer of good news arrived,**[44] **he put it** — Joseph's shirt — **upon Jacob's face, and he reverted to seeing** (12:96).

"Did I not say to you that I surely know from God what you do not know?" (12:96), Jacob (A) exclaimed. Truly, God Most Gracious had vindicated his trust in Him beyond anything he could have hoped for!

The brothers now expressed their remorse and sorrow for what they had done. **"O our father,"** they pleaded, **"ask forgiveness of our sins for us. Indeed, we have been sinners!"** (12:97).

"I will ask forgiveness for you from my Lord," the noble prophet assured them. Like Joseph (A), he uttered no reproach, vented no anger and held no grudge in his heart against his ten sons for all the suffering they had caused him and their brothers. More than that, he comforted and assured them of God's unfailing forgiveness, saying, **"Indeed, it is He who is the Forgiving, the Merciful"** (12:98).

---

[43]Ibn 'Abbas says that the wind stirred up and brought the scent of Joseph to his father from a distance equal to eight nights' journey (said to be 480 kilometers), at which Jacob informed his people that he perceived the scent of Joseph, despite their considering him weak in his mind (Tabari/*H*, II:180).

[44]It is reported that this was Judah, the brother who had long ago brought his father Joseph's shirt with the false blood upon it, so that he might make Jacob glad, as previously he had made him sad.

We must now imagine the departure of the numerous family members of the venerable patriarch from Palestine and their arrival in Egypt.[45] Ibn Kathir reports that when Jacob's family neared Egypt, Joseph went out to receive his parents with honor[46] — according to some accounts, accompanied by many people, possibly including the king and the royal retinue.

And when they came to him, he took his parents to himself — meaning that he embraced them and showed them great respect and honor — **and said, "Enter Egypt, God willing, in safety." And he raised his parents upon the throne, and they bowed to him in prostration**[47] (12:99).

"O my father," Joseph (A) exclaimed, **"this is the interpretation of my earlier vision! My Lord has made it reality. He was certainly good to me when he took me out of the prison and brought you all here from the desert after Satan had incited enmity between me and my brothers. Indeed, my Lord is subtle in what He wills. Indeed, it is He who is the Knowing, the Wise"** (12:100).

Then Joseph (A) uttered one of the most beautiful prayers recorded in the Qur'an, saying,

---

[45]We may well wonder why Joseph did not return to Palestine himself instead of calling his large family to Egypt. There are several possible reasons for this. First, since he was inspired and guided in everything by his Lord, his calling his people to Egypt would have been by divine direction, so that God's plan and purpose for the descendants of Jacob might be accomplished. Second, God had established Joseph in a position of trust and authority in Egypt by which he could benefit great numbers of people during a critical period. He was also in a position to bring God's Message to polytheists who were ignorant of the divine guidance. Third, there was a severe famine in the land of Canaan, with all the hardship it entailed for his family and trip after trip to Egypt to obtain supplies. Further, from a historical perspective, there was nothing unusual about the migration of Jacob's family, for similar migrations occurred in antiquity during periods of drought.

[46]It is not clear who the wife of Jacob was at this time. Although Ibn Kathir asserts that Joseph's mother Rachel was still alive, this is hard to believe since the Qur'anic account makes no mention of her existence — and she would surely have been an actor in the drama of her sons' lives had she been alive. Other commentators hold that she was long since dead, and that the other "parent" whom Joseph raised to the dias was his aunt Leah (Liyyah), his mother's sister (Tabari/*H*, II:182; Ibn Kathir/*T*, 12:100).

[47]Qatadah says that the greeting among people in that time was their bowing down to each other (Tabari/*H*, II:183). Ibn Kathir notes that from the time of Adam up to Jesus, it was permitted to prostrate before one's elders. He also states that in Syria people used to prostrate before the king, even up to Islamic times. Only in the ***Shari'ah*** (divine Law) brought by Muhammad (S) did God prohibit prostrating to anyone other than Him, the Exalted. It is reported in a ***hadith*** that in the early days of Islam, Salman al-Farsi prostrated to the Prophet (S), whereupon the Prophet (S) told him not to do so but to prostrate only to God (Ibn Kathir/*T*, 12:100). However, Muhammad Asad states, on the authority of Ibn 'Abbas, that the words, **"bowed to him in prostration"** refer to God, not to Joseph, since it is unimaginable that Joseph would have allowed his parents to prostrate to him (Asad/*Q*, 12:fn. 98).

"My Lord, You have granted me something of sovereignty and taught me something of the interpretation of events.[48] **Creator of the heavens and the earth, You are my protector in this world and the Hereafter. Cause me to die as a *muslim* and join me with the righteous!"** (12:101).

It is here that this **"best of stories"** comes to an end. And in order to dispel all doubts about its absolute accuracy, its divine Author adds:

> **This is of the tidings of the Unseen which We reveal to you [Muhammad]. And you were not with them [the brothers] when they put together their plan, while they conspired.** (12:102)

God Most High also leaves us with a final word concerning Jacob (A) and his sons, which makes clear the ultimate purpose of the trials suffered by him and Joseph, God's peace and blessings be upon them both, saying:

> **And this Abraham enjoined [on his sons], and so did Jacob, [saying,] "O my sons, indeed, God has chosen the religion for you, so do not die except that you be *muslims.*" Or were you present when death came to Jacob, when he said to his sons, "What will you worship after me?" They said, "We will worship your God and the God of your fathers Abraham and Ishmael and Isaac, the one God, and we are surrendered to Him."** (2:132-33)

From this, it may be perhaps be assumed that after their repentance, Joseph's ten brothers became better men, sincere in faith, and that they continued in God's worship and carried the message of His Oneness to the idol-worshipping Egyptians. This is confirmed by the fact that an Egyptian believer during the time of Moses (A) testified to the legacy of Joseph (A), in the words, **"And Joseph had already come to you previously with clear proofs. . . ."**[49] (40:34).

It is reported that when death approached Jacob (A), he made Joseph (A) his heir, having him promise that he would take his body back to Palestine for

---

[48]We note here the utter absence of egotism in Joseph. Although God had granted him prophethood and revelation, as well as virtually supreme authority in Egypt, resulting in the saving of thousands of lives, in his humility he referred to it as **"something of sovereignty"** and **"something of the interpretation of events,"** attributing everything to his Lord and accepting no share in anything for his ego or *nafs*. Joseph's words echo the words spoken by Jacob when he told him of his vision in childhood: **"And thus will your Lord choose you and teach you the interpretation of events, and complete His favor upon you and upon the family of Jacob, as He completed it previously upon your fathers, Abraham and Isaac. Indeed, your Lord is Knowing and Wise"** (12:6), and the words of the Most High: **And Thus did We establish Joseph in the land, that We might teach him the interpretation of events** (12:21), indicating that the interpretation of events or dreams through divine inspiration was a main attribute of Joseph's prophethood.

[49]This is detailed in the story of Moses in Volume Two, Chapter 22.

burial. Accordingly, Joseph (A) took his father's body home and buried him with Abraham and Isaac (A) in the cave that Abraham had bought for the purpose in Hebron. It is said that Joseph (A) stayed in Hebron and mourned his father for seven days and then returned to Egypt.

Joseph (A) is reported to have been the father of two sons: Ephraim, the father of Nun, the father of Joshua (A), the prophet following Moses, and Manasseh. It is said that Joseph (A) lived for 120 years.[50]

Joseph's high rank with his Lord is made clear by the fact that the Holy Prophet (S) met him in the third heaven during his Ascension (*Me'raj*) to the heavens (*Bukhari*, 4:429, 5:227). It is also reflected in the Prophet's saying,

> The noble one is the son of the noble one, the son of the noble one, the son of the noble one — Joseph son of Jacob, son of Isaac, son of Abraham, the Friend of God. (*Bukhari*, 4:597, 6.211; also 4:596, 4:603, 6:210)

May God's boundless peace and blessings be upon Joseph, about whom God Most High says, **Indeed, he was among Our chosen servants** (12:24), and upon his honored and distinguished forefathers, Abraham, Isaac and Jacob, throughout eternity.

REFERENCES: Qur'an: 12:94-101. Commentaries: Tabari/*H*, II:140, 180-184; Tabari/*H*, III:31-32, 66, 69; Ibn Kathir/*T*, 12:88-90, 100; Ibn Kathir/*Q*, "Musa"; Asad/*Q*, 12:fns. 96, 98; Ali/*Q*, fn. 1777. Other works: Newby/*Pharaohs*, p. 174.

---

[50]In Gen. 50:25 it is stated that Joseph took a promise from his brothers to carry his bones "up from this place" at his death. "And after they embalmed him, he was placed in a coffin in Egypt." Ex. 13:19 reports that "Moses took the bones of Joseph with him" on the Exodus from Egypt, and subsequently his remains were buried in Palestine, presumably in the town of Nablus, where Joseph's Tomb remains to this day. Althought al-Tabari repeats this biblical account (*History*, II:184; III:66), there is some dubiousness concerning it for a number of reasons. First, the reports concerning are of questionable authenticity. Second, the Holy Prophet (S) stated explicitly, "No prophet was ever buried except in the place where he died" (*Muwatta*, 16.10.27). And third, it is an Islamic belief, based on the Prophet's *ahadith*, that the bodies of prophets do not decay in their graves. (The life of the prophets in the spiritual world after death is discussed in Volume Two, Chapters 24 and 52.)

16. Time Out for Reflection

There is certainly a lesson in their [the prophets'] stories for those of understanding. Never was it [the Qur'an] an invented narration, but rather a confirmation of what was before it and a detailed explanation of all things, and a guidance and mercy for people who believe. (12:111)

The story of Joseph (A) is one that may be taken at face value with its most obvious, apparent meanings — the tale of one prophet's life. At the same time, it is a story to ponder and reflect on, a story full of subtleties and metaphors, on which we have remarked in their place. And at its end we may ask, *What is its message? What is God Most High saying to us through this "**best of stories,**" which, if it had not been told in the Qur'an, would never have been accurately known?*[51]

Joseph's story is loaded with powerful, unmistakable symbolism. The ten brothers are unwilling to admit the God-given superiority of their step-brother's nature over their own. Out of envy and readiness to follow Satan's promptings, they conspire to reduce him to the lowest of the low. But the One who, in His infinite wisdom, had granted Joseph (A) his noble nature and chosen him as His prophet, took him, quite literally, out of the depths of degradation and raised him to the height of honor, power, authority and usefulness. And in the end, the brothers had no choice except to admit his superiority and their own sinfulness.

Joseph's story is a striking lesson in forgiveness and generosity. Not only did Joseph (A) not take revenge against his brothers for their wicked behavior, but he did not even reproach them for it, for his aim was to reclaim and reform them, to heal old enmities and wounds, and to bring hearts together. Nor did his father Jacob (A), although anything he or Joseph might have said or done would have been understandable. Thus, Joseph (A) becomes the model of forgiveness, forbearance and generosity for all times.[52]

---

[51]A comparison between the story of Joseph as told in Gen. 37, 39-50 and the Qur'anic account reveals certain striking differences, especially in the personalities of the prophets Jacob and Joseph.

[52]In the tenth year of his prophethood, Prophet Muhammad (S) escaped from his birthplace, Mecca, under threat of his life. When he re-entered the city as a few years later as its undisputed conqueror, he asked its assembled people what they thought he would do to them. They replied, "Good. You are a noble brother, the son of a noble brother [meaning Abraham]." To this he responded, "Indeed, I say as my brother Joseph said, **'No blame is there upon you this day. God will forgive you, and He is the Most Merciful of the Merciful"** (12:92). Always compassionate and generous in the tradition of the prophets who preceded him, Muhammad (S) then pardoned all those who had injured him, apart from a handful of people who were executed for specific crimes or treason, and thus the conquest of Mecca took place virtually without bloodshed (Ibn Ishaq/*M*, p. 553; Martin Lings/*M*, pp. 300-301).

From the affair of Zulaikha, other lessons emerge. Joseph's words and behavior teach us that prohibited deeds and sins can be resisted if there is sufficient fear of God and strong enough determination. And from Zulaikha we learn the lesson of taking honest responsibility and facing the consequences of one's mistakes without lying or making excuses.

But perhaps the central message of this story can best be summed up in the words of Joseph (A) himself: **"Indeed, my Lord is subtle in what He wills"** (12:100) — that is, in the unfathomable and often mysterious workings of the divine Will.

While it was this Will that separated Joseph (A) from his father and brothers, it was the same Will that reunited them many years later. This Will permitted Satan to play with the ten brothers up to the end of the rope that God gave them, and finally it led them to repent and become the righteous carriers of His Message. That Will decreed that Zulaikha would attempt to seduce Joseph (A) and inflict great harm on him. At the same time, it decreed that Joseph (A) would retain his purity and clear sense of direction, carry out his work in prison under the most difficult of circumstances, and emerge from his trial strengthened with prophethood, power and authority, to become a benefactor of mankind. It was also by the divine Will that both Jacob and Joseph, God's peace and blessings be upon them, were granted the assurance of the beneficial outcome of this series of strange and baffling occurrences, enabling them to exercise patience until God had manifested His purpose to them.

Why? we may ask. *Why did God not make everything all right to start with, instead of letting things go wrong and then, years later, correcting them?*

Our answer is that God's wisdom and knowledge are so all-embracing and yet subtle that only He knows the interconnection of events and people within His divine plan. Perhaps we can ask such questions because in our time we are used to instant solutions, quick fixes. But as a result of this mindset, we often fail to understand that the working out of God's Will means that all things reach the destiny appointed for them in a destined manner and in a destined time, and that we must be patient until His Will becomes clear. All things happen in God's time frame, not ours, and according to His infinite knowledge and wisdom, not according to our limited understanding. *He* plans but we think that we are planning; *He* wills but we understand it as our will; *He* guides all things to their decreed destinies and we think that we are choosing, willing and doing.

Within limits, we are correct. We *do* make choices, we *do* intend, we *do* act. But we must know that we **do not will except as God wills** (76:30, 81:29), and that His divine Will, proceeding from His infinite knowledge and wisdom, is above our limited human wills. Therefore, when He wills to test us with adversity and suffering, after doing whatever is in our power to change things — like Joseph, when he asked his prison mate to mention him to his master, and Jacob, when he advised his sons not to enter by a single gate — we must wait for relief to come, in *His* time, for indeed, **there is no refuge from God except in Him** (9:118).

Thus, the ultimate, most important lesson of Joseph's story is summed up in Jacob's words, repeated twice over: **"Patience is most befitting"** (12:18, 83) in relation the working of the divine Will. For while the end and destination are necessarily obscure to our limited and finite vision, **God knows whatever is in heaven and earth** (22:70), and He **is sufficient for us and the best Disposer of affairs** (3:173).

Qur'anic References — Joseph

6:84

And We granted him [Abraham] Isaac and Jacob, each [of them] We guided. And previously We guided Noah, and among his descendants, David and Solomon and Job and Joseph and Moses and Aaron. And thus do We reward the doers of good.

12:1-101

Alif, lam, ra.[54] These are the verses of the clear Book. (1) Indeed, We have revealed it as an Arabic Qur'an, that you may understand. (2) We relate to you [Muhammad] the best of stories in what We have revealed to you of this Qur'an, although you were, before it, among the unaware. (3)

[Mention, O Muhammad,] when Joseph said to his father, "O my father, indeed I saw eleven stars and the sun and the moon — I saw them prostrating to me." (4)

He said, "O my son, do not tell your vision to your brothers, or they will make a plot against you. Indeed, Satan is a clear enemy to the human being. (5) And thus will your Lord choose you and teach you the interpretation of events, and complete His favor upon you and upon the family of Jacob, as He completed it previously upon your fathers, Abraham and Isaac. Indeed, your Lord is Knowing and Wise." (6)

Indeed, in Joseph and his brothers are signs for the enquiring, (7) when they said, "Joseph and his brother are more dear to our father than we, while we are a clan. Indeed, our father is in clear aberration. (8) Kill Joseph or banish him to [another] land. Your father's regard will then be accessible to you, and after that you will be righteous people." (9)

A speaker among them said, "Do not kill Joseph, but, if you must do something, put him into the bottom of the well. Some travelers will pick him up." (10)

They said, "O our father, why do you not entrust us with Joseph, while we are indeed his sincere well-wishers? (11) Send him with us tomorrow that he may enjoy himself and play, and indeed we will be his guardians." (12)

He said, "Indeed, it saddens me that you should take him, and I fear that a wolf may devour him while you are heedless of him." (13)

They said, "If a wolf were to devour him while we are a clan, we would then indeed be losers!" (14)

Then when they took him and banded together to put him into the bottom of the well — and We revealed to him, "You will surely inform them about this affair of theirs while they do not perceive." (15)

---

[54]This *surah* is among many which are prefaced by certain Arabic letters, whose meaning no one knows with certainty except God Most High.

And they came to their father at night, weeping. (16) They said, "O our father, indeed, we went racing and left Joseph with our things, and a wolf devoured him. But you would not believe us, even if we were truthful!" (17) And they produced his shirt with false blood upon it. (18)

He said, "No, but your lower selves have enticed you to something. Therefore, patience is most befitting, and God is the One sought for help against that which you describe." (18)

And there came a company of travelers, and they sent their drawer of water and he let down his pail. He said, "Good news — here is a lad!" And they concealed him as merchandise, and God was Knowing of what they did. (19) And they sold him for a low price, a few dirhams, and they were of those satisfied with little regarding him. (20)

And the one from Egypt who bought him said to his wife, "Make his stay honorable. Perhaps he may benefit us or we may adopt him as a son." And thus did We establish Joseph in the land, that We might teach him the interpretation of events. And God is predominant over His affair, but most people do not know. (21)

And when he reached maturity, We granted him judgment and knowledge, and thus do We reward the doers of good. (22)

And she in whose house he was sought to seduce him. She closed the doors and said, "Come, you!"

He said, "God be my refuge! Indeed, he is my master, who has made my stay good. Indeed, the wrongdoers will not prosper." (23) And she certainly desired him, and he would have inclined toward her if he had not seen his Lord's proof. Thus it was, that We might avert evil and immorality from him. Indeed, he was among Our chosen servants. (24)

And they both raced to the door and she tore his shirt from the back, and they found her husband at the door (25). She said, "What is the recompense of one who intended evil to your wife except that he be imprisoned or a painful punishment?" (25)

He said, "It was she who sought to seduce me." And a witness from her household testified, "If his shirt is torn from the front, then she has told the truth and he is of the liars, (26) but if his shirt is torn from the back, then she has lied and he is of the truthful." (27)

Therefore, when he saw his shirt torn from the back, he said, "This is of your plotting. Terrible indeed is your plotting! (28) Joseph, turn away from this. And, [O my wife,] ask forgiveness for your sin. Indeed, you were of the sinful." (29)

And women in the city said, "The wife of al-'Aziz is seeking to seduce her slave; he has inflamed her with love. Indeed, we see her in clear aberration." (30)

Then when she heard of their scheming, she sent for them and prepared a banquet for them, and she gave each of them a knife and said, "Come out before them!" And when they saw him, they extolled him greatly and cut their hands and said, "How perfect is God! This is not a mortal, this is nothing but a noble angel." (31)

She said, "That, then, is the one concerning whom you blamed me. And I certainly sought to seduce him but he firmly refused. And if he does not do what I order him, he will surely be imprisoned and will be among the debased!" (32)

He said, "My Lord, prison is more to my liking than that to which they are inviting me. And if You do not avert their plot from me, I might incline toward them and be among the ignorant." (33) So his Lord responded to him and averted their plot from him. Indeed, He is the Hearing, the Knowing. (34)

It then occurred to them, after they had seen the signs, that he should certainly imprison him for a time. (35) And there entered the prison with him two young men. One of them said, "Indeed, I have seen myself pressing wine."

The other said, "Indeed, I have seen myself carrying bread upon my head, from which birds were eating. Inform us of the interpretation of it. We surely perceive you to be among the doers of good." (36)

He said, "You will not receive food that is provided to you until I inform you of its interpretation before it comes to you. That is from what my Lord has taught me. Indeed, I have left alone the religion of a people who do not believe in God and they are disbelievers in the Hereafter, (37) and I have followed the religion of my fathers, Abraham, Isaac and Jacob. And it was not for us to associate anything with God. That is from God's favor upon us and upon mankind, but most of mankind are not grateful. (38)

"O two companions of the prison, are separate lords better or God, the One, the Prevailing? (39) You worship, besides Him, mere names [by which] you have named them, you and your fathers, for which God has sent down no authority. The authority is only for God. He has commanded that you worship no one but Him. That is the correct religion, but most of mankind do not know. (40)

"O two companions of the prison, as for one of you, he will pour his master wine, and as for the other, he will be crucified and birds will eat from his head. The matter has been decreed about which you both enquire." (41) And he said to the one whom he supposed would be saved, "Mention me before your master." But Satan caused him to forget the mention to his master, and he remained in the prison a few [more] years. (42)

And the king said, "Indeed, I saw seven fat cows being eaten by seven lean ones, and seven green ears and others dry. O nobles, explain my dream to me, if you are able to interpret dreams." (43)

They said, "A mixture of false dreams, and we are not knowledgeable about the interpretation of dreams." (44)

And the one of the two who was saved but remembered after a time said, "I shall inform you of its interpretation, so send me forth. (45) Joseph, O you truthful one, inform us concerning seven fat cows eaten by seven lean ones, and seven green ears and others dry, so that I may return to the people, that they may know." (46)

He said, "You will plant for seven years consecutively, and what you harvest, leave it in its sheaves, except a little, from which you will eat. (47) Then after that will come seven hard [years] which will consume what you have set aside for them, except a little out of that which you have stored. (48) Then after that will come a year in which the people will have rain and in which they will press [oil and wine]." (49)

And the king said, "Bring him to me."

But when the messenger came to him, he said, "Return to your master and ask him what is the case of the women who cut their hands. Indeed, my Lord is Knowing of their scheme." (50)

He said, "What was your affair when you sought to seduce Joseph?"

They said, "How perfect is God! We know nothing of evil concerning him." The wife of al-'Aziz said, "Now the truth has become evident. It was I who sought to seduce him, and indeed, he is of the truthful." (51)

"That is so he will know that I did not betray him in secret and that God does not guide the scheming of the betrayers. (52) Nor do I absolve myself. Indeed, the *nafs* is a persistent enjoiner of evil, except as my Lord shows mercy. Indeed, my Lord is Forgiving and Merciful." (53)

And the king said, "Bring him to me. I shall appoint him exclusively for myself." And when he spoke to him, he said, "Assuredly, you are this day established and trusted in our presence." (54)

He said, "Appoint me over the storehouses of the land. Indeed, I will be a knowledgeable guardian." (55) And thus did We establish Joseph in the land, to settle therein wherever he willed. We touch with Our mercy whomever We will, and We do not permit the reward of the doers of good to be lost. (56) And the reward of the Hereafter is better for those who believe and are mindful of God. (57)

And Joseph's brothers arrived and came to him, and he recognized them but he was unknown to them. (58) And when he had furnished them with their supplies, he said, "Bring me a brother of yours from your father. Do you not see that I give full measure and that I am the best of hosts? (59) But if you do not bring him to me, no measure shall you have from me, nor shall you approach me." (60)

They said, "We will try to dissuade his father from him, and indeed we shall do so." (61)

And he said to his servants, "Put their property into their saddlebags so they may recognize it when they have gone back to their people, that perhaps they will return." (62)

Then, when they returned to their father, they said, "O our father, measure has been denied to us, so send our brother with us, that we may be given measure. And we will surely be his guardians." (63)

He said, "Shall I entrust you with him except as I entrusted you with his brother previously? But God is the best Guardian and He is the Most Merciful of the Merciful." (64)

And when they opened their baggage, they found their property restored to them. They said, "O our father, what [more] could we desire? This is our property, restored to us. And we will obtain supplies for our families and guard our brother, and obtain an increase of a camel's load; that is an easy measure!" (65)

He said, "Never will I send him with you until you give me a promise by God that you will bring him [back] to me, unless you should be surrounded." And when they had given their promise, he said, "God is Witness over what we say." (66) And he said, "O my sons, do not enter by one gate, but enter by different gates. Yet I cannot avail you against God in the least. The decision is only for God. Upon Him have I relied, and let the relying rely upon Him." (67) And when they went in whence their father had ordered them, it did not avail them against God in the least; it was but a need within Jacob's soul, which he satisfied. And he was surely a possessor of knowledge because of what We had taught him, but most of mankind do not know. (68)

And when they went in to Joseph, he took his brother to himself. He said, "Indeed, I am your brother, so do not grieve over what they used to do." (69)

Then, when he had furnished them with their supplies, he put the cup into his brother's bag. Then a herald called out, "O people of the caravan, indeed, you are thieves!" (70)

They said, while turning toward them, "What is it you are missing?" (71)

They said, "We are missing the king's measure. And he who produces shall have a camel's load, and I am responsible for it." (72)

They said, "By God, you certainly know that we did not come to make corruption in the land, nor are we thieves!" (73)

They said, "Then what should its recompense be if you are liars?" (74)

They said, "Its recompense will be that he in whose bag it is found — he [himself] will be the recompense. Thus do we recompense the wrongdoers!" (75)

So he began with their bags before his brother's bag; then he took it out of his brother's bag. Thus did We plan for Joseph. He could not have taken his brother under the law of the king except that God willed. We raise in degrees whomever We will, but over every possessor of knowledge is one [more] knowing. (76)

They said, "If he steals, a brother of his had stolen previously." But Joseph kept it within himself and did not disclose it to them. He said, "You are worse in position, and God is most knowing of that which you describe." (77)

They said, "O 'Aziz, indeed he has a father, an old man, so take one of us in place of him. We surely perceive you to be among the doers of good." (78)

He said, "God forbid that we should take [anyone] except him with whom we found our property. We would then indeed be unjust." (79)

So when they had despaired of him, they gathered in private consultation. The eldest of them said, "Do you not know that your father has taken an oath from you by God, and previously you failed concerning Joseph. Therefore, I will never leave the land until my father gives me permission or God decides for me, and He is the Best of Judges. (80)

"Return to your father and say, 'O our father, indeed, your son has committted theft, and we do not testify except to what we knew, nor were we guardians of the Unseen. (81) And enquire of the town where we were and of the caravan in which we came. And indeed, we are truthful.'" (82)

He [Jacob] said, "No, rather your lower selves have enticed you to something, so patience is most befitting. Perhaps God will bring them to me, all together. Indeed, it is He who is the Knowing, the Wise." (83) And he turned away from them and said, "Oh, my sorrow over Joseph!" and his eyes became white from grief, for he was a suppressor [of it]. (84)

They said, "By God, you will not cease remembering Joseph until you become fatally ill or become of those who perish!" (85)

He said, "I only complain of my suffering and my grief to God, and I know from God that which you do not know. (86) O my sons, go and seek information about Joseph and his brother, and do not despair of relief from God. Indeed, no one despairs of relief from God except the disbelieving people." (87)

So when they went in to him, they said, "O 'Aziz, adversity has touched us and our family, and we have come with scanty goods, but give us full measure and be charitable to us. Indeed, God rewards the charitable." (88)

He said, "Do you know what you did to Joseph and his brother, when you were ignorant?" (89)

They said, "Are you indeed Joseph?"

He said, "I am Joseph and this is my brother. God has certainly been gracious us. Indeed, the one who fears God and is patient, then surely God does not permit the reward of the doers of good to be lost." (90)

They said, "By God, God has certainly preferred you over us, and indeed we have been sinners!" (91)

He said, "No blame is there upon you this day. God will forgive you, and He is the Most Merciful of the Merciful. (92) Go with this, my shirt, and put it over my father's face; he will become seeing. And come to me with all your family." (93)

And when the caravan departed, their father said, "Indeed, I feel the scent of Joseph, if you do not think me weakened in mind." (94)

They said, "By God, indeed, you are in your old aberration!" (95)

And when the bearer of good tidings arrived, he put it over his face, and he reverted to seeing. He said, "Did I not tell you that I know from God that which you do not know?" (96)

They said, "O our father, ask forgiveness of our sins for us. Indeed, we have been sinners!" (97)

He said, "I will ask forgiveness for you from my Lord. Indeed, it is He who is the Forgiving, the Merciful." (98)

And when they came in to Joseph, he took his parents to himself and said, "Enter Egypt, God willing, in safety." (99) And he raised his parents upon the dias and they bowed to him in prostration. And he said, "O my father, this is the interpretation of my earlier vision. My Lord has made it reality. And He was certainly good to me when He took me out of the prison and brought you [here] from the desert after Satan had incited [enmity] between me and my brothers. Indeed, my Lord is subtle in what He wills. Indeed, it is He who is the Knowing, the Wise. (100)

"My Lord, You have granted me something of sovereignty and taught me something of the interpretation of events. Creator of the heavens and earth, You are my protector in this world and the Hereafter! Cause me to die a ***muslim*** and join me with the righteous." (101)

This is of the tidings of the Unseen which We reveal to you [Muhammad]. And you were not with them when they put together their plan, while they conspired. (102)

40:34

[The Secret Believer of Moses' time said to the Egyptian people:] "And Joseph had already come to you previously with clear proofs . . ."

The Story of Job (Ayyoub)

peace be upon him

Indeed, We have revealed to you [Muhammad] as We revealed to Noah and the prophets after him; and We revealed to Abraham and Ishmael and Isaac and Jacob and the descendants [of Israel], and Jesus and Job and Jonah and Aaron and Solomon, and We granted David the *Zabur*. (4:163)

1. JOB'S GENEALOGY

And We granted him [Abraham] Isaac and Jacob; each [of them] We guided. And previously We guided Noah, and among his descendants, David and Solomon and Job and Joseph and Moses and Aaron. And thus do We reward the doers of good. (6:84-87)

Among the descendants of Abraham (A) was Job (Ayyoub), peace be upon him, the prophet whose steadfastness in the face of the most awesome trials originated the well-known expression, "the patience of Job."

There are differering opinions among the Qur'anic commentators concerning Job's ancestry. The most commonly accepted one is that his mother was Lot's daughter and that his father was Maws, the grandson of Esau, son of Isaac, son of Abraham (A). As for his wife, some commentators state that she was Liyya, who was either the daughter of Jacob (A) or the daughter of Manasseh, son of Joseph (A). Another opinion, held by Ibn 'Abbas (R), is that her name was Rahmah, and that she was the daughter of Ephraim, Joseph's second son.

Job (A) is mentioned four times in the Qur'an. Although he was a prophet, receiving inspirations from God, there is no mention of his having had followers.

REFERENCES: Tabari/*H*, II:140; Ibn Kathir/*Q*, "Ayyoub".

2. The Testing of Job (A)

We will surely test you with something of fear and hunger and loss of wealth and lives and fruits; but give good tidings to the patient, who, when a calamity befalls them, say, "Indeed, to God we belong and indeed, to Him we will return." Those are the ones upon whom are blessings from their Lord and mercy. And it is those who are the [rightly-]guided. (2:155-156)

It is reported that Job, peace be upon him, lived in Syria near Damascus. God Most High had granted him great wealth in the form of lands, herds and servants, and he had a devoted wife and many children. With all that, he was a humble man of great piety, constantly glorifying and devoutly thanking his Lord.

God then willed to test him by a series of calamities. What these were and in what order they occurred is not specified in the Qur'an. However, the classical commentators, taking their information from the Old Testament Book of Job, say that God first tested Job (A) by suddenly stripping away all his considerable wealth and property. But Job (A) remained firm and constant, not shattered or even shaken by this disaster, and continued to glorify his Lord.

God then took the lives of Job's many children. This too did not change him, and he continued to be steadfast in service and devotion to his Lord. God then took away his health, afflicting him with terrible pain and suffering, and such loathesome ailments that people shunned him. Still Job's faith and serenity remained undisturbed, for his heart was with his Lord. It is said that there was no one on the face of the earth more honorable to God than Job, may God's peace and blessings be upon him.

Ibn Kathir, recapitulating the works of earlier scholars, summarizes the matter thus:

> Job was a man with great wealth of all kinds: cattle and slaves and sheep and widely-spreading lands in al-Bathaniyyah in the territory of Harran [in Syria]. He had many children and numbers of relatives. All this was taken from him and his body was afflicted with many kinds of diseases, so there was not a single organ that was sound except his heart and tongue, and with these two he would mention God Most High, for despite all this he was extremely patient, remembering God the Mighty and Glorious night and day, morning and evening. (Ibn Kathir/*Q*, "Ayyoub")

Job's disease lasted so long that his companions left him and visitors were disgusted by him. They expelled him from his city and threw him onto a refuse heap outside the city, and people abandoned him and boycotted him. No one remained sympathetic to him except his wife. She would care for him and always recall his earlier good treatment of her and his love of her.

> So she nursed him and looked after his welfare and helped him to fulfill his needs and stood by him. Her condition deteriorated and her money decreased to the point at which she served people for wages to feed him and provide for his other needs, may God be pleased with her, and she was very patient with all that occurred as their wealth and children were taken away from them. Thus, in addition to the calamity of her husband, she suffered from lack of means and was obliged to serve people after having had wealth and happiness and servants and honor. To God we belong and to Him we return! (Ibn Kathir/*Q*, "Ayyoub")

REFERENCES: Ibn Kathir/*T*, 21:83-84, 38:42-44; Ibn Kathir/*Q*, "Ayyoub"; Tabari/*H*, II:142.

3. The Restoration

Then We responded to him [Job] and removed that which afflicted him of injury. And we granted him his family and their like with them as a mercy from Ourselves and a reminder for the worshippers. (21:84)

And We granted him his family and their like with them as a mercy from Ourselves and a reminder for those of understanding. (38:44)

The story of Job (A) is continued in the following *hadith*, reported by Ibn Kathir:

God's prophet Job remained in his trial for eighteen years, and his near and far friends and relatives left him, excepting two of his brothers[-in-faith] who were special brothers to him. They used to come and go twice a day, and then one of them said to the other, "Know that, by God, Job has committed such a sin as no one has committed in the world."

Then his friend asked, "How so?"

He replied, "For the last eighteen years, God has not shown him any mercy or given him any relief.'"

Then when the other went to Job, he could not restrain himself but told him what his friend had said. Job said, "I cannot understand what you are saying, for indeed, God the Mighty and Glorious knows that if I so much as passed by two disputing people and they mentioned God, I would come home and do expiation on their behalf, fearing that they might have mentioned the name of God Most High in vain."[1]

Job would go out to relieve himself, [the Prophet (S) continued,] and when he had finished, his wife would take his hand and bring him back [to his resting-place, due to his extreme weakness].

One day she was delayed in coming to him. Then God Most High revealed to him at the place where he was, **"Strike** the earth **with your foot. This is a cool bath and drink"** [38:42].

Then presently she returned, looking for him, and he went toward her, and God had removed his affliction from him and he was as sound as he had been [previously]. When she saw him she said, "May God bless you, have you seen the prophet of God who was ill here? And by God

[1]That is, that they might be punished for their careless use of God's holy Name. Job's love and concern for his friends was so great, says Ibn Kathir, that when God restored him to his previous state, He ordered him to strengthen his relations with his companions by sacrificing an animal on their behalf and asking forgiveness for them because they had sinned against Him with regard to Job (Ibn Kathir/Q, "Ayyoub").

> Almighty, I have not seen a man more similar to him when he was healthy than you!"
>
> He said, "Indeed, I am he!"[2] (Ibn Kathir/*Q*, "Ayyoub")

Together with his health, Ibn 'Abbas (R) adds, God Most High also restored Job's wealth and children to their previous state and granted him even more. In this connection, the Holy Prophet (S) said,

> While Job was bathing naked, there fell upon him golden locusts, so Job started to catch them in his garment. Then His Lord called him, [saying,] "O Job, have I not enriched you beyond what you see [here]?" He said, "Certainly, by Your honor, but I cannot be too rich in Your blessings!'" (*Bukhari*, 1:277),

meaning that he treasured the gift his Lord had granted him, not because it would enrich him materially but because it came to him from Him.

Yet one difficulty still remained for Job (A), which is referred to in God's instructing him, **"Take a bundle in your hand and strike with it, and do not break your oath"** (38:44).

In the verse cited previously, God ordered Job (A) to **strike the earth** with his foot for healing. And now, so that he would not violate an oath he had previously taken, He ordered him to take a bundle of something in his hand and strike something or someone with it. And according to the consensus of the classic commentators, that "someone" was his faithful and extraordinarily patient wife.

In the Biblical account, Job's wife has no role except to reproach her husband in his affliction and illness, saying, "Are you still holding on to your integrity? Curse God and die!" (Job 2:9). But in marked contrast to this, the Muslim commentators are unanimous in proclaiming the selflessness and goodness of Job's wife, herself a descendant of prophets. As for the meaning of 38:44 above, they have offered a variety of interpretations.

Because some of these are at variance with the justice and kindness that was clearly due from Job to his long-suffering, loving wife, and with the actions of a prophet about whom God Most High says, immediately after mentioning the matter of the bundle, **"Indeed, We found him patient, an excellent slave"** (38:44), we have not included them here. What can be understood from these interpretations is simply that, for some reason, Job (A), the immensely patient

---

[2]This *hadith* is cited both in Ibn Kathir's *Qasas*, "Ayyoub," and in his *Tafsir*, commentary on 21:83-84. Although Ibn Kathir notes that the *hadith* may not go back all the way to the Prophet (S), Ibn 'Abbas reports something similar, adding that after healing Job, God sent him a garment from Paradise which he was wearing when his wife returned and was unable to recognize him (Ibn Kathir/*Q*, "Ayyoub"; Ibn Kathir/*T*, 21:83-84).

prophet who bore such heavy afflictions without complaint, became angry with his wife for something she had done or said.

The most likely explanation among those offered by the commentators seems to be the following: Without intending any harm, out of her deep compassion for her husband's suffering and her own profound exhaustion as his only caregiver, Job's wife listened to advice from Satan and said something to Job (A) concerning his trials which seemed blasphemous. One opinion is that Satan came to her, asking why this disaster had befallen her husband, as a result of which she asked Job (A), "How long will this last?" as if questioning God's Will. Job (A) advised her to repent and ask forgiveness, but when she seemed to hold back from doing so, he became angry with her for the sake of God, whose right to do whatever He sees fit with His servants he refused to question, vowing that if he recovered he would give her one hundred lashes. Other commentators add that he even refused to let his wife serve him after that.

Then, in his suffering and loneliness, Job (A) cried to his Lord, saying, **"Indeed, adversity has touched me, and You are the Most Merciful of the Merciful!"** (21:83). And because all the afflictions he had experienced were not as great a trial to him as Satan's attempt to turn him away from satisfaction with his Lord and make him ungrateful, impatient and despairing, he added, **"Indeed, Satan has touched me with exhaustion and suffering"** (38:41). Another interpretation of these words is that his bodily afflictions had reached the point at which he feared he might not be able to continue to glorify his Lord with his tongue, which would have been the worst of calamities to him.

Thus it was that when God accepted Job's prayer and removed his affliction, Job (A) was faced with a dilemma in connection with the oath he had taken. If he kept his oath, he would harm the faithful, loving wife who had cared for and supported him throughout the long years of his suffering, and who deserved nothing but the best from him. However, if he did not, he would violate his word, and both of these alternatives were unacceptable and displeasing to his Lord.

God Most High, who knows all the innermost secrets of the hearts, then appointed for Job (A) a way out of his double dilemma, instructing him to **take a bundle [*digtha*] in** his **hand and strike [or touch] with it** in order not to break his oath (38:44). The word ***"digtha"*** means a bundle or bunch of twigs, rushes, straws, or possibly a date palm branch with many fronds. According to the majority of commentators, Job (A) gathered a hundred of these, made a bundle of them, and touched his wife lightly once with the bundle of one hundred, thereby fulfilling the requirement of the one hundred strokes he had vowed.[3]

Other commentators say that he was ordered to take a bundle of wet grasses, which was as heavy as one hundred blades, and touch her body with it.

It is said that Job (A) lived ninety-three years or more. He appointed his son Hawmal as his heir, and after Hawmal, God appointed Bishr, another of Job's sons, as a prophet, calling him Dhul-Kifl (A).

REFERENCES: Qur'an: 4:163; 6:84-87; 21:84; 38:41-44. Commentaries: Ibn Kathir/*T*, 21:83-84, 38:42-44; Ibn Kathir/*Q*, "Ayyoub"; Tabari/*H*, II:143; Maududi/*Q*, 38:fns. 42, 46.

[3]In the books of technicalities of Islamic law, Job's example is cited as a precedent for replacing a severe punishment with a lighter one in cases is which such a proceeding is justified.

4. Time Out for Reflection

If God should touch you with adversity, there is no remover of it but He. And if He touches you with good, then He is able to do all things. (6:117)

And give good tidings to the humble — those who, when God is mentioned, feel fear in their hearts, and the patient toward what has afflicted them. (22:35)

Job's story occupies a unique place among the stories of the prophets, first because it is both a personal history as well as a parable of testing and patience. Second, unlike earlier prophets, there is no evidence that Job (A) was sent with a message to his people or that he had a following. Rather, his prophetic mission consisted of his silent example of steadfastness and devotion to his Lord under the heaviest trials.

Each of the afflictions with which Job (A) was tested, one more difficult than the other, would have been more than enough to shake the faith of a lesser person. Yet throughout the long period of his trial, Job (A) remained steadfast and unwavering in his commitment to God, firmly upholding His right to test him by whatever means He saw fit, while remaining virtually unmoved by the events around him — **an excellent slave . . . who repeatedly turned back** to his Lord (38:44).

One aspect of Job's suffering is especially noteworthy. Many are the people who suffer terrible afflictions but whose human dignity remains intact throughout their ordeal. But Job (A) lost his dignity together with all else. As we have seen, he was afflicted with such a repulsive disease that virtually everyone shunned him except his faithful wife, and he was considered so vile that he was left upon a refuse heap outside the city. Nevertheless, not only did he not complain, but he continued to praise and glorify his Lord with whatever was left of his strength. His example, therefore, is especially relevant to sufferers whose affliction is increased by the loss of their dignity.

Now, in general we human beings are pleased with God when things go well for us, but when they do not, we become impatient, desperate and angry with Him This human propensity for changing our view of God and our relationship with Him according to our circumstances is mentioned in several Qur'anic verses: —

The human being does not tire of supplicating for good things, but if evil touches him, then he is hopeless and despairing. (41:49)

If We give the human being a taste of mercy from Ourselves and then withdraw it from him, indeed, he is despairing and ungrateful. (11:9)

When We bestow favor upon the human being, he turns away and distances himself, and when evil touches him, he is ever despairing. (17:83)

And as for the human being, when his Lord tries him [with good] and is generous to him, he says, "My Lord has honored me." But when He tries him [with difficulty] and restricts his provision, he says, "My Lord has humiliated me. (89:15-16)

But Job, peace be upon him, was different. His devotion to God was absolutely sincere and unconditional, without a trace of self-interest or self-absorption. A reading of the Qur'anic text and commentaries gives one the impression that he is saying something like the following:

"Praise be to my Lord the Most High without regard to transitory conditions and situations. Glory be to Him, whether in ease or hardship, wealth and poverty, health or illness, companionship or solitude, whether He pours out His divine favors or takes them away, for they are His to do with as He pleases. Indeed, He is the Praised and the Glorious, forever and without end!

"Nothing that He may see fit to grant or withhold from me or anyone else, or even from the entirety of His creation, can diminish His glory, praiseworthiness or beneficence in the slightest degree. Nor can it alter my desire to glorify Him as long as there is breath in my body, or detract an iota from the intensity of my love for Him, which has no relationship to anything He may or may not do for me but is purely for the sake of His exalted divine Self alone. Indeed, **there is no refuge from God except in Him** [9:118]. *O my Lord, I am pleased with whatever You are pleased with for me!*"

Job's story therefore contains vital and precious lessons for mankind. One of these is the lesson of fortifying one's heart in trials and sufferings with the constant glorification and remembrance of God Most High (*dhikr-Allah*), according to His saying,

Indeed, God leaves astray whomever He wills and guides to Himself whomever turns [to Him] — those who believe and whose hearts find tranquility in the remembrance of God. Unquestionably, in the remembrance of God hearts do find tranquility. (13:28)

Another lesson is that enduring suffering and affliction with patience and steadfastness provides one of the best opportunities and surest means of strengthening our souls and coming closer to our Lord. This is mentioned a number of Qur'anic verses, such as those cited at the beginning of this section, and in numerous *ahadith*, such as the following:

> If any Muslim who suffers some calamity says that which God has commanded him — **"Indeed, to God we belong and indeed, to Him we will return"** [2:156] — [followed by,] "O God, reward me for my affliction and give me something better in exchange for it," God will give him something better than it in exchange. (*Muslim*, 1999)

> If any Muslim man or woman suffers a calamity and keeps it in his memory, even if it occurred a long time previously, saying, each time it is remembered, **"Indeed, to God we belong and indeed, to Him we will return,"** God the Blessed and Exalted will give a fresh reward each time it is said, equivalent to the reward of when it occurred. (*Mishkat*, 1759)

> No calamity befalls a Muslim but that God forgives some of his sins due to it, even if it is only the prick of a thorn. (*Bukhari*, 7:544)

> The magnitude of the reward goes along with the magnitude of the affliction. When God the Almighty and Glorious loves people He afflicts them, and those who accept it gladly receive God's pleasure, but those who are displeased receive God's displeasure. (*Mishkat*, 1566)

> The believing man or woman continues to be afflicted in person, property and children so that they may finally meet God free of sin. (*Mishkat*, 1567)

When the Prophet (S) was asked which people suffered the greatest affliction, he replied,

> The prophets, then those who come next to them, then those who come next to them. A man is afflicted in keeping his religion. If he is firm in his religion his trial is severe, but if there is weakness in his religion it is made light for him, and it continues like that until he walks on the earth having no sin. (*Mishkat*, 1562)

And, speaking on behalf of his Lord, the Prophet (S) reported that God Most High says:

> When I afflict a servant of Mine who is a believer and he praises Me for the affliction I have brought upon him, he will rise from that bed of his as sinless as he was the day his mother gave birth to him. The Lord, Blessed and Exalted, will say, "I fettered and afflicted My servant, so record for him whatever you were recording for him when he was well." (*Mishkat*, 1579)

> Son of Adam, if you show endurance and seek your reward from Me in the first affliction, I shall be pleased with no less reward than Paradise for you. (*Mishkat*, 1758)

Obviously, when we are preoccupied with this world's life and are happy, healthy, well-off, surrounded by family, friends and good things, we are likely to give less time and attention to God and to our spiritual life. But when this good is taken from us, we turn to Him quickly, crying for help. The fire of suffering then softens and melts our hearts until they are tender and receptive, giving us an opportunity we might otherwise not have had of coming nearer and nearer to our Lord, until, for some servants like Job (A), their beloved Lord occupies their hearts to the exclusion of all else.

May God's best blessings and peace be upon that patient prophet, our example in adversity, about whom He says,

> **Indeed, We found him patient, an excellent slave. Indeed, he was one who repeatedly turned back [to his Lord]. (38:44)**

Qur'anic References — Job

4:163

Indeed, We have revealed to you [Muhammad] as We revealed to Noah and the prophets after him; and We revealed to Abraham and Ishmael and Isaac and Jacob and the descendants [of Israel], and Jesus and Job and Jonah and Aaron and Solomon, and We granted David the *Zabur.*

6:84

And We granted him [Abraham] Isaac and Jacob; each [of them] We guided. And previously We guided Noah, and among his descendants, David and Solomon and Job and Joseph and Moses and Aaron. And thus do We reward the doers of good.

21:83-84

And [mention] Job, when he called ot his Lord, "Indeed, adversity has touched me, and You are the Most Merciful of the Merciful!" (83) Then We responded to him and removed that which afflicted him of injury. And we granted him his family and their like with them as a mercy from Ourselves and a reminder for the worshippers. (84)

38:41-44

And recall Our servant Job, when he called to his Lord, "Indeed, Satan has touched me with exhaustion and suffering." (41) [It was said:] "Strike [the earth] with your foot. This is a cool bath and drink." (42) And We granted him his family and their like with them as a mercy from Ourselves and a reminder for those of understanding. (43) [And it was said:] "And take a bundle in your hand and strike with it, and do not break your oath." Indeed, We found him patient, an excellent slave. Indeed, he was one who repeatedly turned back [to his Lord]. (44)

THE STORY OF SHU'AYB

peace be upon him

Has there not reached them [the pagan Meccans of Muhammad's time] the news of those before them — the people of Noah and the 'Aad and Thamud, and the people of Abraham and the dwellers in Midian and the Overturned Cities? Their messengers came to them with clear proofs. And never would God have wronged them, but [rather] they wronged themselves. (9:70)

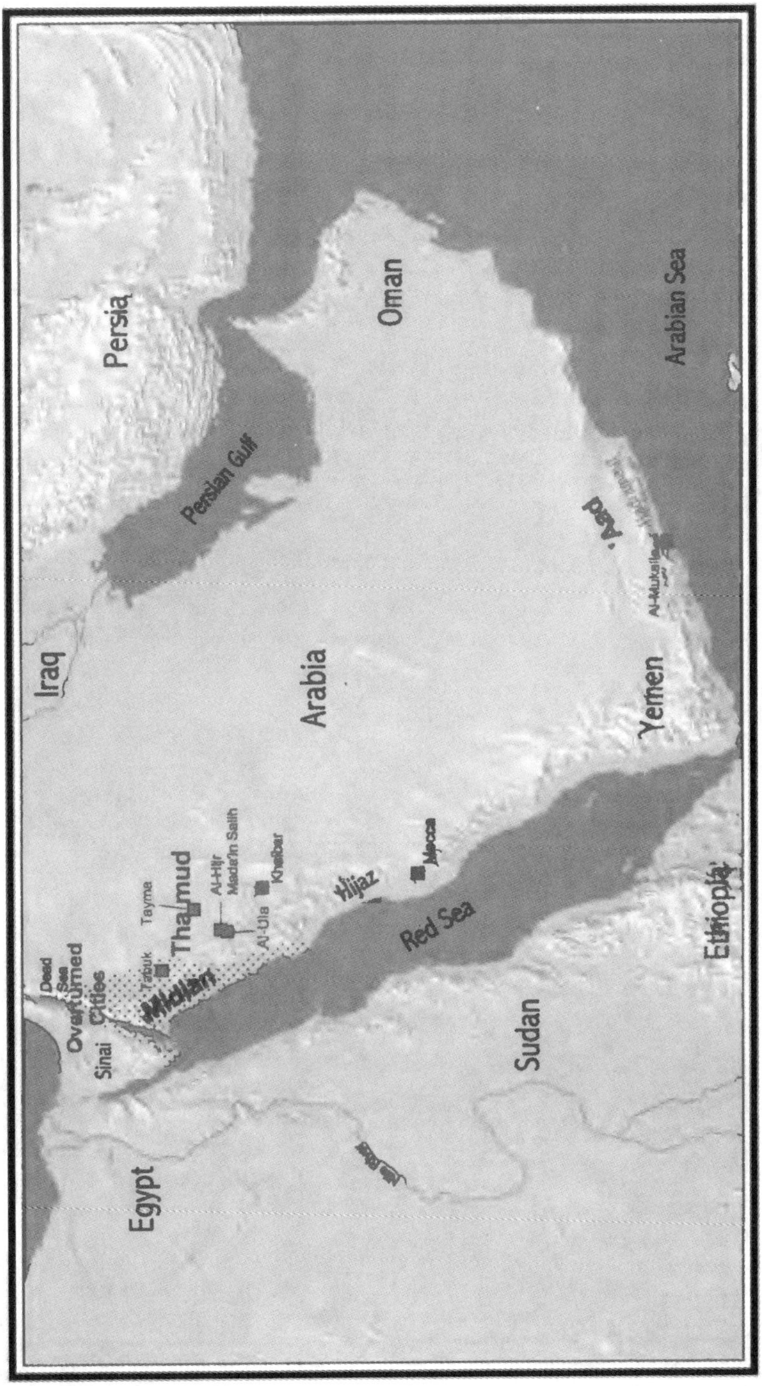
Persia
Iraq
Persian Gulf
Oman
Arabian Sea
Arabia
'Aad
Al-Mukalla
Yemen
Egypt
Sinai
Overturned Cities
Dead Sea
Tabuk
Midian
Thamud
Tayma
Al-Hijr
Mada'in Salih
Al-'Ula
Khaibar
Hijaz
Mecca
Red Sea
Sudan
Ethiopia

Map 9. Midian

1. The Dwellers in Midian and the Thorn Bush

Before them, the people of Noah and the companions of al-Rass[1] and Thamud denied, and 'Aad and Pharoah and the brothers of Lot, and the dwellers in the thorn bush and the people of Tubba'[2] — all denied the messengers, and so My threat was justly carried out. (50:12-14)

We now come to third of the four Arabian prophets, Shu'ayb, peace be upon him, for whose name there is no certain English equivalent.

Just when Shu'ayb (A) lived is a matter of some speculation. What is known with certainty is that he was sent to the people of Midian, an area in the northwestern part of the Arabian peninsula which extended from the present-day Gulf of Aqabah west into the Sinai peninsula and to the mountains of Moab east of the Dead Sea. Its inhabitants were Arabs of the Amorite group of tribes.

The Midianites lived at the crossroads of the great trade route extending from Yemen to Hijaz and northward to Syria, and from Egypt to Iraq, mentioned in the verses,

> **And the dwellers in the thorn bush were wrong-doers, so We took retribution from them, and surely both [their territory and the Overturned Cities] are on a clear road** (15:78-79),

which we discussed earlier in connection with the Overturned Cities. Consequently, because the Meccan trading caravans to Syria and Egypt had to pass both through Midian as well as through the territory of Lot's people, the Midianites too were remembered among the Arab tribes long after their destruction

Shu'ayb's people are referred to in the Qur'an both as Midianites (***Madyan***) (7:85; 9:70; 11:84, 95; 22:44; 29:36) and as the dwellers in the thorn bush or companions of the wood, ***as-hab al-aykah*** (15:78, 26:17, 38:13, 50:14). According to some commentators, the word ***aykah*** means a thick forest or thicket; others say that it means "thorny bush," referring to a kind of twisted or twining tree which grew in the area. Al-Aykah is also said to have been the name of the capital city of Shu'ayb's people, located at the site of Tabuk in what is now Saudi Arabia.

---

[1]A pre-Islamic tribe destroyed by divine punishment, who are also mentioned in the verse, **[We destroyed] 'Aad and Thamud and the dwellers in al-Rass, and many generations between them** (25:38). It is said that this tribe inhabited a village of the Thamud, and that they killed their prophet and threw his body into a *rass* or dry well.

[2]The title of a succession of pre-Christian Himayarite kings, also mentioned in the verse, **Are they bettter or the people of Tubba' and those before them? We destroyed them; indeed, they were sinners** (44:37). It is said that the people of Tubba' ruled over southern Arabia for centuries. The above verses make it clear that both the people of al-Rass and of Tubba', and their appalling fate, were well-known to the Arabs of Prophet Muhammad's time.

The classical commentators differ as to whether the Midianites and the dwellers in the thorn bush were the same or different peoples. However, the fact that the two are never mentioned in the same verse suggests that they were the same; so does the fact that same set of vices are mentioned for both. The most correct opinion seems to be that Madyan and Aykah were two branches descended from the same ancestors, intermarrying and sharing the same language and customs — as well as the same sins. Concerning these people, Ibn Kathir says:

> The people of Midian were unbelievers, worshippers of *al-aykah,* which is a kind of thorny tree growing in thickets. They were also highwaymen, and they gave short weight and measure, measuring more when they took in and less when they gave out.
>
> Then God sent among them a man from themselves, His messenger Shu'ayb, who called them to the worship of God alone, without ascribing partners to Him. And when he prohibited them from doing such abominable deeds as stealing and highway robbery, some of them believed in him but most of them denied him, until God sent upon them a severe punishment. (Ibn Kathir/*T*, 7:85-93)

This informs us that the first and primary sin of Shu'ayb's people was that they ascribed divinity to false gods. Another was that they habitually cheated in trade, giving short measure and weight but taking in more than their due, in spite of the fact that God had given them good provision and made their lives easy. And their third major sin was the practice of highway robbery.

Since the territory of Shu'ayb's people lay on a major trade route, one branch of which connected Yemen with Syria and the other Egypt with the Persian Gulf, they were in a prime position to prey on passing caravans. Indeed, it is said that they would not to let any caravan pass until it had paid a stiff ransom. Ibn 'Abbas (R) reports that they originated the crime of sitting by the roadside and forcibly extracting a payment for its use, while the early commentator al-Suddi says that they used to take one-tenth of the property of passers-by by force. And although we have no clear information concerning this, it may be that they applied it to the extreme of "Your money or your life."

REFERENCES: Tabari/*H*, II:143-145; Ibn Kathir/*T*, 85-93; Ibn Kathir/*Q*, "Shu'ayb"; Maududi/*Q*, 44:fn. 32, 15:fns. 43-45, 7:fn. 69, 25:fn. 52, 26:fn. 115; Asad/*Q*, 44:fn. 20; Ali/*Q*, fns. 1055, 2000, 3485.

2. The Identity of Shu'ayb (A)

And to Midian [We sent] their brother Shu'ayb. (7:85, 11:84, 29:36)

Who was Shu'ayb, peace be upon him? We cannot say with certainty. While the Holy Prophet (S) mentioned him as being among the four Arabian prophets,[3] we do not have clear information about his identity or the time when he lived. However, Shu'ayb's words,

> **"And, O my people, let not dissension with me cause you to sin, lest there befall you something like what befell the people of Noah or the people of Hud or the people of Saleh. Nor are the people of Lot far removed from you"** (11:89),

make it clear that Shu'ayb (A) lived after the time of Lot (A).

A number of Qur'anic commentators maintained that Shu'ayb (A) was Reuel or Jethro, mentioned in the Old Testament as the father-in-law of Moses (Ex. 2:15-21, 3:1). This identification is based on the fact that, after his accidental killing of the Egyptian, Moses (A) fled to Midian, where he lived for several years with the venerable sheikh of the place, whose daughter he married (20:40; 28:22-23, 45).

Other commentators asserted that Shu'ayb (A) was a descendant of Abraham (A) through his Canaanite wife, Keturah (Qaturah or Qanturah), whom he married after the death of Sarah and who bore him six sons. One of these sons was Midian (Madyan), mentioned in Gen. 25:1-2, the ancestor of Shu'ayb's people, the Midianites. Yet another view is that Shu'ayb (A) was not a descendant of Abraham (A) but rather was someone who believed in him, possibly following his ordeal of the fire, and who followed his religion and emigrated with him to Syria. It has also been said that he was a descendant of Lot's daughter. But only God knows the truth.

Shu'ayb's people are mentioned seven times in the Qur'an as **"Madyan,"** and four times as **"the dwellers in the thorn bush"** (or **"the companions of the wood"**), while Shu'ayb (A) himself is mentioned by name eleven times. It is said that he was either weak of vision or blind. And he was granted a special favor — namely, such eloquence in speech and argument that thousands of years later Prophet Muhammad (S) said of him, "And that was the speaker of the prophets [*khatib al-anbiya'*]" (Ibn Kathir/*Q*, "Shu'ayb").

REFERENCES: Tabari/*H*, III:fn.166; Tabari/*H*, II:127, 129, 143-145; Ibn Kathir/*T*, 7:85-93; Ibn Kathir/*Q*, "Shu'ayb"; Maududi/*Q*, 7:fn. 69; Ali/*Q*, fn. 1054; Keller/*R*, x330, p. 1097.

---

[3]See "Hud," footnote 1.

3. Shu'ayb Calls to His People

The dwellers in the thorn bush denied the messengers. (26:176)

Like most of the prophets before him, nothing is known concerning the life of Shu'ayb (A) prior to his appointment as a messenger to his people. And like the earlier prophets, he began his mission by calling his people to their Lord.

"O my people, worship God," he said. **"You have no deity other than Him** (7:85, 11:84, 29:36). **And look forward to the Last Day, and do not do evil in the land, causing corruption"** (29:36).

Thus was initiated a series of dialogues that took place between Shu'ayb (A) and his people over an unspecified period of time. As was the case with the earlier prophets, Shu'ayb's preaching was met with hostility and rejection, and once again there began a conflict of escalating intensity between the forces of falsehood and the representative of the Lord of truth.

After addressing his people's first and gravest sin, polytheism or idolatry, Shu'ayb (A) spoke to them about their sins in relation to their fellow men. Among these were their dishonest and deceitful trade practices, their corrupting the land by highway robbery, and other evil actions. Shu'ayb's preaching and his people's responses are reported in three passages of the Qur'an.

"Will you not be mindful of God?" Shu'ayb (A) admonished, using the identical words of the warner-prophets before him. **"Indeed, I am a trustworthy messenger to you, so be mindful of God and obey me. And I do not ask of you any recompense for it. My recompense rests only upon the Lord of the worlds** (26:177-180).

"Give full measure and do not be among those cause loss to others, **and weigh with an even scale,"** Shu'ayb (A) urged. **"And do not deprive people of their goods or do evil in the land, causing corruption. And be mindful of the One who created you and the former generations"** (26:181-184).

But, unwilling to acknowledge the truth of their prophet's message or to change their way of life and evil habits, his people put forth a number of excuses for not believing in him.

"You are only one of those under a magic spell," they charged. **"And you are nothing but a mortal like ouselves, and indeed, we consider you to be among the liars."** Then, like the peoples of other prophets before them, they threw out an impertinent challenge: **"So cause pieces of the sky to fall upon us, if you are among the truthful!"** (26:187).

"My Lord is most knowing of what you do" (26:188), Shu'ayb (A) replied. It was not for him to compel them to believe and accept guidance, nor to punish them for not doing so, for the decreeing and arrangement of all matters lay with God alone, and he rested his case with Him.

Another Qur'anic passage reports Shu'ayb (A) as saying, **"O my people, worship God; you have no deity other than Him. There has surely come to you clear evidence from your Lord, so give full measure and weight, and do not deprive people of their goods or cause corruption in the land after its improvement. That is better for you, if you are believers!"** (7:85).

Shu'ayb (A) also appealed to his people to give up their other very serious sin, the practice of highway robbery. **"And do not station yourselves on every road, threatening and turning away from God's path those who believe in Him and seeking to make it crooked,"** he pleaded. Then, attempting to make them acknowledge God's favors and bounties to them as a people, he said, **"And recall when you were few but God increased you."** Finally, he reminded them of the divine retribution that had come upon the peoples who preceded them, whose stories they knew only too well, saying, **"And observe what was the end of the corrupters!"** (7:86).

But while Shu'ayb's preaching and warning merely inflamed the enmity of the hardened deniers of truth, among those who listened to him, some nevertheless recognized the validity of his Message and accepted faith, as is clear from his words, **"And if there is a group among you that has believed in that with which I have been sent and a group that has not believed, then be patient until God judges between us. And He is the Best of Judges"** (7:87).

The chiefs of those who were arrogant among his people took up the challenge. **"We will surely drive you and those who believe with you out of our community, O Shu'ayb, unless you return to our religion!"** (7:88), they threatened.

"Even if we detest it?" Shu'ayb (A) retorted. **"We would have made up a lie against God if we returned to your religion after God had saved us from it. And it is not for us to return to it unless God, our Lord, so wills,"** he continued, trying to make clear to the unbelievers that he did nothing by his own will, for his will was totally under the command of the One who had appointed him as their prophet. **"Our Lord encompasses everything in His knowledge. Upon God have we relied."** He then addressed himself to his maker, saying, **"Our Lord, decide between us and our people with truth, and You are the Best of Deciders"** (7:88-89).

But the unbelievers would have none of this. Even though they recognized the truth of what their prophet was saying to them, their pride, stubbornness and love of the life to which they were accustomed would not let them admit it. **"If you were to follow Shu'ayb,"** they said to one other, **"you would then certainly be the losers"** (7:90).

A third dialogue is reported in which Shu'ayb (A) repeated the same condemnation of his people's evil practices, following it with a warning:

"Do not short-change measure and weight," he admonished. **"Indeed, I see you in prosperity, but I surely fear for you the punishment of an all-encompassing Day"** (11:84). That is, while you may now be well-off (perhaps as a result of cheating people), you must not forget that the Day of Accounting is coming, which you cannot possibly escape.

"And, O my people," he repeated, **"give full measure and full weight with justice, and do not deprive the people of their goods nor act wickedly in the land, causing corruption. That which is left by God,"** meaning whatever remains to you as profit when you engage in honest trade, giving people their due rights, **"is best for you, if you are believers. But,"** he concluded, **"I am not a guardian over you"** (11:85-86).

As their prophet continued to preach and warn, the unbelievers wickedly turned his faith and his words against him. **"O Shu'ayb,"** they mocked, **"does your way of prayer** — that is, your religion — **command you that we should renounce what our fathers worshipped or not do what we please with our property? Indeed, you are the tolerant, the rightly-guided!"** (11:87).

"O my people," Shu'ayb (A) replied earnestly, **"have you considered: if I am taking my stand upon clear evidence from my Lord, while He has granted me a goodly provision from Himself,** I would not be saying this to you to advance my own worldly interest, for God has already granted me abundance.[4] **And I do not intend to differ from you in what I have forbidden you,"** meaning that I would never forbid you to do something that I did myself.[5] **"I only intend reform, as much as I am able. And my succcess is not but through God. Upon Him I rely and to Him I turn** (11:88).

---

[4]The sentence here is left incomplete. The completion of it given above is taken from al-Razi and other Qur'anic commentators (Asad/*Q*, 11:fn. 112). However, according to Ibn Kathir, the meaning is related to Shu'ayb's prophethood; namely, "If God Almighty has seen fit to grant me the great blessing of prophethood, then what can your excuse be for not believing in me?" (Ibn Kathir/*T*, 11:88).

[5]One of the worst of sins is hypocrisy; as God says, **"Do you enjoin righteousness on people and forget [to practice it] yourselves?"** (2:44).

"And, O my people," Shu'ayb (A) pleaded out of his deep concern for them, **"do not let dissension with me cause you to sin, lest there befall you something like what befell the people of Noah or the people of Hud or the people of Saleh. Nor are the people of Lot far removed from you"** (11:89).

Then, assuring them of God's readiness to accept repentance and His boundless forgiveness, he added: **"And seek forgiveness from your Lord, then repent to Him. Indeed, my Lord is Merciful and Loving!"** (11:89-90).

"O Shu'ayb," his people flung back at him, **"we do not understand much of what you say, and indeed, we consider you as weak among us.[6] And if it were not for your family, we would have stoned you, for you are not powerful among us!"** (11:91).

"O my people," Shu'ayb (A) replied, **"does my family have more power over you than God, while you have thrust Him behind your backs"** — that is, without regard or fear of Him, whereas fear of my family is keeping you from taking action against me. **"Indeed, my Lord encompasses whatever you do!"** (11:92).

Then, with unshakable trust in God, His Protector, he threw out a bold challenge to the unbelievers:

"And, O my people, act according to your ability; I too am acting. Soon you are going to know upon whom there will come a punishment that will disgrace him and who is a liar. And watch; indeed, I am a watcher with you!" (11:93).

REFERENCES: Qur'an: 7:85-90; 11:84-93; 22:42-44; 26:176-188; 29:36. Commentaries: Tabari/*H*, II:144-147; Ibn Kathir/*T*, 11:88; Asad/*Q*, 11:fn. 112.

---

[6]The Qur'anic commentators state that the "weakness" referred to here was Shu'ayb's poor vision or blindness.

4. The Punishment

But they denied him, so the quaking overtook them and they became prostrate in their homes. (29:37)

When the enmity of the unbelievers toward their prophet had increased beyond all bounds, God's decree went forth against them. With terrible, stunning swiftness, the divine retribution fell.

What was that retribution? God Most High describes it in powerful, image-invoking language, saying:

> **But they denied him, so the punishment of the day of the overcast seized them. Indeed, it was the punishment of a terrible day! In that is surely a sign, but most of them are not believers. And indeeed, your Lord — He is the Almighty, the Merciful.** (26:189-191)
>
> **Then the quaking [*al-rajfah*] overtook them and they became prostrate in their homes. Those who denied Shu‘ayb became as though they had never lived there; those who denied Shu‘ayb — it was they who were the losers!** (7:91-92)
>
> **And the clamor [*al-sayhah*][7] overtook those who had done wrong, and they became prostrate in their homes, as if they had never lived in them. Then away with Midian, just as Thamud was taken away!** (11:94-95)

The details of the calamity are given by Ibn ‘Abbas (R). When asked about the meaning of the words, **So the punishment of the day of the overcast seized them** (26:189), he said:

> God sent upon them fire and extreme heat, which took away their breath. They went into the innermost parts of their houses, but the heat entered there and took away their breath. Then they ran out of their houses into the desert. God Almighty then sent a cloud which protected them from the sun, and they found coolness and pleasure in it, so they called to one other to come there until they had all gathered beneath it, and then God sent fire upon them. So that was **the punishment of the day of the overcast. Indeed, it was the punishment of a terrible day!** [26:189]. (Tabari/*Q*, "Shu‘ayb")

Ibn Kathir likewise states that the people of the thorn bush were destroyed by a variety of interrelated punishments. His comment on 26:189 suggests that they were visited by a heat wave which lasted for seven days. Neither water nor shade nor going underground helped them, and they ran from their houses

---

[7]See "Saleh," page 237 , for a discussion of the terms ***al-rajfah*** and ***as-sayhah***.

toward the desert. There a cloud overshadowed them and they gathered beneath it. God then sent upon them fire and flaming missiles of stone. The earth quaked beneath them, while a thunderous roar came from the sky. **Indeed, it was the punishment of a terrible day!** And thus they perished (Ibn Kathir/*T*, 26:189).

From these accounts, we may speculate that the **"overcast"** (**"*dhullah*,"** meaning shade, covering or canopy) may have been the sort of darkness that often occurs simultaneously with volcanic eruptions and earthquakes, or it may have been a dense cloud of volcanic ash prior to an eruption. Whatever it was, the Midianites were obliterated as a single body, like the communities of unbelievers preceding them.

But the punishment did not come near Shu'ayb (A) and the believers, for **When Our command came, We saved Shu'ayb and those who believed with him by mercy from Ourselves** (11:94). And Shu'ayb (A) turned away from the remains of his community, saying, **"O my people, I certainly conveyed my Lord's Message to you and advised you, so how can I grieve over a disbelieving people?"** (7:93).

It is reported that Shu'ayb (A) and his followers died in Mecca. Ibn Kathir mentions the exact location of their graves on the west side of the K'abah. May God's peace and blessings be upon Shu'ayb, the messenger to the Midianites!

REFERENCES: Qur'an: 7:91-93; 11:94-95; 26:189-191; 29:37. Commentaries: Tabari/*Q*, "Shu'ayb"; Tabari/*H*, II:144-147; Ibn Kathir/*T*, 26:189; Ibn Kathir/*Q*, "Shu'ayb"; Maududi/*Q*, 26:fn.117, 7:fn. 75; Ali/*Q*, fns. 1063, 1597, 3220, 3221; Asad/*Q*, 11:fn. 98, 26:fn. 78.

5. The Traces of Shu'ayb's People

And the dwellers in the thorn bush were [also] wrong-doers, so We took retribution from them, and surely both [their territory and the Overturned Cities] are on a clear road. (15:79)

Whether the Midianites and the people of the thorn bush were a single group or two groups of people, they were eliminated without a trace.

Like the territory of the Thamud, the nearby region of Midian is characterized by unmistakable evidence of volcanic eruptions and earthquakes. Earlier, in the story of Lot (A), we cited Maulana Maududi's comment in connection with 15:79 above, in which he said that in the opinion of geographers, "There is no other land on the surface of the earth which looks as desolate as this territory, especially its southern part" (Maududi/Q, 15:fn. 42). And Muhammad Asad writes:

> Like the *harrah* once inhabited by the Thamud tribe, the adjoining region of Madyan (the Biblical Midian) shows ample evidence of volcanic eruptions and earthquakes. (Asad/ Q, 7:fn. 73)

6. Time Out for Reflection

So relate the stories, that perhaps they may reflect. (7:176)

The story of Shu'ayb (A) is the last of the stories of the five warner-prophets whose entire communities were destroyed by catastrophic divine punishments, the others being Noah, Hud, Saleh and Lot, may God's peace and blessings be upon them all.

Centuries after the last of these prophets had come and gone, God Most High was to reveal to His Last Prophet, Muhammad (S):

> **Those communities — We relate to you some of their tidings. And their messengers certainly came to them with clear proofs, but they would not believe in what they had previously denied. Thus does God seal up the hearts of the unbelievers.** (7:101)

Perhaps these last words, **Thus does God seal up the hearts of the unbelievers [*kafirin*],** may cause us to reflect. The Arabic word ***kufr***, from which ***kafir***[8] is derived, has a number of related meanings: to hide, cover, conceal, to deny or disacknowledge, and to be ungrateful or thankless. And a basic characteristic of the people whom God calls unbelievers was that they hid, covered or concealed the truth, denied God's being the sole Lord of creation, rejected His prophets, and were ungrateful for His favors. The Prophet (S) alluded to this in his divinely-inspired ***hadith:***

> God Most High said: "Jinn and humankind [are troubled] concerning **the tremendous news** [78:2]: [that] I create and [someone] other than Me is worshipped, and I grant provision and [someone] other than Me is thanked." (Al-Bayhaqi)

Earlier, we pointed out that the idolatrous peoples of the prophets whose stories are reported in the Qur'an never denied or questioned God's existence or power. Indeed, the fact that they were well-aware of the identity of the Creator of all things is clear from the following verses:

> **Say, [O Muhammad:] "Who provides for you from the sky and the earth, or who controls hearing and sight, and who brings forth the living from the dead and brings forth the dead from the living, and who arranges the [entire] matter?" They [the unbelievers] will then say, "God," so say: "Will you not then be mindful of Him?"** (10:31)
>
> **Say, [O Muhammad:] "Whose is the earth and whoever is in it, if you know?" They will say, "They are God's." Say: "Will you not**

---

[8]Plural, ***kafirin/kafirun/kufar***, translated, for the sake of simplicity, as "unbeliever(s)".

> **then remember?" Say: "Who is Lord of the seven heavens and Lord of the mighty Throne?" They will say, "They are God's." Say: "Will you not then be mindful of Him?" Say: "In whose hands is the dominion of all things, and He protects, while none can protect against Him, if you know?" They will say, "They are God's." Say: "How then are you deluded?"** (23:84-89)
>
> **If you [Muhammad] asked them [the unbelievers of his time], "Who created the heavens and the earth, and subjugated the sun and moon?" they would surely say, "God." How then are they deluded? . . . And if you asked them, "Who sends down rain from the sky and thereby gives life to the earth after its death?" they would surely say, "God." . . . And when they embark on a ship [and find themselves in danger], they call upon God, sincere to Him in faith, but when He delivers them to the land, then they ascribe partners to Him.** (29:61, 63, 65)
>
> **If you [Muhammad] asked them, "Who has created the heavens and the earth?" they would surely say, "They were created by Almighty, the All-Knowing." . . . But they have assigned to Him a portion of His slaves [as partners in His divinity].** (43:9, 15)
>
> **If you asked them who created them, they would surely say, "God." How then are they deluded?** (43:87)

You may also have noticed that the "disbelieving" peoples of various prophets said such things as, **"If *God/our Lord* had willed, He would have sent angels"** (23:24, 41:14); **"He is nothing but a man who has fabricated a lie *about God*"** (23:38); **"Do you [really] know that Saleh is sent *by his Lord*?"** (7:75); **"Swear *by God* that we will attack him [Saleh] and his family secretly by night"** (27:49); and, **"You are nothing but mortals like ourselves, and *the Most Merciful* has not revealed anything"** (36:15). Obviously, these are not the words of atheists or people who deny God's existence.

All this demonstrates beyond any doubt that when the warner-prophets approached their people with God's Message, the problem was not their inability to believe in Him due to intellectual doubts or questions, especially since traditions concerning the earlier prophets had remained very much alive among them. Rather, the issue was that, after being polytheists, acknowledging the Creator as the sole Deity, with all that implied, would have required major changes which they were completely unwilling to make. It was easier and more convenient for them to deny the truth, *although they knew that it was the truth*, than to admit God's Oneness and Lordship, accept the guidance revealed to them through His prophets, and restructure their entire way of thinking and mode of life accordingly.

This is illustrated by the story of Abraham (A), which gives us an incisive glimpse into the mind-set of his idol-worshipping people. They did not hesitate or feel ashamed to admit, **"We worship idols and remain devoted to them"** (26:71). Yet when Abraham (A) demanded of them whether their idols could speak, they were so completely confounded that they could not offer any reply (21:65). In confusion at having been caught in such a false position, they went aside and said to one another, **"Indeed, you** yourselves **are the wrong-doers"** (21:64). And afterwards, when Abraham (A) forcefully challenged their belief in their fabricated gods, the only response they could muster was to throw him into a fire big enough to burn a whole town.

Such was the invariable response of the warner-prophets' peoples to God's call to them through the messengers He sent among them. By denying truth and defending, cherishing and living by falsehood, they sealed their fate and finally died for it, for ultimately, when their hearts remained closed and their response remained unchanged, God's response to *them* was to decree their destruction.

Afterwards, new generations arose that perhaps benefitted temporarily from the lessons of the past. But little by little these lessons were forgotten and the downward spiral of civilization again began and gathered momentum. New prophets were then sent, were similarly rejected, and their people destroyed in like manner. This recurrent cycle of history is eloquently summarized in the following passages:

> **Then after them [the people of Noah] We brought forth another generation. And We sent among them a messenger from among themselves, [saying,] "O my people, worship God. You have no deity except Him, so will you not be mindful of Him?" And the chiefs among his people who disbelieved and denied the meeting with God in the Hereafter, while We had given them luxury in this world's life, said, "This is nothing but a man like yourselves. He eats of whatever you eat and drinks of whatever you drink, and if you obey a man like yourselves, you will certainly be losers! Does he promise you that when you have died and become dust and bones, you will be brought forth again? How far-fetched, how far-fetched, is that which you are promised! There is nothing except our life of this world. We die and we live [but once], and we will not be resurrected. He is nothing but a man who has fabricated a lie about God, and we are not going to believe in him." He [the prophet] said, "My Lord, support me because they have denied me!" He [God] said, "In a little while, they will surely be regretful!" Then the clamor rightfully overtook them and We made them like stubble. Then away with the wrong-doing people! Then after them We brought forth other generations. No nation will precede its time [of termination], nor will they remain [after it]. Then We sent Our messengers in succession. Each time there came**

to a nation its messenger, they denied him, so We made them follow one another [in destruction] and We made them [mere historical] narratives. So away with a people who do not believe! (23:31-44)

We certainly sent a messenger among every nation, [saying,] "Worship God and avoid false objects of worship." And among them were those whom God guided and among them were those upon whom misguidance was decreed. So travel though the earth and observe what was the end of the deniers. (16:36)

How many of the generations after Noah have We destroyed! And your Lord is sufficient for the sins of His servants, Well-Acquainted and Seeing [all things]. (17:17)

Perhaps in our time we may feel safe and confident in assuming that all that is a thing of the past and that no punishment will ever come upon people or societies in our time. But if we permit ourselves such faulty reasoning, we are not only turning our backs on what the collective history of mankind has to teach us, but also failing to understand one of the most important of all lessons: that actions have consequences, both for individuals and their societies, which must sooner or later be felt.

Sometimes the consequences of our actions are deferred for the Hereafter, but at other times, when God wills, they may be experienced during this life. The message of all the warner-prophets' stories is that when people are admonished and advised by the sources of faith they acknowledge, yet consistently refuse to accept truth and turn away from divine guidance for reasons of self-interest, God's punishment may fall upon them collectively during this life in advance of their individual punishment in the Hereafter.

This may seem to contradict what we observe, for we live in a world in which evil, oppression, violence, cruelty, lust and greed often seem to dominate. However, the stories of the warner-prophets make it clear that, when those who perpetrate evil, immorality, injustice and oppression appear to flourish, even for seemingly long periods, God Almighty, the Lord of all creation, is nonetheless in absolute command and control.

Because His Will is ever above all wills, the reality is that, regardless of the extent and duration of wrong-doing, it can continue only up to the limit that He permits. Therefore, as is demonstrated by these stories, when God, who is endlessly Patient and Forbearing, sends His warnings to a people and they repeatedly disregard and reject them, terrible consequences can be expected. And unfortunately, as so many events in the past and in our own time have shown, those consequences do not come only upon the guilty members of a society but affect everyone in it; as God says:

And fear an affliction which will not exclusively befall those who have done wrong among you, and know that God is severe in penalty. (8:25)

God's punishment can take any and every form, for as He possesses all means to create, so He also possesses every means to destroy. In these stories we have seen some of the means which He employs for eradicating a people whose misdeeds have passed the point of His tolerance. Reminding us of His awesome power and of the fates of peoples before us, He says:

So We seized each for his sin; and among them were those upon whom We sent stones, and among them were those who were overtaken by the clamor, and among them were those whom We caused the earth to swallow, and among them were those whom We drowned. And it was not God who wronged them, but it was they who wronged themselves. (29:40)

Therefore, sometimes He punishes His servants by the awesome array of natural forces that are at His disposal, sending upon them floods, fires, droughts, famines, extreme heat or cold, storms, volcanic eruptions, earthquakes, epidemics or insect infestations. At other times He punishes us by the hand of our fellow humans, who do not lack imagination in inventing means of inflicting pain and death, so that we may repent and return to Him.

As long as revealed scriptures remain among us, the eternal, unchanging Message of the prophets still speaks to our hearts. We do not have the excuse of claiming that no warner or guide came to us to show us the way, for the true histories of God's messengers have been preserved in the Holy Qur'an, which remains, word for word, letter for letter, exactly as it was revealed through the angel Gabriel to the Last Prophet, Muhammad (S), over fourteen hundred years ago. And these stories were revealed, not as clever parables or fanciful tales, but as living lessons of those who walked on this earth before us, sent down for our guidance and well-being, so that a similar fate may not overtake us.

We are living in an extremely difficult time, a time in which unprecedented evils flourish upon the earth. These evils, one following the other, leave their mark upon the planet, upon our hearts and minds and bodies and societies — indeed, upon the very air we breathe. None of us is exempt from their effects.

As long as they continue, we must consider ourselves vulnerable to God's judgment. Today, the earth is giving the strongest possible signals, in the form of frequent violent natural disasters such as earthquakes, volcanic eruptions, fires, floods, storms and the like, that the injustices carried out upon its surface, in its atmosphere, and even in the depths of its seas, has produced a profound disturbance in its equilibrium. As God says:

> **Corruption has appeared in the land and the sea because of what people's hands have earned, and so He will let them taste something [of the consequences] of what they have done, that they may turn back.** (30:41)

Today, as in the time of the prophets and through their tongues, God Most High calls us to return to Him. And safety lies in keeping firmly to the path of faith and goodness, the path of His messengers and their righteous inheritors and followers — all those who keep Him in their hearts and live by His guidance, and who say,

> **Our Lord, You did not create this in vain. May You glorified! Then save us from the punishment of the Fire. Our Lord, indeed, whomever You admit to the Fire, you have disgraced him, and there are no helpers for the wrongdoers. Our Lord, indeed, we have heard a caller calling to faith, [saying,] "Believe in your Lord," and we have believed. Our Lord, then forgive us our sins and remove from us our misdeeds and cause us to die with the righteous. Our Lord, and grant us what You promised us through Your messengers and do not disgrace us on the Day of Resurrection. Indeed, you do not fail in [Your] promise!"** (3:191-194)

Qur'anic References — Shu'ayb and His People

7:85-93

And to Midian [We sent] their brother Shu'ayb. He said, "O my people, worship God; you have no deity other than Him. There has surely come to you clear evidence from your Lord, so give full measure and weight, and do not deprive people of their goods or cause corruption in the land after its improvement. That is better for you, if you are believers! (85) And do not station yourselves on every road, threatening and turning away from God's path those who believe in Him and seeking to make it crooked. And recall when you were few but God increased you, and see what was the end of the corrupters! (86) And if there is a group among you that has believed in that with which I have been sent and a group that has not believed, then be patient until God judges between us. And He is the Best of Judges." (87)

The chiefs of those were arrogant among his people said, "We will surely drive you and those who have believed with you out of our community, O Shu'ayb, unless you return to our religion!"

He said, "Even if we detest [it]? (88) We would have made up a lie against God if we returned to your religion after God had saved us from it. And it is not for us to return to it unless God, our Lord, so wills. Our Lord encompasses everything in His knowledge. Upon God have we relied. Our Lord, decide between us and our people with truth, and You are the Best of Deciders." (89)

And the chiefs of those who disbelieved among his people said, "If you were to follow Shu'ayb, you would then certainly be the losers." (90) Then the quaking overtook them and they became prostrate in their homes. (91) Those who denied Shu'ayb became as though they had never lived there; those who denied Shu'ayb — it was they who were the losers! (92)

Then he turned away from them and said, "O my people, I certainly conveyed my Lord's Message to you and advised you, so how can I grieve over a disbelieving people?" (93)

9:70

Has there not reached them the news of those before them — the people of Noah and the 'Aad and Thamud, and the people of Abraham and the dwellers in Midian and the Overturned Cities? Their messengers came to them with clear proofs. And never would God have wronged them, but [rather] they wronged themselves.

11:84-95

And to Midian [We sent] their brother Shu'ayb. He said, "O my people, worship God; you have no deity other than Him. And do not short-change measure and weight. Indeed, I see you in prosperity, but I surely fear for you the punishment of an all-encompassing day. (84) And, O my people, give full measure and full weight with justice, and do not deprive the people of their goods or act wickedly in the land, causing corruption. (85) Whatever is left by God is best for you, if you are believers. But I am not a guardian over you." (86)

They said, "O Shu'ayb, does your way of prayer command you that we should renounce what our fathers worshipped or that we do what we please with our property? Indeed, you are the tolerant, the rightly-guided!" (87)

He said, "O my people, have you considered: if I am [taking my stand] upon clear evidence from my Lord, while He has granted me a goodly provision from Himself. . . ? And I do not intend to differ from you in what I have forbidden you; I only intend reform, as much as I am able. And my succcess is not but through God. Upon Him I rely and to Him I turn. (88)

"And, O my people, do not let dissension with me cause you to sin, lest there befall you something like what befell the people of Noah or the people of Hud or the people of Saleh. Nor are the people of Lot far removed from you. (89) And seek forgiveness from your Lord and then repent to Him. Indeed, my Lord is Merciful and Loving!" (90)

They said, "O Shu'ayb, we do not understand much of what you say, and indeed, we consider you as weak among us. And if it were not for your family, we would have stoned you, for you are not powerful among us." (91)

He said, "O my people, does my family have more power over you than God, while you have thrust Him behind your backs? Indeed, my Lord encompasses whatever you do! (92) And, O my people, act according to your ability; I too am acting. Soon you are going to know upon whom there will come a punishment that will disgrace him and who is a liar. And watch; indeed, I am a watcher with you!" (93)

And when Our command came, We saved Shu'ayb and those who believed with him by mercy from Ourselves; and the clamor overtook those who had done wrong, and they became prostrate in their homes, (94) as if they had never lived in them. Then away with Midian, just as Thamud was taken away! (95)

15:78-79

And the dwellers in the thorn bush were [also] wrong-doers, (78) so We took retribution from them, and surely both [their territory and the Overturned Cities] are on a clear road. (79)

22:42-44

And if they deny you [Muhammad], thus did the people of Noah and 'Aad and Thamud deny [their prophets] before them, (42) and the people of Abraham and the people of Lot (43) and the dwellers in Midian. (44)

26:176-191

The dwellers in the thorn bush denied the messengers, (176) when Shu'ayb said to them, "Will you not be mindful of God? (177) Indeed, I am a trustworthy messenger to you, (178) so be mindful of God and obey me. (179) And I do not ask of you any recompense for it. My recompense rests only upon the Lord of the worlds. (180)

"Give full measure and do not be among those cause loss [to others], (181) and weigh with an even scale; (182) and do not deprive people of their goods or do evil in the land, causing corruption. (183) And be mindful of the One who created you and the former generations." (184)

They said, "You are only one of those under a magic spell, (185) and you are nothing but a mortal like ouselves, and indeed, we consider you to be among the liars. (186) So cause pieces of the sky to fall upon us, if you are among the truthful!" (187)

He said, "My Lord is most knowing of what you do." (188) But they denied him, so the punishment of an overcast day seized them. Indeed, it was the punishment of a terrible day! (189) In that is surely a sign, but most of them are not believers. (190) And indeeed, your Lord — He is the Almighty, the Merciful. (191)

29:36-37

And to Midian [We sent] their brother Shu'ayb, and he said, "O my people, worship God and look forward to the Last Day, and do not do evil in the land, causing corruption." (36) But they denied him, so the quaking overtook them and they became prostrate in their homes. (37)

38:12-14

Before them, the people of Noah and 'Aad and Pharaoh, possessor of the stakes, (12) denied, and Thamud and the people of Lot and the dwellers in the thorn bush. Those were the factions; (13) each denied the messengers, wherefore My punishment was justified. (14)

50:12-14

Before them, the people of Noah and the dwellers in al-Rass and Thamud denied, (12) and 'Aad and Pharaoh and the brethren of Lot, (13) and the dwellers in the thorn bush and the people of Tubba' — all denied the messengers, wherefore My threat was justly fulfilled. (14)

GLOSSARY OF TERMS

'Abd (pl., *'ibad)* – slave or servant.

Adab – proper manners.

Ahadith – plural of *hadith.*

Al-'alamin – lit., "the worlds," meaning the universes, the species therein, or all mankind.

'Alayhi-s-salam – peace be upon him, the Islamic invocation of blessings upon prophets or angels.

Alhamdulillah – praise be to God.

Alhamdulillahi Rabbi-l-'alamin – Praise be to God, Lord of the worlds.

Allahu akbar – God is Most Great.

'Arafat – the name of a vast, empty plain outside Mecca which is the site of one of the rites of *Hajj.*

Ashhadu an la ilaha illa-Llah wa ashhadu anna Muhammadan 'abduhu wa rasuluhu – I bear witness [or testify] that there is no deity except God, and I bear witness that Muhammad is His slave and His Messenger.

Al-Asma' al-Husna – the Beautiful or Excellent Names of God.

'Asr – lit., time; also the name of third prayer of the day, observed in the latter part of the afternoon.

A'udhu bil-Llahi min ash-Shaytani-r-rajim – I seek refuge in God from Satan, the accursed.

Awliya' (sing., *wali)* – holy people, saints.

'Azazil – the proper name of Iblis or Satan before his fall.

Al-'Aziz – the Exalted, one of God's Holy Names. In the story of Joseph, a title approximately equivalent to "His Excellency".

'Azra'il – the Angel of Death.

Al-Bait al-Ma'mur. – the prototype of the Holy K'abah in the fourth heaven.

Al-Bait al-Maqdis – the Sacred House in Jerusalem, i.e., Solomon's Temple.

Bani Isra'il – the Children of Israel (Jacob), the Israelites.

Barzakh – lit., interval, break, gap, partition, bar, obstruction; the term for the intermediate life between bodily death and the Day of Resurrection.

Bashir, also *mubashir* (pl., *mubashirin*) – a bringer of good tidings, referring to those prophets who brought revelations of God's mercy and forgiveness.

Bismillah/Bismillahi-r-Rahmani-r-Rahim – In the name of God/In the name of God, the Beneficent, the Merciful.

Dahiya – the slaughtering of an animal for charitable purposes.

Dhikr – remembrance of God.

Dhul-Hijjah – the twelfth month of the Islamic (lunar) calendar, the month of the *Hajj*.

Dhulm – injustice, oppression, tyranny, wrong-doing, transgressing proper limits.

'Eid al-Adha – the Festival of Sacrifice, commemorating events in the lives of Abraham, Hagar and Ishmael, observed during the time of the *Hajj*.

'Eid al-Fitr – the Festival of Fast-Breaking, marking the end of Ramadan.

Fajr – dawn; also the name of the first prayer of the day, observed at dawn.

Fitrah – natural disposition or innate, God-given nature.

Al-Ghafur – the Forgiving, one of God's Holy Names.

Al-Ghayb – the Unseen, the spiritual realm.

Hadith (pl., *ahadith*) – a report of a saying or action of the Prophet (S), painstakingly compiled in numerous collections during the first century *Hijrah*.

Hadith qudsi – a *hadith* in which the Holy Prophet speaks about God Most High through divine inspiration; the words are the Prophet's but the meaning is given by God Himself.

Al-Hajar al-Aswad – the Black Stone.

Hajj – the prescribed pilgrimage to Mecca.

Hanif – a believer in pure monotheism, specifically among the pre-Islamic Arabs and other peoples.

Hanifiyyah – pure, pristine monotheism; the true faith.

Haram – prohibited, either in the sense of prohibited things or actions, or a sanctuary in which wrong-doing is prohibited.

Harrah (pl., *harrat*) – a lava flow.

Hijrah – emigration, specifically, the Holy Prophet's emigration from Mecca to Medina in the year 1 of the Islamic (*Hijri*) calendar.

Hikmah – wisdom.

Hira' – the cave near Mecca in which the Holy Prophet (S) received the first revelation of the Qur'an.

Hyksos – a dynasty of kings related to the descendants of Abraham, who ruled Egypt during the time of the prophet Joseph.

Iblis – Satan, the Devil.

Ibn Kathir – an eminent eighth century C.E. Qur'anic commentator and scholar.

Injil – the sacred scripture revealed to Jesus by God.

Israfil – the angel who will blow trumpet on Day of Resurrection.

Al-Isra' wal-Me'raj – the Holy Prophet's Night Journey and Ascension to the Divine Presence.

Jahiliyah – ignorance; specifically, the period of ignorance of the divine guidance prior to Islam.

Jihad – struggle, striving, earnest effort.

Jinn – an unseen order of intelligent beings, which includes both believers and devils.

Jurhum – an Arab tribe dating back to the time of Abraham or earlier.

K'abah – the sacred House of God in Mecca.

Kafir (pl., *kafirin/kafirun/kufar*) – one who disbelieves, covers truth with falsehood, or denies God's favors.

Khalifah – deputy, vicegerent.

Khalil – close, intimate friend; Abraham, the Friend of God, is *Khalil-Allah* or *Khalil ar-Rahman* (the Friend of the Most Merciful).

Al-Kiraman Katibin – the Honored Scribes, the two angels who write down each person's deeds.

Al-Kitab – the Book or Scripture, i.e., the Holy Qur'an.

Kufr – unbelief, covering truth with falsehood, or denying God's favors.

Labbayk – Here I am!

Lailat al-Qadr – the Night of Power, during which the first revelation of the Qur'an was conveyed to the Holy Prophet (S) by the angel Gabriel in Hira' cave.

Al-Lawhi-l-Mahfudh – the Preserved or Guarded Tablet of God's decrees for all eternity.

Maghrib – sunset; also the name of the fourth prayer of the day, observed after sunset.

Malik – the angel who is the the keeper of Hell.

Maqam Ibrahim – the Station or Standing-Place of Abraham, the spot beside the K'abah where Abraham stood in prayer.

Al-Masjid al-Aqsa – the Farthest Mosque, i.e., the Temple of Solomon in Jerusalem.

Al-Masjid al-Haram – the Sacred Mosque in Mecca, enclosing the Holy K'abah.

Me'raj – the Holy Prophet's ascension to the Divine Presence.

Michael – angel in charge of safety, fertility, rain and provision.

Mina – a small town near Mecca, the site of certain rites of the *Hajj*.

Miswak – a natural toothbrush made from the twigs of a tree growing in the Arabian peninsula.

Muharram – the first month of the Islamic (lunar) calendar.

Munkar and Nakir – the two angels who question the souls after death.

Mushrik (pl., *mushrikin/mushrikun*) – those who ascribe divinity or its attributes to anyone or anything other than God.

Al-Mu'tafikat – the Overturned Cities of the prophet Lot.

Nabi (pl., *anbiya'/nabiyin*) – prophet.

Nadhir, also *mundhir* (pl. *mundhirin*) – a prophet who brought a warning of God's punishment to his people.

Nafs – self or soul, also used in the sense of lower self or ego. *Al-nafs al-lawwamah* refers to the self-reproaching soul or conscience.

Nubuwwah – prophethood.

Qada wa qadar – the Divine Decree by which all things are arranged.

Qiblah – direction; specifically, the direction which Muslims face during *salat*.

Rabbi-l-'alamin – the Lord of the worlds, universes, or all species of beings, known and unknown.

Radi-Allahu 'anhu – may God be pleased with him, the Islamic invocation of blessings upon the Companions of the Prophet (S).

Al-Rahim – the Merciful, Beneficent or Compassionate, one of God's Holy Names.

Al-Rahman – the Most Merciful, Most Beneficent or Most Compassionate, one of God's Holy Names.

Rajab – the seventh month of the Islamic (lunar) calendar.

Ar-rajfah – a tremendous quaking, shaking, trembling, rocking or convulsion.

Rak'at – the cycle of movements and words which comprises a unit of *salat*.

Ramadan – the ninth month of the Islamic calendar, the month of obligatory fasting.

Rasul (pl., *rusul/mursalin/mursalun*) – messenger, one who is sent.

Ridwan – the angel who guards the gates of Paradise.

Risalah – the message revealed to a messenger (*rasul*).

Sacred Mosque – *al-Masjid al-Haram*, the vast mosque enclosing the Holy K'abah in Mecca.

Sa'i – hastening; specifically, walking between the two hills of Safa and Marwah as part of the rites of *Hajj* and *'Umrah*.

As-sa'iqah – a strike or blast that stuns, causes unconsciousness or destroys.

Salam – peace.

As-salamu 'alaikum wa rahmat-Allahi – peace be upon you, and God's mercy and His blessings.

Salat – the prescribed Islamic prayer or worship.

Salehin – righteous, holy people.

Sallalahu 'alayhi wa sallam – "God's peace and blessings be upon him," the Islamic invocation of blessings upon Prophet Muhammad.

As-sayhah – a sound, noise, shout, cry or clamor.

Al-Shahadah – lit., "that which is witnessed"; that is, the visible, material world. Also, the declaration of Islamic faith (see *Ashhadu an la ilaha illa-Llah wa ashhadu anna Muhammadan 'abduhu wa rasuluhu*).

Shari'ah – lit., way, a divinely-revealed law.

Shaytan – Satan.

Shirk – ascribing partners or the attributes of divinity to other than God.

Sifat – God's divine attributes.

Subhanallah – glory be to God.

Sujud/sajdah – prostration.

Sunnah – practice; the *sunnah* of the Prophet (S) consists of that which he did, said or approved of in others.

Surah – chapter of the Qur'an.

Al-Tabari – an eminent ninth century C.E. Qur'anic commentator and scholar.

At-taghiyah – a tremendous, destructive outburst.

Taharah – cleanliness, purification

Talbiyah – the special call uttered by pilgrims during the *Hajj.*

Taqwa – mindfulness of God, God-consciousness, fear of God.

Tarbiyah – training, upbringing, rearing, instruction, education.

Taurat/Taurah – the original scripture revealed to Moses by God.

Tawaf – circumambulation of the K'abah, part of the rites of *Hajj* and '*Umrah.*

'Ubudiyat – servanthood.

'Ulu-l-'azm – possessors of determination, denoting the greatest of the prophets and other spiritually outstanding personalities.

Ummah – nation, people, faith community.

'Umrah – the minor pilgrimage to Mecca, performed at any time of the year.

Wudu' – ablution for prayer.

Zakat – the obligatory charity ("poor-due") prescribed through all the prophets, which is one of the five obligatory acts of worship in Islam.

Zamzam – the famed well in Mecca revealed to Hagar during her desperate search for water.

INDEX

A

G

H

I

J

M

Q

V

W

Y

Z